D1331930

COLLINS
GEM
ENCYCLOPEDIA

VOLUME I
A-K

COLLINS GEM
ENCYCLOPEDIA

VOLUME 1
A-K

Collins
London & Glasgow

First Published 1979
Revised Impression 1980
© 1979 William Collins Sons & Co. Ltd.

ISBN: 0 00 458754 5

Typeset by C.R. Barber & Partners, Wrotham, Kent

Printed in Great Britain by
William Collins Sons & Co. Ltd.

Collins Gem Encyclopedia
is based on and abridged from
Collins Concise Encyclopedia

PREFACE

The *Gem Encyclopedia* is a completely up-to-date, easy to use reference guide to all fields of human activity and knowledge. *The Encyclopedia* has been arranged into two compact volumes, containing over 14,000 articles. The entries have been listed alphabetically so that the reader can locate the information required as quickly and easily as possible.

The coverage of the *Gem Encyclopedia* ranges from the birth of civilization in Sumeria to the furthest reaches of space exploration, from ancient Greek tragedy to pop art. Both text and selection strive for impartiality and wherever possible stick to facts rather than opinions. Finally, although the *Encyclopedia* aims at world-wide coverage, it has been particularly tailored to the needs of the English-speaking world.

Ian Crofton

EDITORIAL STAFF

ABBREVIATIONS USED IN THE ENCYCLOPEDIA

AD	anno domini	Dec.	December
admin.	administration, administrated	dept.	department
agric.	agricultural, agriculture	dist.	district
alt.	altitude	E	east
anc.	ancient	eg	for example
anon.	anonymous	Eng.	English
Arab.	Arabic	esp.	especially
at. no.	atomic number	est.	estimated
at. wt.	atomic weight	estab.	established
Aug.	August	etc	and so on
autobiog.	autobiography	excl.	excludes, excluding
auton.	autonomous, autonomy	Feb.	February
av.	average	Finn.	Finnish
b.	born	fl	flourished
BC	before Christ	Flem.	Flemish
biog.	biography	Fr.	French
bor.	borough	ft	foot, feet
C	central	Ger.	German
c	about	Gk.	Greek
cap.	capital	gm	gram
cent.	century	govt.	government
cm	centimetre, centimetres	ha.	hectare, hectares
		Heb.	Hebrew
co.	county, company	h.e.p.	hydro-electric power
co. bor.	county borough	hist.	historical
coll.	college	hr	hour
co. town	county town	hq	headquarters
d.	died	Hung.	Hungarian
		ie	that is

in.	inch, inches
incl.	include, including, included
indust.	industrial, industry
isl.	island
Ital.	Italian
Jan.	January
Jap.	Japanese
jct.	junction
kg	kilogram
km	kilometre, kilometres
kmh	kilometres per hour
L.	Lake
lat.	latitude
lb	pound (unit of weight)
long.	longitude
max.	maximum
mfg.	manuacture, manufacturing
mi	mile, miles
min.	minimum, minute
mm	millimetre
MP	Member of Parliament
mph	miles per hour
Mt.	Mount
Mts.	Mountains
mun. bor.	municipal borough
N	north
Nov.	November
NT	New Testament
Oct.	October
orig.	originally
OT	Old Testament

penin.	peninsula
PM	Prime Minister
Pol.	Polish
pop.	population
Port.	Portuguese
prehist.	prehistoric
prob.	probably
protect.	protectorate
prov.	province
pseud.	pseudonym
pub.	published
R.	River
RC	Roman Catholic
Russ.	Russian
S	south
sec	second
Sept.	September
Span.	Spanish
sq km	square kilometres
sq mi	square miles
St	Saint
St.	Street
str.	strait
Swed.	Swedish
territ.	territory
Turk.	Turkish
TV	television
UK	United Kingdom
UN	United Nations
univ.	university
US	United States
v	against
vol.	volume
WW	World War
W	west
yd	yard, yards

A

Aachen (Fr. *Aix-la-Chapelle*), city of
W West Germany. Pop. 177,000.
Indust. centre in coalmining area,
railway jct. Thermal baths from
Roman times. N cap. of Holy Roman
Empire, cathedral (10th cent.) has
Charlemagne's tomb. Badly
damaged in WWII.

Aalborg, city of NE Jutland, Denmark, on Lim Fjord. Pop. 100,000.
Port, shipbuilding; cement; textiles.

Aalto, Alvar (1899-1976), Finnish
architect, furniture designer. Pioneer of modern architecture, he was
noted for his imaginative use of
materials, esp. wood and brick, and
for relating buildings to the landscape.

aardvark, *Orycteropus afer*, nocturnal burrowing mammal of C and
S Africa, order Tubulidentata. Long
snout, extensible sticky tongue; diet
of ants, termites. Also known as
antbear, earth pig.

aardwolf, *Proteles cristatus*, burrowing hyaena-like mammal of
Protelidae family, inhabiting scrubland of S Africa. Diet of termites,
carrion.

Aargau, canton of N Switzerland.
Area 1404 sq km (542 sq mi); cap.
Aarau (Helvetic cap., 1789-1803).
Crossed by fertile valley of R. Aare.
Cereals, fruit. Mineral springs.

Aarhus, city of E Jutland, Denmark,
on Kattegat. Pop. 199,000. Port;
trade, transport centre; oil refining.

Aaron, in OT, elder brother of Moses
and leader with him of Israelites in
march into 'promised land'. First
high priest of Hebrews.

abacus, calculating device consisting of frame with beads which slide
back and forward on parallel wires
or in slots. Widely used in Middle
East, Orient and Russia.

Abadan, city of SW Iran, on Abadan
isl. at head of Persian Gulf. Pop.
306,000. Oil refining and export
centre.

Abakan, city of USSR, cap. of
Khakass auton. region, SC Siberian
RSFSR. Pop. 107,000. Produces
textiles, metal products. Founded in
1707 as fortress.

abalone, gastropod mollusc, genus
Haliotis, found mainly on Californian coast. Shell, resembling
human ear, source of mother-of-
pearl; flesh commonly eaten. Ormer,
H. tuberculata, found in Channel
Islands.

Abbasids, Arab dynasty of caliphs.
Overthrew OMAYYAD dynasty (750)
and moved cap. from Damascus to
Baghdad. Achieved great fame and
splendour under Harun al-Rashid.
Destroyed (1258) by Mongols under
Hulagu Khan.

Abbas [I] the Great (1557-1628),
Persian shah (1587-1628). Greatly
enlarged empire at expense of Turks
and, with help of English, Portuguese.

abbey, in Christian religion, monastic house in which a community of at least 12 monks or nuns live, ruled by an abbot or abbess. First abbey founded (c 529) by St Benedict at Monte Cassino, Italy.

Abbey Theatre, Dublin home of Irish National Theatre Society, founded during Irish literary revival of early 1900s, by W.B. Yeats, G.W. Russell (A.E.), Lady Gregory. Works by Synge, O'Casey received 1st presentation.

abdication, formal renunciation of high public office or authority, usually by monarch. In UK requires consent of Parliament, most famous example being Edward VIII (1936).

abdomen, in mammals, part of body below the thorax and above the pelvis; separated from thorax by the diaphragm. Contains stomach, intestines, liver, kidney, etc. In insects and crustaceans, hind part of body beyond thorax.

Abdul Hamid II (1842-1918), Ottoman sultan (1876-1909). Dismissed Midhat Pasha whose newly-framed constitution he then suspended (1876). Pursued pro-German policy after CONGRESS OF BERLIN. Deposed by Young Turks.

Abel, in OT, second son of Adam and Eve. Killed by his brother CAIN. A shepherd, his offerings were accepted by God when those of Cain (a tiller of the soil) were refused.

Abel, · Niels Henrik (1802-29), Norwegian mathematician. Independently of Galois, showed impossibility of solving general polynomial of 5th degree by algebraic means. Noted for pioneering work on elliptic functions.

Abelard, Peter or **Pierre Abélard** (1079-1142), French scholar. Held universals to exist only in thought but based in particular objects. Applied Aristotelian logic to faith in *Sic et Non*. Charged with heresy (1121). Remembered through their letters for tragic romance with Héloïse, provoking his castration by her uncle. Regarded as founder of Univ. of Paris. Works incl. autobiog. *Historia calamitatum*.

Abercromby, Sir Ralph (1734-1801), British general. Commanded ably in campaigns against French in Europe (1794-5) and West Indies (1795-7). Killed while defeating French at Aboukir Bay.

Aberdare, urban dist. of Mid Glamorgan, S Wales. Pop. 38,000. Coalmining; cables, electrical goods mfg.

Aberdeen, George Hamilton-Gordon, 4th Earl of (1784-1860), British statesman, PM (1852-5). Helped bring Austria into coalition against Napoleon with Treaty of Töplitz (1813). Failed to keep Britain out of Crimean War, resigned as PM after censure.

Aberdeenshire, former county of NE Scotland, now in Grampian region. Grampian Mts. in SW. Crops, livestock (esp. beef cattle); fishing, granite quarrying. Has offshore oil indust. Co. town was Aberdeen, city on R. Dee. Pop. 182,000. Chief Scottish fishing port, tourism, shipbuilding, oil rig service industs. Became royal burgh (1179). Has univ. (colls. 1494, 1593); cathedral (14th cent.). Called 'Granite City'.

aberration, in astronomy, apparent displacement of position of star or other heavenly body, caused by motion of earth. During earth's annual motion about sun, star appears to move in small ellipse. Effect discovered by Bradley 1725, who used it to estimate speed of light.

aberration, in optics, failure of lens or mirror to form perfect image. In spherical aberration, light rays from a point source are focused at different points. In chromatic aberration, edges of images are coloured because refractive index of lens varies for light of different wavelengths.

Aberystwyth, mun. bor. of Dyfed, W Wales. Pop. 11,000. Tourist resort. Has coll. of Univ. of Wales (1872); National Library of Wales (1911).

Abidjan, cap. of Ivory Coast, on Ebrie Lagoon. Pop. 510,000. Admin., commercial centre; railway terminus; exports coffee, cocoa, timber, fruit via outport at Port Bouet; univ.

abolitionists, in US history, advocates of end to Negro slavery. Influenced by British anti-slavery campaign success (1833). Leaders incl. W.L. Garrison and Wendel Phillips. Fugitive State Law (1850) strengthened UNDERGROUND RAILROAD, activities culminating in John Brown's abortive raid (1859) on Harpers Ferry. Unyielding attitude of abolitionists helped bring about Civil War.

abominable snowman, see YETI.

aborigine (Lat. *ab origine,* from the beginning), inhabitants of a country who are believed to be original natives of the region. Term used esp. to refer to AUSTRALIAN ABORIGINES.

abortion, in medicine, spontaneous or induced expulsion of foetus from the womb before 28th week of pregnancy. Sometimes referred to medically as miscarriage if it occurs after 16th week; this term popularly refers to accidental premature birth at any stage.

Aboukir or **Abukir,** village of N Egypt, on Aboukir Bay. Scene of Nelson's victory (1798) over French fleet in the 'Battle of the Nile'.

Abraham, regarded as father of Jewish nation. In OT received Jehovah's promise of Canaan as land for his descendants. Prob. historical figure, but more important in Bible as archetype of the man of faith. *See* ISAAC.

Abraham, Plains of, see QUÉBEC (city).

abrasive, material used for scouring, grinding or polishing. Natural forms incl. corundum, emery and diamond. Artificial forms incl. carborundum (silicon carbide), boron carbide and synthetic diamond.

Abravanel, Judah Léon, called Leone Ebreo (c 1460-1523), Jewish philosopher, b. Portugal. Expounded classic interpretation of Platonic love in *Dialogues of Love* (1535) describing union of the lover with the idea of the beautiful.

Abruzzi e Molise, region of SC Italy, in Apennine Mts. Sparsely populated, no large towns. Agric. (livestock, cereals, grapes) in fertile valleys.

Absalom, in OT, King David's favourite son. Instigated revolt against his father. After defeat, was killed by Joab while caught in a tree.

abscess, swollen area in body tissue in which pus collects as a result of infection. Occurs in tooth sockets, inner ear, skin, *etc.* Treated by antibiotics, but may require surgical drainage.

absinthe, green-coloured liqueur flavoured with wormwood, anise and other aromatics; contains from 60% to 80% alcohol. Now banned in most countries because of toxic effect of wormwood on nervous system.

absolute zero, temperature zero point on absolute or Kelvin scale, corresponding to −273.15˚ C. Theoretically lowest possible temperature, when molecular motion ceases.

absolutism, doctrine or system of govt. under which the ruler has unlimited power. Absolute monarchy *fl* in Europe 16th-18th cent., was defended by HOBBES.

abstract art, non-representational painting and sculpture, relying on form and colour to achieve aesthetic and emotional impact. Abstract art of 20th cent. derives from fauvism and cubism; early exponents incl. Kandinsky (1st abstract work 1910), whose early work emphasizes expressive use of colour, and Mondrian, who developed pure geometric style out of cubism. Brancusi was noted exponent of abstract sculpture.

abstract expressionism, school of American painting which developed after WWII; characterized by emphasis on artist's spontaneous and self-expressive application of paint in creating abstract work. Leading exponents incl. Pollock, Franz Kline and Rothko.

absurd, philosophical term used by CAMUS to describe meaninglessness of human existence in an irrational world. Precondition of much exist-

entialist philosophy and literature as in novels of SARTRE, plays of Beckett, Ionesco. More personally pessimistic than SCEPTICISM.

Abu Bakr or **Abu Bekr** (573-634), Arab leader. Important early convert to Islam, became devoted follower of Mohammed, who married his daughter. Succeeded Mohammed as 1st caliph (632); expansion of Islam into major world religion began under his rule.

Abu Dhabi, isl. sheikdom of United Arab Emirates, on Persian Gulf. Area c 67,300 sq km (26,000 sq mi); pop. 46,000; cap. Abu Dhabi. Has rich oil reserves.

Abu Simbel, village of S Egypt, on R. Nile. Site of 2 temples built c 1250 BC by Rameses II, rebuilt in sections 1964-8 above flood waters of Aswan High Dam.

Abydos, ancient city of C Egypt, on R. Nile. Former religious centre, with temples to Osiris; burial place of many kings. Remains date from 3100-500 BC.

Abyssinia, see ETHIOPIA.

acacia, genus of tropical and subtropical trees of Leguminosae family. Pinnate leaves with clusters of yellow or white flowers. Many cultivated as ornamentals; yields gum arabic, dyes, tanning aids, furniture woods. Species incl. cooba, *Acacia salicina,* an Australian wattle.

Académie Française, institute estab. 1635 for protection and perfection of French language. Began compilation of definitive dictionary 1639. Awards annual literary prizes.

academies of art, official organizations of artists. First academy, founded by Vasari in Florence (1563) under patronage of Cosimo de'

Medici, was concerned with raising social status of artists. French Academy of Painting and Sculpture founded (1648), later achieved monopoly of teaching and public exhibition, served as organ of official taste and standards. By 1790 over 100 academies throughout Europe, incl. Royal Academy, London (founded 1768). Romantic movement brought opposition to formal 'academism'.

academism, originally olive grove near Athens where Plato and followers met. Modern academy is learned society promoting arts, sciences, often publicly financed.

Academy Awards, prizes awarded annually since 1927 by US Academy of Motion Picture Arts and Sciences for outstanding achievements in cinema, incl. awards for best film, actor, music, *etc*, of year. Prizes in form of statuette known as Oscar.

Acadia (Fr. *Acadie*), hist. region of E Canada, comprising Nova Scotia, Prince Edward Isl., part of New Brunswick. French founded Port Royal, its chief town, in 1605; ceded to British 1713.

acanthus, genus of perennial herbs of Mediterranean region. White or coloured flowers with deeply cut spiny leaves. Stylized form of leaf used as architectural ornament, esp. on capitals of Corinthian columns, from *c* 5th cent. BC.

Acapulco, winter seaside resort of SW Mexico, on Pacific. Pop. 235,000. Has many hotels, excellent beaches; facilities for deep-sea diving, fishing. Fruit, cotton trading.

acceleration, rate of change of velocity. Gravitational acceleration is acceleration of free-falling body caused by gravitational attraction of Earth. Assumed constant near Earth's surface, equals *c* 981 cm/sec². Varies with altitude and longitude.

accelerator, in physics, device used to impart high velocities to charged particles by accelerating them in electric fields. Linear and cyclic are used in nuclear research, esp. investigation of elementary particles of matter. Examples incl. bevatron, betatron, cyclotron, synchrotron.

accentor, sparrow-like Eurasian bird, genus *Prunella*. Species incl. hedge sparrow or dunnock, *P. modularis*.

accessory, in law, a person who, although absent, helps another to break or escape the law. May be an accessory before (or after) the fact, *ie* one who aids the accused before (or after) the commission of the crime.

accipiter, any of genus *Accipiter* of small hawks with short wings, long tails. Species incl. goshawk, *A. gentilis*, and sparrow hawk, *A. nisus*.

accordion, portable reed organ. Wind is supplied by bellows and is directed to the reeds by keys and buttons, which sound accompanying chords. Invention variously attributed to Buschmann of Berlin (1822), Damien of Vienna (1829) and Bouton of Paris (1852).

accountancy, keeping or inspecting of financial data concerning persons and organizations. Data should incl. specific assets, liabilities, income, expenses, net receipts. First chartered body, Society of Accountants in Edinburgh (1854);

American Association of Accountants chartered in 1887.

Accra, cap. of Ghana, on Gulf of Guinea. Pop. 738,000. Admin., commercial centre; railway terminus and port, exports cocoa, hardwoods, gold; Univ. of Ghana nearby. Grew round 2 17th cent. forts; cap. of Gold Coast colony from 1876.

accumulator or **secondary cell,** device used to store electricity. Current is passed between 2 plates in a liquid, causing chemical changes by electrolysis. When plates are electrically connected, reverse chemical changes cause current flow.

acetaldehyde (CH_3CHO), colourless liquid, formed by oxidation of ethanol. Used in dye and hypnotic drug mfg. Occurs in body during decomposition of ingested alcohol.

acetic acid (CH_3COOH), organic acid contained in vinegar. Colourless liquid with pungent smell, obtained by destructive distillation of wood or oxidation of acetaldehyde. Its esters incl. cellulose acetate, used to make plastics.

acetone (CH_3COCH_3), inflammable colourless liquid, the simplest KETONE. Obtained commercially from isopropanol. Used as paint and varnish remover and organic solvent.

acetylcholine, organic chemical secreted at ends of nerve fibres; stimulates adjacent nerve cells, thus transmitting impulses through nervous system.

acetylene (C_2H_2), colourless gas, produced by action of water on calcium carbide or from natural gas. Used in welding and organic synthesis; burns with intense flame when mixed with oxygen in oxyacetylene burner.

acetylsalicylic acid, see ASPIRIN.

Achad Haam, pseud. of Asher Ginzberg (1856-1927), Jewish philosopher, b. Ukraine. Founder of cultural Zionism, believed concern for justice forms basis of Judaism.

Achaea, admin. dist. of S Greece, in Peloponnese, cap. Patras. Currants, olives; sheep, goats. Cities formed powerful Achaean League 280-146 BC, until conquered by Rome.

Acheson, Dean Gooderham (1893-1969), American govt. official. Secretary of state (1949-53), developed policy of Communist containment through aid to W Europe; helped estab. NATO.

Achilles, in Greek legend, warrior and Greek leader in Trojan War. As child, was dipped in R. Styx by his mother, Thetis, to make him invulnerable, but water did not touch heel she held him by. At Troy, killed Hector but was killed by Paris with an arrow which struck his only vulnerable spot, his heel. Hero of Homer's *Iliad*.

Achill Island, Co. Mayo, W Irish Republic. Area 148 sq km (57 sq mi). Mountainous; agric., fishing, tourism. Bridge from mainland.

acid, substance which liberates hydrogen ions in aqueous solution (Arrhenius' theory). Reacts with base to form salts. Strength measured by concentration of hydrogen ions (pH scale); those undergoing complete ionization (*eg* hydrochloric acid) are strong. Most acids corrode metals, turn litmus red and taste sour.

acidosis, condition in which alkalinity of human blood is less than normal. May be caused by failure of lungs to eliminate carbon dioxide, kidney failure, malnutrition, diabetes.

acne, skin disease caused by abnormal activity of sebaceous (grease) glands; common among adolescents and young adults. Characterized by pimples on face, back and chest; alleviated by ultraviolet light (which occurs in sunlight).

Aconcagua, mountain of W Argentina, highest of Andes Mts., close to Chile border and Uspallata Pass. Height 6960 m (22,835 ft).

aconite, see MONKSHOOD.

acorn, ovoid fruit or nut of OAK. Consists of nut itself in cup-shaped base. Formerly used as food for pigs.

acoustics, branch of physics dealing with propagation and detection of sound.

Acre (Heb. *Acco*), port of N Israel, on Bay of Haifa. Pop. 339,000. Steel, chemical indust. Christian centre during 13th cent. Crusades. Mainly Turkish rule (1517-1918), British (1918-48).

acropolis, elevated fortified citadel of ancient Greek cities. Surviving buildings of Acropolis in Athens incl. PROPYLAEA, PARTHENON, Erectheum and temple of Athena Nike, mostly constructed under Cimon and Pericles in 5th cent. BC.

acrostic, composition, usually in verse, in which certain letters in each line (*eg* first or last) spell out a word or words. Used notably by Latin and 16th-17th cent. English poets.

acrylic paint, emulsion paint used by artists, formed by adding pigment to acrylic resin. Can be applied with water to obtain thin washes or directly in thick impasto, imitating oil paint.

Actaeon, in Greek myth, a hunter. Angered Artemis by watching her bathe. She changed him into a stag and he was torn to pieces by his own hounds.

actinides, name given to group of elements with at. nos. from 89 to 103. Incl. uranium, actinium, thorium and 11 man-made transuranic elements. All radioactive and metallic.

actinium (Ac), radioactive metallic element; at. nc. 89, at. wt. 227. Discovered (1899) by Debierne in pitchblende.

action painting, term originally used as synonymous with ABSTRACT EXPRESSIONISM, but has come to imply more extreme examples of painter's spontaneous self-expression, involving apparently random application of paint to canvas. Pollock was leading exponent.

Actium, promontory of NW Greece, opposite modern Préveza. Site of Octavian's naval defeat of Antony and Cleopatra (31 BC).

act of God, in law, unforeseeable, unavoidable accident caused by extraordinary natural event. Injured party cannot normally claim damages.

Acton, John Emerich Edward Dalberg Acton, Baron (1834-1902), English historian. Prominent Liberal and RC, became professor of modern history at Cambridge (1895). Planned *Cambridge Modern History,* wrote many celebrated essays.

Acts of the Apostles, fifth book of NT. Written in Greek *c* AD 60, traditionally ascribed to Luke. Describes growth of early church, incl. missionary journeys of Paul.

actuary, statistician employed by govt. department, insurance company or other business. Calculates possibilities and risks involved in insurance, lotteries, *etc*.

acupuncture, form of medical treatment of ancient Chinese origin. Consists of insertion of needles into determined parts of body to relieve pain and treat disease.

Adam and Eve, first man and woman in creation story of OT book, Genesis. Adam was formed from dust; Eve from one of Adam's ribs taken while he slept. *See* EDEN, GARDEN OF.

Adam, Robert (1728-92), Scottish architect. With brother, James Adam (1730-94), designed numerous public buildings, houses and interiors, in highly refined style derived from Classical architecture. Works incl. London's Adelphi (now destroyed), Syon House, Osterley Park. Also applied principles to furniture design.

Adam de la Halle or **le Bossu** (*c* 1240-88), French poet, dramatist, musician. Works incl. *Le Jeu de Robin et Marion*, dramatized poem of pastoral seduction, with interludes for song. Also composed *rondeaux* of great originality.

Adamov, Arthur (1908-), French dramatist, b. Russia. Plays, eg *Ping-Pong* (1955), *Paolo Paoli* (1957), are satirical indictments of capitalist society.

Adams, prominent American family from Massachusetts. John Adams (1735-1826) was president (1797-1801). A Patriot leader, defended Declaration of Independence (1776) as representative at Continental Congress. Served as vice-president (1789-97) under Washington. As president, retained his political integrity despite Federalist-dominated Congress' attempts (eg Alien and Sedition Acts) to discredit Jeffersonian Republicans. His son, **John Quincy Adams** (1767-1848), was also president (1825-9). While secretary of state (1817-25), promulgated Monroe Doctrine (1823) on foreign policy in the Americas. A Federalist, elected president by House of Representatives over Jackson after neither candidate had obtained majority of electoral coll. votes. Congressman from Massachusetts (1831-48). His son, **Charles Francis Adams** (1807-86), was a diplomat. Minister to Great Britain (1861-8), aided Union cause in Civil War in negotiations over incidents involving *Trent*, *Alabama* ships.

Adams, Ansel (1902-), American photographer. Specialized in photographs of majestic American landscapes, exploiting dramatic light effects. Works incl. *Moonrise over Hernandez, New Mexico* (1941).

Adams, John Couch (1819-92), English astronomer. Independently of Leverrier, predicted position of previously unknown planet Neptune (1845-6) by calculations accounting for perturbations in motion of Uranus.

Adams, Richard (1920-), English author. Known for bestselling children's novel, *Watership Down* (1972). Other works incl. *Shardik* (1974).

Adams, Samuel (1722-1803), American Revolutionary leader. Advocated total separation from Britain, instigated BOSTON TEA

PARTY (1773). Signatory to Declaration of Independence. Second cousin of John Adams.

Adamson, Robert, pioneer photographer. *See* HILL, DAVID OCTAVIUS.

Adana, city of S Turkey, on R. Seyhan. Pop. 383,000. Trade centre; cotton goods, tobacco. Colonized by Romans; revived under Harun al-Rashid *c* 782.

addax, *Addax nasomaculatus,* large antelope of N Africa, esp. Sahara. Has whitish-grey coat, long spiralling horns.

adder, *Vipera berus,* poisonous European snake; bite painful but rarely fatal. Variable colour pattern, normally zigzag band edged by dark spots. Name also applied to African puff adder and various harmless American snakes.

addiction, compulsive uncontrolled use of habit-forming substances, *eg* alcohol or drugs; marked by physical dependence on drug, tolerance to it, and harmful effects on user and society. Sudden cessation may cause withdrawal symptoms, characterized by acute physical and mental distress.

Addington, Henry, *see* SIDMOUTH, HENRY ADDINGTON, VISCOUNT.

Addis Ababa, cap. of Ethiopia. Pop. 881,000. Admin., communications centre, railway to Djibouti; coffee trade, food processing. Hq. of OAU. Cap. of Ethiopia from 1896; cap. of Italian E Africa 1936-41. Has Imperial palace, 2 univs.

Addison, Joseph (1672-1719), English poet, essayist, moralist, politician. Contributed to *Tatler,* collaborated with STEELE in *Spectator* developing Augustan ideals of culture in masterly prose style. Also

wrote hymn 'The Spacious Firmament on High', poetry, blank-verse tragedy *Cato* (1713), literary criticism.

additive, inclusive term for wide range of chemicals added to substances to produce desired effect, *eg* anti-knock agents in petrol, food preservers, mould inhibitors.

Adelaide, city of SC Australia, on Torrens R., cap. of South Australia. Pop. 842,000. Commercial, indust. centre; exports (via Port Adelaide) wheat, wool, wattle bark, fruit, animal products; univ. Settled (1836) by free immigrants. Museum; Anglican, RC cathedrals.

Adélie Land, region of Antarctica, S of 60°S and between 136° and 142° E. Part of French Southern and Antarctic Territs. Discovered 1840. Site of research station.

Aden, port of SW Southern Yemen, on Gulf of Aden. Pop. 225,000. Free port since 1850; oil refining, salt mfg. British colony from 1839, joined Federation of South Arabia (1959) with British protect. of Emirates of South. Became cap. of independent Southern Yemen (1970).

Aden, Gulf of, arm of W Arabian Sea, between Southern Yemen and Somali Republic.

Adenauer, Konrad (1876-1967), West German statesman, chancellor (1949-63). Twice arrested during Nazi regime. Took part in founding (1945) Christian Democratic Union. Championed W European cooperation esp. through formation (1957) of EEC. Advocated German reunification through free elections and supported De Gaulle's policy of European independence of US.

adenoids, masses of lymphoid

tissue in upper part of throat behind the nose. Nasal infection in children resulting from overgrowth sometimes necessitates surgical removal.

Adige (anc. *Athesis*, Ger. *Etsch*), river of N Italy. Flows c 360 km (225 mi) from Resia Pass on Austrian border via Trento, Verona, to Adriatic N of R. Po. Irrigation, h.e.p.

Adirondack Mountains, range of NE New York, US; in S extension of Laurentian Plateau. Rise to 1629 m (5344 ft). Many lakes, waterfalls; extensively forested. Tourist resort area.

Adler, Alfred (1870–1937), Austrian psychologist. After studying with Freud, founded own school of individual psychology. Rejected Freud's emphasis on sexual motive in behaviour in favour of drive for power; believed inferiority complex fundamental to personality problems.

administrative law, laws and judicial decisions made by executive under powers given it by legislature of state. In 20th cent., govts. have increased such powers. In US, Administrative Procedure Act (1946) provided safeguards against them. In UK, ministers of the Crown may make orders, *etc*, amending or overriding statutes. Select Committee on Statutory Instruments acts as watchdog on executive.

admiral, brilliantly coloured butterfly of Nymphalidae family. Species incl. red admiral, *Vanessa atalanta*, common in Europe and North America.

Admiralty, in UK, former govt. dept. for admin. of naval affairs. Absorbed by ministry of defence (1964). Also refers to its hq. (1723-5, with modern additions) in Whitehall.

Admiralty Islands, group of small isls. of SW Pacific, in Bismarck Archipelago, NE of New Guinea. Area c 2070 sq km (800 sq mi); pop. c 22,000. Chief isl. Manus.

Adonis, in Greek myth, handsome youth disputed by Aphrodite and Persephone. When killed by wild boar, Zeus arranged for him to spend summer above ground with Aphrodite and winter in underworld with Persephone. Hence celebrated as symbolic of yearly cycle of vegetation.

Adowa, see ADUWA, Ethiopia.

adrenal gland, either of 2 endocrine glands against upper ends of each kidney. Consists of inner part (medulla) which secretes noradrenaline and adrenaline, and outer layer (cortex) which secretes steroid hormones that influence CARBOHYDRATE formation, sexual development, and control salt and water balance in body.

adrenaline, hormone secreted by medulla of adrenal gland. Stimulates heart action and sympathetic nervous system, raises blood pressure and blood sugar level; used to treat asthma.

Adrian IV, orig. Nicholas Breakspear (c 1115-59), English churchman. Only English pope (1154-9); defended papal supremacy against opponents, incl. Frederick Barbarossa. Prob. gave Ireland as fief to Henry II of England.

Adrian, Edgar Douglas Adrian, Baron (1889–1977), English physiologist. Authority on nervous system; developed electrical methods to investigate sense organs. Shared

Nobel Prize for Physiology and Medicine (1932) with Sherrington for work on nerve impulses.

Adrianople, see EDIRNE.

Adriatic Sea, arm of Mediterranean Sea between Italy (W) and Yugoslavia, Albania (E). Length c 800 km (500 mi); W coast is straight, lowlying; E coast is steep, rocky. Many ports, tourist resorts.

Aduwa or **Adowa,** town of N Ethiopia. Pop. 10,000. Scene of decisive defeat (1896) of Italians by Ethiopians under Menelik II, securing Ethiopian independence.

Adventists, evangelical sects who believe that Second Coming of Christ to Earth is imminent. Largest body is Seventh Day Adventists, formally organized in US in 1863. Observe Saturday as Sabbath.

advertising, informing public of products, services, needs, *etc*, through media of mass communication. Esp. important in 20th cent. commerce, giving rise to specialist agencies. 'Madison Avenue' synonymous with American advertising indust.

advocate, in law, person appointed to plead another's cause, esp. in court or court-martial, *ie* English barrister or counsel, Scottish and French advocate, American attorney. Lord advocate of Scotland is senior law-officer of the Crown responsible for criminal prosecutions; retires with govt. by which appointed.

A.E., see RUSSELL, GEORGE WILLIAM.

Aegean Sea, arm of Mediterranean Sea between Greece and Asia Minor. Linked by Dardanelles with Sea of Marmara and Black Sea. Many isls.

incl. Cyclades, Dodecanese, Euboea, Sporades. Ports, tourism.

Aegina (mod. *Aígina*), small isl. of Greece, in Saronic Gulf. Sponge fishing, olives, vines. Ancient commercial centre (struck 1st Greek coins) until pop. expelled by Athens (431 BC).

Aegisthus, in Greek myth, incestuous son of THYESTES and his daughter Pelopia. Killed his uncle ATREUS to allow his father to regain throne. Lover of Clytemnestra, he slew her husband, Agamemnon, on his return from Troy. Killed in revenge by Orestes.

Aelfric (*c* 955-1020), English churchman, grammarian, homilist. Greatest English scholar and chief Old English prose stylist of period. Many works incl. free vernacular version of 1st 7 books of OT, *Lives of Saints* (996-7), a grammar.

Aeneas, Trojan leader in Homer's *Iliad* and classical legend. Vergil's *Aeneid*, epic poem in 12 books (30-19 BC) develops him into exemplar of Roman virtues and forefather of Rome's founders, using story to celebrate Augustus' empire. After fall of Troy, Aeneas sets out to find new home, is delayed in Carthage by love for DIDO, but eventually reaches Italy to found Alba Longa.

aeolian harp, zither-like instrument made from strings of varying thickness, all tuned to the same note. Placed out of doors, produces series of rising and falling harmonies when the wind blows over it.

Aeolian Islands, see LIPARI ISLANDS, Italy.

Aeolus, in Greek myth, ruler of the winds which he kept in cave on isl. of

Aeolia. Gave Odysseus winds adverse to him tied in leather bag.

aerial or **antenna**, in electronics, a conductor used to transmit or receive radio waves. In transmitter, signal from circuit causes electrons in antenna to oscillate, producing electromagnetic radiation. This radiation induces oscillations in receiving aerial, which are then amplified.

aerodynamics, branch of fluid mechanics dealing with forces (resistance, pressure, *etc*) exerted by air or other gases in motion. Concerned with principles governing flight of aircraft, wind resistance of vehicles, buildings, bridges. One of the basic tools is the wind tunnel.

aeroembolism or **bends**, bodily disorder caused by formation of nitrogen bubbles in blood and body tissues following too rapid decrease in atmospheric pressure. Characterized by nausea, pain in muscles, paralysis. Most commonly suffered by deep-sea divers who return to surface too quickly.

aeronautics, science of the design, construction and operation of all heavier-than-air aircraft. *See* AERODYNAMICS, AVIATION.

aeroplane [UK] or **airplane** [US], powered heavier-than-air aircraft which derives lift from action of air against (normally) fixed wings and is driven forward by a screw propeller or by JET PROPULSION. Stability is provided by vertical and horizontal tailpieces; control by flaps (ailerons) on trailing edge of wings. Designs range from early biplane (double-winged) types, monoplanes incl. delta-wing shapes, and swing-wing types suitable for super-

sonic flight. For history, *see* AVIATION.

aerosol dispenser, container in which gas under pressure is used to aerate and dispense liquid through a valve in the form of spray or foam. Used for insecticides, paints, polishes, *etc*.

Aeschylus (525-456 BC), Greek tragic poet. Founded classical Greek TRAGEDY, introducing 2nd actor and thereby dramatic dialogue. Only 7 of *c* 90 plays survive, of which masterpiece is trilogy *Oresteia*. Also wrote *The Persians*, *Seven against Thebes*.

Aesculaplus, *see* ASCLEPIUS.

Aesir, in Nordic myth, the gods associated with Odin. Fought but later allied themselves with VANIR, preceeding gods. Lived in ASGARD.

Aesop (6th cent. BC), semi-legendary fabulist. Body of native Greek fable ascribed to him. Moral conveyed through stories of animals, *eg The Tortoise and the Hare*. Said to have been freed slave.

aesthetic movement, British artistic movement of 1870s and 1880s, noted for its exaggerated emphasis on artistic sensibility ('art for art's sake'). Influenced by Pre-Raphaelitism, Japanese art, Pater's writing, it sought to improve dress design, book illustration, interior decoration, *etc*.

aesthetics, branch of philosophy concerned with nature of art. Plato contended that beauty lay in object itself; Epicurus that it lay in eye of beholder.

Aethelbert, *see* ETHELBERT.

Aethelred the Unready, *see* ETHELRED THE UNREADY.

Aetolia, region of WC Greece, N of

Gulf of Patras. Part of admin. dist. of Aetolia and Acarnania, cap. Missolonghi. Mainly mountainous. Formed Aetolian League 4th cent. BC against Achaea, Macedonia; defeated by Rome 189 BC.

Afars and the Issas, French Territory of the, see DJIBOUTI.

affinity, in law, relationship by marriage which is not a blood relationship. May affect legal or canonical status of marriage, *eg* person cannot marry stepchild legally; may not marry deceased spouse's sibling in RC church.

Afghan hound, breed of large hunting dog. Long narrow head, prominent hip bones, silky thick hair. Stands *c* 68 cm/27 in. at shoulder.

Afghanistan, republic of SC Asia. Area 647,500 sq km (250,000 sq mi); pop. 18,796,000; cap. Kabul. Language: Afghan. Religion: Islam. Mainly mountainous, dominated by Hindu Kush; agric., stock rearing (karakul) in river valleys and plains. Dry continental climate, cold in winter, hot in summer. Modern Afghanistan estab. in 18th cent; kingdom created 1926. Republic proclaimed after military coup (1973).

Africa, second largest continent of the world. Area *c* 30,262,000 sq km (11,684,000 sq mi); pop. *c* 352,000,000. Bounded by Mediterranean (N), Red Sea (NE), Indian Ocean (SE, S), Atlantic (W); incl. Madagascar, Cape Verde, Ascension, St Helena isls. Largely ancient plateau; Great Rift Valley in E; mountain ranges incl. Atlas, Ethiopian Highlands, Ruwenzori, Drakensberg; highest point Mt. Kilimanjaro (5892 m/19,340 ft). Main rivers Congo, Limpopo, Niger, Nile, Zambezi; main lakes Albert, Chad, Nyasa, Victoria. Has vast inland deserts, incl. Sahara, Libyan, Kalahari; extensive tropical savannah; jungle, rain forests along equator. Widespread subsistence agric., export crops incl. cocoa, groundnuts, cotton, hardwoods. Mineral resources incl. gold, diamonds, copper, petroleum, iron ore. Earliest prehist. man may have lived in E Africa; advanced civilization developed in Egypt before 3000 BC. N coast colonized by Romans after fall of Carthage (146 BC); Arabs introduced Islam from 7th cent. European exploration began 15th cent., led to extensive colonization in 19th cent. by UK, France, Germany, Italy, Belgium; most colonies became independent in mid-20th cent.

Afrikaans, language of West Germanic group of Indo-European family. Developed from Dutch of 17th cent. Boer settlers in S Africa. Contains many Hottentot, Bantu, English loan-words.

Afro-Asiatic, major Near East and N African language family. Formerly known as Hamito-Semitic, but term abandoned as it misleadingly implied non-Semitic languages were as closely interrelated as Semitic. Incl. Berber, Chad, Cushitic, Egyptian in non-Semitic group, divides Semitic into NW and SW branches.

Agadir, town of SW Morocco, on Atlantic Ocean. Pop. 45,000. Port for fertile agric. dist., exports fruit, vegetables; fishing. Visit by German gunboat *Panther* (1911) caused diplomatic crisis with France. Devastated by earthquake (1960).

Aga Khan III, real name Aga Sultan Sir Mahomed Shah (1877-1957), Indian leader. Hereditary head of Ismaili Moslem sect, founded All-India Moslem League (1906). Member of wealthy family, renowned for extravagant life style.

Agamemnon, legendary leader of Greek forces in Trojan War; king of Mycenae. On his return from Troy, was murdered by his wife, Clytemnestra, and her lover, Aegisthus.

agaric, any fungus of Agaricaceae family, esp. of genus *Agaricus*. Blade-shaped gills on underside of the cap. Incl. common edible field mushroom, *A. campestris*.

agate, hard, semi-precious gemstone. Chalcedonic variety of silica, formed mainly of fine-grained quartz. Has bands of 2 or more colours. Major sources in US, Brazil, Mexico, India.

agave, genus of plants native to tropical America and SW US of family Amaryllidaceae. Spirituous liquor (mescal) distilled from agave sap. Some cultivated for their fibre, *eg* sisal.

Agee, James (1909-55), American poet, novelist, film critic. Works incl. *Let Us Now Praise Famous Men* (1941), bitter exposé of Southern poor-white life (with Walker Evans' photographs) and novel, *A Death in the Family* (1957).

aggression, in social psychology, form of behaviour characterized by unprovoked attacks or acts of self-defence. In psychoanalysis, used in special sense by Adler as the manifestation of the 'will to power' over others. In international law, important concept with, as yet, no satisfactory general definition, but used for certain specific acts, *eg* invasion, by one state against another.

Agincourt (mod. *Azincourt*), village of N France. Scene of victory (1415) of Henry V of England over French during Hundred Years War.

Agnew, Spiro Theodore (1918-), American politician. Governor of Maryland (1966-9). Elected vice-president (1968) on Republican ticket with Nixon. Resigned (1973) after corruption charges brought against him; pleaded guilty to tax evasion.

Agnon, Shmuel Yosef, orig. Czaczkes (1888-1970), Israeli writer, b. Galicia. Author of novel trilogy *Bridal Canopy* (1931-5) reflecting E European Jewish life. Shared Nobel Prize for Literature (1966) with Nelly Sachs.

agnosticism, maintenance of position that the human mind cannot know anything beyond material phenomena. Term coined by T.H. Huxley (1869); other agnostics incl. Kant, Comte, Herbert Spencer.

agouti, rabbit-sized rodent, genus *Dasyprocta*, of forests of Central and South America. Tailless, short-haired; destructive of sugar cane.

Agra, city of Uttar Pradesh, NC India, on R. Jumna. Pop. 595,000. Founded 1566, Mogul cap. until 1658; hist. buildings incl. Taj Mahal and Akbar's fort.

Agricola, Gnaius Julius (*c* AD 37-93), Roman general. Elected consul in 77. Became governor in Britain (*c* 78-*c* 85) and extended Roman rule into Scotland.

agriculture, science and art of farming, incl. the cultivation of soil, production of crops and raising of livestock. Use of chemical fertilizers, herbicides and insecticides, fast-ripening and disease-resistant crops with high yields, specialized animal breeding, advanced mechanization leading to large-scale production, have revolutionized modern agriculture.

Agrigento (anc. *Agrigentum*), town of S Sicily, Italy. Pop. 48,000. Formerly called Girgenti. Harbour at Porto Empedocle; sulphur trade. Founded c 580 BC by Greek colonists; taken by Romans 210 BC. Many Greek, Roman remains.

agrimony, plant of genus *Agrimonia* of rose family. Aromatic pinnate leaves with small yellow flowers. Grows wild in N temperate regions and cultivated in herb gardens.

Agrippa, Marcus Vipsanius (c 63-12 BC), Roman general. Adviser of Augustus, helped in defeat (31 BC) of Antony at Actium.

Agulhas, Cape, headland of W Cape Prov., South Africa. Most S point of Africa. Danger to shipping; lighthouse.

Ahab (d. c 853 BC), Israelite king (c 874-c 853 BC). In OT, provoked Hebrew prophet, Elijah, by allowing his wife, Jezebel, to encourage worship of Baal. Politically, consolidated empire; Syrian wars ended with his death in battle.

Ahaggar or **Hoggar Mountains**, highland region of S Algeria, in WC Sahara. Rises to Mt. Tahat (3000 m/9850 ft). Annual rainfall up to 25 cm (10 in); many wadis. Most important oasis town, Tamanrasset.

Ahmedabad, city of Gujarat state, W India. Pop. 1,588,000. Cotton textiles. Cultural and religious cen-

tre; buildings incl. Jama Masjid mosque, Jain temple (1848).

Ahwaz, city of SW Iran, cap. of Khuzistan prov., on R. Karun. Pop. 286,000. Railway jct.; petrochemical indust. An ancient city, revived recently with development of oilfields.

Aidan, St (d. 651), Irish missionary. Estab. monastery on Lindisfarne. Christianized Northumbria under patronage of King Oswald.

Aiken, Conrad Potter (1889-1973), American author. In tradition of Poe, work reflects concern with musicality of poetry, psychological subjects. Also wrote novels.

Ailsa Craig, small granite isl. in Firth of Clyde, W Scotland. Seabird sanctuary.

Aintab, see GAZIANTEP.

Ainu, hairy, European-like aboriginal inhabitants of Japan. Language unrelated to any known linguistic stock. Driven to N islands, fewer than 17,000 remain, supporting themselves by hunting and fishing.

aircraft, any machine designed to travel through the air, whether heavier or lighter than air, incl. AEROPLANE, AIRSHIP, AUTOGYRO, BALLOON, HELICOPTER, glider.

Airdrie, town of Strathclyde region, C Scotland. Pop. 38,000. Engineering, heavy industs.

Airedale, breed of dog, largest of terrier group. Wiry black and tan coat; stands 58 cm/23 in. at shoulder.

air plant, see EPIPHYTE.

airship or **dirigible balloon**, any self-propelled aircraft that is lighter than air and can be steered. Usually a large gas-filled container with attached means of propulsion and steering, and suspended compartment for passengers or freight. German Zeppelin type with rigid gas-carrying hull used for bombing in WWI. After WWI, British and American types used for passenger-carrying, until destruction by fire of several incl. British R101 (1930), German *Hindenburg* (1937). Non-rigid types (blimps) using non-flammable helium rather than hydrogen continue in use.

Aisne, river of N France. Flows c 240 km (150 mi) from Argonne via Soissons to R. Oise near Compiègne. Scene of heavy fighting in WWI.

Aix-en-Provence, town of Provence, SE France. Pop. 94,000. Commercial centre, agric. market. Roman *Aquae Sextiae*, founded 123 BC near thermal springs. Cap. and cultural centre of Provence in Middle Ages. Univ. (1409), town hall, cathedral. Birthplace of *Cézanne*.

Aix-la-Chapelle, *see* AACHEN, West Germany.

Aix-la-Chapelle, Treaty of, settlement (1668) ending French invasion of Spanish Netherlands (War of Devolution). France retained most conquests in Flanders. Also name of treaty (1748) concluding War of AUSTRIAN SUCCESSION (1740-8). Chief result was ceding of Silesia to Prussia. Pragmatic Sanction upheld, confirming Maria Theresa's right to inherit Habsburg possessions from her father Charles VI.

Aix-les-Bains (anc. *Aquae Gratianae*), town of Savoy, SE France, on Lac du Bourget. Pop. 21,000. Spa from Roman times.

Ajaccio, town of W Corsica, France, on Gulf of Ajaccio. Pop. 42,000. Port,

resort, fishing. Birthplace of Napoleon.

Ajanta, village of Maharashtra state, SC India. Buddhist cave temples dating from c 200 BC-AD 700 nearby.

Ajax, legendary Greek hero of Trojan War, second only to Achilles in bravery. Killed himself when beaten by Odysseus in contest for Achilles' armour.

Akbar, orig. Jalal ed-Din Mohammed (1542-1605), Mogul emperor of India (1556-1605). Grandson of BABER. Expanded territ. by conquest of Afghanistan and all N India. Introduced admin. reforms and promoted religious tolerance.

Akhenaton, *see* IKHNATON.

Akron, city of NE Ohio, US, on Little Cuyahoga R.; at highest point of Ohio and Erie Canal. Pop. 275,000. Rubber indust. (major tyre producer); car parts, machinery, chemicals mfg. Founded 1825.

Aksum or **Axum**, ancient town of N Ethiopia. Pop. 10,000. Coffee trade. Cap. of Aksumite empire 1st-8th cent.; religious centre, Ark of the Covenant reputedly brought here by descendant of Solomon.

Alabama, state of SE US. Area 133,667 sq km (51,609 sq mi); pop. 3,444,000; cap. Montgomery; chief city Birmingham. Plateau in N; plain in S (cotton, corn production) stretches to Gulf of Mexico. Drained by Alabama, Tombigbee rivers. Coal mining, quarrying, iron and steel, petroleum industs. Spanish exploration in 16th cent.; French settlement 1702; ceded by French to British 1765. Seat of Confederate govt. 1861-5. Admitted to Union as 22nd state (1819).

Alabama dispute (1871-2), US claim for damages from UK after Civil War losses to Union shipping caused by British-built confederate warships *Florida*, *Alabama*, and *Shenandoah*. Arbitration at Geneva awarded considerable damages to US.

alabaster, fine-grained, translucent variety of gypsum. Light-coloured or white, often streaked. Softer than marble, often used for statues, ornaments. Major sources in Mexico, Italy, France, US.

Alain-Fournier, pseud. of Henri Alban Fournier (1886-1914), French author. Reputation based on novel, nostalgic fantasy *Le Grand Meaulnes* (1913). Killed in WWI.

Alamein, El, village of N Egypt, W of Alexandria. Scene of decisive defeat (1942) of Germans under Rommel by British under Montgomery; prevented Axis occupation of Egypt.

Alamo, *see* SAN ANTONIO.

Alanbrooke, Alan Francis Brooke, 1st Viscount (1883-1963), British general. Commander-in-chief of British Home Forces (1940-1), he was chief of Imperial General Staff (1941-6).

Aland Islands (*Ahvenanmaa*), archipelago of SW Finland, at mouth of Gulf of Bothnia. Area 1505 sq km (581 sq mi); main town Mariehamn. Fishing; barley, flax growing. Incl. c 6000 isls., 80 inhabited. Held by Finland from WWI. Pop. Swedish-speaking.

Alarcón y Mendoza, Juan Ruiz de (c 1581-1639), Spanish dramatist, b. Mexico. Known for comedies of ethics, esp. *The Truth Suspected* (c

1619) adapted by Corneille as *Le Menteur*.

Alaric I (c 370-410), Visigothic king. Served with Visigothic troops of Roman emperor Theodosius I; proclaimed their leader in 395. Invaded and plundered Greece (395-6). Invaded Italy (401, 408); sacked Rome 410.

Alaska, state of US, in NW North America. Area 1,518,776 sq km (586,400 sq mi); pop. 302,000; cap. Juneau; largest town Anchorage. Arctic Ocean in N, Pacific in S. Polar climate in N; tundra region drained by Yukon R.; S volcanic ranges stretch W to Aleutian Isls. Scattered Eskimo pop. Fish, fur, timber, minerals are main resources. Important oil strike in late 1960s. Of strategic importance; has D.E.W. line radar system. Settled by Russians in 18th cent.; bought by US 1867. Gold strikes 1899, 1902. Admitted to Union as 49th state (1959).

Alaska Range, mountain system of SC Alaska, US. Incl. North America's highest peak, Mt. McKinley (6194 m/20,320 ft).

Alba, Fernando, Duque de, *see* ALVA, FERNANDO ALVAREZ DE TOLEDO, DUQUE DE.

Alba Longa, ancient city of C Italy, near Castel Gandolfo. Founded 12th cent. BC, reputed birthplace of Romulus and Remus. Destroyed 7th cent. BC by Rome.

Albania (*Shqipnija*), republic of SE Europe, on Adriatic. Area c 28,500 sq km (11,000 sq mi); pop. 2,416,000; cap. Tirana. Language: Albanian. Religions: Islam, Eastern Orthodox. Mainly mountainous; lower marshy but fertile areas near coast. Cereals, tobacco, olives; slow indust. development Turkish until 1912; Italian occupation in WWII, communist govt. estab. 1946 under Hoxha.

Albany, cap. of New York state, US; on Hudson R. Pop. 116,000. Port and shipping centre; printing and publishing, varied mfg. industs. One of oldest US cities. Dutch settlement estab. 1614; English control 1664; became cap. 1797.

Albany Congress, meeting (1754) of delegates from 7 American colonies at Albany, New York. Benjamin Franklin's Plan of Union, for unifying colonies, later rejected by colonial legislature and Britain. Treaty signed with Iroquois.

albatross, large sea bird of genus *Diomedea,* found in S hemisphere. Long narrow wings, hooked beak; excels in sustained flight. Largest species is wandering albatross, *D. exulans.*

Albee, Edward Franklin (1928-), American playwright. Known for one-act absurdist plays, incl. *The Zoo Story* (1958), and first full length play *Who's Afraid of Virginia Woolf?* (1962).

Albéniz, Isaac (1860-1909), Spanish pianist, composer. One of the 1st Spanish composers to write in a national style, he produced much piano music, incl. suite *Iberia,* songs and operas.

Alberoni, Giulio (1664-1752), Italian churchman. Created chief minister of Spain (1715). Attempted to rescind Treaty of Utrecht and gain control of Austrian possessions in Italy; Spanish claims resisted by QUADRUPLE ALLIANCE. Dismissed in 1719.

Albert I (1875-1934), Belgian king (1909-34). Sponsored resistance to German invasion during WWI. Initiated social reforms in Belgium and Belgian Congo. Killed in climbing accident.

Alberta, Prairie prov. of W Canada. Area 661,188 sq km (255,285 sq mi); pop. 1,627,000; cap. Edmonton; other major city Calgary. Scenic Rocky Mts. in N; mainly forested in N; agric. plains (wheat, cattle) in S. Drained N by Peace, Athabaska rivers. Leading oil, coal producer; large natural gas reserves. Ceded by Hudson's Bay Co. to Canada 1869; became prov. 1905.

Alberti, Leone Battista (1404-72), Italian architect. His *De re aedificatoria,* inspired by Vitruvius, was 1st Renaissance treatise on architecture and influenced Renaissance style. Emphasized use of Classical forms, and scientific methods to obtain perfect proportion.

Albert Nile, *see* BAHR-EL-JEBEL, Sudan.

Albert Nyanza or **Lake Albert,** lake between W Uganda and NE Zaïre. Area 5345 sq km (2064 sq mi); part of Great Rift Valley. Fed by Victoria Nile, Semliki rivers; drained by Albert Nile. Discovered 1864, named after Prince Consort.

Albert [**Francis Charles Augustus Emmanuel**] **of Saxe-Coburg-Gotha, Prince** (1819-61), German prince, consort of Queen Victoria of Britain. Promoted arts and scientific developments, notably Great Exhibition of 1851. Exercised strong influence on foreign policy.

Albigensians, religious group of S France, *fl* 12th-13th cent. Regarded as heretics, adopted Manichaean doctrine of duality of good and evil, held that Jesus lived only in semblance. Supported by Raymond VI of Toulouse; movement killed by Albigensian Crusade proclaimed by Pope Innocent III (1208), and by Inquisition.

albinism, condition in humans, animals and plants, characterized by deficiency of pigmentation. In humans, manifested by white skin, white hair and pink eyes; inherited as a recessive genetic character.

Albinoni, Tommaso (1671-1750), Italian composer, violinist. Wrote over 50 operas and many concertos for solo violin. Work was admired by Bach, who used some of Albinoni's themes.

albumin or **albumen**, in biochemistry, one of group of water-soluble proteins occurring in animal and vegetable fluids and tissues. Found in blood, milk, muscles, egg-white (albumen).

Albuquerque, Alfonso de (1453-1515), Portuguese admiral, administrator. Founded Portuguese empire in East (1503-15), conquering Goa, Malacca, Ceylon. Died at sea after being superseded in office.

Albuquerque, health resort of C New Mexico, US; on Rio Grande. Pop. 244,000; state's largest city. Railway jct.; railway engineering, food processing. Founded 1706. ·

Alcaeus (b. c 620 BC), Greek lyric poet. Prolific and varied writer, greatly influenced Horace among others. Associate of SAPPHO.

Alcamenes (5th cent. BC), Athenian sculptor. Pupil of Phidias, his *Aphrodite of the Gardens* was one of the masterpieces of the ancient world.

Alcatraz, rocky isl. of W California,

US; in San Francisco Bay. Military prison from 1859; federal prison 1933-63, now closed.

alcázar, fortress or palace built by the Moors in Spain. Best known are those in Seville and Toledo.

alchemy, early form of chemistry, with philosophical and magical associations. Came to Europe through Islamic science, which used methods and traditions of Egyptians, Babylonians, and philosophy of Greeks. Based on Aristotelian idea of one 'prime matter' for all substances, sought to change one substance into another. Best known for attempts to make gold from base metals. Developed complex symbolism.

Alcibiades (c 450-404 BC), Athenian statesman. Helped form alliance of Argos, Mantinea and Athens against Sparta; defeated at Mantinea (418). Led Sicilian expedition of 415; accused of sacrilegious mutilation of statues of Hermes in Athens before embarkation, fled to Sparta. Returned to Athens (411), won several battles before naval defeat at Notium (407). Murdered in Phrygia.

Alcock, Sir John William (1892-1919), English aviator. With Sir Arthur Whitten Brown (1886-1948), made 1st Atlantic crossing in an aéroplane (1919).

alcohol, organic compound obtained from HYDROCARBON by replacement of 1 or more hydrogen atoms with hydroxyl (–OH) radicals. Name applies esp. to ETHANOL (ethyl alcohol). Other alcohols incl. METHANOL, GLYCOL, GLYCEROL.

alcoholism, pathological condition caused by excessive consumption of ethyl alcohol. Chronic form leads to vitamin deficiency, gastritis, cirrhosis of liver, brain damage. May be treated by drugs, psychotherapy or by organizations such as Alcoholics Anonymous.

Alcott, Louisa May (1832-88), American author. Semi-autobiog. novels *Little Women* (1868-9), *Little Men* (1871), *Jo's Boys* (1886), describing her unconventional upbringing, are now children's classics.

Aldabra Island, small atoll group in Indian Ocean, NW of Madagascar. Formerly part of British Indian Ocean Territ., now admin. by Seychelles. Noted for rare plants and animals, esp. giant land tortoises.

aldehyde, organic compound of form RCHO where R is an ALKYL or ARYL group. Examples incl. benzaldehyde, C_6H_5CHO, used in perfume and dye mfg., ACETALDEHYDE and FORMALDEHYDE.

alder, deciduous shrub or tree of genus *Alnus* of cool temperate regions. Toothed leaves and conelike fruit. Wood is water resistant; used for pumps, millwheels, bridges, *etc.* Bark yields brownish dye. Species incl. black alder, *A. glutinosa.*

Alderney, northernmost of Channel Islands, UK. Area 8 sq km (3 sq mi). Main town St Anne. Cattle rearing, potato growing.

Aldershot, mun. bor. of Hampshire, S England. Pop. 33,000. Has large military training centre, estab. 1854.

Aldington, Richard (1892-1962), English writer. Member of early group of poets who introduced IMAGISM. Bitterly anti-war novels incl. *The Colonel's Daughter* (1931).

Also wrote lives of T.E. Lawrence and D.H. Lawrence.

Aldridge-Brownhills, town of West Midlands met. county, WC England. Pop. 88,000. Formed from union of 2 towns (1966). Engineering indust.; bricks, tiles mfg.

Aldrin, Edwin, *see* ARMSTRONG, NEIL.

Aldus Manutius (1450-1515), Venetian printer, humanist. Printed works of classical authors, *eg* Aristotle, in inexpensive editions for scholars. Designed a Greek alphabet and introduced italic type (1501). Founded Aldine Press.

Alembert, Jean le Rond d' (1717-83), French mathematician, philosopher. Enunciated D'Alembert's principle (1742), which he used to solve problems in fluid motion. Assisted in writing of Diderot's *Encyclopédie.*

Aleppo (Arab. *Haleb*), city of NW Syria. Pop. 639,000. Trade in wool; produces silk and cotton goods. Once a centre of caravan trade with East, taken by Turks (1517) and held until WWI.

Alessandria, town of Piedmont, NW Italy, on R. Tanaro. Cap. of Alessandria prov. Pop. 105,000. Railway jct., engineering, hat mfg. Founded 11th cent. as stronghold of Lombard League.

Alesund or **Aalesund,** town of W Norway. Pop. 39,000. Major fishing port; whaling, sealing.

Aleutian Islands, chain of c 150 isls. in Bering Sea, between USSR and Alaska, US; extension of Aleutian Range. Pop. c 8000. Incl. Unimak, Unalaska, Andreanof Isls. Mainly mountainous with several volcanoes. Small groups of Russo-Eskimo fishers and fur trappers.

Alexander III, orig. Orlando Bandinelli (d. 1181), Italian churchman, pope (1159-81). Opposed by 3 successive anti-popes, forced to seek refuge in France 1162-5; supported by Lombard League in contest with Frederick Barbarossa, who was defeated at Legnano (1176). Supported Becket against Henry II of England. Summoned Third Lateran Council (1179), which estab. rules for future papal elections.

Alexander VI, orig. Rodrigo Lanzol y Borja (1431-1503), Spanish-Italian churchman, pope (1492-1503). Elected pope by bribery, his papacy was notorious for political intrigue and favouritism shown to his illegitimate children (incl. Cesare and Lucrezia Borgia).

Alexander I (1777-1825), tsar of Russia (1801-25). Succeeded his father, Paul I, at whose murder he prob. connived. Early attempts at domestic reform failed. Joined alliance against Napoleon in 1805; series of defeats resulted in peace with Treaty of Tilsit (1807). Successfully countered Napoleon's invasion of Russia (1812); attended Congress of Vienna (1814-15) to map out political settlement of Europe. Fearing liberalism, promoted Holy Alliance with Austria, Prussia to retain European status quo.

Alexander II (1818-81), tsar of Russia (1855-81). Son of Nicholas I, initiated reform programme that incl. Edict of Emancipation (1861), freeing serfs; failure of changes resulted in increasing terrorism. Adopted expansionist foreign policy in Asia. Assassinated by anarchist.

Alexander III (1845-94), tsar of Russia (1881-94). Son of Alexander II, he took measures, particularly by increasing police powers, to crush liberalism, enforce persecution of Jews and minorities. Advocated peace in foreign policy.

Alexander [III] the Great (356-323 BC), Macedonian king. Son of Philip II of Macedon, succeeded father in 336. After subduing an uprising in Thebes, began conquest of Persian Empire (334). Gained control of most of Asia Minor, defeating Darius III at Issus (333). Occupied Egypt, where he founded Alexandria. Returning to Mesopotamia, destroyed Persian army at Gaugamela on Tigris (331). Pushed on into Bactria and India, reaching Punjab by 326. Army refused to go beyond R. Hyphasis and Alexander returned to Susa (324). Attempted to fuse Greek and Asian cultures by marrying his officers to Asian wives (he married Bactrian princess ROXANA). Died of fever in Babylon.

Alexander I (c 1078-1124), king of Scotland (1107-1124). Son of Malcolm III; succeeded brother Edgar to throne. Crushed Celtic rebellion, continued anglicization policy; built many abbeys eg Scone, Inchcolm. Succeeded by brother David.

Alexander II (1198-1249), king of Scotland (1214-1249). Supported English barons against King John. Invaded England twice, but disputes settled by marriage to Henry III's sister.

Alexander III (1241-86), king of Scotland (1249-86). Victory over Haakon IV of Norway at Largs (1263) led to acquisition of Western Isles and Isle of Man.

Alexander, Harold Rupert Leofric George, Earl Alexander of Tunis (1891-1969), British field marshal. In WWII, directed retreats from Dunkirk (1940) and Burma (1942); led invasion of Italy through Sicily, becoming Allied commander-in-chief of Mediterranean forces. Governor-general of Canada (1946-52).

Alexander, Sir William, *see* STIRLING, WILLIAM ALEXANDER, EARL OF.

Alexander Archipelago, group of c 1000 isls. off SE Alaska, US; part of Alaska Panhandle. Consists of summits of submerged mountain system; densely forested. Pop. mainly Indian.

Alexander Nevski, St (1220-63), Russian national hero. Grand duke of Vladimir-Suzdal, acquired name Nevski after defeating Swedes on the Neva (1240). Victorious over Livonian Knights near L. Peipus (1242).

Alexandra Feodorovna (1872-1918), Russian empress, consort of Nicholas II. Granddaughter of Queen Victoria. Dominated by RASPUTIN, who encouraged royal couple's opposition to reform. Shot with husband and family by Bolsheviks.

Alexandria (*El Iskandarîya*), city of N Egypt, between L. Mareotis and Mediterranean Sea. Pop. 2,032,000. Major port, railway jct., air terminal; exports cotton; cotton industs. Founded 332 BC by Alexander the Great, partly on former Pharos isl. Ancient Jewish, Greek, Arab cultural and educational centre (libraries, univ.); Roman prov. cap. Declined after taken by Arabs (7th cent.); revived 19th cent. when joined to Nile by canal. Remains of ancient city incl. Pompey's Pillar, ruins at Pharos, catacombs.

Alexandrian Codex, Greek manuscript of the Scriptures believed written 5th cent. Presented by patriarch of Constantinople to Charles I of England (1628). Contains Septuagint version of OT. Now in British Museum.

alfalfa or **lucerne,** *Medicago sativa,* European leguminous forage plant. Trifoliate leaves, purple clover-like flowers. Naturalized in most temperate regions and used extensively in US for fodder, pasture and as a cover crop.

Alfieri, Vittorio, Conte (1749-1803), Italian writer. Tragedies show hatred of tyranny, eg *Saul* (1782), *Antigone* (1783). Other works incl. sonnets, political pamphlets, autobiog.

Alfonso [X] the Wise (1221-84), king of Castile and León (1252-84). Son and successor of Ferdinand III. Main ambition to become Holy Roman emperor, failed in election (1257). Took Cádiz from Moors (1262). Patron of learning; systematized legal code with work *Las Siete Partidas.*

Alfonso XIII (1886-1941), king of Spain (1886-1931). Reigned during dictatorship (1923-30) of Primo de Rivera. Estab. of republic under Alcalá forced him into exile.

Alfred the Great (849-99), king of Wessex (871-99). Most of reign spent fighting Danish invaders. Retreat to Somerset (878) gave rise to legend of Alfred and the cakes. Later routed Danes at Ethandun, enabling him to bring in reforms, legal code based on strong centralized monarchy. Created navy. Great interest in culture led to revival of clerical learning, estab. of Old English prose. Translated many Latin works, inspired others. ANGLO-SAXON CHRONICLE begun at his command.

algae, chlorophyll-containing plants of division Thallophyta. Found in fresh and salt water. Range from unicellular forms, usually microscopic, to multicellular forms up to 30 m/100 ft in length. Incl. pond scum, seaweeds.

Algarve, coastal region and prov. of S. Portugal, cap. Faro. Tourism; fruit, fishing. Last Moorish stronghold in Portugal, reconquered 1249.

algebra, branch of mathematics which generalizes operations of ordinary arithmetic by allowing letters or other symbols to stand for unknown quantities. Modern abstract algebra develops axiomatically systems that arise in many branches of mathematics; incl. ring theory and group theory.

Algeciras, town of Andalusia, S Spain, on Algeciras Bay. Pop. 82,000. Port; fishing, tourism. Founded 711 by Moors; new town built 1760. Scene of European powers' conference (1906) on Morocco.

Algeria, republic of N Africa. Area 2,388,000 sq km (922,000 sq mi); pop. 15,772,000; cap. Algiers. Languages: Arabic, French. Religion: Islam. Sahara in S; coastal plain, Atlas Mts. in N. Cereals, dates, wine production; fishing; mineral resources incl. major oil, natural gas fields. Incl. ancient region of Numidia. Arabs introduced Islam in 7th cent.; stronghold of Barbary pirates 16th-18th cent.; occupied by French from 1830. Violent campaign fought by FLN in 1950s, led to independence (1962) after referendum.

Algiers (Arab. *Al-Jezair,* Fr. *Alger*), cap. of Algeria, on Bay of Algiers. Pop. 943,000. Major port, exports wine, fruit; admin., commercial centre, univ. (1879). Founded 10th cent.; base for Barbary pirates 16th-18th cent. Taken by French (1830). Allied N African hq. in WWII. Badly damaged during independence conflict. Has 16th cent. fortress.

Algonkin, *see* ALGONQUIN.

Algonquin or **Algonkin,** North American Indian tribe of Algonquian linguistic stock. Among first tribes to make alliance with French settlers (early 17th cent.). Dispersed by Iroquois, remnants in Québec, Ontario. Little remains of their culture.

algorithm, in mathematics, systematic procedure for solution of a problem in a finite number of steps. Computers may be programmed to use algorithms to solve complicated equations quickly.

Algren, Nelson (1909-), American novelist. Works, *eg Never Come Morning* (1942), *The Man with the Golden Arm* (1949), extract a poetic nihilism from the brutality of Chicago street life.

Alhambra, fortified palace of Moorish rulers of Granada, Spain. Built largely in 14th cent., its interior is richly decorated with geometric ornament and fine honeycomb vaulting.

Ali (c 600-61), 4th caliph (656-61). Married Fatima, daughter of Mohammed. His rule was opposed by Muawiya, who became caliph on abdication of Ali's son, Hasan.

Murdered by fanatics. Shiite-Sunnite division in Islam began after his reign.

Ali, Muhammad, orig. Cassius Marcellus Clay (1942-), American boxer. Famous for his unorthodox style and colourful personality, he won world heavyweight title (1964). Refused to serve in US Armed Forces because of Black Muslim faith; licence to box withdrawn (1967-70). Regained title with defeat of George Foreman (1974). Lost title to Leon Spinks (1978) but regained it same year.

Alicante, city of SE Spain, on Mediterranean Sea, cap. of Alicante prov. Pop. 185,000. Port, exports wine, fruit, tobacco; tourist resort. Castle on hilltop site fortified from Greek times.

Alice Springs, town of SC Northern Territ., Australia, on Todd R. Pop. 11,000. Railway to Adelaide; centre for surrounding cattle raising, mining industs.; tourism; base of Royal Flying Doctor Service. Founded (1889) as Stuart; cap. (1926-31) of former Central Australia.

alien, in law, resident of a country who owes political allegiance to another country. Subject to laws limiting entry to countries, conditions of residence. British Nationality Act (1948) defined as alien anyone unrecognized as British subject in any part of the Commonwealth. May only enter UK by permission of an immigration officer; since 1970, Commonwealth citizens' entry limited by patrial rule. In US, entry subject to scrutiny by Immigration and Naturalization Service. Alien may claim intercession by home country.

alienation, in social sciences, term used to refer to estrangement of part or whole of personality from experience. Used as important concept by Marx for effects of economic production and class system on workers ('alienated labour').

alimentary canal, in mammals, tubular passage from mouth to anus, concerned with intake of food, its digestion and disposal of residual waste products. Incl. pharynx, cesophagus, stomach, intestines, rectum.

alimony, in law, allowance ordered by court to be paid by husband to separated wife. Temporary alimony may be ordered pending divorce, nullity suit, *etc.* After decree, permanent alimony may be ordered usually until remarriage of ex-wife.

aliphatic compounds, organic compounds containing only straight or branched open chains of carbon atoms, as opposed to closed rings of carbon atoms in AROMATIC compounds. Incl. paraffins, olefines, fatty acids.

alkali, soluble hydroxide of a metal, esp. an alkali metal. Term also applies to any strong BASE. Alkalis neutralize acids and turn litmus blue. Used in manufacture of soap, paper, glass.

alkali metals, the univalent metallic elements lithium, sodium, potassium, rubidium and caesium.

alkaloid, any of group of organic bases containing nitrogen, often of plant origin and having medicinal or poisonous effects. Examples are morphine, quinine, caffeine.

alkyl group, in chemistry, univalent hydrocarbon RADICAL of form C_nH_{2n+1}.

Allah, Arabic name for God used by

Moslems and Arabic-speaking Christians.

Allahabad, city of Uttar Pradesh, NC India, near confluence of Jumna and Ganges. Pop. 514,000. Hindu pilgrimage centre.

Allegheny Mountains, W range of Appalachian system, NE US. Extend from N Pennsylvania to Virginia; rise to 1480 m (c 4860 ft) at highest point. Rich coal, iron ore deposits.

allegory, narrative or description in which characters, objects, incidents, form extended metaphor for system of religious, political or social ideas. Characters often treated as universal 'types'. Very strong in medieval Europe, more recent examples range from Bunyan's *Pilgrim's Progress* to Orwell's *Animal Farm*.

Alien, Ethan (1738-89), American Revolutionary leader. Organized Vermont militia, known as Green Mountain Boys; defended region against New York control in boundary dispute. Captured Fort Ticonderoga (1775); seized by British during attempt to invade Canada. Advocated independence for Vermont.

Allen, Bog of, peat bog of EC Irish Republic, between rivers Shannon and Liffey. Peat used to fuel power stations.

Allenby, Edmund Henry Hynman, 1st Viscount Allenby of Megiddo (1861-1936), British field marshal. Commander of British Expeditionary Force (1917-19), invaded Palestine and decisively defeated Turks at Megiddo (1918). High commissioner for Egypt (1919-25).

Allende, Salvador (1909-73), Chilean statesman. Elected president (1970), becoming 1st Marxist head of govt. in South America. Withdrawal of financial credit by West followed agrarian reforms and nationalizing foreign investments. Subversion by CIA and US indust. fuelled domestic discontent. Allende died in military coup.

allergy, hypersensitivity to usually harmless specific substance, *eg* pollen, hair, various foods, or physical conditions (heat and cold). Believed to be caused by antibodies which cause local tissue inflammation by release of histamine while providing little immune protection. Allergic disorders incl. skin rashes, asthma, hay fever.

Alleyn, Edward ('Ned') (1566-1626), English actor-manager. Main rival of BURBAGE. Played in several of Marlowe's plays incl. *Tamburlaine, Doctor Faustus, The Jew of Malta.*

Allier, river of C France. Flows *c* 435 km (270 mi) from Cévennes via fertile Limagne to R. Loire near Nevers.

alligator, large aquatic reptile of crocodile family; 2 species: *Alligator mississippiensis* of S US, and smaller *A. sinensis* of Yangtze valley, China. Leather greatly valued, leading to diminution of species; now protected in US.

allium, genus of bulbous plants of lily family. Strong-smelling leaves; umbellate white, yellow or red flowers. Found in Europe, N Africa, Asia, North America. Species incl. onion, garlic, chives, leek, shallot, all with characteristic odour.

allosaur, extinct carnivorous dinosaur of Jurassic period, genus *Allosaurus.* Over 9.2 m/30 ft long with small forelegs, massive hind legs.

allotropy, property that certain chemical elements have of existing in 2 or more forms, with different crystalline structures and physical properties. Carbon, sulphur and phosphorus exhibit allotropy.

alloy, metallic substance composed of 2 or more metals or of metallic and non-metallic elements. May be a compound, mixture or solid solution. Common alloys are brass (copper, zinc) and steel (iron, carbon).

All Saints' Day, in RC and Anglican churches, feast day (1 Nov.) instituted by Pope Gregory IV in honour of all saints, known and unknown. One of principal feasts in RC calendar.

All Souls' Day, in RC calendar, feast day (2 Nov.) on which church prays for faithful still suffering in purgatory.

allspice, berry of allspice tree, *Pimenta officinalis,* of myrtle family. Yields pungent aromatic spice.

alluvium, sand, silt or gravel transported and deposited by running water. Provides excellent crop-growing conditions on river flood plains or in delta areas, *eg* Nile, Ganges rivers.

Alma-Ata, city of USSR, cap. of Kazakh SSR. Pop. 794,000. Cultural and indust. centre; machinery, textile mfg. Seat of Kazakh Academy of Sciences (1946). Formerly called Verny.

almanac, yearly calendar originally containing astronomical, meteorological and ecclesiastical data, often incl. astrological and prophetic material. Now usually refers to book of useful facts and statistics.

Almería, city of S Spain, on Gulf of Almería, cap. of Almería prov. Pop. 115,000. Port, exports minerals, fruit (esp. grapes). Fl under Moors (8th-15th cent.) as naval base. Medieval castle, cathedral.

almond, *Prunus amygdalus,* tree of warm temperate regions, native to W Asia. Fruit has nut-like edible stone or kernel which yields oil. Sweet almonds used in cooking and confectionery. Bitter almonds used in manufacture of flavouring extracts, cosmetics, medicine.

alpaca, *Lama pacos,* domesticated South American mammal, related to llama. Bred for its fleecy brown **or** black wool.

alphabet, any system of characters used to record a language in which there is (theoretically) a one-to-one relationship between each character and phoneme. Developed by Phoenicians (*c* 1400 BC) possibly from signs derived from Egyptian hieroglyphic writing. Transmitted from NW Semites to Greece (first recorded *c* 8th cent. BC), used in ancient Rome. Forms basis of alphabets in W European and several recently written African and Asian languages. Cyrillic alphabet, also developed from Greek, used in Russian. Hebrew and Arabic alphabets are also still in use.

Alpha Centauri, brightest star of constellation Centaurus, visible in S hemisphere. Has 3 components, incl. Proxima Centauri, nearest star to Earth beyond Sun (4.3 light years away).

alpha particle, positively charged helium nucleus, consisting of 2 neutrons and 2 protons, emitted during spontaneous decay of nucleus of certain radioactive elements, *eg* uranium 238. Relatively low penetrating power.

alpine rose, any of various European and Asiatic alpine RHODODENDRONS.

Alps, mountain system of SC Europe. Extend from Franco-Italian border through Switzerland, Germany, Austria to Yugoslavia. Many glaciers, valleys, snow-capped peaks. C Alps incl. Mont Blanc (highest), Monte Rosa, Matterhorn, Jungfrau. Crossed by many passes incl. Brenner, Great St Bernard, Mont Cenis, Simplon. Dairying, timber, h.e.p., tourism esp. winter sports.

Alsace (Ger. *Elsass*), region of NE France, between Vosges Mts. and R. Rhine. Main towns Colmar, Mulhouse, Strasbourg. Agric. in Rhine plain, vineyards on Vosges foothills, potash mining. Long disputed by France and Germany. Annexed by France in 17th cent.; incorporated, with part of Lorraine, into Germany (1871) as imperial territ. of Alsace-Lorraine. Restored to France after WWI.

alsatian or German shepherd, sheepdog of wolf-like appearance, used in police work and as guide dog for blind. Stands *c* 63 cm/25 in. at shoulder.

Altai, mountain system of USSR (S Siberia), W Mongolia and N China. Reaches 4506 m (14,783 ft) at Belukha. Rich mineral deposits incl. lead, zinc, silver.

Altaic, major European and Asian family of languages. Divided into W and E groups, incl. Turkic, Mongolian and Manchu languages.

Altamira, cave site of Santander prov., N Spain. Cave contains drawings of animals made in late Magdalenian period; discovered 1879.

Altdorfer, Albrecht (*c* 1480-1538), German painter. First European to stress romantic use of landscape. Early works show insignificant figures set in mysterious landscapes; later works incl. pure landscapes.

alternating current (AC), electric current that periodically reverses its direction of flow, changing continuously to reach a maximum in one direction, then in the other. Used extensively because of ease of changing voltage; transmitted at high voltages to minimize energy loss.

alternation of generations, in biology, occurrence of generations of an organism in alternate order, one of which reproduces sexually, the other asexually. Phenomenon exhibited by many coelenterates, which alternate between sedentary asexual polyps and free-swimming sexual medusae (jellyfish).

Althing, legislature of Iceland. Oldest European assembly, convened 930. Dissolved 1800-74 during period of direct rule by Denmark.

altimeter, device used to measure altitude. Types in use incl. aneroid barometer. Absolute altimeter, used by aircraft, works by reflecting radio signals from Earth's surface.

Altman, Robert (1922-), American film director. Achieved international success with *M.A.S.H.* (1970), other films incl. *Nashville* (1976).

alto, in singing, term used for highest male voice; also lowest female voice. In instruments of similar range, usually pitched between soprano and tenor.

alum, hydrated double sulphate of potassium and aluminium, used as mordant in dyeing and fireproofing agent.

alumina or **aluminium oxide** (Al_2O_3), chemical compound occurring naturally in clay, and as main component of bauxite. Also found in almost pure form as corundum.

aluminium or **aluminum** (Al), silvery metallic element; at. no. 13, at. wt. 26.98. Ductile and malleable; good conductor of heat and electricity. Obtained commercially by electrolysis of bauxite and cryolite. Used pure or alloyed where lightness is required, eg in aircraft or cooking utensils.

Alva, Fernando Alvarez de Toledo, Duque de (1508-82), Spanish general, administrator. Commanded armies of Charles V, Philip II. As regent (1567-73) in Netherlands for Philip II, instituted 'Court of Blood' (Alva boasted of c 18,000 executed) to crush rebellion against Spanish tyranny. Conquered Portugal (1580).

alyssum, genus of plants of Cruciferae or mustard family. Greyish leaves, small yellow or white flowers. Native to Eurasia.

AM (amplitude modulation), *see* MODULATION.

Amagasaki, port of Japan, on Osaka Bay, Honshu isl. Pop. 553,000. Indust. centre; iron and steel works, chemical and textile mfg.

amalgam, alloy containing mercury. Gold and silver amalgams occur naturally; tin, copper and other amalgams are man-made. Used in dentistry, mirror mfg.

amanita, genus of widely distributed fungi. Most species have russet cap with white markings and are poisonous. Incl. *Amanita muscaria* or fly agaric.

amaranth, any of genus *Amaranthus* of plants of worldwide distribution. Garden species cultivated for colourful foliage and showy flowers, eg Joseph's coat, love-lies-bleeding. Some species are weeds, eg pigweed, tumbleweed.

Amarna, Tel-el-, *see* TEL-EL-AMARNA.

amaryllis, genus of bulbous plants native to S Africa. Several white, purple or pink flowers on single stem. Species incl. belladonna lily, *Amaryllis belladonna.*

Amaterasu, sun goddess in SHINTO pantheon. She shut herself in the cave of heaven because of her brother's cruelty. Grandmother of Jimmu Tenno, mythical first ruler of Japan.

Amati, family of Italian violin makers in Cremona in 16th and 17th cents. Founded by **Andrea Amati** (c 1505-c 1575), who estab. basic design used by his descendants. Most famous member was **Niccolò Amati** (1596-1684), who taught Antonio Stradivari and Andrea Guarneri.

Amazon, river of South America; main stream of largest river system in world. Formed in N Peru by confluence of Marañón, Ucayali; flows E 6280 km (c 3900 mi) across Brazil to the Atlantic. Main tributaries incl. Negro in N, Tocantins, Xingu, Tapajos in C Brazil. Tropical jungle along banks; major source of rubber during late 19th cent.; inhabited by primitive Indian tribes. Recent economic development in region.

Amazons, in Greek legend, nation of female warriors living around Euxine Sea (Black Sea). As 9th labour Heracles was required to obtain girdle of Amazon queen, Hippolyte. She was captured by Theseus, and bore him Hippolytus.

amber, yellow, often transparent fossil resin, derived from now extinct conifers. In highly polished form, used since prehist. times for beads, amulets, *etc.* Found mainly in Tertiary estuarine deposits on Baltic coast.

ambergris, waxy substance secreted from intestine of sperm whale, found floating in tropical seas. Physiological significance undecided. Used as perfume fixative.

Ambler, Eric (1909-), English thriller writer. Set new standard in genre, with anti-heroes, documentary settings. Works incl. *The Mask of Dimitrios* (1939), *Journey into Fear* (1940).

Ambleside, tourist resort of Cumbria, NW England. Pop. 2000. In Lake Dist. at head of L. Windermere. Nearby · is Grasmere, home of Wordsworth.

Ambrose, St (*c* 340-97), Roman churchman. Elected bishop of Milan (374), denounced Arianism at Synod of Aquileia (381). Wrote doctrinal instructions and reformed ritual; encouraged use of hymns in worship (Ambrosian chant).

ambrosia and nectar, in Greek myth, the food and drink of the gods, giving immortality and eternal youth.

Amenhotep III (*fl* 14th cent. BC), Egyptian pharaoh (*c* 1410-1372 BC). Ruled during an age of great splendour, his empire at peace. Built great monuments at Thebes, incl. temples at Luxor and Karnak. Succeeded by IKHNATON.

America, see NORTH AMERICA, CENTRAL AMERICA, SOUTH AMERICA.

American Federation of Labor and Congress of Industrial Organizations (AFL-CIO), federation of auton. labour unions in US. Estab. by merger (1955) of American Federation of Labor (AFL) and Congress of Industrial Organizations (CIO). AFL formed (1881) as loose-knit association of craft unions, against radicalism of KNIGHTS OF LABOR. This tradition continued until 1935 split, when dissidents set up Congress of Industrial Organizations (CIO), led by J.L. LEWIS. Merger (1955) created AFL-CIO.

American football, eleven-a-side team game played with oval leather ball. Developed from English rugby in 1870s into major college sport. Professional form was organized into leagues in 1920 (National Football League, comprising 28 teams from large cities, dates from 1922).

American Indians, pre-European inhabitants of the Americas. South American cultures incl. MAYA, TOLTEC, AZTEC, INCA, Chibcha, some of which reached high cultural level; all fell during Spanish conquest. North American Indian tribes driven back by westward expansion into Indian Territories. Some 400,000 remain in US and Canada. Extremely diverse culture, but divides loosely into NW coast, Plains, Plateau, E woodlands, Northern, and SW groups. Most tribes were relatively settled farmers, food gatherers or hunters but the advent of the horse in late 17th cent. revolutionized Plains culture; led to nomadic hunting of buffalo from horseback with bow and arrow, and the last serious resistance to white hegemony. Although largely assimilated into Western culture, 20th cent. has seen movement towards preserving Indian culture throughout Americas.

American Revolution (1775-83), uprising resulting in independence from Britain of Thirteen Colonies of North America. By mid-18th cent., colonists had begun demands for limited self-govt.; Stamp Act (1765) caused colonial opposition to 'taxation without representation'. Further resentment after Townshend Acts (1767), levying duty on British manufactured goods, resulted in Boston Massacre (1770) and BOSTON TEA PARTY (1773). Parliament subsequently passed Intolerable Acts (1774); representatives of colonies listed grievances at Continental Congress of 1774. Conflict began (April, 1775) at Lexington. Washington appointed to lead Continental Army; Declaration of Independence adopted July, 1776. Badly prepared volunteer forces of colonists defeated in Québec campaign (1775-6); fighting inconclusive until British defeat (Oct. 1777) at Saratoga, followed by hard winter for colonial army at Valley Forge. French gave rebels crucial aid and British were pushed N from Carolinas (1780-1), leading to Cornwallis' surrender (Oct. 1781)

and conclusion of hostilities. Treaty of Paris (1783) formally recognized independence of US. Conflict also known as American War of Independence.

American Samoa, see SAMOA.

americium (Am), man-made radioactive element, at. no. 95, mass no. of most stable isotope 243. Silvery-white metal, discovered (1944) by bombarding plutonium with neutrons.

Amerindians, term applied to AMERICAN INDIANS, particularly those of South America.

amethyst, semi-precious gemstone, a variety of quartz. Violet or purple in colour. Major sources in Brazil, Uruguay, Sri Lanka, Siberia, US.

Amharic, official language of Ethiopia, belonging to SW Semitic branch of Afro-Asiatic family.

Amherst, Jeffrey Amherst, Baron (1717-97), British army officer. Captured Louisbourg (1758), Montréal (1760) from French during Seven Years War in North America.

amides, organic compounds obtained by replacing hydrogen atoms of ammonia, NH_3, by organic acid radicals, eg acetamide, CH_3CONH_2.

Amiens, city of N France, on R. Somme, cap. of Somme dept. Pop. 118,000. Agric. market; textile centre from 16th cent. Cap. of Picardy until 1790. Scene of Treaty of Amiens (1802) ending French Revolutionary Wars. Cathedral (13th cent.).

Amiens, Treaty of (1802), settlement between Britain, France, Spain and Batavian Republic in which Britain returned most of its gains from French Revolutionary Wars; France agreed to evacuate Naples.

Amin, Idi (1925-), Ugandan political leader. Seized power in 1971 military coup. Nationalized UK-owned firms. Expelled Uganda Asians and ruthlessly suppressed opponents. Head of Organization of African Unity (1975). Deposed 1979.

amines, compounds obtained by replacing hydrogen atoms of ammonia, NH₃ by organic radicals. Divided into primary, secondary or tertiary amines according to whether 1, 2 or 3 hydrogen atoms are replaced.

amino acids, organic compounds in which carboxyl (COOH) and amino (NH₂) groups are linked to central carbon atom. Essential to living tissue as they link to form proteins; 22 occur in animal proteins. In man, 8 cannot be synthesized and must be incl. in diet.

Amirante Islands, dependency of the Seychelles in Indian Ocean. Pop. *c* 100. Exports copra.

Amis, Kingsley (1922-), English writer. One of ANGRY YOUNG MEN. Works incl. satirical novel *Lucky Jim* (1954) attacking academic establishment.

Amman, cap. of Jordan. Pop. 570,000. Commercial, indust. centre. Textile mfg.; noted marble quarries nearby. As Rabbath Ammon, cap. of Ammonites; named Philadelphia in 3rd cent. BC. Great pop. increase after Israeli wars (1949).

ammeter, instrument used for measuring strength of electric current in ampères. DC ammeter contains pivoted coil, which carries current to be measured, and permanent magnet.

ammonia (NH₃), pungent-smelling highly soluble gas. Forms weak base ammonium hydroxide NH₄OH when dissolved in water. Produced from atmospheric nitrogen by Haber process. Used in manufacture of explosives and fertilizers and as refrigerant.

ammoniac or gum ammoniac, gum resin prepared from milky exudation from stem of plant, *Dorema ammoniacum,* native to Iran, India, Siberia. Used in perfumes, manufacture of porcelain cements and in medicine as an expectorant.

ammonite, coiled fossil mollusc of class Cephalopoda. Has elaborately chambered shell. Common in Mesozoic era, extinct by end of Cretaceous period.

amnesia, temporary or prolonged loss of memory. Suppression of memory may be caused by neurosis; permanent loss may result from head injuries.

amoeba, microscopic one-celled animal of class Rhizopoda. Consists of naked mass of protoplasm. Moves and feeds in water by action of pseudopodia (false feet); reproduces by fission. Species incl. *Entamoeba histolytica,* cause of amoebic dysentery.

Amon, in ancient Egyptian pantheon, creator of universe. Represented as ram or man with ram's head and horns. Had oracle (Jupiter Amon) at Siwa in Libyan desert. Identified with Greek Zeus and Roman Jupiter.

Amos, prophetic book of OT, written by shepherd Amos *c* 750 BC. Attacks hypocritical worship, social injustice. Made up of 3 parts, God's judgment on Gentiles and Israel; sermons on fate of Israel; visions of destruction. Final **promise** of redemption is prob. by later writer.

Ampère, André Marie (1755-1836), French physicist. Extended Oersted's findings on interaction of electricity and magnetism; showed that electric currents exert forces on one another. Formulated Ampère's law on strength of magnetic field induced by current flowing in conductor.

ampere or **amp**, SI unit of electric current; defined as current in pair of infinitely long, infinitely thin, parallel wires that produces force of 2×10^{-7} newtons per metre of length.

amphetamine, colourless liquid, used in form of sulphate to stimulate central nervous system. Used to overcome depression, aid slimming by suppression of appetite. Addiction can cause heart damage and mental disturbance.

Amphibia (amphibians), class of cold-blooded vertebrates comprising frogs, salamanders and legless, worm-like caecilians. Larva is aquatic, breathing through gills; undergoes rapid metamorphosis to terrestrial lung-breathing adult.

amphitheatre, circular or oval theatre with an open space surrounded by rising rows of seats. Earliest dates from 1st cent. BC; used by Romans for staging gladiatorial contests. Examples incl. ruined Colosseum in Rome and those in Nîmes and Arles, France.

Amphitrite, in Greek myth, one of the NEREIDS. Wife of Poseidon, by whom she was mother of Triton.

amplitude, in physics, the maximum departure from equilibrium of an oscillatory phenomenon, eg alternating current or swinging pendulum.

Amritsar, city of Punjab state, N India. Pop. 433,000. Carpet mfg.; trade in cotton, skins. Sikh religious centre, site of Golden Temple. Scene of 1919 nationalist massacre by British.

Amsterdam, cap. of Netherlands, at confluence of Ij and Amstel rivers. Pop. 808,000. Major port, indust. centre (shipbuilding, chemicals, diamond cutting and polishing). Built on piles, with radial and concentric canal system, many bridges. Canal links to North Sea, Rhine delta. Chartered c 1300, Hanseatic trade centre; at cultural, commercial height in 17th cent. Taken by French 1795; cap. from 1815 (admin. sits at The Hague). German occupation in WWII. Churches (13th, 15th cent.), Rijksmuseum (1808, with priceless Dutch, Flemish paintings), van Gogh museum, univs. (1632, 1882). Airport at Schiphol.

Amu Darya (anc. *Oxus*), river of C Asia. Length c 2500 km (1550 mi). Rises in Pamir Mts., flows W along Afghanistan-USSR border and NW through Turkmen SSR and Uzbek SSR to enter Aral Sea by long delta.

amulet, object worn as charm to ward off evil influences, sometimes hung on doors or walls. Believed to be source of impersonal power, inherent in object rather than that of deity working through object. Common to many cultures; may be engraved with symbols or magic formulae.

Amundsen, Roald (1872-1928), Norwegian explorer. First to reach South Pole (1911), 35 days ahead of R.F. Scott. First to navigate Northwest Passage (1903-6). Flew over North Pole (1926) with Umberto Nobile, whom he tried to rescue from polar air crash (1928); died in search.

Amundsen Sea, part of S Pacific Ocean, E of Ross Sea, extending into Ellsworth Highlands, Antarctica.

Amur (Heilung-kiang), river of NE Asia. Length c 2900 km (1800 mi). Flows SE forming much of Soviet-Chinese (Manchuria) border before turning NE to Tartar Str. Navigable, ice-free May-Oct.

amylase, enzyme which helps convert starch into sugar. Found in saliva, pancreatic juices and in some plants.

Anabaptists, originally pejorative name for various Protestant sects which deny validity of infant baptism. Applied historically to German followers of Thomas Münzer (d. 1525), who preached separation of church and state, and were persecuted as heretics.

anaconda, Eunectes murinus, semi-aquatic constrictor snake of boa family from tropical South America. Olive green with black spots; reaches lengths of 7.5 m/25 ft.

Anacreon (c 570-c 485 BC), Greek lyric poet. Poems mostly celebrate love and wine.

anaemia, disease resulting from reduction in number, or in haemoglobin content, of red blood cells. Caused by loss of blood by bleeding, excessive destruction of red cells, iron deficiency, etc. Characterized by paleness, weakness, breathlessness.

anaesthetics, drugs which produce loss of sensation, either in restricted area (local anaesthetic) or whole body (general anaesthetic). General anaesthetics in use incl. ether, cyclopropane, sodium pentothal, nitrous oxide. Local anaesthetic acts on peripheral nerve endings in region of application; drugs used incl. procaine and novocaine. Early experimenters in use of anaesthetics incl. C.W. Long (ether, 1842) and J.Y. Simpson (chloroform, 1847).

analgesic, drug used to relieve pain. Those used incl. derivatives of salicylic acid (eg aspirin), phenacetin, phenylbutazone.

analog computer, see COMPUTER.

analysis, in chemistry, decomposition of a substance into its elements or constituent parts to determine either their nature (qualitative analysis) or proportion (quantitive analysis).

analytical or **coordinate geometry**, branch of geometry in which position is defined by reference to coordinate axes and curves described by algebraic equations.

anarchism, in politics, theory that all forms of authority interfere with individual freedom and that state should be replaced by freely-associating communities. Early principles outlined by Zeno of Citium; modern anarchist theories developed by WILLIAM GODWIN, PROUDHON and BAKUNIN, who introduced terrorism as strategic means of resisting organized govt. Theories influenced syndicalists, esp. in Spanish Civil War.

Anastasia (b. 1901), Russian princess. Daughter of Nicholas II, believed assassinated with rest of royal family (1918) after Russian Revolution. Several women, notably Anna Anderson, have since claimed her identity without conclusive proof.

Anatolia, see ASIA MINOR.

anatomy, branch of science concerned with structure of plants and animals, and with their dissection. Pioneers in its study incl. Galen, whose findings dominated medical thought until 16th cent., and Vesalius, who founded modern descriptive anatomy.

Anaxagoras (c 500–c 428 BC), Greek philosopher. Developed dualistic theory of universe composed of particles arranged by an omnipresent intelligence (*nous*). Also studied astronomy, correctly explaining eclipses.

Anaximander (c 611–547 BC), Greek philosopher. Held that world consists of primary matter (*apeiron*) which is eternal and indestructible. Invented sundial, map. Known as 1st Greek author to write in prose.

ancestor worship, religious practices based on belief that souls of the dead continue to be involved with their living descendants. Occurs in many societies, incl. ancient Greeks and Romans.

Anchises, in Greek myth, member of royal house of Troy, father of Aeneas, by Aphrodite. Carried from burning remains of Troy by Aeneas, whom he accompanied on his voyages.

Anchorage, town of SC Alaska, US; at head of Cook Inlet. Pop. 48,000; state's largest, most important town. Transport jct.; fishing, oil, mining centre. Military bases estab. in WWII. Badly damaged by earthquake (1964).

anchovy, small herring-like marine fish of Engraulidae family. *Engraulis encrasicholus*, found in Mediterranean, used as food.

Ancona, city of the Marches, EC Italy, on the Adriatic Sea; cap. of Ancona prov. Pop. 113,000. Port, shipbuilding, sugar refining. Founded 4th cent. BC by Greeks from Syracuse; fl under Romans (triumphal arch erected AD 115 to Trajan). Romanesque cathedral.

Andalusia (*Andalucía*), region and former prov. of S Spain. Incl. Sierra Morena (N), Guadalquivir basin (C), Sierra Nevada (S). Irrigated agric., fruit growing, bull breeding; rich mineral resources, fishing, tourism. Widespread poverty among rural pop. Settled 11th cent. BC by Phoenicians; fl under Moorish rule (8th–15th cent.) esp. at Córdoba, Granada, Seville.

Andaman and Nicobar Islands, union territ. of India, in SE Bay of Bengal. Area: of Andaman Isls. 6500 sq km (2500 sq mi); Nicobar Isls. 1830 sq km (700 sq mi). Pop. 115,000; cap. Port Blair (pop. 26,000). Timber, copra exports.

Andersen, Hans Christian (1805–75), Danish author. His 168 fairy tales (pub. 1835–72), incl. 'The Ugly Duckling', 'The Emperor's New Clothes', 'The Red Shoes', children's classics combining symbolic significance with humour and whimsy. Also wrote plays, poetry, novel *Improvisatoren* (1835).

Anderson, Dame Judith (1898–), Australian actress, appeared mainly in US. Roles incl. Lavinia in O'Neill's *Mourning Becomes Electra*, Gertrude to Gielgud's *Hamlet*, Medea.

Anderson, Lindsay (1923–), British film director. Films, often marked by social or political concerns interwoven with fantasy, incl. *This Sporting Life* (1963), *If* (1968), *O Lucky Man* (1972).

Anderson, Maxwell (1888-1959), American dramatist. Works incl. blank verse *Winterset* (1935), *High Tor* (1936), *Lost in the Stars* (1950), the last with music by Weill and based on Alan Paton's *Cry the Beloved Country*.

Anderson, Sherwood (1876-1941), American author. Themes show pathos of individuals in industrial society reflected in related short stories of *Winesburg, Ohio* (1919) and novels *Poor White* (1920), *Dark Laughter* (1925).

Andes, major mountain system of South America, extending N-S 8000 km (5000 mi) from Venezuela to Cape Horn. Rises to highest point at Aconcagua (6960 m/22,835 ft) on Chile-Argentina border. Forms volcanic plateau in Bolivia, narrow ranges in Ecuador, Colombia. Peruvian Andes was centre of ancient Inca civilizations. Indian pop. in high basins; important deposits of copper, silver, tin. Region subject to earthquakes.

Andhra Pradesh, state of SE India. Area 275,000 sq km (106,000 sq mi); pop. 43,400,000; cap. Hyderabad. Largely plains; mountains (Eastern Ghats) in E. Rice, sugar cane grown. Formed in 1956 to unite Telugu-speaking peoples of Madras and Hyderabad states.

Andorra, republic of SW Europe, in E Pyrenees. Area 495 sq km (191 sq mi); pop. 19,000; cap. Andorra la Vella. Language: Catalan. Religion: RC. Under nominal Franco-Spanish suzerainty. Many high peaks, up to *c*

3050 m (10,000 ft). Pasture (cattle, sheep), tobacco, fruit; tourism.

Andrassy, Julius, Count (1823-90), Hungarian statesman. Supported KOSSUTH during Revolution of 1848-9, exiled until 1850. Helped form AUSTRO-HUNGARIAN MONARCHY (1867); premier of Hungary (1867-71), encouraged Magyar supremacy over Slavs.

Andrew, St (*fl* 1st cent. AD), fisherman, one of Twelve Disciples of Jesus. Traditionally, missionary to Gentiles, crucified on X-shaped cross. Patron saint of Russia, Scotland.

Andrewes, Lancelot (1555-1626), English churchman, scholar. Bishop of Chichester (1605), Ely (1609), Winchester (1619). Opposed Puritanism; helped translate Authorized (King James) Version of Bible. Noted for both learning and piety.

androgen, name given to any male sex hormone which gives rise to secondary sexual characteristics. Natural androgens are steroids produced in testes and adrenal cortex.

Andromache, in Greek myth, wife of Hector of Troy and mother of Astyanax. At fall of Troy Greeks killed her child and she became slave of Neoptolemus, son of Achilles. Later married Helenus, brother of Hector.

Andromeda, in Greek myth, daughter of Cepheus by Cassiopeia. Rescued from sea monster by Perseus, who subsequently married her. Andromeda, Cassiopeia, Cepheus were placed among the stars at their death.

Andromeda Galaxy, spiral galaxy in constellation Andromeda, *c* 2 million light years away; visible to naked eye as dim patch of light.

Andros, Aegean isl. of Greece, northernmost of Cyclades. Area 375 sq km (145 sq mi); main town Andros. Famous for wines from ancient times.

Aneirin (fl c AD 600), Welsh poet. Long heroic poem *Y Gododdin* is contained in *Llyfr Aneirin* ('Book of Aneirin'), 13th cent. manuscript.

anemone, genus of plants of buttercup family, widely distributed in temperate and subarctic regions. Species incl. *Anemone patens,* blue flower of North American prairies, *A. quinquefolia,* spring wild flower with slender stem and delicate whitish blossoms. Cultivated garden varieties have showy variously coloured flowers, eg European pasqueflower *A. pulsatilla.*

aneroid barometer, instrument for measuring atmospheric pressure. Consists of partially evacuated metal container, thin lid displaced by changes in atmospheric pressure, thus causing a pointer to move.

aneurism or **aneurysm,** abnormal bulge of weakened wall of an artery; caused by syphilis, atheroma, injury, high blood pressure. Bulge may burst, resulting in serious internal bleeding; treatment by surgery, eg insertion of tube of synthetic material.

Angarsk, city of USSR, SC Siberian RSFSR; on R. Angara. Pop. 219,000. Produces petrochemicals.

angel (Gk.,=messenger), in theology, immortal being. According to traditions of Judaism, Christianity and Islam, intermediate between God and man. Classified by Dionysius the Areopagite into 3 choirs: seraphim, cherubim, thrones; dominions, virtues, powers; principalities, archangels, angels. Angels of hell are followers of Satan and tempt mankind.

Angel Falls, waterfall of SE Venezuela, on Caroni tributary. Prob. highest waterfall in world. Height 979 m (3212 ft).

angelfish, brightly-coloured fish of Chaetodontidae family. Spiny headed, with laterally-compressed body; inhabits tropical reefs.

angelica or **archangel,** plant of genus *Angelica,* esp. *A. archangelica.* Cultivated in Europe for aromatic odour and root stalks which are candied and eaten, and for roots and seeds yielding oil used in perfume and liqueurs.

Angelico, Fra, orig. Guido di Pietro (1387-1455), Italian painter, Dominican friar. Work, intended to serve religion, is characterized by simple direct style, and purity of line and colour. Painted frescoes *c* 1440 in convent of San Marco, Florence, and in chapel of Pope Nicholas V in Vatican.

Angers (anc. *Juliomagus*), city of W France, on R. Maine, cap. of Maine-et-Loire dept. Pop. 129,000. Wine, glass, textiles; largest French slate quarries nearby. Hist. cap. of Anjou from 9th cent. Castle, cathedral (both 13th cent.).

Angevin, noble family of medieval Europe. Descended from Fulk the Red, 1st count of Anjou, France, whence the name. Comprised 2 main lines: 1) rulers of parts of France (from 9th cent.), Jerusalem (1131-86), PLANTAGENET kings of England (from 1154); 2) branch of CAPETIANS, incl. rulers of parts of France (from

1246), kings of Naples and Sicily (from 1266), Hungary (from 1308), Poland (from 1370).

angina pectoris, disease characterized by sudden attacks of chest pain extending down left arm. Caused by obstruction of coronary arteries, resulting in lack of oxygen to heart muscles.

angiosperm, any plant of class Angiospermae, incl. all the flowering plants, characterized by having the seeds enclosed in an ovary. Opposed to GYMNOSPERM.

Angkor, ruins in W Cambodia. Incl. Angkor Thom, ancient cap. of Indo-Chinese Khmer empire, and Angkor Wat temple. Discovered by French in 1861.

anglerfish, any of Lophiidae family of bottom-dwelling marine fish. Worm-like filament growing from head lures prey to its mouth. Species incl. *Lophius piscatorius*, found in European waters.

Angles, Teutonic people originally inhabiting what is now Schleswig-Holstein (S Denmark, N Germany). Settled in late 5th cent. in E, N and C England in area of later kingdoms of East Anglia, Northumbria and Mercia.

Anglesey, isl. of Gwynedd, NW Wales, separated from mainland by Menai Strait. Area 705 sq km (272 sq mi); main town Holyhead. Agric., *eg* livestock rearing. Tourist industs.

Anglican Communion, informal organization of the Church of England and derived churches with closely related faith and forms, incl. Church of Ireland, Episcopal Church of Scotland, Protestant Episcopal Church in US. Representatives meet every 10 years at Lambeth Conference with archbishop of Canterbury presiding. See ENGLAND, CHURCH OF.

angling, sport of fishing with rod and line. Freshwater fish sought by anglers incl. salmon, trout, bass and pike; saltwater varieties prized incl. tuna, marlin and swordfish. Izaak Walton's *Compleat Angler* (1653) is famous account of angling.

Anglo-Catholicism, see OXFORD MOVEMENT.

Anglo-Saxon Chronicle, annals of English history, begun under Alfred the Great c 891, written in Old English. Simultaneous compilation at 7 different places gives varied picture of English history, incl. Danish invasions, clerical corruption, stories, *eg* 'Cynewulf and Cyneheard'. Peterborough Chronicle continues to 1154.

Anglo-Saxon language, see ENGLISH.

Anglo-Saxon literature, written works in Old English. Poetry unrhymed, using 4-stress line broken into 2 halves, each with internal alliteration, suited to narrative, not lyric. Heroic epic BEOWULF, *Battle of Maldon*, etc, reveal Germanic pagan heritage and oral tradition, although recorded in Christian era. Elegaic verse incl. *Deor*, *The Wanderer*. Hymn of CAEDMON 1st Christian poem, others incl. *The Dream of the Road*, versions of pieces from Bible, *eg Judith*, lives of saints. Literary prose begun in reign of ALFRED with translations from Latin and the ANGLO-SAXON CHRONICLE.

Anglo-Saxons, Teutonic peoples who settled in England in 5th-6th cent. incl. ANGLES, SAXONS and

Jutes. Term also used generally for non-Celtic inhabitants of British Isles before Norman Conquest; recent use for Anglo-American society, its values and attitudes.

Angola, formerly Portuguese West Africa, republic of WC Africa. Area (incl. CABINDA) 1,246,600 sq km (481,300 sq mi); pop. 5,812,000; cap. Luanda. Languages: Bantu, Portuguese. Religions: native, Christian. Narrow coastal strip, interior tableland; main river Cunene. Livestock, fishing; exports coffee, diamonds, oil. Colonized 16th cent. by Portuguese, centre for slave trade until 19th cent. Civil uprisings in 1960s ruthlessly suppressed. Independent 1975; war between competing liberation groups ended in victory (1976) for Marxist forces.

Angora, see ANKARA.

angostura bark, bitter aromatic bark of 2 South American trees, *Galipea officinalis* and *G. cusparia*. Used in medicine and in preparation of liqueurs and bitters.

Angoulême, town of W France, on R. Charente, cap. of Charente dept. Pop. 51,000. Road and rail jct., wine, paper mfg. Seat of counts of Angoumois from 9th cent. Cathedral (12th cent.).

Angry Young Men, applied to several British authors of 1950s, incl. John Osborne, Kingsley Amis, John Braine. Work characterized by resentment of establishment.

Ångström, Anders Jons (1814–74), Swedish physicist. Pioneer in spectroscopy, he investigated solar spectrum, and discovered hydrogen in Sun. Unit of measurement of wavelength of light named after him (1 angstrom = 10^{-10} m).

Anguilla, isl. of E West Indies, in Leeward Isles. Area 91 sq km (35 sq mi); pop. 6000. Exports cotton, salt. Former British colony with St KITTS, Nevis; associate state of St Kitts-Nevis-Anguilla; nationalist unrest led to landing of British troops (1969).

Angus, former county of E Scotland, now in Tayside region. Co. town was Forfar. Grampian Mts. in N; Sidlaw Hills in S; fertile Strathmore in C. Barley, potato growing; livestock rearing. Known as Forfarshire until 1928.

anhydride, in chemistry, non-metallic oxide or organic compound (eg sulphur trioxide) which reacts with water to form an acid; or metallic oxide (eg calcium oxide) which reacts with water to form a base.

aniline ($C_6H_5NH_2$), colourless oily liquid, obtained from coal tar or by reduction of nitrobenzene. Used in manufacture of dyes, plastics and drugs.

animal, any member of animal kingdom, as opposed to plant kingdom. Distinction between plants and animals is largely based on means of feeding; most plants manufacture food from inorganic substances, whereas animals must eat food containing necessary proteins. Animals are also usually capable of independent movement and have nervous systems. Some unicellular organisms, eg *Euglena*, possess chlorophyll but have certain animal characteristics. Animals are classified into c 20 phyla ranging from unicellular Protozoa to Chordata, which incl. all vertebrates. See CLASSIFICATION.

animism, in primitive religion, belief that material objects and natural phenomena contain a spiritual force which governs their existence. In philosophy, doctrine that the essential force of life is irreducible to the mechanistic laws of natural science.

anise, *Pimpinella anisum,* herbaceous plant of Mediterranean regions. Small white or yellow flowers. Its seed (aniseed) is used medicinally to expel intestinal gas and in cookery for its liquorice-like flavour.

Anjou, hist. region of NW France, cap. Angers. Drained by R. Loire. County from 9th cent., finally annexed (1481) to French crown by Louis XI. Plantagenet rulers of England descended from counts of Anjou.

Ankara, cap. of Turkey, in C Anatolia; formerly Angora. Pop. 1,461,000. Commercial centre; trade in mohair from Angora goats; leather goods, textile mfg. Cap. of Roman province of Galatia in 1st cent AD; has ruined marble temple. Replaced Constantinople (1923) as Turkish cap. Atatürk mausoleum is notable building.

Annaba, city of NE Algeria, on Mediterranean Sea. Pop. 169,000. Formerly called Bône. Port, exports phosphates, iron ore; iron, chemical industs. Important city of ancient Numidia, Roman *Hippo Regius.* Episcopal see of St Augustine 396-430.

Annam, hist. kingdom and French protect. of SE Asia. Dominated by Annam Highlands. Part of VIETNAM after 1954.

Annapolis, cap. of Maryland, US; near mouth of Severn R. Pop. 30,000.

In fruit- and vegetable-growing region. Became colonial cap. 1694; US cap. 1783-4. Mainly residential with many hist. buildings; has US Naval Academy.

Annapurna, mountain range in Nepalese Himalayas. Has 2 high peaks: Annapurna I, height 8078 m (26,502 ft), and Annapurna II, height 7938 m (26,041 ft).

Ann Arbor, town of SE Michigan, US; on Huron R. Pop. 100,000. Research, educational, indust. centre in farming, fruit-growing region. Varied mfg. industs. Has Univ. of Michigan (1841).

Anne (1665-1714), queen of England, Scotland and Ireland (1702-14). Daughter of James II, last Stuart monarch. Act of Union (1707) made her 1st queen of Great Britain and Ireland. Reign dominated by War of Spanish Succession (1701-14), in which British forces were commanded by MARLBOROUGH, a leading favourite. Succeeded by George I under Act of Settlement (1701), none of her children having survived her.

annealing, process by which materials, esp. metals, are relieved of strains, rendering them less brittle. Involves application of heat and slow controlled cooling.

Anne Boleyn, see BOLEYN, ANNE.

Annecy, town of SE France, on L. Annecy, cap. of Haute-Savoie dept. Pop. 57,000. Resort, textiles, paper mfg.; bell foundry at nearby Annecy-le-Vieux. Birthplace of St Francis of Sales.

Annelida (annelids), phylum of worms, incl. earthworms, leeches and aquatic worms, *eg* ragworm, lugworm. Body made of jointed segments.

Anne of Austria (1601-66), queen of France, daughter of Philip III of Spain. Wife of Louis XIII, acted as regent (1643-61) for son Louis XIV. Regency dominated by MAZARIN, whom she may have married secretly.

Anne of Cleves (1515-57), English queen, fourth wife of Henry VIII. Marriage (1540), arranged by Thomas Cromwell to build alliance with Germany, nullified 6 months later.

annual, plant which germinates, flowers, seeds and dies within 1 year, eg zinnia. Biennial completes life cycle in 2 years, flowering in 2nd year. Many crop vegetables are biennials which are harvested after 1 year when they have produced a food store but have not yet run to flower, eg cabbage, carrot. Perennial has life cycle of more than 2 years, eg tulip.

Annunciation, Feast of the, or **Lady Day,** holy day (25 March) commemorating announcement to the Virgin Mary, by angel Gabriel, that she was to be the mother of Jesus.

anoa, *Anoa depressicornus,* smallest member of buffalo family, found in Celebes. Stands c 1 m/39 in. high at shoulder; horns almost straight.

anode, *see* ELECTRODE.

anomie or **anomy,** individual's lack of ethical values, rules, resulting from personal disorganization or from inability to find solution to contradictory norms in society (*see* DURKHEIM). Also applied to social structure without norms.

Anouilh, Jean (1910-), French dramatist. Plays revolve on problem of purity v worldly maturity, eg *Antigone* (1942), *L'Alouette* (1953) on Joan of Arc, *Becket* (1959) on Becket's relationship with Henry II.

Anschluss (Ger., = joining), term referring to German annexation of Austria (1938). Policy developed by Hitler and advocated in Austria by National Socialists although contravening peace treaties of 1919.

Anselm, St (c 1033-1109), Italian churchman, theologian, archbishop of Canterbury (1093-1109). Denied right to appoint bishops claimed by William II, Henry I of England. Exiled; reconciled in compromise agreed by pope. First to incorporate Aristotelian logic into theology, promulgated ontological proof of God's existence.

Anshan, city of Liaoning prov., NE China. Pop. 1,500,000. Metallurgical centre; major iron and steel plant, chemicals mfg. Developed under Japanese in 1930s.

Anson, George Anson, Baron (1697-1762), British admiral. Circumnavigated world (1740-4), inflicting heavy damage on Spanish ships. Instigated admin. reform in navy as first lord of the Admiralty in 1750s.

ant, insect of Formicidae family, comprising thousands of widely-distributed species. Lives mainly in underground colonies with various castes maintaining division of social activities, eg cultivating fungi, 'milking' aphids, guarding colony. Most ants winged sterile workers; adult males winged and short-lived. Fertile females (queens) shed wings and start colonies after nuptial flight.

Antakya or **Antioch,** town of S Turkey, on R. Orontes. Pop. 58,000. Founded c 300 BC, became important commercial city under Romans and early centre of Christianity. Changed hands often; fell to Crusaders (1098) and Mamelukes (1268). Declined in importance; attached to Syria after 1919, restored to Turkey in 1939.

Antarctica, continent surrounding South Pole, completely covered by ice shelf. Area c 13,000,000 sq km (5,000,000 sq mi). Comprises 2 geologically distinct regions, E and W Antarctica, joined by immensely thick ice cap. Ellsworth Highlands rise to 5140 m (16,860 ft) at Vinson Massif, highest point on continent. Early explorations made by Bellingshausen (1819-21), Weddell (1823), Ross (1841-2); Amundsen reached South Pole first (1911), month before Scott; Byrd first flew over Pole (1929). Area S of 60°S reserved for international scientific research. *See* AUSTRALIAN ANTARCTIC TERRITORY, BRITISH ANTARCTIC TERRITORY, NORWEGIAN ANTARCTIC TERRITORY, ROSS DEPENDENCY, ADÉLIE LAND. Chile, Argentina, USSR and US also maintain bases. Unassigned area incl. Ellsworth Highlands, Marie Byrd Land, Bellingshausen and Amundsen seas.

antbear or **giant anteater**, *Myrmecophaga jubata*, South American mammal, order Edentata. Shaggy grey coat, long snout; diet of ants, termites.

anteater, one of several mammals, eg pangolin, echidna, antbear, characterized by long snout, sticky tongue and ant diet.

antelope, hoofed ruminant of Bovidae family, found mainly in Africa. Species incl. bushbuck, bongo;

largest is giant eland. Horns hollow and unbranched.

antenna, *see* AERIAL.

antennae, in zoology, flexible jointed appendages on heads of most arthropods. Function mainly sensory (touch, smell), but used by some crustaceans for swimming or attachment.

Anthony, St or **Anthony of Egypt** (c 251-c 356), Egyptian ascetic. Traditionally, founder of 1st Christian monastery.

anthracite, hard, shiny black variety of COAL. Has high carbon content, burns with smokeless flame and has good heat-producing capacity; widely used as domestic fuel. Dates mainly from Carboniferous period.

anthrax, infectious disease of cattle, sheep, *etc*; can be transmitted to man as localized inflammation of skin producing pustules, or as fulminating pneumonia. Caused by *Bacillus anthracis*; treated by penicillin and other antibiotics. Vaccine developed by Pasteur.

anthropology, scientific study of man and his societies. Developed in early 19th cent. Deals with evolution, distribution, social organization, cultural relationships. Distinguished from sociology in its tendency to concentrate on data from non-literate peoples, and historical emphasis.

Antibes, town of SE France, on Côte d'Azur. Pop. 48,000. Port, resort, flower-growing centre; perfume, chocolate mfg. Greek colony founded 4th cent. BC. Roman remains; Château Grimaldi has works by Picasso.

antibiotic, chemical substance, produced by bacteria, moulds, fungi, *etc*, which in dilute solution has capacity of inhibiting growth of or destroying bacteria or other microorganisms. First observed and named was penicillin (by Alexander Fleming, 1928); those used to treat infectious diseases incl. streptomycin, aureomycin, chloromycetin.

antibody, protein produced in vertebrate cells to counteract presence in body of specific antigens (enzyme, toxin) associated with invading bacteria or viruses. By combining chemically with antigens, antibodies form defence mechanism against disease-producing organisms and provide immunity to later attacks.

Anti-Comintern Pact, agreement between Germany and Japan (1936). Stated policy of opposition to international communism. Enlarged (1941) to incl. most AXIS countries.

Anti-Corn Law League, *see* CORN LAWS.

anticyclone, area of relatively high atmospheric pressure, normally creating dry, cloudless conditions, warm in summer, cold in winter. Air moves spirally outwards to areas of lower pressure; deflection by Earth's rotation causes clockwise wind circulation in N hemisphere, anticlockwise in S hemisphere.

antifreeze, substance of low freezing point added to a liquid to depress its freezing point. Ideally should be stable, non-corrosive, non-volatile and good conductor of heat but not of electricity. Ethylene glycol is used in cooling systems of water-cooled engines.

Antigone, in Greek myth, daughter of OEDIPUS and Jocasta; sister of Polynices and Eteocles. Accompanied her father in exile to Colonus, returned to Thebes after his death. Despite prohibition of Creon, she performed funerary rites over Polynices. As punishment, buried alive in rock tomb where she committed suicide.

Antigonus [I] Cyclops (382-301 BC), Macedonian soldier, ruler. Served under Alexander the Great, after whose death he attempted to gain control of all Asia. Held Asia Minor and Syria by 316. Failed to conquer Egypt. Defeated and killed at Ipsus in Phrygia.

Antigua, isl. of E West Indies, in Leeward Isls. Area 280 sq km (108 sq mi); pop. 70,000; cap. St John's (pop. 24,000). Sugar cane, cotton growing; exports sugar, molasses, rum. Has important tourist industs. Discovered by Columbus (1493). Settled by British in 17th cent.; became associate state (1967) with dependencies Barbuda, Redonda.

antihistamine, name given to drugs which neutralize effects of histamine in human body. Used in treatment of allergies.

Anti-Lebanon, mountain range on Syria-Lebanon border. Highest point Mt. Hermon 2814 m (9232 ft). Once noted for timber, now barren.

Antilles, isl. group of Caribbean, incl. all West Indies except Bahamas. Greater Antilles consist of Cuba, Jamaica, Hispaniola, Puerto Rico. Lesser Antilles consist of Leeward and Windward Isls., Netherlands Antilles.

anti-matter, hypothetical matter composed of ANTI-PARTICLES. Ordinary matter and anti-matter brought in contact should annihilate each other, liberating radiation energy. Thus anti-matter cannot exist long in our universe.

antimony (Sb), brittle silver-grey semi-metallic element: at. no. 51, at. wt. 121.75. Occurs as oxide or as stibnite Sb_2S_3. Produced by roasting ore and reducing oxide with iron. Used in making alloys, esp. type metal, and in medicine.

antinomianism, in Christian theology, doctrine that faith alone, not obedience to moral law, is necessary for salvation. Heresy prevalent in Middle Ages; upheld by Anabaptists.

Antioch, see ANTAKYA.

Antiochus [III] the Great (d. 187 BC), Syrian king (223–187 BC). Reconquered much of earlier Seleucid empire. Invaded Greece but was defeated by Romans at Thermopylae (191). Following him into Asia Minor, Romans destroyed his army at Magnesia (190).

anti-particles, particles analogous to ELEMENTARY PARTICLES of matter but having opposite charge and magnetic moment. Brought into contact, an elementary particle and its anti-particle annihilate each other, producing radiation and other elementary particles. Anti-particle of electron is POSITRON.

antipodes, places diametrically opposite in location on the globe, ie separated by 180° of longitude and by the Equator. Term commonly used in UK to refer to Australia or New Zealand.

antipope, pope set up by a group within RC church against the one chosen by church laws and whose election has subsequently been declared uncanonical. See SCHISM, GREAT.

anti-Semitism, antipathy towards Jews. Manifested from Roman times to 19th cent. through persecution and restriction (see GHETTO). Religious cause stressed until 19th cent., subsequently practised for political, social or economic gains, reaching its height in Nazi Germany. Hitler instigated extermination of c 6 million Jews (1939–45). In E Europe, esp. USSR, Poland, Jews have suffered restrictive laws, recurrent violence, eg Kishinev massacre (1903), pogroms.

antiseptic, chemical used to curb growth of or destroy micro-organisms, usually on living tissue, and thus to prevent infection. LISTER introduced use in surgery following Pasteur's research. Modern development is technique of asepsis, ie production of germ-free conditions for surgery.

Antisthenes (c 444–c 370 BC), Greek philosopher. Sophist in early life, but subsequently disciple of Socrates. Founded school of CYNICS at Athens.

antitoxin, antibody formed in body to neutralize poisons (toxins) released into bloodstream by bacteria. Can be given by injection for short-term effect against toxins, eg those of diphtheria and tetanus.

anti-trust legislation, see MONOPOLY.

Antofagasta, port of N Chile, on Pacific coast. Pop. 126,000. Nitrates, copper exports. Its occupation by Chileans initiated war (1879–84) with Bolivia, which ceded territ. to Chile. Has artificial harbour; railway link with Bolivia.

Antonescu, Ion (1882–1946), Romanian military and political leader.

Became premier (1940) before estab. dictatorship. Allied Romania with Axis powers in WWII, but was overthrown 1944. Executed for war crimes.

Antonine Wall, Roman wall, C Scotland. Length 60 km (37 mi), extending from R. Forth to R. Clyde; marked Empire's northern frontiers. Abandoned *c* 185; remains still visible.

Antoninus Pius (AD 86-161), Roman emperor (138-161). Adopted by Hadrian as his successor in 138. Encouraged art, science and building during peaceful reign. Had Antonine Wall built between firths of Clyde and Forth in Scotland (142).

Antonioni, Michelangelo (1912-), Italian film director. Films, tending to replace narrative with character study and (often) unexplained happenings, incl. *L'Avventura* (1959), *Blow-Up* (1967), *Zabriskie Point* (1969).

Antony, Mark or **Marcus Antonius** (*c* 83-30 BC), Roman soldier, political leader. Served with Caesar in Gaul, taking his side during civil war. After Caesar's assassination (44), aroused the people to expel conspirators from Rome. After conflict with Octavian, joined him and Lepidus in 2nd Triumvirate, which ruled the empire for 5 years. He and Octavian defeated Brutus and Cassius at Philippi (42). While in Asia Minor, fell in love with Cleopatra. Deprived of power by senate, was defeated by Octavian at Actium (31). Joined Cleopatra in Egypt, where he killed himself.

Antrim, former county of NE Ireland, co. town was Belfast. Low basalt plateau; scenic valleys ('Glens of Antrim'); Giant's Causeway on N coast. Main industs., agric., fishing, linen mfg., shipbuilding. **Antrim,** town on Lough Neagh. Pop. 2000. Has 10th cent. round tower. **Antrim,** district; area 563 sq km (217 sq mi); pop. 27,000. Created in 1973, formerly part of Co. Antrim.

Antwerp (Fr. *Anvers*), city of N Belgium, cap. of Antwerp prov. Pop. 234,000. Port and commercial centre on R. Scheldt. Sugar, oil refining; shipbuilding, textiles; diamond trade. Gothic cathedral (1352). Trade centre of 16th cent. Europe, declined after sack by Spaniards (1576), closure of Scheldt (1648-1795). Prosperity regained from 19th cent. Damaged in both WWs.

Anubis, in ancient Egyptian pantheon, god who led the dead to judgment. Depicted with head of a jackal. Sometimes identified with Greek Hermes.

anus, in mammals, posterior opening of alimentary canal, through which waste is excreted.

anxiety, in psychology, reaction ranging from uneasiness to complete panic when individual is faced with real or apparent threat. Classified normal and neurotic; latter often said to be core of neuroses, characterized by helpless response to threat.

Anzio (anc. *Antium*), town of WC Italy, on Tyrrhenian Sea. Pop. 16,000. Fishing port. Birthplace of Caligula, Nero. Scene of Allied landings (1944).

aorta, main artery of body, conveying blood from left ventricle of the heart to all parts of body except the lungs.

Aosta, town of NW Italy, in the

Alps, on R. Dora Baltea. Cap. of Valle d'Aosta prov. Pop. 39,000. Tourist centre; metals, chemicals. Roman ruins, medieval cathedral.

aoudad or **Barbary sheep**, *Ammotragus lervia*, wild N African sheep with large curved horns. Resembles goat; highly adaptable to climatic extremes.

Apache, North American Indian tribes of Nadene linguistic stock. Warlike hunters of SW. Successfully resisted advance of Spanish colonization but inter-tribal warfare reduced numbers. Some 80,000 still live in reservations, mainly in Arizona.

apartheid, racial segregation on grounds of colour, practised in South Africa from 1948. In Afrikaans, word means 'apartness'; policy aimed at achieving separate development of races, effectively restricting residence, movements, occupations of non-whites. Rather than change its racist policy, South Africa withdrew from Commonwealth (1961).

ape, any of Pongidae family of Old World tailless monkeys, particularly those most closely related to man (gibbon, orangutan, gorilla and chimpanzee).

Apeldoorn, city of EC Netherlands. Pop. 128,000. Railway jct. Paper mfg. Royal family summer residence nearby.

Apelles (*fl* 4th cent. BC), Greek painter. Reputed to be leading painter of antiquity, none of his work survives. Court painter in Macedon to Philip and Alexander; his portrait of Alexander holding a thunderbolt was in Temple of Diana at Ephesus.

Apennines, mountain range of Italy. Extends *c* 1300 km (800 mi) from Maritime Alps to Calabria and Sicily. Livestock, agric. on lower slopes; marble quarries. Formerly widely forested. Highest peak Monte Corno (2913 m/9560 ft) in Gran Sasso d'Italia, C Italy. Earthquakes, esp. in S; volcanoes, incl. Vesuvius.

aphelion, point furthest from Sun in orbit of planet about Sun. Opposite is perihelion.

aphid or **plant louse**, small softbodied insect of Aphididae family. Causes much damage to plants by sucking sap and carrying virus disease. Common greenfly, pest of roses, is an aphid.

Aphrodite, in Greek myth, goddess of love, beauty, fertility. Daughter of Zeus and Dione, or sprung from sea into which a severed member of Uranus had been thrown. Unfaithful wife of Hephaestus, being variously connected with Ares, Dionysus, Hermes, Poseidon and the mortals Anchises, Adonis. Had power of granting beauty and charm. Identified by Romans with Venus.

apocalypse, form of prophetic writing common in ancient Hebrew and Christian literature. Depicts end of the world in visions of triumph of good over evil; characterized by rich and obscure symbolism. NT book of REVELATION is often known as the Apocalypse.

Apocrypha, Jewish writings of *c* 300 BC – *c* AD 100 not incl. in the canon of sacred scripture by the Council of Jamnia (AD 90) and now excluded by most Protestant churches. Consists of 14 books included in SEPTUAGINT and VULGATE.

apogee, point furthest from Earth in orbit of Moon or satellite about Earth. Opposite is perigee.

Apollinaire, Guillaume, orig. Wilhelm Apollinaris de Kostrowitski (1880–1918), French poet, b. Rome. His art criticism established CUBISM as a movement, which influenced poetry *Alcools* (1913), *Calligrammes* (1918). Also wrote surrealist drama *Les Mamelles de Tirésias* (1917), modernist manifesto, *L'esprit nouveau et les poètes.*

Apollo or **Phoebus Apollo,** in Greek myth, son of Zeus and Leto, born with his sister Artemis at Delos. God of social and intellectual attributes of Greek civilization, eg prophecy, healing, purification, music, archery. Represented as ideal of youthful beauty. Cult centred at Delphi where oracular utterances were given by his priestess, Pythia.

Apollodorus (*fl* 415 BC), Athenian painter. First painter to use light and shade to model figures, step towards illusionistic painting.

Apollonius Rhodius (*c* 295 BC–after 247 BC), Alexandrian scholar, poet. Librarian of Museum in Alexandria, wrote epic *Argonautica* about Jason and the Golden Fleece.

Apollo programme, see SPACE EXPLORATION.

apologetics, the branch of theology which deals with the formal defence of a religious belief. Major Christian apologists incl. Augustine, Aquinas, Pascal, Karl Barth. Since 19th cent., principal attacks on belief have come from psychology, Darwinism, historical criticism of Gospels.

apoplexy or **stroke,** sudden paralysis with total or partial loss of consciousness and sensation, pos-

sible loss of speech, and other aftereffects of varying severity. Caused by bleeding from arteries in brain, thrombosis or embolism.

apostle, name given to TWELVE DISCIPLES of Jesus (sometimes excluding Judas Iscariot), and also to other early missionaries of Christian church, eg St Paul, St Barnabas.

Apostles' Creed, one of the three basic statements of Christian faith. Used in RC and various Protestant churches. Formerly ascribed to the Apostles; prob. dates in present form from 6th cent.

apostolic succession, doctrine that the religious authority and mission conferred by Jesus on St Peter has come down through an unbroken succession of bishops. Basis of religious authority in RC, Eastern Orthodox and Anglican churches, but not accepted by Presbyterian churches.

Appalachian Mountains, system of E North America. Extend 2570 km (c 1600 mi) from Québec (Canada) to C Alabama. Incl. White, Green, Catskill, Allegheny, Blue Ridge, Black Mts. Mt. Mitchell is highest point (2037 m/6684 ft). Rich in mineral resources, esp. coal.

appeasement, policy of acceding to demands of hostile power in attempt to maintain peace. Used by British, French towards Axis powers in late 1930s; culminated in MUNICH PACT.

appendix or **vermiform appendix,** in man, outgrowth of large intestine in lower right abdomen. No known function. Infection may result in appendicitis which usually necessitates removal of appendix.

Appian Way (anc. *Via Appia*), ancient road of Italy, begun 312 BC, extending c 560 km (350 mi) from Rome to Brindisi. Part of Roman route to Greece, Asia.

apple, any tree of genus *Malus* of rose family. The common apple *M. sylvestris* has hard, round, red, yellow or green edible fruit. Economically important esp. in North America, Europe and Australia. Several thousand varieties of cultivated apples incl. eating, cooking and cider types.

apple of discord, in Greek myth, golden apple inscribed 'for the fairest' thrown among guests at wedding of Peleus and Thetis by Eris. Claimed by Athena, Hera and Aphrodite, and awarded by PARIS to Aphrodite who in return helped him kidnap Helen, thus starting the Trojan War.

Appleton, Sir Edward Victor (1892-1965), English physicist. Investigated reflection of radio waves by ionized particles in upper atmosphere; located Kennelly-Heaviside layer and discovered Appleton layers above this. Awarded Nobel Prize for Physics (1947).

Appomattox Courthouse, building near Appomattox, S Virginia, US. Scene of Confederate General Lee's surrender to Union on 9 April, 1865, marking end of Civil War.

apricot, *Prunus armeniaca,* tree with downy, orange-coloured edible fruit. Native to Far East, introduced into Europe and US.

a priori, in logic, term denoting that which comes before experience, as opposed to *a posteriori* denoting that which comes after experience. Hence formal logic is *a priori* while scientific information is *a posteriori*.

apse, vaulted semicircular or poly-gonal projection at sanctuary end of church.

Apuleius, Lucius (*fl* 2nd cent. BC), Roman writer, orator. Known for *Metamorphoses* or *Golden Ass,* prose romance which greatly influenced development of novel in post-Renaissance fiction.

Apulia (*Puglia*), region of SE Italy. Hilly in C, plains in N and S; cereals, olives, vines, almonds. Prone to drought. Part of medieval Norman kingdom of Sicily.

Aqaba, Gulf of, thin arm of NE Red Sea. Jordan's only sea outlet. Blockade by Egypt in 1967 war failed on Israeli capture of Sinai Penin.

aquamarine, semi-precious gemstone, a variety of beryl. Transparent, blue or blue-green in colour; used in jewellery. Major sources in US, Brazil, Siberia, Malagasy Republic.

Aquarius, see ZODIAC.

aquatint, method of etching by tone rather than line, giving effect similar to water colour or wash drawing. Transparent tones are obtained by biting printing plate with acid through porous ground. Much used by Goya.

aqueduct, artificial channel constructed for conducting water. Name often applies to bridge built in series of arches to carry water across a river or valley, *eg* Pont du Gard, Nîmes.

aquilegia, genus of herbs of buttercup family. Species incl. COLUMBINE.

Aquinas, Thomas, see THOMAS AQUINAS, ST.

Aquitaine, region of SW France. Fertile plain drained by R. Garonne; main cities Bordeaux, Toulouse. Cereals, vineyards, fruit and vegetable growing. Roman prov. from 56 BC; powerful medieval duchy, (name corrupted to *Guienne*) under English rule from 1152; retaken by France (1451).

Arabia, penin. of SW Asia, between Red Sea and Persian Gulf. Mainly desert inhabited by pastoral nomads; rich oil deposits in E. Tribes united (6th cent.) by Mohammed who founded Islamic religion. Under control of OTTOMAN Turks until 1918, Saudi Arabia emerged as dominant country of region after 1925.

Arabian Nights, also known as *The Thousand and One Nights*, series of stories in Arabic, linked by story of Scheherazade, who keeps her husband in suspense by telling him stories over 1001 nights, thus escaping death, fate of all his previous wives. Incl. tales of Ali Baba, Sinbad and Aladdin. Only partly Arab in origin, the collection draws on all leading Eastern cultures. First European translation into French 1704–17, English translations incl. Burton's unexpurgated version (16 vois., 1885–8).

Arabian Sea, part of NW Indian Ocean; lies between Arabia and India.

Arabic, SW Semitic language of Afro-Asiatic family. Spoken in most of N Africa, Sudan, Arabian peninsula, Lebanon, Syria and Iraq.

Arabic literature, began with lyric poetry in pre-Islamic period (4th cent.). Only form was ode, 30–100 lines long, on love, fighting, hunting, as in Muallaqat. 8th–9th cent. saw change of subject to town life, abandonment of ode form by leading poets, eg Abu Nuwas. Poetry superseded by prose romances, eg ARABIAN NIGHTS. Also historical, geographical, theological and philosophical writing, latter esp. by Spanish Arab writers. Little writing of world note since 1300.

Arabic numerals, number signs 0 1 2 3 4 5 6 7 8 9; of Hindu origin, they were introduced into Europe by translation of Arabic texts during Middle Ages.

Arab-Israeli wars, series of conflicts, culminating on 4 occasions in outright war between Israel and Arab countries over existence in Palestine of independent Jewish state of Israel. Its proclamation (1948) led to immediate invasion by neighbouring Arab states; ended (1949) by UN armistice. Resulted in increased territ. for Israel, Egypt and Jordan. Egyptian seizure (1956) of Suez Canal precipitated Sinai campaign in which Israel succeeded in occupying Gaza Strip and most of Sinai; Israel gave these up on agreeing to UN cease-fire (Nov. 1956). Third war broke out in June, 1967, after Egypt blockaded Gulf of Aqaba to Israeli shipping. Israel extended frontiers to control W R. Jordan, E bank of Suez Canal, Sinai and Jordanian sector of Jerusalem. Fourth war (Yom Kippur war), Oct. 1973, involved Israeli crossing of Suez Canal after early Egyptian successes, as well as repulse of Syria at Golan Heights. UN supervised ceasefire following intervention by KISSINGER. Israel withdrew from Egyptian side of Suez Canal and relinquished control of Sinai strategic positions to UN.

Arab League, organization of Arab states formed (1945) to promote cooperation, esp. in defence and economic affairs; attempted joint Arab action against existence of state of Israel. Original members were Egypt, Syria, Lebanon, Jordan, Iraq, Saudi Arabia, Yemen; 11 more subsequently joined. Collective security agreement came into force 1952; failures in 1960s, esp. 1967 war, resulted in decline in League's importance as unifying force in Arab world.

Arabs, name given to large group of Arabic-speaking people in W Asia and N Africa bound by common tradition, Islamic religion and Arabic language. Main Arab countries are Egypt, Saudi Arabia, Iraq, Lebanon, Syria, Sudan, Libya, Tunisia and Yemen. Divided into settled Arabs and Bedouin nomad herdsmen.

Arachne, in Greek myth, Lydian girl who challenged Athena to contest in weaving. Depicted love of the gods, thus angering Athena who destroyed the work. Hanged herself and was turned into spider by Athena.

Arachnida (arachnids), class of arthropods incl. spiders, scorpions, mites, ticks, king crabs. Mainly terrestrial, but king crab is aquatic. Characterized by 2 body sections and 6 pairs of appendages, 4 being locomotory.

Arafat, Yasser, pseud. of Mohammed Abed Ar'ouf Arafat (1929-), Palestinian resistance leader. Head (since 1968) of more moderate resistance groups, Palestine National Liberation Movement (Al Fatah) and Palestine Liberation Organization.

Arafura Sea, extension of W Pacific Ocean, between Australia and New Guinea. Linked to Coral Sea by Torres Str.

Aragon, Louis (1897-), French writer. After early associations with DADA wrote surrealist novel *Le Paysan de Paris* (1926). Became Communist; later works incl. poetry, eg *Le Crève-Coeur* (1941) inspired by participation in Resistance.

Aragón, region and former prov. of NE Spain. Incl. Pyrenees foothills, Ebro valley, part of C plateau; arid, sparsely pop. Main towns Saragossa, Huesca. Sheep rearing, irrigated agric., mineral deposits. Independent kingdom from 1035; united with Catalonia 1137, with Castile 1479 by marriage of Ferdinand and Isabella.

Aral Sea, inland sea of USSR, on Kazakh-Uzbek SSR border; 4th largest lake in world. Area c 67,000 sq km (26,000 sq mi). Slightly saline; no outlet. Fished for carp, perch.

Aramaic, language of Syria belonging to NW Semitic branch of Afro-Asiatic family. Now dead, widely spoken in centuries before and after Christ. Superseded by Arabic.

Aran Islands, small, rocky isl. group of Co. Galway, W Irish Republic, in Galway Bay. Largest is Inishmore. Fishing.

Ararat, Mount (*Agri Dagi*), mountain of NE Turkey, near border with Iran and Soviet Armenia. Has 2 main peaks; higher is Great Ararat, height 5156 m (16,916 ft), traditional resting place of Noah's Ark.

arbitration, see CONCILIATION, INDUSTRIAL.

Arbroath, town of Tayside region, E Scotland. Pop. 23,000. Formerly Aberbrothock. Fishing indust. (famous for smoked haddock); tourist resort; cloth mfg. Has 12th cent. abbey; scene of Robert I's Declaration of Independence (1320).

Arbuthnot, John (1667-1735), Scottish satirist and scientific writer, court physician to Queen Anne. Founded Scriblerus Club with Pope and Swift. Principal author of the *Memoirs of Martinus Scriblerus* (1741), satire on false taste. Political satire, the *History of John Bull* (5 pamphlets, 1712) estab. John Bull as national type.

arbutus, genus of trees or shrubs of the heath family with dark-green leaves, clusters of pinkish flowers and strawberry-like berries. Widely grown as ornamental.

arc, electric, luminous and intensely hot discharge produced when current flows through a gap between 2 electrodes; characterized by high current and low voltage. Carbon arcs used as sources of very bright light; heating effect utilized in electric arc furnace.

Arcadia, admin. dist. of S Greece, in C Peloponnese. Mainly mountainous. Isolated; pastoral farming from ancient times.

arch, curved structure, *eg* of bricks or stone blocks, which supports weight of material over an open space. Keystone (inserted in centre of arch) pushes stress outwards. Types used incl. pointed arch, characteristic of Gothic buildings, and semi-circular arch, employed by Romans and revived in Renaissance.

Archaean era, *see* PRECAMBRIAN.

archaeology, the study of human past by systematic examination and tabulation of excavated relics. Little interest was shown in ancient remains until Renaissance, when Greek and Roman pottery, coins became highly prized. Systematic classification dates from concept of THREE AGE SYSTEM, introduced in 1818 by Thomsen. Scientific contributions to modern archaeology incl. radiocarbon dating methods.

archaeopteryx, earliest known fossil bird (Jurassic period), probably descended from dinosaur. Feathers on tail and wings; possession of teeth and claws on wings indicates reptilian origin. Flightless.

Archangel (*Arkhangelsk*), city of USSR, port of NW European RSFSR; at mouth of N R. Dvina. Pop. 355,000. Port icebound much of year, kept open by icebreakers; exports timber. Sawmilling and fishery centre. Founded 1553 with estab. of Muscovy Co.; only Russian seaport until St Petersburg founded (1703).

archangel, chief ANGEL. Best known are Michael, Gabriel, Raphael.

archbishop, high dignitary in episcopal churches. The archbishops of Canterbury and York are principal dignitaries of Church of England.

archerfish, *Toxotes jaculator,* freshwater fish of East Indies. Captures insect prey by spitting jets of water at them.

archery, art of shooting with bow and arrow, formerly practised in hunting and warfare, today solely a sport. Origins reach back over 50,000 years; bow-making techniques were improved in Near East from c 2500 BC. Decisive in battles in Middle Ages (Crécy, Agincourt) until introduction of gunpowder. Official sport at Olympic Games since 1972.

Archimedes (c 287-212 BC), Greek

mathematician, physicist, inventor. Created science of hydrostatics and worked out the principle of the lever. Determined areas under curves and volumes of solids by methods akin to calculus; obtained accurate approximation for π. Enunciated Archimedes' principle – upward thrust exerted on body immersed in fluid equals weight of fluid displaced.

archipelago, group or chain of islands. Ancient name for Aegean Sea and formerly used for any sea with many isls.

architecture, art of designing and constructing buildings, ideally aiming for maximum beauty and utility. Styles are influenced by climate, materials and techniques available, social and cultural settings. History of architecture is largely concerned with religious buildings, reaching back beyond 3000 BC to tombs of ancient Egypt. In 20th cent. techniques such as steel frame and reinforced concrete have revolutionized architecture.

arctic fox, *Alopex lagopus,* small fox of Arctic region. Valued for slate-grey fur which turns white in winter.

Arctic Ocean, ocean surrounding North Pole, lying entirely above Arctic Circle (66½°N). Area c 14,300,000 sq km (5,500,000 sq mi). Connected to Atlantic by Greenland Sea, to Pacific by Bering Strait. Largely covered by ice, which breaks into drifting pack-ice in summer.

Arden, John (1930-), English playwright. Works, incl. *Live like Pigs* (1958), *Serjeant Musgrave's Dance* (1959), reflect ambivalent sympathies by mingling song, prose and verse dialogue.

Arden, Forest of, Warwickshire, WC England. Remnant of once extensive Midlands forest. Scene of Shakespeare's *As You Like It.*

Ardennes, plateau of SE Belgium, NE France, Luxembourg. Extensive woodland, some agric. Battlefield in both WWs.

Areopagus, Athenian council of elders with political and judicial powers in 6th and 5th cents. BC. Power reduced to jurisdiction in homicide cases by 462 BC. Named after hill near Acropolis where council met.

Arequipa, town of S Peru, alt. 2380 m (c 7800 ft). Pop. 195,000. Wool market; tourism. Founded (1540) by Pizarro on ancient Inca site. Damaged by frequent earthquakes.

Ares, in Greek myth, son of Zeus and Hera; god of war. Loved by Aphrodite. Appears as instigator of violence or as tempestuous lover. Identified by Romans with Mars.

Aretino, Pietro (1492-1557), Italian writer, adventurer. Known for venomous and bawdy satire, called by Ariosto 'scourge of princes'. *Letters* give uninhibited picture of 16th cent. Italy.

Argenteuil, suburb of Paris, N France, on right bank of R. Seine. Aero and vehicle industs., market gardens. Grew around convent founded 7th cent. by Charlemagne, at which Héloïse was abbess (12th cent.).

Argentina, federal republic of S South America, on Atlantic. Area 2,776,889 sq km (1,072,157 sq mi); pop. 23,364,000; cap. Buenos Aires. Language: Spanish. Religion: RC. W boundary formed by Andes; cotton growing in Chaco plain (N); pop. and wealth in Pampas (beef, wheat produce); arid Patagonia plateau in S (sheep rearing, oil); indust. concentrated in Buenos Aires. Spanish colonization in 16th cent.; independence struggle led by San Martín (achieved 1816); republic estab. 1852. Ruled by successive dictatorships in 20th cent., esp. Perón (1946-55, 1973-4).

argon (Ar), inert gaseous element; at. no. 18, at. wt. 39.95. Found in air (0.9%); obtained by distillation of liquid air. Used to fill electric lamps, fluorescent tubes and as inert atmosphere for welding. Discovered (1894) by Rayleigh, Ramsay.

argonaut or **paper nautilus**, marine cephalopod mollusc, genus *Argonauta*, related to octopus. Female builds itself thin translucent shell to incubate eggs.

Argonauts, in Greek myth, band of heroes led by JASON, sent to bring GOLDEN FLEECE from king of Colchis to Greece. Sailed in ship *Argo* suffering many trials on outward and homeward journey, *eg* the Symplegades (clashing rocks), Scylla and Charybdis.

Argonne, hilly woodland of NE France, in Champagne and Lorraine. Strategic WWI battleground.

Argos, ancient city of S Greece, in NE Peloponnese. Pop. 17,000. Occupied from Bronze Age; 'Diomed' of Homer's *Iliad*. Centre of Argolis, dominated Peloponnese from 7th cent. BC; taken by Sparta *c* 494 BC, by Rome 146 BC. Heraeum temple nearby.

Argyll, Archibald Campbell, 8th Earl of (1607-61), Scottish nobleman. Led Covenanting forces against royalists in Civil War. After execution of Charles I, supported Charles II who had agreed to introduce Presbyterianism to England. Submitted to Cromwell (1652); beheaded after Restoration. His son, **Archibald Campbell, 9th Earl of Argyll** (1629-85), was beheaded for aiding Monmouth's rebellion. **John Campbell, 2nd Duke of Argyll and Duke of Greenwich** (1678-1743), was general responsible for quelling Jacobite rebellion of 1715.

Argyllshire, former county of W Scotland, now in Strathclyde region. Incl. some of Inner Hebrides; co. town was Inveraray. Mountainous; indented coast. Sheep, forestry, fishing, distilling, tourism.

aria, in music, composition for voice, esp. solo with orchestral accompaniment. A feature of operas, cantatas, oratorios since 1600.

Ariadne, in Greek myth, daughter of King Minos and Pasiphaë, who gave THESEUS the skein of thread by which he found his way out of the labyrinth after slaying the Minotaur. Fled with Theseus, but deserted by him on Naxos, she was found by Dionysus who married her.

Arianism, *see* ARIUS.

Aries, *see* ZODIAC.

Ariosto, Ludovico (1474-1533), Italian poet. Famous for epic poem *Orlando Furioso* (1532) on Roland, sometimes called greatest Renaissance poem. Also wrote lyrics, satires, dramas.

Aristarchus of Samos (3rd cent. BC), Greek astronomer. Reputed to be 1st to hold theory that Earth revolves about Sun. Devised trigonometrical methods to determine relative distances of Sun and Moon from Earth.

Aristides [the Just] (c 530-c 468 BC), Athenian statesman, general. Ostracized (483 BC) by Themistocles, he fought at Salamis and commanded army in victory over Persians at Plataea (479 BC). Organized Delian League against Persia.

Aristippus (c 435-c 356 BC), Greek philosopher. Pupil of Socrates. Founder of Cyrenaics, holding pleasure to be the greatest good, virtue to be the ability to enjoy. Thus opposed to Cynics in first coherent statement of HEDONISM.

aristocracy, in political theory, term used for govt. by elite, usually hereditary, designated as best equipped to rule. Usage has widened to denote class from which governing elite is drawn, or those who by birth or wealth occupy privileged position compared with rest of community.

Aristophanes (c 450-c 385 BC), Greek comic poet. Although not innovative, plays are greatest of Greek comedies, mixing political, social and literary satire, vigorous rather than savage. Only 11 plays extant, incl. *The Clouds*, *The Wasps*, *The Birds*, *Lysistrata*, and *The Frogs*.

Aristotle (384-322 BC), Greek philosopher. Pupil of Plato, tutor of Alexander the Great. Founded Peripatetic school of Athens (335 BC). Established the methods of Western philosophy in *eg*, *Analytics*, *Metaphysics*, *Ethics*, *Politics*, *Poetics*. Believed in Divine Being, but unlike Plato did not posit separate world of ideal essences. Held that happiness, goodness in man come from use of reason, *ie* fulfilment of intended function. Enlightened monarchy with aristocracy was his political ideal.

arithmetic, branch of mathematics dealing with real numbers, their addition, subtraction, multiplication, and division. Term also applies to study of whole numbers (integers), esp. prime numbers.

Arius (c 256-336), Libyan theologian. Advanced theory (Arianism) that Christ was not co-equal or co-eternal with God, thus renouncing Trinity. Condemned as heretic at 1st Council of Nicaea (325). Arianism persisted in N Africa and Spain until 6th cent.

Arizona, state of SW US. Area 295,024 sq km (113,909 sq mi); pop. 1,771,000; cap. Phoenix; other major city Tucson. Forested Colorado Plateau in N (incl. Grand Canyon), desert in S. Agric. irrigated by several dams (*eg* Roosevelt, Coolidge); fruit, vegetables, wheat, beef, cotton farming. Copper, silver mining. Largest Indian pop. in US (many reservations). First explored in 16th cent. by Spanish; purchased by US (1848). Admitted to Union as 48th state (1912).

ark, in OT, *see* NOAH.

Arkansas, state of SC US. Area 137,539 sq km (53,104 sq mi); pop. 1,923,000; cap. Little Rock; other major cities Fort Smith, Hot Springs. Ozark Mts. in NW; Mississippi R. forms E border; crossed by White, Arkansas, Ouachita rivers. Agric. incl. cotton, soya bean growing, livestock farming; important bauxite mines. Part of French Louisiana Purchase (1803). Admitted to Union as state (1836).

Arkansas, river of C US. Rises in Rocky Mts. of C Colorado. Flows SE

2330 km (c 1450 mi) through Kansas, Oklahoma, Arkansas to Mississippi. Chief tributary Canadian R.

Arklow, town of Co. Wicklow, E Irish Republic, at mouth of R. Avoca. Pop. 7000. Fishing; fertilizers; tourism.

Arkwright, Sir Richard (1732–92), English inventor. Developed mechanical spinning process (patent, 1769) which provided basis for mass-production in cotton indust.

Arlberg Pass, W Austria. Height 1801 m (5912 ft); links Vorarlberg (W) and Tyrol (E) by road and rail (latter uses tunnel, built 1884).

Arles, town of Provence, SE France, on Rhône delta. Pop. 46,000. Agric. market, wines, silk mfg. Important Roman, Gaulish centre; archbishopric from 4th cent. Cap. of kingdom of Arles (933–1378). Roman remains incl. arena, theatre; has cathedral (11th cent.).

Arlington National Cemetery, burial ground of US war dead (estab. 1864). Opposite Washington, DC, on Potomac R. Incl. tomb of Unknown Soldier and also notable citizens, eg J.F. Kennedy.

arm, in man, upper limb of body, extending from shoulder to wrist. Skeleton is formed by humerus in upper arm, radius and ulna in forearm. ..

Armada, Spanish, fleet of 130 ships sent (1588) by Philip II of Spain to carry invasion force against England. Attacked by English fleet under Howard and Drake off Plymouth, and later broken up by fire ships off Calais. Suffered heavy losses through storm damage while escaping via Scotland and W coast of Ireland; less than half of fleet reached Spain.

armadillo, burrowing mammal of Dasypodidae family found from S US to South America. Body armourplated with bony discs; rolls up into ball when threatened. Species incl. ninebanded armadillo, *Dasypus novemcinctus*, found in Texas.

Armageddon, in Bible, esp. Book of Revelation, scene of last, decisive battle between forces of good and evil, to be fought before the Day of Judgment. Name prob. refers to the 'hill of Megiddo' which was a proverbial symbol of war because of its many ancient battles.

Armagh, former county of S Northern Ireland. Low-lying in N; hilly in S. Agric.; cattle rearing; linen mfg. Co. town was Armagh. Pop. 12,000. Ecclesiastical cap. of Ireland from 5th cent. Has Protestant, RC cathedrals. Armagh, district; area 675 sq km (260 sq mi); pop. 47,000. Created 1973, formerly part of Co. Armagh.

Armagnac, former French province in Gascony, cap. Auch. Noted for brandy.

Armenia, hist. region and former kingdom, now divided between Turkey, Iran and USSR. Mainly plateau, incl. Mt. Ararat and sources of Tigris and Euphrates. Embraced Christianity (303); changed hands repeatedly, with Russia taking what is now Armenian SSR from Persia in 19th cent. Turkish attempts to suppress Armenian nationalism led to massacres (1894–1915).

Armenian Soviet Socialist Republic, constituent republic of SW USSR, bounded on S and W by Iran and Turkey. Area 29,800 sq km

(11,500 sq mi); pop. 2,493,000. Cap. Yerevan. Mainly mountainous with high plateaus; produces cotton, tobacco, wine; minerals incl. copper, molybdenum, zinc. Region seized by Russia from Persia (1828); incorporated by USSR (1920).

Arminius (d. AD 21), German chieftain. Organized rebellion against Romans and destroyed (AD 9) legions under Quintilius Varus. Defeat led Romans to withdraw from territ. E of Rhine.

Arminius, Jacobus, orig. Jacob Harmensen (1560-1609), Dutch reformed theologian. Opposed Calvinist teaching of absolute predestination. Teachings formulated (1622) by Simon episcopus became known as Arminianism.

armistice, truce before signing of peace treaty; temporary stopping of hostilities by mutual agreement. Armistice Day (11 Nov.) anniversary of WWI armistice (1918), commemorated by National Day of Remembrance (UK), Veterans Day (US).

Armory Show, international art exhibition held at 69th Regiment Armory, New York, in 1913. Introduced modern European art into US; cubist, fauvist, post-impressionist and symbolist works were shown.

Armstrong, Louis ('Satchmo') (1900-71), American jazz trumpeter, band leader, singer. First musician to develop a solo style in jazz, he created stunning improvisations that defined the role of the soloist. Known internationally for his ability to entertain audiences.

Armstrong, Neil (1930-), American astronaut. As member of *Apollo XI* mission (July, 1969), became 1st man to set foot on Moon; accompanied by (Edwin) 'Buzz' Aldrin (1930-), while Michael Collins (1930-) remained in Moon orbit in command module.

army, organized body of men, trained and armed for military combat on land. Professional standing army developed with growth of Roman Empire. In feudal Europe, military service was obligatory among knights and yeomanry. System declined with increased use of mercenaries. Conscription was introduced during French Revolutionary Wars. During peacetime, modern army often made up of enlisted volunteers.

army ant or **driver ant**, nomadic ant, esp. of genus *Eciton* found in South American tropics. Travels in long columns, devouring animals in its path.

Arne, Thomas Augustine (1710-78), English composer. Wrote many operas, but best known for his tuneful songs, incl. 'Rule Britannia' and several Shakespeare settings.

Arnhem, city of EC Netherlands, on R. Rhine, cap. of Gelderland prov. Pop. 134,000. Railway jct., engineering, textiles. Scene of defeat (1944) of British airborne assault.

Arnhem Land, aboriginal reserve of NE Northern Territ., Australia. Pop. *c* 4000; white settlement confined to mission stations. Mainly swamp and grassland; monsoon climate. Bauxite development at Gove.

Arnim, Ludwig Joachim von (1781-1831), German poet. With brother-in-law Brentano, pub. folksong collection *The Boy's Magic Horn* (1805-8). Wife, Bettina von Arnim (1785-1859), pub. *Goethe's*

Correspondence with a Child (1835), semi-fictitious memoir of her childhood correspondence with Goethe.

Arno, river of NC Italy. Flows 240 km (150 mi) from Apennines via Florence, Pisa to Ligurian Sea. Fertile, scenic valley.

Arnold, Benedict (1741-1801), American general. Held commands during American Revolution, but plotted to betray West Point garrison. Discovered but escaped and later fought for British.

Arnold, Malcolm Henry (1921-), English composer. Compositions, melodious and often humerous, incl. 6 symphonies, concertos for horn and clarinet, chamber and film music.

Arnold, Thomas (1795-1842), English educator. As headmaster of Rugby (1827-42), he reformed English public school system, creating modern pattern. Also a classical scholar, historian. His son, **Matthew Arnold** (1822-88), was a poet and critic. Held that poetry should be 'criticism of life', saw culture as the only means to save society from Victorian materialism. Poems incl. 'The Scholar Gypsy' (1853), 'Thyrsis' (1866), criticism incl. *Essays in Criticism* (2 series 1865, 1888). Major figure in English critical tradition.

aromatic compounds, in chemistry, organic compounds derived from benzene. Many such compounds, esp. those discovered first, have recognizable odours.

Arp, Jean or **Hans** (1887-1966), French sculptor and painter. Associated with dada and surrealist groups. Produced 2-dimensional works, incl. collages, flat reliefs, and sculpture in the round; sculpture of 1930s suggests organic forms while remaining abstract.

arquebus or **harquebus,** small-calibre gun operated by matchlock, precursor of the musket. Prominent in 16th cent. Italian wars.

Arrabal, Fernando (1932-), French novelist, playwright. Plays, eg *Pique-nique en campagne* (1959), *Fando et Lis* (1962), inhabited by childlike characters, are examples of 'theatre of cruelty'. Novels incl. *L'enterrement de la sardine* (1961).

arrack, alcoholic liquor made mainly in Asian countries from fermented rice, molasses or coconut palm juice.

Arran, isl. of Strathclyde region, W Scotland. Area 430 sq km (166 sq mi); pop. 4000; main town Brodick. Tourism, hill-walking.

Arras, town of N France, on canalized R. Scarpe, cap. of Pas-de-Calais dept. Pop. 54,000. Agric. market, engineering. Medieval tapestry indust. Hist. cap. of Artois, under Spanish rule 1493-1640. Birthplace of Robespierre.

Arras, Treaty of, agreement (1482) between LOUIS XI of France and MAXIMILIAN of Austria. Maximilian was to cede duchy of Burgundy, Artois and Franche-Comté (inherited at death of his wife, MARY OF BURGUNDY) to France.

arrest, seizure and taking into custody of person by authority of law. In civil law, can only take place on issue of court order. Arrest may be made with or without warrant when a crime is thought to have been committed; both law officers and private individuals are empowered and have duty to arrest

person suspected of committing felony or breach of the peace in their presence.

arrowhead, any aquatic perennial of genus *Sagittaria* of water plantain family. Arrow-shaped leaves, small, white, cup-like flowers.

arsenic (As), chemical element; at. no. 33, at. wt. 74.92. Exists in 3 allotropic forms, commonest being grey crystalline arsenic. Occurs as realgar (As_2S_3), white arsenic (As_2O_3) and arsenopyrite (FeAsS). Its extremely poisonous compounds used in weed and insect killers, also medicinally.

art, visual, branch of human activity, divided into PAINTING, SCULPTURE and ARCHITECTURE. Individual articles in this encyclopedia on styles of painting incl.: MANNERISM, IMPRESSIONISM, FAUVISM, CUBISM, POP and OP ART, FUTURISM, ABSTRACT EXPRESSIONISM, POST-IMPRESSIONISM, ABSTRACT ART, SOCIAL REALISM. For various articles on architectural styles *see*: BAROQUE, ROCOCO, ROMANESQUE, NORMAN ARCHITECTURE, GOTHIC, EARLY ENGLISH, PERPENDICULAR, DECORATED STYLE, NEO-CLASSICISM, GOTHIC REVIVAL.

Artaud, Antonin (c 1895-1948), French avant-garde dramatic theorist, producer. In *The Theatre of Cruelty* (1935), *The Theatre and Its Double* (1938) stressed that theatre should interpret experience in primitive images.

art deco, decorative style of late 1920s and 1930s, deriving its name from Exposition Internationale des Arts Décoratifs et Industriels Modernes (1925) in Paris. Characterized by geometric design, bright metallic surfaces, it attempted to express 'machine' aesthetic. Popular again in presence.

Artemis, in Greek myth, daughter of Zeus and Leto; sister of Apollo. Virgin goddess of hunting, wildlife, chastity, childbirth. Associated with the moon because of its supposed influence on organic life. Identified by Romans with Diana.

artemisia, genus of perennial herbs of Compositae family. Native to temperate and arctic regions. Scented foliage and small rayless flowers. Species incl. wormwood, mugwort, sagebrush, tarragon.

arteriosclerosis, hardening and thickening of walls of the arteries. Usually caused by deposition of fatty material, *eg* cholesterol, in linings of arteries. Frequently occurs in old age.

artery, any vessel carrying blood from heart to body tissues. Arteries have thick walls, lined with elastic fibres and muscles to withstand blood pressure.

artesian well, drilled well which relies on hydrostatic pressure to force water to surface. Pressure created within syncline, which comprises water-bearing layer (aquifer) sandwiched between impermeable strata. Named after Artois, France, where 1st such well was drilled.

arthritis, inflammation of joints. Rheumatoid arthritis, most severely crippling form, is characterized by inflammation of connective tissue around joints, esp. those of wrist and hand; often leads to deformity of joints. Cause unknown. Osteoarthritis is degeneration of joints, with loss of cartilage lining and growth of bone. Occurs mainly in elderly people, esp. in joints of leg and spine.

Arthropoda (arthropods), largest phylum of animal kingdom, incl. arachnids, crustaceans, insects, centipedes, millipedes. Segmented body, horny outer skeleton, primitive brain; various jointed appendages serve as limbs, gills or jaws.

Arthur, see ARTHURIAN LEGEND.

Arthur I (1187-c 1203), duke of Brittany (1196-c 1203). Posthumous son of Geoffrey, 4th son of Henry II of England. Rival to Prince John in claim for English throne after death of Richard I (1199). Captured by John; imprisoned at Rouen, prob. murdered there.

Arthurian legend, mass of interrelated stories prob. drawn from Celtic legend centring on King Arthur and his court. Arthur first mentioned in Celtic literature, c 600, as leader of Britons. GEOFFREY OF MONMOUTH's *Historia* (c 1135) portrayed Arthur as conqueror of W Europe. Wace's *Roman de Brut* (c 1155) first treated story as courtly romance, introduced Round Table. CHRÉTIEN DE TROYES (12th cent.) wrote 5 romances dealing with Arthur's knights. First treatment of Tristram and Isolde story was by German poet GOTTFRIED VON STRASSBURG. After 1225 literary tradition continued only in England, with anon. *Sir Gawain and the Green Knight* (c 1370) and MALORY's *Morte d'Arthur*. Full story makes Arthur illegitimate son of King Uther Pendragon, who demonstrates royal blood by removing sword from stone. Later receives invincible sword Excalibur from Lady in the Lake, and estab. court at Camelot,

marrying Guinevere and gathering around his Round Table best knights of Christendom. Decline begins with Holy Grail quest (dispersing knights), with Sir Lancelot's love for Guinevere, and ends with Sir Mordred (Arthur's son) fatally wounding Arthur. He is taken to Avalon, whence he will return in time of national peril. Other figures incl. Sir Galahad and Sir Percival, pure heroes of Holy Grail quest; Sir Gawain, Arthur's nephew; Merlin, magician and adviser to Arthur; Morgan le Fay, Arthur's half-sister and enchantress.

artichoke, name for 2 different garden vegetables of Compositae family. *Cynara scolymus*, native to Africa, is French or globe artichoke. Jerusalem artichoke, *Helianthus tuberosus*, is perennial sunflower with tuberous roots used as vegetable or livestock food.

Articles of Confederation, see CONFEDERATION, ARTICLES OF.

artificial insemination, method of introducing semen from male into female artificially to facilitate fertilization. Widely used in propagation of animals, esp. livestock. Sometimes used in humans when normal fertilization impossible.

artificial kidney, mechanical device which substitutes for lost kidneys. Blood is led from arteries by cellophane tube and waste products removed by DIALYSIS. Used 2 or 3 times per week.

artificial respiration, restoration or maintenance of breathing by manual or mechanical means. Mechanical devices used incl. IRON LUNG. Mouth-to-mouth method involves forcing breath into patient's mouth, while holding his nostrils shut.

artillery, originally any form of armament involving discharge of a projectile, incl. bow, catapult. Now any type of heavy firearm fired from carriage or platform.

art nouveau, term used to describe style of decorative art, at its height in Europe and North America *c* 1890-1910. Characterized by flat curvilinear designs based on natural forms. Applied in architecture and interior design (by Horta, van de Velde, Mackintosh), jewellery, book illustration (by Beardsley), glassware (by Louis Tiffany).

Artois, region and former prov. of N France, cap. Arras. Mainly agric., incl. part of Franco-Belgian coalfield. Disputed by France and the Habsburgs, finally taken by France 1640. Scene of many battles in WWI. Gave name to artesian wells, first sunk here in 12th cent.

arts and crafts movement, artistic and social movement, originating in late 19th cent. England, which tried to revive standard of decorative arts and restore creative dignity of craftsmen in reaction to debased quality of manufactured goods. Influenced by work and theories of William Morris, cooperative workshops were founded to produce furniture, textiles, wallpaper, pottery.

Arundel, mun. bor. of West Sussex, SE England, on R. Arun. Has 11th cent. castle, seat of dukes of Norfolk.

Aryan, Sanskrit word used for peoples speaking Indo-European languages. The Aryans originally spread (from *c* 2000 BC) throughout Mesopotamia from S Russia and Turkestan. Term used, with little scientific basis, in Nazi ideology to designate Indo-European race.

aryl group, in chemistry, organic RADICAL or group of atoms derived from aromatic compounds, *eg* phenyl radical C₆H₅.

asbestos, silicate mineral with fibrous structure. Common forms are chrysotile (type of SERPENTINE), crocidolite; often found as veins in other rock. Resistant to fire and acid, fibres may be pressed into plasterboard, woven into ropes, clothing, pipe insulation, *etc.* Major sources in Canada, South Africa, Rhodesia.

Ascension, isl. in S Atlantic, NW of St Helena. Area 88 sq km (34 sq mi). Site of American satellite tracking station. Dependency of St Helena since 1922.

Ascension, Christian festival, celebrating the bodily ascent of Jesus into heaven on the 40th day after Resurrection.

asceticism, doctrine that man can reach a higher spiritual state by rigorous self-discipline and self-denial. Has been common in the major monotheistic religions, also Hinduism, Buddhism and among the CYNICS. May involve prolonged fasting, self-mutilation, flagellation.

Asclepius, mythical Greek physician, son of Apollo. Learned art of medicine from CHIRON. Killed by Zeus for raising Hippolytus from the dead. Worshipped as god of healing, esp. at Epidaurus. Serpent was sacred to him. Known as Aesculapius by Romans.

ascorbic acid or vitamin C, crystalline water-soluble solid, occurring in fruit and vegetables. Necessary in diet of humans and guinea pigs to form fibres of connective tissue (absence causes scurvy). Identified 1932. Held to be effective in counteracting colds.

Ascot, village of Berkshire, S England. Has famous racecourse at Ascot Heath estab. 1711.

asdic, see SONAR.

Asgard, in Norse myth, home of the gods (Aesir) and slain heroes. Consisted of many great banqueting halls, incl. VALHALLA. Entered via rainbow bridge, Bifrost, guarded by Heimdal, watchman of the gods.

ash, any tree of genus *Fraxinus*. Pinnate leaves, winged fruit, tough elastic wood. Source of valuable timber. Incl. common European ash, *F. excelsior*, as well as white ash *F. americana* and black ash *F. nigra* of US.

Ashanti, admin. region of S Ghana. Hilly and forested, produces cocoa, hardwoods; noted for gold working. Hist. stronghold of Ashanti tribe, cap. Kumasi; wars against British in 19th cent. led to annexation by Gold Coast colony (1901), break-up of Ashanti confederation. Region of Ghana from 1957.

Ashcan School, popular name for group of American painters, called 'The Eight', who exhibited in New York in 1908. Attempted to portray contemporary scene in realistic terms. Led by Robert Henri, group incl. Arthur Davies, William Glackens. Organized ARMORY SHOW.

Ashcroft, Dame Edith Margaret Emily ('Peggy') (1907-), English actress. Notable in Shakespearian roles and as Margaret in *Dear Brutus*, Miss Madrigal in *The Chalk Garden*.

Ashes, the, mythical cricket trophy said to be held by the winning team of test series between England and Australia. Name derives from mock obituary of English cricket written in *Sporting Times* (1882), stating that 'the body will be cremated and the ashes taken to Australia'.

Ashkhabad, town of USSR, cap. of Turkmen SSR; near Iran border. Pop. 266,000. Textile mfg. Founded 1881, almost destroyed by earthquake in 1948.

Ashtart, see ASTARTE.

Ashton, Sir Frederick William Mallandaine (1906-), British choreographer, dancer, b. Ecuador. Founder choreographer to the Royal Ballet, director (1963-70). Ballets incl. *Façade, Enigma Variations, Tales of Beatrix Potter* (film, 1971).

Ash Wednesday, first day of Christian LENT, seventh Wednesday before Easter. Name derived from custom of rubbing ashes on the forehead as sign of penitence.

Asia, largest and most populous continent of the world. Bounded by Pacific (E), Arctic (N), Indian (S) oceans; stretches from Ural Mts. (USSR) and Asia Minor in W to Bering Str., Japan and Indonesia in E. Area *c* 43,300,000 sq km (16,700,000 sq mi). Pop. *c* 2,060,000,000. Mountain ranges incl. Himalayas, whose peaks, *eg* Mt. EVEREST, are highest in world. Major rivers Yenisei, Ob in Siberia; Yangtze, Mekong, Amur (S, SE); Indus, Ganges (S), Tigris, Euphrates (SW), centres of earliest known civilizations. Cold Siberian tundra merges in S with coniferous forestland; wooded steppes merge into desert regions of W China. In SE are fertile monsoon coastlands and river valleys of China, Japan, India, Indonesia and Indo-China, all densely populated and supported by rice crops. Vast oil reserves in SW desert regions (Arabia) now exploited; mineral resources in Siberia being developed.

Asia Minor or **Anatolia**, penin. of W Asia, between Black Sea, Mediterranean and Aegean; comprises Asiatic Turkey. High plateau crossed by Taurus Mts. in S; dry interior with many salt lakes. Scene of ancient cultures and numerous invasions; fell to Ottoman Turks 13th-15th cent.

Asimov, Isaac (1920-), American scientist and writer, b. Russia. Author of science fiction, eg I, Robot (1950), and scientific books for layman, eg The Intelligent Man's Guide to Science (1960).

Aske, Robert (d. 1537), English lawyer. Leader of PILGRIMAGE OF GRACE. Although tried to prevent 2nd revolt, was arrested and executed for high treason.

Asmara, city of N Ethiopia, cap. of Eritrea prov. on plateau. Pop. 241,000. Trade centre in agric. region; textiles, ceramics mfg.; univ. (1958). Railway link to Massawa. Cap. of Italian colony of Eritrea from 1890 until taken in 1941 by British.

Asoka (d. c 230 BC), Indian emperor of Maurya dynasty. Extended his empire over Afghanistan, Baluchistan and most of India. Abandoned wars after conversion to Buddhism, which he made state religion. Sent Buddhist missionaries abroad.

asp, one of several species of small poisonous snakes incl. Vipera aspis of S Europe, and Egyptian cobra.

asparagus, Asparagus officinalis, perennial garden vegetable native to Eurasia, cultivated in Britain, US. Tender shoots considered delicacy. Decorative species incl. A. plumosus.

aspen, any of several species of poplars with flattened leaves. Incl. Populus tremula of Europe as well as P. tremuloides and P. grandidentata of North America. Soft wood of some species is source of pulp.

asphalt, brown or black tar-like substance composed of various hydrocarbons. Occurs in asphalt lakes; obtained as residue of petroleum distillation. Used in road making and water-proofing.

asphodel, hardy stemless plant of genera Asphodelus and Asphodeline of lily family, native to Eurasia. Has showy flower spikes.

aspidistra, genus of Asiatic herbs of lily family. Has stiff, glossy, evergreen leaves, dark inconspicuous flowers near ground. Cultivated as house plant.

aspirin or **acetylsalicylic acid**, white crystalline solid used to reduce fever and relieve pain. Dangerous in excessive doses as it may cause bleeding in stomach.

Asquith, Herbert Henry, 1st Earl of Oxford and Asquith (1852-1928), British statesman, PM (1908-16). Headed Liberal govt. which introduced national insurance scheme after depriving Lords of veto power in 1911 PARLIAMENT ACT. Attempt to estab. Irish Home Rule failed. Resigned in favour of Lloyd George following WWI reverses.

ass, small horse-like mammal, genus Equus, found wild in semi-desert areas of Africa and Asia. Species incl. African ass, E. asinus, and

Asian ass, *E. hemionus*. Noted for endurance; domesticated varieties, incl. donkey, used as pack animals. Mule is offspring of jackass with horse mare, hinny offspring of she-ass with horse stallion; both sterile.

Assad, Hafiz al- (1928-), Syrian political leader and soldier. Became president (1971), led Syria into 1973 war with Israel. Sent troops to establish ceasefire in Lebanese civil war (1976).

Assam, state of NE India. Area *c* 77,700 sq km (30,000 sq mi); pop. 14,952,000; cap. Shillong. Almost enclosed by mountains; pop. concentrated in fertile river valleys, *eg* Brahmaputra. Heavy rainfall; produces timber, tea, rice. Incl. Northeast Frontier Agency union territ.

Assassins, members of a secret sect in Islam, founded *c* 1090 by Hasan Sabbah in Persia. Distinguished by total obedience to their leader, supposedly while under the influence of hashish. Regarded murder as sacred duty to eliminate enemies, incl. Crusaders. Purged by Mongols (from 1256).

Assent, Royal, in UK law, formal consent given by sovereign to bill after its passage through Parliament, condition of its becoming an act of Parliament. Last refused by Queen Anne (1702).

Assiniboine, river of Canada. Rises in E Saskatchewan, flows SE 950 km (590 mi) into Manitoba to join Red R. at Winnipeg.

Assisi, town of Umbria, C Italy. Pop. 24,000. Religious, tourist centre, overlooking Spoleto valley. Birthplace of St Francis; churches (frescoed by Cimabue, Giotto) built (13th cent.) over his tomb.

assizes, in England, court sessions held periodically by judges of High Court in regions to try civil and criminal cases. Assize towns grouped in 7 circuits, with 2 judges travelling each circuit.

association, in psychology, principle according to which ideas, feelings are connected in mind of the individual because of their previous occurrence together. In sociology, basic social unit, esp. one with common goal(s).

Association football or **soccer**, eleven-a-side team game played with round leather ball. Follows rules set down by Football Association in London (1863). Played worldwide, esp. on professional basis in Europe and South America. First professionals in England (1880s), League estab. 1888. International competition is controlled by FIFA (founded 1904) which organizes World Cup every 4 years (first held 1930).

Assuan, *see* ASWAN, Egypt.

Assyria, ancient empire of SW Asia, centred on Ashur on upper R. Tigris. *Fl* 9th-7th cents. BC when it gained ascendancy in Middle East esp. under Sargon II and Sennacherib. Conquered Egypt 671 BC under Esarhaddon and reached height of its power under Assurbanipal. Empire declined rapidly and cap. Nineveh was destroyed 612 BC by Medes and Babylonians.

Astaire, Fred, pseud. of Frederick Austerlitz (1899-), American dancer, singer, film actor. Known for films, esp. with Ginger Rogers, expressing 1930s' elegance, wit, *eg Top Hat* (1935), *Swing Time* (1936).

Astarte or **Ashtart**, Semitic goddess of fertility and love. Associated with planet Venus. Identified with Babylonian Ishtar and Greek Aphrodite.

astatine (At), radioactive element of halogen group; at. no. 85, mass no. of most stable isotope 210. Half-life 8.3 hrs. First prepared 1940 by bombarding bismuth with alpha particles.

aster, large genus of perennial plants of Compositae family. Purplish, blue, pink or white daisy-like flowers. Most garden varieties derived from North American autumn-blooming species. Cultivated as Michaelmas daisies in Europe.

asteroid or planetoid, minor planet of Solar System. Over 1600 recognized, most of which lie in belt between Mars and Jupiter. Largest and 1st discovered (1801) is Ceres, diameter 686 km (427 mi).

asthma, chronic disorder characterized by difficulty in breathing. Results from spasm of muscles in bronchial tubes and is accompanied by accumulation of mucus. Often caused by allergy or emotional stress.

Asti, town of Piedmont, NW Italy, cap. of Asti prov. Pop. 77,000. Distilleries; famous for sparkling wines (Asti Spumante).

astigmatism, irregularity in curvature of lens (incl. eye lens); results in inability to bring whole of an image into focus and consequential distortion. Use of cylindrical lens corrects astigmatism of eye.

Astor, John Jacob (1763-1848), American millionaire, b. Germany. Amassed immense fortune after start as fur trader, estab. family as prominent New Yorkers. Great-

grandson, William Waldorf Astor, 1st Viscount Astor (1848-1919), moved to England in 1890, founded English branch of family, known for philanthropy. His daughter-in-law, Nancy Witcher Astor, née Langhorne (1879-1964), was 1st woman to sit in House of Commons (1919-45). Famous political hostess, influenced govt. policy through 'Cliveden set', Conservative group who met at her Cliveden house parties.

Astrakhan, city of USSR, SE European RSFSR; on Volga Delta. Pop. 427,000. Centre of river transport; shipbuilding, fish processing (esp. caviare). Cap. of Tartar khanate, taken by Ivan the Terrible 1556.

astringent, drug used to contract body tissue and check bleeding, mucus secretion, etc. Examples incl. aluminium salts, tannin, silver nitrate.

astrolabe, ancient and medieval scientific instrument used to measure altitude of heavenly bodies. Consisted of graduated metal disc with pivoted sighting arm. Replaced by quadrant and sextant.

astrology, form of divination based on theory that all events on Earth are determined by movements of heavenly bodies. Basis of ancient astronomy, from which it diverged after Copernicus. Individual's fate predicted by use of horoscope, map of heavens at time of birth, drawing on chart of ZODIAC.

astronomy, scientific study of nature, position and motion of heavenly bodies. Of ancient origin, fl under Greeks; their findings, summarized by Ptolemy, were displaced by Copernican theory in 16th cent.

Newton's laws of motion and gravitation provided basis for later study. Branches incl. astrophysics, cosmology, radio and X-ray astronomy.

astrophysics, branch of astronomy dealing with physical properties of heavenly bodies and also their origin and evolution.

Asturias, Miguel Angel (1899–1974), Guatemalan author, diplomat. Novels incl. *El Señor Presidente* (1946), *Mulata de tal* (1963, *The Mulatta and Mr Fly*), use technique of 'magical realism'. Nobel Prize for Literature (1967).

Asturias, region and former kingdom of NW Spain, hist. cap. Oviedo. Cantabrian Mts. in S; hilly woodland, pasture. Coalmining from Roman times, metal industs.; cattle raising, apple orchards. Christian stronghold during Moorish conquest; kingdom joined with León (866), later with Castile. Principality 1388-1931.

Asunción, cap. of Paraguay, port on Paraguay R. Pop. 437,000. Major commercial, transport centre; food processing, textile mfg. Founded *c* 1536. Centre of Spanish colonization in S of continent.

Aswan or **Assuan** (anc. *Syene*), city of S Egypt, just below First Cataract of the Nile. Pop. 202,000. Trade, tourist centre; chemicals indust.; syenite quarries. Nearby are Aswan Dam (completed 1902); Aswan High Dam (completed 1970), 111 m (365 ft) high, 4.8 km (3 mi) wide, has created L. Nasser, reservoir (area *c* 5180 sq km/2000 sq mi) providing irrigation, h.e.p. for Egypt and Sudan. Construction required raising of ABU SIMBEL temples.

Atacama Desert, arid region of N Chile-S Peru, between Andes and Pacific coast. Alt. 610 m (*c* 2000 ft). Has rich nitrate, copper, iron ore deposits. One of driest areas in world, with almost no vegetation.

Atahualpa (d. 1533), last Inca ruler of Peru. Seized whole empire after defeating half-brother Huáscar. Captured (1532) by Spanish conquistador Pizarro, who had him killed.

Atalanta, in Greek myth, huntress famed for speed and skill. Took part in Calydonian hunt, was first to wound the boar. Ran race with suitors on condition that she would marry first man to outstrip her; the others would be killed. Hippomenes, or Melanion, won race by dropping 3 golden apples which Atalanta stopped to pick up.

Ataturk, Kemal, orig. Mustafa Kemal Pasha (1881-1938), Turkish military and political leader. Participated in Young Turks revolt (1908). Estab. rival govt. in Asia Minor (1919) against Allied-controlled Constantinople regime after Turkey's collapse in WWI. Repulsed Greek invasion from Anatolia (1919-22); re-estab. Turkish sovereignty over occupied territs. First president of Turkey (1923-38), ruled as dictator. Introduced Westernizing reform programme.

Athabaska, river of NC Alberta, Canada. Rises in Rocky Mts., flows NE 1230 km (765 mi) to Lake Athabaska (on N Alberta-Saskatchewan border); area 8100 sq km (*c* 3120 sq mi). Rich oil-bearing sands along lower course of river.

Athanasian Creed, statement of

Christian belief maintaining belief in the Trinity, as opposed to Arianism (see ARIUS). Formerly attributed to Athanasius, now believed to date from 6th cent.

Athanasius, St (c 296-373), Egyptian theologian, patriarch of Alexandria. Maintained consubstantiality of Jesus with God, opposing ARIUS at 1st Council of Nicaea (325) and in *Defence against the Arians* (348). Influential in shaping Catholic doctrine.

atheism, denial of existence of God or gods: Occurs in ancient times, *eg* in Socrates' attack on religious orthodoxy of Athens; again in 19th cent. with belief in an inherent conflict between science and religion. *See* AGNOSTICISM.

Athelstan (c 895-939), king of England (924-39). Consolidated and built upon work of his grandfather, Alfred; defeated union of Scots, Danes and Welsh at Brunanburh (937).

Athena or **Pallas Athena**, in Greek myth, patron goddess of Athens, personification of wisdom, patron of intellectual and practical skills. Represented as warlike virgin goddess, having sprung fully-armed from the head of Zeus. PARTHENON erected to her on Acropolis. Identified by Romans with Minerva.

Athens (*Athinai*), cap. of Greece, on Plain of Attica. Pop. 2,540,000 (incl. Piraeus). Admin., indust., cultural centre; univ.; Greek Orthodox archbishopric. Foremost Greek city state from 5th cent. BC, esp. under Pericles. Won Persian Wars, but defeated by Sparta (404 BC); decline followed defeat by Philip of Macedon (338 BC); sacked by Rome (86

BC). Fell to Turks 1458, rebuilt as cap. of independent Greece (1834). Buildings incl. Acropolis, Parthenon, Erechtheum. Now forms one city with Piraeus, largest Greek port. Exports wine, olive oil. Built c 450 BC, once linked to Athens by Long Walls, destroyed by Sulla (86 BC).

atherosclerosis, type of arteriosclerosis associated with deposits of fatty material, usually cholesterol, in lining of arteries. Factors linked to its cause incl. eating of animal fat, tobacco smoking, lack of exercise.

athlete's foot, *see* RINGWORM.

athletics, physical games and contests, divided into field (throwing, jumping, vaulting) and track (running) events. History can be traced as far as Greek games of 13th cent. BC. Modern athletics date from 19th cent. and received considerable impetus from estab. of international competitions, esp. Olympic Games (1896).

Athlone, town of Co. Westmeath, C Irish Republic, on R. Shannon. Pop. 10,000. Military station; broadcasting centre.

Athos or **Akti**, penin. of NE Greece, easternmost part of Chalcidice penin., Macedonia. Rises to Mt. Athos (*Hagion Oros*: 'Holy Mountain'), 2032 m (6670 ft) high; incl. 20 Basilian monasteries (founded 10th cent.), created an autonomous state 1927.

Atkinson, Sir Harry Albert (1831-92), New Zealand political leader, b. England. Premier of colony (1876-7, 1883-4, 1887-91).

Atlanta, cap. of Georgia, US. Pop. 497,000. Transport and commercial centre; textiles, steel products. Founded 1837 as Terminus, renamed

1843. City burned by W. T. Sherman during Civil War.

Atlantic Cable, submarine telegraph cable linking Britain and US. Successfully laid (1866) through efforts of Cyrus Field (1819-92). Telephone cable link between UK and Canada completed 1961.

Atlantic Charter, programme drawn up (Aug. 1941) by Churchill (Britain) and F.D. Roosevelt (US), stating general aims for post-WWII peace. Goals incl. in UN declaration (1942).

Atlantic City, resort of SE New Jersey, US; on Absecon Beach (sand bar). Pop. 48,000. Has board walks, luxury hotels, auditorium; holds political conventions.

Atlantic Ocean, world's 2nd largest ocean. Area 82,362,000 sq km (c 31,800,000 sq mi). Extends from Arctic to Antarctic, between Americas and Europe and Africa. Greatest depth at Milwaukee Deep (8530 m/28,000 ft) just N of Puerto Rico. Chief ocean currents Equatorials and subsidiaries: Gulf Stream and Labrador in N, Brazil and Guinea in S. N Atlantic is world's busiest passenger and freight waterway.

Atlantis, legendary large island in western sea. Plato describes it as a Utopia, destroyed by earthquake. Solon identified it with Santorin in Cyclades isls., which erupted c 1500 BC causing destruction of Minoan civilization by fire and tidal wave.

Atlas, in Greek myth, a Titan, son of Iapetus and Clymene. For his part in Titans' revolt against Olympians, condemned to hold up sky. Identified with Atlas Mts. in N Africa.

Atlas Mountains, system of NW Africa. Extend c 2400 km (1500 mi) from SW Morocco to N Tunisia. Incl. Tell Atlas, Saharan Atlas (Algeria); High Atlas (Morocco) rise to 4163 m/13,664 ft at Djebel Toubkal. Resources incl. phosphates, coal, oil, iron ore.

atmosphere, combination of gases surrounding a celestial body. For Earth, it consists mainly of nitrogen (78%), oxygen (21%). Extends up to c 950 km (600 mi), becomes rarer with distance from Earth's surface, 99% of mass of atmosphere being within 80 km (50 mi). Layers, in ascending order, are TROPOSPHERE, STRATOSPHERE, mesosphere, thermosphere, exosphere. Atmosphere forms protective shield; absorbs and scatters harmful radiation, causes solid matter to burn up. Also see IONOSPHERE

atoll, form of CORAL REEF. Circular or horseshoe-shaped, encloses a lagoon.

atom, in chemistry, smallest particle of an element which can take part in chemical reaction. Atom consists of positively charged nucleus, where its mass is concentrated, surrounded by orbiting electrons; nucleus is composed of protons and neutrons, the number of protons equal to number of electrons. See ELEMENT.

atomic bomb, weapon deriving explosive force from nuclear fission. Detonated by rapidly bringing together 2 subcritical masses of fissile material (eg uranium 235 or plutonium 239), with total mass exceeding critical mass. Ensuing chain reaction releases nuclear energy, yielding intense heat and shock waves, gamma and neutron radiation. Developed during WWII and first used on Hiroshima.

atomic clock, extremely accurate clock utilizing vibrations of atoms and molecules. Originally ammonia and caesium used; now hydrogen maser gives accuracy of c 1 part in 10^{13}.

atomic energy, see NUCLEAR ENERGY.

Atomic Energy Commission, US body set up (1946) to supervise peaceful uses of atomic energy. Five members appointed by president, subject to Senate's approval.

atomic mass unit or **amu,** unit of mass, 1/12 of mass of most abundant isotope of carbon (mass no. 12). Equals c 1.66×10^{-27} kg.

atomic number, number of protons in atomic nucleus of an element.

atomic theory, study of structure of fundamental components of matter. Early contributors incl. DEMOCRITUS (5th cent. BC) who held that matter is composed of minute indivisible particles (atoms) in motion. Modern theory began with JOHN DALTON (1808) who held that elements are made of identical atoms, whose physical and chemical properties are different from those of atoms of other elements. A theory of internal structure of atoms was formulated by RUTHERFORD and improved by BOHR, who used quantum theory to describe electron orbits about central nucleus. Most recent theories rely on probabilistic methods of WAVE MECHANICS.

atomic weight, average mass of atom of specified isotopic composition of an element, measured in atomic mass units. Usually natural isotopic composition taken.

atonality, in music, absence of a key or tonal centre. Much of modern 'classical' music has moved away from definite tonal centres. Developed in work of Ives, Schoenberg, Webern, Bartók.

atonement, in Christian theology, the effect of Jesus' sufferings and death in bringing about the reconciliation of man to God. First made explicit by St Anselm in *Cur Deus Homo?*

Atonement, Day of (Heb. *Yom Kippur*), most important Jewish holy day on 10th day of 7th month, Tishri (late Sept. or Oct.). Day of prayer for forgiveness; liturgy begins with Kol Nidre prayer.

Atreus, in Greek myth, king of Mycenae; father of Agamemnon and Menelaus. To avenge treachery of his brother, THYESTES, he killed Thyestes' sons and served their flesh to him at a banquet. Killed by AEGISTHUS.

atrium, in anatomy, either of two upper chambers on each side of heart. Left atrium receives oxygenated blood from lungs; right atrium receives venous blood from rest of body.

atrium, in architecture, inner central court of Roman house, usually open to sky and surrounded by dwelling rooms. Name also applies to open court in front of early Christian and medieval churches.

Attenborough, Sir Richard (1923–), English actor, film producer. Roles incl. Pinkie in *Brighton Rock* (1947); directed and produced *Oh What a Lovely War* (1969).

Attica (*Attiki*), admin. dist. of EC Greece, cap. Athens. Cereals, olive oil, wine. In legend, Ionian state formed by Theseus; dominated by Athens from 5th cent. BC.

Attila (c 406-53), king of the Huns (434-53). Ruled over most of area between the Rhine and Caspian. Forced Rome to pay tribute and invaded Gaul when tributes ceased. Defeated at Châlons (451). Later invaded Italy but withdrew N after abandoning plan to capture Rome (452).

Attis, in Phrygian pantheon, god of vegetation. After death, caused by self-castration, spirit passed into pine tree; violets grew from his blood, symbolizing rebirth of plant life. Spring festival celebrated death and resurrection.

Attlee, Clement Richard Attlee, 1st Earl (1883-1967), British statesman, PM (1945-51). Rose to Labour Party leadership (1935), after serving in 1924 and 1929 Labour govts. Deputy leader in Churchill's wartime coalition cabinet (1942-5). His own admin. inaugurated nationalization of major industs., created National Health Service; concluded Palestinian mandate and granted independence to India. After 1951 election loss, led opposition until retirement (1955).

attorney, in law, person empowered to act as agent for or in behalf of another, esp. a lawyer. *See* ADVO-CATE.

Aube, river of NE France. Flows c 240 km (150 mi) NW from Langres Plateau to R. Seine.

aubergine, deep purple fruit of eggplant, *Solanum melongena,* native to India. Cultivated widely esp. in Mediterranean region.

aubretia, genus of plant of Cruci-ferae family. Showy purplish flowers, often cultivated in rock gardens. Native to Middle East.

Aubrey, John (1626-97), English writer. Known for his collection of vivid biog. sketches, pub. (1813) as *Brief Lives.*

Auch, town of SW France, on R. Gers, cap. of Gers dept. Pop. 24,000. Agric. market, wine, brandy. Major city (*Auscorum*) of Roman Gaul; cap. of Armagnac from 10th cent., of Gascony from 17th cent. Cathedral (15th cent.).

Auckland, city of N North Isl., New Zealand, on isthmus between 2 harbours. Pop. 152,000. Major port for overseas trade; exports dairy produce, fruit, timber. Shipbuilding, engineering industs.; food processing. Has major airport; univ. (1882); RC, Anglican cathedrals. Former cap. of New Zealand (1840-65). Seven extinct volcanoes in area.

Auden, W[ystan] H[ugh] (1907-73), English poet. Led left-wing literary movement in 1930s. Plays with Isherwood incl. *The Dog Beneath the Skin* (1935), *The Ascent of F.6* (1937). *Collected Poetry* (1945) contains best-known verse. Also wrote opera libretti (incl. text for Stravinsky's *The Rake's Progress*) and criticism; edited anthologies and lectured. Settled in US 1939.

Audenarde, see OUDENAARDE, Belgium.

Audubon, John James (c 1785-1851), American ornithologist, artist. Conducted first bird-banding experiments in US. Visited Britain (1826) to obtain publication of *The Birds of America* and *Ornithological Biography* (with William Mac-Gillivray), works featuring his drawings of bird life.

Augsburg, city of S West Germany,

on R. Lech. Pop. 213,000. Railway jct., textile centre. Roman colony founded 14 BC by Augustus. Important commercial centre 15th-16th cent., home of Fugger banking family.

Augsburg, League of, European alliance (1686) against Louis XIV of France formed by Habsburgs, Sweden and various German states. Joined by England and Holland (1689) to form Grand Alliance which fought France until 1697. *See* RYSWICK, TREATY OF.

Augsburg, Peace of, settlement (1555) of problems created within Holy Roman Empire by Reformation. Estab. principle that choice between Lutheranism and Catholi-' cism was to be made by individual princes.

Augsburg Confession, official statement of Lutheran beliefs. Presented to Charles V at Diet of Augsburg (1530). Mainly the work of Melanchthon and endorsed by Luther.

Augurs or **Augures,** college of officials in ancient Rome who interpreted signs (*auspicia*) of divine approval or disapproval in natural phenomena, *eg* eclipse, meteors, flight or feeding of birds.

Augusta, town of E Georgia, US; on Savannah R. Pop. 60,000. Cotton market; indust., trade centre. Estab. as trading post 1735; state cap. 1785-95.

Augusta, cap. of Maine, US; on Kennebec R. Pop. 22,000. Trading post estab. 1628. Mfg. industs. developed with damming of river (1837).

Augustine, St (354-430), Numidian churchman, theologian. Brought up as Christian, but not baptized until 387 after period of great doubt recorded in spiritual autobiog. *Confessions.* Bishop of Hippo in N Africa (396-430), defended Christianity against heretical beliefs incl. Manichaeism, Pelagianism. Other works incl. *City of God,* defending Christianity against pagan critics and giving Christian view of history.

Augustine of Canterbury, St (d. *c* 605), Roman Benedictine missionary, 1st archbishop of Canterbury. Sent (596) by Pope Gregory I to England, converted Ethelbert of Kent and introduced Roman doctrines, calendar into England.

Augustinians, religious orders in RC church which live according to Rule of St Augustine of Hippo. First organized in 11th cent. Most famous house is hospice on Great St Bernard Pass.

Augustus, full name Gaius Julius Caesar Octavianus (63 BC-AD 14), 1st Roman emperor. Adopted as son and heir by Caesar. On Caesar's death, entered into ruling coalition (2nd Triumvirate) with Lepidus and ANTONY. Subsequent conflict with Antony and Cleopatra culminated in his victory at Actium (31 BC), leaving him master of Rome. Assumed leadership (28 BC), given title Augustus. Took control of the army and estab. frontiers of the empire. Reorganized admin. of the provinces. Rule marked by prosperity, flourishing of the arts.

auk, diving bird of Alcidae family of N hemisphere, with webbed feet, short wings. Flightless great auk, *Pinguinus impennis,* was largest species; became extinct in mid-19th cent. through hunting.

Auld Alliance, long-standing alliance between Scotland and France against common enemy, England, from 12th to 16th cent. Often worked against Scottish interests.

Aurangzeb (1618-1707), Mogul emperor of India (1658-1707). Seized throne by imprisoning father, Shah Jehan. Extended empire through military conquests. Fanatical supporter of Islam, destroyed Hindu temples and antagonized Sikhs.

Aurelian, full name Lucius Domitius Aurelianus (c 212-75), Roman emperor (270-5). Successful military leader, acclaimed emperor by his troops. Secured Danube and Rhine frontiers against barbarians and defeated ZENOBIA of Palmyra; recaptured Gaul.

Aurelius, Marcus, see MARCUS AURELIUS ANTONINUS.

Aurora, in Roman religion, goddess of dawn, identified with Greek Eos.

aurora, coloured light phenomenon visible at night in near-polar regions. Aurora borealis (northern lights) seen in N hemisphere, aurora australis in S. Believed to be caused by collisions of air molecules and charged particles from Sun, deflected towards poles by Earth's magnetic field. Occurs esp. during periods of sunspot activity.

Auschwitz, see OŚWIECIM, Poland.

Austen, Jane (1775-1817), English novelist. Works reflect experience as unmarried daughter of a country rector, but her ironically witty analysis of character and moral problems is profound and universal. *Emma* (1816) and *Pride and Prejudice* (1813) are most popular, but *Sense and Sensibility* (1811), *Mansfield Park* (1814), *Northanger Abbey* and *Persuasion* (both pub. 1818) all show the same skilful construction.

Austerlitz (*Slavkov*), town of SC Czechoslovakia. Pop. 4000. Scene of battle (1805) in which French under Napoleon defeated combined Austro-Russian force.

Austin, Herbert Austin, 1st Baron (1866-1941), English pioneer automobile manufacturer. Designed 1st Wolseley automobile (1895); began production of Austin in 1906.

Austin, cap. of Texas, US; on Colorado R. Pop. 250,000. In irrigated agric. region; food processing industs. Educational and artistic centre. Estab. as cap. 1839. Has Univ. of Texas (1883).

Australasia, term referring normally to Australia, New Zealand, New Guinea and adjacent isls. May also refer to all Oceania.

Australia, smallest continent, between Indian Ocean (W) and Pacific Ocean (E). Forms, with Tasmania, Commonwealth of Australia. Area 7,690,000 sq km (2,970,000 sq mi); pop. 12,728,000; cap. Canberra. Language: English. Religions: Anglican, RC. Comprises 6 states: New South Wales, Queensland, South Australia, Tasmania, Victoria, Western Australia; also Capital Territ., Northern Territ. Narrow coastal lowlands, except for Nullarbor Plain in S; Great Dividing Range in E; vast arid tableland in W. Climate varies from tropical monsoon in N to temperate in S. Isolation led to distinct flora and fauna *eg* giant eucalyptus, marsupials. Agric. incl. sheep rearing, wheat and fruit growing; minerals incl. gold, lead, copper, zinc, uranium, bauxite, oil, iron, coal; industs. incl. iron and steel, chemicals. E coast claimed (1770) for Britain by Cook. Originally used as penal settlement; pop. increased greatly after gold discoveries c 1850. Separate colonies federated 1901 to form Commonwealth.

Australian aborigines, ethnic group of Australian mainland (mainly N and NE). Nomadic hunters, they have primitive material culture but complex social system with totemic worship. Weapons incl. boomerang. Est. pop. is 70,000 mostly on reservations, largest being Arnhem Land, Northern Territ.

Australian Alps, mountain range of SE New South Wales and NE Victoria, Australia. Incl. Snowy Mts.; highest peak Mt. Kosciusko. Winter sports area.

Australian Antarctic Territory, all isls. and mainland S of 60°S and between 45° and 160°E (with exception of Adélie Land); comprises almost half of Antarctica. Incl. Enderby, MacRobertson, Princess Elizabeth, Wilhelm II, Queen Mary, Wilkes, George V lands and parts of Victoria Land.

Australian Capital Territory (ACT), territ. of SE Australia, enclave within New South Wales. Area, incl. Jervis Bay port, 2432 sq km (939 sq mi); pop. 144,000; cap. Canberra. Mainly grassy or forested upland; drained by Molonglo R. ACT created 1911 to incl. site of new federal cap.

Australian rules football, eighteen-a-side team game played with an oval ball. Dates from 1858, rules being revised in 1866. Derived from soccer, rugby and Gaelic football. Most popular in S and W states.

Australopithecus, extinct genus of hominid family from which modern man may have evolved. Earliest discovered was *Australopithecus africanus* (South Africa, 1925). Tool-making form *A. boisei* (formerly known as *Zinjanthropus*), c 1.8 million years old, was discovered (1959) by Leakey in OLDUVAI GORGE.

Austria (*Osterreich*), republic of C Europe. Area 83,851 sq km (32,375 sq mi); pop. 7,521,000; cap. Vienna. Language: German. Religion: RC. Mainly mountainous, fertile Danube plain in NE. Agric. (cereals, cattle, pigs), timber, coal, iron ore, h.e.p. Indust. centres Vienna, Graz, Linz. Ruled by Habsburgs 1282-1918, centre of Holy Roman Empire; incorporated Hungary, expanded with Partitions of Poland (18th cent.). Became Austrian empire (1804); unrest in Hungary led to dual monarchy (1867), collapsed 1918. Forcibly made part of Nazi Germany 1938-45; occupied by Allies 1945-55.

Austrian Succession, War of the (1740-8), European conflict precipitated by Maria Theresa's succession to Habsburg lands, by PRAGMATIC SANCTION, challenged by Bavarian elector (later Emperor Charles VII). Frederick II of Prussia, by claiming and invading Silesia, started war; withdrew (1745) after obtaining most of Silesia, through Treaty of Dresden. Bavaria withdrew from war after death of Charles VII (1745) when it was overrun by Austrians. Subsequent hostilities inconclusive, war concluded by Treaty of AIX-LA-CHAPELLE.

Austro-Hungarian Monarchy or **Dual Monarchy**, reorganized form of Habsburg empire, estab. (1867) to placate Hungarian nationalist aspirations. Hungary given control of internal affairs, union of crowns of Hungary and Austria maintained. Dissolved 1918.

Austro-Prussian War, conflict (June-Aug. 1866), between Prussia, supported by Italy, and Austria, allied with several German states. Prussia won quick victory over German states and defeated Austrians at Sadowa. Peace of Prague resulted in Austria ceding Venetia to Italy; Prussia annexed Frankfurt, Hanover and Hesse-Kassel. War provided 2nd stage in estab. of German Empire in 1871. Also known as Seven Weeks War.

authoritarianism, in psychology, tendency in individual to be obsequious to those hierarchically superior, and to be dominant over those inferior. In sociology, the theory and practice of administration by means of commands, punishment, without recourse to justification, consultation, persuasion.

Authorized Version, English translation of the Bible, pub. in 1611 with the authorization of King James I (also called King James Bible). Prepared by committee of Protestant scholars under direction of Lancelot Andrewes.

autism, psychosis, esp. of children, characterized by withdrawal from contact with other humans and disregard for external reality.

autobiography, person's account of own life. Mainly a post-Renaissance form, *Confessions* of St Augustine could be regarded as a precursor. Later exponents incl. Casanova, Ben Franklin, Rousseau. Forms range from poetry (Wordsworth's *Prelude*) to Hitler's political *Mein Kampf*.

auto da fé (Port., = act of faith), ceremonial burning of heretics in public. In widest use during Inquisition in Spain and Portugal; last known use in Mexico (1815). Also refers to trial and sentencing of alleged heretics by Inquisition.

autogiro or **gyroplane**, aircraft that moves forward by means of a powered propeller and is supported in air mainly by a revolving horizontal aerofoil turned by air pressure and not motor power. Used for its ability to make short take-offs and landings.

Autolycus, in Greek myth, grandfather of Odysseus. Accomplished thief and trickster with special powers.

automation, in industry, automatic control of processes by self-regulating machinery. Such machinery makes use of part of its output effect to modify and correct input (feedback), using *eg* electronic sensing devices.

automobile or **motor car**, self-propelling passenger vehicle usually powered by INTERNAL COMBUSTION ENGINE. Wheels driven via GEARBOX and DIFFERENTIAL. Developed in Germany by Karl Benz (c 1885), Gottlieb Daimler, and in US by Henry Ford.

autonomy, in politics, freedom to act without external constraint, specifically referring to limited self-determination; often granted as prelude to complete independence, *eg* UK granted extensive internal legislative powers to Canada, Australia before their independence.

autumn crocus, *see* MEADOW SAFFRON.

Auvergne, region and former prov. of C France, in Massif Central, cap. Clermont-Ferrand. Cereals, livestock, cheese mfg.; mineral springs. Mainly mountainous, range of extinct volcanoes runs N-S. Hist. part of Aquitaine, part of France from 1527.

auxin, plant hormone, produced in actively growing parts, which regulates amount, type and direction of plant growth. Synthetic auxins are important in agriculture to promote growth, *etc.*

avalanche, swiftly descending mass of ice and snow, often with accumulated rock and vegetation, common in mountain areas. Causes incl. melting of base of snow mass, sudden shocks (*eg* noise, earth tremors).

Avalon, in Celtic myth, isle of blest or paradise, sometimes identified with Glastonbury (Somerset). *See* ARTHURIAN LEGEND.

Avebury, village in Wiltshire, England, SW of Swindon. Site of Neolithic stone circle, older and larger than that at Stonehenge. Many stones removed in earlier times for building material.

Ave Maria (Lat., = hail, Mary), prayer to Virgin Mary, fixed in present form by Pope Pius V (16th cent.). Main prayer of the ROSARY.

Averroës, Arabic name Ibn Rushd (1126-98), Spanish Moslem philosopher. Made Aristotle known in Europe by commentaries which were translated into Latin. Dealt with the demarcation of faith and reason, but felt that they were not opposed.

Avesta or **Zend-Avesta,** collection of writings sacred to Zoroastrians and Parsees. Incl. creation myth, litanies, laws of ritual purification. Written in old Iranian and survives only in fragmentary and much corrupted form. *See* ZOROASTRIANISM.

aviation, operation of heavier-than-air aircraft. History of aviation highlighted by Wright brothers' 1st flight in heavier-than-air craft (US, 1903); Louis Blériot's flight across English Channel (1909); Alcock and Brown's transatlantic flight (1919); Charles Lindbergh's solo Atlantic crossing (1932). First transatlantic passenger service begun by Pan American Airways (1939). Years following WWII saw development of jet propulsion and supersonic flight for military and civilian purposes.

Avicebron, *see* IBN GABIROL, SOLOMON BEN JUDAH.

Avicenna, Arabic name Ibn Sina (980-1037), Persian philosopher, physician. Estab. classification of sciences used in medieval schools of Europe. Known for his *Canon of Medicine.*

Avignon, town of Provence, S France, on R. Rhône. Cap. of Vaucluse dept. Pop. 89,000. Wine trade, silk mfg., tourist centre. Papal see during 'Babylonian Captivity' (1309-77), remained under papal control until 1791. Town walls, papal palace (both 14th cent.); ruins of 12th cent. bridge.

Avila, town of C Spain, on R. Adaja,

cap. of Avila prov. Pop. 25,000. Tourist and religious centre. Cathedral, town walls (both 11th cent.). Birthplace of St Teresa.

avocado or **avocado pear**, tropical American tree, *Persea americana*, esp. cultivated varieties originating in West Indies, Guatemala, Mexico. Yields fleshy, green or purple, pear-shaped edible fruit. Also called alligator pear.

avocet, long-legged wading bird related to snipe, genus *Recurvirostra*, with worldwide distribution. Feeds by sweeping upward-curving bill through water.

Avogadro, Amadeo, Conte di Quaregna (1776-1856), Italian physicist. Formulated Avogadro's hypothesis, that equal volumes of gases at same temperature and pressure contain equal numbers of molecules, thus explaining Gay-Lussac's law of combining volumes.

avoirdupois, systems of weights used in UK and US: 16 drams = 1 ounce, 16 ounces = 1 pound, 28 pounds = 1 quarter, 4 quarters = 1 hundredweight, 20 hundredweights = 1 ton.

Avon, Anthony Eden, 1st. Earl of, see EDEN, ANTHONY.

Avon, county of SW England, on Bristol Channel. Area 1337 sq km (516 sq mi); pop. 914,000; co. town Bristol. Created 1974, incl. parts of Gloucestershire, Wiltshire, Somerset.

Avon, several rivers of UK. **1,** flows 154 km (96 mi) from Northamptonshire via Stratford into R. Severn at Tewkesbury. **2,** flows 120 km (75 mi) from Gloucestershire via Bath, Bristol into Bristol Channel at Avonmouth. Also name of other rivers in Scotland, Wales.

Axis, coalition of states (1936-45), active in WWII. Grew out of German-Italian alliance (1936); joined by Japan in Berlin Pact of 1940. Later incl. Hungary, Romania, Bulgaria, Slovakia, Croatia. Also *see* ANTI-COMINTERN PACT.

axolotl, aquatic larval salamander, genus *Ambystoma*, of SW US and Mexico. Does not develop into terrestrial adult amphibian, but can breed.

Axum, see AKSUM, Ethiopia.

Ayer, Sir A[lfred] J[ules] (1910-), English philosopher. Brought LOGICAL POSITIVISM to attention of English readership in *Language, Truth and Logic* (1936). Other works incl. *The Foundations of Empirical Knowledge* (1940), *The Problem of Knowledge* (1956).

Ayesha (c 611-678), favourite wife of Mohammed. Helped father, Abu Bakr, succeed to caliphate on Mohammed's death. Fomented revolt against ALI, 4th caliph.

Aylesbury, mun. bor. of C England, co. town of Buckinghamshire. Pop. 41,000. Main indust. food processing.

Ayrshire, former county of SW Scotland, now in Strathclyde region. Hills in SE. Dairying (Ayrshire cattle) potato growing; coalmining industs. Co. town was Ayr, royal burgh on R. Ayr. Pop. 48,000. Small port, resort; textile, engineering industs. Alloway, birthplace of Burns, is nearby.

Ayub Khan, Mohammed (1907-74), Pakistani army officer, statesman. Became president after military coup (1958). Introduced land reforms; ended martial law (1962).

Resigned 1969 amidst mounting opposition.

azalea, widely distributed genus of shrubs or trees, now usually considered a subgenus of genus *Rhododendron.* Deciduous leaves and funnel-shaped flowers of various colours. Many varieties cultivated as house plants. Species incl. American flame azalea, *R. calendulaceum.*

Azaña, Manuel (1880-1940), Spanish statesman. Premier of republic (1931-3, 1936), attempted to introduce social reform. President (1936-9), fled to France on Franco's victory in Civil War.

Azerbaijan Soviet Socialist Republic, constituent republic of SW USSR; on Iran border. Area *c* 86,600 sq km (33,400 sq mi); pop. 5,111,000; cap. Baku. Crossed by Caucasus Mts. in N; C plain watered by R. Kura and tributaries. Produces cotton, wheat; major oil deposits in Apsheron penin., centred on Baku. Territ. ceded to Russia in 19th cent. by Persia, incorporated by USSR (1920).

azimuth, in astronomy, arc of horizon between its N or S point and vertical circle passing through zenith and centre of heavenly body.

Azores (*Açores*), archipelago of N Atlantic, admin. dist. of Portugal *c* 1450 km (900 mi) W of Lisbon. Area 2300 sq km (888 sq mi); largest isl. São Miguel, has chief town Ponta Delgada. Volcanic, rises to 2315 m (7600 ft). Fruit, vegetables grown; winter resort. Settled by Portuguese mid-15th cent.

Azov, Sea of (Latin *Palus Maeotis*), N arm of Black Sea, to which it is connected by Kerch str. Area *c* 37,700 sq km (14,500 sq mi). Shallow, with many sandbanks and low salinity; receives R. Don near town of Azov. Important fisheries.

Aztec, American Indian people of C Mexico. Ruling group at time of Spanish conquest (16th cent.). Noted for highly sophisticated civilization, centred on cap. Tenochtitlán on site of modern Mexico City. Spoke a Uto-Aztecan language.

Aztec civilization, culture of Aztec people developed (from 12th cent.) on Mayan and Toltec foundations. Characterized by use of irrigation for agriculture, fine weaving, intricate metalwork (esp. gold), massive buildings erected by slave labour. Religion was pantheistic, latterly involving human sacrifice.

B

Baal, fertility god of N Semites, worship spread to Carthage and Egypt; name later applied to gods of particular towns. BEL of OT.

Baal-Schem-Tov, orig. Israel ben Eliezer (1700-60), Russian Jewish teacher. Founded HASIDISM movement, preaching belief in joyous religious expression rather than academic rabbinical formalism.

Babbitt, Irving (1865-1933), American critic, essayist. One of founders of early 20th cent. 'New Humanism' movement, influencing T.S. Eliot through advocacy of return to classical ideals. Works incl. *The New Laokoön* (1910), *Rousseau and Romanticism* (1919), *Democracy and Leadership* (1924).

Babel, Tower of, in OT, structure erected by Noah's descendants in Babylonia. Symbol of pride of city-dwellers who sought to rebel against God by building a tower to heaven. Thwarted by God's confusing their language so that they could not understand each other.

Baber or **Babar,** title given to Zahir ed-Din Mohammed (*c* 1482-1530), Indian emperor, founder of Mogul dynasty. Conquered most of N India (1526), invading from Afghanistan. Distinguished for his writings, cultural interests.

Babeuf, François Noël (1760-97), French revolutionary. Advocate of economic equality and early form of communism. Leader of cell-based group which plotted overthrow of the DIRECTORY. Betrayed and executed.

babirussa, *Babirussa babirussa,* wild pig of Celebes. Has backward-curving tusks; inhabits marshy forest.

baboon, large short-tailed monkey, genus *Papio,* found mainly in Africa. Fierce, with dog-like teeth and snout; lives in large social groups. Arabian baboon, *P. hamadryas,* once sacred to Egyptians.

Babylon, ancient city of Babylonia, on N bank of Euphrates. Its ruins are in C Iraq, S of Baghdad. Important under Hammurabi (*c* 1750 BC) who made it cap. of Babylonia. Destroyed *c* 689 BC by Assyrians, rebuilt and achieved great splendour under Nebuchadnezzar. Its Hanging Gardens were one of the Seven Wonders of the World.

Babylonia, ancient empire of S Mesopotamia. Grew to power in 18th cent. BC under Hammurabi, who took Babylon as his cap. Conquered and ruled by the Kassites until *c* 1150. Recovered under Assyrian rule, which it later overthrew with capture of Nineveh (612). Under Nebuchadnezzar, empire was extended over Mesopotamia, Egypt, Palestine. Absorbed into Persian empire after Cyrus' conquest (539 BC).

Babylonian Captivity, in history of Israel, period from fall of Jerusalem to Babylonians (586 BC) until creation of new Jewish state (538 BC) in Palestine. Many Jews were removed to Mesopotamia at this time. Term also applied to period in Middle Ages when papacy moved from Rome to Avignon, France. Began (1309) under Clement V, ended (1377) under Gregory XI; all popes of this period were French.

Bacchanalia, ancient Roman festivals in honour of Bacchus, god of wine. Excesses caused them to be banned by the Senate (186 BC), although they were continued secretly.

Bacchus, Roman name for Greek god DIONYSUS.

Bach, Johann Sebastian (1685-1750), German composer, leading member of family of musicians. Music director in several royal courts, supreme organist of his time. Bach's music came when the adoption of equal temperament made great harmonic movement possible; combined this with immense contrapuntal skill to produce some of the most assured music ever composed. His work consists mainly of keyboard works, pieces for instruments and orchestra, and religious music. Works incl. *Magnificat, Mass in B minor, St John Passion, The Well-tempered Clavier, Brandenburg Concertos.* His son, Carl Philipp Emanuel Bach (1714-88), was also a composer, as well as a noted keyboard player and improviser. Compositions characteristic of mid-18th cent., in reaction against his father's polyphonic style. His half-brother, **Johann Christian Bach**

(1735-82), lived in London from 1762, where he enjoyed royal patronage. First to play piano as solo instrument in Britain. Wrote operas, symphonies, piano concertos.

backgammon, game played on a special board by two people. Each has 15 pieces which are moved according to the throw of dice. Played by Greeks and Romans and still common in countries of E Mediterranean; enjoyed popularity in West in mid-20th cent.

Bacon, Francis (1910-), British painter, b. Dublin. Works, characterized by lurid colour, distorted figures and use of photographs, emphasize repulsiveness and horror of human condition. Incl. *Velázquez' Innocent X* and *Three Studies for Figures at the Base of a Crucifixion* (1944).

Bacon, Francis, Baron Verulam (1561-1626), English philosopher, statesman. In *The Advancement of Learning* (1605), *Novum Organum* (1620), developed INDUCTIVE METHOD as replacement for deduction from Aristotelian authority. Also known for *Essays* (1597-1625) on religious, ethical matters. Lord Chancellor (1618); removed from office (1621) for corruption.

Bacon, Roger (c 1215- c 1292), English scholar, scientist. Believed scientific experiment and learning necessary complement to faith. Credited with discovery of gunpowder; worked in optics. Wrote encyclopedic *Opus majus, Opus minor* and *Opus tertium* for Pope Clement IV.

Baconian theory, argument first advanced in mid-18th cent. by W.H. Smith that Shakespeare lacked the education to write plays attributed to him, proposing Francis Bacon as true author. Now generally discredited.

bacteria, large group of usually one-celled micro-organisms, found in soil, water, plants and animals. Considered plant-like, they lack chlorophyll and multiply rapidly by simple fission. Of 3 typical shapes: rod-shaped (*bacillus*), spherical (*coccus*) and spiral (*spirillum*). Many are active in fermentation, promotion of decay of dead organic material and fixing of atmospheric nitrogen. Pathogenic (parasitic) bacteria, 'germs', produce wide range of plant and animal diseases.

bacteriophage, virus that is parasitic upon certain bacteria, whose synthetic machinery it uses to replicate itself.

Bactrian camel, see CAMEL.

Badajoz, city of W Spain, on R. Guadiana, cap. of Badajoz prov. Pop. 102,000. Food processing, border trade centre. Former seat of Moorish emirate. Moorish citadel, 13th cent. cathedral.

Badalona, city of Cataonia, NE Spain. Pop. 163,000. Forms conurbation with Barcelona; textiles, chemicals, glass industs. Nearby 15th cent. monastery.

Baden, region of SW West Germany. Former state, from 1952 part of Baden-Württemberg. Incl. picturesque Black Forest and part of Jura; vineyards, minerals, tourism.

Baden-Baden, town of SW West Germany, in Black Forest. Pop. 40,000. Tourism; thermal springs in use from Roman times.

Baden-Powell, Robert Stephenson Smyth, 1st Baron Baden-

Powell of Gilwell (1857-1941), British army officer. Defended Mafeking (1899-1900) during Boer War. Founded BOY SCOUTS.

badger, *Meles meles*, nocturnal burrowing carnivore of Europe and N Asia, with black and white striped head. Diet of rodents, insects. American badger, *Taxidea taxus*, is smaller species.

badminton, game played by volleying a light shuttle, either of feathers or nylon, over a net using gut-strung rackets. Played by 2 or 4 persons. Rules were drawn up in 1870s; said to have originated at Badminton, seat of duke of Beaufort.

Badoglio, Pietro (1871-1956), Italian field marshal. Commanded conquest (1935-6) of Ethiopia. After fall of Mussolini (1943) formed non-fascist govt. Signed armistice with Allies, declared war on Germany.

Baedeker, Karl (1801-59), German publisher. Introduced famous series of Baedeker travel guides, reliability of which based on his own observations.

Baekeland, Lee Hendrik (1863-1944), American chemist, b. Belgium. Developed photographic paper using Velox process. Synthesized bakelite, phenol-formaldehyde resin used for electrical insulation.

Baer, Karl Ernst von (1792-1876), Estonian naturalist. Regarded as founder of comparative embryology, he discovered notochord and mammalian egg. Originated theory of embryonic germ layers which develop to form various vertebrate organs and tissues.

Baffin, William (c 1584-1622), English explorer. Piloted 2 unsuccessful expeditions (1615-16) to find Northwest Passage. Baffin Bay and Baffin Isl. named after him.

Baffin Island, largest and most E island in Canadian Arctic; in SE Franklin Dist., Northwest Territs. Area 476,068 sq km (c 183,810 sq mi). Eskimo pop.; whaling, fur trapping. Separated from Greenland by Baffin Bay, connected by Davis Str. to Atlantic.

Bagehot, Walter (1826-77), English economist, social and literary critic. Author of classic interpretation of govt., *The English Constitution* (1867); other works incl. *Physics and Politics* (1872). Editor (1860-77) of *The Economist*.

Baghdad, cap. of Iraq; on R. Tigris. Pop. 2,970,000. Road, rail, air route jct.; produces textiles and cement. Founded 763, *fl* under caliph Harun al-Rashid as centre of commerce and learning. Declined after sack by Mongols (1258). Became cap. of independent Iraq (1921).

Baghdad railway, railway linking Istanbul with Baghdad, Iraq. Financed by German capital, Turkish section to Konya was completed by 1896. Because of its strategic importance, German plans to extend line to Baghdad were opposed by Britain (1911). Completed in 1940.

bagpipe, musical wind instrument consisting of bag inflated either by bellows or by player's breath blown through pipe; bag is squeezed by arm to force air out into several reedpipes. Chanter pipe has finger holes to produce melody; drones produce continuous bass notes. Of ancient Asiatic origin, bagpipes were introduced to Europe by Romans.

Bagpipe playing as art form is esp. developed in Scotland.

Baguio, summer cap. of Philippines, mountain resort in NC Luzon isl. Pop. 85,000. Gold mining centre.

Bahaism, religion founded in 19th cent. by Baha Ullah (1817-92), Persian religious leader. Bahaists believe in the unity of all religions, universal education, equality of the sexes and world peace.

Bahamas, coral isl. state of *c* 700 isls. in N West Indies; member of British Commonwealth. Incl. Andros (largest), New Providence, SAN SALVADOR. Area 11,404 sq km (4403 sq mi); pop. 168,000, mostly Negro; cap. Nassau. Subsistence agric.; some timber, fish, salt, exports. Important tourist industs. Subject to hurricane damage. Settled by English in 17th cent.; crown colony until independence in 1973.

Bahia, *see* SALVADOR, Brazil.

Bahrain or **Bahrein,** isl. group of E Arabia, in Persian Gulf. Area *c* 595 sq km (230 sq mi); pop. 225,000; cap. Manama. Important oil reserves; dates grown. Sheikdom under British protection until 1971; allied with United Arab Emirates.

Bahr-el-Jebel, section of R. White Nile, S Sudan. Called Albert Nile from L. Albert (Uganda) to Sudan border, flows *c* 960 km (600 mi) N to join Bahr-el-Ghazal at L. No.

Baikal, Lake, freshwater lake of USSR, SC Siberian RSFSR. Area *c* 31,500 sq km (12,200 sq mi). World's deepest lake, reaching depth of 1742 m (5714 ft). R. Angara only outlet.

bail, in law, temporary release of an arrested person on giving bond to court, with assurance that he will appear at subsequent proceedings.

Usually granted in civil cases, may be withheld in criminal.

Baird, John Logie (1888-1946), Scottish inventor. Pioneer of television, gave 1st transmission demonstration (1926) using mechanical scanning disc. Demonstrated colour television 1939.

Baja California (Lower California), narrow penin. of NW Mexico, between Gulf of California and Pacific. Mainly mountainous, arid climate; vegetation and pop. concentrated in irrigated region near US border.

bakelite, see BAEKELAND.

Baker, Sir Samuel White (1821-93), English explorer. Explored Nile and tributaries from 1861, met J.H. Speke at Gondokoro (1863). First European to reach Albert Nyanza (1864). Later worked to suppress slave trade on upper Nile.

Bakst, Léon, orig. Lev Nikolayevich R_enberg (1868-1924), Russian painter. Gained international reputation for stage and costume design while working with Diaghilev's Ballets Russes. His work, noted for exotic motifs and intense colour, was influenced by Russian folk art.

Baku, city of USSR, cap. of Azerbaijan SSR; on Caspian Sea. Pop. 1,314,000. Centre of oil producing area of Apsheron penin. from 1870s; importance has diminished since WWII. Under Persian control 16th-18th cent., incorporated by Russia (1806).

Bakunin, Mikhail Aleksandrovich (1814-76), Russian anarchist. An aristocrat, active in Revolution of 1848; eventually exiled in Siberia but escaped 1861.

Expelled (1872) from First INTERNATIONAL for opposition to Marxists. Believed in complete freedom, with violence as revolutionary means.

Balakirev, Mili Alekseyevich (1837-1910), Russian composer. Leader of nationalist Russian school of music; founded group of composers called 'the Five'. Works incl. symphonic poem *Tamara* and overture *King Lear*.

Balaklava, suburb of Sevastopol, USSR, Ukrainian SSR; on Crimean penin. Scene of charge of Light Brigade on 25 Oct. 1854 during battle of Crimean War.

balalaika, Russian guitar, usually with three strings, fretted fingerboard and triangular body.

balance of payments, statement of account of a country comprising record of all public and private transactions between that country and all other countries. Takes into account all gifts, foreign aid, loans, interest on debts, payments for goods and received payments for exports, shipping and commercial services abroad, interest on overseas investments.

balance of power, policy of preventing one nation from gaining sufficient power to threaten security of other nations. Formulated by Metternich at Congress of Vienna (1815), served as basis for 19th cent. foreign policy of European nations. Again underlay post-WWII relations between US and USSR.

Balanchine, George, orig. Georgi Melitonovich Balanchivadze (1904-), American choreographer, dancer, teacher, b. Russia. Co-director with Diaghilev of Ballets Russes in

Paris (1924-8). Directed New York City Ballet from 1948. Known for choreography of Stravinsky's music.

Balaton (Ger. *Plattensee*), shallow lake of WC Hungary, largest in C Europe. Area 596 sq km (230 sq mi). Vineyards around shores; tourism.

Balboa, Vasco Nuñez de (c 1475-1519), Spanish conquistador. Joined in conquest of Darién; crossed isthmus (1513) accompanied by Indians, becoming first to reach Pacific. Claimed coast for Spain. Beheaded for treason.

bald eagle, *Haliaeetus leucocephalus*, North American bird of prey. Black, with white head, neck and tail. Feeds on dead fish, rodents. National emblem of US.

Balder, in Norse myth, son of Odin, god of light, peace, virtue, wisdom. Killed by the trickery of Loki after attempt by his mother to make him invulnerable.

Baldwin, James (1924-), American author. Best known for first novel, *Go Tell it on the Mountain* (1953), but essays on Negro problems incl. equally important *Notes of a Native Son* (1955). Also wrote plays, eg *Amen Corner* (1955).

Baldwin, Robert (1804-58), Canadian statesman. Co-leader with LaFontaine of ministry (1848-51) which achieved responsible govt. for Prov. of Canada (modern Québec and Ontario).

Baldwin, Stanley Baldwin, 1st Earl (1867-1947), British statesman, PM (1923-4, 1924-9, 1935-7). Leader of Conservative Party (1923-37). First term ended on protectionist tariff issue; later instrumental in ending General Strike (1926). Rise of fascism in Europe and constitutional crisis over Edward VIII's abdication marked 3rd term.

Bâle, *see* BASLE, Switzerland.

Balearic Islands (*Islas Baleares*), archipelago of W Mediterranean Sea, forming Baleares prov. of Spain. Area 5012 sq km (1935 sq mi); cap. Palma. Incl. Majorca, Minorca, Iviza, Formentera. Tourism, agric., fishing. Inhabited from prehist. times; under Moorish rule 10th cent.-1235; united with Aragón 1349.

Balfour, Arthur James Balfour, 1st Earl of (1848-1930), British statesman, PM (1902-5). His Conservative govt. resigned after cabinet split over Joseph Chamberlain's proposals for tariff reform (1905); party heavily defeated in 1906 election. As foreign secretary, drew up BALFOUR DECLARATION (1917).

Balfour Declaration (1917), assurance of British protection for Jewish settlement of Palestine after its capture by British forces. Drawn up by foreign secretary Balfour and contained in letter to Rothschild of British Zionist Federation. Jews allowed into Palestine under limited quota system between world wars.

Bali, isl. of Indonesia, just off E Java. Area c 5700 sq km (2200 sq mi); pop. 2,250,000. Mountainous, with fertile soil and good climate; produces rice, copra, coffee. Balinese are Hindus, having been converted in 7th cent.

balkanization, breakup of territ. into small, mutually hostile political units. Term derived from post-WWI treaties of Trianon and Sèvres, in which Allies estab. new boundaries for Balkan countries.

Balkan Peninsula, SE Europe. Extends S from rivers Danube, Sava.

Comprises Albania, Bulgaria, Greece, Turkey (Europe), Yugoslavia. Includes Balkan Mts. (Bulg. *Stara Planina*), range of C Bulgaria. Rise to 2372 m (7785 ft); crossed by Shipka Pass.

Balkan Wars (1912-13), two short wars for possession of Ottoman Empire's European territ. Serbo-Bulgarian alliance (1912) led to First War (Oct.), in which Turkey lost all European possessions except Constantinople area. Austria, Hungary and Italy, at a meeting of Great Powers in London, created (1913) an independent Albania, thwarting ambitions of Serbia, which then demanded greater share of Macedonia from Bulgaria. Latter attacked Serbia (June, 1913), only to be attacked by Romania, Greece and Turkey. Second Balkan War ended with Treaty of Bucharest (Aug. 1913), in which Bulgaria lost territ. to all its enemies. Serbian territ. ambitions contributed to outbreak of WWI.

Balkhash, Lake, shallow lake of USSR, in SE Kazakh SSR. Area *c* 18,200 sq km (7000 sq mi). E part saline; W part, fed chiefly by R. Ili, fresh; no outlet. On N shore, Balkhash, is copper-mining centre. Pop. 70,000.

Ball, John (d. 1381), English priest. Expounded Wycliffe's doctrines; excommunicated (1376) and imprisoned. Released by rebels, became leader of PEASANTS' REVOLT (1381); caught and executed.

ballad, orig. (medieval British) narrative song in short stanzas, often with refrain, usually of popular origin, and orally transmitted, though sometimes composed by minstrels for noble audience. Now incl. narrative poems, eg Rossetti's *Sister Helen*.

ballade, poetic form set to music, *fl* 13th and 14th cent. In Provence and Italy. Composers, esp. Chopin and Brahms, used term for dramatic piano pieces.

Ballance, John (1839-93), New Zealand politician, b. Ireland, premier (1891-3). His Liberal govt. introduced widespread constitutional and social reforms.

Ballantyne, R[obert] M[ichael] (1825-94), Scottish writer of boy's adventure stories. Works incl. *Martin Rattler* (1858) and *Coral Island* (1858).

Ballarat, city S Victoria, Australia. Pop. 58,000. Railway Australia. indust. centre; trade in wool, wheat, fruit. Mining town from 1851 gold rush; scene of 'Eureka Stockade' miners' revolt (1854).

ballet, dramatic entertainment combining music, dance, mime, spectacle. Ballet as known today descends from court festivities of French, Italian Renaissance. Developed by French, esp. at Louis XIV's court where Lully and Molière created *comédies-ballets,* combination of dance and speech. The 5 classical foot positions were adopted in 18th cent., classical white dress and *en pointe* style in 19th cent. In 20th cent., rigid traditions attacked by Isadora Duncan and Diaghilev's Ballets Russes. With latter were associated Fokine, Nijinsky, Pavlova, Massine, Balanchine. Modern choreographers incl. Martha Graham, Frederick Ashton, and companies incl. New York City

Ballet, Bolshoi (Moscow), Royal Ballet (London).

Balliol, or de Baliol, John (1249-1315), king of Scotland (1292-6). Disputed succession with Robert the Bruce. Edward I of England invited to arbitrate; Balliol chosen, but had to swear fealty. Later revolted; was captured by Edward, who then annexed Scotland. His mother founded Balliol College, Oxford (1269).

balloon, non-powered aircraft obtaining lift from bag filled with lighter-than-air gas or hot air. Montgolfier brothers credited with invention (hot-air type, 1783). Hydrogen type first flown (1783) by J. Charles. Used for military observation since Napoleonic Wars: in WWII, balloons anchored by cables were used to obstruct low-flying aircraft. Now used for meteorological research, normally filled with helium for its non-flammability.

Ballymena, town of E Northern Ireland, in former Co. Antrim. Pop. 16,000.· Linen mfg.

balm or bee balm, *Melissa officinalis,* many branched lemon-scented perennial of thyme family with white, lipped flowers. Favourite plant of bees.

balsa or corkwood, *Ochroma lagopus,* tree of Central and South America and West Indies. Strong, light wood used in model-making. Raft in Kontiki expedition (1947) was made of balsa trunks.

balsam, several trees, shrubs and plants of family Balsaminaceae which yield aromatic balsam. Species incl. orange balsam, *Impatiens capensis,* of North America; Himalayan balsam, *I. grandulifera,*

showiest of the genus, grows wild beside rivers.

Baltic, branch of Indo-European family of languages, close to Slavic. Incl. Lettish (Latvian), Lithuanian, Old Prussian; last now dead. Said to be closest of modern Indo-European languages to ancient parent tongue.

Baltic Sea (Ger. *Ostsee*), sea of N Europe. Bordered by Denmark, Germany, Finland, Poland, Sweden, USSR. Linked to North Sea by Oresund, Great and Little Belt, Kiel Canal. Shallow; small tides. Hist. area of Hanseatic trade. Intensive fishing.

Baltic States, hist. name for countries on E shores of Baltic Sea, incl. LIVONIA, Estonia, Latvia, Lithuania (all now in USSR).

Baltimore, port of N Maryland, US; on Chesapeake Bay inlet. Pop. 906,000. Has natural harbour; exports coal and grain. Commercial, indust., railway centre; shipbuilding, steel indust., oil refining. Built 1729, with growth based on shipbuilding ('Baltimore' clippers famous in 19th cent.). Terminus of 1st US railway. RC bishopric (Primate of US); Johns Hopkins Univ. (1876).

Baltimore oriole, *Icterus galbula,* North American insectivorous bird. Male black and orange; nest is woven hanging bag.

Baluchistan, region of SW Pakistan bounded by Iran, Afghanistan and Arabian Sea. Arid and mountainous; inhabited by Baluchis, Baluchas. N controlled by British after Afghan wars of 19th cent.

Balzac, Honoré de (1799-1850), French novelist. Best known for *La Comédie humaine,* extensive series of novels incl. *Eugénie Grandet*

(1833), *Père Goriot* (1834), *Cousine Bette* (1846), which attempted to represent contemporary French society by creating a complete, detailed fictional world.

Bamako, cap. of Mali, on R. Niger. Pop. 197,000. Admin., commercial centre; river port, railway to Dakar. Former cap. of French Sudan.

bamboo or **cane,** semitropical or tropical grasses of the genera *Bambusa, Arundinaria, Phyllostachys.* Rapidly growing clump plant propagated by spreading underground roots. Some attain 35 m/120 ft. *Bambusa arundinacea,* hard, durable, with hollow stems, is used in buildings, furniture, utensils, paper making. Young bamboo shoots of some species are edible.

banana, *Musa sapientum,* large perennial Asian plant, now widely cultivated in tropical regions of W hemisphere. Simple leaves, clustered flowers with edible fruits growing in large pendent bunches. Rich in carbohydrates.

band, a group of musicians, usually smaller than an orchestra. A brass band consists principally of brass instruments; a percussion or rhythm band mainly of percussion instruments. Bands are also named by the kind of music they play, *eg* dance band, military band. A 'big band' is large dance band consisting of sections of saxophones, trombones and trumpets overlying a rhythm section; it developed with the swing music of the 1930s.

Banda, Hastings Kamazu (1902-), Malawi statesman. Campaigned against Federation of Rhodesia and Nyasaland; imprisoned 1959-60. Became PM (1963), and president (1966) after Nyasaland had become republic as Malawi.

Bandaranaike, Sirimavo (1916-5, 1970-77). Entered politics following her husband Solomon Bandaranaike's assassination (1959) while PM. She hosted Conference of Non-aligned Nations (1976).

bandicoot, nocturnal Australasian marsupial of Peramelidae family, comprising *c* 20 species. Rat-like, with pointed muzzle; digs for insects, worms, roots.

Bandung, city of W Java, Indonesia. Pop. 1,202,000. Textile, rubber product mfg. Resort in beautiful surroundings.

Banff, resort town of SW Alberta, Canada. Pop. 4000. Nearby is Banff National Park; area 6641 sq km (2564 sq mi). Scenic lakes, glaciers, hot springs.

Banffshire, former county of NE Scotland, now in Grampian region. Cairngorm Mts. in S, fertile coastal plain in N. Cattle, fishing, distilling. Co. town was Banff, royal burgh (chartered 1163) on Moray Firth. Pop. 8000. Resort.

Bangalore, city of S India, cap. and railway jct. of Karnataka state. Pop. 1,648,000. Textile indust., electrical apparatus, machinery mfg. Tata Institute of Science (1911). Founded 16th cent.; ruins of Tippoo Sahib's palace.

Bangkok (*Krung Thep*), cap. of Thailand, port near mouth of R. Chao Phraya. Pop. 1,867,000. Exports teak, rice, rubber; rice milling, oil refining. Transport in old city mainly by canal boats. Became cap. 1782; royal temple (1785) has famous image of Buddha.

Bangladesh, republic of SC Asia, at N end of Bay of Bengal. Area *c* 143,000 sq km (55,200 sq mi); pop. 71,614,000; cap. Dacca. Language: Bengali. Religion: Islam. Consists mainly of deltas of Ganges, Brahmaputra and Meghna rivers; densely populated. Agric. economy based on rice, tea and esp. jute. Subject to flooding and cyclones. Was East Pakistan from 1947 until civil war led to independence (1971).

Bangor, port of E Northern Ireland, on Belfast Lough. Pop. 35,000. Tourist resort; former shipbuilding indust. Has ruins of 6th cent. abbey.

Bangor, city of Gwynedd, NW Wales, on Menai Strait. Pop. 15,000. Tourist resort. Has Univ. of Wales coll. (1893); 16th cent. cathedral.

Bangui, cap. of Central African Empire, on R. Ubangi. Pop. 187,000. Port and trade centre, textile indust. Univ. (1970). Founded 1889, formerly cap. of Ubangi-Shari territ.

Banjermasin or **Bandjarmasin,** cap. of Kalimantan prov. (Borneo), Indonesia. Pop. 282,000. Port near mouth of R. Barito. Exports oil, rubber.

banjo, stringed musical instrument with a circular parchment resonator and open back. Of African origin but developed in US, where it was brought by black slaves.

Banjul, cap. of Gambia, at mouth of R. Gambia. Pop. 39,000. Admin., commercial centre; port, exports groundnuts, hides. Founded 1816, known as Bathurst until 1973.

banking, conduct of financial transactions through institutions primarily devoted to accepting deposits (subject to transfer and withdrawal by cheque) and making loans. Thus banks do not necessarily own the total of the funds they may use. Practised in classical times; large-scale banking in Middle Ages dominated by Italian families. Modern banking developed during 18th-19th cent. in W Europe and US with expansion of trade and indust. *See* BANK OF ENGLAND, FEDERAL RESERVE SYSTEM.

Bank of England, central bank of Britain, founded (1694) as commercial bank. Bank Charter Act (1844) estab. present system. Responsible for issue of bank notes, funding of national debts, *etc.* Nationalized 1946.

bank rate [UK] or **discount rate** [US], minimum rate at which Bank of England or US Federal Reserve Bank makes loans to commercial banks and other prime borrowers. As other lending rates are closely related to bank rate, high rate restricts borrowing and lending, low rate encourages expansion of credit. Thus used as instrument of monetary control.

Banks, Sir Joseph (1743-1820), English naturalist. Accompanied Cook in expedition around the world (1768-71), accumulating remarkable plant collection. Leading figure in development of Kew Gardens. President of the Royal Society (1778-1820).

banksia or **bottle brush,** genus of evergreen trees and shrubs of Protraceae family named after Sir Joseph Banks. Widely distributed in S hemisphere, esp. Australia.

Banks Island, SW Franklin Dist., Northwest Territs., Canada. Area 67,340 sq km (*c* 26,000 sq mi). First explored 1851.

Bannister, Sir Roger Gilbert (1929–), English physician. First man to run the mile in under 4 min. (Oxford, 1954). Best time was 3 min. 58.8 sec.

Bannockburn, town of Central region, C Scotland. Site of battle (1314) in which Robert the Bruce's victory over Edward II of England secured Scottish independence.

Banting, Sir Frederick Grant (1891–1941), Canadian physician. With C.H. Best, isolated (1921) insulin from pancreas; later purified it for use in treating human diabetes. Shared Nobel Prize for Physiology and Medicine (1923).

Bantry Bay, inlet of SW Irish Republic, 40 km (25 mi) long. Anchorage; oil storage. Scene of attempted French landing (1796). At head is port, Bantry (pop. 2000).

Bantu, African ethnic and linguistic group, c 70 million. Stretch from Equator south, except for extreme SW Africa. Physically diverse, classified mainly on language. Highly developed pre-European conquest; developed protective confederations in 19th cent., incl. ZULU and Basuto. Name, meaning 'the people', commonly used in South Africa for all native people. See BANTU LANGUAGES.

Bantu languages, group of African languages, most important within NIGER-CONGO branch, although considered part of Benue-Congo subgroup. Contains hundreds of languages, spoken throughout C and S Africa; incl. SWAHILI, Zulu, Xhosa, Sotho, Kikuyu.

banyan, E Indian fig tree, *Ficus benghalensis*. Branches send out aerial roots which reach ground to form new trunks, creating large sheltered area. Sacred among Hindus.

baobab or boojum, *Adansonia digitata*, large tree native to Africa, India. Broad trunk adaptable to storage of water. Yields edible fruit (monkey bread). Bark used in making paper, cloth, rope. Leaves used medicinally.

baptism, in most Christian churches, sacrament admitting a person into Christianity. Involves ritual purification with water and invocation of grace of God to free the soul from sin. Baptism of Jesus by John the Baptist is considered part of founding of Christian church.

Baptists, Christian denomination holding that BAPTISM should be given only to believers after confession of faith, and by immersion in water rather than by sprinkling. First English Baptist congregation formed (c 1608) in Amsterdam under John Smyth. Baptist World Alliance (1905) holds regular congresses.

Barabbas, in NT, prisoner chosen by the mob, in accordance with Passover custom, to be released by Pilate in place of Jesus.

Barbados, low-lying isl. state, in British Commonwealth. Most E of West Indies. Area 430 sq km (166 sq mi); pop. 238,000; cap. Bridgetown. Has fertile agric. soil; sugar cane growing; molasses; rum mfg. Winter tourist resort. Claimed by English 1605; independence 1966. Subject to severe hurricanes.

barbary ape, *Macaca sylvanus*, tailless monkey of N Africa, S Spain and Gibraltar. Only monkey native to Europe.

Barbary Coast, coast of N Africa from Morocco to Libya. Named after

Berbers, the chief inhabitants. Notorious for piracy on European shipping (16th-19th cent.), ended by French capture of Algiers (1830). Name also applied to waterfront dist. of San Francisco, US, after 1849 gold rush.

Barbary sheep, *see* AOUDAD.

barbastelle, *Barbastella barbastellus*, common European bat, with almost black fur. Roosts in large colonies.

barbel, freshwater fish of carp family, genus *Barbus*, found in Asia, Africa, Europe. Thread-like growths (barbels) hanging from jaws act as organs of touch. European variety, *B. barbus*, is coarse fish.

Barber, Samuel (1910-), American composer. Work inclines to contemporary European idioms and is written mainly in traditional forms. Best-known piece is *Adagio For Strings*.

barberry, any deciduous shrub of genus *Berberis*. Spiny leaves, sour red berries, yellow flowers. Ornamental species, often used in hedges, incl. Japanese barberry, *B. thunbergii*. The common European barberry, *B. vulgaris*, is also found in North America.

barbet, brightly-coloured bird of Capitonidae family of Old World tropical forests. Thick solid beak with whiskers growing at base.

Barbirolli, Sir John (1899-1970), British conductor. Gained renown in 1936 on succeeding Toscanini as conductor of the New York Philharmonic Orchestra; best known as the conductor of the Hallé Orchestra (Manchester) from 1943 to 1968.

barbiturates, group of drugs derived from barbituric acid, used to promote sleep and as sedatives. Overuse may lead to addiction.

Barbizon School, group of French landscape painters who made their centre at Barbizon in Forest of Fontainebleau in 1840s. Members incl. Millet, Daubigny. Aimed at exact rendering of country life and scenery, painted directly from nature.

Barbour, John (*c* 1316-95), Scottish poet and churchman. Known for chronicle-poem *The Bruce* (1375).

Barbuda, *see* ANTIGUA.

Barcelona, city of Catalonia, NE Spain, on Mediterranean Sea. Cap. of Barcelona prov. Pop. 1,745,000. Major port; indust., commercial centre; univ. (1430). Founded by Carthaginians; taken (801) by Charlemagne, independent countship from 9th cent. Fl after union (1137) of Aragón and Catalonia. Catalan cultural centre, focus of radical movements. Seat of govt. (1938-9) in Civil War. Cathedral (13th cent.), palaces.

Bardot, Brigitte (1933-), French film actress. Known for 'sex kitten' roles, but has taken more serious parts. Films incl. *And God Created Woman* (1956), *Vie Privée* (1961), *Viva Maria* (1965).

Barebone, Praise-God (*c* 1596-1679), English nonconformist lay preacher. Member of provisional assembly (Barebone's Parliament) nominated by Cromwell (1653) after dissolution of Rump Parliament.

Barents or **Barentz, Willem** (d. 1597), Dutch explorer. Made 3 unsuccessful attempts to find Northeast Passage, reached Spitsbergen and Novaya Zemlya. Barents Sea named after him.

Barents Sea, extension of Arctic Ocean, lying N of Norway and bounded in part by Franz Josef Land and Novaya Zemlya. Ice-free ports, eg Murmansk, and fisheries in S.

barge, large boat, usually flat-bottomed, used for transportation on sheltered waters. Common on Nile in ancient Egypt. Modern barges towed by tugs. Self-propelled steel barges used on Great Lakes of North America for bulk transport. Recent developments incl. ships which can take barges aboard to unload them.

Bari, city of Apulia, SE Italy, on Adriatic Sea. Cap. of Bari prov. Pop. 365,000. Major port; oil refining, textiles; univ. (1924). Roman colony (*Barium*); taken (1071) by Normans, embarkation point for medieval Crusades. Cathedral (12th cent.), basilica with relics of St Nicholas.

barite, barytes or **heavy spar** (Ba SO$_4$), heavy, white or colourless mineral. Consists of orthorhombic-shaped crystals; occurs in massive or granular forms. Uses incl. paint pigment, medical radiology. Major deposits in England, Romania, US.

baritone, in singing, high bass voice, midway between bass and tenor.

barium (Ba), silvery metallic element; at. no. 56, at. wt. 137.34. Occurs as BARITE and as carbonate; prepared industrially by reduction of barium oxide. Compounds used in glass, paint and fireworks; sulphate taken internally to help obtain X-ray pictures of digestive tract.

bark, outer covering of the stems and roots of trees and woody plants. Consists of 2 layers; the inner of living flexible cork-like material, the outer a dead inflexible shell. Many barks have economic uses eg as in hemp, flax, jute or as flavourings, eg cinnamon or drugs, eg quinine, cocaine.

bark beetle or **engraver beetle,** insect of Scolytidae family. Tunnels between bark and wood of trees, creating elaborate gallery system; major pest of timber.

Barker, George Granville (1913-), English poet. Contemporary of Auden and wrote on Spanish Civil War, but more akin to Dylan Thomas. Many works incl. *Collected Poems* (1957).

Barker, Harley Granville, see GRANVILLE-BARKER.

Barking, bor. of NE Greater London, England. Pop. 160,000. Has large power station. Motor vehicles indust. Created 1965 from Barking, Dagenham.

barley, genus *Hordeum* of grass family, probably originating in Asia Minor. Cultivated since prehistoric times. Most common cultivated form is *H. vulgare*. Unbranched stems rise in clumps and bearded seed heads extend from the grains. Used to make malt and to feed livestock.

barnacle, sedentary crustacean of subclass Cirripedia, found on rocks, piers and boat hulls. In some species, eg acorn barnacle, *Balanus*, body enclosed in limy plates. Other naked varieties parasitic on marine invertebrates.

barnacle goose, *Branta leucopsis,* European goose with black and white plumage. Eaten on fast days in Middle Ages, as it was believed to be fish, hatching from barnacle.

Barnard, Christiaan Neethling (1922-), South African surgeon.

Performed 1st human heart transplant operation (Cape Town, Dec. 1967); patient died after 18 days.

Barnardo, Thomas John (1845-1905), British social reformer, b. Ireland. Known for founding 'Dr Barnardo's Homes', refuges for destitute children. Also instrumental in securing legislation to protect children.

Barnaul, city of USSR, SC Siberian RSFSR. Pop. 459,000. Railway jct. and port on R. Ob. Textile, machinery mfg. Founded in 18th cent. as mining centre.

Barnes, see RICHMOND-UPON-THAMES, England.

Barnet, bor. of W Greater London, England. Pop. 304,000. Created 1965 from parts of Middlesex, Hertfordshire. Scene of Yorkist victory (1471) in which Warwick the Kingmaker was killed.

barn owl, long-legged pale owl of Tytonidae family with worldwide distribution, esp. *Tyto alba*. Lives in farm buildings; hunts mainly by sound.

Barnsley, town and administrative centre of South Yorkshire met. co., N England, on R. Dearne. Pop. 75,000. Coalmining; engineering; textiles industs.

Barnum, Phineas T[aylor] (1810-91), American showman. Exploited public taste for sensational, eg exhibiting midget Tom Thumb. Estab. circus 'The Greatest Show on Earth' (1871).

Baroda, city of Gujarat state, W India. Pop. 467,000. Railway jct.; textile mfg. Cap. of former princely state of Baroda. Name changed to Vadodara (1976).

barometer, instrument used to measure atmospheric pressure. Comprises mercury-filled tube closed at upper end and held inverted in mercury-filled vessel. Height of mercury in tube gives atmospheric pressure. *See also* ANEROID barometer.

Barons' War (1263-7), in English history, war between Henry III and his barons, led by de MONTFORT. Henry's defeat at Lewes (1265) led to summoning of Great Parliament. De Montfort was defeated and killed at Evesham (1265).

Baroque, in art and architecture, style characterized by much dramatic ornamentation and use of curved, rather than straight lines. Flourished from c 1580-1730; high Baroque style of Bernini was designed to impress beholders both physically and emotionally by enormity and vigour of its figures.

Barquisimeto, city of NW Venezuela. Pop. 291,000. In agric. region (coffee, sugar, cattle exports); textile, cigarettes, leather mfg. Founded (1552) as Nueva Segovia.

Barra, isl. of Outer Hebrides, W Scotland. Chief town Castlebay.

barracuda, voracious tropical fish of Sphyraenidae family. Great barracuda, *Sphyraena barracuda*, is largest, c 1.8 m/6 ft long. Popular game fish.

Barranquilla, port of N Colombia, near mouth of Magdalena R. Pop. 656,000. Sugar refining, textile, chemical mfg.

Barras, Paul François Jean Nicolas, Vicomte de (1755-1829), French Revolutionary. Jacobin activist, later helped overthrow Robespierre during THERMIDOR, ending Reign of Terror (1794). Leading member of Directory, lost power after supporting Napoleon's coup of 18 Brumaire (1799).

Barrault, Jean-Louis (1910-), French actor-director. Renowned mime, director of Théâtre de France (1959-68); films incl. *Les Enfants du Paradis* (1944), *La Ronde* (1950).

barrel organ, mechanical organ in which a barrel armed with pins rotates and trips levers that admit air to organ pipes, to produce a single piece of music. Barrel is usually turned by hand as in the mobile street piano, often wrongly called a barrel organ because it has a similar barrel-and-pin mechanism.

Barrès, [Augustin-] Maurice (1862-1923), French novelist. Known for trilogies *Le Culte du moi* (1888-91) about an egoist who discovers his need for others, *Le Roman de l'énergie national* (1897-1903) based on his public life.

Barrett Browning, Elizabeth, *see* BROWNING, ROBERT.

Barrie, Sir J[ames] M[atthew] (1860-1937), Scottish author. Plays incl. classic nostalgic fantasy *Peter Pan* (1904), also *The Admirable Crichton* (1902), *Dear Brutus* (1917). Wrote novels eg *The Little Minister* (1891), *Sentimental Tommy* (1896).

barrister, in England, qualified member of legal profession who presents and pleads cases in courts. In higher courts has exclusive right to appear on behalf of litigant, but (with few exceptions) can do so only on solicitor's instructions. To qualify, student must join one of four INNS OF COURT; becomes 'junior', then King's (or Queen's) Counsel. *See* ADVOCATE.

barrow, in archaeology, mound erected over burial place. European barrows, dating from Neolithic times, are usually long or round. Building of barrows for burial of important people lasted into Saxon and Viking times.

Barrow-in-Furness, bor. in Furness area of Cumbria, NW England. Pop. 64,000. Iron and steel mfg., shipbuilding, engineering industs.

Barry, Sir Charles (1795-1860), English architect. With Pugin, designed Houses of Parliament at Westminster (1840-6).

Barry, mun. bor. and port of S Glamorgan, S Wales, on Bristol Channel. Pop. 42,000. Exports coal, steel.

Barrymore, Lionel (1878-1954), American stage and film actor. Film roles incl. Rasputin in *Rasputin and the Empress* (1932). His sister, **Ethel Barrymore** (1879-1959), was a leading American actress, appearing on Broadway stage until 1944, then moved to Hollywood to play 'character' parts in films. Their brother, **John Barrymore** (1882-1942), also acted on stage (*Richard III, Hamlet*), and in film. Known for 'profile' as young matinée idol, then romantic star of 1920s (*Raffles*, 1917, *Beau Brummell*, 1924).

Barth, John (1930-), American author. Known for fanciful philosophical fiction eg *The Sotweed Factor* (1960) an extravagant historical novel, *Giles Goat-Boy* (1966) satirizing the concept of education.

Barth, Karl (1886-1968), Swiss Protestant theologian. Believed authority of God is revealed in Jesus and biblical study is superior to philosophy. Early opponent of Nazism. Works incl. *The Word of God and the Word of Man* (1924).

Bartók, Béla (1881-1945), Hungarian composer, pianist. Collected folk music, which influenced much of his work; compositions subsequently became more dissonant. His 6 string quartets greatly extended quartet medium; other works incl. *Concerto for Orchestra*, opera *Bluebeard's Castle*.

Bartolommeo [del Fattorino], Fra (1475-1517), Italian painter of Florentine school. Worked with Raphael in development of high Renaissance style; influenced Raphael in handling of drapery and colouring. Works incl. *Pietà* (Florence).

Barton, Sir Edmund (1849-1920), Australian statesman, PM (1901-3). Leader of movement for federation of Australian colonies, became 1st PM with independence.

Barton, Elizabeth (c 1506-34), English nun, called the Maid of Kent. Uttered 'prophecies' denouncing Henry VIII's proposed divorce of Catherine of Aragon. Executed for treason.

baryon, in physics, one of class of elementary particles, comprising protons, neutrons, and HYPERONS. All experience STRONG NUCLEAR INTERACTION and obey Fermi-Dirac statistics, *ie* are FERMIONS.

barytes, *see* BARITE.

basalt, fine-grained igneous rock, occurring abundantly in volcanic lava. Usually black or dull grey in colour. Basalt flows underlie sediments beneath all oceans, and form many land masses, *eg* Deccan of India, Columbia R. plateau of US.

base, in chemistry, substance which yields hydroxyl (OH) ions if dissolved in water. Reacts with acids to form salt and water. Inorganic bases obtained by adding water to metal oxide; strength depends on degree of ionization. More generally, base defined as substance that accepts protons (thus amines are organic bases).

baseball, nine-a-side team game played with bat and ball, mainly in US. Invention is sometimes attributed to Abner Doubleday (1839). First organized team was New York Knickerbockers (1845); 1st professional team Cincinnati Red Stockings (1869). Major League baseball is played by 26 teams divided between National and American Leagues. Leading teams from the 2 leagues meet annually in World Series to determine champion.

Basel, *see* BASLE, Switzerland.

Bashkir, auton. republic of E European RSFSR, USSR. Area *c* 144,000 sq km (55,000 sq mi); pop. 3,820,000; cap. Ufa. Plateau and mountainous area in S Urals; extensively forested. Forms E part of Volga-Ural oilfields, connected by pipeline to refineries at Omsk. Natural gas, coal, metal ores (iron, copper, manganese).

Basic English, acronym for British American Scientific International Commercial English. Artificial international language, formulated by C.K. Ogden and I.A. Richards (*c* 1928). It is claimed that its vocabulary of 850 English words is capable of expressing any concept and is intended to be an auxiliary language.

basil, several aromatic, perennial herbs or shrubs of Labiatae (mint) family, native to Asia. Leaves of sweet basil, *Ocimum basilicum*, and bush basil, *O. suave*, are used in cookery.

Basildon, urban dist. of Essex, SE England. Pop. 129,000. Engineering, printing industs. Designated new town (1955) incorporating 4 Essex bors.

basilica, large Roman building used as public meeting place; usually rectangular with an interior colonnade and aisles on each side. With advent of Christianity, many were converted into churches.

Basingstoke, mun. bor. of Hampshire, S England. Pop. 53,000. Market town, transport jct.

Baskerville, John (1706-65), English printer. Important designer of typefaces; produced books of quality using high-grade paper and specially prepared black ink. Pub. quarto edition of Vergil (1757) and a Bible (1763).

basketball, five-a-side team ball game. Devised 1891 by James Naismith at Springfield, Mass., US, as an indoor game for YMCA. Extremely popular sport in US colleges; professional National Basketball Association was formed 1949. Olympic event since 1936.

basking shark, *Cetorhinus maximus*, large shark, reaching length of 9.7 m/35 ft; common to N Atlantic. Harmless, feeds on plankton. Cruises on ocean surface.

Basle (Fr. *Bâle*, Ger. *Basel*), city of NW Switzerland, on R. Rhine. Pop. 213,000. Commercial, indust. centre at head of Rhine navigation; railway jct. Roman *Basilia*; joined Swiss Confederation 1501. Oldest Swiss univ. (1460). Cathedral is burialplace of Erasmus.

Basle, Council of, RC reform council (1431-49). Beginning at Basle, with splinter groups moving to Ferrara and Florence, it attempted and failed to replace papal authority with that of the council.

Basque Provinces (Basque *Euzkadi*), region of NE Spain, incl. Alava, Guipúzcoa, Vizcaya provs. Name sometimes incl. Basque areas of Navarre, Gascony (France). Chief cities Bilbao, San Sebastian, Guernica (hist. seat of Basque parliaments). Iron, lead, zinc mining, engineering, fishing. Basques are an ancient people of obscure origin; unique language, distinctive customs. Settled here 9th cent., estab. kingdom of Navarre; later lost independence to Castile. Autonomous Basque govt. in Civil War defeated (1937) after Guernica bombed. Basque nationalism remains source of unrest.

Basra (Arab. *Al Basrah*), city of SE Iraq. Pop. 371,000. Port on Shatt-al-Arab. Oil refining. Exports petroleum products, dates. Cultural centre under Harun al-Rashid.

bass, in singing, the lowest adult bass voice. Also applied to instruments of similar range.

bass, marine and freshwater fish, incl. sea bass (Serranidae) and sunfish (Centrarchidae) families, found in North America, Europe. Popular game and food fish.

basset, breed of short-legged long-eared hound, used in hunting. Stands *c* 36 cm/14 in. at shoulder.

bassoon, orchestral woodwind instrument of oboe family. Wooden or metal tube is bent back on itself, double reed being brought within reach of player's mouth by curved metal tube. Contrabassoon is lower in pitch.

Bass Strait, channel between Tasmania and mainland Australia; greatest width *c* 240 km (150 mi). Furneaux Isls. at E end. Has major oil, natural gas deposits.

basswood, tree of genus *Tilia* of linden family, esp. *T. glabra.* Soft, strong wood is valued for furniture building.

Bast, in ancient Egyptian pantheon, goddess of fire. Represented as cat or cat-headed. Known by Greeks as Bubastis.

Bastia, town of NE Corsica, France, on Tyrrhenian Sea. Pop. 50,000. Port, exports wine, fish, timber; cigarette mfg.; tourist centre. Founded 14th cent. by Genoese, cap. of Corsica until 1791. Citadel (16th cent.).

Bastille, former state prison in Paris. Long used as prison, inmates incl. Voltaire, Fouquet. Stormed as 1st act of French Revolution by Parisian mob (1789) and razed to ground. Anniversary of destruction, 14 July, is national holiday.

Basutoland, see LESOTHO.

bat, nocturnal mammal of order Chiroptera, found in tropical and temperate regions. Only true flying mammal, elongated fingers are joined by membranous wing. Some tropical species are fruit-eating; most others insectivorous, locating prey and navigating by echo sounding. Blood-sucking varieties, eg vampire bat, in South America. Gregarious, living in groups in caves, *etc*; sleeps upside down suspended by claws.

Batavia, see DJAKARTA.

Bates, Daisy Mary, née O'Dwyer Hunt (1861-1951), Australian journalist, b. Ireland. Lived among Aborigines; accumulated knowledge in *The Passing of The Aborigines* (1938), which revealed long neglect of inherent race problems.

Bates, H[erbert] E[rnest] (1905-74), English author. Known for novels of rural life, incl. *My Uncle Silas* (1939), *The Darling Buds of May* (1958). Also wrote short-stories of service life under pseud. 'Flying Officer X'.

Bath, city of Avon, SW England, on R. Avon. Pop. 85,000. Roman *Aquae Sulis* built *c* AD 50 on site of thermal springs. Medieval wool indust. Fashionable 18th cent. spa. Famous Georgian architecture of Nash, Wood, eg Royal, Lansdown Crescents.

batholith or **bathylith,** mass of intrusive igneous rock. Usually granite, forms substructure to many mountain or upland regions. Steepsided, descends to unknown depths. Examples incl. Idaho, US, and Dartmoor, England.

Bathsheba, in OT, wife of Uriah the Hittite. David sent Uriah to death in battle and then married her. She bore him Solomon.

Bathurst, see BANJUL, Gambia.

bathyscaphe, see SUBMERSIBLE.

bathysphere, see SUBMERSIBLE.

batik, Indonesian method of applying coloured designs to cloth. Parts not to be dyed are coated with wax which can be removed after immersion of cloth in dye. Introduced into Europe in 19th cent. by Dutch.

Batista [y Zaldívar], Fulgencio

(1901-73), Cuban political leader. Military coup (1933) brought him to power; became president 1940. Exiled to US (1945), reinstated after leading 2nd coup 1952. Discontent and corrupt regime resulted in overthrow (1959) by CASTRO. Fled to Dominican Republic.

Baton Rouge, cap. of Louisiana, US; port and indust. town on Mississippi R. Pop. 166,000. Cotton, sugar exports; oil refining. Fort estab. by French (1719). Became cap. 1849.

Battersea, part of Wandsworth bor., S London, England, on S bank of R. Thames. Has power station, amusement park, famous dogs' home.

battery, group of cells used as source of electric power. Common dry battery usually consists of Leclanché cells.

battle cruiser, see CRUISER.

battleship, large, armoured warship equipped with heavy guns. Evolved from ironclad warship of 19th cent., built of steel by 1870s. Britain's *Dreadnought* (1906) introduced the 'all-big-gun' class of warship. Extensively used during WWI, became obsolete in WWII with development of aerial tactics, esp. dive-bombing.

Baudelaire, Charles Pierre (1821-67), French poet, important SYMBOLIST. His single collection *Les Fleurs du Mal* (1857) in nuances of imagery attempts to evoke the mystery of life and temper morality with aesthetics. Known also for doctrine of correspondences, *ie* interrelation of senses. Also translated his great influence, Poe.

Baudouin (1930-), king of Belgium (1951-). Son of Leopold III, on whose abdication he became king.

Bauhaus, school of design, architecture and craftsmanship, founded (1919) by Walter Gropius in Weimar, Germany; aimed at union of creative arts and technology of modern mass-production. Artists associated with Bauhaus incl. Klee, Kandinsky, Moholy-Nagy. Moved to Dessau, then to Berlin; closed by the Nazis (1933). Its ideas and teaching influenced both art and industrial design.

bauxite, clay-like mineral deposit, a mixture of hydrated aluminium oxides. Colour varies from white to reddish-brown. Chief source of aluminium and its compounds; major deposits in France, USSR, West Indies.

Bavaria (*Bayern*), state of SE West Germany. Area 70,531 sq km (27,232 sq mi); cap. Munich. Uplands, plains, valleys; principal rivers Danube, Main. Agric., forestry, tourism. Indust. centred in Munich, Nuremberg, Augsburg. Duchy then kingdom, under Wittelsbach dynasty 1180-1918. Stronghold of Nazi party before WWII. Hist. separatist region, joined Federal Republic 1949.

Bax, Sir Arnold (1883-1953), British composer. Master of King's Musick (1942-53). Work shows Celtic influence; incl. *The Garden of Fand, Tintagel* and *A Garland for the Queen.*

Bayern, see BAVARIA, West Germany.

Bayeux Tapestry, piece of embroidery depicting invasion of England by William the Conqueror (1066). Length *c* 70 m/230 ft; prob.

made in 11th cent. Preserved in Bayeux Museum, France.

Bay of Pigs, see PIGS, BAY OF.

bayonet, blade clipped on to end of musket or rifle. Introduced in late 17th cent. Said to have originated at Bayonne.

Bayreuth, town of EC West Germany. Pop. 65,000. Textiles, metals, pottery mfg. Home of Wagner, who designed the opera house (built 1876); annual Wagner festival.

bay tree or bay laurel, see LAUREL.

Bazaine, Achille François (1811-88), French marshal. Surrendered entire force at Metz (1870) during Franco-Prussian War after being out-manoeuvred. Imprisoned (1873) for treason, escaped to Spain.

BBC, see BROADCASTING.

BCG vaccination, preventive vaccination against tuberculosis, usually administered to children at c 13 yrs. Initials stand for bacillus of Calmette and Guérin.

Beadle, George Wells (1903-), American geneticist. Shared Nobel Prize for Medicine and Physiology (1958) with E.L. Tatum for work on bread mould which showed that genes control cell's synthesis of enzymes and other proteins.

Beachy Head, English headland 162 m/531 ft high, at E end of South Downs, nr. Eastbourne.

beagle, small hound with short legs and drooping ears, developed in England to hunt hares. Stands c 33 cm/13 in. at shoulder.

Beaker People, people of early Bronze Age, arrived in Britain c 2000-1800 BC, bringing first metal weapons and tools. Prob. built part of stone circles at Avebury and Stonehenge.

Beale, Dorothea (1831-1906), British educator. Pioneered women's education, esp. as head of Cheltenham Ladies' Coll. (1858-1906).

bean, large kidney-shaped edible seed of several plants of Leguminosae family. Inexpensive source of protein. Species incl. runner bean, soya bean, haricot or navy bean.

bear, large mammal of Ursidae family of Europe, Asia, America. Shaggy fur, short tail; walks flat on soles of feet. Solitary, sleeps through winter in cold climates. Eats little flesh, diet mainly vegetable. Varieties incl. BROWN, BLACK, POLAR bears.

Bear, Great and Little, see URSA MAJOR and URSA MINOR.

bearded lizard, *Amphibolurus barbatus*, agamid lizard of Australia. Inflates beardlike membrane of scales around throat when aroused.

Beardsley, Aubrey Vincent (1872-98), English artist, illustrator. His highly stylized, often grotesque, black and white drawings epitomized art nouveau. Art editor of *Yellow Book* (1894-6); illustrated *Rape of the Lock* and Wilde's *Salomé.*

beat generation, in literature, term for certain US writers active in the 1950s, incl. Kerouac, Burroughs, Ginsberg. Characterized by anarchic life-style, use of drugs, rejection of middle-class values; influenced by Zen Buddhism, music of Charlie Parker, poetry of Whitman.

Beatitudes, in NT, eight blessings given by Jesus at the opening of the Sermon on the Mount.

Beatles, the, British rock musicians, one of most successful groups ever. Comprised John Lennon (1940-), Paul McCartney (1942-), George Harrison (1943-) and Ringo Starr, orig. Richard Starkey (1940-). Gained worldwide following in the 1960s, developing rock music to new musical heights, esp. in *Sergeant Pepper's Lonely Hearts Club Band*. Disbanded c 1970, subsequently active individually.

Beaton, Sir Cecil Walter Hardy (1904-), English photographer, designer, writer. Noted for portrait-studies; designs for theatre, cinema, incl. *My Fair Lady*.

Beaton or Bethune, David (1494-1546), Scottish churchman, cardinal-archbishop of St Andrews. On basis of a dubious will of James V, attempted to assume regency for Mary Queen of Scots. As chancellor (1543), opposed Henry VIII's plans for subjugation of Scotland. His persecution of Protestants led to burning of George Wishart. Murdered in revenge.

Beatty, David Beatty, 1st Earl (1871-1936), British admiral. Led squadron in defeat of German navy at Jutland (1916). Commander of British fleet (1916-19). First sea lord at the Admiralty (1919-27).

Beaufort, Henry (c 1377-1447), English prelate, statesman; half-brother of Henry IV of England. Chancellor to Henry IV (1403-4), Henry V (1413-17) and during regency of Henry VI (1424-26). Made cardinal 1426, he attempted to lead a crusade against the Hussites (1429).

Beaufort Scale, measure of wind velocity; varies from 0 for calm to 12 for hurricane force. Devised in 1805 by Sir Francis Beaufort.

Beaufort Sea, part of Arctic Ocean, bounded by Banks Isl. (N Canada) in E and N Alaska in S.

Beaumarchais, assumed name of Pierre Augustin Caron (1732-99), French dramatist. Best known for comedies *The Barber of Seville* (1775), *The Marriage of Figaro* (1784).

Beaumont, Francis (1584-1616), English dramatist. Wrote mainly in collaboration with FLETCHER; thought to be sole author of *The Woman Hater* (1606), burlesque *The Knight of the Burning Pestle* (1607).

Beaune, town of Burgundy, E France. Pop. 17,000. Agric. market, centre of Burgundy wine trade. Hôtel-Dieu (1443) contains van der Weyden polyptych *Last Judgment*.

Beauvais, town of N France, cap. of Oise dept. Pop. 49,000. Agric. market. Scene of heroic defence (1472) against Charles the Bold. Centre of Gobelins tapestry indust. until WWII. Cathedral (1227) has highest Gothic choir vault.

Beauvoir, Simone de (1908-), French novelist, essayist, member of EXISTENTIALIST movement. Works incl. *Les Mandarins* (1954) fictionalized account of Sartre circle, *Le Deuxième Sexé* (1949) analysing position of women in society.

beaver, large rodent of Europe and North America, genus *Castor*. Amphibious; webbed hind feet and broad flattened tail. Colonial, lives in 'lodges' in river banks; constructs dams in rivers, streams. Species incl. Canadian *C. canadensis* and European *C. fiber*. Numbers depleted by fur hunters.

Beaverbrook, William Maxwell Aitken, 1st Baron (1879-1964),

British statesman, newspaper owner, b. Canada. Already wealthy on arrival in England, bought *Daily Express*, *Evening Standard*, founded *Sunday Express*. Advocate of imperialism; later organized munitions production while in Churchill's war cabinet (1940-5).

Bechuanaland, see BOTSWANA.

Becket, Thomas à, see THOMAS À BECKET, ST.

Beckett, Samuel (1906-), Irish author, settled in France 1932; works in English and French. Best known for tragi-comedy *Waiting for Godot* (1954). Also wrote novels *eg Murphy* (1938), *Molloy* (1951). Nobel Prize for Literature (1969).

Beckford, William (1759-1844), English writer. Known for Gothic romance *Vathek: An Arabian Tale* (1786). Also wrote travel books.

Beckmann, Max (1884-1950), German painter. Painted large allegorical pictures in 1930s, often savage in form, depicting hopelessness and brutality of human situation. Works incl. 9 large triptychs.

Becquerel, Antoine Henri (1852-1908), French physicist. Discovered radioactivity (1896) when he observed clouding of photographic film by uranium salt. Shared Nobel Prize for Physics (1903) with the Curies.

bedbug, small parasitic insect of Cimicidae family with flattened wingless body. Infests beds, walls, feeding on warm blood of mammals, birds. Extremely resistant, can withstand months of fasting.

Bede or Baeda (*c* 673-735), English historian, theologian. Known as the Venerable Bede, spent life as Benedictine monk teaching and

writing. Best known for *Ecclesiastical History of the English Nation*, in Latin, often translated.

Bedfordshire, county of SC England. Area 1234 sq km (476 sq mi); pop. 481,000. Wheat growing, market gardening; indust. centre Luton. Co. town Bedford, mun. bor. on R. Ouse. Pop. 73,000. Agric. equipment mfg., light industs.

Bedlam, popular name for oldest English lunatic asylum (St Mary of Bethlehem). Founded *c*1400 in London; removed to near Croydon 1930.

Bedouin, nomadic ARABS of Saudi Arabia, Syria, Jordan, Iraq, N Africa. Dependent on camel, sheep breeding. Land divided into tribal orbits under a sheik.

bedstraw, any plant of genus *Galium*. Square stem, stalkless whorled leaves, small white or coloured flowers. Formerly used as straw for beds.

bee, four-winged hairy insect of worldwide distribution, order Hymenoptera. Bees are social or solitary. Solitary bees nest in soil or hollow stems. Social bees, incl. bumble bee, cuckoo bee, honey bee, live in colonies, usually operating caste system of queen, workers (infertile females) and male drones. Agents of flower pollination when seeking nectar.

bee balm, see BALM.

beech, large, widespread family of trees incl. the beeches, oaks and chestnuts, but esp. genus *Fagus* with smooth, grey bark, hard wood, pale green leaves and edible 3-corned nuts. Wood is used in furniture and building. Common species are European *F. sylvatica*, copper beech, *F.*

stropunicea, and American *F. grandifolia*.

Beecham, Sir Thomas (1879-1961), English conductor. Founded London Philharmonic Orchestra (1932) and Royal Philharmonic Orchestra (1947). Popularized works of Richard Strauss, Delius. Remembered for his boisterous personality.

bee-eater, small brightly-coloured bird of Meropidae family, found in tropical areas of Old World. Feeds on bees, other insects; nests in holes in river bank, road cuttings, *etc.*

beefwood, hard, heavy, dark red wood from tropical tree, *Manilkara bidentata*, used in flooring and furniture.

Beelzebub (Hebrew, = 'Lord of the Flies'), name applied to SATAN.

beer, alcoholic beverage made by brewing aqueous extract of cereals, esp. malted barley, with hops. Malted barley is crushed and mixed with warm water, which allows enzymes present in malt to convert its starch into sugar. Solution obtained (wort) is boiled with hops, which provide flavouring. Liquid is cooled, mixed with yeast and allowed to ferment. Quantity of malt and water, as well as length of fermenting, determine alcoholic content (usually from 3% to 6%). Britain, Germany, Czechoslovakia and US are major beer producers.

Beerbohm, Sir [Henry] Max-[imilian] (1872-1956), English writer, caricaturist. Known for witty theatre criticism, only novel *Zuleika Dobson* (1911) fantasy set in Oxford.

Beersheba, commercial town of SC Israel. Pop. 84,000. Trade centre for tribes of Negev desert. Pottery, glass

mfg. Hist. associated with Abraham, Elijah.

beet, several varieties of biennial plants of genus *Beta* with edible leaves, thick fleshy white or red roots, widely cultivated as food crop. The sugar beet, *B. vulgaris*, native to Europe and grown in North America, provides *c* 30% of world's sugar. The garden beet or beetroot has red-veined leaves, edible root. Variety *cicla* is cultivated for leaves, known as beet spinach or Swiss chard.

Beethoven, Ludwig van (1770-1827), German composer, pianist. In early life, had some teaching from Mozart, Haydn; concert debut 1795. One of most original and influential composers, bridged Classical and Romantic eras in creating music of great emotional impact and formal qualities. Suffered increasing deafness from 1801 onwards. Among best-known works are orchestral, choral, chamber works and piano sonatas, *eg Third* (*Eroica*), *Fifth*, *Sixth* (*Pastoral*) and *Ninth* (*Choral*) symphonies, as well as *Moonlight Sonata, Mass in D,* string quartets and opera *Fidelio*.

beetle, any insect of order Coleoptera (comprising *c* 250,000 species). Biting mouthparts; horny forewings cover membranous hind wings and protect body. Undergoes complete METAMORPHOSIS.

Beeton, Isabella Mary, née Mayson (1836-65), English writer on cookery. Best remembered for *Mrs Beeton's Book of Household Management* (1859-60), guide to cookery and domestic economy.

Begin, Menachem (1913-), Israeli political leader, b. Russia. Premier (1977-). Led Likud party to victory in 1977 elections, ending 30 years of Labour party dominance. Signed peace treaty with Egypt (1979). Nobel Peace Prize (1978).

begonia, genus of succulent herbs with ornamental leaves and clustered red, pink or white flowers. Native of tropics. Cultivated varieties are divided into fibrous-rooted types which are mainly houseplants for winter blooming, and bulbous, tuberous and rhizomatous begonias.

Behan, Brendan (1923-64), Irish playwright. Known for black comedies, *The Quare Fellow* (1956), *The Hostage* (1959). Autobiog. *Borstal · Boy* (1958) describes his formative years in IRA.

behaviourism, in psychology, doctrine that valid data consists only of the observable and measurable in individual's responses, not valuing subjective or introspective accounts.

Behn, Aphra (1640-89), first English woman professional writer. Works incl. exotic romances and plays, *eg* novel *Oroonoko* (1688). Spy for Charles II in Antwerp (1666-7).

Behrens, Peter (1868-1940), German architect. Pioneer in evolution of modern architectural style and industrial design. Designed factories, houses, offices in functionalist manner employing modern materials. Taught Gropius, Mies van der Rohe, Le Corbusier.

Beida, town of NE Libya in Cyrenaica. Pop. 32,000. Govt. offices, univ. Built from 1961, designated as future national cap.

Beira, town of SC Mozambique, on Mozambique Channel. Pop. 50,000. Port, exports·copper, tobacco, tea; large transit trade, rail links with Malawi, Rhodesia (closed 1976), Zambia.

Beirut, cap. of Lebanon. Pop. 720,000. Port on Mediterranean. Trade centre since Phoenician times. Focus of foreign education; 4 univs. Financial centre; food processing. Became cap. of Lebanon under French mandate (1920). Badly damaged in civil war in late 1970s.

Bel, in OT, prob. refers to Babylonian god Marduk, and BAAL of Phoenicians.

Belém, seaport of NE Brazil, cap. of Pará state, on Pará R. Pop. 603,000. Exports nuts, timber, jute. Centre of early 20th cent. rubber export boom.

Belfast, cap. and port of Northern Ireland, on Belfast Lough. Pop. 359,000. Admin., commercial centre. Shipbuilding; linen, tobacco mfg. Has Queen's Univ. (1845). Severely damaged by bombs and fires in religious conflict from 1969.

Belfort, town of E France, cap. of Territ. of Belfort dept. Pop. 56,000. Commands Belfort Gap between Vosges and Jura. Cotton mills, metal working. Successful resistance of Prussian siege (1870-1) commemorated by *Lion of Belfort* statue; remained French when Alsace ceded (1871) to Germany.

Belgae, tribes of mixed Celtic-Germanic origin, described by Julius Caesar. Occupied parts of Belgium and NE France, whence they spread to S England *c* 100 BC. Introduced coinage, potter's wheel, improved standards of agric. in England.

Belgian Congo, see ZAIRE.

Belgium (Fr. *Belgique*, Flem. *België*), kingdom of NW Europe. Area 30,510 sq km (11,780 sq mi); pop. 9,756,000; cap. Brussels. Languages:

Flemish (N), Walloon French (S). Religion: RC. Main rivers Meuse, Scheldt. Sandy area in N (Flanders), fertile plain in C; forested plateau in SE (Ardennes). Intensive agric. (cereals, flax, livestock). Extensive trade along North Sea coast and canal network. Heavy indust. (metals, textiles) on SC coalfield. Named after Celtic *Belgae*, divided into independent duchies, counties in Middle Ages. Ruled by Burgundy, Habsburgs, Spain, France, Netherlands; independent monarchy from 1830. Colonized Congo (*see* ZAÏRE). German occupation in both WWs.

Belgrade (*Beograd*), cap. of Yugoslavia and of Serbia, at confluence of Danube and Sava. Pop. 770,000. River port, railway jct.; commercial, indust. centre, esp. textiles, chemicals, electrical goods; univ. (1863). Fortified (3rd cent. BC) by Celts. Held by Turks 1521-1867; became cap. of Serbia 1882, of Yugoslavia 1918. Has Turkish citadel.

Belisarius (*c* 505-65), Byzantine general. Served under Justinian I, for whom he suppressed the Nika revolt (532). Defeated Vandals in Africa (534). Fought against Goths in Italy, capturing Ravenna (540). Thwarted Bulgarian attack on Constantinople (559).

Belize, British crown colony of Central America, on Caribbean. Area 22,965 sq km (8867 sq mi); pop. 120,000; cap. Belmopan. Mainly flat with dense forests (valuable timber exports); Maya Mts. in interior. Tropical climate. Sugar cane, citrus fruit growing. English settlement (17th cent.) disputed by Spanish; colony estab. 1884; name changed from British Honduras (1973). Former cap. Belize, port at mouth of Belize R. Pop. 39,000. Timber exports; fish packing.

Bell, Alexander Graham (1847-1922), American scientist, inventor, b. Scotland. Gave 1st successful transmission of sound by telephone (1876). Patented device (1876) and organized Bell Telephone Co. (1877). Estab. laboratory which produced 1st successful phonograph record.

bell, (1) orchestral percussion instrument made of long tubes of brass, suspended in same arrangement as a keyboard; struck with mallet; (2) hollow cup-like vessel, usually made of metal, which rings when struck by an internal clapper or external hammer. Bells are often hung in sets and can be played by mechanical means to produce tunes (*see* CARILLON) or by groups of ringers who go through permutations of the diatonic scale, called change-ringing.

belladonna, *see* NIGHTSHADE.

Bellay, Joachim du (1522-60), French poet. Wrote manifesto of PLÉIADE, *Défense et illustration de la langue française* (1549).

Bellerophon, in Greek myth, hero who slew the CHIMAERA with help of winged horse, Pegasus. Angered Zeus by attempting to fly to heaven on Pegasus. Was thrown to earth and crippled or killed.

bellflower, *see* CAMPANULA.

Bellingshausen, Fabian Gottlieb von (1778-1852), Russian naval officer, explorer. Circumnavigated Antarctica (1819-21), possibly being 1st to sight continental Antarctica.

Bellingshausen Sea, part of S Pacific Ocean, W of British Antarctic Territ. Named after leader of Russian expedition (1819-21).

Bellini, Jacopo (*c* 1400-70), Italian painter. Few of his paintings survive, but his 2 surviving sketchbooks were used by his 2 sons and Mantegna. **Gentile Bellini** (*c* 1429-1507) was prominent portraitist and painter of processions and ceremonies. Worked at court in Constantinople (1479-81). **Giovanni Bellini** (*c* 1430-1516) taught Giorgione and Titian. Works, characterized by lyrical handling of landscape, influenced subsequent Venetian artists. Painted many large altarpieces, small devotional works and portraits.

Bellini, Vincenzo (1801-35), Italian composer. Known for lyrical operas *Norma* and *La sonnambula*.

Belloc, [Joseph] Hilaire [Pierre] (1870-1953), English writer, b. France. Known for collections of gruesome humorous verse, *eg The Bad Child's Book of Beasts* (1896), *Cautionary Tales* (1908). Also wrote novels, historical biog.

Bellow, Saul (1915-), American novelist, b. Canada. Works incl. *The Adventures of Augie March* (1953), *Herzog* (1964), estab. him as major figure. Deals with individual's problems in urban democratic society. Nobel Prize for Literature (1976).

bell-ringing, *see* BELL.

Belmopan, cap. of Belize. Pop. 5000.

Belo Horizonte, city of E Brazil, cap. of Minas Gerais state. Pop. 1,235,000. Centre of mining area (iron, manganese); agric. centre (cotton, cattle); steel indust., textile mfg., diamond cutting. Brazil's 1st planned city, built at end of 19th cent.

Belorussia, *see* BYELORUSSIAN SOVIET SOCIALIST REPUBLIC.

Belsen; village of NE West Germany, in Lower Saxony. Site of concentration camp under Nazi regime.

Belshazzar, in OT, son of Nebuchadnezzar, last king of Babylon. During debauched feast, writing appeared on wall which Daniel saw as ill omen. That night Cyrus captured Babylon.

Belt, Great and **Little,** strs. of Denmark, linking Kattegat with Baltic Sea. Great Belt (*Store Baelt*) separates Zealand and Fyn Isl.; Little Belt (*Lille Baelt*) separates Fyn Isl. and Jutland.

Beltane, *see* MAY DAY.

beluga or **white whale,** *Delphinapterus leucas,* whale of Arctic seas, *c* 4.6 m/15 ft long. Diet of fish, crustaceans; skin of excellent quality.

Bembo, Pietro (1470-1547), Italian churchman, humanist. Edited Petrarch, Dante. Helped estab. Tuscan as literary language of Italy.

Benares, *see* VARANASI.

Benbecula, isl. of Outer HEBRIDES, NW Scotland.

Ben Bella, Ahmed (1919-), Algerian political leader. Joined Algerian nationalist movements, founder (1954) of FLN in Cairo. Twice arrested by the French, returned to become premier (1962). Elected president (1963), ousted in coup (1965).

Benbow, John (1653-1702), English naval officer. Hero of 4-day fight with French in Caribbean (1702) when his flagship was deserted by rest of squadron. Died of his wounds.

bends, in medicine, *see* AERO-
EMBOLISM.

Benedict, St (*c* 480-*c* 547), Italian
monk. Founded BENEDICTINES, formulating chief rule of Western
monasticism, based on communal
living with time for work and prayer.

Benedict XV, orig. Giacomo della
Chiesa (1854-1922), Italian churchman, pope (1914-22). Maintained
strict Vatican neutrality in WWI,
concentrated on relief of war
suffering.

Benedictines, RC monastic order,
estab. by ST BENEDICT at Monte
Cassino (*c* 529). Stressing communal living and physical labour,
they also did much to preserve
learning in early Middle Ages;
Notable Benedictines were St
Gregory the Great and St Augustine
of Canterbury who introduced the
order into England.

Benelux, economic union of Belgium, Netherlands, Luxembourg.
Estab. (1958) after customs union
ratified in 1948.

Benes, Eduard (1884-1948), Czech
statesman, president (1935-8, 1945-
8). Served as foreign minister under
Masaryk; architect of Czech-French
alliances after WWI. Exiled during
WWII, headed provisional govt. in
London, re-elected president after
Czech liberation. Resigned after
Communist coup of 1948.

Benet, Stephen Vincent (1898-
1943), American poet. Epic poems,
John Brown's Body (1928), *Western
Star* (1943), examine roots of
American culture. Other works incl.
famous 'American Names' (1927),
short stories, novels.

Bengal, region of NE India and
Bangladesh in Ganges-Brahmaputra
delta. Under British control follow-
ing victory at Plassey (1757).
Divided (1947) into largely Hindu
West Bengal and Moslem East
Bengal (now in BANGLADESH). Bay of
Bengal is arm of Indian Ocean
between E India and Burma.

Bengali, Indic language belonging to
Indo-Iranian branch of Indo-
European. Spoken in Bangladesh,
Calcutta region.

Benghazi or **Bengasi,** city of NE
Libya, in Cyrenaica on Gulf of Sidra.
Pop. 170,000. Port, admin. centre,
railway jct. Founded by Greeks.
Centre of Italian colonization from
1911 until taken by British in WWII.
Cap. of Cyrenaica prov. 1951-63;
joint cap. (with Tripoli) of Libya
1951-72.

Ben-Gurion, David (1886-1973),
Israeli statesman, b. Poland. Supported British pledges to help Jewish
settlement of Palestine. Leader of
Mapai party, 1st premier (1948-53)
of Israel; returned for 2nd term
(1955-63). Broke away from Mapai
(1965).

Benin or **Dahomey,** republic of W
Africa. Area 112,700 sq km (43,500
sq mi); pop. 2,912,000; cap. Porto
Novo. Official language: French.
Religions: native, RC. Mainly subsistence agric.; exports coffee,
cotton, palm oil. Native kingdom
17th-19th cent. with cap. at Abomey,
promoted slave trade. Colonized
(1892-3) by French; territ. of French
West Africa from 1899. Independent
from 1960, has had unstable govt.

Benin, city of S Nigeria. Pop.
122,000. Centre of rubber, palm and
timber producing area. Fl 14th-17th
cents. as cap. of Benin kingdom;

famous for iron, ivory, bronze carvings. Taken (1898) by Britain.

Benjamin, in OT, youngest son of Jacob and Rachel. His descendants (tribe of Benjamin) incl. Israel's 1st king, Saul, and St Paul.

Benjamin, Judah Philip (1811-84), Confederate statesman. Led defence of Southern policy before and during US Civil War (1861-5); known as 'the brains of the Confederacy'. After defeat of South, escaped to England; became prominent barrister.

Benn, Gottfried (1886-1956), German poet, critic. Collections of expressionist verse incl. *Flesh* (1916), *Rubble* (1919). Autobiog. (1950) reflects agony of Nazi era.

Bennett, [Enoch] Arnold (1867-1931), English author. Known for realistic novels set in industrial Staffordshire, *eg Anna of the Five Towns* (1902), *The Old Wives' Tale* (1908).

Bennett, R[ichard] B[edford]

Bennett, 1st Viscount (1870-1947), Canadian statesman, Conservative PM (1930-5). Successfully advocated adoption of preferential imperial tariff.

Ben Nevis, *see* NEVIS, BEN, Scotland.

Benoni, city of S Transvaal, South Africa. Pop. 163,000. Goldmining, engineering centre in Witwatersrand.

Benson, Sir Frank (1858-1939), British actor-manager. Estab. Stratford-on-Avon Shakespeare festival.

Bentham, Jeremy (1748-1832), English philosopher. Trained in law, early exponent of UTILITARIANISM in *Introduction to the Principles of Morals and Legislation* (1789); taught that govt. should consider 'the greatest good for the greatest number'. Founded (1824) *Westminster Review* with James Mill.

Benue, river of N Cameroon and E Nigeria. Flows c 1450 km (900 mi) W from Adamawa Highlands via Makurdi to R. Niger at Lokoja.

Benz, Karl (1844-1929), German engineer. Credited with building 1st automobile with internal combustion engine (c 1885). Engine was water-cooled and had electric ignition. In 1926 his company merged as Daimler-Benz.

benzene (C_6H_6), colourless liquid hydrocarbon; found in coal tar and produced from petroleum by cracking. Structure as hexagonal ring of 6 carbon atoms, linked by alternate double and single bonds, with hydrogen atom joined to each carbon atom, described by Kekulé. Used as solvent and as starting point of numerous aromatic compounds.

Beograd, *see* BELGRADE, Yugoslavia.

Beowulf, Old English epic. Composed 8th cent., tells story derived from folk tale and Scandinavian history. In first part, young Beowulf rescues Danish court from water monster Grendel and Grendel's mother. In second part, after long and honourable life, Beowulf is called on to defend country from dragon, does so but dies and is given hero's funeral. Celebrates both Germanic pagan and Christian values.

Berbera, town of N Somalia, on Gulf of Aden. Pop. 40,000. Port, exports livestock, hides.

Berbers, Hamitic peoples of N Africa, of unknown origin. Previously Christian they became Moslem by 10th cent. under Arab domination. Apart from the TUAREG they are now settled agriculturists with local industries, eg metalwork, pottery, weaving.

Berchtesgaden, town of SE West Germany, in Bavarian Alps. Pop. 5000. Tourism, salt mining, wood-carving. Site of Hitler's mountain retreat.

Bérenger or **Berengarius of Tours** (c 998-1088), French ecclesiastic, head of Tours Cathedral school. Held radical views on Eucharist, rejected transubstantiation. Accused of heresy after quarrel with Lanfranc; eventually reconciled with Church.

Berenson, Bernard (1865-1959), American art critic, b. Lithuania. Expert on Italian art, he advised collectors and authenticated works for dealers. Writings incl. *Italian Painters of the Renaissance* (1930).

Berg, Alban (1885-1935), Austrian composer. Disciple of Schoenberg; developed 12-note technique to greater heights of expression than his master. Works incl. 2 operas, *Wozzeck* and *Lulu*, violin concerto and *Lyric Suite* for string quartet.

Bergamo, city of Lombardy, N Italy, cap. of Bergamo prov. Pop. 131,000. Engineering, textiles. Incl. old walled hilltop town, with 12th cent. cathedral, Renaissance chapel.

bergamot, several plants incl. species of *Monarda*, native to North America, with oval leaves aromatic when crushed. Sweet bergamot, *M. didyma*, is common in gardens and used to make infusion, Oswego tea. European bergamot is *Mentha aquitica.* Bergamot also designates a type

of pear-shaped orange, *Citrus bergamia*, rind of which yields an oil used in perfumery.

Bergen, city of SW Norway. Pop. 113,000. Port, fishing, shipbuilding, tourism. Founded 1070, *fl* in Middle Ages, member of Hanseatic League. Rebuilt after fire (1916); German naval base in WWII, severely damaged.

Bergman, [Ernst] Ingmar (1918-), Swedish stage, film, TV writer-director, producer. Internationally famous from late 1950s for expressionist films with themes of alienation of individual from God, problems of personal relationships. Films incl. *The Seventh Seal* (1956), *Wild Strawberries* (1957), *Persona* (1966).

Bergman, Ingrid (1917-), Swedish actress. Best known for films made after move to Hollywood (1938), incl. *Casablanca* (1943); career broken by public reaction to affair with ROSSELLINI (1948), returned to Hollywood (1956).

Bergson, Henri (1859-1941), French philosopher. Anti-rationalist, believed in direct intuition as basis of knowledge. Saw evolution as opposition of 'life-force' (*élan vital*) to intransigence of matter. Influenced Proust in theories of memory. Nobel Prize for Literature (1927). Works incl. *Matter and Memory* (1896), *Creative Evolution* (1907).

Beria, Lavrenti Pavlovich (1899-1953), Soviet political leader. Powerful head of Russian secret police (1938-53); tried and executed during post-Stalin power struggle.

beriberi, deficiency disease caused by lack of vitamin B_1 (thiamin) in diet. Characterized by neuritis, swelling of body, *etc.* Occurs mostly in Far East where diet is largely of polished rice.

Bering, Vitus Jonassen (1681-1741), Danish explorer. Employed by Peter I to explore N Siberia; proved that Asia and America not connected. Died on Bering Isl. while leading Great Northern Expedition (1733-41). Bering St. and Sea also named after him.

Bering Sea, extension of N Pacific, between E Siberia and Alaska. Navigable only in summer. Explored by Dane, Vitus Bering c 1728. Bering Strait connects it to Arctic Ocean.

Berkeley, Busby, orig. William Berkeley Enos (1895-1976), American song-and-dance director. Known for spectacular, kaleidoscopic sequences, using great many chorus girls, in 1930s films, incl. *Gold Diggers* series (1933-8), *Dames* (1934).

Berkeley, George (1685-1753), Irish philosopher. Leading antimaterialist, saw the existence of perceived world as dependent on act of the perceiver ('being is being perceived'). Major work, *Treatise concerning the Principles of Human Knowledge* (1710).

Berkeley, Sir Lennox (1903-), English composer. Has written works in traditional forms, esp. for human voice. Compositions incl. chamber music, operas, symphonies.

Berkeley, residential town of W California, US; on E San Francisco Bay. Pop. 117,000. Mfg. industs. Has most famous part of Univ. of California (1873).

berkelium (Bk), transuranic element of actinide series; at. no. 97,

mass no. of most stable isotope 247. First prepared 1949 by bombarding americium with alpha particles.

Berkshire, county of SC England. Area 1255 sq km (484 sq mi); pop. 645,000; co. town Reading. In Thames basin; rich agric. incl. dairying, pigs, wheat, oats. Chalk downs cross C.

Berlin, Irving, orig. Israel Baline (1888-), American composer, b. Russia. Popular songs and musicals incl. 'Alexander's Ragtime Band', 'I'm Dreaming of a White Christmas', *Annie Get Your Gun, Call Me Madam.*

Berlin, city of NE Germany, on R. Spree, divided into East and West Berlin. East Berlin (pop. 1,088,000) is cap. of East Germany; West Berlin (pop. 2,122,000) is West German enclave, connected to west by specified land routes and air 'corridors'. Indust. and mfg. centre. City was cap. of Prussia, then of United Germany 1871-1945. Severely damaged in WWII, military occupation divided city after 1945. Soviet blockade of Berlin by W sectors (1948-9), erection of Berlin wall (1961).

Berlin, Congress of (1878), called to review terms imposed on Turkey by Russia at end of RUSSO-TURKISH WARS; chaired by Bismarck, incl. Disraeli, Andrassy. Revised boundary between Greece and Turkey, placed Bosnia and Hercegovina under Austro-Hungary; Serbia, Montenegro, Romania recognized as independent.

Berlin airlift, supply by Western powers of foodstuffs, *etc,* to, and removal of exports from, Berlin in 1948. Followed imposition of blockade by USSR during period of increasing tension. Blockade ended 1949.

Berliner Ensemble, state theatre company of German Democratic Republic estab. (1948) by BRECHT.

Berlinguer, Enrico (1922-   ), Italian politician. Secretary of Communist party from 1972, his attempts to redefine party role within Western democracy resulted in electoral gains.

Berlin Pact, see AXIS.

Berlin Wall, division between East and West Berlin, erected by East Germany (1961). Followed failure of USSR to gain withdrawal of Allies from city. Use of 12 crossing points requires authorization.

Berlioz, [Louis] Hector (1803-69), French composer. Wrote many large-scale works, often with a literary basis, in which he made innovations in orchestration. Works incl. *Symphonie fantastique, Romeo et Juliet, La Damnation de Faust.*

Bermuda, coral isl. group of c 300 isls. in NC Atlantic. British crown colony, Bermuda largest isl. Area 52 sq km (20 sq mi); pop. 53,000; cap. Hamilton. Indust. based on year-round US tourism. Discovered by Spanish (1515); settled by English (1609).

Bern (Fr. *Berne*), cap. of Switzerland and Bern canton, on R. Aare. Pop. 162,000. Knitwear, chocolate mfg.; printing, publishing. Hq. of Universal Postal Union; univ. (1834). Founded 1191, medieval town remains. Cap. from 1848.

Bernadette, St, orig. Marie Bernarde Soubirous (1844-79), French visionary. As a girl claimed to see visions of Virgin Mary at Lourdes, now a centre of RC pilgrimage. Canonized in 1933.

Bernadotte, Jean Baptiste Jules, see CHARLES XIV, king of Sweden.

Bernanos, Georges (1888-1948), French novelist. Works incl. *Diary of a Country Priest* (1936), deal with struggle between good and evil in exceptional souls. Also known for anti-Vichy essays, *eg Lettre aux Anglais* (1942).

Bernard, Claude (1813-78), French physiologist. Considered founder of experimental medicine, his numerous investigations incl. work on chemistry of digestion and functions of pancreas. Discovered function of glycogen in liver. Wrote *Introduction à l'étude de la médecine expérimentale* (1865).

Bernard of Clairvaux, St (1090-1153), French churchman, scholar. Founded Cistercian monastery of Clairvaux (1115). Influential in contemporary politics, securing recognition for Pope Innocent II. Mystical in theology, opposed rationalism of Abelard, Arnold of Brescia. Inspired 2nd Crusade (1146).

Bernard of Menthon or **Montjoux, St** (c 996-c 1081), Savoyard churchman. Founded hospices in St Bernard passes to aid travellers. Patron saint of mountaineers.

Bern Convention, see COPYRIGHT.

Bernese Oberland, Swiss mountain group, incl. Eiger, Mönch, Jungfrau. Interlaken and Grindelwald are main resorts.

Bernhardt, Sarah, pseud. of Rosine Bernard (1844-1923), French actress. Famous for performances at Comédie Française. Best-known roles incl. Phèdre, Hamlet; played latter with wooden leg.

Bernini, Giovanni Lorenzo (1598-1680), Italian sculptor, architect. Greatest practitioner of the Italian Baroque style; under papal patronage in Rome he designed churches, tombs, statues, fountains, *etc.* Appointed architect to St Peter's (1629), he created colonnades and piazza in front of the church. Works incl. *Ecstasy of St Theresa* (1645-52) and tomb of Urban VIII.

Bernoulli, Jacob or **Jacques** (1654-1705), Swiss mathematician. Developed Leibnitz's calculus; contributed to calculus of variations; estab. principles of probability theory in *Ars Conjectandi*; discovered Bernoulli numbers. His brother **Johann Bernoulli** (1667-1748), was a pioneer of calculus of variations. His son, **Daniel Bernoulli** (1700-82), worked on fluid motion (Bernoulli's principle), kinetic theory of gases and probability theory. Wrote *Hydrodynamica* (1738).

Bernstein, Eduard (1850-1932), German political theorist. In exile (1878-1901); leader of 'revisionist' faction of Social Democratic party after writing *Evolutionary Socialism* (1898), a denial of Marxist prognosis of revolution.

Bernstein, Leonard (1918-), American pianist, composer, conductor. Music makes fresh use of American idioms, esp. musicals *On the Town*, *West Side Story*. Works also incl. religious music, eg *Chichester Psalms* and *Mass*, fusing contemporary serious and popular idioms.

Berryman, John (1914-1972), American poet. Distinctive, complex, highly-wrought poetry incl. *Homage to Mistress Bradstreet* (1956), *77 Dream Songs* (1964), *Berryman's Sonnets* (1968).

Berthelot, [Pierre Eugène] Marcelin (1827-1907), French chemist. Pioneer of modern organic chemistry; synthesized acetylene, ethanol, *etc*, thus dispelling notion of vital force necessary for organic synthesis. Later worked in thermochemistry, devising special calorimeter.

Bertolucci, Bernardo (1940-), Italian film director. Films combine awareness of politics and history with problems of illusion and reality, eg *Before the Revolution* (1965), *The Conformist* (1970), *Last Tango in Paris* (1972).

Bertran de Born (c 1140-c 1214), French troubadour. Involved in struggles between Henry II and his sons, known for verses in praise of war.

Berwick, James Fitzjames, Duke of (1670-1734), French marshal. Illegitimate son of James II of England, whom he supported at Battle of the Boyne (1690). Fought in Wars of Spanish and Polish Succession. Killed in latter.

Berwick-on-Tweed, mun. bor. of Northumberland, NE England, at mouth of Tweed. Pop. 11,000. Salmon fishing. Long disputed by Scotland, became national territ. 1551; incorporated 1885.

Berwickshire, former county of SE Scotland, now in Borders region. Lammermuir Hills in N (sheep); Merse lowland in S (cereal growing). Co. town was Duns.

beryl, very hard mineral, silicate of

beryllium and aluminium. Comprises hexagonal crystals which may be extremely large. Gem forms are EMERALD, AQUAMARINE.

beryllium (Be), hard corrosion-resisting metallic element; at. no. 4, at. wt. 9.01. Occurs as BERYL; obtained by electrolysis of fused salts. Used for making light alloys and in windows for X-ray tubes.

Berzelius, Jöns Jakob, Baron (1779–1848), Swedish chemist. Worked in several branches of chemistry; gave composition of numerous compounds and compiled table of atomic weights. Discovered selenium, thorium, cerium. Introduced modern chemical symbols and formulae.

Besançon, city of E France, on R. Doubs, cap. of Doubs dept. Pop. 116,000. Watchmaking centre, textiles; univ. (1691). Hist. cap. of Franche-Comté. Roman remains, 12th cent. cathedral, palace. Birthplace of Victor Hugo.

Besant, Annie, née Wood (1847–1933), English theosophist, social reformer. Tried, but acquitted, for immorality after pub. birth control pamphlet (1877). Disciple of Helena BLAVATSKY; went to India, where she helped further nationalist cause. President of Theosophical Society (1907–33), wrote much on THEOSOPHY.

Bessarabia, hist. region of Moldavian SSR and W Ukrainian SSR. Disputed by Russia and Turkey; ceded to Russia (1812). Declared itself independent (1918) and joined in union with Romania; recovered by USSR in WWII.

Bessel, Friedrich Wilhelm (1784–1846), German astronomer. In 1838, was 1st to determine accurately parallax of a star (61 Cygni), thus finding its distance from Earth. Compiled star catalogue and introduced Bessel's function in mathematics.

Bessemer, Sir Henry (1813–98), English industrialist, inventor. Developed (c 1856) Bessemer process in mfg. of steel in which impurities (eg carbon, manganese, silicon) are removed by oxidation when air is blown through molten pig iron.

bestiary, medieval allegorical prose or verse catalogue of animals, real and mythical. Descriptions convey Christian or moral message. In later Middle Ages often richly illustrated. Name also applied to early popular treatises on natural history.

beta particle, electron or positron emitted by radioactive nucleus. Electron emitted when neutron spontaneously decays into proton, an anti-neutrino being produced as well. Penetration power c 100 times that of alpha particle.

betatron, cyclic accelerator used to obtain high energy beam of electrons by accelerating them in rapidly increasing magnetic field.

Betelgeuse, red supergiant star in constellation Orion. Of variable brightness, due to pulsation; c 500 light years away.

betel palm, *Areca catechu*, palm native to SE Asia. Source of betel nut, an astringent, orange, nut-like fruit, widely chewed in E for its stimulant effect.

Bethlehem (Arab. *Beit-Lahm*), town of W Jordan. Pop. 24,000. Considered birthplace of Jesus. Emperor Constantine built basilica

(333) on traditional site of Nativity; rebuilt by Justinian in 6th cent.

Betjeman, Sir John (1906-), English poet and architectural authority. Known for light, witty verse, eg *New Bats in Old Belfries* (1940), autobiog. *Summoned by Bells* (1960). Works on architecture, eg *Ghastly Good Taste* (1933) reflect love of Victoriana. Poet laureate (1972).

Betterton, Thomas (c 1635-1710), English actor. Member, subsequently manager of Davenant's company. Most famous actor of Restoration stage esp. in Shakespearian roles.

Betti, Ugo (1892-1953), Italian dramatist, poet. Known for plays on problems of justice and religious faith, eg *The Queen and the Rebels* (1951), *The Burnt Flowerbed* (1953).

Bevan, Aneurin (1897-1960), British politician. As minister of health (1945-51), inaugurated nationalized health service. Resigned over social services cuts, became leader of the left within Labour Party; later, advocated nuclear disarmament.

bevatron, cyclic accelerator used to accelerate protons and other particles up to 6 GeV. Used at Univ. of California (Berkeley) to discover anti-proton.

Beveridge, William Henry (1879-1963), British economist, b. India. Supervised estab. of labour exchanges, wartime food rationing while in civil service (1908-19). Director of London School of Economics (1919-37). Prepared govt. report proposing social security system (1942), planned spending for full employment (1944).

Beverley, mun. bor. of Humberside, N England. Pop. 17,000. Former co.

town of East Riding of Yorkshire. Has 13th cent. minster.

Beverley Hills, town of S California, US; suburb of Los Angeles. Pop. 33,000. Home of Hollywood film stars.

Bevin, Ernest (1881-1951), British politician and labour leader. Instrumental in union merger creating Transport and General Workers' Union. Minister of labour in wartime cabinet (1940-5); foreign secretary (1945-51), worked for closer ties with US through anti-Soviet policy.

Bewick, Thomas (1753-1828), English wood engraver. Illustrated natural history books, eg *History of British Birds* (pub. 1797 and 1804). Helped revive standards of wood engraving, introducing new expressive techniques.

Bexley, bor. of SE Greater London, England. Pop. 216,000. Created 1965 from several Kent towns.

Béziers, town of Languedoc, S France, on Canal du Midi. Pop. 82,000. Wine, brandy trade; cork, barrel mfg. Inhabitants massacred (1209) by Simon de Montfort for harbouring Albigensian heretics.

Bhagavad-Gita (Sanskrit, = song of the blessed one), philosophical dialogue contained in the Mahabharata epic. Sacred text incl. much of basis of Hindu thought and philosophy.

Bharat, ancient Hindi name for India, now used officially.

Bhopal, cap. of Madhya Pradesh, C India. Pop. 392,000. Textile mfg. Cap. of former princely state of Bhopal. Had women leaders (19th cent.).

Bhutan, kingdom of SC Asia. Area c 47,000 sq km (18,000 sq mi); pop.

1,146,000; cap. Thimbu. Language: Tibetan variant. Religion: Mahayana Buddhism. In E Himalayas, bordered by India, Tibet. Parts of S annexed by British in 19th cent; British, then Indian protect.

Bhutto, Zulfikar Ali (1928-79), Pakistani political leader. Succeeded to presidency (1971) on overthrow of YAHYA KHAN. PM (1973-77), effected reconciliation with independent Bangladesh. Re-elected 1977, but deposed by military coup; executed for murder of political opponent (1979).

Biafra, see NIGERIA.

Bialik, Haggim Nahman (1873-1934), Russian · poet. Work in Hebrew, eg 'In the City of Slaughter' (1903), influential in renaissance of the language. Also translated classics from many languages. Lived in Berlin and Israel.

Bialystok, city of NE Poland, cap. of Bialystok prov. Pop. 170,000. Railway jct.; textile mfg., machinery. Founded 14th cent.; under Russian rule 1807-1919.

Biarritz, town of SW France, on Bay of Biscay. Pop. 30,000. Developed in 19th cent. from fishing village into fashionable resort, through patronage of Napoleon III, Queen Victoria.

Bible, sacred book of Christianity. The canon, or standard list, of books making up OLD TESTAMENT is accepted by most churches and is also sacred book of Judaism. The APOCRYPHA, some books of which are accepted by the Eastern Orthodox church, is recognized by the RC church apart from 2 books of Esdras and the Prayer of Manasses. The canon of 27 books of NEW

TESTAMENT is same for all Christian churches. Bible was 1st book to be printed by GUTENBERG, in Latin (see VULGATE). Translators into English incl. WYCLIFFE, TYNDALE; AUTHORIZED VERSION most famous translation. RC scholars pub. DOUAY version (1582-1610).

bibliography, study of editions, dates, authorship etc, of books and other literature, or book containing such study; list of books or other literature related to particular author or subject. National bibliographies incl. literature pub. in one language or country, often in specified time period, eg British National Bibliography (1950-), Cumulative Book Index (US, 1898-) and Bibliographie de la France (1811-). Universal bibliographies attempt listing of all printed material, usually as catalogues of biggest libraries, eg Catalogue général des livres imprimés (1900-49, Bibliothèque Nationale, Paris), Catalogue of Printed Books (1881-1900, British Museum), Library of Congress Catalog (1942-).

bicycle, light, two-wheeled vehicle driven by pedals. First bicycle (with treadles and driving rods) built (1840) in Scotland by Kirkpatrick MacMillan. The 'boneshaker' with rotary cranks built (c 1865) in Paris. Subsequently, light spoked wheels with rubber tyres introduced. Pennyfarthing had large, driven front wheel (up to 163 cm/64 in. diameter) giving higher gear ratio, with rear wheel as small as 30 cm (12 in.). Safety bicycle with equal-sized wheels and sprocket-chain drive first manufactured by James Starley (c 1885) in Coventry. Developments incl. free-wheeling rear hub, variable ratio gears.

Biddle, John (1615-62), English religious leader, founder of UNITARIANISM. Despite official attempts to suppress his work, continued to publish and preach. Died in prison.

Biedermeier style, name given to German style of furniture and decoration of period 1818-48. Resembled French Empire style, but simpler and more suited to bourgeois needs.

Biel, see BIENNE, Switzerland.

Bielefeld, city of N West Germany. Pop. 168,000. Indust. centre, esp. linen, silk, sewing machines, vehicles.

Bienne (Ger. *Biel*), town of NW Switzerland, on L. Bienne. Pop. 64,000. Watch mfg.; machine tools. Ancient lake dwellings nearby. Funicular railway to Jura resorts.

biennial, see ANNUAL.

big-bang theory, in cosmology, hypothesis that universe evolved from highly dense concentration of matter which underwent enormous explosion. This accounts for expansion of universe observed by Hubble. Its plausibility increased with observation in 1960s of uniform background radiation emanating from outer space. Opposed by STEADY-STATE THEORY.

Bighorn, river of Wyoming, US; tributary of Yellowstone R. Battle between Colonel Custer and Sioux forces took place at jct. of Bighorn and Little Bighorn rivers (1876).

bighorn or **Rocky Mountain sheep**, large wild sheep of NW North America, incl. *Ovis canadensis*. Male has heavy curling horns, female small upright horns.

Bihar, state of NE India. Area 174,000 sq km (67,000 sq mi); pop. 56,332,000; cap. Patna. N fertile plain crossed by Ganges; rice grown. Important producer of coal, iron ore. Buddhist centre (see BUDDH GAYA).

Bikini Atoll, in Marshall Isls., C Pacific Ocean. Uninhabited; pop. removed prior to US atomic bomb tests (1946-58).

Bilbao, city of N Spain, at mouth of R. Nervión, cap. of Vizcaya prov. Pop. 410,000. Port, exports wine, iron ore; shipbuilding, iron and steel indust. Seat of Basque autonomous govt. (1936-7) in Civil War.

bilberry, blaeberry or **whortleberry**, *Vaccinium myrtillus*, small shrub native to N Europe and Britain. Has small, globular, bluish-black, edible fruit. Similar species are cultivated in US (see BLUEBERRY).

Bildungsroman (Ger., = novel of education), novel tracing development of hero, *eg* Goethe's seminal *Wilhelm Meister*, Mann's *The Magic Mountain*.

bile, bitter yellow-brown fluid secreted by the liver. Found in gall bladder, from which it is discharged into duodenum to aid digestion, esp. of fats. Colour results from carrying waste products of haemoglobin destruction.

bilharzia or **schistosomiasis**, disease caused by infestation of veins by flukes of genus *Schistosoma*. Larvae in water penetrate skin and adult worms settle in urinary bladder. Eggs cause inflammation of tissue, leading to degeneration of bladder, liver, *etc*.

billiards, game played with cue and 3 balls (1 white cue ball, 1 red and 1 white object ball) on oblong cloth-covered slate table, edges of which are cushioned. Scoring is by pocketing object or cue ball, or by cannons (striking the 2 object balls successively with cue ball). Played in England and France from 16th cent.

bimetallic strip, strip of 2 different metals bonded together in such a way that strip buckles when heated (as metals expand at different rates). Used in thermostats.

bimetallism, use of two metals (usually gold and silver) as monetary standard with fixed values in relation to each other. Both metals circulate as legal tender. Term does not apply to systems where other metals (eg copper, nickel) are used as token coinage.

binary number system, representation of integers by powers of 2, using only digits 0 and 1. In this system, 2 is represented by 10, 3 by 11, etc. Used in computers.

binary star, star consisting of 2 components, revolving about common centre of gravity under effect of mutual gravitation. Very common; c 50% of stars in our galaxy are binaries.

binding energy, in physics, energy required to decompose atomic nucleus into constituent protons and neutrons. Binding energy of neutron is energy required to remove neutron from nucleus.

bindweed, widely distributed family of plants with long climbing stems. Species incl. greater bindweed, *Calystegia sepium,* and lesser or field bindweed, *Convolvulus arvensis* with white or pink flowers. Black bindweed, *Polygonum convolvulus,* of dock family is widespread.

Binet, Alfred (1857-1911), French psychologist. With Théodore Simon, developed Binet-Simon scales (1905-11), series of tests of intelligence forming basis of modern intelligence testing.

binocular, optical instrument for viewing distant objects. Consists of 2 telescopes (binoculars) mounted so that a separate image enters each of viewer's eyes giving greater perception of depth than single image. Normally uses prisms to reduce length.

binomial theorem, in mathematics, theorem giving expansion of powers of $x + y$ in terms of powers of x and y.

Binyon, [Robert] Laurence (1869-1943), English poet. Known for translation of Dante's *Divine Comedy* into English terza rima. Other works incl. *The Burning of the Leaves* (1944), essays on Far Eastern art.

biochemistry, chemistry of living things. Two main branches: determination of structure of organic compounds present in living organisms, eg plant pigments, vitamins, proteins; elucidation of chemical means by which substances are utilized or made in living organisms.

biography, account of person's life by another. Classical biographies incl. Xenophon, Suetonius, Plutarch; medieval writers adapted biog. to give account of miracles performed by saints (hagiography); Renaissance emphasized concern for individual and realism, eg Roper's life of Thomas More, Vasari's lives of Italian artists (1550); biog. at height in 18th cent., eg Boswell's *Life of Samuel Johnson* (1791),

Johnson's own *Lives of the Poets* (1779-81). New developments in 20th cent. incl. use of psychology (*eg* Strachey's *Eminent Victorians*) and fictional biog., combining hist. and creative writing, *eg* Maurois's works on Shelley, Byron *etc*, Irving Stone on Michelangelo, van Gogh.

biology, science and study of living things, comprising BOTANY and ZOOLOGY. Study of form and structure of an organism is morphology; of the functions, physiology; of reproduction and early growth, embryology; of fossil remains, palaeontology. For division of plants and animals into series according to similarities and relationships, *see* CLASSIFICATION.

biosphere, that part of the Earth's crust and atmosphere which contains living organisms.

birch, family of deciduous trees comprising ALDERS and birches, genus *Betula*. Latter is hardy, with papery white bark; yields hard wood. Aromatic oil from sweet birch, *B. lenta*, used as wintergreen oil.

bird, any of class Aves of warm-blooded, egg-laying, feathered vertebrates, with forelimbs modified into wings; *c* 8700 living species. Believed to have evolved from reptiles; *see* ARCHAEOPTERYX.

bird of paradise, bird of Paradisaeidae family of New Guinea and adjacent isls. Males brightly coloured with elongated tail feathers, brilliant ruffs.

Birkenhead, Frederick Edwin Smith, 1st Earl of (1872-1930), British politician. Led Conservative opposition to Irish Home Rule, later prosecuted CASEMENT as attorney general (1915-19). Served as lord chancellor (1919-22).

Birkenhead, co. bor. of Merseyside met. county, NW England, on Wirral penin. Pop. 138,000. Port on R. Mersey, docks opened 1847. Has tunnel link with Liverpool.

Birmingham, city of West Midlands met. county, NW England. Pop. 1,013,000; 2nd largest British city. Transport centre; metal working, esp. vehicles, firearms. Main expansion during Indust. Revolution. Has 2 univs.

Birmingham, city of NC Alabama, US; at S end of Appalachian Mts. Pop. 301,000; state's largest city. Iron and steel centre; cement, textile, chemical mfg. Railway jct. Founded 1871.

Birobidzhan or **Birobijan**, town of USSR, Khabarovsk territ., RSFSR. Pop. 56,000. Sawmilling, clothing mfg. Cap. of Birobidzhan Jewish auton. region, formed 1928 as centre for Soviet Jews. Mainly agric., with mining and forestry.

birth control, *see* CONTRACEPTION.

birthmark, congenital skin blemish. Types incl. pigmented naevus or mole, caused by cluster of pigment cells; strawberry mark and port-wine stain, composed of small blood vessels.

Biscay, Bay of, inlet of N Atlantic Ocean, lying between Ushant Isl., NW France, and Cape Ortegal, NW Spain. Noted for strong currents, heavy seas.

Bishop Auckland, urban dist. of Durham, N England. Pop. 33,000. Seat of Durham bishopric from 12th cent.

Bismarck, Otto Eduard Leopold, Fürst von (1815-98),

BISMARCK

German statesman, chief minister of Prussia (1862-90), architect of German Empire. War with Denmark (1864) resulted in acquisition of Schleswig; friction over Holstein led to Austro-Prussian War (1866), in which Prussian leadership in Germany was consolidated. Provoked French into Franco-Prussian War (1870-1), in which Prussia annexed Alsace-Lorraine. With formation (1871) of German Empire, he became its 1st chancellor. Ruled autocratically (known as 'iron chancellor'), controlling domestic and foreign policies. Engaged in struggle (Kulturkampf) between state and Catholic church, but, as with his opposition to socialism, it eventually failed. Resented by William II; dismissed 1890.

Bismarck, cap. of North Dakota, US; railway jct. on Missouri R. Pop. 35,000. Agric. market (esp. spring wheat). Cap. from 1883.

Bismarck Archipelago, volcanic isl. group in SW Pacific; part of Papua New Guinea. Area c 49,700 sq km (19,200 sq mi). Incl. New Britain, New Ireland, Admiralty Isls.

bismuth (Bi), metallic element; at. no. 83, at. wt. 208.98. Occurs as metal or as oxide Bi_2O_3; obtained by reducing oxide with carbon. Used in metal castings and making alloys of low melting point; compounds used in medicine.

bison, hoofed mammal of cattle family with shaggy mane, short horns, humped back. American bison or buffalo, Bison bison, once numerous on Great Plains; now protected after over-hunting. European bison or WISENT very rare.

Bissau (Port. Bissão), cap. of Guinea-

Bissau, on Geba estuary. Pop. 62,000. Admin. centre; port, exports hardwoods, copra, palm oil. Cap. of Portuguese Guinea from 1942.

bittern, wading bird of heron family, with speckled plumage, long pointed bill. Species incl. nocturnal common European bittern, Botaurus stellaris, and American B. lentiginosus. Male emits booming call.

bittersweet, see NIGHTSHADE.

bitumen, name given to various mixtures of hydrocarbons, esp. solid or tarry mixtures obtained as residues on distilling coal tar, petroleum, etc.

Bivalvia (bivalves), aquatic molluscs of class Lamellibranchiata. Shell formed from 2 hinged halves. Incl. oysters, mussels, clams.

Bizet, Georges, orig. Alexandre César Léopold Bizet (1838-75), French composer. Best known for orchestral pieces L'Arlésienne and Jeux d'Enfants, and opera Carmen. Bizet's lyrical qualities were unrecognized in his lifetime.

Björnson, Björnstjerne (1832-1910), Norwegian author. Known for novels reflecting interest in Norwegian people and legends, eg The Fisher Maiden (1868). Also wrote poetry, incl. words of Norwegian national anthem, social dramas. Nobel Prize for Literature (1903).

Black, Joseph (1728-99), Scottish physician and chemist, b. France. Showed that carbon dioxide is produced when calcium carbonate is heated and investigated its properties. Investigated specific and latent heat.

Black-and-Tans, nickname of irregular force in UK, enlisted for service in Ireland as auxiliaries to Royal Irish Constabulary during disturbances of 1919-22. Name arose from khaki colour of uniform worn with black accessories of Royal Irish Constabulary.

black bear, *Ursus americanus*, most widespread and numerous North American bear, smaller than brown bear. Lives in forests; diet of roots, berries. Himalayan black bear, *Selenarctos thibetanus*, forest-dwelling bear found from Persia to Himalayas.

Blackbeard, see TEACH, EDWARD.

blackberry or **bramble,** *Rubus fructicosus*, low, rambling shrub with white flowers and black fruit. North American species incl. *R. allegheniensis*. Edible berries made into jam or jelly. Once valued for orange dye yielded by roots, and as remedy for swellings and burns.

blackbird, one of various thrush-like birds, males black with yellow beak. Common European variety is *Turdus merula*. Redwinged blackbird most abundant bird of America.

black body, in physics, ideal surface or body which absorbs completely all radiation falling on it. Must also be perfect emitter of radiation, total depending only on absolute temperature. Planck's attempts to explain spectral distribution of black body radiation led to quantum theory.

blackbuck, *Antilope cervicapra*, long-horned antelope of W India. Male black above, white on belly. Female fawn and white.

Blackburn, co. bor. of Lancashire, NW England. Pop. 102,000. Cotton weaving, textile machinery, chemicals, paint mfg.

Black Country, indust. area of WC England, centred in S Staffordshire. Formerly affected by smoke and soot from foundries, factories, *etc.*

Black Death, outbreak of plague which affected Europe *c* 1346-9. Catastrophic effect on pop., killing over ⅓ of inhabitants of many areas.

black earth or **chernozem,** fertile black or dark brown soil. Consists of modified form of LOESS, rich in HUMUS. High nutrient content, good structure make it very suitable for agric., as in *eg* USSR, NC North America.

Blackett, Baron Patrick Maynard Stuart (1897-1974), English physicist. Used cloud chamber to photograph nuclear disintegration (1925). Awarded Nobel Prize for Physics (1948) for this work and for subsequent improvements of Wilson cloud chamber.

black fly, small biting fly of Simuliidae family, found worldwide. Larvae inhabit running water. Females persistent blood-suckers; in Africa transmit roundworm to humans, causing 'river blindness'.

Blackfoot, North American Indian tribes of Algonquian linguistic stock. Settled in 19th cent. on upper Missouri and N Saskatchewan rivers and W to Rocky Mts. Plains buffalo hunters, noted for hostility to settlers and complex ritual. A few remain on reservations in Alberta, Montana.

Black Forest (*Schwarzwald*), wooded mountain region of SW West Germany. Highest peak is Feldberg (*c* 1490 m/4900 ft). Tourism, forestry, woodcarving, clock mfg. Source of Danube, Neckar rivers.

black-headed gull, see GULL.

Black Hills, mountains of NC US, in SW South Dakota, and NE Wyoming. Rise to 2207 m (7242 ft). Forestry, tourism, mineral resources (esp. gold). Gold rush in 1873. Famous sculptures of 4 US presidents at Mt. Rushmore.

black hole, hypothetical state of sufficiently massive star that undergoes gravitational collapse within a certain (Schwarzchild) radius. Region of space around black hole is so distorted that light cannot escape from black hole and so it can never be observed. Certain X-ray stars are believed to be binary companions of black holes.

Black Hole of Calcutta, name given to small room in which British garrison of Calcutta were imprisoned overnight (1756) after successful attack by nawab of Bengal. Most prisoners died of suffocation.

blackjack, see VINGT-ET-UN.

Blackmore, Richard Doddridge (1825-1900), English novelist. Known for classic historical romance, *Lorna Doone* (1869).

Blackpool, co. bor. of Lancashire, NW England. Pop. 151,000. Leading English coastal resort; has famous tower (158 m/520 ft), illuminations.

black power, economic and political power sought by American blacks in struggle for civil rights. Incl. variety of specific movements. Arose as reaction to limited success of non-violent civil rights movement in 1950s and 60s. Increasingly radical, violent action advocated by black urban groups. Militants incl. Black Panther party (estab. 1966), MALCOLM X, Eldridge Cleaver.

Black Prince, see EDWARD THE BLACK PRINCE.

black rat, *Rattus rattus,* common rat of Middle Ages in Europe, largely displaced by brown rat. Carried plague from Asia.

Black Sea (anc. *Pontus Euxinus*), inland sea of SE Europe, bounded by USSR, Turkey, Bulgaria, Romania. Area c 414,000 sq km (160,000 sq mi). Linked to Sea of Azov (NE) by Kerch Str.; to Aegean (SW) by Dardanelles. Almost tideless; marine life in upper levels only.

blackshirts, members of fascist organization. Refers specifically to militant units of Italian Fascist party (estab. 1919) which had black-shirted uniform. March on Rome (1922) brought MUSSOLINI to power. Term also refers to Hitler's elite bodyguard (*Schutzstaffel* or SS).

black swan, *Cygnus atratus,* only swan native to Australia, unique to that country.

blackthorn or **sloe,** *Prunus spinosa,* European deciduous spiny shrub of rose family. Short spikes of small, white flowers are followed by small, astringent fruits (sloes or sloe plums) which are used to flavour sloe gin. Stems used to make shillelaghs in Ireland.

black widow, black venomous spider of tropics and subtropics, genus *Latrodectus.* Female, much larger than male, often eats it after mating. Bite of female intensely painful, rarely fatal.

Blackwood, Algernon (1869-1951), English author. Known for short stories, *eg Tales of the Uncanny and Supernatural* (1949).

Blackwood's Magazine, British literary magazine, first pub. Edinburgh (1817) by William Blackwood (1776-1834). Known for strong Tory feeling and savagery towards 'Cockney School' of poets, eg Keats, Hazlitt. Editors incl. John Gibson Lockhart, James Hogg.

bladder, see GALL BLADDER and URINARY BLADDER.

bladderwort, plant of genus *Utricularia* of Eurasia and N America, esp. *U. vulgaris,* water bladderwort with finely-divided leaves and small bladders. These capture minute water animals and digest them.

blaeberry, see BILBERRY.

Blake, Robert (*c* 1599-1657), English admiral. Defeated Prince Rupert's fleet (1650), Tromp and Dutch navy (1653).Estab. English sea power in the Mediterranean (1654) with victory at Tunis. Captured Spanish treasure fleet (1657). Helped organize Commonwealth's navy.

Blake, William (1757-1827), English poet, engraver, artist. Known for intensely personal vision, abandonment of conventions in poetry and engravings. Translated Biblical symbolism into his own mythology, in works incl. *Songs of Innocence* (1789), *Songs of Experience* (1794), and long, complex 'prophetic books', eg *The Marriage of Heaven and Hell* (1793). Precursor of Romanticism in belief in imagination, individual liberty, simplicity. Illustrated own work but most famous for etchings for Book of Job.

Blanc, Louis (1811-82), French political leader. A socialist, he advocated system of cooperative workshops in *Organisation du travail* (1840). Fled to England after fall

of provisional govt. of 1848 (of which he had been a member), remaining until estab. of Third Republic (1871).

Blanc, Mont, see MONT BLANC.

Blanchard, Jean Pierre or **François** (1753-1809), French balloonist. With John Jeffries, made 1st crossing by air (1785) of English Channel in a balloon.

Blankers-Koen, Fanny (1918-), Dutch athlete. Won 4 Olympic titles in 1948: 100 and 200 m sprints, 80 m hurdles and 4 × 100 m relay.

blank verse, unrhymed verse; in English usually of iambic pentameters. Used in dramatic and epic poetry from Shakespeare and Milton to present.

Blanqui, Louis Auguste (1805-81), French revolutionary socialist. Leader in Revolution of 1848, Paris Commune (1871). Social theories, eg dictatorship of proletariat, influenced Marx; wrote *Critique sociale* (1885).

Blantyre, city of S Malawi, in Shiré Highlands. Pop. 169,000. Commercial, indust. centre on Mozambique-L. Malawi railway. Founded (1876) as mission by Livingstone, named after his birthplace. Joined to nearby Limbe in 1956.

Blarney, village of Co. Cork, S Irish Republic. Castle (15th cent.) contains Blarney Stone, kissing of which reputedly gives one persuasive speech ('blarney').

blast furnace, tower-like furnace used to smelt metals, esp. iron, from their ores. Mixture of ore, coke and limestone is placed in furnace and heated by a blast of air introduced from below. Molten metal separates from slag produced and both are drained off from bottom of furnace.

Blaue Reiter, Der, name given to group of expressionist painters, incl. Marc, Kandinsky, Macke and Klee, working in Munich 1911-14.

Blavatsky, Helena Petrovna, née Hahn (1831-91), Russian occultist. Founded Theosophical Society in New York (1875). Her *Isis Unveiled* (1887) is the textbook of THEOSOPHY.

bleaching, decolorization of coloured matter by chemicals. Common bleaches incl. sodium hypochlorite solution (NaOCl), which acts by oxidation, and sulphur dioxide (SO_2), which acts by reduction.

bleeding heart, any plant of genus *Dicentra* with fern-like leaves and drooping clusters of pink, heart-shaped flowers, esp. *D. spectabilis*, a widely cultivated garden variety, native to Japan.

Blenheim (*Blindheim*), village of SC West Germany. Scene of defeat (1704) of French by Prince Eugène and Marlborough in War of Spanish Succession.

Blériot, Louis (1872-1936), French aviator, inventor. Designed monoplane in which he made (1909) 1st English Channel crossing in heavier-than-air machine.

Bligh, William (1754-1817), British admiral. Remembered for mutiny (1789) on his ship, *Bounty,* while on an expedition in Pacific. Governor of New South Wales (1805-8). Deposed during Rum Rebellion.

blight, general term for many diseases of plants esp. those caused by fungi of family Erysiphaceae which are seen as a white dust on leaves of plant. Also refers to attack by bacteria or insects, eg greenfly.

blimp, see AIRSHIP.

blindness, partial or complete loss of sight. Often results from degenerative diseases associated with ageing; other causes incl. glaucoma, cataracts, etc. Trachoma is a common cause of blindness in tropical countries.

blindworm, see SLOW-WORM.

Bliss, Sir Arthur (1891-1975), British composer. Master of the Queen's Musick (1953-75). His music, vigorous and romantic, incl. *Colour Symphony,* ballets *Checkmate, Miracle in the Gorbals* and film music.

blister beetle, soft-bodied beetle of Meloidae family, often of bright metallic colouring. Some varieties harmful to crops. Cantharides, a blistering agent, formerly extracted from wings of Spanish fly, a S European species.

Blitzkrieg (Ger., = lightning war), form of large-scale surprise attack involving motorized forces with air support. Developed by Germans in WWII.

Bloch, Ernest (1880-1959), American composer, b. Switzerland. Often used Jewish themes in compositions, eg rhapsody *Schelomo.* Other works incl. opera *Macbeth.*

Blocksberg, see BROCKEN, East Germany.

Bloemfontein, judicial cap. of South Africa and cap. of Orange Free State. Pop. 180,000. Commercial, transport, educational centre; univ. (1855). Founded 1846.

Blois, town of Orléanais, NC France, on R. Loire. Cap. of Loir-et-Cher dept. Pop. 45,000. Wine and brandy trade. Château (13th cent.) was residence of counts of Blois, and later of French kings.

Blok, Aleksandr Aleksandrovich (1880-1921), Russian poet; leader of Russian SYMBOLISTS. Works incl. mystical celebration of eternal feminine, *Songs of the Beautiful Lady* (1904), masterpiece of Revolution *The Twelve* (1918). Also wrote increasingly pessimistic plays *eg The Stranger*.

Blondin, Charles, pseud. of Jean François Gravelet (1824-97), French tightrope walker. Famous for crossing of Niagara Falls on rope at height of *c* 50 m (160 ft).

blood, principal fluid of circulatory system in higher vertebrates. Carries oxygen and cell-building material to body tissues and disposes of carbon dioxide and other wastes. Composed of plasma (55%) and cells (45%). Red blood cells (erythrocytes) contain haemoglobin which combines with oxygen in lungs and thus enables oxygen to circulate to tissues. White blood cells (leucocytes) destroy bacteria and form antibodies to neutralize poisons. Smaller blood platelets (thrombocytes) help initiate blood clotting.

blood groups, classification of human blood into groups according to compatibility of red cells of one group with plasma of another. Incompatibility results in agglutination (clumping) of cells which must be avoided in transfusions Four main groups, A, AB, B and O, used in system devised by LANDSTEINER (1900).

bloodhound, large black and tan dog, with drooping ears, wrinkled forehead, keen sense of smell. Stands *c* 69 cm/27 in. at shoulder. Used in tracking fugitives.

blood poisoning, name given to 3 conditions: toxaemia, presence in bloodstream of toxin produced by pathogenic bacteria; septicaemia, spread of bacteria through bloodstream; cellulitis, spread of bacteria from a wound to nearby tissue.

blood pressure, pressure exerted by blood on walls of arteries. Varies with heartbeat between *c* 120 mm/4.72 in. of mercury (systolic pressure) and 80 mm/3.15 in. (diastolic pressure); increases with age. Obesity, arteriosclerosis cause high blood pressure.

bloodstone or **heliotrope,** semi-precious gemstone, a variety of chalcedony. Mostly dark green, speckled with red jasper. Major sources in US, Brazil, India, Australia.

blood transfusion, transfer of blood from one mammal to another of same species. BLOOD GROUPS of donor and patient must be determined to avoid destroying transferred red cells. Tests should also be made for organisms causing disease, *eg* malaria, serum hepatitis.

blood vessels, in higher vertebrates, system of vessels through which blood circulation takes place. They comprise: arteries, carrying blood away from heart; veins, carrying blood towards heart; capillaries, minute vessels which form subdivisions of arteries and then form first small veins. Exchange of material between blood and tissue occurs through thin walls of capillaries.

Bloody Assizes, see JEFFREYS, GEORGE.

Bloomfield, Leonard (1887-1949), American linguist. In major work, *Language* (1933), held that linguistic phenomena should be studied as a formal whole in isolation from their environment or history.

Bloomsbury group, name given to group of English writers, artists, intellectuals who met in Bloomsbury district of London from 1906. Incl. Virginia and Leonard Woolf, Lytton Strachey, E.M. Forster, Duncan Grant, Keynes, Bertrand Russell. 'Bloomsbury' values represented an elitist sensitivity to art and friendship.

blowfly, two-winged fly of Calliphoridae family, commonly called bluebottle or greenbottle. Maggots develop in and feed on living tissue or decaying matter.

Blücher, Gebhard Leberecht von (1742-1819), Prussian field marshal. Contributed to Allied victories against Napoleon at Leipzig (1813), Waterloo (1815).

Bluebeard, villain of traditional tale best known in Perrault's version (1697), prob. based on murderer, Gilles de Rais. Many versions of tale incl. Maeterlinck's *Ariane et Barbebleue* (1901) and operas by Offenbach, Bartók.

bluebell, plant of many species, esp. of genera *Campanula* and *Mertensia*, bearing blue, drooping, bell-shaped flowers. Species incl. *C. rotundifolia*, bluebell of Scotland or harebell and *Endymion nonscriptus* or wild hyacinth, found in Europe and North America. See SQUILL.

blueberry, several plants of genus *Vaccinium*, esp. the high-bush blueberry, *V. corymbosum*, a profusely-branched North American shrub with sweet, edible berry.

bluebird, small North American songbird of thrush family, genus *Sialia*. Male has blue plumage, red breast.

bluebottle fly, blue-coloured BLOWFLY, notorious for spreading dirt and germs.

blue collar, grouping of workers in semi-skilled or unskilled occupations, usually manual labour. Term derived from traditional colour of workshirts. See WHITE COLLAR.

bluefish, *Pomatomus saltatrix*, food fish common to Atlantic coast of North America; occurs also in Indian Ocean, Mediterranean. Travels in dense, voracious shoals.

bluegrass, several grasses of the genus *Poa*, important in lawns and pastures. Known as meadow grass in Britain. Kentucky bluegrass, *P. pratensis*, is particularly valuable as food for horses.

blue-green algae, any of the division Cyanophyta of microscopic ALGAE that contain a blue pigment which masks the green chlorophyll. Widely distributed in unicellular or colonial bodies on moist soil, rocks and trees and in fresh or salt water. Help maintain soil fertility by fixing atmospheric nitrogen and preventing erosion.

Blue Nile, see NILE.

blues, fundamental form of American vocal music, deriving from Negro work songs, and usually melancholy and reflective in mood. Its melodic inflections (blue notes) have influenced much of today's popular music.

bluestocking, female intellectual,

esp. with literary tastes and often pedantic. Originally applied c 1750 to social circle incl. Elizabeth Montagu.

blue tit or **tom tit**, *Parus caeruleus*, European titmouse with yellow underparts and blue cap. Acrobatic when feeding, mainly insectivorous.

blue whale, *Balaenoptera musculus*, whalebone whale of worldwide distribution, now rare from over-fishing. Plankton diet. Largest known mammal, reaching length of 30 m/100 ft.

Blum, Léon (1872-1950), French statesman. Headed 1st POPULAR FRONT govt. (1936-7), instituted sweeping labour reforms. Arrested (1940) by Vichy govt., imprisoned by Germans (1942-5). Again premier 1946-7.

Blunden, Edmund Charles (1896-1974), English poet and critic. Known for prose and verse memories, *Undertones of War* (1928), collections, *The Shepherd* (1922), *Shells by a Stream* (1944).

Blunt, Wilfrid Scawen (1840-1922), English author, diplomat, explorer. Known for poetry, *eg Love Sonnets of Proteus* (1880). Bitter anti-imperialist propaganda caused by travels in Egypt, Arabia.

Blyton, Enid (1897-1968), English writer. Wrote many best-selling children's books, incl. 'Noddy', 'The Famous Five', 'The Secret Seven' series.

boa, large tropical constrictor snake of Boidae family. Best known is boa constrictor, *Constrictor constrictor*, of Central and South America. Arboreal, terrestrial, burrowing varieties exist. Young are born live.

Boadicea, *see* BOUDICCA.

boar, strictly, male pig. Wild boar, *Sus scrofa*, of Europe, N Africa, Asia, probably forerunner of domestic pig; coarse hair and enlarged canine tusk.

Boas, Franz (1858-1942), American anthropologist, b. Germany. Developed rigorous methodology in cultural and physical anthropology. Pioneered linguistics. Wrote classic studies of Eskimos, North American Indians.

bobcat or **wildcat**, *Felix rufa*, small lynx of North America, with reddish-brown coat. Nocturnal hunter. Also called bay lynx.

bobolink, *Dolichonyx oryzivorus*, North American songbird, related to blackbird, oriole. Plumage black and white. Winters in South America; may eat rice crops on flight south.

bobsledding, winter sport in which two or four persons descend course of icy, steeply-banked twisting inclines aboard a bobsled, an open, steel-bordered vehicle with sled-like runners. A development of tobogganing, it originated (19th cent.) in Switzerland. Olympic event since 1924.

bobwhite, *Colinus virginianus*, small North American quail, often called a partridge. Favourite game bird.

Boccaccio, Giovanni (1313-75), Italian poet, b. France. Friendship with PETRARCH influenced him greatly. Best known for secular classic *Decameron*, also wrote prose romance *Filocolo* (c 1340), verse tales *Filostrato* (c 1335), *Teseida* (1339-40).

Boccherini, Luigi (1743-1805), Italian composer, cellist. Prolific composer, noted for chamber music;

wrote over 100 each of string quartets and quintets. Best-known piece is a minuet that comes from one of the string quartets.

Boccioni, Umberto (1882-1916), Italian sculptor, painter. One of the original futurists; work, influenced by cubism, attempted to translate motion, light and sound into form. Works incl. painting *The City Rises* (1910), sculpture *Unique Forms of Continuity in Space* (1913).

Bochum, city of W West Germany, in Ruhr. Pop. 342,000. Indust. centre, esp. iron, steel, engineering, chemicals. Badly damaged in WWII.

Bodensee, *see* CONSTANCE, LAKE, Switzerland.

Bodh Gaya, *see* BUDDH GAYA.

Bodhisattva, in Mahayana Buddhism, a potential Buddha who, despite enlightenment, postpones his apotheosis to assist others.

Bodleian Library, Oxford Univ., England, library famous for collection of rare books and manuscripts. Named after Sir Thomas Bodley, who restored it in late 16th cent. after original library (estab. 15th cent.) destroyed. Receives copy of every book pub. in UK under Copyright Act (1911).

Bodoni, Giambattista (1740-1813), Italian printer. Working in Parma, he produced editions of the classics famous for their typographical elegance. Designed many new typefaces.

Boeotia (*Voiotía*), region of EC Greece. Ancient cap. Thebes, led Boeotian League 6th cent. BC. Modern admin. dist., cap. Levadia.

Boerhaave, Hermann (1668-1738), Dutch physician. Estab. method of clinical teaching at Leiden

Univ., helping to make it leading medical centre in Europe.

Boer War or **South African War** (1899-1902), conflict between Britain and Transvaal Republic-Orange Free State alliance; result of protracted dispute between British and Boers over British territ. ambitions. Aggravated by discovery of gold (1886) and arrival of prospectors. Immediate cause was Britain's refusal to withdraw troops from Transvaal following Jameson Raid (1895). British forces were besieged at Ladysmith, Kimberley and Mafeking by superior Boer army. Ascendant after arrival of heavy reinforcements under Roberts and Kitchener, British relieved Mafeking, invaded Transvaal and occupied Pretoria by July, 1900. Boers adopted guerrilla tactics, led by Botha and Smuts, but were forced to submit (1902). Peace signed May, 1902, in Treaty of Vereeniging.

Boethius, Anicius Manlius Severinus (c 480-c 525), Roman philosopher. Minister under Emperor Theodoric; wrote *The Consolation of Philosophy* while awaiting execution for treason. Greatly influential in transmitting Greek philosophy to Middle Ages.

Bogarde, Dirk, pseud. of Derek Niven van den Bogaerde (1921-), British film actor. Known for roles in films such as *The Servant* (1963) and *The Damned* (1969).

Bogart, Humphrey [De Forest] (1899-1957), American film actor. Famous in tough, cynical roles of 1940s, esp. as private eye in *The Maltese Falcon* (1941), *The Big Sleep* (1946), and as Rick in *Casablanca*

(1942). Later films incl. *The African Queen* (1952).

Bognor Regis, mun. bor. of West Sussex, S England. Pop. 34,000. Seaside resort; many small hotels, convalescent homes.

Bogotá, cap. of Colombia, in E Andean valley; alt. 2610 m (c 8560 ft). Pop. 1,966,000. Cultural, financial centre; textile, chemical mfg.; tobacco, food products. Has international airport. Founded by Spanish (1538) on Chibcha Indian site; cap. from time of Colombian independence. Has Univ. (1572), OAS hq.

Bohemia (*Cechy*), region and former prov. of W Czechoslovakia. Mainly plateau; chief rivers Elbe, Moldau. Agric. (cereals, fruit); minerals (esp. uranium); spas. Indust. centred in Prague, Plzeň (beer). Hist. kingdom; Czech from 1918.

Böhme, Jakob (1575-1624), German mystic. Described all existence as a manifestation of the creative will of God. Evil results from effort to make single element assume the whole. Influenced Hegel. Works incl. *De signatura rerum*.

Böhmerwald or **Bohemian Forest** (*Český Les*), wooded mountain range of Czech-West German border. Highest peak Mt. Arber, alt. 1456 m (4780 ft). Timber; coal, lignite deposits.

Bohr, Niels Henrik David (1885-1962), Danish physicist. Used quantum theory to explain hydrogen atom spectrum, postulating that electron moves in restricted orbits about atomic nucleus. Theory superseded by wave mechanics. Awarded Nobel Prize for Physics (1922). His son, Aage Bohr (1922-), shared Nobel Prize for Physics (1975) for work on ellipsoidal shape of atomic nucleus.

boil, in medicine, inflamed nodule around root of a hair or in a sweat gland. Often caused by infection with *Staphylococcus aureus*. Can be treated by antibiotics.

Boileau [-Despréaux], Nicolas (1636-1711), French critic, poet. Most famous critic of neoclassical age. Works incl. verse treatise *L'Art poétique* (1674), *Satires* after Juvenal.

Boise, cap. of Idaho, on Boise R. Pop. 75,000; state's largest city. Trade, transport centre. Grew after 1863 gold rush; became agric. centre after building of Arrowrock Dam (1911-15).

Bokhara, *see* BUKHARA.

Boksburg, city of S Transvaal, South Africa. Pop. 105,000. Major gold and coalmining centre in Witwatersrand.

Boldrewood, Rolf, pseud. of Thomas Alexander Browne (1826-1915), Australian novelist. Known for adventure stories, esp. *Robbery Under Arms* (1888), celebrating outback.

boletus, genus of fleshy fungi, with thick stems and caps, often brightly coloured. Widely distributed; several species are poisonous but the cèpe, *Boletus edulis*, is edible.

Boleyn, Anne (c 1507-36), English queen, 2nd wife of Henry VIII. Mother of Elizabeth I; she was executed for alleged adultery.

Bolingbroke, Henry St John, Viscount (1678-1751), English politician. Tory secretary of state under Robert Harley, whom he ousted (1714). Opposed George I's accession, was impeached and fled to France. Helped plan Jacobite uprising of 1715. Pardoned (1723), intrigued against Walpole.

Bolivar, Simón (1783-1830), South American revolutionary, b. Caracas; called the 'Liberator'. Rose to leadership during revolution against Spain (1810). After victory at Boyacá (1819), elected president of Greater Columbia. After meeting with SAN MARTÍN at Guayaquil, helped liberate Ecuador (1822), Peru (1824), created Bolivia. His vision of united Spanish America was promoted at meeting in Panama (1826), which accomplished little. Resigned from presidency (1830).

Bolivia, landlocked republic of C South America. Area 1,098,580 sq km (424,162 sq mi); pop. 5,250,000; cap. Sucre; admin. cap. La Paz. Languages: Spanish, Quechua, Aymará, Guaraní. Religion: RC. Andes and tableland (incl. L. Titicaca) in W; tropical rain forests in NE, Chaco plain in SE. Important tin, silver, copper mines (esp. at Potosi) are main source of wealth. Native Indians (Inca ruled) overrun by Spanish (16th cent.); gained independence under Sucre (1824). Wars with Chile, Brazil, Paraguay reduced territ.

Böll, Heinrich (1917-), German author. Works critical of modern society incl. *Letter to a Young Catholic* (1958), novels *eg Billiards at Nine-thirty* (1959). Nobel Prize for Literature (1972).

boll weevil, *Anthonomus grandis,* grey weevil which lays eggs in cotton bolls; larvae feed on cotton fibres. Major pest of S US, Mexico.

Bologna, Giovanni da (1529-1608), Flemish sculptor. Leading sculptor in Florence after death of Michelangelo, his *Rape of the Sabines* (1579-83) is considered a high point of mannerism. Other works incl. *Flying Mercury* (1564).

Bologna, city of Emilia-Romagna, N Italy, cap. of Bologna prov. Pop. 502,000. Engineering, printing, foodstuffs. Roman *Bononia,* on Aemilian Way. Leading medieval centre of learning, with law school, univ. (1200); scholars incl. Dante, Petrarch. Under papal rule from 1560, united with Sardinia 1860. Many medieval buildings.

Bolshevism, Russian revolutionary movement which seized power (Oct. 1917). Term originated at Russian Social Democratic Congress (1903) in London, when radical wing led by LENIN prevailed in dispute over strategy and split from moderates headed by PLEKHANOV, whose followers were called Mensheviks. Russian word *bolshe* means larger; Menshevism, contending faction, comes from *menshe,* smaller. Bolsheviks became Russian Communist party (1918), Mensheviks losing all support by 1921.

Boishoi Theatre, principal opera, ballet theatre in Moscow.

Bolt, Robert Oxton (1924-), English playwright. Best known for *A Man for All Seasons* (1960, filmed 1967) on the martyrdom of Sir Thomas More, and screenplays.

Bolton, bor. of Greater Manchester met. county, NW England. Pop. 154,000. Cotton spinning, woollens, textile machinery mfg.

Bolzano (Ger. *Bozen*), city of Trentino-Alto Adige, NE Italy, on R.

Isarco. Cap. of Bolzano prov. Pop. 105,000. Tourist centre on route to Brenner Pass; textiles, engineering. Passed to Italy from Austria (1919).

Bombay, cap. of Maharashtra state, W India, on Arabian Sea. Pop. of greater city 5,969,000. Indust. centre, major port; exports cotton, cotton goods. Under Portuguese control (1534), ceded to Charles II of England; passed to East India Co. Has extensive university (1857).

Bon, Cape or Ras Addar, headland of NE Tunisia, projecting c 80 km /50 mi into Mediterranean Sea. Hilly, fertile; fruit, vineyards, tobacco. Last German forces in N Africa surrendered here (1943).

Bonaparte, Corsican family, from which NAPOLEON I was descended. His father, **Carlo Buonaparte** (1746-85), was pro-French Corsican lawyer; married Letizia Ramolino (1750-1836). Among their children were: **Joseph Bonaparte** (1768-1844), king of Naples (1806-8) and of Spain (1808-13), forced to abdicate; **Lucien Bonaparte** (1775-1840), contributor to Napoleon's success in coup d'état of 18 Brumaire (1799); **Louis Bonaparte** (1778-1846), king of Holland (1806-10), removed by Napoleon for defying anti-English Continental System; **Caroline Bonaparte** (1782-1839), wife of French marshal MURAT and queen of Naples (1808-15); **Jérôme Bonaparte** (1784-1860), king of Westphalia (1807-13). His marriage (1803) to an American was annulled by Napoleon.

Bonar Law, Andrew, see LAW, ANDREW BONAR.

Bonaventure, St, orig. Giovanni di Fidanza (1221-74), Italian philosopher, called the Seraphic Doctor.

Influential head of Franciscan order. Attempted to reconcile Aristotelian philosophy with Christianity but placed emphasis on the mystical. Works incl. *The Journey of the Mind to God.*

bonds, see SHARES.

Bône, see ANNABA, Algeria.

bone, hard tissue which forms skeleton in vertebrates. Consists of cells held in a matrix of protein fibres and inorganic salts (mainly calcium phosphate). Cells are connected by network of blood vessels and nerves (Haversian canals). Blood-forming marrow is contained in cavities of long bones.

bongo, *Boocercus eurycerus,* large spiral-horned antelope of equatorial African forests. Elusive, travels in small groups; favourite big-game.

Bonhoeffer, Dietrich (1906-45), German Lutheran theologian. Led Church's resistance to Nazism; headed secret theological school (1935-40). Hanged.

Boniface, St, orig. Winfrid (c 675 - c 754), English Benedictine monk, missionary in Germany. Created archbishop of Mainz (745). Estab. bishoprics, abbeys; checked growth of Celtic Christianity. Killed by pagans in Friesland.

Boniface VIII, orig. Benedetto Caetani (c 1235-1303), Italian churchman, pope (1295-1303). Quarrelled with Philip IV of France over taxation of clergy and papal supremacy; issued bulls *Clericis laicos* (1296), *Unam sanctam* (1302). Attacked by Philip's supporters at Anagni (1303), died soon after.

Bonington, Richard Parkes (1802-28), English painter. Known for landscapes in water colour and historical scenes, influenced artists in France and England.

Bonin Islands (*Ogasawara-gunto*), volcanic isl. group of Japan, in Pacific *c* 960 km (600 mi) S of Tokyo. Japanese military base in WWII; occupied by US (1945-1968).

Bonn (anc. *Castra Bonnensia*), cap. of West Germany, on R. Rhine. Pop. 279,000. Admin. centre; publishing, pharmaceuticals, furniture, univ. (1784). Became cap. 1949; has Bundeshaus (Parliament building). Birthplace of Beethoven.

Bonnard, Pierre (1867-1947), French painter. Member of the Nabis group; his early work, influenced by Gauguin and Japanese prints, was characterized by decorative colour and simplified flat form. Later work often depicts intimate domestic interiors and landscapes, using heavier paint, bright colours.

bonsai, art of dwarfing trees in small containers by pruning roots and branches. Technique, first practised in China, pre-dates 13th cent. Specimens can be 300-400 years old and are heirlooms in Japan.

booby, large tropical seabird of Sulidae family, related to gannet. Dives underwater to catch fish. Peruvian booby, *Sula variegata*, is principal producer of guano.

boogie woogie, type of piano jazz style popular in 1930s in US. The left hand keeps up a constant rhythmic phrase while the right executes series of simple variations, often improvised.

boojum tree, *see* BAOBAB.

bookkeeping, systematic recording of money transactions. In double entry bookkeeping, assets are recorded in one column with liabilities in another.

Book of Changes, *see* I CHING.

Book of the Dead, ancient Egyptian religious text, collection of incantations, prayers and spells. Prob. intended as guide for the dead on their journey through the underworld.

Boole, George (1815-64), English mathematician, logician. Known for *An Investigation of the Laws of Thought* (1854), in which logic is treated symbolically, using operations akin to those of algebra. Ideas influenced subsequent work in mathematical philosophy and are important in computer technology.

Boone, Daniel (1734-1820), American frontiersman. Explored and settled Kentucky in 1770s. His adventures became part of American folklore.

Booth, Charles (1840-1916), English social investigator. Pioneered social survey methods through immense, scrupulous work, *Life and Labour of the People in London* (17 vols., 1889-1903).

Booth, John Wilkes (1838-65), American actor. Confederate sympathizer, shot President Lincoln in Ford's Theatre, Washington; killed 2 weeks later. His brother, **Edwin Booth** (1833-93), was a well known actor in Shakespearian roles.

Booth, William (1829-1912), English evangelist preacher. Developed Salvation Army (1878) from missionary work among poor in London. Eldest son, **Bramwell Booth** (1856-1929), succeeded him in 1912 as general of Salvation Army. Fought white slave trade; promoted Criminal Law Amendment Act

(1885). Daughter, **Evangeline Cory Booth** (1865-1950), directed Salvationist movement in Canada and US. General of international movement (1934-9).

Boothia, low-lying penin. of S Franklin Dist., Northwest Territs., Canada. Area 32,331 sq km (12,483 sq mi). Most N part of mainland; has magnetic N pole. First explored (1829-33) by Sir James Ross.

Bootle, bor. of Merseyside met. county, NW England. Pop. 74,000. Seaport on R. Mersey; extensive timber trade.

bootleggers, persons, esp. during PROHIBITION in US, engaged in illegal trade in alcoholic beverages.

Bopp, Franz (1791-1867), German philologist. Author of *Comparative Grammar* (1833-52) demonstrating relationship of Indo-European languages.

borage, any of Boraginaceae family of hairy herbs, shrubs and trees of Asia and Europe, esp. Mediterranean region. Esp. *Borago officinalis*, annual herb with deep blue flowers. Leaves are used in salads.

Borås, town of SW Sweden, on R. Viske. Pop. 73,000. Textiles centre. Founded (1632) by Gustavus Adolphus.

borax or **sodium tetraborate** ($Na_2B_4O_7.10H_2O$), crystalline salt, found naturally as tincal. Used in borax bead test to detect the presence of certain metals, as antiseptic and in glass mfg.

Bordeaux, city of SW France, on R. Garonne, cap. of Gironde dept. Pop. 267,000. Port, centre of Bordeaux wine trade; univ. (1441). Hist. cap. of Aquitaine and Guienne, under Eng-

lish rule (1154-1453). Hq. of Girondists in French Revolution. Has attractive 18th cent. architecture.

Borden, Sir Robert Laird (1854-1937), Canadian statesman, Conservative PM (1911-20). Led Canada through WWI, introducing conscription 1917.

Borders, region of SE Scotland. Area 4670 sq km (1803 sq mi); pop. 99,000. Created 1975, incl. former Berwickshire, Peeblesshire, Selkirkshire, Roxburghshire.

bore, tidal wave found in many river estuaries. Caused by inrush of water, opposed by river current, into progressively narrower and shallower channel. Occurs in *eg* Seine, Severn, Hooghly, Bay of Fundy.

Borges, Jorge Luis (1899-), Argentinian author. Known for personal form of semi-fictional essay 'Ficcione' reflecting interest in philosophical subjects, collected in translated *Labyrinths* (1962). Also wrote verse, criticism.

Borgia, Cesare (1476-1507), Italian political leader. Son of Rodrigo y Borja (later Pope Alexander VI), who made him a cardinal at age of 17. Resigned after murder (1498) of brother at which he prob. connived. Schemed with the French to capture cities of Romagna and estab. his own principality. Fell ill (1503), then lost power as Julius II forced him to restore possessions to papacy. Died fighting for king of Navarre. Considered archetype of Renaissance prince. His sister, **Lucrezia Borgia** (1480-1519), was alleged to be involved in her brother's intrigues. Married Alfonso d'Este (1501) who became duke of Ferrara; made court centre of artistic and intellectual life.

boric or **boracic acid** (H_3BO_3), crystalline soluble solid, with weak acid properties. Used in eyewash and in making enamels.

Boris III (1894-1943), Bulgarian ruler (1918-43). Ruled dictatorially from 1935; brought Bulgaria into Axis group (1941). Died mysteriously shortly after visit to Hitler.

Boris Godunov, *see* GODUNOV, BORIS.

Bormann, Martin (1900-45), German political leader. One of Hitler's chief associates, gained prominence in Nazi party, esp. after 1941. Disappeared at end of WWII, long sought for war crimes. Declared dead (1973) by West German govt.

Born, Max (1882-1970), British physicist, b. Germany. Shared Nobel Prize for Physics (1954) for work on statistical interpretation of wave 'functions, which helped describe electron behaviour.

Borneo, largest isl. of Malay Archipelago. Area *c* 743,000 sq km (287,000 sq mi). Largely dense jungles and mountains; interior sparsely populated by Dyaks. Important oilfields; rubber and copra exports. Divided into 4 sections: Indonesian Kalimantan, former British colonies of Sabah and Sarawak (now part of Malaysia), and British protect. of B.unei.

Bornholm, isl. of Denmark, in Baltic Sea off S Sweden. Area 588 sq km (227 sq mi); main town Rönne. Mainly hilly; tourism, agric., fishing. Danish since 1660.

Borodin, Aleksandr Porfirevich (1833-87), Russian composer. Member of Russian nationalist group of composers 'the Five'. Works incl. 2 symphonies, opera *Prince Igor*, from which came 'Polovtsian Dances', 3 string quartets. Was also professor of chemistry.

Borodino, Battle of, fought (Sept. 1812) during Napoleonic Wars, at Borodino, near Moscow. Russian forces under Kutuzov engaged Napoleon's army in defence of Moscow. French entered Moscow one week later.

boron (B), non-metallic element, existing as brown amorphous powder or dark crystals; at. no. 5, at. wt. 10.81. Occurs in borax and boric acid. Steel alloy used as moderator in nuclear reactors. Borazon (BN), prepared at high temperature and pressure, used in indust. grinding; harder than diamond and more resistant to heat.

Borromini, Francesco (1599-1667). Italian architect. With Bernini, leading architect of Roman Baroque style. Works in Rome incl. San Carlo alle Quattro Fontane, noted for its dynamic spatial composition, and Sant' Ivo della Sapienza. Influenced subsequent work in Italy, Austria and S Germany.

Borrow, George Henry (1803-81), English writer. Known for part fantasy, part biog. works on travel and Gypsies, *eg The Bible in Spain* (1843), *The Romany Rye* (1857). Also wrote Romany lexicon, translations.

borzoi, long-haired Russian wolfhound. Silky whitish coat, narrow head. Stands *c* 76 cm/30 in. at shoulder.

Bosanquet, Bernard (1848-1923), English philosopher. Idealist, reacted against English empiricism. Works incl. *The Philosophical Theory of the State* (1899), *Value and Destiny of the Individual* (1913).

Bosch, Carl (1874-1940), German chemist. Adapted HABER process to indust. production. Invented Bosch process for large scale production of hydrogen. Shared Nobel Prize for Chemistry (1931).

Bosch, Hieronymus (c 1450-1516), Flemish painter. Famous for his fantastic allegorical and religious scenes, painted in minute detail and bright colour; depicted grotesque half animal, half human creatures and strange plants. His symbolism remains obscure. Works incl. *Seven Deadly Sins* (Madrid).

Bose, Sir Jagadis Chandra (1858-1937), Indian physicist, botanist. Demonstrated that plants respond to stimuli in similar way to animals. Invented crescograph to measure plant growth.

Bosnia and Hercegovina, auton. republic of WC Yugoslavia. Area 51,115 sq km (19,735 sq mi); cap. Sarajevo. Mountainous, mainly within Dinaric Alps; main river Sava. Agric. (cereals, fruit, tobacco) in valleys. Bosnia annexed Hercegovina (14th cent.), fell to Turks 1463; ceded to Austria-Hungary 1878; focus of pre-WWI conflict with Serbia, Russia. Part of Yugoslavia from 1918.

boson, in physics, elementary particle, *eg* photon and certain mesons, that does not obey Pauli exclusion principle. Said to obey Bose-Einstein statistics.

Bosporus or **Bosphorus**, narrow str. separating European and Asiatic Turkey; 32 km (20 mi) long, links Black Sea with Sea of Marmara. One of its inlets, the Golden Horn, forms harbour of Istanbul. Of great strategic importance, controlled by Turks since 1452.

Bossuet, Jacques Bénigne (1627-1704), French churchman, noted orator. Attacked Protestantism, quietism (esp. that of FÉNELON) and the Jesuits. In *Histoire universelle* (1681), defended divine authority of civil institutions.

Boston, cap. of Massachusetts, US; on Massachusetts Bay. Pop. 641,000. Atlantic seaport; financial, trade, cultural, education centre. Machinery, textiles, publishing indust. Settled by Puritans 1630. Focus of pre-Revolution activity (Boston Massacre 1770; Boston Tea Party 1773; Bunker Hill 1775); Lexington and Concord battles fought nearby (1776); Boston anti-slavery movement (1831). Indust. growth with 19th cent. shipping. Has many hist. buildings incl. State Capitol, Christ Church, Boston Museum of Fine Arts. Symphony Orchestra.

Boston Tea Party, pre-American Revolution incident (1773) caused by British govt.'s retention of tea tax after repeal of Townshend Acts imposing duty on specified goods. Group of angry Boston citizens, disguised as Indians, threw tea from ships into harbour.

Boston terrier, small dog, bred in US from bulldog and bull terrier. Brindled or black coat. Stands *c* 41 cm/16 in. at shoulder.

Boswell, James (1740-95), Scottish author. Known for masterly biog. of friend Dr Samuel Johnson (1791). Also wrote many miscellaneous articles, *eg Private Papers*, discovered in 20th cent.

Bosworth Field, scene of last battle of Wars of Roses (1485) in which Richard III was defeated and killed by forces of Henry of Richmond, later Henry VII. Near Market Bosworth, Leicestershire.

botany, branch of BIOLOGY, science that deals with plants, their life, structure, growth and classification. Systematic plant CLASSIFICATION begun by Aristotle and his pupil Theophrastus, and improved upon by Linnaeus. Studies of plant anatomy, embryology and reproduction made by 18th cent. Classification now made according to structure, environment and functions.

Botany Bay, inlet of Tasman Sea, E New South Wales, Australia. Site of landing (1770) by Cook and Banks. Now surrounded by Sydney suburbs; oil refinery, airport on shores.

Botha, Louis (1862-1919), South African soldier and statesman. Commanded Boers in war with Britain (1899-1902). Premier of Transvaal (1907-10), 1st PM of Union of South Africa (1910-19). During WWI, conquered German South West Africa.

Botha, Pieter (1916-), South African political leader. Defence minister (1965-); succeeded Vorster as PM (1978-), while holding onto former post. Introduced apartheid reforms.

Bothnia, Gulf of, N arm of Baltic Sea between Sweden (W) and Finland (E). Aland Isls. at mouth. Icebound in winter.

Bothwell, James Hepburn, 4th

Earl of (c 1536-78), Scottish nobleman, 3rd husband of Mary Queen of Scots. Mary's confidant after murder of Rizzio (1566), responsible for assassination (1567) of DARNLEY. After abducting and marrying Mary, he was forced by Scottish nobles to flee to Denmark.

bo tree, name given by Buddhists to *Ficus religiosa*, the pipal or sacred fig tree under which Buddha was enlightened.

Botswana, republic of S Africa; formerly Bechuanaland. Area 600,000 sq km (231,000 sq mi); pop. 709,000; cap. Gaborone. Languages: Tswana, English. Religions: native, Christian. Mainly dry plateau, Okavango Swamp in N, Kalahari Desert in S; nomadic pastoralism, exports cattle, hides. Main food crops maize, millet. Created Bechuanaland Protect. 1885; independent as Botswana from 1966; member of British Commonwealth.

Botticelli, Sandro, orig. Alessandro del Filipepi (c 1445-1510), Italian painter. One of the leading Florentine painters of the Renaissance, his work is noted for delicacy, expressive line and its slight archaism. Most famous works are *Primavera* and *Birth of Venus*.

bottlenosed dolphin, *Tursiops truncatus*, Atlantic cetacean, with short snout. Larger than common dolphin, c 3.6 m/12 ft long. Sociable, responsive to human contact; has been much studied.

bottlenosed whale, *Hyperoodon rostratus*, N Atlantic beaked whale, related to sperm whale. Eats mainly cuttlefish; c 6.4 m/21 ft long.

botulism, rare type of food poisoning caused by toxin produced by bacterium *Clostridium botulinum*, sometimes found in improperly preserved or canned food. Characterized by muscular paralysis; often fatal.

Boucher, François (1703-70), French painter. His work is considered the embodiment of French 18th cent. rococo taste. Made many tapestry designs and paintings of mythological scenes; director of Gobelins factory from 1755.

Boudicca or **Boadicea** (d. AD 62), British queen of Iceni in East Anglia. Led revolt (61) against Romans following brutal annexation of her dead husband's territ. Burned Colchester and London. Her army was defeated by Paulinus; she took poison.

Boudin, Eugène Louis (1824-98), French painter. Painted numerous coastal and harbour scenes, noted for their luminous skies. Advocate of painting directly from nature, influenced Monet.

Bougainville, Louis Antoine de (1729-1811), French navigator. Circumnavigated globe 1767-9, after which he wrote *Description d'un voyage autour du monde*. Largest of Solomon Isls. and bougainvillea plant named after him.

Bougainville, largest of Solomon Isls., SW Pacific; part of Papua New Guinea. Area *c* 10,050 sq km (3880 sq mi). Mountainous, rises to *c* 2590 m (8500 ft) at Mt. Balbi, an active volcano.

bougainvillea, small genus of ornamental, tropical American evergreen vines with brilliant red or purple flowers. Named after French explorer Bougainville.

Boulanger, Georges Ernest Jean Marie (1837-91), French general. War minister (1886-7); gained great popular support as leader of Boulangist movement. Suspected of dictatorial ambitions, fled to Belgium and London (1889). Settled in Jersey where he committed suicide.

Boulanger, Nadia (1887-1979), French music teacher. Her analytical gifts and insistence on creativity have inspired many modern composers, incl. Copland, Berkeley.

boulder clay or **till**, unstratified mixture of clay, sand, gravel and boulders, transported and deposited by retreating glacier. Type of DRIFT, laid down directly from glacier without water transport.

Boulez, Pierre (1925-), French composer. Extended 12-note technique of Schoenberg to fixed organization of all musical elements, eg in *Le Marteau sans maître*. Also a noted conductor, esp. of 20th cent. composers.

Boulogne (-sur-Mer), town of Picardy, N France, on English Channel. Pop. 50,000. Port, ferry services to Dover and Folkestone (England); fishing indust. Badly damaged in WWII.

Boult, Sir Adrian Cedric (1889-), British conductor. Formed BBC Symphony Orchestra in 1930 and was its principal conductor until 1949; moved to London Philharmonic Orchestra until 1957. Championed music of Holst, Vaughan Williams, Elgar.

Boulton, Matthew (1728-1809), English engineer, manufacturer. Financed Watt's steam engine, becoming (1775) his partner in its production. In 1797 he produced new copper coinage for Britain.

Boumedienne, Houari (c 1932-1978), Algerian political leader. Became chief of staff in FLN in fight for Algerian independence (achieved 1962). Overthrew Ben Bella (1965), became chief of state as head of revolutionary council.

bouncing Bet, see SOAPWORT.

Bounty, naval ship, see BLIGH, WILLIAM.

Bourbon, royal house of Europe. Ruled France, Spain, Two Sicilies and Parma. Line traced from Robert of Clermont's marriage (1272) into Bourbon family, his son becoming 1st duke of Bourbon. Title died with CHARLES, DUC DE BOURBON, but branch of family founded line of Bourbon-Vendôme. Antoine de Bourbon (1518-62) became king of Navarre; his son became Henry IV, 1st Bourbon king of France, whose descendants reigned until 1830 (except 1792-1814). Line of Bourbon-Spain started in 1700 with accession of grandson of Louis XIV, Philip V of Spain. Bourbon-Sicily came from Spanish house, founded (1759) by Ferdinand I of the Two Sicilies, ending with Francis II in 1861. Bourbon-Parma (1748-1860) was founded by younger son of Philip V of Spain.

Bourbon, Charles, Duc de (1490-1527), French nobleman. Created Constable of France after victory at Marignano (1515). Later joined Emperor Charles V; helped drive French from Italy, killed while leading attack on Rome.

bourgeoisie, the mercantile or shopkeeping middle class of any country. Prominent from end of medieval period, when they successfully opposed feudal nobility. In Marxist theory, class which, since end of Middle Ages, rose to power, overcoming nobles, monarchs, to reach exclusive political sway in modern state. Thus is one of two elements, the other being the proletarian, in modern dialectical struggle.

Bourges, town of C France, cap. of Cher dept. Pop. 74,000. Route centre, armaments mfg. Hist. cap. of Berry. Cathedral (13th cent.).

Bourguiba, Habib ben Ali (1903-), Tunisian political leader. Led struggle for independence from France, involved in peace negotiations (1954). Elected premier (1956), then president (1959).

Bournemouth, co. bor. of Dorset, S England (formerly in Hampshire). Pop. 153,000. Resort on Poole Bay; has many hotels, convalescent homes.

Bouts, Dierick or **Dirk** (c 1410-75), Netherlandish painter. Noted for his sense of colour and the beauty of his landscape backgrounds. Works incl. *Justice of the Emperor Otto* (Brussels).

Bouvet Island, isl. in S Atlantic, c 2900 km (1800 mi) SSW of Cape Town. Discovered 1739, Norwegian dependency since 1930.

Bovidae, family of even-toed UNGULATES, order Artiodactyla, incl. cattle, sheep, goats, antelopes.

bow, see ARCHERY.

Bowdler, Thomas (1754-1825), English physician, editor. Expurgated literary texts, esp. those of Shakespeare, of anything 'which cannot with propriety be read aloud in a family'; hence to 'bowdlerize'.

Bowen, Elizabeth Dorothea Cole (1899-1973), Irish novelist. Best known for sensitive novels esp. *The Death of the Heart* (1938). Also wrote short stories, essays.

bowerbird, small bird of Australia, New Guinea, family Ptilonorhynchidae. Male builds bower, decorated with feathers, shells, to attract female.

bowfin, *Amia calva*, freshwater fish of eastern North America. Primitive, shows features of fish of Mesozoic era. Voracious predator, lives in overgrown backwaters.

bowling, tenpin, indoor game played by rolling a ball at 10 wooden 'pins'. Game consists of 10 frames, a player being allowed to bowl twice if necessary in a frame. Modernized form of game believed to have been originally introduced into America by Dutch settlers in 17th cent.

bowls or **lawn bowling**, outdoor game dating at least from 13th cent. in England. Played on green, divided into 6 rinks. Opponents alternately roll balls close to small white ball and attempt to dislodge those previously rolled. Rules governed by International Bowling Board (founded 1905), comprising 18 countries.

Bowra, Sir [Cecil] Maurice (1898-1971), English Classical scholar and critic. Known for wit and wide learning. Works incl. *Heroic Poetry* (1952), *Primitive Song* (1962).

box, evergreen shrub of genus *Buxus* of Europe and N Asia. Common variety, *B. sempervirens*, is slow growing and used for clipped hedges.

boxer, short-coated dog of German origin. Fawn or brindle coloured, with protruding jaw. Stands *c* 58 cm/23 in. high at shoulder.

Boxer Rebellion (1898-1900), uprising in China by the Boxers, secret society dedicated to removal of foreign influence. Encouraged by dowager empress Tzu Hsi. Revolt crushed by joint European, Japanese, American forces. China forced to pay heavy indemnities (1901), to allow foreign troops to be stationed in Peking and to alter trade agreements to advantage of foreign nations.

boxing, sport of fighting with the fists. Boxing with soft leather coverings on fists was incl. in ancient Olympic games. Bare fisted boxing revived in 18th cent. England in form of prize fighting. Rules for boxing with gloves were devised *c* 1867 under patronage of Marquess of Queensberry. In modern Olympics since 1908; has also become a major professional sport in Europe and America.

Boyce, William (1711-79), English composer. Master of the King's Musick from 1755. Wrote several symphonies, church and stage music; songs incl. 'Hearts of Oak'.

Boyd Orr, John Boyd Orr, 1st Baron (1880-1971), Scottish biologist. First director-general (1945-8) of UN Food and Agriculture Organization. Awarded Nobel Peace Prize (1949) for contributions to study of nutrition and world food problems.

Boyle, Robert (1627-91), Irish chemist. Enunciated Boyle's law, that volume of a gas kept at constant temperature is inversely proportional to its pressure, following experiments with air. Published *The*

Sceptical Chymist (1661), in which he forwarded atomic view of matter, and distinguished between elements and compounds.

Boyne, river of NE Irish Republic, flows 130 km (80 mi) from Bog of Allen via Kildare, Meath to Irish Sea near Drogheda. Scene of battle (1690) in which William III of England defeated Jacobites under James II.

Boy Scouts, non-military, non-political international organization of boys over 12 years old. Estab. (1908) in UK by Baden-Powell, whose book *Scouting for Boys* (1908) led to incorporation of association by royal charter (1912), and spread of movement worldwide. Introduced into US (1910) by W. Boyce. Parallel organizations for girls are Girl Guides (UK; estab. 1910) and Girl Scouts (US; estab. 1912).

Brabant, area of Belgium and Netherlands. Former prov. of Low Countries, duchy from 12th cent. Prosperous medieval wool, textiles trade centred in Antwerp, Brussels, Louvain. Ruled from 15th cent. by Habsburgs. Divided 1830; Brabant, Antwerp are Belgian provs., North Brabant is Dutch prov.

Bracegirdle, Anne (c 1663-1748), English actress. Protégée of Betterton, friend of Congreve, becoming famous in his plays, esp. as Millamant in *The Way of the World.*

Brachiopoda (brachiopods), phylum of marine invertebrates, often called lampshells (resemble ancient Roman lamp). Brachiopod has bivalve shell enclosing soft body; feeds by means of lophophore. Fossil species of Palaeozoic, Meso-zoic eras are common; c 250 living species, c 30,000 extinct.

bracken or **brake,** several species of FERN, esp. European and American *Pteridium aquilinum,* with coarse, sharp stem and branched spreading fronds. In some places a pernicious weed. Roots once used in tanning and the fronds in thatching.

Bradbury, Ray Douglas (1920-), American science fiction writer. Works incl. novels *eg Fahrenheit 451* (1953), short stories *eg The Martian Chronicle* (1950), and poetry.

Braddock, Edward (1695-1755), British general. During French and Indian War, commanded expedition (1755) to capture Fort Duquesne, losing more than half his troops and his own life.

Bradford, William (1590-1657), English colonist. Founder and long-time governor of Plymouth Colony. Author of *History of Plimoth Plantation.*

Bradford, city of West Yorkshire met. county, N England. Pop. 294,000. Woollens, worsteds, textiles, engineering industs. Church (15th cent.) now cathedral.

Bradlaugh, Charles (1833-91), English social reformer. Championed women's suffrage, birth control, trade unionism. Associate of ANNIE BESANT.

Bradley, Andrew Cecil (1851-1935), English literary critic. Best known for *Shakespearean Tragedy* (1904) stressing an understanding of Shakespeare's characters as a key to the plays.

Bradley, Francis Herbert (1846-1924), English philosopher. Opposed logical empiricism by differentiating between the psychological event and formal meaning in thought. Works incl. *Ethical Studies* (1876), *Appearance and Reality* (1893).

Bradley, Omar Nelson (1893-), American general. Led US troops in Normandy invasion (1944). Chairman joint chiefs of staff (1949-53).

Bradman, Sir Donald George (1908-), Australian cricketer. A prolific run scorer, he played for Australia (1928-48), captain from 1936. His aggregate of 974 runs (1930) is highest for England-Australia test series.

Bradstreet, Anne (c 1612-72), American poet, b. England. Wrote first book of original verse published in Massachusetts Bay Colony, *The Tenth Muse Lately Sprung Up in America* (1650); best known for expression of sexual tenderness.

Bragg, Sir William Henry (1862-1942), English physicist. Researched into penetrating power of alpha particles. Shared Nobel Prize for Physics (1915) with his son, Sir William Lawrence Bragg (1890-1971), for working out theory of X-ray diffraction and using it to determine X-ray wavelengths and crystal structure.

Brahe, Tycho (1546-1601), Danish astronomer. Improved astronomical instruments, thus obtaining positions of heavenly bodies with unprecedented accuracy. Built 2 observatories on isl. of Hven. Kepler made extensive use of Brahe's observations in formulating laws of planetary motion.

Brahma, in Hinduism, supreme and eternal spirit of the universe. Personified as creator in divine triad (*see* also VISHNU, SIVA).

Brahman or Brahmin, in Hinduism, member of priestly (highest) Hindu CASTE. Only Brahmans may interpret the sacred Vedic texts.

Brahmaputra, river of NE India, *c* 2900 km (1800 mi) long. Rises in Himalayas of SW Tibet as Tsangpo, flows through fertile Assam valley; merges with Ganges in Bangladesh.

Brahms, Johannes (1833-97), German composer, pianist. Helped by Joachim and Liszt; close friend of Schumann. Settled in Vienna (1863). Despite romantic inclinations, he worked in classical forms. Works incl. 4 symphonies, a Requiem, piano and violin concertos, choral and orchestral compositions, and chamber music.

Braille, Louis (*c* 1809-52), French inventor. Blind from the age of three, he devised (1829) the system of raised point writing and printing named after him, enabling the blind to read and write.

brain, in vertebrates, that part of central nervous system enclosed in skull. Divided into 3 main sections: hindbrain, midbrain and forebrain. Hindbrain contains brain stem, extending from spinal cord; anterior to this is cerebellum, which co-ordinates muscular movements. Midbrain contains control network for senses of sight and hearing. Forebrain contains: thalamus, which receives and distributes incoming sensations and perceives sensation of pain; hypothalamus, which regulates body temperature, heart beat, metabolic rate, *etc*; relatively huge cerebrum, divided into 2 hemispheres with 4 paired lobes. Cerebrum controls sensations of vision, hearing, touch, *etc*, and higher mental processes.

Braine, John Gerard (1922-). English novelist. Known for *Room at the Top* (1957) a pessimistic view of provincial life. One of the ANGRY YOUNG MEN.

brake, *see* BRACKEN.

Brakpan, city of S Transvaal, South Africa. Pop. 113,000. At height of 1650 m (5400 ft); goldmining centre in Witwatersrand.

Bramante, Donato (1444-1514), Italian architect. Major architect of high Renaissance; engaged by Julius II to rebuild St Peter's, Rome (1503). Other works in Rome incl. Tempietto in courtyard of San Pietro in Montorio.

bramble, *see* BLACKBERRY.

Branchiopoda, subclass of primitive aquatic crustaceans, with many pairs of flattened, leaf-like limbs. Well-known example is daphnia or waterflea.

Brancusi, Constantin (1876-1957), Romanian sculptor. Pioneer of abstract sculpture; his work, in wood, stone and highly-polished metal, is noted for its simplification of natural forms. Works incl. *Bird in Space*.

Brandan, St., *see* BRENDAN, ST.

Brandenburg, town of C East Germany, on R. Havel. Pop. 90,000. Agric. machinery, textiles. Cathedral, town hall (both 14th cent.). Cap. of former Brandenburg prov. of Prussia.

Brandes, Georg Morris Cohen (1842-1927), Danish literary critic. Formulator of Scandinavian naturalism, esp. in *Critical Studies* (1899) incl. study of Ibsen.

Brando, Marlon (1924-), American stage and film actor. First known for 'primitive male' roles, as in play *A Streetcar Named Desire* (1947), film *On the Waterfront* (1954). Later developed range in films with *The Godfather* (1972), *Last Tango in Paris* (1973).

Brandt, Bill (1905-). English photographer. Started as student of Man Ray in Paris. In 1930's concentrated on documenting social contrasts in Britain. After WWII turned to portraiture, landscapes and nudes, often using heightened perspective.

Brandt, Willy, orig. Herbert Ernst Karl Frahm (1913-), German statesman. Active in Norwegian resistance during WWII. Mayor of West Berlin (1957-66) until joined coalition govt. First Social Democrat chancellor (1969-74). Awarded Nobel Peace Prize (1971) for policies of seeking to improve relations with E European countries.

brandy, name for alcoholic spirit distilled from any wine. Best-known grape wine brandy is cognac, made from white grapes in Charente (France). Kirsch is distilled from fermented cherry juice, and slivovitz, of E Europe, from plums. Characteristic light tawny colour acquired when left to mature in oak casks.

Brantford, town of S Ontario, Canada; on Grand R. Pop. 64,000. Electrical equipment mfg., agric. implements. Alexander Graham Bell developed 1st telephone here (1876).

brant goose, *see* BRENT GOOSE.

Braque, Georges (1882-1963), French painter. Early work was in fauve style. Collaborated with Picasso in development of cubism until 1914; originated use of collage in his paintings. Later work incl. still lifes and landscapes in more realistic style.

Bras d'Or, tidal lake of E Nova Scotia, Canada. Area 930 sq km (c 360 sq mi). Almost divides Cape Breton Isl.

Brasilia, cap. of Brazil, in C federal dist. Pop. 538,000. Built as cap. with intention of stimulating growth in undeveloped interior; inaugurated 1960.

Brașov, city of SC Romania, in Transylvanian Alps. Pop. 193,000. Commercial, indust. centre (textiles, machinery); tourism. Founded (1211) by Teutonic Knights; passed from Hungary to Romania in 1920.

brass, name applied to various alloys of zinc and copper; sometimes containing other metal components. Ductile, resists corrosion.

brassica, see CABBAGE; TURNIP.

brass instruments, instruments in which sound is produced by vibration of the lips within a mouthpiece, eg FRENCH HORN; TROMBONE; TRUMPET; TUBA.

Bratislava (Ger. *Pressburg*), city of S Czechoslovakia, on R. Danube. Pop. 284,000. River port; agric. market, oil refinery (pipeline from Ukraine 1962). Cap. of Hungary 1541-1784 and Slovakia 1918-45. Gothic cathedral, town hall (13th cent.).

Braunschweig, see BRUNSWICK, West Germany.

Brautigan, Richard (1935-), American author. Novels reflecting the life of the Pacific coast incl. *Trout Fishing in America* (1967), *In Watermelon Sugar* (1968).

Bravo, Río, Mexican name for RIO GRANDE.

Brazil (*Brasil*), republic of E South America. Area 8,511,965 sq km (3,286,470 sq mi); pop. 79,000,000; cap. Brasilia; major cities Rio de Janeiro; São Paulo. Language: Portuguese. Religion: RC. Covers nearly ½ of South American continent. Has extensive Atlantic coastline; mainly agric. esp. coffee, cotton, sugar cane growing. Tropical forested Amazon basin produces rubber. Mato Grosso plateau in undeveloped interior (mineral resources eg iron ore, manganese). Drained by Amazon (W), Paraná-Paraguay (S), São Francisco river systems. Indust. concentrated in São Paulo, Minas Gerais regions (esp. cotton, steel, chemicals, engineering). Portuguese settlement began in 16th cent.; pop. gradually mixed. Independence gained (1822); republic estab. 1889. Govt. instability of 20th cent. broken by Vargas' dictatorship (1930-45).

brazilnut, edible seeds of tree *Bertholletia excelsa*, of nettle family, native to Brazil. Large woody fruits contain c 20 three-sided edible oily nuts.

Brazos, river of SC US. Rises in E New Mexico, flows SE 1410 km (870 mi) to Gulf of Mexico. Provides irrigation, h.e.p. for N Texas.

Brazzaville, cap. of the Congo, on Stanley Pool of R. Congo, opposite Kinshasa (Zaïre). Pop. 250,000. Admin., commercial centre. River port, railway to Pointe Noire; trade in wood, rubber, minerals from interior to coast. Founded by Brazza (1880); cap. of French Equatorial Africa 1910-60.

bread, food baked from kneaded

dough made from flour, water and yeast (used as raising agent). Unleavened bread contains no raising agent. Wheat flour is generally used, but rye is sometimes employed. White bread is made from grain from which husk has been removed.

breadfruit, large, round, pulpy fruit of Malayan tree, *Artocarpus altilis*, found throughout S Pacific and tropical America. When baked the fruit can be used as bread substitute.

Breakspear, Nicholas, see ADRIAN IV.

bream, *Abramis brama*, European freshwater food fish of carp family. Protruding mouth used for feeding on bottom.

breast, in human female, either of 2 milk-secreting (mammary) glands. Develops with onset of puberty, increasing in size and changing shape. Towards end of pregnancy, hormones from pituitary gland stimulate secretion of milk. Corresponding male glands are undeveloped.

breccia, rock composed of small angular fragments, bound together in matrix of cementing material. Normally formed close to origin of constituent fragments, unlike CONGLOMERATE. Examples incl. cemented scree deposits, fault breccias, volcanic breccias.

Brecht, [Eugen Friedrich] Bertolt (1898-1956), German dramatist. Early work expressionist; best known for Marxist dramas, *eg The Threepenny Opera* (1928) with music by Weill, *Mother Courage and Her Children* (1939), *The Caucasian Chalk Circle* (1945). Applied anti-illusionistic 'alienation' theory in own theatre company, the Berliner Ensemble, from 1948.

Breconshire or **Brecknockshire,** former county of SC Wales, now in Powys. Mountainous in S, incl. Brecon Beacons (National Park). Coalmining; agric. Brecon or Brecknock, mun. bor. and co. town of Powys. Pop. 6000. Has cathedral (1923) formerly Priory Church.

breeder reactor, nuclear reactor which, in addition to creating atomic energy, produces more nuclear fuel by neutron bombardment of suitable radioactive elements, *eg* uranium 238.

breeding, attempt to improve genetic strains of plants and animals by careful selection of parent stock. Cattle are bred to improve meat or milk yield; cereals are bred to be more disease resistant and give larger and more rapid yields.

Bregenz (anc. *Brigantium*), town of NW Austria, on L. Constance, cap. of Vorarlberg prov. Pop. 23,000. Tourism, h.e.p.

Bremen, city of N West Germany, on R. Weser, cap. of Bremen state. Pop. 595,000. Major port; indust., commercial centre. Hanseatic League member from 1358; has medieval cathedral, town hall. Badly damaged in WWII.

Bremerhaven, city of N West Germany, at mouth of R. Weser. Pop. 145,000. Outport for Bremen; major fishing, ferry port. Founded 1827.

Brendan or **Brandan, St. ['the Voyager']** (c 486-578), Irish churchman, explorer. Fame spread by 10th cent. tale, *Brendan's Voyage*, telling of travels, esp. to beautiful Land of Promise in Atlantic, identified with Canary Islands, but thought by some to be North America.

Brennan, Christopher John (1870-1932), Australian poet. Known for idiosyncratic melancholic verse, *eg* 'The Wanderer'. *The Verse of Christopher Brennan* (1958) is definitive collection.

Brenner Pass (Ital. *Passo Brennero*), on Austro-Italian border. Height 1370 m (4500 ft); road (1772), railway (1867) connect Innsbruck with Bolzano.

Brent, bor. of W Greater London, England. Pop. 279,000. Created 1965 from Wembley, Willesden mun. bors.

Brentano, Clemens Maria (1778-1842), German poet. Created 'legend' of 'Lorelei' in novel *Godwi* (1800-1). Collaborated with Achim von ARNIM in *The Boy's Magic Horn* (1805-8). Wrote much romantic verse, novellas.

Brentano, Ludwig Joseph ('Lujo') (1844-1931), German economist. Known for study of guilds and trade unions in England. Leading opponent of German militarism. Awarded Nobel Peace Prize (1927).

brent goose or **brant goose**, *Branta bernicla*, small, dark goose with black head. Breeds in Arctic, winters along Atlantic coasts of North America and Europe.

Brescia, city of Lombardy, N Italy, cap. of Brescia prov. Pop. 215,000. Indust. centre; iron, munitions, textiles. Roman *Brixia*, has temple of Vespasian (AD 73); medieval cathedrals.

Breslau, see WROCLAW, Poland.

Brest, city of Brittany, NW France, on Atlantic Ocean. Pop. 154,000. Port, fishing; major French naval base. Harbour built (1631) by Richelieu. German submarine base in WWII, town badly damaged by Allied bombing.

Brest, city of USSR, transport centre of SW Byelorussian SSR. Pop. 128,000. Cap. of Polish-Lithuanian state from 1569, passed to Russia 1795. Formerly Brest-Litovsk; site of Soviet-German treaty (1918) in WWI. Belonged to Poland (1921-45).

Brest-Litovsk, Treaty of, peace treaty in WWI, signed (1918) by Soviet Russia and Central powers at Brest, after 1917 armistice. Russia recognized independence of Ukraine and Georgia, confirmed independence of Finland, gave up Poland, Baltic states and part of Byelorussia to Germany and Austro-Hungary; also made some concessions to Turkey. Terms renounced at end of WWI.

Brétigny, Treaty of (1360), concluded second phase of Hundred Years War between England and France. King John II was to be ransomed, Edward III was granted countships in France but abandoned claim to French throne.

Breton, André (1896-1966), French author. Involved in DADA, later founded SURREALISM in 3 manifestoes (1924-42). Also wrote novel, *Nadja* (1928), love poetry.

Breton, language, see CELTIC.

Bretton Woods Conference, name given to UN Monetary and Financial Conference (July, 1944), held at Bretton Woods, New Hampshire, US. Resulted in creation of INTERNATIONAL MONETARY FUND and INTERNATIONAL BANK FOR RECONSTRUCTION AND DEVELOPMENT.

brewing, *see* BEER.

Brewster, Sir David (1781-1868), Scottish physicist. Noted for discovery that beam of light reflected from glass is completely polarized when reflected and refracted rays are at right angles.

Brezhnev, Leonid Ilyich (1906-   ), Soviet political leader. President (1960-4) until he succeeded Khrushchev as first secretary of Communist party's Central Committee. Policies incl. DÉTENTE with US, growing estrangement from China, extension of Soviet influence in developing countries. Supported invasion (1968) of Czechoslovakia. Formally acknowledged as head of state after changes to Soviet constitution (1977).

Briand, Aristide (1862-1932), French statesman. Began as Socialist, heading several govts. (1909-29). Foreign minister (1925-32), helped conclude Locarno (1925) and Kellogg-Briand (1928) pacts, aimed at maintaining European peace. Shared Nobel Peace Prize (1926) with Stresemann.

Briansk, *see* BRYANSK.

briar, sweetbriar or **eglantine,** *Rosa eglanteria,* European species of bush rose. Hooked white or pink single flowers, scarlet fruit (hips) which are rich in vitamin C. Now naturalized in North America.

Bridge, Frank (1879-1941), English composer. Compositions incl. symphonic poems, much chamber music. Early works in romantic tradition; later works dispense with traditional tonality. Taught composition to Benjamin Britten.

bridge, card game for four players derived from WHIST. Most popular form is contract bridge, invention of which is credited to Harold Vanderbilt (1925); popularized by Culbertson, Charles Goren. Rules governing tournament play determined by Portland Club, London, European Bridge League, and American Contract Bridge League.

bridge, structure to carry road, railway or canal over gap or barrier. Most common types are cantilever, suspension and arch bridges. Some of world's best-known bridges incl. Forth Railway Bridge, Scotland (cantilever); Brooklyn Bridge, New York (suspension); Sydney Harbour Bridge, Australia (steel arch); Golden Gate Bridge, San Francisco (suspension).

Bridgeport, town of SW Connecticut, US; on Long Isl. Sound. Pop. 157,000. Munitions mfg., engineering, plastics indust. First settled as fishing community (1639).

Bridges, Robert Seymour (1844-1930), English poet. Friend of G.M. Hopkins, editor of his work. Own work incl. *Shorter Poems* (1890), *The Testament of Beauty* (1929). Poet laureate (1913).

Bridget or **Birgitta of Sweden, St** (c 1300-73), Swedish nun, patron saint of Sweden. On death of her husband founded Order of the Holy Saviour (Bridgettines). Went to Rome (1349), where she became famous for advocating reform. Visions famous in Middle Ages.

Bridget, St (c 453-c 523), Irish abbess. Regarded as founder of 1st women's religious community in Ireland at Kildare. Also called Brigid, Bride.

Bridgetown, cap. and seaport of Barbados, on Carlisle Bay. Pop. 9000. Popular tourist resort. Exports sugar, rum, molasses.

Bridgewater, Francis Egerton, 3rd Duke of (1736-1803), pioneer of British inland navigation. Had canal constructed to carry coal from his Worsley estate to Manchester; later had canal extended to the Mersey (1772).

Bridie, James, pseud. of Osborne Henry Mavor (1888-1951), Scottish playwright. Known for *The Anatomist* (1931) on Burke and Hare, *A Sleeping Clergyman* (1933) on heredity, and *Daphne Laureola* (1949).

Brie, region of N France, E of Paris. Cereals, cattle rearing; noted for dairy produce, esp. cheese. Early medieval county, cap. Meaux.

Brigantes, early people of N England. Under queen Cartimandua became client-state of Rome, but defeated in AD 71 by Agricola. Unsuccessful revolt (155) led to estab. of many more Roman forts and settlements.

Bright, John (1811-89), British politician. Noted orator, joined by COBDEN in leading Anti-Corn Law League, advocating free trade; Corn Laws repealed (1846). Championed middle classes on basis of laissez-faire doctrines.

Brighton, co. bor. of East Sussex, S England. Pop. 166,000. Seaside resort, popular since Royal Pavilion built 1817 by Prince Regent (George IV). Has Roedean School for girls; Univ. of Sussex (1959) is nearby.

brill, *Scophthalmus rhombus,* European marine flatfish of turbot family. Valued as food.

Brindisi, town of Apulia, SE Italy, on Adriatic Sea, cap. of Brindisi prov. Pop. 85,000. Port; petrochemicals, engineering. As Roman *Brundisium* was naval station, terminus of Appian Way. Medieval castle, cathedral.

Brisbane, city of E Australia, cap. of Queensland; on Brisbane R. Pop. 866,000. Admin., commercial centre; port, exports wool, wheat, fruit, minerals. Founded (1824) as penal colony; first free settlers came 1838; state cap. from 1859. Univ. of Queensland (1909).

bristletail, primitive, wingless insect with long antennae. Divided into 2 orders: 1) Diplura, eyeless with 2 long tail filaments, represents link with ancestral insect type; 2) Thysanura, with compound eye, body scales, lives among stones, dead leaves. Species incl. SILVERFISH.

Bristol, city of Avon, SW England, on R. Avon. Pop. 425,000. Seaport, food processing, aircraft mfg., tobacco indust. Medieval wool trade; 17th-18th cent. slave trade. Has Church of St Mary Redcliffe (14th cent.), univ. (1909). Bombed in WWII.

Bristol Channel, inlet of Atlantic between SW England and Wales, c 136 km (85 mi) long. Chief river is Severn; extreme tidal range.

Britain, Battle of, German air offensive (Aug.-Oct. 1940), intended to destroy British defences prior to invasion. Luftwaffe lost 1733 aircraft and abandoned tactic in mid-Oct., though night raids continued.

British Antarctic Territory, all isls. and mainland S of 60°S and between 20° and 80°W. Incl. Graham Land, parts of Coats Land

and Weddell Sea, South Shetland and South Orkney Isls.

British Columbia, coastal prov. of W Canada; incl. Vancouver, Queen Charlotte Isls. Area 948,600 sq km (366,255 sq mi); pop. 2,185,000; cap. Victoria; major city Vancouver. Mainly mountainous. Coast Mts. rise to Rockies in interior; main rivers Fraser, Columbia; h.e.p. Major timber indust; dairy, fruit, mixed farming; fisheries; copper, lead, zinc mining; aluminium smelting. Acquired by Hudson's Bay Co. (1821), became prov. 1871; linked with E by railway (1885).

British Commonwealth of Nations, see COMMONWEALTH, BRITISH.

British Guiana, see GUYANA.

British Honduras, see BELIZE.

British Indian Ocean Territory, colony formed (1965) from Chagos archipelago, Des Roches, Farquhar and Aldabra isls. Pop. 2000. Last 3 isls. part of Seychelles from 1976.

British Isles, archipelago of NW Europe in Atlantic Ocean, comprising GREAT BRITAIN, IRELAND. Incl. Hebrides, Orkneys, Shetland, Isle of Man, Isle of Wight, Scilly Isles, Channel Isls.

British Museum, national museum in London, founded (1753) on basis of Sir Hans Sloane's collection; opened to public 1759. Collection incl. coins and stamps, books and manuscripts, eg Lindisfarne Gospels, Egyptian antiquities, eg Rosetta Stone, classical sculpture, eg Elgin Marbles.

British North America Act (1867), constitution of Canada, passed by British Parliament, embodying plans for federal govt.

agreed at Québec Conference (1864). Provided for division of provincial (enumerated) and federal (residual) legislative powers; safeguarded independence of courts and special language and educational status for Québec prov. Also allowed for admission of further provs.

British Standards Institution (BSI), originally Engineering Standards Committee, formed by various engineering bodies (1901, granted charter 1929) who voluntarily prepared and pub. agreed mfg. standards for their products. The BSI now covers over 60 major industs. in UK.

British thermal unit (BTU), quantity of heat required to raise temperature of 1 pound of water by 1° F; equals c 252 calories.

Brittany (*Bretagne*), region of NW France, occupying penin. between English Channel and Bay of Biscay; hist. cap. Rennes. Rocky coast, natural harbours (eg Brest), interior largely moorland. Agric., esp. fruit, vegetables; fishing, tourism. Ancient *Armorica*; settled by Celts from Britain c 500 AD. Medieval duchy, incorporated (1532) into France. Breton language still spoken in rural areas, distinctive customs retained.

Britten, [Edward] Benjamin (1913-76), English composer. Highly personal composer, worked in traditional idioms and forms, principally opera and vocal music. Works incl. operas *Peter Grimes* and *Billy Budd*, oratorio *A War Requiem*, symphonic work *The Young Person's Guide to the Orchestra*.

Brno (Ger. *Brünn*), city of C Czechoslovakia. Pop. 336,000. Commercial and indust. centre, esp.

textiles, engineering. Produced Bren gun. Besieged by Swedish (1645). Hist. hilltop prison-fortress until 1857. Cap. of Moravia (1938-45).

broadcasting, public transmission of sound and images by radio and television. Sound broadcasting began c 1920 in US; 1st public TV service begun by British Broadcasting Corporation (1936). Developments since incl. use of high frequencies (VHF) to increase available radio space, and colour TV, begun in US (1953), in Europe later.

Broads, The, see NORFOLK, England.

Broadway, street of New York City. Passes through theatre district, hence synonymous with American commercial theatre. Off Broadway, term used for small N.Y. theatres putting on 'art' productions.

broccoli, Brassica oleracea, plant related to the cauliflower but bearing tender shoots with greenish buds cooked as vegetable. Native to S Europe and cultivated widely in N temperate zones.

broch, circular dry-stone tower, up to 15 m (50 ft) high, found mostly in N and NW Scotland. Used as fortified homestead in early Christian times.

Brocken or **Blocksberg,** mountain of East Germany, highest of Harz Mts. (1142 m/3747 ft). Traditional meeting place of witches on Witches' Sabbath (May 1). Scene in Goethe's Faust.

Brocken spectre, natural phenomenon, named after highest of Harz Mts., in which greatly enlarged shadow of observer is projected onto bank of cloud or mist below him. May be accompanied by 'glory',

circular rainbow bands seen round shadow, caused by diffraction.

Broglie, Louis Victor, Prince de (1892-), French physicist. Awarded Nobel Prize for Physics (1929) for theory of wave nature of electron, starting point of wave mechanics.

Broken Hill, city of W New South Wales, Australia. Pop. 30,000. Silver, lead, zinc, gold mining; market town for large pastoral area.

Bromberg, see BYDGOSZCZ, Poland.

bromine (Br), reddish-brown volatile liquid element of halogen family; at. no. 35, at. wt. 79.91. Vapour has choking, irritating smell. Occurs in salts found in sea water and mineral deposits. Used in organic synthesis; compounds used in photography (silver bromide) and formerly in medicine.

Bromley, bor. of SE Greater London, England. Pop. 304,000. Created 1965 from Bromley, Beckenham mun. bors., 4 NW Kent towns incl. Orpington.

bronchitis, inflammation of airpassages (bronchial tubes) in lungs. Acute form may be caused by viral or bacterial infection. Chronic form, characterized by regular coughing with mucus, may be caused by smoking, air pollution, etc.

Bronowski, Jacob (1908-74), English scientist, writer, b. Poland. Attempted to fuse cultural, scientific history, esp. in The Ascent of Man (1973).

Brontë sisters, three English novelists. Although daughters of a Yorkshire clergyman, living circumscribed lives, produced some of most famous fiction of early 19th cent. Charlotte Brontë, pseud. Currer Bell

(1816-55), wrote semi-autobiog. works incl. *Jane Eyre* (1847), *Villette* (1853), *The Professor* (1857). **Emily Jane Brontë**, pseud. Ellis Bell (1818-48), wrote single novel, masterpiece *Wuthering Heights* (1847), imaginative verse. **Anne Brontë**, pseud. Acton Bell (1820-49), known for *The Tenant of Wildfell Hall* (1848), also collaborated with sisters in poetry and juvenilia. Their works show effect on powerful imaginations of wild surroundings and intense isolated family life.

brontosaurus, extinct semi-aquatic herbivorous dinosaur, genus *Apatosaurus*. Over 21.3 m/70 ft long, with long neck and tail, it weighed *c* 30 tons. Bones have been found in Jurassic strata of US.

Bronx, see NEW YORK CITY.

bronze, alloy consisting mainly of copper and tin; may contain zinc and aluminium. Used to make medals, bells, *etc*; phosphor bronze used in springs, aluminium bronze in bearings.

Bronze Age, archaeological period characterized by use of bronze weapons and tools. Dates from before 3500 BC in Middle East, is associated with beginning of recorded history. Placed between Stone and Iron Ages.

Bronzino, Angelo, real name of Cosimo Allori (1503-72), Italian painter. Noted for his portraits in mannerist style; his sitters were rendered in unemotional, elegant manner. Works incl. *Venus, Cupid, Time and Folly*.

Brook, Peter Stephen Paul (1925-), English director. Known for innovative productions using stage and actors to full, eg *The Perse-cution and Assassination of Marat ...* (1964), *A Midsummer Night's Dream* (1970).

Brooke, Alan Francis, see ALAN-BROOKE, ALAN FRANCIS BROOKE, 1ST VISCOUNT.

Brooke, Rupert Chawner (1887-1915), English poet. Known for romantic, patriotic (often on war) verse, esp. 'Grantchester' and *1914 and Other Poems* (1915). Also wrote perceptive criticism. Died of septicaemia on Dardanelles expedition.

Brookeborough, Basil Stanlake Brooke, 1st Viscount (1888-1973), Irish statesman, PM of Northern Ireland (1943-63). Advocated strong links with Britain.

Brooklyn, see NEW YORK CITY.

Brooks, Van Wyck (1886-1963), American literary historian. Works, *eg The Wine of the Puritans* (1909), *America's Coming of Age* (1915), *Makers and Finders* (series 1936-52), helped estab. sense of autonomy and unity in American culture.

broom, shrubs of 3 related genera *Cytisus*, *Genista*, *Spartium* of Leguminosae family, with yellow, white or purple flowers. Common or Scotch broom is native to temperate Europe, Asia and is naturalized in North America.

Brouwer, Adriaen (*c* 1605-38), Flemish painter. Known for genre scenes of peasant life, often set in taverns; later work was usually monochromatic.

Brown, Sir Arthur Whitten, see ALCOCK, SIR JOHN WILLIAM.

Brown, Ford Madox (1821-93), English painter, b. France. Associated with the Pre-Raphaelites, and profoundly influenced by them.

Works incl. *Work* and *The Last of England.*

Brown, John (1800-59), American abolitionist. Belief in need for armed intervention to free slaves led to his capture of govt. arsenal at HARPERS FERRY (1859). It was retaken and Brown was hanged.

Brown, Lancelot ('Capability') (1716-83), English landscape gardener. Laid out gardens at Chatsworth, Blenheim, *etc,* using clumps of trees, serpentine lakes, undulating lawns to achieve informal effect.

brown algae, any of the division Phaeophyta of large ALGAE that contain a brown pigment which masks the green chlorophyll. Often have air bladders and a gelatinous surface, eg bladder wrack, *Fucus vesiculosus.* Mainly marine group abundant in colder latitudes. Some species are 70 m/230 ft long.

brown bear, *Ursus arctos,* omnivorous bear of Europe, Asia, North America. Variations in size of species, with Kodiak bear of Alaska largest; also incl. GRIZZLY BEAR. Gives birth to 1 or 2 tiny helpless cubs. Rare in Europe, now protected.

Browne, Hablot Knight, pseud. Phiz (1815-82), English illustrator. Works incl. illustrations for many of novels by Charles Dickens and cartoons for *Punch* magazine.

Browne, Sir Thomas (1605-82), English author. Known for individual, sonorous prose style, esp. in *Religio Medici* (1643), *Hydriotaphia, Urn Burial* (1658), ranging over science, philosophy, mysticism.

brown earth or **brown forest soil,** widely distributed group of soils associated with deciduous forests.

Brownian motion, unceasing random movement of small particles suspended in fluid. Described by Scottish botanist Robert Brown (1827) when observing motion of pollen grains in water. Caused by bombardment of particles by continuously moving fluid molecules; theoretical explanation given by Einstein (1905).

Browning, Robert (1812-89), English poet. Known for long poem, *The Ring and the Book* (1868-9), earlier poetry 'Pippa Passes', 'My Last Duchess'. Work notable for metric innovation, dramatic monologue allowing shifting viewpoint. His wife, **Elizabeth Barrett Browning** (1806-61), was also a poet, known for *Sonnets from the Portuguese* (1850), addressed to husband. Known for their love affair, overcoming her jealous father and her own invalidism.

brown rat, *Rattus norvegicus,* large rodent of Muridae family. Of Asian origin, reached Europe, US in 18th cent. Destruction of foodstuffs, spread of disease make it major pest.

brownshirts (*Sturmabteilung* or SA), paramilitary force (storm troops) of Nazi party, founded in 1922. Wore brown uniform, distinct from black of the *Schutzstaffel* (SS) or elite corps.

Bruce, Robert, see ROBERT THE BRUCE.

Bruce, Stanley Melbourne, 1st Viscount Bruce of Melbourne (1883-1967), Australian statesman, PM (1923-9). Treasurer (1921-3) before becoming leader of National

Party, headed coalition govt. with Country Party.

Bruce, Sir William (c 1630-1710), Scottish architect. Influential in introduction of Palladian style to Scotland. Works incl. Kinross House, remodelling of Holyrood Palace, Edinburgh.

brucellosis, see UNDULANT FEVER.

Bruch, Max (1838-1920), German composer. Best known for violin concerto in G minor, still popular in concert repertory. Also wrote *Kol Nidre* for cello and orchestra.

Brücke, Die ('the bridge'), group of German expressionist painters, incl. Kirchner, Schmidt-Rottluff and Heckel, founded in Dresden (1905). Work, characterized by vivid symbolic colour, distortion, was influenced by primitive art and van Gogh, Gauguin, Munch, *etc.* Disbanded 1913.

Bruckner, Anton (1824-96), Austrian composer. Influenced by Wagner in producing grandiose works, albeit principally for orchestra in classic forms. Major compositions incl. 9 symphonies, several masses and *Te Deum*.

Brueghel or **Bruegel,** family of Flemish painters. His son, **Pieter Bruegel** (c 1525-69) was noted for his painting of landscape, peasant village scenes and religious subjects; in allegorical works, made use of fantastic images of Bosch. Works incl. series *The Months.* His son, **Pieter Brueghel** (1564-1638), known as 'Hell Brueghel' copied many of his father's works. Another son, **Jan Brueghel** (1568-1625), known as 'Velvet Brueghel', painted landscapes and still life.

Brugge (Fr. *Bruges*), town of NW Belgium, cap. of West Flanders prov. Pop. 51,000. Agric. market, lace mfg.; ship canal to Zeebrugge. Prosperous medieval wool trade, Hanseatic centre. Cloth Hall, belfry (13th cent.) with carrillon; art treasures incl. works of Michelangelo, van Eyck.

bruise, bleeding into injured skin following a blow, *etc.* Discoloration results when red blood pigment loses its oxygen and later breaks down into bile pigments.

Brumaire, second month of French Revolutionary Calendar (officially operating 1793-1805). Coup of 18 Brumaire (9-10 Nov. 1799) overthrew DIRECTORY and created consulate under Napoleon.

Brummell, George Bryan ('Beau') (1778-1840), English dandy. Close associate of the prince regent (later George IV), he became recognized arbiter of fashionable dress in Regency period. Died in squalor following quarrel with the prince and loss of his fortune through gambling.

Brunei, sultanate of N Borneo. Area *c* 5760 sq km (2200 sq mi); pop. 136,000. Cap. and main seaport, Bandar Seri Begawan (formerly Brunei), pop. 37,000. Rubber, fruit grown; rich oil deposits. Became British protect. 1888.

Brunel, Sir Marc Isambard (1769-1849), British engineer, b. France. Built old Bowery Theatre, New York, Thames tunnel, London (1825-43). His son, **Isambard Kingdom Brunel** (1806-59), an authority on rail traction, steam navigation and civil engineering, was responsible for building of much of Great Western Railway. Designed steamships *Great Western* (1838), *Great Eastern* (1858).

Brunelleschi, Filippo (1377-1446), Italian architect. Pioneer in scientific study of perspective and the creation of controlled space, based on mathematical proportion. Most famous for design of dome of Florence cathedral (1420).

Brunhild, Brynhild or **Brünn-hilde,** in Germanic myth, great female warrior. In NIBELUNGENLIED defeated by SIEGFRIED, and causes his death. In *Volsungsaga*, is chief of Valkyries, loved by Sigurd, whom she kills for infidelity, then commits suicide. Story adapted by Wagner in *Ring of the Nibelung*.

Brüning, Heinrich (1885-1970), German politician. Leader of Catholic Centre party, chancellor (1930-2) during economic crisis stemming from unemployment and inflation. Introduced harsh financial measures, disbanded Hitler's storm troops. Dismissed by Hindenburg, in exile (1934-52).

Bruno, Giordano (1548-1600), Italian philosopher. Rejected dogma on grounds that knowledge is infinite and final truth cannot be established. Formulated monadic theory of universe. Influenced Spinoza, Leibnitz. A Dominican, burned as heretic.

Bruno of Cologne, St (c 1030-1101), German monk. Founded order of CARTHUSIANS.

Brunswick (*Braunschweig*), city of NE West Germany, on R. Oker. Pop. 223,000. Food processing, machinery, publishing industs. Hanseatic League member from 13th cent. Has medieval cathedral, town hall, fountain.

brush turkey, *Alectura lathami,* large bird of E Australia. Eggs laid in mound of plant matter and hatched by heat of fermentation.

Brussels (Fr. *Bruxelles*), cap. of Belgium, on R. Senne. Pop. 1,075,000. Commercial, indust. centre (textiles, esp. lace); railway jct. Gothic cathedral, Grand' Place, town hall (15th cent.), Atomium (1958); univ. (1834). Hq. of EEC, NATO. Cap. of Brabant from 15th cent., of Belgium from independence (1830), German occupation in WWs.

Brussels sprouts, *Brassica oleracea gemmifera,* vegetable of CABBAGE family. Small edible heads are borne on stem.

Brutus, Marcus Junius (c 85-42 BC), Roman political leader. Sided with Pompey against Caesar in civil war; pardoned after battle of Pharsala. Joined Cassius in assassination of Caesar (44), but had to flee to Macedonia. Defeated by Antony and Octavian at Philippi (42); committed suicide.

Bryansk or **Briansk,** city of USSR, WC European RSFSR. Pop. 338,000. Railway jct.; machine mfg., ironworks. Founded 1146, passed to Russia in 17th cent.

bryony, any of a genus, *Bryonia,* of perennial vines of the gourd family with large fleshy roots and greenish flowers.

Bryophyta, small phylum of plant kingdom comprising mosses and liverworts. Widely distributed on moist soil and rocks. Reproduction is normally by spores.

Bubastis, *see* BAST.

bubble chamber, vessel filled with superheated transparent liquid used to study nature and motion of charged atomic particles. Passage of particle through liquid causes string of bubbles to appear, which are then photographed.

Buber, Martin (1878-1965), Austrian philosopher. Exponent of religious existentialism; influenced by Kierkegaard and HASIDISM. Works, esp. *I and Thou* (1923), explore the individual's personal dialogue with God. Worked to infuse political Zionism with ethical values. Settled in Jerusalem (1938).

Buchan, John, 1st Baron Tweedsmuir (1875-1940), British author, statesman. b. Scotland. Best known for adventure novels, esp. *The Thirty Nine Steps* (1915), *Greenmantle* (1916). Governor-general of Canada (1935-40).

Buchanan, James (1791-1868), American statesman. As Democratic president (1857-61), pursued moderate policy on slavery issue. Efforts to achieve compromise met with suspicion by both North and South, and Civil War followed end of his admin.

Bucharest (*Bucureşti*), cap. of Romania, on R. Dambrovita. Pop. 1,529,000. Cultural, commercial, indust. centre. Orthodox patriarchal see. Cathedral (17th cent.), former royal palace, univ. (1864). Cap. of Walachia from 1698; of Romania from 1861.

Buchenwald, village of SW East Germany, near Weimar. Site of Nazi concentration camp in WWII.

Büchner, Georg (1813-37), German dramatist. Inspired by French Revolution, wrote 2 stark, realistic tragedies, *Danton's Death* (1835), *Woyzeck* (pub. 1879). Latter made into opera by Berg.

Buck, Pearl S[ydenstricker] (1892-1973), American novelist. Wrote novels based on experiences as daughter of missionaries in China, eg trilogy *The House of Earth* (1935), translations from Chinese. Nobel Prize for Literature (1938).

Buckingham, George Villiers, 1st Duke of (1592-1628), English courtier. Royal favourite under James I, arranged Charles I's marriage to Henrietta Maria of France. Expeditions against France during Charles' reign met with little success. Assassinated. His son, **George Villiers, 2nd Duke of Buckingham** (1628-87), was powerful courtier under Charles II. Member of CABAL ministry.

Buckingham Palace, official London residence of British sovereigns since Queen Victoria's reign. Built (1703) for the dukes of Buckingham; bought as private residence by George III. Reconstructed (1825-36) by John Nash.

Buckinghamshire, county of SC England. Area 1882 sq km (726 sq mi); pop. 496,000; co. town Aylesbury. Chiltern Hills in S; fertile valley in N. Cereals, fruit, vegetable growing, livestock rearing. Buckingham, mun. bor. on R. Ouse. Pop. 5000. Market town, dairy produce. Stowe House public school (1923) nearby.

buckthorn, family of deciduous and evergreen trees and shrubs, Rhamnaceae, native to Europe and N Asia. Some species have thorny branches. Fruit has purgative properties and yields dye, Chinese green. Common buckthorn, *Rhamnus cathartica*, is hedge plant in America.

buckwheat, any of several plants of

genus *Fagopyrum,* grown for their black tetrahedral grains from which a dark nutritious flour can be made.

Budaeus, see BUDÉ, GUILLAUME.

Budapest, cap. of Hungary, on R. Danube. Pop. 2,027,000. Admin., commercial centre; heavy industs.; food processing, agric. market (grain, wine, cattle). Formed from union of Buda and Pest (1872). Roman *Aquincum,* 13th cent. church, univ. (1635), 19th cent. basilica. Damaged during Russian siege (1945) and in revolution (1956).

Buddha (Sanskrit,=the enlightened one), title given to Siddhartha Gautama (*c* 563–483 BC), Indian ascetic, founder of BUDDHISM. Renounced luxury for asceticism following prophetic vision and after 6 years' contemplation found perfect enlightenment under sacred bo tree in Buddh Gaya, thus becoming the Buddha. Life then devoted to teaching of path to enlightenment.

Buddh Gaya or **Bodh Gaya,** village of Bihar state, NE India, S of Gaya. Site of Buddha's enlightenment under sacred bo tree.

Buddhism, religion of followers of BUDDHA, widespread in SE Asia, China and Japan; originally related to Hinduism, it was in part reaction against its formalism. The 'four noble truths' are: life is sorrow; origin of sorrow is desire; sorrow ceases when desire ceases; desire is ended by following the 'noble eightfold path'. That path comprises: right belief, right resolve, right speech, right conduct, right occupation, right effort, right contemplation, right meditation. Final goal is Nirvana, the annihilation of all desires and passions and cessation of rebirth. *See* MAHAYANA and ZEN BUDDHISM.

Budé, Guillaume (1467–1540), French scholar, known by Latinized name Budaeus. Leading humanist and scholar of Renaissance. Persuaded Francis I of France to found Collège de France, furthered classical scholarship both by teaching and writing.

Budge, [John] Donald (1915–), American tennis player. First man to achieve the 'grand slam' of tennis by winning British, US, French and Australian singles championships (1938).

budgerigar, *Melopsittacus undulatus,* Australian parakeet, with many domestic varieties. In wild, green with yellow head. Colour variations produced by selective breeding. Lives in nomadic flocks; diet of seed, grain. Popular pet and excellent mimic, introduced to Europe in 1840s.

budget, govt. statement (usually issued annually) of revenue and expenditure of previous year and estimated revenue and expenditure of forthcoming year. In UK, presented by chancellor of the exchequer to Commons, sitting as Committee of Ways and Means. In US, executive budget recommendations supervised by Bureau of the Budget (estab. 1921) after Congressional approval.

Budweis, see CESKÉ BUDEJOVICE, Czechoslovakia.

Buenaventura, seaport of W Colombia, on Pacific. Pop. 179,000. Coffee, hides, sugar, platinum and gold exports. Founded *c* 1540, grew with building of railway to Cali (1914).

Buenos Aires, cap. of Argentina, on W Rio de la Plata estuary. Pop. 2,972,000, greater city pop. 8,353,000; incl. suburbs La Matanza, Lanús, Morón, General San Martín, Lomas de Zamóra, Quilmes, Vicente López. Railway terminus; country's chief port, indust., commercial centre. Beef, wheat, wool exports. Settled permanently 1580; became cap. 1880. Prospered with development of Pampas in 19th cent. Has San Martín's tomb, opera house, cathedral, univ. (1827).

Buffalo, city of N New York, US; on L. Erie and Niagara R. Pop. 463,000. Major Great Lakes port and transport jct. serving Middle West. Grain, iron, coal shipping; iron and steel, chemical mfg., flour milling. First settled 1803; burned by British in War of 1812. President W. McKinley assassinated here (1901).

buffalo, any of various large forms of cattle. Species incl. Cape buffalo, and Indian WATER BUFFALO. Name also popularly applied to American bison.

Buffalo Bill, see CODY, WILLIAM FREDERICK.

Buffet, Bernard (1928-), French painter. Known for his austere portrayal of figures, religious scenes and city life; work characterized by cold tonality and prominent black lines.

Bug or **Western Bug,** river of E Europe. Rises in NW Ukrainian SSR, flows c 800 km (500 mi) NW into Poland to join R. Vistula below Warsaw. Forms part of Poland-USSR frontier. **Southern Bug** flows c 850 km (530 mi) SE through Ukrainian SSR into Black Sea.

bug, any insect of suborder Heter-

optera of order Hemiptera. Sucking mouthparts; front wings half membranous, half thickened. Wingless varieties also exist. Term also popularly applied to any insect or insect-like animal.

Buganda, see UGANDA.

bugle, any plant of genus *Ajuga*. Perennial, with numerous running stems and spikes of white, pink or blue flowers.

bugle, valveless form of trumpet which produces only notes of the harmonic series; all bugle calls are confined to these notes.

building society [UK] or **savings and loan association** [US], financial organization that accepts savings from the public to be placed in share accounts on which dividends are paid and from which mortgage loans on homes are made. Orig. directly controlled building of houses. First estab. Birmingham, England (1781), first in US estab. 1831.

Bujumbura, cap. of Burundi, on L. Tanganyika. Pop. 107,000. Admin. centre; port, exports coffee, cotton, hides. Estab. as German military post (1889). Formerly called Usumbura, was cap. of Ruanda-Urundi.

Bukavu, or E Zaïre, on L. Kivu, cap. of Kivu prov. Formerly called Costermansville. Pop. 156,000. Port, commercial centre; coffee, pharmaceuticals indust.

Bukhara or **Bokhara,** town of USSR, S Uzbek SSR. Pop. 114,000. Centre of cotton producing area; once famous for carpets. Centre of Islamic learning under Arab rule in 8th cent. Cap. of emirate of Bukhara until 1920.

Bukharin, Nikolai Ivanovich

(1888-1938), Soviet political leader. Leading Bolshevik theorist after Lenin's death, advocated gradualist policies on collectivizing agric. Executed in Stalinist party purges.

Bukovina, region of NE Romania and SW USSR (Ukraine), in Carpathian foothills. Main town Chernovtsy; main rivers Siret, Prut. Ceded by Turkey to Austria (1775); Romanian from 1918, N part to USSR (1940).

Bulawayo, city of SW Rhodesia. Pop. 297,000. Indust., commercial centre, agric. market, railway engineering. Founded 1893. Cecil Rhodes tomb in nearby Mátopo Hills.

bulb, underground storage and reproductive structure of certain plants. Formed by swelling of leaf bases, constructing sheath round embryo flower. Distinct from corm which is formed by swelling of stem, as in crocus; rhizome which is an elongated underground swelling of stem, as in iris; and tuber which is a swollen underground branch, as in potato, or root as in dahlia.

Bulgakov, Mikhail Afanasyevich (1891-1940), Russian author. Known for *The White Guard* (1925) which he dramatized as *The Days of the Turbins* (1926) portraying a family hostile to the revolution, *The Master and Margarita* (pub. 1967) a fantasy set in modern Moscow.

Bulganin, Nikolai Aleksandrovich (1895-1975), Russian military and political leader. Helped plan 1941 defence of Moscow against German invasion. Armed forces minister (1947-9), premier (1953-8), succeeded by KHRUSHCHEV.

Bulgaria, republic of SE Europe, on Balkan Penin. Area 110,899 sq km

(42,818 sq mi); pop. 8,619,000; cap. Sofia. Languages: Bulgarian, Turkish. Religions: Eastern Orthodox, Islam. Balkan Mts. run E-W across C, Rhodope Mts. in SW. Lowland in N (Danube basin), SE; Black Sea in E. Continental climate; vines, tobacco, wine, attar of roses. Agric. increasingly mechanized. Coal, oil industs. developing. Invaded 7th cent. AD by Bulgars from Russia; Turkish rule (1395-1878) ended by Russia; independent monarchy (1908). Lost territ. in Balkan Wars (1912-13), WWs. Communist govt. estab. (1946).

Bulge, Battle of the, popular name for last German offensive (in the Ardennes) of WWII on Western Front (Dec. 1944-Jan. 1945).

Bull, John (1563-1628), English composer, organist. Lived in Low Countries from 1613. Compositions incl. church music and keyboard music of considerable virtuosity and individuality.

Bull, John, see JOHN BULL.

bull, papal pronouncement, more solemn than a brief or encyclical, traditionally sealed with lead. Famous bulls incl. *Exsurge Domine* (1520) against Luther, *Pastor aeternus* (1871) on papal infallibility. Also used to proclaim canonization of a saint.

bulldog, breed of dog once used in bull-baiting. Square-jawed, with powerful grip. Stands between 33-38 cm/13-15 in. at shoulder.

bullfighting, national spectacle of Spain (where it is known as *corrida de toros*), also popular in S France and Latin America. Matador, aided by banderilleros and picadors, makes passes with cape and manoeuvres bull to tire it for the kill. Earliest dated public bullfight in Spain was in 1080.

bullfinch, *Pyrrhula pyrrhula,* timid bird of finch family found in woodlands of Europe, North America, Asia. Male has pink breast, black wings.

bullfrog, *Rana catesbeiana,* largest North American frog, up to 20 cm/8 in. long. Catches prey (mice, insects) with tongue. Male emits deep croak as mating call.

bullhead, any of several marine and freshwater fish of Cottidae family, found in N hemisphere. European bullhead or miller's thumb, *Cottus gobio,* is mainly nocturnal river species. Often called sculpin in North America.

Bull Moose Party, see PROGRESSIVE PARTY.

Bull Run, stream of N Virginia, US. Scene of 2 Confederate victories during Civil War (1861, 1862).

Bülow, Hans von (1830-94), German pianist, conductor. Considered 1st virtuoso conductor; advocated Liszt, Wagner, Brahms. Directed premières of Wagner's *Tristan,* and *Die Meistersinger,* after which his wife Cosima, daughter of Liszt, left him for Wagner.

bulrush, several species of perennial sedge of genus *Scirpus,* growing in wet land or water. Slender, round or triangular stems tipped with brown spikelets of minute flowers. Species incl. *S. lacustris* of Europe, and *S. validus* of US.

Bulwer-Lytton, Edward George Earle Lytton, 1st Baron Lytton (1803-73), English author. Known for novels, eg *Pelham* (1828), *The*

Last Days of Pompeii (1834), plays incl. *Richelieu* (1839).

bumble bee, social bee of worldwide distribution, usually of genus *Bombus.* Yellow and black hairy body, rounder than honey bee. Often nests in holes in ground; in temperate regions, only queen survives winter. Also called humble bee.

Bunin, Ivan Alekseyevich (1870-1953), Russian author. Known for short story, *The Gentleman from San Francisco* (1916); novels esp. *The Village* (1910) depicting brutality of peasant life. Settled in France (1919). Awarded Nobel Prize for Literature (1933).

Bunker Hill, Battle of (June, 1775), in American Revolution, conflict in which British victory failed to break colonists' siege of Boston. Actually fought on nearby Breed's Hill (Charleston, Mass.).

Bunsen, Robert Wilhelm (1811-99), German scientist. With Kirchhoff, pioneered spectrum analysis, thus discovering elements caesium and rubidium. Worked on arsenic-containing organic compounds. Contributions to chemical apparatus incl. Bunsen burner and zinc-carbon battery.

bunting, any of various small, brightly-coloured birds of Emberizidae family. Species incl. YELLOWHAMMER, SNOW BUNTING. Name applied in US to birds of finch family.

Buñuel, Luis (1900-), Spanish film writer-director. First known for surrealist films (using Dali's sets), incl. *Un Chien andalou* (1928); later films mock bourgeois and religious hypocrisy, eg *Viridiana* (1961), *The*

Discreet Charm of the Bourgeoisie (1972).

Bunyan, John (1628-88), English author and preacher. Known for classic religious allegory *The Pilgrim's Progress* (1678) which exerted great influence on English prose. Imprisoned (1660-72) for unlicensed preaching.

Burbage, Richard (c 1567-1619), English actor-manager. First to play many major parts in plays of Shakespeare, Jonson, Fletcher, incl. Hamlet, Othello, Lear. With his brother, Cuthbert, estab. Globe Theatre at Southwark, London.

burbot, *Lota lota,* freshwater fish of cod family, widely distributed in Europe, Asia, North America. Barbels on nose and chin; broad, flat head. Sometimes called ling.

Burckhardt, Jacob Christoph (1818-97), Swiss historian. Author of classic *The Civilization of the Renaissance in Italy* (1860), expressing view that each culture is peculiar to its era.

Burckhardt, Johann Ludwig (1784-1817), Swiss explorer. Supported by the African Association (London), he visited Syria and Egypt, rediscovering Petra (1812). Joined pilgrimage to Medina and Mecca, disguised as Moslem. Works incl. *Travels in Arabia* (pub. 1829).

burdock, *Arctium lappa,* tall spreading large-leaved perennial plant native to Europe, found in North America. Purple flower heads are surrounded by hooked bristles which dry to form burrs. An essence made from plant is used in a soft drink and formerly in medicine.

bureaucracy, literally 'rule by officials', used in sociology to describe a form of administrative organization, typified, according to WEBER, by rational decision-making, impersonal social relations, routinization of tasks, and centralized authority.

Burgas, town of E Bulgaria, on Black Sea. Pop. 142,000. Port, exports wool, tobacco; chemicals indust., oil refining. Founded 18th cent.

Burgess, Anthony, pseud. of John Burgess Wilson (1917-), English novelist, critic. Best known for novels criticizing modern society, eg *A Clockwork Orange* (1962), *Inside Mr Enderby* (1966).

Burgh, Hubert de (d. 1243), English statesman. Chamberlain to King John, became chief justiciar (1215) until charged with treason (1231). Later pardoned, restored to earldom of Kent.

Burghley, William Cecil, 1st Baron (1520-98), English statesman. Chief adviser as member of privy council to Elizabeth I, instrumental in consolidation of Protestantism and in execution of Mary Queen of Scots (1587).

burglary, in law, breaking and entering any building with intent to commit a FELONY. 'Breaking' is not limited to forcible entry, but can incl. entry by use of threat, fraud, etc.

Burgos, city of N Spain, cap. of Burgos prov. Pop. 120,000. Textiles, leather goods; tourism. Founded 9th cent., cap. of Castile until 11th cent. Franco's cap. during Civil War (1936-9). Famous Gothic cathedral (1221) contains tomb of El Cid.

Burgoyne, John (1722-92), British army officer, playwright. During American Revolution led poorly trained troops in invasion from Canada, was forced to surrender at Saratoga (1777). Wrote several comedies, eg *The Heiress* (1786).

Burgundy (*Bourgogne*), region of E France, hist. cap. Dijon. Famous for wines (esp. in Chablis, Côte d'Or). Medieval duchy, at cultural and commercial height in 14th-15th cent.; ruled most of NE France, Low Countries. Passed to France (1477).

Burke, Edmund (1729-97), British statesman, writer, b. Ireland. Prominent Whig orator, pamphleteer, wrote *Thoughts on the Present Discontents* (1770), attacking George III's influence in politics, and *Conciliation with American* (1775). Instigated impeachment and trial (1787-94) of HASTINGS. Broke with party (1791) over French Revolution, which he denounced in *Reflections on the Revolution in France* (1790).

Burke, John (1787-1848), Irish genealogist. Published dictionary of peerage, baronetage which became British annual, widely known as *Burke's Peerage.*

Burke, Robert O'Hara (1820-61), Irish soldier, policeman, explorer. With W.J. Wills, crossed Australia from Melbourne to Gulf of Carpentaria as leader of Victorian expedition (1860-1). Both died of starvation on return journey.

Burke, William (1792-1829), Irish murderer. Notorious for killing, with fellow-Irishman William Hare, at least 15 people to sell bodies to Edinburgh anatomist. Burke was hanged on Hare's evidence.

Burlington, Richard Boyle, 3rd Earl of (1694-1753), English architect and patron. Leading advocate of Palladianism in English architecture, he patronized Kent, Campbell, *etc* and encouraged their writings on the style. Own work incl. his villa at Chiswick.

Burma, Union of, republic of SE Asia. Area *c* 678,000 sq km (262,000 sq mi); pop. 30,310,000; cap. Rangoon. Official language: Burmese. Religion: Buddhism. Agric. concentrated around Irrawaddy valley; major rice growing area separated from India and Bangladesh by mountain ranges. Exports incl. teak, petroleum, rubies. Annexed by Britain in 19th cent.; became prov. of India (1885-1937); independent republic (1948).

Burmese cat, breed of short-haired domesticated cats. Originally brown, now blue and cream varieties bred.

Burne-Jones, Sir Edward Coley (1833-98), English painter. Known for his paintings of medieval subjects, which have a dream-like romantic quality. Designed tapestry and stained glass for William Morris' company.

Burney, Fanny, pseud. of Mrs Frances Burney D'Arblay (1752-1840), English author. Known for *Early Diary: 1768-78* (1889) with sketches of Dr Johnson, Reynolds, *etc*, and *Diary and Letters: 1778-1840* (pub. 1842-6) giving account of Court. Also wrote domestic novels, *eg Evelina* (1778).

Burnham, [Linden] Forbes [Sampson] (1923-), Guyanese politician. PM (1964-). Succeeded Jagan as PM of British Guiana (1964) and led country to independence as Guyana (1966).

burning bush, *Euonymus attro-*

purpureas, North American tree widely cultivated as ornamental for its brightly coloured autumn foliage.

burning bush, in OT, bush out of which voice of God spoke to Moses on Mt. Horab (Exodus 3: 2), assuring Moses of deliverance of Israel from Egypt. Emblem of Presbyterian church in remembrance of its early persecution.

Burnley, co. bor. of Lancashire, NW England. Pop. 76,000. In coalmining area; cotton weaving, textiles; machinery mfg.

Burns, John (1858-1943), British labour leader. Helped lead London dock strike (1889) for higher wages. Socialist advocate, served as Independent Labour MP (1892-1918).

Burns, Robert (1759-96), Scottish poet. Gained fame with *Poems, Chiefly in the Scottish Dialect* (1786). Best known works incl. 'Tam o'Shanter', 'The Jolly Beggars', 'Holly Willie's Prayer', 'To a mouse', reflect background as tenant-farmer's son but encompass witty anti-clericalism, political radicalism.

Burr, Aaron (1756-1836), American political leader. Tied with JEFFERSON in 1800 presidential election, elected vice-president by House of Representatives. Killed HAMILTON in duel (1804) after being defeated in election for governor of New York. Involved in plan to invade Mexico, tried for treason (1807) and acquitted.

Burroughs, Edgar Rice (1875-1950), American novelist. Created Tarzan in *Tarzan of the Apes* (1914). Also wrote science fiction.

Burrourghs, William (1914-), American novelist. Works incl. *Junkie* (1953), *The Naked Lunch*

(1959), using experimental forms to convey a world at mercy of technology, drugs.

Bursa, city of NW Turkey. Pop 318,000. Agric. trade; textile, carpet mfg. Cap. of Ottoman Turks (1326-1402), until sacked by Tamerlane. Has mosques and tombs of early sultans.

Burt, Sir Cyril Lodowic (1883-1971), English psychologist. Pioneer in use of intelligence tests to predict achievement in schoolchildren. Recent doubt about validity of data he used to support his theories.

Burton, Sir Richard Francis (1821-90), English explorer, writer. Visited Mecca and Medina (1853) in Moslem disguise. Attempted, with J.H. Speke, to find source of Nile; reached L. Tanganyika (1858). Later explored W Africa, Brazil. Wrote accounts of travels, translated *Arabian Nights* (1885-8).

Burton, Robert (1577-1640), English author. Known for compendium of wide-ranging erudition, *The Anatomy of Melancholy* (1621), cataloguing every cause and form of melancholy, written under pen-name of Democritus Junior.

Burundi, republic of EC Africa. Area 27,800 sq km (10,750 sq mi); pop. 3,615,000; cap. Bujumbura. Languages: Bantu, French. Religions: native, Christian. Mainly high broken plateau; L. Tanganyika in SW. Cattle rearing, tin mining, exports coffee. Formerly a kingdom, part of German East Africa from 1899, of Belgian colony of Ruanda-Urundi after WWI. UN Trust territ. from 1946; independent 1962, became republic 1966. Has traditional rivalry between Tutsi and Hutu.

Bury St Edmunds, mun. bor. of Suffolk, E England. Pop. 26,000. Market town; sugar refining, brewing industs. Ruined abbey is burial place of St Edmund (d. 870). Has two 15th cent. churches, one now cathedral.

bus, public passenger-carrying vehicle of large seating capacity. Horse-drawn form originated in France in early 19th cent. and was introduced to London in 1829. Motorized form dates from early 20th cent.

bushbaby, small arboreal mammal of tropical Africa, genus *Galago*. Nocturnal, with large eyes, bushy tail; capable of great leaps. Mainly insectivorous; some species make good pets.

bushido (Jap., = way of the warrior), ancient code of honour, conduct of Japanese nobility. Emphasizes loyalty, courage, self-sacrifice, preferring death to dishonour. Scorned commerce, profit. Code of the SAMURAI

bushmaster, *Lachesis muta*, large poisonous snake of pit viper family, found in Central and South America. Unlike other pit vipers, lays eggs. Reaches lengths of 3.7 m/12 ft.

Bushmen, remnants of aboriginal race of S Africa, now confined to C and N Kalahari Desert. Nomadic hunters living in groups of 50-100. Noted for cave paintings. Language has same 'clicks' as that of Hottentots.

bushrangers, Australian robbers of 19th cent. Originally escaped convicts living in bush, raiding settlements. Later, gold discoveries led to incentive for organized gangs raiding highways, banks, *eg* KELLY gang.

Busoni, Ferruccio Benvenuto (1866-1924), Italian pianist and composer. Best known for his music editing, *eg* of Bach and Liszt, and teaching, notably of Kurt Weill. Made piano transcriptions, esp. of Bach; wrote opera *Doktor Faust*.

Bustamante, Sir [William] Alexander, orig. Clarke (1884-1977), Jamaican statesman. As Labour Party leader, was chief minister (1953-5). First PM (1962-7) of fully independent Jamaica.

bustard, any of Otididae family of Old World birds, related to crane. Ground-living, can run quickly. Large size makes flight difficult. The great bustard, *Otis tarda*, largest European land bird.

butane (C_4H_{10}), gaseous hydrocarbon of paraffin series. Obtained from natural gas and petroleum. Used as fuel, stored under pressure.

butcherbird, any of genus *Cracticus* of Australasian birds with strong hooked bills. Preys on insects, birds, lizards; impales bodies on thorns to store them.

Bute, John Stuart, 3rd Earl of (1713-92), British statesman, PM (1761-3). George III's chief exponent of Tory policies against Whig supremacy. Resigned after unpopular treaty ending Seven Years War (1763).

Buteshire, former county of W Scotland, now in Strathclyde region. Incl. isls. in Firth of Clyde (Bute, Arran, Great and Little Cumbrae). Agric., tourism. Isl. of Bute (area 145 sq km/ 56 sq mi) has the former.co. town, Rothesay.

Butler, James, *see* ORMONDE, JAMES BUTLER, 1ST DUKE OF.

Butler, R[ichard] A[usten], Baron Butler of Saffron Walden (1902–), British politician. Minister of education (1941-5), sponsored 1944 Education Act. In Conservative govts. (1951-64), he was chancellor of the exchequer (1951-5), foreign secretary (1963-4).

Butler, Samuel (1612-80), English poet. Known for *Hudibras*, mock-epic satirizing Puritan cant and hypocrisy.

Butler, Samuel (1835-1902), English author. Known for autobiog. novel, *The Way of all Flesh* (1903), condemning his Victorian upbringing; *Erewhon* (1872) satirizing received opinions.

butter-and-eggs, *see* TOADFLAX.

buttercup, herbs of Ranunculaceae family with alternate leaves and glossy yellow flowers. Native to cooler regions of N hemisphere. Pernicious weed, species incl. tall perennial meadow or bitter buttercup, *Ranunculus acris*; creeping buttercup, *R. repens*, and bulbous buttercup, *R. bulbosus*.

butterfly, insect of group comprising, with moths, order Lepidoptera. Scales on body, wings (2 pairs, often brightly coloured). Uses proboscis to suck nectar. Four stage life cycle: egg, larva, pupa, adult. Larva is caterpillar, usually herbivorous. Mainly diurnal, unlike moth.

butternut, oily, edible fruit of white walnut tree, *Juglans cinerea*, of E North America. Kernel is used in candy, ice cream, and is pickled.

buttress, projecting structure of brick or masonry, built against a wall to give additional strength. Flying buttresses are arches or parts of arches, which support distant walls and are themselves supported by buttresses.

Buxtehude, Dietrich (1637-1707), Danish composer, organist. Organist at Lübeck from 1668. Organ compositions influenced Bach, who walked over 320 km (200 mi) to hear Buxtehude play.

buzzard, any of numerous heavily-built hawks, esp. genus *Buteo*, with short broad wings, soaring flight. Species incl. European buzzard, *Buteo buteo*. In US, name applied to various hawks and vultures.

Byblos, chief city of Phoenicia in 2nd millennium BC. Trade centre with Egypt as early as 2800 BC. Gave name to Greek word for book *biblos*, on account of papyrus fields. At site of modern Jebail.

Bydgoszcz (Ger. *Bromberg*), city of NC Poland, on R. Brda and Bydgoszcz canal, cap. of Bydgoszcz prov. Pop. 283,000. River port, railway jct.; textile mfg., machinery. Founded 14th cent.; under Prussian rule 1772-1919.

Byelorussian or **Belorussian Soviet Socialist Republic,** constituent republic of W USSR. Area *c* 208,000 sq km (80,000 sq mi); pop. 9,003,000; cap. Minsk. Mainly low-lying, with Pripet marshes in S; large areas forested. Peat major source of power. Region disputed by Poland, Russia until it passed to Russia (1795); joined USSR 1922. Area greatly increased by acquisitions from Poland in 1945. Has seat in UN. Also called White Russia.

Byng, John (1704-57), British admiral. Failure to relieve Minorca

(1756) from French siege resulted in his court martial and execution.

Byng, Julian Hedworth George, 1st Viscount Byng of Vimy (1862-1935), British general. Commanded capture of Vimy Ridge (1917) during WWI. Governor-general of Canada (1921-6), refused to grant Mackenzie King's request to dissolve Parliament, precipitating constitutional crisis.

Byrd, Richard Evelyn (1888-1957), American explorer, aviator. Made 1st flight to North Pole (1926), to South Pole (1929). Led 5 US expeditions to Antarctica 1928-56. Writings incl. *Skyward* (1928), *Alone* (1938).

Byrd, William (*c* 1543-1623), English composer. Composed both Anglican and RC music, incl. motets and 3 Masses. Also wrote string and keyboard music, madrigals. A master of polyphony, regarded as one of foremost early English composers.

Byron, Lord George Gordon Noel, 6th Baron Byron of Rochdale (1788-1824), English poet. Best known for *Childe Harold's Pilgrimage* (1812-18), 'Vision of Judgment' (1822), *Don Juan* (1819-24). Regarded as embodiment of Romanticism, left England (1816) for Italy. Died at Missolonghi while aiding Greek fight for independence.

Bytom (Ger. *Beuthen*), city of S Poland. Pop. 187,000. Lead and zinc mining from 12th cent., metal works. Under Prussian rule 1742-1945.

Byzantine art, style of art blending Oriental and Hellenistic traditions, fl in (Christian) Byzantine Empire from 5th cent. In architecture, substituted circular church building and pendentive cupola for straight lines of Roman basilica and introduced 3 aisles, apse, altar, bell tower. Mosaics and painting marked by use of rich colours (esp. gold), stylised figures, geometrical designs. Much Christian symbolism originated in forms developed during this period. Cimabue and Giotto were first painters to break with Byzantine formalism, turning to more naturalistic style. Main centres and remains are at Constantinople (modern Istanbul), Ravenna, and in E, Trebizond and Mistra.

Byzantine Empire, former empire of SE Europe and Asia Minor. Named after Byzantium, rebuilt as cap. and renamed Constantinople (AD 330) after Constantine I. Territ. incl. (at various times) Asia Minor, Balkan Penin. incl. Macedonia, Thrace, Greece, Illyria. Main language Greek; main religion Orthodox Christianity. State estab. as direct successor to Roman Empire; suffered barbarian invasions 4th-6th cents. Fl as centre of art, architecture, education, law, esp. under JUSTINIAN I. Involved in political schism with West (800), religious schism (1054); suffered Turkish, Norman attacks in 11th cent. Fourth Crusade diverted to sack Constantinople (1204). Empire partially recovered under Palaeologus family; finally fell (1453) to Turks.

Byzantium, ancient city on shores of Bosporus, on one of 7 hills of modern ISTANBUL.

C

cabal, term for secret group of policy-makers, originating from Charles II of England's advisers. Name from initials of members – Clifford, Arlington, Buckingham, Ashley and Lauderdale.

cabala, cabbala or **kabbala,** occult religious philosophy developed by certain Jewish rabbis in Middle Ages. Adherents believed that every letter and number in Scripture was part of a significant mystical system, accessible only to the initiate. Became basis of letter and number formulae of medieval magic. Chief works incl. *Zohar* and *Sefer Yezira.*

cabbage, *Brassica oleracea capitata,* leafy vegetable of mustard family from which cauliflower, broccoli, kohlrabi, Brussels sprouts and KALE are derived. Native to E Europe, it has been cultivated for more than 4000 years. Varieties are green, white or red, with various leaf forms.

cabbage white butterfly, *Pieris brassicae,* insect whose larvae feed on cabbage, other plants. Commonest British butterfly.

cabbala, see CABALA.

Cabinda, exclave of Angola, W Africa. Area 7250 sq km (2800 sq mi); pop. 51,000; main town Cabinda. Exports coffee, hardwoods, oil. Separated from Angola (1886) when mouth of R. Congo ceded to Belgian Congo (now Zaïre).

cabinet, in govt., group of advisers responsible to head of state, who themselves usually head executive depts. of govt. Evolved out of English PRIVY COUNCIL to become a body of ministers selected by prime minister from major party in House of Commons. Cabinet is responsible for executing govt. policy, and is answerable to Parliament. Also, it coordinates activities of state's depts. In UK, depts. represented incl. Foreign Office, Home Office, Treasury. Most Commonwealth countries have imitated system. In US, cabinet comprises heads of the 12 executive depts. of govt. and ambassador to UN. Appointed by and responsible to president alone. Members of US cabinet not drawn from either house of Congress.

Cabot, John, English form of Giovanni Caboto (c 1450–98), Italian navigator, explorer. Led English expedition (1497) in search of W sea route to Orient. Landed in E Canada, laying basis for English claims to North America. His son, **Sebastian Cabot** (c 1485–1557), explored Rio de la Plata region (1526–30) for Spain; later entered service of Henry VIII. Founded 'Merchant Adventurers' which estab. trade with Russia.

cacao, see COCOA.

cachalot, see SPERM WHALE.

cactus, plant of family Cactaceae comprising several hundred species, mainly native to tropical regions of North and South America. Most species adapt to drought by storing water in fleshy stem. Largest species is the *Opuntia*, distinguished by its jointed pads, sharp spines. Other genera incl. night-blooming cactus, *Cereus*; Christmas cactus, *Zygocactus*; orchid cactus, *Epiphyllum*.

Cadbury, George (1839-1922), English chocolate manufacturer, social reformer. Assumed control of father's Birmingham factory, and, with his brother Richard, greatly expanded its business. Moved factory to Bournville (1879), where he set up model workers' village.

Cadbury Hill, hill-top site in SE Somerset, England, of great archaeological interest. Traces of Neolithic, Bronze Age, Iron Age, post-Roman and late Saxon settlements. Thought by some to be Camelot of ARTHURIAN LEGEND.

caddis fly, any insect of Trichoptera order with hairy wings and body, very reduced mouth-parts. Nocturnal, resembles moth. Larvae aquatic, living in tubular cases of twigs, sand, *etc.*

Cade, Jack (d. 1450), English rebel. Leader of Kentish uprising (1450) against Henry VI. Rebels defeated royal force and occupied London, but were pardoned and dispersed. Cade was hunted down and killed.

cadenza, an interlude in a piece of music, usually a concerto, in which a soloist plays unaccompanied to demonstrate his virtuosity. Cadenzas were once improvised but now most performers play standard written cadenzas.

Cadiz, city of SW Spain, on Bay of Cadiz, cap. of Cadiz prov. Pop. 136,000. Port, exports wine, fruit; shipyards, naval base. Founded *c* 1100 BC by Phoenicians; held 8th-13th cent. by Moors; *fl* in colonial era (16th-18th cent.), centre of New World trade. Has 2 cathedrals (13th, 18th cent.).

cadmium (Cd), soft silvery-white metallic element; at. no. 48, at. wt. 112.4. Occurs in zinc ores and as greenockite (yellow sulphide); obtained during production of zinc. Used in alloys, accumulators and as moderator in nuclear reactors; compounds used as pigments in paint.

Caedmon (*fl* 7th cent. AD), English poet. First English Christian poet to be known by name, his story is told by BEDE, who gives Latin translation of only extant poem, on the Creation.

Caen, city of Normandy, N France, on R. Orne. Cap. of Calvados dept. Pop. 110,000. Port; agric. market, textiles (esp. lace) mfg. Important medieval centre; has three 11th cent. churches. Much destruction, incl. univ. (1432), during WWII.

Caernarvonshire, former county of NW Wales, now in Gwynedd. Mountainous except for Lleyn Penin. in SW; incl. SNOWDON. Sheep farming, slate quarries; tourism. Caernarfon, mun. bor. and co. town of Gwynedd, on Menai Strait. Pop. 9000. Port, tourist resort. Castle (13th cent.) was site of investiture of Prince of Wales (1969).

Caerphilly, urban dist. of S Glamorgan, S Wales. Pop. 41,000. Coalmining; cheese mfg. Has largest Welsh castle (13th cent.).

Caesalpinus, Andreas, orig. Cesalpino (1519-1603), Italian botanist, physician. Anticipated Linnaean system by devising classification of plants based on comparative study of fruit and flowers. Described a theory of blood circulation.

Caesar, [Gaius] Julius (c 102–44 BC), Roman soldier, statesman. Governor of Further Spain (61), estab. military reputation. Formed 1st Triumvirate with Crassus and Pompey on return to Rome (60). Appointed ruler of Gaul, greatly enlarged the empire by subjugating the Gauls (58-51). Struggle for power with Pompey and the senate culminated in civil war (49) when Caesar's armies crossed the Rubicon into Italy. Routed Pompey at Pharsala (48) and pursued him into Egypt; there he met Cleopatra, by whom he had a son. Created dictator for 10 years (46), began to restore order to empire. Appointed dictator for life (44), he was assassinated by group of former supporters under Brutus, Cassius. Wrote *Gallic Wars*, *Civil War*.

Caesarean section, surgical operation for delivery of baby by cutting through mother's abdominal wall and front of uterus. In legend, Julius Caesar was said to have been born this way.

caesium or **cesium** (Cs), soft metallic element, at. no. 55, at. wt. 132.91. Highly reactive; ignites in air and combines vigorously with water to form powerful alkali. Used in photoelectric cells. Discovered (1860) by Bunsen and Kirchhoff.

Caetano, Marcello (1906–), Portuguese political leader. Succeeded Salazar as premier (1968). Exiled 1974 following military coup under Spinola.

caffeine, alkaloid drug present in coffee, tea, *etc*; stimulates heart and increases alertness when subject is tired.

Cage, John (1912–), American composer, writer, mycologist. Known for experimental, controversial works, esp. those using random elements, eg *Music of Changes*, electronic and silent music. Created 1st 'happening' (Black Mountain Coll. in 1952).

Cagliari, town of S Sardinia, Italy, on Gulf of Cagliari. Cap. of Cagliari prov. Pop. 232,000. Port, exports salt, metal ores, fish; univ. (1626). Carthaginian city, taken (238 BC) by Romans. Held by Pisa 11th-14th cent. Roman remains incl. amphitheatre; 2 Pisan towers.

Cagney, James (1899–), American film actor. Known for mannered playing in gangster roles, esp. in *The Public Enemy* (1931), *The Roaring Twenties* (1939).

Caicos Islands, see TURKS AND CAICOS.

caiman, reptile of alligator family of Central and South America. Species incl. black caiman, *Melanosuchus niger*; can reach length of 4.6m/15ft.

Cain, in OT, elder son of Adam and Eve. Killed his brother ABEL in jealousy when Abel's offerings were accepted by God. Condemned to wander the earth.

Cainozoic era, see CENOZOIC.

Cairngorms, mountain range of NE Scotland, in GRAMPIANS. Highest point Ben Macdhui (1309 m/ 4296 ft). Has nature reserve; tourist industs., incl. climbing, winter sports (esp. at Aviemore).

cairn terrier, small shaggy dog of Scottish origin. Bred to chase vermin from burrows. Stands 25 cm/10 in. high at shoulder.

Cairo (*El Qâhira*), cap. of Egypt, at head of Nile delta. Pop. 4,961,000, largest city in Africa. Admin., commercial, indust. centre; cement, textile mfg., brewing. Site of Roman *Babylon;* Old Cairo (*El Fustât*) founded 7th cent., New Cairo founded 969. Ruled by Ottoman Turks 1517-1798. Hist. Islamic religious, educational centre, has c 200 mosques, El Azhar Univ. (972), Saladin's citadel (12th cent.), many museums, eg Museum of Antiquities. Pyramids of Giza nearby.

Caithness, former county of N Scotland, now in Highland region. Has infertile moorland and hills. Sheep farming, crofting, fishing. Co. town was Wick.

Calabria, region of SW Italy, penin. between Tyrrhenian, Ionian seas. Main town Reggio, cap. Catanzaro. Underdeveloped region, mainly mountainous, partly forested. Vines, fruits, olives; h.e.p. in La Sila mountains. Ancient *Bruttium;* part of medieval Norman kingdom of Sicily, of kingdom of Naples from 1822.

Calais, town of Nord, N France, on English Channel. Pop. 75,000. Port, fishing, ferry service to Dover (England). Under English rule (1347-1558) following long siege by Edward III. Badly damaged in WWII.

calcite (CaCO₃), mineral form of calcium carbonate. Consists of hexagonal crystals; white, often slightly coloured by impurities. Forms incl. chalk, limestone, marble. Used in building, cement and fertilizer mfg.

calcium (Ca), soft white metallic element; at. no. 20, at. wt. 40.08. Occurs as carbonate (limestone, marble, chalk) and sulphate (gypsum). Obtained by electrolysis of fused calcium chloride. Essential constituent of living organisms, found in bones and teeth.

calculator, electronic, numerical calculating device employing a microprocessor incorporated into a single chip of semiconducting material. Series of keys are used to enter numbers or commands into the calculator; results of calculations usually appear on electronic display panel. More advanced calculators possess keys for special mathematical functions, have memories and can be programmed.

calculus, branch of mathematical analysis dealing with continuously varying functions and their rates of change. Concerned with such problems as drawing tangents, calculating velocity, determining area and volume, *etc.* Divided into DIFFERENTIAL and INTEGRAL CALCULUS.

Calcutta, cap. of West Bengal, E India. Pop. 7,005,000. Major port, exports raw materials; indust. centre, jute milling, textiles. Founded c 1690 by East India Co.; scene of 'Black Hole' massacre of British garrison (1756). Cap. of India 1833-1912. Univ. (1857).

Calder, Alexander (1898-1976), American sculptor. Invented the mobile, form of kinetic sculpture, consisting of cut-out shapes connected by wire. His static sculpture uses simple shapes of flat metal welded together.

Calderón [de la Barca], Pedro (1600-81), Spanish playwright. Known for classic of Spanish theatre, *Life is a Dream* (c 1636).

Also wrote many classical comedies, religious plays.

Caldwell, Erskine [Preston] (1903-　), American author. Novels, eg *Tobacco Road* (1932), *God's Little Acre* (1933), deal with poverty in South, as dramatic but accurate social documentaries.

Caledonia, Roman name (from 1st cent. AD) for Britain N of Antonine Wall. Now used poetically for whole of Scotland.

Caledonian Canal, waterway of N Scotland. Length 97 km (60 mi), connects Loch Linnhe with Moray Firth via lochs Lochy, Oich and Ness. Completed 1847, now of little importance.

calendar, systematic division of year into months and days. Ancient Chinese and Egyptian calendars based on phases of moon with adjustments to fit solar year. Julius Caesar introduced Julian calendar (45 BC), dividing year into 365 days and inserting additional day every 4th year. Inaccurate by 10 days in 1582 when Pope Gregory XIII ordered readjustment, not adopted by Britain until 1752.

Calgary, city of S Alberta, Canada; on Bow R., in foothills of Rockies. Pop. 403,000. Railway jct.; oil refining, meat packing, flour milling. Founded 1883. Has annual Calgary Stampede.

Cali, city of SW Colombia, in W Andean valley. Pop. 951,000. Indust., agric. centre; sugar refining, textiles, footwear, soap mfg. Founded 1536; grew after railway to Buenaventura built (1914).

calico, form of plain weave cotton cloth, originating in Calicut, India. Imported into England in 17th cent.,

it was produced there in large quantities in 18th cent.

Calicut, *see* KOZHIKODE.

California, state of W US. Area 411,000 sq km (158,690 sq mi); pop. 19,953,000; cap. Sacramento; chief cities Los Angeles, San Francisco, San Diego. Most populous state in US. Bounded by Pacific in W, Sierra Nevada in E, Coast Range shelters fertile Central Valley. Varied climate. Irrigation widely used for agric.; fruit, cotton, vegetables, cattle and dairy produce. Seasonal labour, mostly Mexican, employed for picking and packing. Fisheries, defence industs; fuel minerals esp. oil. Spanish settled in 18th cent.; republic estab. after Mexican War (1846); ceded to US (1848); gold rush (1849) resulted in great pop. increase. Admitted to Union as 31st state (1850).

California, Gulf of, narrow arm of Pacific, separating Lower California from W Mexico. Fishing, pearl diving.

California, University of, univ. under state support since estab. (1868). On 9 campuses, incl. Berkeley, Los Angeles, San Diego, Santa Barbara, Santa Cruz.

California Institute of Technology, Pasadena, California, US. Privately supported college, founded (1891) as the Throop Polytechnic Institute. Incl. Jet Propulsion Laboratory and Guggenheim Aeronautical Laboratory.

californium (Cf), transuranic element; at. no. 98, mass no. of most stable isotope 251. First prepared (1950) at Univ. of California by bombarding curium with alpha particles.

Caligula, real name Gaius Caesar Germanicus (AD 12-41), Roman emperor (37-41). Ruled tyrannically after an illness which is believed to have left him insane. Said to have made his horse a consul. Assassinated by one of his guards.

caliph, name given to successors of Mohammed who assumed leadership of Islam. First caliph was ABU BAKR. Dispute over right of descendants of ALI to succeed to caliphate led to split between SHIITES and SUNNITES. Muawyaa estab. Omayyad dynasty in Damascus; it was destroyed by Shiites (750), who set up Abbasid dynasty in Baghdad. Abbasid rule lasted until capture of Baghdad (1258) by Mongols.

Calixtus II, orig. Guy de Vienne (d. 1124); Burgundian churchman, pope (1119-24). Expelled antipope Gregory VIII. Settled investiture dispute with Emperor Henry V by Concordat of Worms (1122), called 1st Lateran Council.

Calixtus III, orig. Alonso de Borja (1378-1458), Spanish churchman, pope (1455-8). Estab. Borgia family in Italy through nepotism. Sponsored partly successful crusade against Turks.

Callaghan, [Leonard] James (1912-), British statesman, PM (1976-79). Posts in Labour govt. incl. chancellor of the exchequer (1964-7), foreign secretary (1974-6). Succeeded Wilson as PM in Labour leadership election. Term marked by efforts to combat high inflation.

Callao, major seaport of W Peru. Pop. 335,000. Pacific depot for Lima, handling most of Peru's imports. Fish processing, agric. related

industs. Founded 1537; occupied by Chile (1881-3). Destroyed by earthquake (1746).

Callas, Maria, née Calogeropoulou (1923-1977), American soprano. Born in New York of Greek parents, trained in Athens. Became internationally renowned opera singer in 1950s. Famous roles in *Madame Butterfly, Norma, Aida.*

Callicrates (5th cent. BC), Greek architect. With Ictinus, built the Parthenon at Athens (447-432 BC). Also designed temple of Athena Nike on the Acropolis.

calligraphy, art of fine writing. Practised by Chinese from 5th cent. BC, it was regarded as equal to painting; also important in Japanese art from 7th cent. AD. In Islamic art, which forbids portrayal of living forms, decoration of Koran represents highly refined development of calligraphy.

Callimachus (c 305-c 240 BC), Greek poet and scholar. Prolific writer, best known for *Aetia,* elegiac verse account of religious practices. Profound influence on later writers.

Calliope, in Greek and Roman myth, Muse of epic poetry. Represented as carrying a writing tablet and stylus.

calorie, unit of heat energy; defined as quantity of heat required to raise temperature of 1 gram of water by 1° C. Equals 4.1855 joules.

Calvary (Lat., *calvaria* = skull; translation of Aramaic *golgotha*), scene of Jesus' crucifixion outside walls of Jerusalem. Traditionally believed to be near site of the Holy Sepulchre.

Calvin, John (1509-64), French theologian, Reformation leader. Converted to Protestantism (c 1533); systematized Protestant theology in

Institutes of the Christian Religion (1536), rejecting papal authority. Estab. theocratic republic in Geneva as centre of CALVINISM. Taught doctrine of predestination, salvation for the elect, justification by faith alone and subservience of state to church. Encouraged thrift, industry and sobriety.

Calvinism, Protestant doctrine formulated by CALVIN. Distinguished from Lutheranism by doctrine of PREDESTINATION. Adopted by Huguenots in France, spread to Scotland through teachings of John Knox and influenced Puritans in England and New England. Associated with PRESBYTERIANISM.

Calypso, in Greek myth, nymph, daughter of Atlas. In Homer's *Odyssey* she entertained ODYSSEUS for 7 years when he was shipwrecked on Ogygia.

calypso, humorous song, often extemporized on topical or amatory theme, sung to traditional Caribbean melody and accompaniment.

Camargue, La, region of Rhône delta, S. France. Mainly marsh, lagoons in S. Fishing, marine salt indust.; horse and bull rearing, some agric. (incl. rice) on reclaimed land. Frequented by many species of wild bird.

Cambacérès, Jean Jacques Régis de (1753-1824), French revolutionary, statesman, legislator. Second consul (1799-1804); helped prepare Code Napoléon (1800-4), developing and codifying civil law. Created duke of Parma (1808).

Camberwell, see SOUTHWARK, England.

Cambodia, state of SE Asia. Area *c* 181,300 sq km (70,000 sq mi); pop. 8,354,000; cap. Phnom Penh. Language: Khmer. Religion: Hinayana Buddhism. Large plain drained by Mekong. Mainly agric. (rice); Tonlé Sap is base for fisheries. Formerly French protect. of Cambodia (1863-1955), part of INDO-CHINA. Independent constitutional monarchy (1955), Khmer republic estab. 1970. Involved in Vietnam War with US invasion (1970). Five year civil war ended in 1975 by victory of Communist Khmer Rouge forces. Now known as Kampuchea. Khmer Rouge overthrown by Vietnamese-backed forces (1979).

Cambrai, town of Nord, NE France, on R. Escaut (Scheldt). Pop. 40,000. Hist. textile centre, gave name to cambric. Scene of formation of League of Cambrai (1508) against Venice. Under Spanish rule 1595-1677.

Cambrian Mountains, mountain system of Wales. Runs N-S, incl. SNOWDON, Cader Idris, Plynlimmon.

Cambrian period, first geological period of Palaeozoic era; began *c* 570 million years ago, lasted *c* 70 million years. Extensive seas. Typified by trilobites, graptolites, brachiopods; some algae, lichens. Also *see* GEOLOGICAL TABLE.

Cambridge, city of E Massachusetts, US; near Boston on Charles R. Pop. 100,000. Has Harvard and Radcliffe Univs., Massachusetts Institute of Technology. Industs. incl. scientific instruments, printing and publishing. First settled 1630.

Cambridgeshire, county of E England. Area 3409 sq km (1316 sq mi); pop. 533,000. Incl. Isle of Ely. Fertile fens, artificial drainage;

cereals, sugar beet, fruit, vegetable growing. Co. town **Cambridge**, city on R. Cam. Pop. 99,000. Univ. has 23 residential colls. (oldest Peterhouse, 1284). Medieval trading centre. Electronics indust.

Cambridge University, Cambridge,, UK, one of two oldest English univs. Estab. (c 1209) by dissident Oxford scholars. Since 1st college, Peterhouse, founded (1284), the univ. has grown to comprise 23 residential colleges for undergraduates, 3 of which are women's. Women were only allowed full membership in 1948. Has led in modern literature, philosophy, science, with Cavendish Laboratory for experimental physics. Also noted are King's College Chapel, Fitzwilliam Museum.

Camden, bor. of NW Greater London, England. Pop. 201,000. Created 1965 from Hampstead, Holborn, St Pancras met. bors.

camel, mammal of Camelidae family, related to llama, order Artiodactyla. Arabian camel or dromedary, *Camelus dromedarius,* has 1 hump; Bactrian camel, *Camelus bactrianus,* of C Asian deserts, has 2 humps, shaggy coat. Fat stored in humps helps desert survival. Strong pack animal, but some dromedaries used only for riding.

camellia, genus of flowering evergreen shrubs and small trees of Theaceae family, native to Asia. Cultivated in warm climates and greenhouses. Most important economically is tea plant, *Camellia chinensis,* from India and China. Garden varieties belong to *C. japonica* and *C. reticulata,* and incl. greenhouse and outdoor species.

Camelot, see ARTHURIAN LEGEND.

Camembert, village of Normandy, N France. Gave name to a cheese, first made here in 18th cent.

cameo, carving in relief on hard or precious stones or on shells. Agate and sardonyx are used so that raised design can be cut in a lighter layer than background. Cameos, esp. portrait heads, were highly developed in ancient Greek and Roman eras.

camera, light-proof container with lens that focuses optical image to be recorded on light-sensitive FILM. Developments incl. adjustable focus lens to allow objects at various distances to be recorded sharply, variable aperture settings (*f* stop) to control amount of light entering camera, high-speed shutters to photograph moving objects and linked light meters to control these variables automatically. The motion picture camera takes a series of photographs (usually 24 per sec) which when projected at same rate gives impression of movement.

Cameron, Richard (d. 1680), Scottish leader of extreme sect of COVENANTERS. Strongly opposed efforts to re-estab. Episcopal church in Scotland after Restoration. Denied the authority of Charles II. Killed by royalist forces. Followers (Cameronians) became Reformed Presbyterian Church (1743).

Cameroon (Fr. *Cameroun*), republic of WC Africa, on Bight of Biafra. Area 474,000 sq km (183,000 sq mi); pop. 6,531,000; cap. Yaoundè. Languages: French, English. Religions: Christianity, Islam. Savannah in N; tropical forest in W; elsewhere mainly plateau. Produces cocoa, coffee, bananas, groundnuts; bauxite mining. Formerly German (Kamerun); taken by Allies in WWI. Divided (1919) into British, French Cameroons; both UN Trust Territs. from 1946. French Cameroons independent from 1960; S part of British Cameroons joined to form federal republic (1961); N part joined Nigeria.

Cameroon, Mount, volcano of W Cameroon. Highest peak of W Africa, reaches 4067 m/ 13,350 ft. Rainfall on W slopes exceeds 1016 cm/400 in. per year.

Camões or **Camoens, Luis Vaz de** (c 1524-80), Portuguese poet. Best known for epic *The Lusiads* (1572) celebrating Portuguese history and exploits of Vasco da Gama. Also wrote sonnets and lyrics.

camomile or **chamomile,** any plant of genera *Anthemis* or *Matricaria* of aster family. Common European species, *A. nobilis,* is used for the astringent and bitter camomile tea.

camouflage, in warfare, disguise of troops, ships, guns, aircraft etc by making them blend with their surroundings. Greatly developed in WWI, subsequently declined in importance with development of radar, although retains usefulness in guerrilla campaigns.

Campania, region of S Italy, main town Naples. Largely fertile, produces hemp, fruit, tobacco; mountainous interior. Many coastal resorts. Roman region much smaller, incl. sites of Pompeii, Herculaneum.

campanile, in architecture, Italian bell-tower usually built separately from main building, eg church or town hall. Examples incl. that of Florence, built by Giotto (1334), and the leaning tower of Pisa.

campanula, genus of plants of bellflower family with bell-shaped flowers. Found in temperate parts of N hemisphere and widely cultivated. Harebell, *Campanula rotundifolia,* and Canterbury bell, *C. medium,* are well-known species.

Campbell, Scottish noble family, *see* ARGYLL, ARCHIBALD CAMPBELL, 8TH EARL OF.

Campbell, John, 1st Earl of Breadalbane (c 1635-1717), Scottish chieftain. Led massacre (1692) of Macdonald clan at Glencoe for delay in swearing allegiance to William III.

Campbell, Sir Malcolm (1885-1949), British motor racing enthusiast. Broke world speed record on land (1935) in *Bluebird* and on water (1939) in boat of same name. His son, Donald Malcolm Campbell (1921-67), broke world water record in turbo-jet hydroplane and land record (both 1964). Died in attempt on water record.

Campbell, Mrs Patrick, née Beatrice Stella Tanner (1865-1940), English actress, friend of Wilde, Shaw. Known for role of Eliza Doolittle in Shaw's *Pygmalion.*

Campbell, Roy Dunnachie (1901-57), South African poet. Known for poetry celebrating danger, vitality eg *Flaming Terrapin* (1924), and *Flowering Rifle* (1939), satire celebrating Franco in whose army he fought.

Campbell, Thomas (1777-1844), Scottish poet. Remembered for war songs, eg 'Ye Mariners of England'. Also wrote discursive verse essay

The Pleasures of Hope (1799), criticism.

Campbell-Bannerman, Sir Henry (1836-1908), British statesman, PM (1905-8). Liberal leader, his admin. was marked by self-govt. for South African colonies and growth of conflict between Commons and Lords.

Camperdown (*Kamperduin*), village of North Holland prov., NW Netherlands. Naval battle fought offshore (1797) in which British defeated Dutch.

camphor, volatile, crystalline substance with strong, characteristic odour, derived from wood of camphor laurel, *Cinnamomum camphora*. Used to protect fabrics from moths, in manufacturing cellulose plastics, and in medicine as an irritant and stimulant.

Campion, Edmund (c 1540-81), English Jesuit martyr. Favourite of Elizabeth 1 before his conversion to Catholicism. Became Jesuit (1573) after studying at Douai. Returned to England as missionary (1580), preached with effect until captured; executed for treason.

Campion, Thomas (1567-1620), English poet, musician. Best known for songs for the lute.

campion, various flowering plants of genera *Lychnis* and *Silene* of the pink family. Species incl. red campion, *L. dioica*, pink-flowered hairy perennial of Britain, moss campion, *S. acaulis*, perennial alpine plentiful in Scotland, and sea campion, *S. maritima*.

Campo Formio, Treaty of (Oct. 1797), French-Austrian settlement of Napoleon's campaign in Italy. Austria ceded Austrian Netherlands to France and secretly promised left bank of Rhine; Venetian Republic dissolved and most of it ceded to Austria, the rest to France and Cisalpine Republic (N Italy).

Campsie Fells, range of Scottish hills, runs E-W just N of Glasgow, in Strathclyde and Central Regions. Rise to over 500m (1600 ft).

Camus, Albert (1913-60), French writer, b. Algeria. In essay *Le Mythe de Sisyphe* (1942), outlined theory of ABSURD which permeates novels, *eg L'Etranger* (1942), *La Peste* (1947). Member of SARTRE circle but parted from him on thinking. Awarded Nobel Prize for Literature (1957).

Canaan, OT name for region W of R. Jordan. The 'promised land' occupied by Israelites after Exodus from Egypt. Subsequently known as Palestine.

Canada, federal country of N North America, independent member of British Commonwealth. Area 9,976,128 sq km (3,851,787 sq mi); pop. 23,143,000; cap. Ottawa; major cities Montréal, Toronto. Languages: English, French. Religions: Protestant, RC. Stretches from Pacific to Atlantic, from Arctic to the Great Lakes; extreme climate. Comprises 10 provs. as well as Yukon and Northwest Territs. Rocky Mts. divide coastal British Columbia (timber, wood pulp, h.e.p.) and agric. Prairies (wheat); Ontario, Québec (major concentrations of pop. and indust.); Maritimes, Newfoundland (fisheries); C Laurentian Plateau (copper, nickel, oil). Explored 1534 by Cartier, settled by French in 17th cent.; competing claims to sovereignty resolved by British victory at Québec (1759).

Independence (1867) uniting Upper (Ontario) and Lower (Québec) Canada with Nova Scotia, New Brunswick; subsequently enlarged by W expansion.

Canadian Pacific Railway (CPR), privately owned and operated railway system. First Canadian transcontinental railway, completed in 1885. Built as one of conditions on which British Columbia agreed to enter confederation in 1871.

canal, artificial waterway used for transportation, drainage and irrigation. GRAND CANAL of China, completed in 13th cent., is longest in world. Transportation canals may be provided with locks so that level of water can be changed to raise or lower boats. St Lawrence Seaway network of canals connects Great Lakes with Atlantic.

Canaletto, properly Antonio Canale (1697-1768), Italian painter. Specialized in topographically accurate views of Venice; visited England (1746-55) where he produced several fine landscapes and views of London.

canary, *Serinus canarius,* small singing finch of Canary Islands, Azores. Grey or green in wild; yellow varieties bred in captivity. Popular pet.

Canary Islands, isl. group of Atlantic Ocean, off NW Africa, comprising 2 provs. of Spain. Isls. incl. Grand Canary, Lanzarote, Tenerife. Area 7270 sq km (2807 sq mi); main towns Las Palmas, Santa Cruz de Tenerife. Volcanic, rise to c 3700 m (12,100 ft). Banana, tobacco growing, fishing, tourism. Possibly the ancient 'Fortunate Islands'; Spanish from 1476.

canasta, card game, a variation of rummy, for two to six players, using a double deck of cards. Originated in Montevideo (1949).

Canaveral, Cape, E Florida, US. Missile-testing centre, launch point of satellites, spacecraft. Known as Cape Kennedy 1963-73.

Canberra, cap. of Australia, in Australian Capital Territory, on Molonglo R. Pop. 159,000. Admin. centre; national library, univ. (1929). Founded 1913, replaced Melbourne as cap. 1927.

Cancer, see ZODIAC.

cancer, group of diseases resulting from disorder of cell growth. Cancer cells grow without control or need, locally at first, but later they may spread to other parts of body via lymph vessels or veins. Causes incl. chemical agents, *eg* dyes and hydrocarbons, cigarette smoke, radiation, viruses, hereditary factors. Treatments incl. X-rays and radioactive sources, hormones, surgery and chemotherapy.

Cancer, Tropic of, parallel of latitude 23½° N of Equator. Marks most N position at which Sun appears vertically overhead at noon. At this line, Sun shines directly overhead at June solstice (summer in N hemisphere).

candela (cd), SI unit of luminous intensity, equivalent to 1/60 of intensity of 1 sq cm of blackbody radiator at temperature of solidification of platinum (2046° K).

Candia, see IRÁKLION, Greece.

candle, mass of tallow or wax surrounding a wick, used as source of light when burned. Known since Roman times, candles, usually of tallow, became widespread in Europe during Middle Ages. Modern candles are usually machine-moulded from paraffin wax.

Candy, see KANDY.

candytuft, annual or perennial herb of cabbage family, native to S and W Europe. Globe candytuft, *Iberis umbellata*, is cultivated species.

cane, see BAMBOO; RATTAN; SUGAR CANE.

Canidae, the dog family. Carnivorous mammals, incl. wolf, fox, jackal, dog.

canna or Indian shot, genus of plants of Cannaceae family, native to tropical America and Asia. Many varieties cultivated for striking foliage and brilliant flowers. *Canna indica* and *C. edulis* yield kind of arrowroot.

cannabis, see HEMP..

Cannae (modern *Canna*), town of Apulia, S Italy, on R. Aufidus (modern *Ofanto*). Scene of Hannibal's victory (216 BC) over Romans.

Cannes, town of Provence, SE France, on Côte d'Azur. Pop. 68,000. Resort, casinos; fruit and flower growing, perfume mfg. Annual international film festival.

cannibalism, practice in certain societies of eating human flesh. Has occurred among many peoples at many times. Normally associated with the ritual attempt to transfer properties of victim to other members of group.

Canning, George (1770-1827), British statesman, PM (1827). Tory foreign secretary (1807-9), planned capture of Danish fleet (1807). Supported Spanish American and Greek independence movements after succeeding CASTLEREAGH as foreign secretary (1822). Advocated free trade and Catholic Emancipation.

canning, process of preserving cooked food by sealing it in airtight containers, afterwards subjected to heat. Method was invented in early 19th cent. France by N. Appert, who used glass bottles. Use of tin cans was patented in 1810, but mass-production of tin-coated steel cans began in 1840s.

cannon, a smooth-bore piece of artillery, used until the 19th cent., firing shot of 24-47 lb (11-21 kg). The term also now refers to large machine guns carried by fighter aircraft.

Cano, Juan Sebastian del (c 1476-1526), Spanish navigator. Sailed (1519-22) with Magellan, on whose death he took command, becoming first to circumnavigate globe.

canoe, narrow, light boat ending in a point at each end. Usually propelled by paddles but sail or motor may be used. Important in the culture of several primitive peoples, eg in South Pacific, among North American Indians. The Indian birchbark canoe was adopted by Europeans for explorations and trapping expeditions in North America. *See* CANOEING, KAYAK.

canoeing, sport of propelling a canoe through water. Divided into various activities: slalom, down river or wild-water racing, long distance and sprint racing. Popularized by John McGregor who founded Canoe Club in England (1866). Olympic event since 1936.

canon, musical form in which a melody is repeated note for note so that it overlaps itself. A catch or round is a simple vocal canon.

canonization, process by which RC church gives official sanction to veneration of dead person as a saint. Formal canonization dates from enactments of Pope Urban VIII in 1634. After careful investigation of a candidate's life, case may be brought by Church with objections raised by the *promotor fidei* (popularly known as 'devil's advocate'). Case for canonization consists of proof of 4 miracles and evidence of an exemplary life.

canon law, body of laws governing the ecclesiastical affairs of a Christian church. In RC church, systematized in *Codex juris canonici* (1918). In Church of England, based on canons pub. in 1604 and subsequently revised. Only clergy are bound by it, unless laws are authorized by Parliament or declared old custom. Rejected in Scotland after Reformation, but retained in laws of marriage, legitimacy and succession.

Cantabrian Mountains, range of N Spain, extending *c* 480 km (300 mi) E-W parallel to Bay of Biscay coast. Rise to 2648 m (8687 ft) at Peña Cerredo. Rich in coal and iron. Source of R. Ebro.

cantaloupe, *see* MELON.

cantata, sacred or secular piece of music of several movements for chorus and orchestra, usually with vocal soloists; similar to oratorio but shorter.

Canterbury, city of Kent, SE England, on R. Stour. Pop. 33,000. Roman *Durovernum*; hist. cap. of Saxon Kent. Abbey founded 597 by St Augustine who was 1st archbishop. Seat of Anglican primate. Pilgrimage centre since Becket's murder in cathedral (1170). Focus of Chaucer's *Canterbury Tales*. King's School (*c* 600, refounded 1541). University of Kent (1965).

Canterbury, region of EC South Isl., New Zealand. Area 36,000 sq km (13,900 sq mi); pop. 398,000; chief city Christchurch. Extends from Pacific coast (E) to Southern Alps foothills (W). Sheep, dairy farming on Canterbury Plains; tourism, h.e.p. in mountains.

cantilever, in architecture, horizontal beam supported at one end only and carrying a load at free end or evenly distributed along exposed portion. Used in bridge building for large spans, *eg* Forth Railway Bridge, Scotland.

Canton, China, *see* KWANGCHOW.

Canton and Enderbury Islands, in Phoenix Isls., C Pacific Ocean. Jointly admin. from 1939 by US, UK; others of Phoenix Isls. part of Gilbert and Ellice Isls. colony. Originally source of guano for US, also export copra. Canton was air refuelling base, now disused.

Cantonese, *see* CHINESE.

Canute or **Knut [II] the Great** (*c* 995-1035), king of England, Denmark and Norway. Invaded England 1015, sole ruler from 1016; estab. more efficient admin., codified law. King of Denmark from 1018, of Norway after invasion in 1028.

canvas, strong unbleached fabric made from flax, hemp etc. Used for sails, tents and as surface in oil-painting.

canvasback, *Aythya valisneria,* North American duck. Brown head, dark back; hunted as game.

canyon, deep, narrow gorge, often with steep sides. Usually formed in arid areas by rivers cutting into soft rock, low rainfall preventing erosion of canyon walls. Grand Canyon, US, is largest in world.

capacitance, in electronics, property of CAPACITOR which determines how much charge can be stored in it for given potential difference between its terminals; measured, in farads, as amount of charge required to increase potential by 1 unit.

capacitor, device for storing electric charge, usually consisting of 2 or more conducting plates separated by insulating material (dielectric). Used in electrical devices, *eg* radios. Formerly called condenser.

Cape Breton, isl. of Canada, forms E part of Nova Scotia. Area 10,282 sq km (*c* 3970 sq mi). Rugged terrain, fishing, lumbering, coal mining at Sydney-Glace Bay, steel production. French colony 1713-58; joined with Nova Scotia 1820.

Cape hunting dog, *Lycaon pictus,* wild dog of S and E Africa. Hunts in packs; can kill much larger animals.

Čapek, Karel (1890-1938), Czech playwright. Known for *R.U.R.* (1921) about a fantasy state where robots revolt against man. Also wrote novels, short stories. Collaborated with his brother, Josef Čapek (1887-1945), in social allegory *The Insect Play* (1921).

Cape of Good Hope, *see* GOOD HOPE, CAPE OF.

Cape [of Good Hope] Province, prov. (largest) of SW South Africa. Area 720,000 sq km (278,000 sq mi); pop. 4,235,000; cap. Cape Town. Plateau, drained by R. Orange. Produces cereals, tobacco, fruit, vines; diamond (Kimberley), copper (Okiep) mining. Settled from 1652 by Dutch at Table Bay, by Huguenots (1689). Annexed 1806 by Britain; became prov. of Union of South Africa (1910).

caper, any plant of genus *Capparis,* esp. a prickly, trailing Mediterranean bush, *C. spinosa,* tiny green flower buds of which are pickled and used to flavour sauces.

capercaillie or **capercailzie,** *Tetrao urogallus,* large grouse-like bird of N Europe. Grey-coloured; usually seen on ground.

Capet, Hugh (*c* 938-96), French king (987-96). Son of Hugh the Great; elected successor to Louis V in preference to Charles, duke of Lorraine. First of Capetians.

Capetians, dynasty of French kings, named after Hugh Capet (*c* 938-96), 1st Capetian ruler. Direct descendants of his ruled 987-1328, last was Charles IV. Throne then passed to House of Valois.

Cape Town or **Capetown,** legislative cap. of South Africa and cap. of Cape Prov. Pop. 1,096,000. Port on Table Bay, at foot of Table Mt. Admin., commercial centre, univ. (1918). Founded (1652) by Dutch; cap. of Cape Colony until 1910. Dutch colonial architecture, botanic gardens. Oldest South African white settlement.

Cape Verde Islands, country of EC Atlantic. Area 4040 sq km (1560 sq mi); pop. 303,000; cap. Praia. Incl. 10 isls. of volcanic origin. Stock raising, fishing; exports coffee, fruit. Colonized 15th cent. by Portuguese. Independent 1975, retains links with Guinea-Bissau.

Cape York Peninsula, penin. of N Queensland, Australia, between

Coral Sea and Gulf of Carpentaria. Aboriginal reserves; cattle ranching, bauxite mining. First part of Australia sighted by Europeans (Jansz, 1606).

capillaries, in physiology, *see* BLOOD VESSELS.

capillary action, force resulting from adhesion, cohesion and surface tension in liquids which are in contact with solids. Accounts for water rising in capillary tube, because adhesive force between glass and water exceeds cohesive force between water molecules.

capital, in architecture, the top part of a column, pilaster or pier, which transmits the weight of the superstructure to the supporting column. Gothic and Romanesque capitals were often richly carved with animal forms, grotesque heads, *etc.*

capital, in economics, originally interest-bearing money; now all means of production and distribution, *eg* land, plant, transport, raw materials, potentially yielding income. Ownership of capital is both private and public in most indust. countries, although in Communist countries nearly all capital is state-owned. *See* CAPITALISM, CORPORATE STATE.

capitalism, economic system in which means of production and distribution (land, factories, transport) are privately owned and operated for profit. Importance dates from Industrial Revolution, characterized by free competition and great concentrations of wealth; later by large corporations and varying degrees of govt. regulation, often as technocratic state capitalism (*see* CORPORATE STATE). As term,

capitalism developed by Marx in historical analysis (DIALECTICAL MATERIALISM) as stage in evolution of society.

capital punishment, legally sanctioned taking of life as punishment for crime. Once recognized penalty for sacrilege and offences against property, in 20th cent. usually reserved for treason, murder. In 1970s only W European countries retaining it were France, Spain. In US, Supreme Court ruled (1972) that death penalty violated 8th, 14th Amendments, but left way open for it to be imposed by new legislation passed by Congress or specific states, as it was in same year by Congress (for hijacking) and by most states.

Capone, Al[fonso] (1899-1947), American gangster, b. Italy. Notorious for leadership of crime syndicate in Chicago during prohibition era of 1920s.

Capote, Truman (1924-), American author. Early work, *eg Other Voices, Other Rooms* (1928), has gothic elements. *Breakfast at Tiffany's* (1958) reflects New York chic; *In Cold Blood* (1966) is leading example of 'documentary fiction'.

Capp, Al (1909-), American cartoonist, known for burlesque, satirical strip cartoon, 'Li'l Abner'.

Cappadocia, mountainous region of Asia Minor, in C Turkey. Independent kingdom in 3rd cent. BC, with cap. at Mazaca; became Roman prov. in AD 17.

Capra, Frank (1897-), American film writer-director, b. Sicily. Known for stylish comedies of 1930s-40s, conveying belief in redeemable human nature, incl.

Platinum Blonde (1932), *It Happened One Night* (1934), *Mr Deeds Goes to Town* (1936).

Capri, isl. of S Italy, in Bay of Naples. Area 10 sq km (4 sq mi). Tourist centre with famous Blue Grotto. Site of ruined villas of emperors Augustus, Tiberius.

Capricorn, *see* ZODIAC.

Capricorn, Tropic of, parallel of latitude 23½° S of Equator. Marks most S position at which Sun appears vertically overhead at noon. At this line, Sun shines directly overhead at December solstice (summer in S hemisphere).

Capua (anc. *Casilinum*), town of Campania, S Italy, on R. Volturno. Pop. 18,000. Strategic Roman site on Appian Way; sacked by Arabs (AD 841), inhabitants moved to present site.

capuchin, commonest monkey of Central and South America, genus *Cebus*, incl. *c* 12 species. Hair resembles monk's cowl. Lives in troops led by dominant male.

capybara, *Hydrochoerus hydrochoeris,* largest rodent, up to 1.2 m/4 ft long, resembling giant guinea pig. Lives in groups, good swimmer; found on river banks of South America.

car, *see* AUTOMOBILE.

Caracas, cap. of Venezuela, linked to Caribbean port La Guaira. Pop. 2,175,000; alt. 945 m (c 3100 ft). Oil refining, textile mfg. Founded 1567. Scene of declaration of Venezuelan independence (1811); birthplace of Bolívar. Cap. from 1829. Wealth derived from oil has facilitated growth of modern city.

Caractacus or **Caradoc** (*fl* AD 50), British chieftain. Led resistance against Romans (43-51). Captured and taken to Rome, where his life was spared by Claudius.

carat, unit describing quantity of gold in an alloy: 1 carat is 24th part of pure gold, thus 15 carat gold contains 15 parts gold and 9 parts alloy.

Caravaggio, Michelangelo Amerighi da (1573-1610), Italian painter. Famous for his revolutionary use of light and shade, contemporary costume and rejection of idealization to achieve previously unknown degree of realism. Had great influence on subsequent artists. Works incl. *Martyrdom of St Matthew.*

caraway, white-flowered biennial herb, *Carum carvi,* of parsley family with spicy, strong-smelling seeds which are used as flavouring and a carminative. Leaves are eaten as vegetables and in soup.

carbide, compound of an element, usually metal, with carbon. Incl. calcium carbide (CaC_2), used to make acetylene, and silicon carbide or carborundum (SiC_2), used as abrasive.

carbohydrate, organic compound of carbon, hydrogen and oxygen with general formula $C_x (H_2O)_y$, incl. sugars, starches and cellulose. Formed in green plants by PHOTOSYNTHESIS; starch essential to human diet, providing energy during its oxidation.

carbolic acid, *see* PHENOLS.

carbon (C), non-metallic element; at. no. 6, at. wt. 12.01. Exists in 3 allotropic forms: crystalline diamond graphite, and amorphous carbon (charcoal, lampblack, coke). Numerous compounds subject of organic chemistry. Used in electrodes; activated charcoal, specially treated to remove hydrocarbons, absorbs gases.

Carbonari ('charcoal burners'), Italian political secret society originating in Naples. Aimed at expulsion of foreign rulers and estab. of democracy. Active in uprisings (1820, 1831), later merged with Young Italy movement of MAZZINI.

carbon dioxide (CO_2), colourless gas, found in atmosphere; formed by combustion of carbon or heating carbonates. Dissolves in water to form weak unstable carbonic acid. Exhaled by animals and absorbed by plants, which convert it into carbohydrates and oxygen by photosynthesis. Used in production of mineral water, in fire extinguishers; solid carbon dioxide known as 'dry ice' used as refrigerant.

carbon fibre, material composed of extremely fine filaments of pure carbon bonded together. Great strength-to-weight ratio and heat resistance; valuable in reinforcing components of jet engines.

Carboniferous period, fifth geological period of Palaeozoic era; began c 345 million years ago, lasted c 65 million years. Divided into Lower Carboniferous or Mississippian, and Upper Carboniferous, or Pennsylvanian. Many crinoids, brachiopods; increasing amphibians, fish, insects, 1st reptiles. Club mosses, horsetails led to development of vast COAL seams. Also *see* GEOLOGICAL TABLE.

carbon monoxide (CO), colourless inflammable gas, formed by incomplete combustion of carbonaceous fuels. Extremely poisonous, as it combines with haemoglobin of blood, making this unavailable to carry oxygen. Occurs in exhaust fumes of petrol engines, coal gas.

carborundum, *see* CARBIDE.

carboxylic acid, organic acid containing 1 or more carboxyl (COOH) groups, *eg* formic acid.

carbuncle, inflammation of tissue beneath the skin, of same kind as a BOIL, but larger and with several heads through which pus is discharged.

Carcassonne, town of Languedoc, S France, on R. Aude. Cap. of Aude dept. Pop. 46,000. Tourist centre, wine trade. Divided by R. Aude into ancient hilltop 'Cité' (castle, cathedral, town walls) and 'Ville Basse' (founded 1247).

Carchemish, ancient city of S Turkey, on Euphrates near Syrian border. Centre of neo-Hittite culture c 1000 BC; scene of victory of Nebuchadnezzar II over Necho II (605 BC) which ended Egyptian power in Asia.

carcinogen, any substance that produces cancer. In 1775 Pott showed that soot causes cancer in chimney sweeps. Isolation of carcinogens started (1915) when Yamagima and Ichikawa showed that repeated applications of coal tar to skin of rabbits produces cancer.

cardamom or **cardamon**, spice from seed capsules of E Indian plant, *Elettaria cardamomum*, used in curries and pickling.

Cárdenas, Lázaro (1895-1970), Mexican political leader. President (1934-40); his policy incl. land reform reallocating private holdings to individuals and collectives, expropriation of foreign assets.

Cardiff, cap. city and port of Wales, in S Glamorgan. Near Bristol Channel on R. Taff. Pop. 278,000. Major coal, iron, steel exports. Admin., commercial centre; has coll. of Univ. of Wales. Site of Roman station; 11th cent. castle.

Cardigan, James Thomas Brudenell, 7th Earl of (1797-1868), British army officer. Led the disastrous cavalry charge at Balaklava (1854) in the Crimean War, immortalized by Tennyson. The woollen garment called a cardigan is named after him.

Cardiganshire, former county of W Wales, now in Dyfed. Main town Aberystwyth. Plateau in E (livestock rearing), lowland along coast (oats, barley growing). Has many British, Roman remains. Co. town was Cardigan, mun. bor. on R. Teifi. Pop. 4000. Agric. market.

cardinal, any of several North American crested songbirds of scarlet plumage, esp. *Richmondena cardinalis* of E US.

Carew, Thomas (*c* 1594-1640), English poet. Known for Cavalier lyric verse in manner of Jonson, *eg* 'Ask me no more where Jove bestows', 'Mediocrity in love rejected'.

Carib, South American Indians of separate Carib language family, formerly inhabiting Lesser Antilles. Named by Columbus, noted for their ferocity (a corruption of Carib gives English word 'cannibal'); also expert navigators. Some 500 pure-blooded Caribs remain on Dominica.

Caribbean, sea of W Atlantic Ocean, bounded by Venezuela, Colombia, Central America. Area 1,942,500 sq km (*c* 750,000 sq mi).

Linked with Gulf of Mexico by Yucatán Channel. Has many isls. *eg* West Indies, Greater and Lesser Antilles. Named after Carib Indians who once inhabited coastal areas.

caribou, large North American deer, resembling reindeer, genus *Rangifer*. Native of Arctic and subarctic. Both sexes have antlers. Two main types: barren-ground group of Alaska, N Canada; woodland group of E Canada.

carillon, set of bells worked by keyboard and pedals, or automatically. The world's largest carillon, at Cincinnati, Ohio, contains 83 bells in a tower 91m (300 ft) high. Originated in Low Countries, *c* 16th cent.

Carinthia (*Kärnten*), prov. of S Austria. Area 9531 sq km (3680 sq mi); cap. Klagenfurt. Mountainous, incl. GROSSGLOCKNER, many lakes. Timber, mining. Incorporated into Austria 14th cent.

Carlisle, city and co. bor. of Cumbria, N England, on R. Eden. Pop. 71,000. Railway jct., textile mfg. Roman *Luguvallum*; hist. strategic site in border wars; has castle (1092), cathedral (12th cent.).

Carlists, supporters of descendants of Don Carlos de Bourbon (1788-1855), 2nd son of Charles IV of Spain, as pretenders to Spanish throne. Defeated in civil war (1833-9) by forces of Isabella II, and failed in uprisings (1860, 1869, 1872). Also lost civil war of 1873-6 despite gains in Basque provs., Catalonia. Supported fascists under FRANCO in Spanish Civil War (1936-9).

Carlow, county of Leinster prov., SE Irish Republic. Area 896 sq km (346 sq mi); pop. 34,000. Mountains in SE. Agric., dairying, livestock. Co.

town Carlow, pop. 9000. Market town. Theological coll. (18th cent.), RC cathedral (19th cent.).

Carlyle, Thomas (1795-1881), Scottish writer. Translated Goethe, Schiller. Distrust of democracy, belief in divinely-informed hero expressed in *French Revolution* (1837), *On Heroes, Hero-Worship* (1841). Also wrote biog. *Frederick the Great* (1858-65). *Sartor Resartus* (1833-4) is spiritual autobiog.

Carman, [William] Bliss (1861-1929), Canadian poet. Known for bohemian 'vagabond' verse, esp. *Low Tide on Grand Pré* (1893). Also wrote essays, *The Kinship of Nature* (1906).

Carmarthenshire, former county of S Wales, now in Dyfed. Mountainous in NE (livestock rearing), agric. in lowlands. Coalmining, metal industs. centred in Llanelli in SE. Carmarthen, mun. bor. and co. town of Dyfed, on R. Towy. Pop. 13,000. Dairy centre, on site of Roman town *Maridunum*.

Carmel, Mount, mountain of NW Israel, rising 546 m (1792 ft) from Haifa. Associated in Bible with prophet Elijah. Carmelite order was founded here in 12th cent.

Carmelites, in RC church, mendicant friars of the order of Our Lady of Mt. Carmel. Founded as order of hermits in Palestine *c* 1150. Stress contemplative aspects of religious life and have incl. several mystics, *eg* ST THERESA OF AVILA, St John of the Cross. Known as White Friars.

Carnac, town of Brittany, NW France, on Quiberon Bay. Pop. 4000. Site of *c* 3000 menhirs arranged in rows, among which are ancient burial chambers.

Carnap, Rudolf (1891-1970), German philosopher, settled in US 1936. Pioneer of LOGICAL POSITIVISM, claiming object of philosophy is description and criticism of language. Works incl. *The Logical Syntax of Language* (1934).

Carnarvon, *see* CAERNARVONSHIRE, Wales.

carnation, *Dianthus caryophyllus*, perennial herbaceous plant with many cultivated varieties. White, pink or red flowers popular as buttonholes. *See* PINK.

Carné, Marcel (1903-), French film director. Known for subtly-characterized films, incl. *Le Jour se lève* (1939), *Les Enfants du Paradis* (1944).

Carnegie, Andrew (1835-1919), American industrialist, b. Scotland. Estab. steel business based in Pittsburgh which produced by 1900 one quarter of total US steel. Sold out (1901) to US Steel Corporation and devoted his fortune to funding of libraries, univs.

Carnegie, Dale (1888-1955), American writer. Famous for self-improvement manuals, esp. *How to Win Friends and Influence People* (1936).

Carnivora (carnivores), order of flesh-eating mammals with large canine teeth. Terrestrial group, Fissipedia, incl. dog, cat, otter, bear, lion. Marine group, Pinnipedia, incl. seal, walrus.

Carnot, Lazare Nicolas Marguerite (1753-1823), French revolutionary soldier. Organized republican armies, reforming methods and supply systems. Exiled (1815) after restoration. His son, Nicolas Léonard Sadi Carnot (1796-1832), was a physicist. Helped found thermodynamics with work on heat, mechanical energy. His nephew, [Marie François] **Sadi Carnot** (1837-94), was a statesman. President (1887-94), countered Boulanger's populist movement. Assassinated by Italian anarchist at Lyons.

carob, leguminous tree, *Ceratonia siliqua,* of E Mediterranean, bearing leathery brown pods with sweet pulp which are sometimes used as fodder.

Carol II (1893-1953), king of Romania (1930-40). Renounced right to succession (1925), but deposed son Michael (1930) and took throne. Overthrown by ANTONESCU (1940), fled to Mexico.

carol, song of annual religious festivals, esp. Christmas. Some of the tunes originate in folk song while others are borrowed from secular music or specially composed.

Caroline Islands, archipelago of W Pacific Ocean. Area 900 sq km (350 sq mi); chief isls. PALAU, Ponape, Truk, Yap. Main crops copra, sugar cane, tapioca; also produce bauxite, phosphate, guano. Discovered 1526 by Spain, bought (1899) by Germany. Occupied by Japanese from WWI; part of US Trust Territ. of the Pacific Isls. from 1947.

Caroline of Brunswick (1768-1821), German princess, consort of George IV of England. Married (1795) prince of Wales, but they were separated 1796. She refused to renounce her rights at his accession; George's subsequent divorce proceedings were abandoned.

Carolingians, dynasty of Frankish rulers, succeeding Merovingians (751) through Pepin the Short. His

son, Charlemagne, crowned Western emperor (800); empire split by Treaty of Verdun (843) among his grandsons who founded dynasties ruling Germany until 911 and France until 987. Succeeded by Capetians.

carp, freshwater fish of Cyprinidae family, esp. *Cyprinus carpio,* of worldwide distribution. May be cultivated as food fish. Goldfish is domestic variety of golden carp.

Carpaccio, Vittore (c 1460-1526), Italian painter. Influenced by Gentile Bellini, his narrative paintings, filled with anecdotal detail, describe pageantry of Venice. Works incl. *Legend of St Ursula* series.

Carpathians, mountain range of EC Europe, curving from Czechoslovakia through SW Ukraine to Romania. Rise to 2662 m (8737 ft) in Tatra Mts. (Czechoslovakia). Forests; minerals; tourism.

Carpentaria, Gulf of, shallow inlet of Arafura Sea, N Australia, between Arnhem Land and Cape York Penin.

carpet or rug, thick fabric, usually of wool, used as a floor covering, *etc.* Carpet making reached a high point of artistry in Turkey, Persia and C Asia in 16th cent. European production dates from 17th cent. at such centres as the Savonnerie in Paris. In England, Axminster, Wilton and Kidderminster were important centres. Power loom introduced 1841 made mass-production possible.

carpetbagger, American political term popularized in post-Civil War period. Referred to speculators and entrepreneurs who started business in devastated Southern states with no more than they could carry in a carpetbag.

Carpini, Giovanni de Piano (c 1180-1252), Italian Franciscan monk. Sent by Pope Innocent IV in 1245 to Mongol court of Karakorum. Crossed Russia and Asia in c 106 days. Journal was 1st European record of Mongols.

Carracci, Ludovico (1555-1619), Italian artist. Founded teaching Academy in Bologna with cousins, Agostino Carracci (1557-1602) and Annibale Carracci (1560-1609). Annibale's decoration of Farnese Gallery in Rome is esp. famous for its use of illusionism and feigned architectural, sculptural forms.

Carrantuohill, mountain of Co. Kerry, SW Irish Republic. Highest in Ireland (1040 m/3414 ft).

Carranza, Venustiano (1859-1920), Mexican political leader, president (1914-20). Contested leadership with Huerta, Villa and Zapata after overthrow of Diaz (1911). Reform programme of nationalization of mineral assets (1917) was never implemented.

Carrara, town of Tuscany, NC Italy. Pop. 68,000. Centre of Italian marble indust. Has medieval cathedral.

carriage, non-self-propelling wheeled vehicle, used esp. for carrying passengers; strictly refers to 4-wheel types. Covered horse- or mule-drawn carriage dates from c 15th cent. Public stagecoach much used in 17th and 18th cent. Hansom cab (2-wheel) plying for hire introduced in London (1834). Other 2-wheeled carriages incl. stanhope, tilbury, gig, sulky, dog-cart. Private 4-wheeled carriages widely used in 19th cent. incl. brougham, landau, victoria. Open 4-wheeled carriages incl. phaeton, wagonette, brake.

Carrickfergus, town of E Northern Ireland, on Belfast Lough. Pop. 15,000. In former Co. Antrim. Fishing port; linen mfg.

Carrick-on-Shannon, co. town of Leitrim, NW Irish Republic, on R. Shannon. Pop. 2000. Agric. market; fishing.

carrion crow, see CROW.

Carroll, Lewis, pseud. of Charles Lutwidge Dodgson (1832-98), English writer, mathematician. Known for classics of inverted logic, ostensibly for childern, eg *Alice's Adventures in Wonderland* (1865), *Through the Looking-glass* (1872). Also wrote nonsense verse incl. *The Hunting of the Snark* (1876).

carrot, *Daucus carota*, widely distributed biennial plant of parsley family, with fleshy, orange-coloured edible roots. Derived from Queen Anne's lace or wild carrot.

Carson, Christopher ('Kit') (1809-68), American frontiersman. Renowned Indian fighter, acted as guide in Frémont's Western expeditions in 1840s. Aided in Mexican War (1846).

Carson, Edward Henry Carson, Baron (1854-1935), Irish politician. Opposed Irish Home Rule and rallied Ulster in support of British govt. during WWI, serving in wartime cabinets. Denounced creation (1921) of independent Irish Free State.

Carson City, cap. of Nevada, US; near California border. Pop. 15,000. Grew in late 19th cent. after nearby silver strike at Comstock Lode. Resort town. Named after Kit Carson.

Cartagena, seaport of N Colombia,

on Caribbean. Pop. 257,000. Has canal link to Magdalena R. Oil pipeline terminus; exports govt. produce. Founded (1533) by Spanish, it was shipping centre for precious stones and metals of New World; frequently sacked and invaded.

Cartagena, city of Murcia, SE Spain, on Mediterranean Sea. Pop. 147,000. Port, exports iron and lead; metallurgical centre, naval base. Founded *c* 225 BC by Hasdrubal; major port under Romans. *Fl* 16th-18th cent. with New World trade.

Carte, Richard D'Oyly, see D'OYLY CARTE, RICHARD.

cartel, in economics, association of manufacturers or traders to fix prices, sales quotas or to divide markets. Shares many characteristics of MONOPOLY.

Carter, Elliott (1908-), American composer. His complex works usually employ traditional forms; esp. noted for chamber music. Compositions incl. *Variations for Orchestra,* 3 string quartets.

Carter, Howard (1873-1939), English archaeologist. Working with Lord Carnarvon in Valley of Kings in Egypt, discovered (1922) tomb of Tutankhamen, only Egyptian royal tomb to be discovered intact with all its treasure.

Carter, James Earl ('Jimmy') (1924-), American statesman, president (1977-). Upheld human rights abroad. Helped bring Israel and Egypt to peace table. Energy policy aimed at conservation.

Carteret, John, 1st Earl Granville (1690-1763), British statesman. Foreign minister (1721-4), clashed with Walpole. Leader of opposition (1730-42), instrumental in Walpole's downfall; became virtual head of govt. (1742-4). Supported George II's unpopular Hanoverian policy.

Carthage, ancient city of N Africa, near modern Tunis. Founded 9th cent. BC by Phoenicians; estab. colonies in Sardinia, Sicily, Spain. Trade rivalry with Rome led to PUNIC WARS, city finally destroyed 146 BC. New colony founded 44 BC by Romans; Vandal cap. from AD 439. Totally destroyed (698) by Arabs.

Carthusians, order of monks in RC church. Most austere order, each member living in individual cell, scarcely meeting others unless in public worship. Founded (1084) by St Bruno at Chartreuse, France. Chartreuse liqueur first made here.

Cartier, Sir George Etienne (1814-73), Canadian statesman. First minister (1858-62) of Lower Canada in Cartier-Macdonald ministry, largely responsible for French-Canadian interest in confederation.

Cartier, Jacques (1491-1557), French navigator, explorer. In search of Northwest Passage, made 2 voyages (1534, 1535-6) exploring E Canada, Gulf of St Lawrence. Reached St Lawrence R.; visited Stadacona (now Québec), Hochelaga (now Montréal); proclaimed French sovereignty. Colonizing expeditions (1541, 1543) failed.

Cartier-Bresson, Henri (1908-), French photographer. Known for extreme naturalism, as well as news photographs of important international events. Worked with Jean Renoir, founded Magnum-Photos (1947).

cartilage or **gristle,** tough whitish tissue which forms part of skeletal systems. Lines moving surfaces of joints and forms external ear, nose, *etc.* Skeletons of embryos are largely formed of cartilage, which gradually turns to bone.

cartography, the art and science of map making, now generally applied to all stages from field survey to finished map. Ancient Babylonians produced earliest known map (c 2500 BC); Greeks, esp. Eratosthenes and Ptolemy, estab. principles of cartography little altered until 17th cent. First world atlas produced by Mercator (1569). Modern cartography founded by Delisle and d'Anville; 1st systematic national survey pub. 1756 in France, followed 1801 by British Ordnance Survey.

cartoon, in art, full-size preliminary drawing of a design or painting, usually worked out in detail. Name also applies to drawing with humorous or satirical intention.

Cartwright, John (1740-1824), English reformer. Refused to fight American colonists. Campaigned for abolition of slavery, vote by secret ballot, other reforms. His brother, **Edmund Cartwright** (1743-1823), invented the powerloom (1785) and wool-combing machines.

Caruso, Enrico (1873-1921), Italian operatic tenor. Achieved fame in Europe and America. One of 1st singers to exploit gramophone recording successfully.

Cary, [Arthur] Joyce [Lunel] (1888-1957), English novelist, b. Ireland. Early works, *eg Mister Johnson* (1939), reflect experiences in Nigerian colonial services, later novels, *eg The Horse's Mouth*

(1944), *A Prisoner of Grace* (1952), deal comically with individual's isolation, with artist, politician as hero.

caryatid, in Greek architecture, supporting column in form of draped female figure (said to represent woman of Caryae). Famous examples found on porch of Erechtheum, Athens.

Casablanca (Arab. *Dar-al-Baida*), city of N Morocco, on Atlantic Ocean. Pop. 1,371,000. Indust., commercial centre; major port, exports phosphates, manganese. Founded 16th cent. by Portuguese on site of ancient *Anfa.* Scene of Roosevelt-Churchill meeting (1943).

Casals, Pablo or **Pau** (1876-1973), Spanish cellist; conductor. Founder and musical director of Barcelona orchestra (1919-36). Renowned for interpretation of Bach's cello pieces, he raised status of cello as a solo instrument.

Casanova de Seingalt, Giovanni Giacomo (1725-98), Italian adventurer, writer. Known for *Mémoires* (1826-38) which recount his fluctuating affairs, both financial and sexual, on travels across Europe.

Cascade Range, N extension of mountain system of W US; from California through Oregon, Washington to S British Columbia (Canada). Mt. Rainier in Washington is highest point (4392 m/14,410 ft). Heavily forested on slopes.

casein, main protein of milk, precipitated by addition of acid or rennet. Chief constituent of cheese; used to make plastics, adhesives.

Casement, Sir Roger David (1864-1916), Irish nationalist. Served in British consular service in

Belgian Congo and Peru. Attempted to gain German aid for Irish rebellion (1916), returning to Ireland in German submarine. Captured and hanged for treason. Regarded as martyr by Irish.

Casey, Richard Gardiner Casey, Baron (1890-1976), Australian statesman. Liberal minister (1949-60) in Menzies govt. Governor-general of Australia (1965-9).

Caslon, William (1692-1766), English typefounder. Designed 'old-style' types, legibility of which made their use widespread with printers until end of 18th cent.

Caspian Sea, salt lake between Europe and Asia, world's largest inland sea. Area *c* 373,000 sq km (144,000 sq mi). Almost entirely in USSR, part of S shore in Iran. Receives R. Volga and R. Ural, no outlet; 27m (90 ft) below sea level, its level decreases by evaporation. Sturgeon fisheries.

Cassander (*c* 350-297 BC), Macedonian king. Son of Antipater, fought against Polyperchon who had succeeded Antipater as regent of Macedonia. Master of Macedonia by 316, strengthened his position by murdering Alexander the Great's widow and son. Defeated Antigonus I at Ipsus (301).

Cassandra, in Greek legend, daughter of King Priam of Troy. Prophetess of Apollo, who caused her prophecies never to be believed. After fall of Troy, captive of Agamemnon; killed with him by his wife Clytemnestra.

Cassatt, Mary (1845-1926), American painter, etcher. Allied to impressionist group, she was influenced by Degas. Later work,

influenced by Japanese prints, relied on line and pattern. Excelled in mother-and-child scenes.

cassava or **manioc**, any of several tropical American plants of genus *Manihot* of the spurge family, having edible starchy roots used to make tapioca.

Cassel, see KASSEL, West Germany.

cassia, the bark of a tree, *Cinnamomum cassia*, of the laurel family, native to SE Asia. Used as a cinnamon substitute. Also a genus, *Cassia*, of herbs, shrubs and trees of Leguminosae family, common in tropical countries. The cathartic drug senna is prepared from the leaves of *C. acutifolia* and *C. angustifolia*.

Cassino, town of Latium, C Italy, at foot of Monte Cassino. Pop. 19,000. Monastery on summit founded 529 by St Benedict; used as stronghold by Germans (1944), destroyed by Allied bombing. Restored 1964.

Cassirer, Ernst (1874-1945), German philosopher. Known for Kantian critique of culture leading to conception of man as the 'symbolic animal'. Works incl. *Philosophy of Symbolic Forms* (1923-9).

Cassius [Longinus], Galus (d. 42 BC), Roman soldier. Pardoned by Caesar after supporting Pompey in civil war (48 BC). He became a leading figure in the conspiracy to assassinate Caesar (44 BC). With Brutus, he was defeated by Mark Antony at Philippi, where he committed suicide.

Cassivellaunus (*fl c* 55 BC), British chieftain. Led resistance against Roman invasion under Caesar, but was defeated and forced to pay tribute.

Casson, Sir Hugh Maxwell (1910-), British architect. Director of Architecture for Festival of Britain (1948-51). Works incl. *Homes by the Million*, *An Introduction to Victorian Architecture* (1947). President of the Royal Academy (1975).

cassowary, *Casuarius casuarius*, large flightless bird of N Australia, New Guinea, with brightly coloured neck and head, capped by bony crest; related to emu. Male incubates eggs.

castanets, percussion instrument consisting of a pair of shell-shaped wooden blocks joined by a piece of string; held between thumb and fingers and clicked rapidly together. A pair is usually held in each hand. Characteristic to Spain.

caste, in Hindu population of India, exclusive social grouping. Classified by Brahmans (*c* AD 200) into 4 divisions with Untouchables below these; now *c* 3000 castes. Traditionally, no member of any caste may marry outside it; rules may also regulate occupation and diet. Discrimination against castes made illegal (1947).

Castel Gandolfo, village of Latium, C Italy, in Alban Hills. Castle (17th cent.) is papal summer residence; Vatican astronomical observatory estab. 1936.

Castellammare di Stabia, town of Campania, S Italy, on Bay of Naples. Pop. 69,000. Resort (mineral springs), naval dockyard, engineering. Roman *Stabiae*, destroyed by Vesuvius eruption AD 79. Ruined 13th cent. castle.

Castiglione, Baldassare, Conte (1478-1529), Italian author. Wrote *Libro del Cortegiano* (1528; English translation, *The Courtier*, 1561), lively collection of dialogues on Renaissance courtly morals and manners.

Castile (*Castilla*), region and former kingdom of C Spain. Largely arid plateau, drained by Douro, Tagus rivers; divided by mountains into Old (N) and New (S) Castile. Limited agric. incl. cereals, fruit, sheep; mining. Independent from 10th cent.; led fight against Moors. United with León (1230), Aragón (1479) to found Spain. Language became standard Spanish.

castle, fortified dwelling characteristic of medieval times. Principal features of Norman castle were: rectangular donjon or keep, which served as living quarters; inner bailey (courtyard) surrounding the keep and separated from outer bailey by a wall; outer walls of masonry, from which round towers (bastions) projected; moats, crossed by drawbridges, which protected outer walls.

Castlebar, co. town of Mayo, NW Irish Republic. Pop. 6000. Agric. market. Scene of French-Irish rout of English garrison ('Races of Castlebar' 1798).

Castlereagh, Robert Stewart, 2nd Viscount (1769-1822), British statesman, b. Ireland. As Irish secretary crushed French-backed revolt (1795). Secretary of war during Napoleonic wars, helped plan Peninsular campaign. Fought duel with George CANNING after alleged political betrayal, resigned 1803. Foreign secretary (1812-22), helped organize 'Concert of Europe' opposing Napoleon. Favoured moderate settlement at Congress of

VIENNA (1814-15), maintenance of conservative interests in Europe. Committed suicide.

Castor and Pollux, in classical myth, *see* DIOSCURI.

castor oil, extracted from seeds of Palma Christi shrub, *Ricinus communis,* native to subtropical regions, but widely cultivated as ornamental. The oil is used medicinally as a quick-acting laxative; also used in paint and varnish indust.

castration, removal of sex glands (testicles) of male animal. Results in sterility and curbing of secondary sex characteristics when practised on children. Used to improve meat quality and decrease aggressiveness of farm animals.

Castro [Ruz], Fidel (1927-), Cuban revolutionary and political leader, premier (1959-). Chief figure in '26th of July' movement; organized Cuban revolutionary forces while in Mexico and returned to lead successful guerrilla campaign (1956-9), which overthrew BATISTA. Proclaimed (1961) allegiance to Communist bloc; supported revolutionary movements in Latin America. Collectivized agriculture, expropriated indust.

casuistry, originally, branch of ethics which deals with delicate moral questions by applying general principles. Term also refers to arguing away of ambiguous acts with hair-splitting subtleties.

cat, any animal of Felidae family, incl. lion, leopard, tiger. Carnivorous, with sharp claws used for climbing trees, holding prey. Numerous varieties of domestic cat, *Felis catus,* probably derived from African wildcat, *F. lybica.*

catacombs, early Christian subterranean cemeteries arranged in vaults and galleries; those in Rome date mainly from 3rd and early 4th cents. and cover *c* 600 acres. Also served as places of refuge during Christian persecutions; later became shrines of pilgrimage. Others, besides Rome, were in Naples, Syracuse, Paris, *etc.*

Catalan, Romance language of Italic branch of Indo-European family. Spoken in Catalonia, Valencia, Balearic Islands, Roussillon region of SE France, and is Andorran official language.

catalepsy, unconscious fit, resulting in temporary loss of feeling and rigidity of muscles. May occur in epilepsy, schizophrenia, hysteria.

Catalonia (Cataluña), region of NE Spain, hist. cap. Barcelona. Hilly, drained by R. Ebro. Almond, fruit growing, wine mfg.; metal, textile industs. based on h.e.p. Frankish county from 9th cent.; united with Aragón (12th cent.), with Castile (15th cent.). Autonomous govts. (1932-4, 1936-9) reflect hist. strong Catalan nationalism. Catalan language suppressed after 1939.

catalyst, any substance which speeds up or slows down rate of chemical reaction, but is itself unchanged at end of reaction. Plays important role in indust. preparation of ammonia, sulphuric acid, *etc.* Platinum, nickel, manganese dioxide are catalysts.

Catania, city of E Sicily, Italy, on Gulf of Catania. Cap. of Catania prov. Pop. 402,000. Port, shipbuilding, sulphur refining, food processing; univ. (1434). Founded 8th cent. BC by Greek colonists.

Often damaged by eruptions of Mt. Etna.

cataract, in medicine, disease of eye in which lens becomes opaque, causing partial or total blindness. Commonly results from ageing; treated by surgery.

catarrh, obsolete term for inflammation of mucous membrane, esp. of nose, causing a discharge of mucus. Rhinitis now describes such inflammation of nose.

catastrophe theory, mathematical theory that uses topology to describe ways in which a dynamic system can pass through a point of instability eg the point at which water being heated turns into steam. Applications in many subjects, incl. economics, sociology, biology.

catastrophism, in geology, theory that features of Earth's crust change by means of isolated catastrophes. Rejects theory of evolution implicit in UNIFORMITARIANISM. Widely held from ancient times, upheld by Cuvier in early 19th cent.; now generally discarded.

catchment area, area in which all water drains into a particular river, lake or reservoir. Separated from adjacent catchment area by high land forming a WATERSHED.

caterpillar, worm-like, segmented, larva of butterfly or moth. Usually herbivorous, has strong jaws. Moults skin c 5 times to allow growth. Pupates in cocoon spun from silk thread.

catfish, any of a large group of scaleless freshwater and marine fish, abundant in New World. Whisker-like sensory barbels around mouth.

Cathari, generic name for adherents

of dualistic heresies in medieval Europe, esp. ALBIGENSIANS.

Catherine I (c 1683-1727), tsarina of Russia (1725-7). Originally Martha Skavronskaya, a Livonian peasant girl; became mistress of Peter the Great and married him (1711). Chosen as his successor.

Catherine [II] the Great (1729-96), tsarina of Russia (1762-96), b. Germany. Married (1744) the future Peter II, whom she had deposed by conspiracy headed by the Orlovs shortly after his accession. Reforming zeal unfulfilled after peasant rebellion (1773-5) and French Revolution. Her reign was marked by territ. expansion at expense of Poland, ascendancy in Near East after wars (1768-74, 1787-92) with Turkey and annexation of Crimea. A monarch of the Enlightenment, encouraged development of Russian literature. Lovers incl. Orlov, Potemkin.

Catherine de' Medici, see MEDICI.

Catherine of Alexandria, St (d. c 307), Alexandrian martyr. Traditionally, broke spiked wheel on which she was being tortured; subsequently beheaded. Patron saint of virgins.

Catherine of Aragon (1485-1536), queen of England, 1st wife of Henry VIII. Daughter of Ferdinand and Isabella of Spain. Discontent with their marriage and lack of a male heir led Henry to seek annulment on grounds of illegality. Pope's refusal led to English Reformation.

Catherine of Braganza (1638-1705), Portuguese princess, consort of Charles II of England. Dowry for marriage (1662) incl. Bombay, Tangier. Lived away from court, but protected by Charles when accused of complicity in Popish Plot (1678).

Catherine of Genoa, St (1447-1510), Genoese mystic. Broke from life of society in order to nurse sick. Thoughts contained in *Treatise on Purgatory and Spiritual Dialogue*.

Catherine of Siena, St (1347-80), Italian Dominican nun, mystic. After vision of united Church, convinced Pope Gregory XI to leave Avignon for Rome; subsequently defended Urban VI against antipope Clement VII. Teachings contained in *A Treatise on Divine Providence*.

Catherine of Valois (1401-37), French princess, consort of Henry V of England. Gave birth to Henry VI (1421). Secret marriage to Owen Tudor after Henry V's death (1422) provided basis for subsequent Tudor claims to English throne.

cathode, see ELECTRODE.

cathode rays, stream of electrons emitted from cathode when electrical discharge takes place in tube containing gas at very low pressure.

cathode ray tube, vacuum tube in which cathode rays are directed by electric fields to strike fluorescent screen and produce illuminated traces, visible outside tube. Used in oscilloscopes and television picture tubes.

Catholic Emancipation, name given to series of acts passed in Britain. Culminated in Catholic Emancipation Act (1829) which relieved British RCs from the legal and civil disabilities accumulated since time of Henry VIII, eg restrictions on land inheritance, debarment from forces, judiciary, univs.

Catiline, full name Lucius Sergius

Catilina (c 108-62 BC), Roman politician. Twice failed to be elected consul (66, 63); after his 2nd failure, when defeated by Cicero, formed scheme to take power by force. Conspiracy exposed by Cicero in 4 orations; Catiline killed in subsequent battle.

catmint or **catnip,** *Nepeta cataria,* plant of mint family, with downy leaves, spikes of bluish flowers. Native to Britain and Europe. Tea, made of leaves and flowers is old medicinal remedy.

Cato, Marcus Porcius or **Cato the Elder** (234-149 BC), Roman statesman. Appointed censor (184), tried to restrict entry to senate to those he considered worthy. Opposed introduction of Greek culture in favour of ancient Roman simplicity. Campaigned for the destruction of Carthage. Wrote *De Re Rustica,* treatise on agric.

Cato Street conspiracy, see THISTLEWOOD, ARTHUR.

Catskill Mountains, range of E New York, US; part of Appalachian Mts. Rise to 1231 m (4040 ft). Area provides water for New York City. incl. locale of Rip van Winkle tale. Popular tourist area.

cattail or **reed mace,** any of genus *Typha* of tall marsh plants with reed-like leaves and long, brown, fuzzy, cylindrical flower spikes. Incl. species *T. latifolia, T. angustifolia* which are used in making baskets and matting.

cattle, ruminant mammals of genus *Bos.* In particular domestic cattle, *Bos taurus,* used for dairy products, meat, hides. Milk breeds incl. Ayrshire (brown and white), Friesian and Holstein (black and white),

Guernsey (fawn and white), Jersey. Meat producers incl. Aberdeen Angus (black), Hereford (red with white face). Normandy and shorthorn are dual purpose.

Catullus, Gaius Valerius (c 84–c 54 BC), Roman poet. Describes unhappy love for 'Lesbia' in superb lyrics. Other poems incl. satires, epigrams. Personal approach, intense feeling and colloquial style make him major influence on European literature.

Caucasus, mountain system of SW USSR, between Black and Caspian seas. Its peaks incl. Mt. Elbrus. Separates N Caucasia from Transcaucasia.

cauliflower, variety of cabbage, *Brassica oleracea botrytis.* Has a dense white mass of fleshy flower stalks which form edible head. Introduced from Cyprus in 16th cent., now grown extensively as commercial or garden crop.

Cavafy, Constantinos (1863–1933), Greek poet, b. Egypt. Works incl. ironic narrative poems on Greek past, homosexual love lyrics, collected in *The Complete Poems of Cavafy* (pub. 1961).

Cavalcanti, Guido (c 1255–1300), Italian poet. Friend of Dante, wrote *canzoni,* ballads and sonnets, all on theme of love, notably in *Canzone d'amore.*

Cavaliers, in English Civil War (1642–8), supporters of Charles I in his struggle with Parliament's forces (Roundheads).

Cavalli, Pietro Francesco (1602–76), Italian composer. Active in the early development of opera. He composed over 40 operas, in which song achieved greater importance.

cavalry, mounted soldiers, important from classical times down to the 18th cent. because of their speed and mobility. Declined during the 19th cent. but were still used for reconnaissance and skirmishing in the early part of WWI. Now all UK cavalry regiments are armoured units except for the Household Cavalry, retained for ceremonial purposes.

Cavan, county of Ulster prov., NC Irish Republic. Area 1891 sq km (730 sq mi); pop. 53,000. Hilly moorland, largely infertile; many lakes. Some agric., livestock; distilling. Co. town Cavan, pop. 3000. Ruined abbey; modern RC cathedral.

cave, natural chamber or cavity in Earth's crust. Sea-caves formed by wave action or by abrasion due to pebbles, boulders, *etc* being hurled against cliff. Inland caves usually found in limestone areas, formed by running water dissolving rock.

Cavell, Edith (1865–1915), English nurse. Matron of nurses' training institute in Brussels. Shot by the Germans for helping Allied soldiers to escape over Dutch frontier in WWI.

Cavendish, Henry (1731–1810), English scientist, b. France. Investigated properties of hydrogen ('inflammable air') and carbon dioxide. Researched into composition of water and air. Measured density of Earth.

Cavendish, Thomas (c 1555–92), English navigator. Commanded 3rd circumnavigation of globe (1586–8), destroying Spanish shipping and settlements on W coast of South America. Died attempting similar voyage.

cave paintings, see ALTAMIRA; LASCAUX.

caviare, salted eggs of sturgeon prepared, mainly in USSR and Iran, as a table delicacy. Black Sea and Caspian are major areas for catching the sturgeon.

Cavour, Camillo Benso, Conte di (1810-61), Italian statesman. Premier of Sardinia (1852-9, 1860-1), secured French alliance which brought Sardinia's union with Lombardy after war with Austria (1859). Sponsored Garibaldi's campaign leading to unification (*Risorgimento*) of Italy under VICTOR EMMANUEL II.

Cawnpore, see KANPUR.

Caxton, William (c 1422-91), first English printer. Learned printing trade in Cologne and then printed in Bruges (1475) his own translation of *Recuyell of the Historyes of Troye,* 1st book pub. in English. Returned to England to set up press in Westminster, where he printed 1st dated book in England, *Dictes or Sayengis of the Philosophes* (1477).

Cayenne, cap. of French Guiana, Atlantic port on isl. at mouth of Cayenne R. Pop. 20,000. Original source of Cayenne pepper. Exports rum, gold. Had penal settlement 1854-1938.

cayenne, very hot red pepper made from dried pods of several species of *Capsicum,* native to South America.

Cayman Islands, coral group of West Indies, NW of Jamaica. Area 260 sq km (100 sq mi); pop. 11,000; cap. Georgetown. Comprise Grand Cayman, Little Cayman, Cayman Brac. Famous for turtles; turtle products, shark skin exports.

Admin. by Jamaica until 1962; British colony.

CBI, see CONFEDERATION OF BRITISH INDUSTRY.

Ceauşescu, Nicolae (1918-), Romanian political leader, president (1974-). Succeeded Gheorghiu-Dej as Communist Party general secretary (1965), continued policy of independence within Soviet bloc.

Cebu, isl. of Philippines. Area c 4400 sq km (1700 sq mi). Grows corn, sugar cane, peanuts; coal and copper mined. Cebu is chief town and port; pop. 385,000. Cap. of Spanish colony (1565-71). Has cross erected by Magellan (1521).

Cecil, Lord [Edward Christian] David [Gascoyne] (1902-), English literary critic and biographer. Works incl. biog. of Cowper *The Stricken Deer* (1929), *Early Victorian Novelists* (1934), *The Young Melbourne* (1939).

Cecil, Robert, see SALISBURY, ROBERT CECIL, 1ST EARL OF.

Cecil, William, see BURGHLEY, WILLIAM CECIL, 1ST BARON.

cedar, coniferous tree of genus *Cedrus* of pine family, with short needle leaves arranged in close spiral on spine-like branches. Has durable wood with characteristic fragrance. Species incl. notable cedar of Lebanon, *C. libani.*

celandine, name of 2 unrelated plants. Lesser celandine, *Ranunculus ficaria,* of buttercup family is small herb with heart-shaped leaves and yellow flowers. Greater celandine, *Chelidonium majus,* of poppy family is erect, branched herb with divided leaves and yellow flowers.

Celebes or **Sulawesi,** isl. of

Indonesia. Area *c* 186,000 sq km (72,000 sq mi); pop. *c* 9,000,000. Irregular shape comprises 4 penins; largely mountainous with forests. Exports coffee, timber, copra, spices. Under Dutch control to 1670.

celery, *Apium graveolens,* biennial plant of parsley family, native to Europe and America. Blanched stem used in salads and as vegetable, dried leaves as flavouring.

celesta, orchestral keyboard instrument invented (1886) by Auguste Mustel in Paris. Hammers strike steel bars attached to wooden resonators.

cell, fundamental unit of living matter. Consists of mass of protoplasm bounded by a membrane and, in case of plants, additional rigid cell wall. Usually contains central NUCLEUS surrounded by cytoplasm, in which enzyme systems which control cell's metabolism are situated. Plant cells also contain chloroplasts in which photosynthesis takes place. Cells reproduce themselves by various methods of division. *See* MEIOSIS *and* MITOSIS.

cell, voltaic, device for producing electric current by chemical action. Two main types: primary cell and secondary cell or ACCUMULATOR. Primary cell usually irreversible in action. Variety of Leclanché cell, in which electrodes are carbon and zinc and electrolyte is ammonium chloride, used in common dry cell.

Cellini, Benvenuto (1500-71), Florentine sculptor, goldsmith. Famous works incl. gold salt-cellar and bronze statue *Perseus*. Best known for *Autobiography* giving vivid picture of artistic life in Rome and Florence.

cello or **violoncello,** low-pitched member of violin family. Developed in 17th cent., it gradually replaced bass viol as bass line in orchestras and chamber groups, and as solo instrument.

cellulose, chief constituent of cell walls or fibres of all plant tissue. White polymeric carbohydrate, insoluble in water. Nearly pure in the fibre of cotton, linen, hemp. Basis of nitrocellulose, celluloid, collodion and guncotton. Used in manufacture of rayon, plastics, explosives.

Celsius, Anders (1701-44), Swedish inventor, astronomer. Devised (1742) Celsius or centigrade temperature scale. Took boiling point of water as 0° and freezing point as 100°; order later reversed.

Celtic, branch of Indo-European language family. Spoken throughout Europe before Roman conquest, now exists as 2 subgroups: Brythonic (Breton, Welsh, and extinct Cornish); Goidelic or Gaelic (Irish Gaelic, Scottish Gaelic and extinct Manx). Continental, 3rd subgroup, now extinct.

Celtic Sea, area of NE Atlantic between SE coast of Ireland, Pembrokeshire coast, Cornwall, W coast of Brittany.

Celts, ancient people who inhabited W and C Europe. Associated with La Tène culture (beginning in 5th cent. BC), which saw development of iron working and characteristic linear art. Invaded N Italy in early 4th cent. BC and later reached Greece and Asia Minor. Romans gained control of their territs. in Italy by 222 BC and most of their territ. in France and Belgium during Gallic Wars (58-51 BC).

cement, material which bonds together 2 surfaces. Portland cement made by mixing powdered limestone and clay and heating product; mixed with water and sand to make mortar, or with sand, gravel and water to make concrete.

Cenozoic or **Cainozoic era,** fourth and most recent geological era, incl. time from end of Mesozoic era to present day. Began c 65 million years ago. Comprises Tertiary and Quaternary periods. Alpine, Himalayan mountain building; extensive glaciation; formation of deserts. Typified by evolution of modern flora and fauna; dominance of mammals, emergence of *Homo sapiens.* Also see GEOLOGICAL TABLE.

censorship, system in which circulation of writings, presentation of plays, films, TV programmes, works of art, *etc,* may in whole or part be prohibited. In UK, films are voluntarily submitted to British Board of Film Censors, sale of publications may be banned under Obscene Publications Act (1857); in US, there is film censorship in some states. Censorship is feature of totalitarian states.

census, official, usually periodic, count of population and recording of economic status, age, sex, *etc.* Estab. in ancient times amongst Jews, Romans for tax purposes. Census of England and Scotland first took place in 1801, has been done every 10 years since. In US, federal census began 1790, Bureau of Census estab. 1902.

centaur, in Greek myth, one of race of beings with upper body of human, lower of horse. Represented as tending to riotous living and wine, as in fight with Lapiths. See CHIRON.

centigrade temperature, see TEMPERATURE.

centipede, any carnivorous many-legged arthropod of class Chilopoda. Flat segmented body with poison claws on first segment; c 35 pairs of legs. Widely distributed; largest species c 30 cm/12 in. long.

CENTO, see CENTRAL TREATY ORGANIZATION.

Central, region of C Scotland. Area 2621 sq km (1012 sq mi); pop. 263,000. Created 1975, incl. former Stirlingshire, Clackmannanshire, SW Perthshire.

Central African Republic, republic of C Africa. Area 623,000 sq km (241,000 sq mi); pop. 2,370,000; cap. Bangui. Languages: Sangho, French. Religions: native, Christian. Largely savannah-covered plateau, tropical forest in S; drained by Ubangi, Shari rivers. Cotton, coffee growing; diamond, uranium mining. Formerly Ubangi-Shari territ. of French Equatorial Africa, independent from 1960. Member of French Community. Known as Central African Empire (1976-9).

Central America, isthmus connecting North and South America, comprising Guatemala, Costa Rica, Nicaragua, Honduras, Belize, El Salvador, Panama, and some Mexican states. Area 584,000 sq km (c 230,000 sq mi). Has many volcanic mountains, coastal plains; tropical climate. Subject to earthquakes. Bananas, coffee, cotton produce. Panama Canal links Caribbean, Pacific. Had ancient Maya civilizations. Region comprised

Central American Federation (1825-38).

Central American Common Market (CACM), body estab. (1960) by treaty to facilitate trade between members. Members originally Honduras, Nicaragua, Guatemala, Salvador, later joined by Costa Rica. Honduras withdrew after 1969.

Central Committee of the Communist Party, in USSR, executive, possessing real power over Supreme Soviet legislative structure. Its members elected from Party Congress, who, in turn, elect Politburo and Secretariat. Central Committee role reduced during Stalinist era.

Central Intelligence Agency (CIA), independent executive bureau of govt. of US estab. by National Security Act (1947) as centre for all foreign intelligence operations. Allen Dulles, director (1953-61), strengthened CIA and emboldened tactics. Scandal broke (1974) with discovery that CIA had been massively involved in illegal domestic espionage. Senate Intelligence Committee found (1975) CIA, from 1950s, had policy to assassinate foreign leaders, also attempted to block Allende's accession to power in Chile.

Central Treaty Organization (CENTO), defensive military alliance, formed 1955 by Iraq (withdrew 1958), Iran, Turkey, Pakistan and UK on basis of Baghdad Pact; US interests represented. Also provides for social and economic cooperation. Known as Middle East Treaty Organization until 1959.

centre of gravity, in physics, point on body where its weight can be considered as concentrated. Centre of mass defined similarly. These correspond in constant gravitational field.

centrifugation, means of separating solid, whose particles are too fine to be filtered, from a liquid. Liquid spun at high velocity so that centrifugal force moves denser material, eg suspended solids, to sides of tube containing liquid. Ultracentrifuge, working at greater speeds, used to determine particle size and molecular weights in polymers.

Cephalonia (*Kefallinia*), isl. of Greece, largest of Ionian Isls. Area 925 sq km (357 sq mi); main town Argostolion. Mountainous; fruit, wine. Disastrous earthquake 1953.

Cephalopoda (*cephalopods*), class of molluscs, incl. squid, octopus, cuttlefish, with prehensile tentacles around mouth. Usually no shell (*see* ARGONAUT). Numerous fossil species.

Ceram, isl. of Indonesia, in S Moluccas. Area *c* 17,000 sq km (6600 sq mi). Mountainous with dense forests in interior; produces copra, sago.

ceramics, art and science of making POTTERY.

Cerberus, in Greek myth, three-headed dog which guarded passage to and from the underworld (Hades). Dead were buried with honey cake to appease him on their journey. Last labour of Heracles was to capture him.

cereal, variety of annuals of grass family cultivated for edible fruit, known as grain. Cereal crops cover *c* ½ world's arable land, chief in order of acreage being wheat, rice, millet, sorghum, maize, barley, oats, rye. Some cereals fermented to make alcohol.

Ceres, Roman fertility goddess of the earth and growing corn, identified with Greek goddess DEMETER. Her temple on the Aventine Hill was centre of a plebeian cult.

cerium (Ce), soft metallic element of lanthanide group; at. no. 58, at. wt. 140.12. Alloyed with iron, used in lighter flints. Compounds used to make gas mantles.

Cervantes [Saavedra], Miguel de (1547-1616), Spanish novelist. Known for satire of chivalric romance, *Don Quixote* (1605-15), influential in development of novel. Also wrote pastoral romances, eg *Novelas ejemplares* (1613), many plays.

cervix, *see* UTERUS.

Ceske Budejovice (Ger. *Budweis*), town of SW Czechoslovakia, on R. Moldau. Pop. 78,000. Beer mfg.; timber, graphite industs. Noted for Baroque architecture.

Cestoda (cestodes), class of ribbon-like flatworms without gut or mouth. Body divided into numerous segments. Parasitic in intestinal canals of vertebrates. Species incl. TAPEWORM.

Cetacea (cetaceans), order of aquatic fish-like mammals. No hind limbs; front limbs modified into flippers. Divided into toothed whales, eg dolphin, porpoise, sperm whale, and toothless whales, eg blue whale.

Cetewayo or **Ketchwayo** (c 1836-84), Zulu chieftain. Led determined resistance to British advances into his territ. until defeated (1879) at Ulundi.

Ceuta, Spanish enclave in NW Morocco. Area 18 sq km (7 sq mi); pop. 88,000. Free port and military post. Spanish from 1580, now part of Cádiz prov.

Cévennes, mountain range of S France, SE of Massif Central. Runs SW-NE for c 240 km (150 mi), highest peak Mont Mézenc (1754 m/ 5755 ft). Source of many rivers, incl. Loire, Allier, Lot. Largely barren limestone. Sheep rearing.

Ceylon, SEE SRI LANKA.

Cézanne, Paul (1839-1906), French painter. Encouraged by Pissarro, he abandoned a violent romantic style for impressionist landscape technique. Later work was distinguished from impressionism by emphasis on structural analysis and use of tone and colour to express form. His attempts to reduce forms to their geometric equivalents influenced cubism. Works incl. sequence of bathers, portraits, still life.

c.g.s. system of units, system of physical units based on centimetre, gram and second. Superseded by SI units for scientific works.

Chabrier, [Alexis] Emmanuel (1841-94), French composer. Best-known work is the rhapsody *España*, written after a visit to Spain in 1882. His opera *Le Roi malgré lui* is still performed.

Chabrol, Claude (1930-), French film director, critic. Credited with starting *nouvelle vague* cinema technique. Early films incl. *Le Beau Serge* (1958), later ones, often centred around murder, incl. *The Beast Must Die* (1969), *The Butcher* (1970).

Chaco or **Gran Chaco**, large lowland plain of C South America, stretching from S Bolivia through Paraguay to N Argentina. Sparse pop.; unexploited resources. Bolivia and Paraguay warred for regional control (1932-5).

Chad, republic of NC Africa. Area 1,284,000 sq km (495,000 sq mi); pop. 4,116,000; cap. Ndjamena. Official language: French. Religions: native, Christian, Islam. Savannah in S; desert, Tibesti Mts. in N. Main river Shari, flows into L. Chad in SW. Cotton, peanut growing in S; nomadic pastoralism in N. Crossed by trans-Saharan caravan routes. Former territ. of French Equatorial Africa, independent from 1960. Member of French Community.

Chad, Lake, lake of NC Africa. Mainly in SW Chad, partly in NE Nigeria, SE Niger, NW Cameroon. Area varies with season, up to c 26,000 sq km (10,000 sq mi); fed by R. Shari, no outlets. Now much smaller than when discovered (1823).

Chadwick, Sir James (1891-1974), English physicist. Discovered neutron during bombardment of beryllium by alpha particles (1932); awarded Nobel Prize for Physics (1935).

Chadwick, Lynn (1914-), English sculptor. Began sculpting career with mobiles. Later produced 'balanced sculpture' consisting of figures with thin legs, bulky bodies and bird-like heads.

Chaeronea, ancient town of Boeotia, EC Greece. Athens and Thebes defeated here (338 BC) by Philip II of Macedon; Mithradates VI defeated (86 BC) by Sulla. Birthplace of Plutarch.

chaffinch, *Fringilla coelebs*, finch common in European woodlands. Male has pinkish breast, white bars on brown wings.

Chagall, Marc (1889-), Russian painter. His imaginative, richly coloured art is based on reminiscences of Russian-Jewish village life; has designed stained glass and murals. Fantasies influenced surrealists. Lived mainly in France from 1910.

Chagos Archipelago, isl. group in C Indian Ocean, NE of Mauritius; part of British Indian Ocean Territ. Exports copra.

Chain, Sir Ernst Boris (1906-), British biochemist, b. Germany. Shared Nobel Prize for Physiology and Medicine (1945) with Fleming and Florey for initiating work on penicillin.

chain reaction, in physics, self-sustaining nuclear reaction of FISSION type. Occurs when neutrons emitted from uranium 235 cause fission of further uranium nuclei. Basis of atomic bomb and nuclear reactors.

chalcedony, variety of silica, consisting mainly of extremely fine crystals. Occurs in many different forms, some semi-precious, eg agate, bloodstone, chrysoprase, onyx.

Chalcidice (*Khalkidiki*), penin. of NE Greece, on Aegean Sea; modern admin. dist., cap. Polygyros. Incl. ATHOS. Wheat, olives, wine; magnesite mining. Colonized 7th cent. BC from Chalcis (below name).

Chalcis (*Khalkis*), town of E Greece, cap. of Euboea admin. dist. Pop.

24,000. Port, agric. trade. Active colonizer (*eg* Chalcidice, Sicily) from 8th cent. BC. Called Negropont in Middle Ages.

Chaldaeans, Semitic people who inhabited S Babylonia from *c* 1000 BC. Empire flourished under Nebuchadnezzar II but fell to Cyrus the Great (539 BC). Astrology reached high development in this period, hence term used loosely to denote astrologers.

Chaliapin, Feodor Ivanovich (1873-1938), Russian bass singer. Famous as Boris Godunov in Mussorgsky's opera. Also known for his recitals, at which he popularized the famous Russian folk song 'Song of the Volga Boatmen'.

chalk, soft, fine-grained limestone, white in colour. Consists mainly of calcareous skeletal material, laid down in Cretaceous period. Used to make putty, plaster, quicklime, cement.

Challoner, Richard (1691-1781), English RC churchman. Revised Douay Bible, his version becoming standard for English-speaking Catholics. Attacks by Protestant opponents culminated in flight from London during Gordon riots (1780).

Chalmers, Thomas (1780-1847), Scottish theologian. Leader of seceding Church of Scotland ministers who broke (1843) to form Free Church.

Chalon-sur-Saône, town of Burgundy, EC France, on R. Saône and Canal du Centre. Pop. 53,000. River port, wine and grain trade. Cap. of kingdom of Burgundy in 6th cent.

Chamberlain, Houston Stewart (1855-1927), Anglo-German writer, b. England. Known for *Foundations of the Nineteenth Century* (1899), forming doctrine of Teutonic superiority and anti-Semitism. Son-in-law of Richard Wagner.

Chamberlain, Joseph (1836-1914), British politician. Reform mayor of Birmingham (1873-6). Resigned (1886) from Gladstone's cabinet over Irish Home Rule policy, leading Liberal Unionist revolt. Colonial secretary (1893-1903), his imperial expansionist policies helped precipitate Boer War. Championed imperial preference tariffs, resigned 1903; this split coalition with Conservatives, leading to 1906 election defeat. His son, Sir [Joseph] Austen Chamberlain (1863-1937), was Conservative chancellor of exchequer (1903-6, 1919-21). Helped negotiate Irish settlement (1921). Foreign secretary (1924-9), instrumental in signing of LOCARNO PACT (1925) guaranteeing German borders; awarded Nobel Peace Prize (1925). His half-brother, [Arthur] Neville Chamberlain (1869-1940), was PM (1937-40). Chancellor of exchequer before succeeding Baldwin at head of National govt. Used 'appeasement' policy in attempting to limit Hitler in E Europe, signing MUNICH PACT (1938) over Czechoslovakia. Led Britain into WWII, resigning (1940) after German invasion of Norway.

chamber music, music for performance by a small number of singers or players, *eg* a string quartet. Originally intended for performance in a private house but now mainly to be heard in smaller concert halls.

Chambers, Sir William (1723-96), British architect. Leading official architect of his day, his works incl.

Somerset House, London (1776-86), and the pagoda in Kew Gardens.

Chambéry, town of SE France, cap. of Savoie dept. Pop. 54,000. Tourist centre; vermouth, silk mfg. Hist. cap. of Savoy. Cathedral (14th cent.).

chameleon, any of Chamaeleontidae family of lizard-like Old World reptiles. Long prehensile tail, eyes capable of independent movement. Extends tongue to catch insects. Undergoes colour change to match surroundings.

chamois, *Rupicapra rupicapra,* ruminant mammal intermediate between antelope and goat. Agile jumper, found in mountains of Europe and SW Asia. Name also applied to leather of animal.

chamomile, *see* CAMOMILE.

Chamonix, town of Savoy, E France, in Chamonix valley. Pop. 8000. Alpine resort, base for ascent of mountains in Mont Blanc region.

Champagne, region and former prov. of NE France, cap. Troyes. Divided into 3 by parallel ridges; dairying in E, sheep rearing in C, champagne in W (esp. around Rheims, Epernay). Main rivers Aisne, Marne, Seine. Powerful medieval county, scene of famous trade fairs, *eg* Provins, Troyes. Incorporated into France (1314). Battleground in many wars.

champagne, sparkling white wine produced around Rheims and Epernay in Champagne district of France. Sparkling quality is obtained by adding cane sugar to wine which has been bottled following initial fermentation; this induces a secondary fermentation in the bottle.

Champlain, Samuel de (1567-1635), French explorer. Made several voyages to E Canada and NE US; sailed up St Lawrence R. (1603), founded Port Royal (1605) and led 1st colonists to Québec (1608). Initiated fur trade; laid basis for French claims in North America.

Champlain, Lake, on New York-Vermont border, NE US; extends into S Québec (Canada). Length 201 km (125 mi). Fishing resort. Strategic region in Seven Years War, American Revolution (Fort Ticonderoga). Named after French explorer.

Champollion, Jean François (1790-1832), French archaeologist. Regarded as founder of science of Egyptology, deciphered Egyptian hieroglyphics (1822) with aid of ROSETTA STONE.

chancel, part of E end of church around altar, reserved for clergy and choir. Often separated by railings or screen from main body of church.

Chancellorsville, E Virginia, US. Site of Confederate General Lee's last great victory of American Civil War (1863) which led to his invasion of North in Gettysburg Campaign.

Chandigarh, joint cap. of Punjab and Haryana states, N India. Pop. 233,000. Built in 1950s to designs by Le Corbusier.

Chandler, Raymond Thornton (1888-1959), American detective story writer. Created cynical private detective, Philip Marlowe. Crime novels incl. *The Big Sleep* (1939), *Farewell, My Lovely* (1940).

Chanel, Gabrielle ('Coco') (1883-1971), French fashion designer. Founded fashion house in Paris (1914), dominating fashion world by 1924. Noted for successful scent

(Chanel No. 5) and design of comfortable clothes.

Chaney, Lon (1883-1930), American film actor. Known for macabre disguises in horror films, eg *The Hunchback of Notre Dame* (1923), *The Phantom of the Opera* (1925), *The Unholy Three* (1930).

Changchun, cap. of Kirkin prov., NE China. Pop. 1,500,000. Railway jct.; major motor vehicle production centre, esp. trucks, tractors; film studios. Cap. of Manchukuo under Japanese (1934-45).

Changkiakow (*Kalgan*), city of Hopeh prov., N China. Pop. 1,000,000. Trade centre, food processing. Military centre in Manchu dynasty, on caravan route between Peking and Ulan Bator.

Channel Islands (Fr. *Iles Normandes*), UK isl. group in S English Channel. Area 194 sq km (75 sq mi); pop. 126,000. Main isls. Jersey, Guernsey, Alderney, Sark; main town St Helier (Jersey). Separate laws, taxes; languages incl. English, French, Norman dialects. Market gardening, dairying, tourism. Isls. English from Norman Conquest (1066). German occupation (1940-5).

Channel swimming, sport of swimming across English Channel, first accomplished by M. WEBB (1875). First to make two-way crossing was Argentinian Antonio Abertondo (1961).

chansons de geste, medieval French epic poems (late 11th-early 14th cent.). More than 80 survive of which most important are in cycle *Geste du Roi*, on Charlemagne and vassals. Best known and oldest is *Chanson de Roland* (c 1098-1100). *See* ROLAND.

chant, a vocal melody usually sung as part of a ritual, often religious and often unaccompanied. The melody is usually sung in unison. PLAINSONG is a medieval religious chant from which Western art music grew.

Chantilly, town of Picardy, N France. Pop. 10,000. Horse racing centre; popular Parisian resort near Forest of Chantilly. Former lace mfg. centre. Hist. château.

Chaos, in Greek myth, disordered void from which sprang GAEA, mother of all things earthly and divine.

Chapala, Lake, WC Mexico. Length 80 km (c 50 mi). On C plateau; largest lake in Mexico. Important tourism in surrounding area and isls. Waters are rapidly receding.

Chaplin, Sir Charles Spencer ('Charlie') (1889-1977), British film actor, producer, director. Famous for creation of tramp-like clown figure, with baggy pants, toothbrush moustache, distinctive walk. Worked first with Mack Sennett's Keystone Cops, later appeared in full-length features, eg *The Gold Rush* (1924).

Chapman, George (c 1560-1634), English poet, dramatist, translator. Best known for sophisticated verse translation *The Whole Works of Homer* (1616) which inspired Keats's sonnet. Also wrote philosophical tragedies, eg *Bussy d'Ambois* (1604), comedies.

char, food fish of salmon family, genus *Salvelinus*, inhabiting deep cold lakes. Arctic char, *S. alpinus*, is European variety, found in Norway. Also incl. brook trout of North America.

charcoal, *see* CARBON.

Charcot, Jean Martin (1825-93), French neurologist. Estab. major neurological clinic in Paris. Studied treatment of hysteria by hypnosis and influenced Freud, his pupil, in his early thinking on subject.

Chardin, Jean Baptiste Siméon (1699-1779), French painter. Noted for his still lifes and genre scenes of simple domestic interiors, devoid of sentimentality. Developed exceptional use of light and colour. Works incl. 2 self-portraits in pastel.

Charente, river of WC France. Flows c 355 km (220 mi) from Haute-Vienne dept. via Angoulême to Bay of Biscay opposite Oléron Isl. Region of cattle raising, cognac production.

charge, electric, fundamental attribute of elementary particles of matter. By convention, electron carries 1 negative unit of electric charge, proton 1 positive unit; matter containing excess of electrons is negatively charged, etc. Like charges repel each other, unlike charges attract each other. Measured in coulombs.

Chari, see SHARI.

chariot, earliest form of horse-drawn vehicle, with 2 wheels and waist-high guard at front of car. Originated in Mesopotamia c 3000-2000 BC; widely used in ancient world for war, passenger-carrying and races.

Charites or **Graces**, in Greek myth, three sister goddesses, daughters of Zeus. Personification of charm and beauty in human life and nature. They are Aglaea (Brilliance), Euphrosyne (Joy), Thalia (Bloom).

Charlemagne or **Charles I** (742-814), king of the Franks (771-814), emperor of the West Romans (800-14). Son of Pepin the Short. Sole ruler of Franks on death of brother Carloman (771). In support of pope, defeated Lombards and became their king (774). Led campaign aginst Moors of NE Spain (778); subjugated Saxons (772-804), forced their conversion to Christianity. Crowned emperor by Leo III, whose papal ambitions he had supported; created strong empire by estab. marches, efficient admin. His court at Aachen (Fr. *Aix-la-Chapelle*) became centre of learning, classical studies; famous scholars incl. Alcuin, Einhard. Life became centre of medieval cycle of romance and legend, notably in the *Chanson de Roland* (prob. written 11th cent.).

Charleroi, town of S Belgium, on R. Sambre. Pop. 24,000. Coalmining, steel mfg. Canal link with Brussels.

Charles [II] the Bald (823-77), king of West Franks (843-77), Holy Roman emperor (875-7). With brother, Louis the German, defeated Lothair I at Fontenoy (841); became West Frankish king by Treaty of Verdun (843). Succeeded Louis II as emperor (875).

Charles [III] the Fat (839-888), king of West Franks (884-7), Holy Roman emperor (881-7). Son of Louis the German; also king of Italy from 879. Deposed 886 by Arnulf following weakness in fighting Norse invaders.

Charles IV or **Charles of Luxembourg** (1316-78), king of Bohemia (1346-78), king of Germany (1347-78), Holy Roman emperor (1355-78). Son of John of Luxembourg. Founded univ. at Prague (1348); issued Golden Bull (1356) on matter of imperial elections.

Charles V (1500-58), Holy Roman emperor (1519-58), king of Spain as Charles I (1516-56). Son of Philip I of Castile, became greatest Habsburg and most powerful ruler in Europe. Wars against France during 1520s ended in consolidation of influence over papacy. Promoted Catholic reform with Council of Trent (1545). Enlarged Spanish empire in Americas, conquering Mexico and Peru. After 1530, increasingly delegated powers in Germany to his brother, later Ferdinand I. Fierce opponent of Protestantism, broke power of Reformation princes in Germany (1547), but later signed Peace of Augsburg (1555) allowing choice of religion to be made by individual princes. Retired to monastery (1556).

Charles VI (1685-1740), Holy Roman emperor (1711-40), king of Hungary as Charles III. Unsuccessfully claimed Spanish throne, instigating war (1701-14). Had no male heir, circumvented succession problem by issuing PRAGMATIC SANCTION, passing Habsburg lands on to his daughter, Maria Theresa.

Charles VII (1697-1745), Holy Roman emperor (1742-5). Elector of Bavaria as Charles Albert (1726-45). Disputed succession (1740) under PRAGMATIC SANCTION; joined alliance against Maria Theresa, elected to throne (1742), losing his own Bavarian territ.

Charles (1887-1922), emperor of Austria (1916-18), also king of Hungary (as Charles IV). Succeeded great uncle Francis Joseph; deposed after unsuccessful attempt to make separate peace with Allies in WWI. Twice failed in coups to regain Hungary. Died in exile.

Charles I (1600-49), king of England, Scotland and Ireland (1625-49). Succeeding father James I, offended public by Catholic marriage. Struggle with Puritan-dominated Parliament led to Petition of Right (1628) asserting Parliament's supremacy. Charles ruled repressively without Parliament (1629-40) until Scottish wars forced him to recall. Long Parliament of 1640 had STRAFFORD beheaded and ended arbitrary taxation and Star Chamber courts. Defeated in ensuing CIVIL WAR (1642-6), captured 1646. Tried by Puritan-controlled court, convicted of treason and beheaded.

Charles II (1630-85), king of England, Scotland and Ireland (1660-85). Fled to France (1646), crowned king in Scotland (1651) after father Charles I's death; escaped again when defeated by Cromwell. Restored as king (1660), aided ' by CLARENDON, his chief minister. CABAL ministry replaced Clarendon in 1667. Charles entered 2 Dutch wars to assert commercial supremacy. Secretly allied with France (1670), promising to restore Catholicism. Forced to approve TEST ACT (1673), directed against Catholics; later blocked Exclusion Act (1681) against his brother James by dissolving Parliament, after which he ruled absolutely. No legitimate heirs, succeeded by brother. Important features of reign incl. development of political parties, advances in trade and sea power, territ. expansion and growth of Parliament's power.

Charles [V] the Wise (1337-80), king of France (1364-80). Served as regent during father John II's captivity, suppressing Jacquerie (peasant uprising). Reformed taxation, strengthened army and navy; his general, du Guesclin, warred successfully against Navarre, English forces in France.

Charles [VI] the Well Beloved (1368-1422), king of France (1380-1422). Under power of regent until 1388; insane after 1392. Rival factions fought for power, leading to civil war between houses of Orléans (Armagnacs) and Burgundy. Invasion and victory of Henry V of England at Agincourt (1415) led to Treaty of Troyes (1420) recognizing Henry as Charles's successor.

Charles VII (1403-61), king of France (1422-61). Excluded from succession by father Charles VI, ruled from Bourges until Joan of Arc raised siege of Orléans and had him crowned at Rheims (1429). During reign, English expelled from all France except Calais, ending Hundred Years War.

Charles X (1757-1836), king of France (1824-30). Led ultra-royalist group before following his brother, Louis XVIII, to throne. Abdicated after liberal-inspired July Revolution. Died in exile.

Charles II (1661-1700), king of Spain (1665-1700). Last of Spanish Habsburgs, constantly at war with Louis XIV. Died childless, precipitating WAR OF THE SPANISH SUCCESSION.

Charles III (1716-88), king of Spain (1759-88). King of Naples and Sicily after 1735, succeeded Ferdinand VI on Spanish throne. Brought Spain into SEVEN YEARS WAR and American Revolution against British (1779).

Charles IV (1748-1819), king of Spain (1788-1808). Reign dominated by chief minister, Godoy, who favoured involvement in French Revolutionary Wars; Spain withdrew 1795. Alliance with France (1796) led to disastrous Peninsular War (1807). Forced to abdicate in favour of his son, Ferdinand, after which both were held captive by Napoleon until 1814.

Charles [Gustavus] X (1622-60), king of Sweden (1654-60). Invaded Poland (1655), captured Warsaw and Kraków; forced to withdraw after unsuccessful siege of Czestochowa. Wars with Denmark (1658-60) resulted in territ. expansion into Danish lands in Sweden.

Charles XII (1682-1718), king of Sweden (1697-1718). Challenged by alliance of Denmark, Poland and Russia, routed Danes and defeated Peter the Great at Narva (1700), crushed Poland. Campaign in Russia (1708-9) ended in defeat at Poltava; fled to Turkey, failed to gain continued support from Ahmed III after Russo-Turkish peace (1711). Invaded Norway (1716), killed during siege of Fredrikssten. Despite strategic flair, failed to consolidate successes and Sweden entered decline as major power.

Charles XIV (1763-1844), king of Sweden and Norway (1818-44). Born in France as Jean Baptiste Jules Bernadotte, became one of Napoleon's marshals. Adopted (1810) as heir to Swedish throne by Charles XIII, for whom he ruled. Joined alliance against Napoleon; secured union of Sweden and Norway (1814) before ascending throne. Economic progress during his reign; lost popular support through anti-liberal policy.

Charles [Philip Arthur George], Prince of Wales (1948-), heir to British throne. Son of Elizabeth II and Prince Philip.

Charles, Jacques Alexandre César (1746-1823), French physicist. Evolved Charles' law: at constant pressure volume of gas is directly proportional to its absolute temperature. Made 1st successful ascent in hydrogen balloon.

Charles Albert (1798-1849), king of Sardinia (1831-49). Avoided revolution by granting constitution (1848). Warred with Austria in Italy; defeated at Novara, abdicated in favour of his son, Victor Emmanuel II.

Charles Martel (*c* 688-741), Frankish ruler. Grandfather of Charlemagne. United Merovingian kingdoms of Austrasia, Neustria under his rule. Thwarted Moslem invasion of Europe with victory at Poitiers (732).

Charles the Bold (1433-77), last duke of Burgundy (1467-77). Son of Philip the Good, father of Mary of Burgundy. Confirmed opponent of Louis XI of France. Aimed to restore Lotharingian kingdom; killed while fighting Swiss after he had annexed Lorraine.

Charleston, port of S South Carolina, US; on Atlantic inlet. Pop. 67,000. Naval depot; timber, fruit, cotton exports. Settled by English (1670). Civil War opened with Confederates firing on Fort Sumter (1861); besieged by Union forces (1863-5). Has famous botanical gardens.

Charleston, cap. of West Virginia,

US; on Kanawha R. Pop. 230,000. Rail, trade and indust. centre. Oil refining; chemical, glass mfg. Expanded around Fort Lee; became permanent state cap. 1885. Home of Daniel Boone.

charlock, *Brassica arvénis*, plant of mustard family with yellow flowers, seedpods. Pernicious weed in Britain. Seeds can lie dormant for *c* 50 years.

Charlotte, city of SC North Carolina, US; in Piedmont region. Pop. 241,000; state's largest city. Transport jct.; cotton, textiles, chemical mfg.

Charlottetown, seaport of Canada; cap. of Prince Edward Isl., on S coast. Pop. 19,000. Exports dairy produce, potatoes. Settled 1768; scene of Canadian confederate conference (1864). Has RC St Dunstan's Univ. (1855).

Charlton, Robert ('Bobby') (1937-), English footballer. Outstanding forward for Manchester United and England; played 106 times for England (1958-70). Renowned for sportsmanship.

charm, in nuclear physics, supposed fundamental attribute of elementary particles, manifested by non-zero charm quantum number. First predicted theoretically, its status was enhanced by discovery (1974) of the psi (J) particle, believed to be composed of a new type of charmed QUARK and corresponding antiquark.

Charon, in Greek myth, boatman of R. Styx who ferried souls of the dead to underworld (Hades). A coin was placed in the mouth of the dead to pay for this service.

Charpentier, Gustave (1860-

1956), French composer. Best known for orchestral piece *Impressions of Italy* and opera *Louise*.

Chartism, movement in Britain for social and political reform, estab. 1838. Roots lay in decline in working class conditions during economic depression of 1830s. Principles contained in 'People's Charter', submitted to Parliament: universal manhood suffrage, equal election dists., vote by ballot, annual parliaments, abolition of property qualification for MPs, payment of MPs. Petition's rejection followed by riots; movement declined in 1840s, esp. after 1848. Brought about some legislation but important indust. reform was to come with abandonment of trade unions.

Chartres, town of N France, on R. Eure, cap. of Eure-et-Loir dept. Pop. 37,000. Market town; tourist and pilgrimage centre. Medieval county, duchy from 1528. Famous Gothic cathedral (12th–13th cent.) with 2 spires, 13th cent. stained-glass windows.

Chartreuse, Grande, mountain group of SE France, in Dauphiné Alps. Highest peak Chamechaude (2085 m/6847 ft). Monastery (1084), principal seat of Carthusian order until 1903, produces famous liqueur.

Charybdis, in Greek myth, see SCYLLA.

Chase, Salmon Portland (1808–73), American statesman. Opposed slavery while serving in Senate. As treasury secretary (1861–4), originated national bank system. Chief justice of Supreme Court (1864–73), presided over impeachment trial of President Johnson (1868).

chat, insectivorous bird of thrush family, esp. of genera *Cercomela* and *Saxicola*. Whinchat and stonechat are species. Yellow-breasted chat is largest North American warbler.

château, term originally denoting a French medieval castle. With development of castles into places of residence rather than defence in 15th and 16th cents., name came to describe large country houses and estates. Famous examples found in Loire valley.

Chateaubriand, François René, Vicomte de (1768–1848), French author, diplomat. Forerunner of French romanticism through egoism, impassioned prose, interest in the exotic. Works incl. novels *Atala* (1801), *Les Natchez* (1826) dealing with Red Indians, autobiog. *Mémoires d'Outre-tombe* (1848-50).

Chatham, 1st Earl of, see PITT, WILLIAM.

Chatham, mun. bor of Kent, SE England. Pop. 57,000. Naval base, estab. by Henry VIII; has naval barracks (1897), hospital (1907).

Chattanooga, town of SE Tennessee, US; on Tennessee R. Pop. 119,000. Timber products, machinery mfg. Centre of Tennessee Valley Authority irrigation and h.e.p. schemes. Strategic area (1863) during Civil War.

Chattanooga campaign, a series of engagements (1863) in the American Civil War, notably Chickamauga, Lookout Mt., and Missionary Ridge (Nov.) where Grant defeated the Confederates, who withdrew to Georgia.

Chatterton, Thomas (1752-70), English poet. Known for 'forgeries' of poetry by imaginary 15th cent. priest, Thomas Rowley. Work has considerable imaginative, poetic power, eg 'An Excelente Balade of Charitie'. His suicide made him a hero of later Romantics.

Chaucer, Geoffrey (c 1340-1400), English poet. Member of king's household, holder of various official posts, employed on missions to Continent. First important poems derived from French works, in content or style, eg *Romaunt of the Rose* (c 1370) and *Boke of the Duchesse* (1369). After visiting Italy influenced by Dante (*House of Fame*, c 1379-80) and Boccaccio, whose *Filostrato* he used for *Troilus and Criseyde* (c 1385-6). Best known for unfinished cycle *Canterbury Tales* (c 1387), collection of 23 tales narrated by pilgrims en route from London to Canterbury. Works preeminent in estab. of modern English as literary language.

Cheboksary, town of USSR, cap. of Chuvash auton. republic, E European RSFSR. Pop. 227,000. Agric. centre on Volga; h.e.p. station.

check, *see* CHEQUE.

checkers, *see* DRAUGHTS.

cheese, food made from curds of soured milk. Numerous varieties of cheese are usually divided into hard cheeses, eg Cheddar, Edam and Gouda, and soft cheeses, eg Brie and Camembert. Various micro-organisms introduced into cheese produce characteristic flavours, eg those of Stilton. Leading cheese producers incl. England, Holland, Switzerland, Italy, France.

cheetah, *Acinonyx jubatus,* dog-like cat of grasslands and semi-deserts of Africa, SW Asia. Small head, long legs, black-spotted tawny coat.

Fastest of all land mammals, reaching speeds of 95 km/60 mph.

Chekhov, Anton Pavlovich (1860-1904), Russian dramatist and short story writer. Known for plays dealing with hopelessness of communication, eg *The Seagull* (1896), *Uncle Vanya* (1899), *Three Sisters* (1901), *The Cherry Orchard* (1904), now classics. Stories incl. *Ward No. 6* (1892), and *The Lady with the Dog* (1899).

Chekiang, maritime prov. of E China. Area c 103,600 sq km (40,000 sq mi); pop. (est.) 31,000,000; cap. Hangchow. Contains fertile Yangtze delta (rice). Mountainous, densely populated. Rice, tea, wheat, cotton grown.

Chelmsford, mun. bor. and co. town of Essex, SE England. Pop. 58,000. Light industs. Church (1424, rebuilt 19th cent.) now cathedral.

Chelsea, *see* KENSINGTON AND CHELSEA, England.

Cheltenham, mun. bor. of Gloucestershire, W England. Pop. 70,000. Spa from 18th cent.; has famous racecourse, public school (1841).

Chelyabinsk, city of USSR, SW Siberian RSFSR. Pop. 810,000. Railway jct.; indust. centre; produces steel, zinc, agric. machinery.

chemical engineering, branch of ENGINEERING dealing with design, construction and operation of plants and machinery for industrial mfg. of chemicals, eg acids, dyes, synthetic plastics.

chemical warfare, the use of POISON GAS or liquids as a weapon, started by the ancient Greeks with sulphur fumes. Prohibited by the Hague Declaration (1899) but employed with deadly effect on the

Western Front in WWI, using chlorine, phosgene and mustard gas. Again outlawed at the Washington Conference (1922) it was not used in WWII.

chemistry, science concerned with composition of substances and their reactions with one another. Usually divided into organic, inorganic and physical chemistry. Organic chemistry deals with compounds of carbon, excluding metal carbonates and oxides and sulphides of carbon. Inorganic chemistry deals with elements and their compounds, excluding organic carbon compounds. Physical chemistry is application of physical measurements and laws to chemical systems and their changes.

Chemnitz, *see* KARL-MARX-STADT, East Germany.

Chengchow, cap. of Honan prov., EC China. Pop. 1,500,000. Rail jct.; textile centre; meat packing, fertilizer mfg.

Chengtu, cap. of Szechwan prov., SC China. Pop. 2,000,000. Port on R. Min. Textile, paper mfg. Cultural, commercial centre; 2 univs. Ancient cap. of Shu Han dynasty 3rd cent.

Chénier, André Marie de (1762-94), French poet, b. Istanbul. *Bucoliques, Elégies,* reflect love of Greek antiquity. Also wrote philosophical poetry, *eg L'Invention* (1819). Supporter of Revolution but executed during Reign of Terror.

Cheops, *see* KHUFU.

cheque or **check,** written order to a bank to pay the stated amount of money from one's account. Used in Italy in 15th cent., now principal medium of exchange.

Chequers, Tudor mansion and estate near Wendover, Buckinghamshire, England. Official country residence of UK prime minister. Presented to nation in 1921.

Cherbourg, town of Normandy, N France, on N coast of Cotentin penin. Pop. 40,000. Transatlantic port; major fortified naval base from 17th cent.

Cherenkov, Pavel Alekseyich (1904-), Soviet physicist. Discovered Cherenkov effect when high energy charged particles move through medium at velocity exceeding that of light in the medium; used in detection of subatomic particles. Shared Nobel Prize for Physics (1958).

Cherokee, North American Indian tribe of Hokan-Siouan linguistic stock. Largest tribe in SE US. Settled farmers with advanced culture. Frequently fought Iroquois and were valuable allies of British against the French. Estab. (1827) Cherokee Nation with govt. modelled on that of white colonists. Became US citizens (1906), a few remain in North Carolina.

cherry, tree of genus *Prunus* of rose family. Smooth stone enclosed in fleshy, usually edible fruit. Native to Asia Minor. Most varieties are derived from sweet-cherry, *P. avium.*

Cherubini, [Maria] Luigi (1760-1824), Italian composer. Lived in Paris from 1788 and became director of Paris Conservatoire in 1822. Composed several operas, incl. *Medea* and *The Water-carrier* (French title *Les deux journées*).

chervil, *Anthriscus cerefolium,* annual herb of parsley family with sweet, aromatic leaves used for flavouring in cookery. Native to

Russia, reaching Mediterranean area c 300 BC.

Chesapeake Bay, largest Atlantic inlet of US; separates E Maryland and part of Virginia from mainland. Length 320 km (c 200 mi). Important oyster, crab fisheries.

Cheshire, county of NW England. Area 2322 sq km (896 sq mi); pop. 896,000; co. town Chester. Wirral penin. in NW; low-lying, drained by Mersey, Dee. Dairying, esp. cheese; shipbuilding; salt, chemical industs.

chess, game for 2 players, each with 16 pieces, played on a board divided into 64 squares, alternately black and white. Pieces are moved according to conventional rules. Prob. originated in India, later spreading to Persia and Middle East. Popular in W Europe by 13th cent.

chest, in human anatomy, same as THORAX.

Chester, city and co. town of Cheshire, NW England, on R. Dee. Pop. 63,000. Railway jct.; metal goods mfg. Roman *Devana Castra;* only English city with medieval walls intact. Cathedral dates from Norman times; has 16th-17th cent. timbered houses.

Chesterfield, Philip Dormer Stanhope, 4th Earl of (1694-1773), English statesman, man of letters. Remembered for *Letters to His Son* (pub. 1774), written to his bastard son.

Chesterton, G[ilbert] K[eith] (1874-1936), English author. Known for novels of ideas, eg *The Napoleon of Notting Hill* (1904), *The Man Who Was Thursday* (1908); 'Father Brown' detective stories. Also wrote literary criticism, RC apologia, eg *St Thomas Aquinas* (1933).

chestnut, tree of genus *Castanea* of beech family found in N temperate regions. Species incl. edible sweet or Spanish chestnut, *C. sativa*, American chestnut, *C. dentata*, and Japanese chestnut *C. crenata*. Fruit is burr-like, containing 2-3 nuts. Wood is strong and durable. See HORSE CHESTNUT.

Chevalier, Maurice (1888-1972), French film actor, singer. Achieved fame in Paris revues of 1920s, became international film star in 1930s; known for accent, boater, charm. Films incl. *Love Me Tonight* (1932), *Gigi* (1958).

Cheviot Hills, range on Scotland-England border, rising to 815 m (2676 ft) on The Cheviot. Sheep rearing (Cheviot breed).

chevrotain or mouse deer, mammal of Tragulidae family of forests of Asia, Africa. Resembles deer, but has no antlers. Smallest of ruminants, reaches heights of 30 cm/1 ft.

chewing gum, gummy substance usually made from chicle, with added flavouring and sweeteners. Patented in US in 1869.

Cheyenne, North American Indian tribe of Algonquian linguistic stock. Originally farmers on Cheyenne R., became nomadic buffalo hunters after introduction of horse (c 1760). Colorado gold discovery (1858) forced Cheyenne into reservation where govt. neglect provoked raids by the Indians, many were then massacred by US army at Sand Creek (1864). A few remain in Montana.

Cheyenne, cap. of Wyoming, US; in extreme S of state. Pop. 41,000. Transport jct., commercial centre in cattle rearing region. Territ. cap. 1869; grew with cattle, gold booms of 1870s.

Chiang Kai-shek (1887-1975), Chinese military and political leader. Emerged as head of revolutionary Kuomintang in 1920s, leading expedition (1926-8) in N resulting in overthrow of Peking govt. Leader (1928-48), ruled with extensive power. Fought local warlords and, with Communists, resisted Japanese invasions; later driven from mainland (1950) in civil war with Communists. After 1950, challenged Communists from Taiwan-based Nationalist govt., pledged to return to mainland.

Chianti, Monti, small mountain range of Tuscany, C Italy, W of R. Arno. Grapes for Chianti wine grown on slopes.

Chicago, port of NE Illinois, US; on SW shore of L. Michigan. Transport and indust. hub of US Middle West. Pop. 3,369,000. Shipping, railway centre; important grain market; large meatpacking indust., machinery mfg. Growth began after completion of Erie Canal. Became a city (1837); devastated by fire (1871). Has Univ. of Chicago (1892); Art Institute.

Chichén Itzá, ruin of E Mexico, ancient Mayan city state on Yucatán penin. Founded in 6th cent. by the Itzá. Important archaeological site with pyramids, temples, statues.

Chichester, Sir Francis (1901-72), English yachtsman, aviator. Made 1st E-W solo flight across Tasman Sea (1931). Best known for sailing around world single-handed in *Gipsy Moth IV* (1966-7).

Chichester, city and co. town of West Sussex, SE England. Pop. 21,000. Agric. market. Roman remains incl. amphitheatre; has church (11th cent.) with separate bell tower. Goodwood racecourse nearby.

chicken, *see* FOWL.

chickenpox, infectious virus disease, usually of young children. Characterized by eruption of small spots which later become blisters. Incubation period of 2 to 3 weeks.

chickpea, bushy annual plant, *Cicer arietinum*, of Leguminosae family. Cultivated in India for edible seeds contained in pods.

chickweed, low annual or perennial herb of genus *Stellaria* of pink family, native to temperate regions. Small, white flowers. Old World weed, *S. media*, is well-known species of lawns and gardens.

chicle, gum-like substance derived from latex of tropical American trees, esp. sapodilla, *Achras sapota*, of Yucatán and Guatemala. Introduced into US as rubber substitute and basis of chewing gum.

chicory, *Cichorium intybus*, European annual plant, also grown in US. Leaves used in salads; root ground and roasted as coffee substitute. *See* ENDIVE.

Chicoutimi, port and lumber town of EC Québec, Canada; at confluence of Saguenay and Chicoutimi rivers. Pop. 34,000. Pulp and paper centre (with nearby Jonquière; pop. 28,000).

chiffchaff, *Phylloscopus collybita*, European bird of warbler family. Olive-green and brown; distinctive song, giving rise to name.

chiffon, sheer lightweight fabric made of silk, rayon or cotton.

Delicate and transparent, it is used in scarves and blouses, *etc.*

Chifley, Joseph Benedict (1885-1951), Australian statesman, PM (1945-9). Railway union activist, entered Parliament 1928. Held several Labor cabinet posts incl. treasurer from 1941 before becoming leader. His govt. strengthened position of central bank as means of countering depression.

Chihli, *see* HOPEH and POHAI, GULF OF.

Chihuahua, town of N Mexico, cap. of Chihuahua state. Pop. 289,000. On C plateau in cattle-raising, mining region; textile mfg., smelting indust.

chihuahua, small dog, probably descended from the Techichi of the Toltecs of Mexico. Large pointed ears; stands 13 cm/5 in. high at shoulder.

chilblain, painful inflammation of skin of hands and feet, caused by contraction of blood vessels in response to cold.

Chile, republic of W South America. Area 756,945 sq km (292,256 sq mi); pop. 10,454,000; cap. Santiago. Language: Spanish. Religion: RC. Comprises narrow coastal strip W of Andes extending S to Tierra del Fuego, with outlying Easter, Juan Fernández isls. Important mining in Atacama Desert region (copper, nitrates, iron ore). Agric. in SC valleys (sheep, cattle rearing). Conquered by Spanish in 16th cent.; Indian resistance until 19th cent. Independence gained under San Martín (1818); gained N region in war with Bolivia, Peru (1879-84). First South American country to elect Marxist govt. (1970); fell in military coup (1973).

chili, *see* PEPPER.

Chillon, fortress at E end of L. Geneva, Switzerland. Mainly built 13th cent.; scene of Byron's *Prisoner of Chillon.*

Chiltern Hills, SC England. Chalk range *c* 88 km (55 mi) long, running SW-NE through Oxfordshire, Buckinghamshire, Hertfordshire.

Chimaera, in Greek myth, fire-breathing monster with lion's head, goat's body, dragon's tail. Killed by Bellerophon.

chimes, set of bells, usually sounded as a signal, *eg* of the hour. The chimes heard in an orchestra consist of a set of tubular bells which are struck with hammer.

chimpanzee, *Pan troglodytes,* ape of African tropical forests. Black hair, naked face; diet of fruit, small animals. Walks on all fours. Most intelligent ape, can use simple tools. Stands *c* 1.5 m/5 ft tall.

China, People's Republic of, state of E Asia. Area *c* 9,561,000 sq km (3,691,500 sq mi); pop. (est.) 852,133,000; cap. Peking, largest city Shanghai. Official language: Peking Chinese; religions: Confucianism, Buddhism, Taoism. Comprises 21 provs., 5 auton. regions. Mountainous in N (Manchuria) and W (TIBET), descends to fertile valleys, plains in E. Chief rivers incl. Hwang Ho, Yangtze. Climate extreme in N, subtropical in S. Agric. economy, esp. rice, wheat; textile mfg. Great mineral potential, coal mining. China ruled by succession of imperial dynasties until 1912. Chiang Kai-shek's rule (1928-49) ended by estab. of Communist govt. under Mao Tse-tung. Joined UN 1971.

china clay or **kaolin,** fine, whitish

clay. Consists mainly of kaolinite (hydrous aluminium silicate). Used in pottery, paper, rubber mfg., medicine. Major sources in US, France, England.

chinchilla, small squirrel-like rodent of Chinchillidae family found in South American Andes. Bred on farms in North America, Europe for its valuable fur.

Chinese, chief language group of Sino-Tibetan family. Has largest number of speakers in world. Official language of China is Mandarin, from N China, on which is based new 'national tongue', *Kno-yu*, renamed by Communists *p'u t'ung hua*. Other forms incl. Wu (Kiangsu and Chekiang provs.), Fukienese (Fukien prov., Taiwan, SE Asia), Cantonese (Kwangsi, Kwangtung provs., Hong Kong, SE Asia, US), Hakka (Kwangtung, Kiangsi provs.). Debatable whether mutually unintelligible forms are dialects or languages. All variants share literary language *wenyen*, which is very different from vernaculars, and *paihua*, vernacular adopted by Communist regime for all writing.

Chinese lantern or **winter cherry,** *Physalis alkekengi,* plant of nightshade family of Eurasian origin. Bears fruit in inflated orange calyx which is dried to form floral decoration.

Chinese literature, oldest extant works written in late Chou dynasty (c 1027-256 BC), although written records date from c 1400 BC. Important early works incl. *Wu Ching,* traditionally attributed to Confucius, made up of 5 books on chronology, divination (I CHING), ritual, history, poetry; *Shih Ching;*

Tao Te Ching and *Chuang-Tze,* both associated with TAOISM. Greatest poetry written in T'ang period (AD 618-906) using special literary language; poets incl. Wang Wei, Li Po, Tu Fu, Po Chü-I; poems short, allusive, non-intellectual, influenced IMAGISTS. Narrative vernacular prose begun in T'ang, developing through drama of Yüan period (AD 1260-1368) to great novels of Ming, eg *Hsi Yu Chi* (translated as *Monkey,* 1943), and later works, eg *Hung Lou Meng* (18th cent.). Post-1949 literature governed by criterion of socialist realism, although some early works used as political allegory, esp. those attacking Confucius.

Chinghai, *see* TSINGHAI.

Chioggia, town of Veneto, NE Italy, on isl. in lagoon of Venice. Pop. 48,000. Port, resort; fishing, metal indust. Scene of naval battles (1379-80) between Venice and Genoa.

Chios *(Khios),* isl. of Greece, in Aegean Sea off Turkey. Area 870 sq km (336 sq mi). Wine, figs, mastic. Pop. massacred by Turks 1822. Main town, Chios, is a port; pop. 24,000. Ancient Ionian city state; Turkish held 1566-1912, taken by Greece. Traditional birthplace of Homer.

chip, small slice of semi-conducting material, eg germanium or esp. silicon, used in transistors and INTEGRATED CIRCUITS. *See* SILICON CHIP.

chipmunk, burrowing North American rodent of squirrel family. Common chipmunk of E North America, *Tamias striatus,* has cheek pouches, striped markings on head, back. Diet of nuts, berries. Chipmunks of genus *Eutamias* found in W North America, Asia.

Chippendale, Thomas (1718-79), English cabinet maker. Pub. *The Gentleman and Cabinet Maker's Director* (1754), important book of furniture designs, primarily in the rococo style, but sometimes inspired by contemporary taste for Gothic or Chinese style. Worked mainly with dark mahogany.

Chirac, Jacques (1932-), French political leader. Gaullist leader, was PM (1974-6) under Giscard d'Estaing. Elected mayor of Paris (1977), first since THIERRY.

Chirico, Giorgio de (1888-1978), Italian painter, b. Greece. Precursor of surrealism, his early work conveys mood of mystery and unease by use of empty spaces, steep perspective and objects taken out of context. Adopted more romantic realistic style after WWI.

Chiron, in Greek myth, wisest and kindliest of the CENTAURS. Skilled in medicine, prophecy, taught Asclepius, Achilles, Jason.

chiropractic, system of treatment of disease based on theory that disease is caused by interference to normal nerve function, which can be restored by manipulation, esp. of backbone. Originated by D. D. Palmer (1895).

Chittagong, cap. of Chittagong division, SE Bangladesh. Pop. 469,000. Major seaport on R. Karnaphuli. Exports jute, tea. Oil refinery, iron and steel works. Hindu temples.

chivalry, system of organization and code of personal conduct pertaining to medieval knighthood. Reached zenith at time of Crusades (12th-13th cents.). In ideal form involved knightly class in strict observance of qualities of loyalty, piety, valour, honour; also emphasized nobility of womanhood. Battlefields and tournaments served as arenas for displaying these virtues. Mixture of military and Christian ideals, seen most clearly in formation of military-religious orders, *eg* Knights Templars, Knights Hospitallers. Large body of literature grew around chivalric ideals, *eg* CHANSONS DE GESTE, epic poems of the TROUBADOURS. Also *see* ARTHURIAN LEGEND, CHRÉTIEN DE TROYES.

chives, *Allium schoenoprasum*, perennial plant of onion family. Tubular leaves used in salads and as flavouring.

chlorella, genus of unicellular green algae. Several species are rich sources of proteins, carbohydrates and fats. Used in study of photosynthesis.

chlorine (Cl), greenish-yellow gaseous element; at. no. 17, at. wt. 35.45. Occurs in sodium chloride (common salt) in sea water and rocks; obtained by electrolysis of brine. Used in manufacture of hydrochloric acid, bleaches, and much organic synthesis; also used to purify water.

chloroform (CHCl₃), volatile liquid with sweet smell. Produced by action of chlorine on methane. Used as industrial solvent and formerly as anaesthetic.

chlorophyll, complex pigment existing only in plants which make their own food by PHOTOSYNTHESIS, *ie* autotrophs. Molecule similar to blood pigment, haemoglobin.

Chlorophyll is green, but colour may be masked by other pigments. Absent from all heterotrophs, *eg* fungi, animals.

chocolate, see COCOA.

choir, trained body of singers. A full choir is divided into 4 ranges of voices (sopranos, altos, tenors and basses) and each group normally sings a separate line from the others.

cholera, acute infectious disease caused by bacterium *Vibrio cholerae*; contracted from food or water contaminated by human faeces. Characterized by severe diarrhoea, muscular cramps, dehydration. Controlled by proper sanitation.

cholesterol, white fatty alcohol of STEROID group, found in body tissue, blood and bile. Assists in synthesis of vitamin D and various hormones. Excessive deposits of cholesterol on inside of arteries are associated with arteriosclerosis and coronary heart disease.

Cholon, see HO CHI MINH CITY.

Chomsky, [Avram] Noam (1928-), American linguist. In *Syntactic Structures* (1957) set out theory of transformational-generative grammar. Theory began revolution in linguistics by positing a 'deep structure' (possibly common for all languages) from which innumerable syntactic combinations may be generated using transformational rules resulting in 'surface structure' (different for each language). Later wrote political commentaries.

Chopin, Frédéric François (1810-49), Polish composer, pianist. Lived in France from 1831. A leader of the Romantic movement, Chopin composed almost entirely for piano. Expanded harmonic concepts in his

mazurkas, ballades, nocturnes, études, *etc.* Lived with George Sand from 1837 to 1847.

chorale, hymn of Protestant church, usually written in 4 parts for choir but generally sung in unison by congregation. Tunes often used in German Baroque music as themes for larger choral works. Chorale prelude, for organ, is based on chorale tune.

chord, in music, any group of notes that are heard at the same time, but usually 3 or more. The formation of chords is studied in HARMONY.

Chordata (chordates), phylum of animals possessing a NOTOCHORD at any stage of development. Incl. vertebrates, hemichordates, tunicates.

Chorzów (Ger. *Königshütte*), city of S Poland. Pop. 152,000. Coalmining, iron and steel works, nitrate plant, engineering. Under Prussian rule 1794-1921.

Chou, Chinese imperial dynasty (*c* 1000-249 BC). Period marked by great expansion of realm and mediocrity of emperors; by end of dynasty, China had broken up into semi-independent states. Many advances in agriculture, use of metals, literature, education, commerce and industry.

Chou En-lai (1898-1976), Chinese political leader, premier 1949-76). Helped found (1922) Chinese Communist Party. Cooperated with Chiang Kai-shek against Japanese invasions, but fought against him (1930) after split with Kuomintang. Participated in LONG MARCH (1934-5). First premier and also foreign minister (1949-58), remaining in power despite ideological differences with Chairman Mao Tse-tung.

chough, mainly European bird of crow family, genus *Pyrrhocorax*, with black plumage and red feet. Species incl. *P. pyrrhocorax*, with long red beak, and yellow-billed Alpine chough, *P. graculus*, of mountain habitat.

chow chow, breed of dog developed in China. Thick brown or black coat, black tongue. Stands 50 cm/20 in. high at shoulder.

Chrétien de Troyes or **Chrestien de Troyes** (*fl* 1170), French poet. Wrote verse romances, 1st treatments of ARTHURIAN LEGEND, eg *Yvain, Erec et Enide, Lancelot, Perceval,* using elements of legend, Christian thought, code of courtly love.

Christ, see JESUS CHRIST.

Christchurch, city of E South Isl., New Zealand, on Canterbury Plains. Pop. 165,000. Outport at Lyttelton exports wool, meat, dairy produce; food processing. Founded 1850 as church settlement. Has Anglican cathedral, univ. (1873).

Christian I (1426-81), king of Denmark (1448-81). United Norway with Denmark (1450); union lasted until 1814. King of Sweden (1457-64), but defeated in his attempts to subdue the country (1471).

Christian IV (1577-1648), king of Denmark and Norway (1588-1648). Championed Protestant cause during Thirty Years War; invaded Germany (1625), defeated (1626) and signed separate peace in 1629. Re-entered war (1643-5) opposing Sweden, lost 2 Norwegian territs.

Christian IX (1818-1906), king of Denmark (1863-1906). Annexed Schleswig (1863), precipitating war against Prussia and Austria in which Denmark lost Schleswig and Holstein.

Christian X (1870-1947), king of Denmark (1912-47). Figurehead of national resistance during German occupation of WWII. Lost Iceland (1944) after public referendum.

Christiania, see OSLO, Norway.

Christianity, religion of those who believe that Jesus is the realization of the Messiah prophesied in OT and who base their faith on his life and teachings, as recorded in the NT and on Jewish myth and history of OT. Early Church tended to be highly organizational and this tendency, coupled with geographic spread of Christianity, soon resulted in variety of churches (eg RC, Eastern Orthodox, Coptic). Subsequent reformed churches (see REFORMATION) were reaction against what was felt to be formalism and authoritarianism of traditional RC church.

Christian Science, religion founded by MARY BAKER EDDY, and practised by the Church of Christ, Scientist. Adherents believe that evil and disease can only be overcome by the individual's awareness of spiritual truth in his own mind. Promulgated in international daily paper, *Christian Science Monitor.*

Christie, Agatha Mary Clarissa, Lady Mallowan (1891-1976), English author. Known for *c* 50 works of detective fiction, eg *The Murder of Roger Ackroyd* (1926), and plays, esp. *The Mousetrap* (1952). Created private detective Hercule Poirot.

Christie's, popular name for Christie, Manson and Woods, Ltd.,

London firm of art auctioneers and appraisers. Estab. by James Christie (1766).

Christina (1626-89), queen of Sweden (1632-54). Succeeded her father Gustavus II, OXENSTIERNA ruling during her minority. Patronized arts and scholars, but ruled extravagantly. Refused to marry, abdicated (1654) in favour of cousin Charles X. Settled in Rome, became a Catholic; failed in attempts to regain throne.

Christmas, in Christian calendar, celebration (on 25 Dec.) of the birth of Jesus Christ. Not widely celebrated until Middle Ages, although its near coincidence with the winter solstice links it with many ancient festivals.

Christmas Island, territ. of Australia, in Indian Ocean S of Sunda Trench. Area 142 sq km (55 sq mi); pop. 3500. Large phosphate deposits. British from 1888; admin. from Singapore after 1900; transferred to Australia 1958.

Christmas Island, one of Line Isls., C Pacific Ocean, part of Gilbert and Ellice Isls. colony. Area 577 sq km (223 sq mi); largest atoll in the Pacific. Produces copra. Sovereignty disputed by US.

Christmas rose, see HELLEBORE.

Christopher, St (Gk.,=Christ bearer), possibly a Christian martyr of Asia Minor (3rd cent.). Legendary carrier of infant Jesus over a river, sins of the world borne by Jesus making burden almost impossible. Patron saint of travellers, often represented on medallions.

chromatography, method of analysis or separation of chemical mixtures by allowing solution of mixture to flow through column of adsorbent material. Components are adsorbed in different layers, appearing as distinct bands or spots.

chromium (Cr), hard white metallic element; at. no. 24, at. wt. 51.996. Occurs as chrome iron ore (chromite); obtained by reducing oxide with aluminium. Used in manufacture of stainless steel and as protective coating on steel.

chromosome, microscopic threadlike structure found in nucleus of living cells. Consists of linear arrangement of genes, which control hereditary characteristics of organism; DNA is basic constituent. Body cells in each species contain same number of chromosomes, usually occurring in pairs. There are 46 in human cells.

chromosphere, see SUN.

Chronicles 1 and 2, in OT, books detailing history of David, thus paralleling and supplementing Kings 1 and 2. Incl. detailed descriptions of worship in the Temple.

chronometer, highly accurate clock, used esp. at sea to determine longitude. First successful marine chronometer constructed by John Harrison (1761).

chrysanthemum, genus of annual or perennial herbs of daisy family. Native to Orient, but widely cultivated. Late blooming red, yellow, or white flowers. Floral emblem of Japan.

Chrysostom, John, see JOHN CHRYSOSTOM, ST.

Chuang Chou (c 369-c 286 BC), Chinese philosopher. Leading Taoist, stressed the relativity of ideas. Advocated union with universal Tao or nature principle.

chub, fish of carp family. Species incl. *Leuciscus cephalus*, European freshwater fish; in America, river chub, *Hybopsis kentuckiensis*.

chuckwalla, *Sauromalus obesus*, herbivorous lizard of iguana family of NW Mexico, W US desert regions. Reaches lengths of 40 cm/16 in.

Chungking, city of Szechwan prov., SC China on jct. of Yangtze-Chialing rivers. Pop. 3,500,000. Major commercial, indust. centre; shipyards; produces steel, motor vehicles, textiles. Cap. of China during Sino-Japanese War (1937). Former treaty port, opened 1891.

Chur (Fr. *Coire*), town of E Switzerland, cap. of Graubünden canton. Pop. 31,000. Wine market, tourist centre. Roman *Curia Rhaetorum*; cathedral, town hall.

Churchill, John, see MARL-BOROUGH, JOHN CHURCHILL, 1ST DUKE OF.

Churchill, Lord Randolph Henry Spencer (1849-95), British statesman. Drafted Conservative policy for increased democracy, but resigned (1886) as chancellor of the exchequer over high military expenditure. His son, Sir Winston Leonard Spencer Churchill (1874-1965), was PM (1940-5, 1951-5). Journalist and soldier before election to Parliament (1900), he headed Admiralty ministry (1911-15) until failure of Dardanelles campaign in WWI discredited him. Served in Lloyd George's govt. (1917-21), Conservative chancellor of the exchequer (1924-9). Regained influence by opposing 'appeasement' policies towards Germany and replaced Neville Chamberlain at head of wartime coalition govt.

Became symbol of British resistance during WWII; attended series of international conferences (Yalta, Potsdam, *etc*) to oversee settlement of the War. After 1945 leader of the Opposition until returned to power in 1951; retired 1955. Written works incl. *The Second World War* (6 vols., 1948-53), for which he was awarded Nobel Prize for Literature (1953).

Churchill, 1, river of WC Canada. Rises in NW Saskatchewan, flows E 1600 km (1000 mi) through Manitoba to Hudson Bay. Main tributary, Beaver R. H.e.p. at Island Falls. **2,** river of S Labrador, E Canada. Flows 970 km (*c* 600 mi) from Grand Falls to L. Melville; Churchill Falls is site of one of world's largest h.e.p. plants. Formerly called Hamilton R., renamed after Sir Winston Churchill (1965).

Church of England, see ENGLAND, CHURCH OF.

Church of Scotland, see SCOT-LAND, CHURCH OF.

Chu Teh (*c* 1886-1976), Chinese military and political leader. With Mao Tse-tung led the Long March (1934-5). Commanded Chinese Communist forces during WWII and ensuing civil war. Appointed deputy chairman of People's Republic 1949. Denounced during 1967 'cultural revolution'.

Chuvash, auton. republic of EC RSFSR, USSR; in middle Volga valley. Area *c* 18,300 sq km (7070 sq mi); pop. 1,244,000; cap. Cheboksary. Wooded steppeland; main occupations agric. and forestry; notable woodworking. Chuvashes, descended from ancient Bulgars, are Finno-Tartar people.

CIA, see CENTRAL INTELLIGENCE AGENCY.

Cibber, Colley (1671-1757), English actor-manager, playwright. Wrote *Love's Last Shift* (1690), first of the 'sentimental comedies'. Known for foppish roles, as manager of Drury Lane and for brilliant autobiog. Created poet laureate (1730).

cicada, any 4-winged insect of Cicadidae family of warm areas. Eggs laid in holes bored in twigs or plant stems; larvae live several years in ground. Males make loud noise by vibrating tymbal organ.

Cicero, Marcus Tullius (106-43 BC), Roman orator, statesman. Appointed consul (63) in opposition to CATILINE. Exposed Catiline's conspiracy to seize power by force in 4 famous orations. Sided with Pompey during civil war; pardoned by Caesar. Attacked Antony in 2 *Philippics*; on reconciliation of Octavian and Antony he was executed on orders of Antony. Famous for series of letters, giving picture of Roman life. Philosophical and rhetorical works are masterpieces of Latin prose.

Cid, El, see DÍAZ DE VIVAR, RODRIGO.

cider, fermented apple juice containing from 4% to 7% alcohol. Major areas of production are Normandy and Brittany in France, Norfolk and SW of England. In US, cider refers to unfermented apple juice (hard cider is fermented form).

cigar, compact roll of tobacco leaves for smoking. Indians of West Indies and parts of South America smoked cured tobacco leaves in pre-Columbian times; cigar smoking was introduced into Spain and rest of Europe in late 16th cent. Cigars have been machine-made since c 1900 but finest cigars, eg those of Havana, are hand-made.

cigarette, roll of finely cut tobacco wrapped in thin paper. Popular tobaccos are those grown in Virginia, Georgia, the Carolinas in US, and in Turkey, Syria and Greece. Cigarette smoking has grown enormously in popularity in 20th cent. but its links with lung cancer have led to anti-smoking campaigns.

Cilicia, region of Asia Minor, in SE Turkey between Taurus Mts. and Mediterranean. Cilician Gates is pass through mountains important for access to interior. Armenian state (Little Armenia) founded here 1080; taken by Turks 1375.

Cimabue, Giovanni, orig. Cenni di Pepo (c 1240-c 1302), Italian painter. Regarded as founder of modern painting; fame due to mention in Dante's *Divine Comedy*. Forms link between Byzantine style and more realistic style of early Renaissance. Works incl. frescoes, mosaics.

cinchona, genus of tropical South American trees from the bark of which quinine and related medicinal alkaloids are obtained. Widely cultivated in Asia and East Indies.

Cincinnati, city of SW Ohio, US; on Ohio R. Pop. 453,000. Transport jct., commercial centre. Industs. incl. machine tools, chemical mfg., meat packing. Founded 1788; focus of shipping in 19th cent.

Cincinnatus, Lucius Quinctius (*fl* 5th cent. BC), Roman soldier. Appointed dictator (458 BC) he defeated the Aequi, then resumed life as a farmer 16 days later.

cinema, art and business of making

films or motion pictures; term often used for motion pictures alone. Nineteenth cent. developments in CAMERA, FILM, projectors resulted in public screening by 1896. First film theatre built (1905) in Pittsburgh, US. Film-making in US at first estab. in New York, with Hollywood becoming centre after 1913. Films were silent, accompanied by piano or organ, until *The Jazz Singer* (1927) introduced dialogue. Colour perfected with Technicolor (1932). Genres of Hollywood's 'golden age' (1930s and 1940s) incl. westerns, musicals, detective thrillers. Postwar developments incl. Italian social realism (late 1940s), *nouvelle vague* (France, late 1950s), Western appreciation of Japanese film and maturation of film criticism.

cineraria, ornamental blooming plants of genus *Senecio*. Varieties incl. popular garden plant, dusty miller, and greenhouse *S. cruentus*.

Cinna, Lucius Cornelius (d. 84 BC), Roman politician. Consul (87–84), expelled from Rome when he tried to introduce reforms during Sulla's absence. Captured Rome with Marius and ruled alone when Marius died. Killed in mutiny when embarking to fight Sulla.

cinnabar (HgS), mercury ore mineral. Heavy, red or brown in colour; consists of mercuric sulphide. Major sources in Spain, Italy, US.

cinnamon, sweet spice from dried inner bark of E Indian evergreen tree, *Cinnamomum zeylanicum*, used in cookery and medicine.

cinquefoil, plant of genus *Potentilla* of rose family, with yellow or white flowers and fruit like small, dry strawberry. Most species are perennial herbs from N temperate and subarctic regions. Species incl. creeping cinquefoil, *P. reptans*, and silvery cinquefoil, *P. argenta*.

Cinque Ports, originally ports of Hastings, Romney, Hythe, Dover, Sandwich, S England. From 11th cent. given extensive Crown privileges for supplying warships. Winchelsea, Rye, others added later.

CIO, see AMERICAN FEDERATION OF LABOR AND CONGRESS OF INDUSTRIAL ORGANIZATIONS.

circulation (blood), see BLOOD VESSELS; HEART; LUNGS.

Cirencester, urban dist. of Gloucestershire, W England. Pop. 13,000. Agric. market. Roman *Corinium*, remains incl. amphitheatre. Has ruined 12th cent. abbey.

cirrhosis, degenerative disease of liver, marked by excessive formation of fibrous scar tissue. Often caused by chronic alcoholism or malnutrition.

cirrus cloud, see CLOUD.

Cistercians, in RC church, monks of order founded (1098) by St Robert of Molesme and St Stephen Harding. Derived from Benedictine order, stressed asceticism. Influential in introducing new agric. techniques in Europe. Made great use of lay brothers in their farms. Notable members incl. St Bernard of Clairvaux. See TRAPPISTS.

citric acid, soluble crystalline organic acid, found in lemons, oranges, *etc.* Obtained by fermentation of glucose. Used in flavouring effervescent drinks.

citrus, genus of evergreen trees and shrubs of family Rutaceae, native to Asia. Bear oranges, lemons, limes, citron, grapefruit, *etc.*

Città Vecchia (*Mdina*), town of Malta. Cap. until 1570; severely damaged by earthquake 1693. Cathedral (12th cent.), palace of Knights Hospitallers, catacombs.

Ciudad Juárez, *see* JUÁREZ.

Ciudad Real, town of C Spain, cap. of Ciudad Real prov. Pop. 42,000. Agric. market, textile mfg., brandy distilling. Founded 13th cent.; Gothic cathedral.

Ciudad Trujillo, *see* SANTO DOMINGO.

civet, small cat-like carnivore of Viverridae family of Africa, SE Asia. Species incl. Indian civet, *Viverra zibetta*. Possesses scent producing glands, secretion used in perfume mfg.

civil disobedience, non-violent opposition to law or govt. policy by refusing to comply with it, usually on the grounds of conscience. Advocated by M.L. King while leading black civil rights movement in US (1950s, 1960s). More extreme form of opposition pursued by GANDHI in campaign of passive resistance, involving fastings and mass public demonstrations in Indian struggle for independence.

civil engineering, branch of ENGINEERING dealing with planning, designing and construction of *eg* bridges, harbours, tunnels. Also incl. alteration of landscape to suit particular needs. Professional institutions estab. in UK (1818), US (1852).

civil law, body of codified law governing individual's private rights, distinct from public and CRIMINAL LAW. Based on Roman law, esp. as laid down in *Corpus juris civilis* and revived 11th-12th cent. Adopted by continental Europe, Latin America, some Asian states. Most English-speaking countries have COMMON LAW.

civil rights, rights guaranteed to individual by law. Universal Declaration of Human Rights, passed (1948) by UN, incl. list of basic civil rights which should be available to all people in world. In US, set out in 13th, 14th, 15th and 19th Amendments to Constitution. Extended by acts of Congress to give minority groups, esp. blacks, equal rights. Four acts passed 1866-75, further three in 1957, 1960, 1964, latter three as result of civil rights movement's opposition to racial discrimination. Voting Rights Act (1965), originally aimed at protection of blacks' voting rights, extended to foreign-language minorities (1975). Feminists have since taken advantage of 1964 Civil Rights Act's provisions on employment, *etc.* In UK, Race Relations Acts (1965, 1968) set up Race Relations Board, to which cases of discrimination made illegal by acts can be referred. Equal Pay Act (1970), Sex Discrimination Act (1975) gave women rights in employment, education, services.

civil service, body of those employed by central govt. other than those in armed forces, judiciary. Term originally applied to part of East India Co.'s administration, later (mid-19th cent.) assumed modern meaning. US Civil Service Commission estab. (1883) as result of anti-patronage reform movement. Governs entry into service through examinations, as in UK civil service (since 1855).

Civil War, in English history, conflict (1642-6, 1648) between supporters of Charles I (Royalists or Cavaliers) and of Parliament (Roundheads). Struggle was culmination of Parliament's attempt to limit king's powers, *eg* by PETITION OF RIGHT (1628); central to dispute was Charles' belief in divine right to rule as opposed to Parliament's legislative rights, esp. over taxation. King was supported by majority of nobles, Catholics, Anglicans, and Parliament by merchants, gentry, Puritan movement and initially by Scottish Presbyterians. Parliamentary forces, organized (1644-5) into New Model Army, gained decisive victories at Marston Moor (1644), Naseby (1645) under CROMWELL and Fairfax. First phase of war ended with king's surrender to Scots (1646). Second phase, following king's escape and Scottish intervention on his side, ended with Cromwell's victory at Preston (1648).

Civil War, in US history, conflict (1861-5) between Union (Northern states) and Confederacy (Southern states). Causes incl. disagreement over prohibition of slavery in W territs. (*see* KANSAS-NEBRASKA BILL), also issue of STATES' RIGHTS. Southern states seceded from Union (1860-1), during which time LINCOLN was elected president; fighting started with Confederates firing on Fort Sumter (April, 1861). Early Southern successes, esp. under R.E. LEE, reversed in Gettysburg campaign (June-July, 1863). Gradual Union military ascendancy under U.S. GRANT culminated in retreat of Southern troops towards Richmond

and Sherman's advance into Georgia (May-Sept. 1864). Lee eventually surrendered at Appomattox Courthouse (April, 1865). Union victory marred by assassination of Lincoln, whose EMANCIPATION PROCLAMATION (1862) abolishing slavery was upheld; seceding states were readmitted to Union under RECONSTRUCTION.

Civitavecchia, town of Latium, WC Italy, on Tyrrhenian Sea. Pop. 38,000. Port of Rome from 1st cent. AD; fishing, cement. Citadel designed by Michelangelo.

Clackmannanshire, former county of Scotland, now in Central region. Ochil Hills in N; plain of R. Forth in S. Coalmining, brewing, distilling. Co. town was Clackmannan, pop. 2000.

Clair, René, orig. René Chomette (1898-), French film director known for sophisticated comedy, *eg Sous les toits de Paris* (1929), *À Nous la liberté* (1931), *Les Belles de nuit* (1952).

clam, one of various bivalve molluscs, living in sand or mud. Round clam or quahog, *Venus mercenaria*, of NW Atlantic coast, common edible species.

clan, form of social group whose members trace descent from common ancestor. Term originally used in Scottish Highlands but extended to similar groups elsewhere. The clan includes several families but traces descent through one line only and is exogamous.

Clare or **Clara, St** (c 1193-1253), Italian nun. Disciple of St Francis of Assisi, founded (c 1212) order of Franciscan nuns, 'Poor Clares', strictly upholding ideal of poverty.

Clare, John (1793-1864), English poet. Known for *Poems Descriptive of Rural Life and Scenery* (1820), *The Shepherd's Calendar* (1827) on changing countryside, vanishing customs. Went insane in middle age, died in asylum.

Clare, county of Munster prov., W Irish Republic. Area 3188 sq km (1231 sq mi); pop. 75,000; co. town Ennis. Hilly in E, N; rugged coast. Many bogs, lakes; low-lying, fertile along Shannon estuary. Agric., salmon fishing; prehist. remains.

Clarendon, Edward Hyde, 1st Earl of (1609-74), English statesman. After death of Charles I, became Charles II's chief adviser in exile. Appointed lord chancellor at Restoration (1660), favoured religious toleration; later, however, enforced Clarendon Code (1661-5), statutes strengthening Church of England. Lived in exile after dismissal (1667).

clarinet, single-reed woodwind instrument with cylindrical bore, invented late 17th cent. Usually pitched in B flat and A. Occasionally used as a solo instrument. Also found in military bands; plays a very characteristic role in traditional jazz.

Clark, [Charles] Joseph (1939-), Canadian statesman. Progressive Conservative PM (1979-).

Clark, Jim (1937-68), Scottish racing driver. Twice world champion (1963, 1965), he won Indianapolis 500 (1965). His total of major Grand Prix wins exceeded that of Fangio. Died in crash at Hockenheim circuit.

Clark, Kenneth Mackenzie Clark, Lord (1903-), British art historian. His writings incl. *Leonardo da Vinci* (1939), *Landscape into Art* (1949), and *Civilisation* (1970), based on popular lecture series for television.

Clark, Mark Wayne (1896-), American general. In WWII, commanded in N African and Italian invasions. Supreme commander of UN forces in Korea (1952-3).

class, social, *see* SOCIAL CLASS.

Classicism, in the arts, adherence to qualities regarded as characteristic of ancient Greece, Rome, incl. rationality, restraint, formal precision. *See* ROMANTICISM.

classification, in biology, systematic grouping of animals and plants into categories according to similarities and evolutionary relationships. Broadest division is into 2 kingdoms, Plantae (plants) and Animalia (animals); 3rd kingdom, Protista, consisting of all protozoans, algae, fungi and bacteria, is sometimes used. Kingdoms are divided into 6 taxa: phylum (equivalent in botany is division), class, order, family, genus, species (from most to least inclusive). Species is smallest unit of classification, usually defined as those animals or plants capable of interbreeding only among themselves. Closely related species are grouped into same genus. Binomial nomenclature used in international scientific descriptions of animals employs genus name, whose initial letter is capitalized, followed by specific name, uncapitalized. Man belongs to species *Homo sapiens*, genus *Homo*, family Hominidae, order Primates, class Mammalia, phylum Chordata.

Claudel, Paul [Louis Charles Marie] (1868-1955), French dramatist, poet and diplomat. Known for poetic dramas with religious inspiration, eg *Tête d'or* (1890), *La Ville* (1890), showing symbolist influence, *Le Soulier de satin* (1929), using Japanese no conventions. Also wrote lyric verse, prose impressions of China.

Claude Lorraine, pseud. of Claude Gellée (1600-82), French painter. Famous for his poetic treatment of landscape, depicting mythical seaports and country around Rome. Works incl. *Liber Veritatis*, book of drawings of his own paintings.

Claudian (c AD 370-404), Latin poet. Last major classicist of Rome, wrote epic *Rape of Proserpine*, idylls, epigrams.

Claudius I (10 BC-AD 54), Roman emperor (AD 41-54). Nephew of Tiberius, succeeded Caligula as emperor through support of Praetorian guard. Reign marked by territ. expansion; made Britain a province (43). Poisoned, prob. at instigation of wife Agrippina, who persuaded him to accept her own son Nero as his heir.

Clausius, Rudolf Julius Emanuel (1822-88), German mathematician, physicist. Developed concept of entropy and introduced 2nd law of thermodynamics: heat does not flow of itself from colder to hotter bodies. Contributed to kinetic theory of gases.

Claverhouse, John Graham of, see DUNDEE, JOHN GRAHAM OF CLAVERHOUSE, 1ST VISCOUNT.

clavichord, small keyboard instrument, developed in 15th cent. Small tangents (blades) of brass, activated by keys, press against strings,

simultaneously sounding them and stopping them.

Clay, Cassius, see ALI, MUHAMMAD.

Clay, Henry (1777-1852), American politician. Congressman from Kentucky, leader of 'war hawks' before War of 1812. Instrumental in passages of Compromises (1820, 1850), maintaining balance of slave and free states. Opposed extremists in N and S, supported claims of Union. Unsuccessful presidential candidate (1832, 1844).

clay, fine-grained earth, consisting mainly of hydrous aluminium silicate. May be residual (found in place of origin) or transported. Sticky and plastic when wet, hardens when dry or fired. Used for making bricks, tiles, pottery, drainage pipes.

Cleanthes (c 300-220 BC), Greek philosopher. Pupil of Zeno, subsequently leader of Stoics. See STOICISM.

Clearances, the, mass evictions of tenants in 18th and 19th cents. by Scottish Highland landowners to clear overcrowded estates for sheep pasture, deer stalking *etc.* Carried out with much brutality. Many emigrated to Canada, Australia.

clef, sign at the beginning of a staff of music that defines the pitches of the lines and spaces making up the staff.

cleft palate, congenital defect caused by failure of 2 halves of palate to unite; often associated with divided or hare lip. Repair may be effected by surgery carried out in infancy.

cleg, see HORSEFLY.

Cleisthenes (fl 510 BC), Athenian statesman. Member of Alcmaeonidae family, continued work of Solon in making Athens a democracy. Divided citizens into 10 tribes, each tribe subdivided into demes. Introduced system of ostracism.

Cleland, John (1709-89), British author. Known for *Fanny Hill - Memoirs of a Woman of Pleasure* (1749), which was suppressed as pornography.

clematis, genus of perennial plants and woody vines of the buttercup family usually with brightly coloured flowers. Garden varieties incl. Jackman clematis and Japanese clematis. Wild variety, *Clematis vitalba*.

Clemenceau, Georges (1841-1929), French statesman, premier (1906-9, 1917-20), known as the 'Tiger'. Headed coalition govt. that helped secure victory in WWI. Opposed President Wilson in postwar settlement at Versailles (1919); resigned amidst criticism for his moderate stand towards Germany.

Clement V, orig. Bertrand de Got (1264-1314), French churchman, pope (1305-14). Estab. papal seat at Avignon (1308). Dominated by Philip IV of France, he supported dissolution of the Knights Templars.

Clement VII, orig. Giulio de' Medici (1478-1534), Italian churchman, pope (1523-34). Supported Francis I of France against Emperor Charles V, who besieged Rome (1527) and imprisoned him. Refused to sanction Henry VIII's divorce from Catherine of Aragon.

Clement XI, orig. Giovanni Francesco Albani (1649-1721), Italian churchman, pope (1700-21). Renowned in youth for his learning. As pope, prosecuted Jansenism in the Church, esp. in bull *Unigenitus* (1713).

Clementi, Muzio (1752-1832), Italian composer, pianist. Lived mainly in England. First composer to write specifically for the piano, composing a famous collection of studies, *Gradus ad Parnassum*, and many sonatas.

Clement of Alexandria, orig. Titus Flavius Clemens (c 150-c 215), Greek Christian theologian. Taught at Alexandrian catechetical school, where ORIGEN was his pupil. Attempted to reconcile Christianity with Greek thought by showing Christ to be culmination of all philosophies.

Cleopatra (69-30 BC), Egyptian queen. At age of 17, became joint ruler with brother, Ptolemy XII. Deprived of power, she was reinstated with aid of Julius Caesar, by whom she bore a son in Rome. Returned to Egypt after Caesar's death, later to become mistress of Mark Antony. Their union was opposed by Octavian, who destroyed their fleet at Actium (31 BC). They retired into Egypt and both committed suicide.

Cleopatra's Needles, popular name for 2 ancient Egyptian obelisks in red granite, originally erected at Heliopolis (c 1475 BC). Later removed to Alexandria (c 14 BC), one was presented to Britain (1878), the other to America (1880); they stand on Thames Embankment, London, and in Central Park, New York.

clerihew, form of verse invented by Edward Clerihew Bentley, having two couplets humorously characterizing person whose **name** is one of the rhymes.

Clermont-Ferrand, city of SC France, in Massif Central, cap. of Puy-de-Dôme dept. Pop. 149,000. Rubber mfg. centre, metal goods; univ. (1808). Hist. cap. of Auvergne; scene of church council (1095) leading to the Crusades. Gothic cathedral (13th cent.).

Cleveland, [Stephen] Grover (1837-1908), American statesman, president (1885-9, 1893-7). Reform mayor of Buffalo (1882-3) and New York governor (1883-5) before assuming presidency. Alienated radical Democrats in 2nd term by upholding gold standard. Sent troops into Illinois to break Pullman railway strike (1894).

Cleveland, county of NE England. Area 583 sq km (225 sq mi); pop. 567,000; co. town Middlesbrough. Centred on R. Tees. Iron, steel mfg.; heavy indust. Created 1974 incl. parts of N Yorkshire, Durham.

Cleveland, port of NE Ohio, US; on L. Erie at mouth of Cuyahoga R. Pop. 751,000; state's largest city. Major iron ore shipping centre; steel mfg., oil refining (Rockefeller), chemicals mfg. First settled 1796. Canal and railway spurred growth in 19th cent.

Cleves, see KLEVE, West Germany.

climate, average meteorological conditions of a place or region, taken over a period of years. Dependent on many factors, eg latitude, nearness to sea. Studied as climatology.

Clive, Catherine ('Kitty'), née Rafter (1711-85), English actress. Known for comedy roles. Friend of Horace Walpole.

Clive, Robert, Baron Clive of Plassey (1725-74), British soldier,

administrator. In military service of East India Co., won series of victories, notably at Arcot (1751), Calcutta, Plassey (1757). Consolidated British power in India, ousting French. As governor of Bengal promoted reform. On return to England (1767), charged with accepting bribes; acquitted but committed suicide.

cloisonné, enamel decoration, esp. used in Chinese and Japanese art, in which solid metal outlines are filled with enamel paste or powder, baked, and finally ground smooth.

Clonmel, co. town of Tipperary, S Irish Republic, on R. Suir. Pop. 12,000. Sporting centre (hunting, horseracing); livestock market.

closed shop, organization hiring only labour union members as employees, either throughout or for particular jobs. Subject of indust. and political conflict in US and UK. In former, unions adopted closed shop policy c 1840, but strikes to support it were declared illegal until 1935 Wagner Act. Many states passed 'right-to-work' laws outlawing closed shop. In UK, Industrial Relations Act (1971) made closed shop agreement void at law, but law overturned by following Labour govt.

Cloth of Gold, Field of, place near Calais, France, where Henry VIII of England met Francis I of France (1520) to discuss possible alliance against Charles V. Name given because of lavish display of wealth by both retinues.

cloud, mass of water droplets or ice crystals suspended in the atmosphere. Formed by condensation of water vapour, normally at considerable height. The 3 primary cloud types (*cirrus, cumulus, stratus*) first recognized by Luke Howard (1803). International classification now identifies 10 basic forms, distinguished by height. High clouds (over *c* 6100 m/20,000 ft) incl. *cirrus, cirrostratus, cirrocumulus.* Intermediate clouds (*c* 2000 m/6500 ft to *c* 6100 m/20,000 ft) incl. *altocumulus, altostratus.* Low clouds (below *c* 2000 m/6500 ft) incl. *stratus, nimbostratus, stratocumulus.* Clouds growing vertically upwards incl. *cumulus, cumulonimbus.* Certain clouds are associated with particular weather conditions, *eg* nimbostratus with continuous rain or snow, *cumulus* with fair weather, *cumulonimbus* with thunderstorms.

cloud chamber, in physics, enclosed chamber containing supersaturated vapour used to detect paths of charged particles. Particle produces ions as it passes through chamber; path seen as row of droplets formed by condensation of liquid on these ions.

clouded leopard, *Neofelis nebulosa,* nocturnal carnivore of cat family of SE Asian forests. Arboreal, with long heavy tail.

Clough, Arthur Hugh (1819-61), English poet. Known for hexameter verse *Bothie of Toper-na-Fuosich* (1848), lyrics, esp. 'Say not the struggle nought availeth'. Arnold's *Thyrsis* commemorates his death.

clove, pungent dried flower bud of evergreen shrub, *Eugenia caryophyllata,* of myrtle family, native to East Indies. Used whole for pickling and flavouring, ground for confectionery; oil used medicinally.

clover, any plant of genus *Trifolium* of Leguminosae family. Low-growing trifoliate plant with small flowers in dense heads. Widespread in temperate regions. Used as forage crop and to allow NITROGEN FIXATION in soil.

Clovis I (*c* 466-511), Frankish king (481-511). Son of Childeric I; founded Merovingian monarchy· in Gaul and SW Germany. Defeated Romans at Soissons (486), Alemanni at Tolbiarum (496), Visigoths at Vouillé (507). Converted to Christianity (496), estab. court at Paris; thus laid foundations of Charlemagne's empire and modern France.

club foot, hereditary deformity of the foot, in which the sole is turned inwards and the heel drawn up. May be cured by manipulation or surgery.

club root, disease of plants of cabbage family, caused by a slime mould, *Plasmodiophora brassicae,* and characterized by swellings of the roots.

Cluj (Hung. *Kolozsvár*), city of WC Romania. Pop. 213,000. Commercial, indust. centre of Transylvania. Prob. dates from Roman times. Gothic church (14th cent.); seat of 4 bishoprics.

Cluny, town of Burgundy, E France. Pop. 4000. Grew around large Benedictine abbey (founded 910) which became major religious and cultural centre in Middle Ages.

Clwyd, county of NE Wales. Area 2425 sq km (936 sq mi); pop. 354,000; co. town Mold. Created 1974, incl. former Denbighshire, Flintshire.

Clyde, river of W Scotland. Flows 170 km (105 mi) from S Lanarkshire via fruit-growing areas (Lanark,

Carluke) and heavy indust. areas (Glasgow, Clydebank) to Firth of Clyde. Has shipbuilding industs., ports, tourist resorts.

Clydebank, town of Strathclyde region, W Scotland, on R. Clyde. Pop. 48,000. *Queen Mary, Queen Elizabeth, QE2* built in shipyards. Sewing machine mfg. Damaged in WWII air raids.

Clytemnestra, in Greek myth, daughter of Leda and Tyndareus. Unfaithful wife of Agamemnon, whom she murdered on his return from Troy; lover of Aegisthus. Mother by Agamemnon of Orestes, Electra and Iphigenia. Killed with Aegisthus when Orestes avenged his father's death.

Cnossus, see KNOSSOS, Greece.

coal, dark brown or black combustible mineral. Occurs in bands or seams in sedimentary rock. Formed over millions of years by heating and compaction of partly decayed vegetable matter; various stages, in order of increasing carbon content, are peat, lignite, bituminous coal, anthracite. Coals occur from Devonian period on, with max. in Carboniferous. Used as fuel, also in production of coke, coal gas, plastics. Major sources in US, UK, France, Australia, China, USSR.

coal gas, gas made by destructive distillation of coal. Main constituents are hydrogen (50%), methane (30%). Used for heating, illumination. Poisonous, as it contains carbon monoxide.

coal tar, thick black liquid obtained by destructive distillation of coal. Distillation and purification yield such compounds as xylene, toluene,

benzene, phenol. Pitch remains as a residue.

coastguard, govt. organization employed to defend nation's coasts, aid vessels in distress, prevent smuggling, *etc.* In UK was estab. after Napoleonic Wars to prevent smuggling, but now concerned mainly with lifesaving. In US, is special naval branch, formed (1915) with wide duties, incl. maintenance of lighthouses, enforcement of law and order at sea.

Coast Mountains, range of W British Columbia, Canada. Run parallel to Pacific Coast for 1610 km (1000 mi). Rise to highest point at Mt. Waddington 4042 m (13,260 ft). Extensively wooded; heavy rainfall; h.e.p.

Coast Range, volcanic mountain range of W US, parallel to Pacific coastline. Extends S from Washington, Oregon to California.

Coatbridge, town of Strathclyde region, WC Scotland. Pop. 52,000. Coalmining; iron and steel industs.

coati, any of genus *Nasua* of arboreal mammals, related to raccoon, found in Central and South America. Long snout; omnivorous.

cobalt (Co), hard silvery-white metallic element; at. no. 27, at. wt. 58.93. Occurs combined with arsenic and sulphur; obtained by reducing oxide with carbon or aluminium. Used in alloys; radioactive cobalt 60 used to treat cancer. Compounds used in pigments (esp. blue).

Cobbett, William (1762-1835), English political journalist. Campaigned for social, economic reform in his *Weekly Political Register* (1802-35). Best known for *Rural*

Rides (1830) describing conditions in the country.

Cobden, Richard (1804-65), British politician. With John Bright, leader of Anti-Corn Law League; fought for repeal of Corn Laws, achieved (1846) under Peel. Negotiated tariff treaty (1859-60) with French.

Cóbh, town of Co. Cork, S Irish Republic. Pop. 6000. Port of Cork; yachting. Formerly called Queenstown.

Coblenz, *see* KOBLENZ, West Germany.

cobra, highly venomous snake of Elapidae family, found in Africa and Asia. Opens hood of skin around neck when angered. Species incl. Indian cobra, *Naja naja*, and Egyptian cobra, *N. haja*, often used by snake charmers. Largest is king cobra, *N. hannah*, reaching 5.5 m/18 ft.

coca, tropical South American shrub, *Erythroxylon coca*, dried leaves of which are the source of the alkaloid drug, cocaine.

cocaine, white crystalline alkaloid obtained from leaves of coca plant. Formerly used as local anaesthetic, it is a habit-forming drug, causing temporary elation and hallucinations.

Cochabamba, town of WC Bolivia, cap. of Cochabamba dept. Pop. 160,000. in grain, fruit-growing region. Oil refining, furniture, footwear, tyre mfg. Has univ. (1832).

Cochin, seaport of Kerala state, SW India, on Arabian Sea. Pop. 438,000. Exports coconut products. Chief port of former princely state of Cochin. Earliest European settlement in India (1503) following visit of Vasco da Gama.

Cochin China, former French colony of SE Asia. Contained within South VIETNAM after 1954.

cockatoo, easily domesticated crested parrot of Australia, New Guinea, Philippines. Plumage mainly white, edged with yellow or pink.

cockchafer, *Melolontha melolontha*, European species of beetle with black head, thorax and reddish-brown wing cases. Lifespan of c 3 years. Larvae are root feeders.

cocker spaniel, small dog, developed in England. Silky hair, drooping ears. Stands 36 cm/14 in. at shoulder.

cock-fighting, sport of setting trained cocks, usually bearing metal spurs, to fight against each other. Can be traced back as far as 12th cent. in England. Banned in Britain and America in mid-19th cent. Still popular in parts of Asia and Latin America.

cockle, one of group of edible bivalve molluscs, genus *Cardium*. Body enclosed by 2 heart-shaped ribbed shells with scalloped edges.

cockroach, any insect of suborder Blattaria, found worldwide, esp. in tropics. Flat, brownish body, long antennae; emits unpleasant odour. Omnivorous, pest of foodstores. *Blatta orientalis* is cosmopolitan domestic species.

cocoa or cacao, *Theobroma cacao*, spreading tree of Sterculia family, found in forests of South America. Grows to av. height of 10 m/30 ft and has large, round fruits each containing 20-40 seeds or beans (cacao). These when roasted and powdered (cocoa) are used in chocolate and as a beverage.

coconut, *Cocos nucifera*, tropical

tree bearing large, brown, hard-shelled fruit. Edible white kernel (copra) and 'milk' used in confectionery. Yields oil used in soap; husk provides fibre for matting; leaves used as roof covering.

Cocos or Keeling Islands, group of 27 small coral isls., S of Sumatra; under Australian admin. since 1955. Area 13 sq km (5 sq mi); pop. 600. Discovered (1609) by Captain Keeling of East India Co. Exports copra.

Cocteau, Jean (1889-1963), French author, film director. Avant-garde works deal with theme of poet as defier of destiny, risking destruction. Known for ballets for Diaghilev; novels, *eg Les Enfants terribles* (1929, film 1950); plays, *eg La Machine infernale* (1934) on Oedipus myth; films, *eg Le Sang d'un Poète* (1932); autobiog., poetry.

Cod, Cape, narrow sandy penin. of SE Massachusetts, US. Famous holiday resort, fishing area. Pilgrim Fathers landed here (1620).

cod, food fish of Gadidae family of N Atlantic, N Pacific. Atlantic cod, *Gadus morhua,* found esp. off coasts of Newfoundland and Iceland, commercially important. Cod-liver oil source of vitamins A, D.

codeine, alkaloid drug derived from opium and similar to morphine. Used medicinally to relieve pain and suppress coughs.

Code Napoléon, first modern law code, promulgated (1804) by Napoleon I. Important in development of CIVIL LAW, model for many nations' codes.

cod liver oil, oil obtained from liver of cod and other fish. Rich in vitamins A and D, it was much used in treatment of vitamin deficiency diseases, *eg* rickets.

Cody, William Frederick (1846-1917), American showman. Known as 'Buffalo Bill'. Worked as frontier scout. After 1883 toured US, Europe with his 'Wild West Show'.

coeducation, system of education in which students of both sexes are instructed together. Early examples in Scotland and American colonies (17th cent.), spread with W expansion in US (c 1840s) and extension of public education. Elsewhere, widespread coeducation, esp. in univs. and colleges, did not come until early 20th cent. with increasing participation of women in indust., professions.

Coelacanthidae (coelacanths), order of primitive marine fish, known from fossils of Devonian period. Believed to be ancestors of land animals. Living specimen of genus *Latimeria* discovered (1938) off E Africa; other species found since then.

Coelenterata (coelenterates), phylum of aquatic, mainly marine, animals. Life cycle generally involves alternation between asexual sedentary polyp and free-swimming sexual medusa (jellyfish). Polyp stage dominant in some members, *eg* corals, sea anemones, but medusa stage in others, *eg* true jellyfish. Many polyps colonial; some solitary, *eg* HYDRA.

coffee, *Coffea arabica,* evergreen shrub native to Arabia, grown extensively in Brazil, Africa and Asia. Seeds roasted and ground to make beverage. Unknown in Europe until 17th cent. World production *c* 4,000,000 metric tons.

Cognac, town of W France, on R. Charente. Pop. 23,000. Produces famous brandy; barrel mfg., bottling.

cognac, *see* BRANDY.

Cohn, Ferdinand Julius (1828-98), German botanist. Regarded as founder of bacteriology. Studied plant pathology, investigating the lower algae, fungi and bacteria.

Coimbra, city of C Portugal. Pop. 46,000. Wine, grain market. Univ. (1537), 2 cathedrals. Flourished from Roman times; cap. of Portugal 1139-1260.

coins, *see* NUMISMATICS.

Coke, Sir Edward (1552-1634), English jurist, statesman. Appointed attorney-general (1594); as chief justice of Common Pleas (1606-16), championed Parliament, common law, principles of personal liberty against James I's assertion of royal prerogative. Leader of parliamentary opposition from 1620, under Charles I drew up Petition of Right (1628). Wrote *Institutes,* a legal classic.

Coke, Thomas William, Earl of Leicester of Holkham (1754-1842), English agriculturist. Remembered for systematic improvement of methods of arable farming and of breeding livestock, esp. sheep.

coke, residue from destructive distillation of coal; contains *c* 80% carbon. Used as smokeless fuel and in preparation of metals from their ores in blast furnaces.

cola or **kola,** *Cola acuminata,* tree of W tropical Africa, West Indies and Brazil. Nuts yield caffeine and extract used in flavouring soft drinks.

Colbert, Jean Baptiste (1619-83), French statesman. Chief adviser to Louis XIV after 1661, leading exponent of mercantilist policies to develop nation's wealth. Protected indust. with subsidies and tariffs, price regulation. Had road and canal network built, encouraged trade and colonization, increased naval power.

Colchester, mun. bor. of Essex, SE England, on R. Colne. Pop. 76,000. Market town, famous oyster fisheries; has Univ. of Essex (1961). Ancient British cap., Roman *Camulodunum,* part of town wall remains; has Norman castle, now museum.

cold, common, acute inflammation of mucous membranes of nose and throat; believed to be caused by any of *c* 50 different viruses. Most common human ailment. Lack of immunity to common cold prob. caused by new strains of virus developing from earlier ones.

Cold War, economic and political rivalry between nations, without actual military conflict. Popularly used for post-WWII struggle between Communist nations and West. Also term for ideological split between USSR and China, and competition with West for prestige in developing countries by use of aid programmes.

Cole, G[eorge] D[ouglas] H[oward] (1889-1959), English economist. Chairman of Fabian Society (1939-46); president from 1952. Also leading advocate of guild socialism. Author of many works, eg *The Simple Case for Socialism* (1935), *History of Socialist Thought* (1953-8).

cole, *see* KALE.

Coleoptera, largest order of insects; *see* BEETLE.

Coleraine, town of N Northern

Ireland, on R. Bann. Pop. 15,000. In former Co. Londonderry. Fishing; whiskey distilling. Has seat of Univ. of Ulster (1968).

Coleridge, Samuel Taylor (1772-1834), English poet, critic. Estab. English Romanticism in publication, with Wordsworth, of *Lyrical Ballads* (1798) incl. 'The Rime of the Ancient Mariner'. Other works incl. 'Kubla Khan' (1816), philosophical, critical reflections in *Biographia Literaria* (1817).

Coleridge-Taylor, Samuel (1875-1912), British composer. Born of English mother and W African father. Best known for his 3 choral works on the subject of Longfellow's *Hiawatha*. Also wrote orchestral and chamber music, incidental music for stage.

Colet, John (*c* 1467-1519), English humanist. Noted for his exegesis of Pauline theology at Oxford (1497-1504). Dean of St Paul's (1505); refounded and endowed St Paul's School (1509).

Colette, [Sidonie Gabrielle] (1873-1954), French novelist. Known for analytical studies of women, eg 'Claudine' series (1900-3) of semi-autobiog. novels written with 1st husband, and for *Chéri* (1920), *Gigi* (1945).

Coll, isl. of Inner HEBRIDES, W Scotland.

collage, art form in which bits of paper, cloth or other objects are stuck to a canvas or other surface. Much used by cubists who introduced strips of newspaper into otherwise conventionally painted compositions.

collar bone or **clavicle,** part of shoulder extending from shoulder blade (scapula) to breastbone (sternum).

collective bargaining, in indust. relations, term for negotiations between employer and employees' representatives, usually labour union, to agree pay, conditions of work, union rights. Term coined by Beatrice Webb for process first used in 19th cent. Britain.

collective farming, agric. cooperative movement. In USSR, Stalin instituted (1929) *kolkhoz* method in which land, farm equipment were pooled and profits shared among members. Although almost all Soviet agric. was collectivized by 1938, state farms, paying the workers, were later introduced. Chinese cooperatives place greater emphasis on communal living and encourage participation of indust. workers. Israeli kibbutzim also place great emphasis on communal living.

college, institution of higher education. Generally, smaller in size and spread of curriculum than UNIVERSITY; several colleges may constitute university. Earliest were in Paris (12th cent.), preceding famous centres of learning at Oxford and Cambridge univs. Industrial Revolution led to need for scientific and technical training (technical colleges); late 19th cent. brought colleges of education (teachers' training). In US, colleges may grant degrees in specialized courses of study, eg liberal arts, law, medicine, architecture.

Collège de France, institution of higher learning estab. (1529) in Paris by Francis I. Has no fees, no examinations, no degrees, and no state supervision.

collie, breed of long-haired sheepdog, developed in Scotland. Long narrow head; stands 56-66 cm/22-26 in. at shoulder. Kelpie is Australian sheepdog developed from collie or dingo-collie cross.

Collingwood, Cuthbert Collingwood, Baron (1750-1810), British admiral. Distinguished himself at St Vincent (1797) and took command at Trafalgar (1805) after Nelson's death.

Collingwood, Robin George (1889-1943), English philosopher. Believed philosophy originates in history, not science. Works incl. *Principles of Art* (1937), *The Idea of History* (1945).

Collins, Michael (1890-1922), Irish Sinn Fein leader. Organized guerrilla warfare against British. With Arthur Griffith, estab. (1921) Irish Free State. Briefly (1922) head of state and army, before he was assassinated.

Collins, Michael, see ARMSTRONG, NEIL.

Collins, [William] Wilkie (1824-89), English novelist, associate of Dickens. Known for thriller *The Woman in White* (1860), *The Moonstone* (1868), regarded as 1st English detective novel. Also wrote plays.

colloid, solid, liquid or gaseous substance made up of very small insoluble particles that remain in suspension in solid, liquid or gas medium of different matter. Examples incl. solutions of starch and albumen. Suspension of colloidal particles in gas is called an aerosol, *eg* fog and smoke.

collotype, method of printing by which inked reproductions are transferred directly to paper from an image formed on a gelatine-coated glass plate. Used for printing high quality colour illustrations.

Colman, George, ('the Elder') (1732-94), English dramatist. Known for comedies, esp. *The Clandestine Marriage* (1766) written with Garrick, *The Jealous Wife* (1761).

Colman, Ronald (1891-1958), British actor. Played 'English gentleman' roles in films, as in *Bulldog Drummond* (1929), *The Prisoner of Zenda* (1937), *A Double Life* (1948).

Colmar or **Kolmar**, town of Alsace, E France, cap. of Haut-Rhin dept. Pop. 63,000. Major textile mfg. centre, wine trade. Free imperial city from 1226, annexed by France (1681). Many medieval buildings, incl. 13th cent. convent.

colobus monkey, genus of slender African monkeys, usually with long black and white fur, and no thumbs. Treetop dwelling; diet of leaves, fruit. Fur hunting has diminished numbers.

Cologne (*Köln*), city of NW West Germany, on R. Rhine. Pop. 846,000. River port, railway jct.; indust., banking centre; univ. (1388). Perfume mfg., incl. 'eau-de-Cologne'. Roman *Colonia Agrippinensis*; powerful medieval archbishopric, Hanseatic League member from 1201. Gothic cathedral (begun 1248). Badly damaged in WWII.

Colombia, republic of NW South America. Area 1,138,900 sq km (439,700 sq mi); pop. 24,372,000; cap. Bogotá. Language: Spanish. Religion: RC. Has Pacific and

Caribbean coasts; Andes in W; tropical forests, grasslands in E; uninhabited lowland in interior. Chief rivers are Cauca, Magdalena. Coffee, bananas are chief crops; important mineral resources incl. platinum, oil. Spanish colony from 16th cent. Independence gained under Bolivar in 1819; known as New Granada until 1863. Panama seceded in 1903; civil war 1949-53.

Colombo, cap. and chief port of Sri Lanka. Pop. 562,000. Commercial centre; exports rubber, tea. Univ. (1870). Under Dutch control in 17th cent., ceded to British (1796). Site of Colombo Plan conference (1950), on Commonwealth-US aid to S and SE Asia.

colon, the large INTESTINE.

Colorado, state of WC US. Area 270,000 sq km (104,247 sq mi); pop. 2,207,000; cap. Denver. Mainly in Rocky Mts., mean alt. 2070 m (c 6800 ft), plains in E. Has sources of Rio Grande, Arkansas, Colorado rivers. Agric. incl. potato, sugar beet, alfalfa, wheat growing, stock raising. Coal, uranium, molybdenum mining. Part of Louisiana Purchase of 1803; had gold, silver strikes in 19th cent. Admitted to Union as 38th state (1876).

Colorado, two rivers of SW US, 1, rises in Rocky Mts., N Colorado, flows SW 2334 km (1450 mi) through Utah, Arizona (Grand Canyon). Forms much of Californian border. Continues into Mexico to Gulf of California. Provides h.e.p. and irrigation from numerous dams, eg Hoover. **2,** rises in NW Texas, flows SE 1439 km (894 mi) to Gulf of Mexico. Also has several dams.

Colorado beetle or potato

beetle, **Leptinotarsa decemlineata,** leaf-eating beetle originally of W North America, now found wherever potatoes cultivated. Yellow, with black stripes. Serious pest of potatoes, other garden vegetables.

Colorado Springs, town of C Colorado, US; at foot of Pikes Peak. Pop. 135,000. Health and holiday resort (nearby is Garden of the Gods sandstone region). Has US Airforce Academy.

Colosseum or Coliseum, largest amphitheatre of ancient Rome, built c AD 75-80. A 4-storied oval building, it held c 45,000 people on tiers around the arena. Still largely extant.

Colossians, Epistle to the, NT book, traditionally attributed to St Paul while in prison at Rome (c AD 62). Warns the church at Colossae of dangers of false teaching, asserts pre-eminence of Christ.

Colossus of Rhodes, bronze statue of sun god, Helios, which stood in Rhodes harbour. Built by Chares c 292-280 BC, it was c 30 m (100 ft) high. One of seven wonders of the ancient world, it was destroyed by an earthquake (224 BC).

colour, sensation resulting from stimulation of retina of the eye by light of certain wavelengths. Any colour can be produced by combining beams of primary colours, red, green and blue. Pigmented objects produce colour by absorbing certain wavelengths and reflecting others; primary pigment colours are red, yellow and blue.

colour blindness, inability to distinguish between certain colours, esp. red and green. Red-green form is a sex-linked character, being transmitted from women to their sons; thus it is much more common in men. See SEX CHROMOSOME.

Colt, Samuel (1814-62), American inventor. Patented the revolving-breech pistol (1836) and set up a large arms factory at Hartford, Conn.

coltsfoot, *Tussilago farfara,* plant of daisy family. Common weed of N temperate regions. Large heart-shaped leaves, hairy, scaly stalk, yellow spring flower.

Colum, Padraic (1881-1972), Irish poet. Associated with Irish Renaissance. Works incl. *Wild Earth* (1907), autobiog. *Our Friend James Joyce* (1959), classic song 'She Passed through the Fair'.

Columba or **Columcille, St** (c 521-97), Irish missionary. Estab. Celtic monasteries in Ireland at Derry, Durrow, Kells. Set up monastery on Iona (563) as centre for the conversion of N Scotland. Made extensive and successful missionary journeys among the Picts.

Columbia, cap. of South Carolina, US; on Congaree R. Pop. 114,000. Cultural, education centre. Agric. industs. esp. cotton, textile mills. Founded 1786. Chosen as cap. 1786.

Columbia, river of W US and Canada. Rises in Rocky Mts. (SE British Columbia). Flows 1950 km (c 1210 mi) to US border; then SW through Washington, which lower course separates from Oregon, before reaching Pacific. Snake R. is chief tributary. Supplies irrigation for surrounding agric. regions from Grand Coulee, Bonneville dams. Source of h.e.p.

Columbia, District of, *see* DISTRICT OF COLUMBIA.

Columbia University, New York City, US. Estab. (1754) as King's College by grant of George II. Became Columbia Univ. (1896) after additions and enlargements. Incl. Barnard Coll. for Women, many graduate and research schools.

columbine, plant of genus *Aquilegia* of buttercup family, incl. *c* 70 species found in temperate regions. Native European species, *A. vulgaris,* is purple or white. *A. caerulea,* a blue and white variety, is state flower of Colorado.

columbium, *see* NIOBIUM.

Columbus, Christopher, English form of Cristoforo Colombo (1451-1506), Italian navigator, b. Genoa. Engaged for many years in Portuguese sea trade; sailed westward (1492) for Ferdinand and Isabella of Spain in *Santa Maria, Niña,* and *Pinta,* landing on Watling Isl. in Bahamas. On 3 subsequent voyages reached Leeward Isls., Puerto Rico, Cuba, Jamaica, Hispaniola, and American mainland from Orinoco to Panama, believed by him to be East Indies.

Columbus, town of W Georgia, US; on Chattahoochee R. Pop. 155,000. Indust., transport centre; cotton, textiles, agric. implement mfg. Founded as trading post (1828).

Columbus, cap. of Ohio, US; on Scioto R. Pop. 533,000. Indust. and transport centre; produces aircraft, car parts, mining machinery. Founded as state cap. 1812.

column, in architecture, slender upright structure generally consisting of cylindrical or polygonal shaft, with base and capital; used as a support or ornamental member in a building. Greeks perfected design of columns in temples, *eg* Parthenon. *See* ORDERS OF ARCHITECTURE.

Colwyn Bay, mun. bor. of Clwyd, N Wales. Pop. 26,000. Seaside resort.

coma, state of complete and prolonged unconsciousness from which patient cannot be aroused. Caused by brain disturbance, *eg* injury, poisoning, lack of oxygen.

Comanche, North American Indian tribe of Uto-Aztecan linguistic stock. Separated from SHOSHONE and settled (*c* 1680) in S Texas and W Oklahoma. Nomadic plains warriors, fiercely opposed to white man. Greatly reduced by war and disease to *c* 1500 (1904), when confined to Oklahoma reserve.

Combination Acts (1799, 1800), in UK, laws outlawing trade unions. Unions went underground until laws were repealed 1824.

COMECON, *see* COUNCIL FOR MUTUAL ECONOMIC ASSISTANCE.

Comédie-Française, French national theatre in Paris estab. 1681 from a company of Molière's actors. Renamed *Théâtre Français* (1791).

comedy, originally drama or narrative with happy ending and non-tragic theme (*eg* Dante's *Divine Comedy*), now usually given humorous treatment. In England, tradition goes back through Latin writers, *eg* Plautus, to Greek drama of Aristophanes, Menander. In France, Molière combined *commedia dell'arte* with classical influence in Comedy of Manners, which developed in England into Restoration comedy (Congreve), and later into satirical character comedies of Goldsmith, Sheridan, Wilde; 20th cent. social comedies written by G.B. Shaw, Noël Coward.

Comenius, Johann Amos, Latinized form of Jan Amos Komenský (1592-1670), Czech educator, Moravian churchman. Advocate of universal education, coeducation. Revolutionized Latin teaching, relating it to everyday life, through textbook *The Visible World in Pictures* (1658).

comet, heavenly body moving under influence of Sun. Consists of bright nucleus, surrounded by hazy gaseous mass (coma). When passing near Sun, tail of gaseous material may be formed, pointing away from Sun. Generally follows elongated elliptical orbit, returning at calculable intervals, *eg* Halley's comet. Others have completely disintegrated, *eg* Biela's comet.

Cominform (Communist Information Bureau), coordinating organ of Communist parties of USSR, its E European allies, France and Italy. Estab. in Belgrade (1947), hq. moved to Bucharest after expulsion of Yugoslavia (1948). Became instrument of oppression for Stalin, dissolved in 1956.

Comintern (Communist International), also known as Third International, association of world Communist parties estab. by Lenin (1919). Leading members incl. Zinoviev, Trotsky, Radek, Bukharin. Founded to give leadership to more extreme elements of world socialist movements, dominated by Russian Communists. Anti-Comintern Pact formed (1936) by Germany and Japan. USSR dissolved Comintern in 1943 as goodwill gesture to Allies in WWII.

commedia dell'arte, Italian dramatic genre dating from 16th cent.

Travelling actors improvised on stock characters (Harlequin, Scaramouche, *etc.*). Conventions influenced Shakespeare, Jonson, Molière, de Vega, Goldoni, later developed into pantomime.

commerce, the buying and selling of goods, esp. on large scale, eg between countries. Carried on in ancient times around Mediterranean by Egyptians, Sumerians, Phoenicians. Crusades stimulated European trading aspirations, trade superiority eventually passing to cities of N Italy. Exploitation of New World by Spain gave her brief hegemony. The 18th cent. was marked by rivalry between Dutch, British and (later) French. Industrial Revolution gave Britain superiority in 19th cent. Recent developments incl. European Economic Community and growing trade between Communist and capitalist blocs. *See* MERCANTILISM. FREE TRADE.

commodity, in economics, term for anything which is limited in supply and thus has a value in exchange.

common law, law of nation based on custom, usage, and legal precedent. Distinct from but complementary to statute law. Important in England where it became estab. in 13th cent., influenced English-speaking countries.

Common Market, Central American, *see* CENTRAL AMERICAN COMMON MARKET.

Common Market, European, *see* EUROPEAN COMMUNITIES.

Commons, House of, *see* HOUSE OF COMMONS.

Commonwealth, govt. of England under Cromwell and Parliament (1649–60); *see also* PROTECTORATE.

Commonwealth, British, free association of UK and ex-colonies. Evolved from dominions, estab. as autonomous by STATUTE OF WESTMINSTER (1931) after Imperial Conference (1926). Commonwealth Relations Office estab. 1947, with which Colonial Office was merged (1966). Member states incl. Canada, Australia, New Zealand, India, many African, Asian, Caribbean states. South Africa withdrew (1961), Pakistan (1972). Territs. dependent on UK incl. Hong Kong, Gibraltar, Bermuda.

Commune of Paris, (18 March–29 May, 1871), Parisian revolutionary govt. Set up at end of FRANCO-PRUSSIAN WAR after premier Adolphe Thiers' attempt to crush armed national guard of Paris. Socialist govt. elected (26 March). Thiers' siege succeeded, and *c* 20,000 prisoners killed.

Communion, Holy, *see* EUCHARIST.

Communism, Mount, highest peak of USSR, in Pamir Mts., Tadzhik SSR; height 7495 m (24,590 ft).

Communism, modern, international movement advocating revolutionary overthrow of capitalism (*see* MARXISM), arising out of Marx and Engels' *Communist Manifesto* (1848). Guided by principles of communal ownership of means of production, everyone receiving according to his need and working according to his capacity. Marxian Communism spread through founding of First INTERNATIONAL and rise of Social Democratic parties in Europe. Radical form taken (1903) in Russia when Bolsheviks, under Lenin, urged immediate violent revolution to overthrow CAPITALISM and estab. world socialist state. Bolsheviks triumphed in RUSSIAN REVOLUTION (1917). Leninists urged workers' union for international revolution; stateless, universal Communism with no class distinction would theoretically follow 'dictatorship of proletariat'. Stalin consolidated Communist power in USSR during 1930s. Soviet victory in WWII brought addition of E European satellites to Communist bloc. Links with China after estab. of Communist state (1949) under Mao Tse-tung; in early 1960s China's accusations of Soviet conciliation with West brought rift. Western powers involved in conflicts in attempts to contain spread of Communism, esp. Korea (1950-3), and US in Vietnam (1965-73).

communism, social or economic system or theory in which property (esp. means of production) is held in common by all members of society, not by individuals. As theory of govt. and social reform, communism can be attributed to Plato who in *Republic* outlined society with communal property. In England, forms of communism manifested in Sir Thomas More's *Utopia* and the DIGGERS. Recent attempts based upon principles of communism incl. Israeli *kibbutzim*, 'drop-out' settlements in US. Movement tends toward agric. based communities, although modern COMMUNISM developed as reaction to capitalist enterprise following Industrial Revolution, in protest against appalling labour conditions.

Communist Manifesto, *see* MARX, KARL.

Communist Party, a political organization based on principles of Communism, as developed by Marx and Engels; modified by Lenin, Stalin and others, dedicated to estab. state socialism. In USSR developed from Bolshevik-Menshevik split (1903), gained power during Russian Revolution (1917). Later centralized, wielding real power through CENTRAL COMMITTEE. In China founded 1921, developed under Mao Tsetung; protracted struggle with Kuomintang, interrupted by WWII, civil war, ended with Communist triumph and estab. of People's Republic (1949). In Americas, Communist Party govts. incl. that under Castro in Cuba and short-lived one under Allende in Chile. Communist parties in West have attempted to gain power through electoral process and trade union activities.

Como, town of Lombardy, N Italy, at S end of L. Como. Cap. of Como prov. Pop. 99,000. Tourist resort. Famous in Middle Ages for craftsmen (silk, *etc*). Marble cathedral, Gothic town hall.

Comorin, Cape, southernmost point of India, near Nagercoil (Tamil Nadu).

Comoro Islands, republic in Indian Ocean, at N end of Mozambique Channel; comprise group of volcanic isls. Area 2170 sq km (838 sq mi); pop. 314,000; cap. Moroni. Language: French. Religions: Islam, Christianity. Produce-vanilla, copra, cocoa, coffee. Formerly French overseas territ., became independent 1975.

company, limited, in UK,

organization, public or private, and legally registered, formed to carry out activities (usually on profit basis). Each partner is liable under 1855 Limited Liabilities Act for only the amount of his investment. Act brought British practice in line with that of Continent. In US, corporations are functionally and legally similar.

compass, name given to 2 instruments: mathematical compass is used to draw circles and measure distance; magnetic compass is used to determine direction by allowing magnetic needle to swing freely on a pivot.

competition, in economics, term for the degree to which the market can be influenced by buyers and sellers. Perfect competition is a theoretical model, in which many producers with no control over price produce goods which are sold to competing buyers. In fact, market limited by industrial cooperation, patents, *etc. See* MONOPOLY, SUPPLY AND DEMAND.

Complègne, town of Ile-de-France, N France, on R. Oise. Pop. 33,000. Tourist resort, sawmilling, glassworks. Scene of siege (1430) in which Joan of Arc captured by English. Armistice of 1918 and French surrender of 1940 both signed in nearby forest.

complex, in psychology, idea or group of ideas arising in the mind as result of highly emotional experience, and repressed partly or wholly, as result of conflict with other ideas accepted by individual. Most famous example is Oedipus complex.

complex number, in mathematics,

number expressed as formal sum $a + bi$, where a and b are real numbers and i is square root of -1. Complex numbers form an extension of real number system in which all polynomials have roots.

Compositae, largest and most highly advanced family of flowering plants. Characterized by flower heads composed of dense clusters of small flowers surrounded by a ring of small leaves, *eg* daisy, thistle, artichoke, chrysanthemum.

comprehensive education, system of state-financed education combining various types of SECONDARY SCHOOL, drawing all pupils from surrounding catchment area. Its implementation in UK by local authorities from 1960s aroused opposition in many areas among advocates of separation of pupils by ability (*see* GRAMMAR SCHOOL).

Compromise of 1850, measures passed by US Congress balancing interests of slave and free states. Provided for California's admission as free state, abolished slavery in Dist. of Columbia. Estab. strict fugitive slave law, boundary of Texas. Bills failed ultimately to resolve slavery question.

Compton-Burnett, Dame Ivy (1892-1969), English novelist. Known for stylized, formal dialogue novels, *eg Brothers and Sisters* (1929), *Elders and Betters* (1944), *Mother and Son* (1955), dealing with claustrophobic family power struggles.

computer, device which, by means of stored instructions and information, performs large numbers of calculations at great speed or may be used to compile, correlate and select data (data processing). Two types; **digital**, which processes information in numerical form, usually in BINARY SYSTEM, and **analog**, which represents information in terms of quantities (eg current or voltage) rather than by digital counting. Sequence of calculations controlled by program, ie series of precisely defined instructions fed into machine. Specialized programming 'languages' evolved to describe operations which machine will carry out. Early examples incl. calculating machines designed by Babbage (1834).

Comte, [Isidore] Auguste [Marie François Xavier] (1798-1857), French philosopher. Disciple of Saint-Simon. Founder of POSITIVISM. Delineated 3 stages (theological, metaphysical, positive) in all fields of knowledge; rejected metaphysics in favour of modern science. Works incl. *Cours de Philosophie Positive* (1830-42).

Conakry or **Konakry,** cap. of Guinea, on Tombo Isl. Pop. 197,000. Admin., commercial centre; railway terminus and deepwater port, exports alumina, iron ore, bananas.

Conan Doyle, see DOYLE, SIR ARTHUR CONAN.

concentration camp, institution for detention of elements of population deemed dangerous by regime. Term first applied to British examples in Boer War. Used esp. by Germans during WWII against 'undesirables', eg Jews, Poles; notorious examples incl. Buchenwald, Dachau, Oswiecim. Associated with single-party state.

Concepción, town of SC Chile, near mouth of Bío-Bío R. Pop. 190,000. Textile, leather, glass mfg. Export centre through port of Talcahuano. Major coalfields nearby. Founded 1550. Has suffered many earthquakes.

concertina, a form of accordion in which both sets of fingers operate buttons or studs, so that the hands do not have to move over a keyboard while squeezing and expanding the bellows. Invented by the scientist Sir Charles Wheatstone in 1829.

concerto, music for one or more soloists and orchestra, usually in 3 movements or sections. A *concerto grosso* features a group of instrumentalists with orchestra. A concerto for orchestra is a display piece to demonstrate virtuosity of the entire orchestra.

conch, marine mollusc, with spiral one-piece shell. Species incl. *Strombus gigas* of West Indies. Shell used for ornaments or as simple trumpet.

conciliation, industrial, means of settling labour disputes by means of seeking involvement and recommendations of 3rd party, often govt. agency, eg UK Advisory, Conciliation and Arbitration Service, US Federal Mediation and Conciliation Service. If parties do not come to voluntary settlement, arbitration may follow to impose compulsory decision.

Concord, see BOSTON, Massachusetts.

Concord, cap. of New Hampshire, US; on Merrimack R. Pop. 30,000. Granite quarrying nearby; printing indust. Settled c 1725.

concordance, alphabetical list of important words used in a book or by a particular writer, with references to the passages in which they occur. First examples inspired by conviction of thematic links between passages of Bible, eg Córcordantiae Morales on Vulgate, attributed to Anthony of Padua. Notable examples of Biblical concordances incl. those of Alexander CRUDEN.

Concorde, first supersonic (Mach 2.2) passenger aircraft developed jointly by France and UK. Maiden flight, Toulouse (March, 1969). Services inaugurated (1976), despite protests in US, UK by environmentalists, because of excessive noise.

concrete, building material made of sand and gravel, bonded with cement; dries to form hard stone-like substance. May be strengthened by introducing steel rods (reinforced concrete). Used by Romans for construction of roads and buildings. Modern concrete dates from discovery of portland cement in early 19th cent.

Condé, Louis [I] de Bourbon, Prince de (1530-69), French nobleman. Huguenot leader, led Protestant forces in religious wars of 1560s. Army defeated by Catholic forces, killed at Jarnac. His great-grandson, **Louis [II] de Bourbon, Prince de Condé** (1621-86), known as the 'Great Condé', won major battles at Nördlingen (1645), Lens (1648) during Thirty Years War. Led FRONDE uprising, commanding army of princes (1651) and Spanish forces (1653-9) against Louis XIV; defeated in battle of the Dunes by Turenne (1658). Pardoned, later fought successfully for Louis against the Dutch.

condenser, in chemistry, device for condensing vapour into liquid, con-

sisting of glass tubes cooled by air or water.

condenser, in electricity, see CAPACITOR.

condor, New World vulture, inhabiting high mountain regions. Black plumage with white markings on wings, neck. Feeds mainly on carrion. Two species: nearly extinct Californian condor, *Gymnogyps californianus*, and Andean condor, *Vultur gryphus* (wingspan c 3 m/ 10 ft).

Condorcet, [Marie Jean] Antoine Nicolas de Caritat, Marquis de (1743-94), French philosopher, mathematician. Girondist member of legislative assembly, laid foundation for state education. Outlawed by Jacobins. Wrote *Esquisse d'un tableau historique de progrès de l'esprit humain*, describing man's progress and heralding perfection of human state to follow French Revolution. His concept of progress influenced later social theorists, esp. Comte.

conduction, thermal, transfer of heat from hotter parts of a medium to colder parts by passage of energy from particle to particle. In metals, heat flow is largely due to motion of energetic free electrons towards colder regions.

Confederacy or **Confederate States of America** (1861-5), govt. estab. by Southern states of US which seceded from Union. After election of Lincoln as president, 7 states left Union (early 1861) followed by 4 more after Lincoln's declaration of war. Jefferson Davis was elected president; Judah P. Benjamin was outstanding cabinet member. For subsequent history, see CIVIL WAR (US).

Confederation, Articles of (1781), pre-constitutional formulation of how American colonies were to be governed. Proved unsatisfactory as central govt. too dependent on states for money, executive powers. Superseded by Constitution (1789). Confederation in Canada embodied in BRITISH NORTH AMERICA ACT (1867).

Confederation of British Industry, organization representing the interests of British employers, particularly on economic questions. Founded 1965 out of Federation of British Industries (founded 1916), British Employers' Confederation, and National Association of British Manufacturers.

Confederation of the Rhine, see RHINE, CONFEDERATION OF THE.

confession, in RC, Orthodox and High Anglican churches, disclosure of sin to priest to obtain absolution. See PENANCE.

Confucius, latinized form of K'ung Fu-tzu (c 551–c 479 BC), Chinese philosopher and social reformer. Advocate of ethical system founded on absolute justice and moderation with the aim of stabilizing society. Teachings became basis of Confucianism, developed as state religion with adherence to traditional values.

conger eel, any of Congridae family of scaleless saltwater eels. Long dorsal fin, sharp teeth, powerful jaws. European conger, *Conger conger*, reaches length of 2.1 m/7 ft. *C. oceanica*, of Atlantic coast of North America, is smaller.

conglomerate, in geology, rock composed of rounded fragments, bound together in matrix of cementing material. Normally formed of transported pebbles, unlike breccia. Examples incl. single pebble type, mixed pebble type, and glacial conglomerates.

Congo (Brazzaville), republic of WC Africa. Area 342,000 sq km (132,000 sq mi); pop. 1,390,000; cap. Brazzaville. Languages: Bantu, French. Religions: native, Christian. Mainly tropical forest, exports hardwoods, sugar, tobacco, coffee; main food crops cassava, yams. Lead, potash mining; aluminium indust. Coast explored 15th cent. by Portuguese, interior 19th cent. by Brazza. Base of French trading (17th–19th cent.). Territ. (Middle Congo) of French Equatorial Africa from 1910; independent 1960. Member of French Community.

Congo (Kinshasa), see ZAÏRE.

Congo or **Zaïre,** river of WC Africa, 2nd longest (c 4800 km/3000 mi) in Africa. Rises in SE Zaïre, called R. Lualaba until reaching Stanley Falls; middle course curves SW, forming part of Zaïre-Republic of Congo border, widening at Stanley Pool. Enters Atlantic by wide estuary, forms part of Zaïre-Angola border. Navigable for ocean-going vessels to Matadi. Mouth discovered (1482), explored by Livingstone (1871); 1st descent made by Stanley (1874–7).

Congregationalism, faith and form of organization of a Protestant denomination in which each member church is self-governing. Based on belief that each congregation has Christ alone at its head. First appeared in 16th cent. England as revolt against state control of Established church; principles formulated by Robert Browne (c 1550-1633). Important in development of New England. Congregations now loosely organized in unions.

Congress of Industrial Organizations, *see* AMERICAN FEDERATION OF LABOR AND CONGRESS OF INDUSTRIAL ORGANIZATIONS.

Congress of the United States, legislature of US federal govt., as distinct from executive and judiciary, estab. (1789) by Article I of Constitution. Comprises an upper house (SENATE) and a lower house (HOUSE OF REPRESENTATIVES).

Congress Party (Indian), *see* INDIAN NATIONAL CONGRESS.

Congreve, William (1670-1729), English playwright. Known for Restoration comedies, esp. *Love for Love* (1695), *The Way of the World* (1700). Tragedy *The Mourning Bride* (1697) was his most popular play in own day.

conic sections, in geometry, curves produced by intersection of a plane with a right circular cone. Consist of ellipse, circle, parabola, hyperbola and degenerate cases of these. Much studied by ancient Greek geometers.

conifer, class of woody perennials comprising 6 families, c 500 species. Mainly evergreen trees bearing cones. Trees cultivated for timber, pulp, resin and turpentine. Incl. PINE, cypress, yew, sequoia.

Coniston Water, lake of Cumbria, NW England. In Lake Dist. at foot of Old Man of Coniston. Length 8 km (5 mi). Scene of Campbells' water speed records (1939, 1959).

conjunctivitis, inflammation of membrane covering inside of eyelids and front of eye. Caused by infection with viruses or bacteria; usually treated by antibiotics.

Connacht or **Connaught,** prov. of W Irish Republic. Area 17,122 sq km (6611 sq mi); pop. 390,000. Comprises cos. Galway, Leitrim, Mayo, Roscommon, Sligo.

Connecticut, New England state of US. Area 12,973 sq km (5009 sq mi); pop. 3,032,000; cap. Hartford. Mainly lowland with indented coastline; divided by Connecticut R. Agric. incl. tobacco growing, dairy, poultry farming. Granite, sandstone quarrying. Mfg. industs. incl. machinery, tools, firearms, textiles, clocks and watches; defence industs. First settled by Dutch, later by Puritans from Massachusetts in 17th cent. One of original 13. colonies of US.

Connemara, region of Co. Galway, W Irish Republic. Lakes, mountains (incl. 'Twelve Pins'). Tourism.

Connolly, Cyril Vernon (1903-74), English author, critic. Known for essays in *Enemies of Promise* (1938), *Ideas and Places* (1953). *The Unquiet Grave* (1944) explores his theme of the 'will-to-failure'.

Connolly, James (1870-1916), Irish nationalist. A Socialist, he supported labour movements in US and Ireland. Captured and shot helping to lead 1916 Easter Rebellion.

Connolly, Maureen ('Little Mo') (1934-69), American tennis player. First woman to achieve 'grand slam' of winning all 4 major tennis championships (1953). Won Wimbledon and US titles 3 times, French twice.

Conquistador (Span.,=conqueror), name given Spanish leaders in conquest of Americas. Suppressed and exploited Indian pop. in search for gold and silver, esp. during Pizarro's conquest of Inca empire. Expeditions estab. Spanish empire and Golden Age of late 16th and 17th cent.

Conrad, Joseph, orig. Teodor Józef Konrad Nalecz Korzeniowski (1857-1924), English novelist, b. Ppland. Works, often set at sea, concerned with man's ability to cope with testing situations, eg *Lord Jim* (1900), *Typhoon* (1903), *Victory* (1915). Short stories, (eg 'Heart of Darkness' (1902), often contain his most intense work.

consanguinity, relationship by descent from same ancestor. Of legal importance in laws relating to marriage (*see* INCEST) and inheritance.

conscientious objector, a term first used in WWI for those who objected to combatant service for moral or religious reasons. They were given legal status in UK by the Military Service Act (1916) and in WWII the Military Training Act (1939) prescribed alternative forms of service. Similar schemes exist in US.

conscription, compulsory enrolment of citizens for military purposes. Recorded in Greece and Rome, it was first used in modern times by Napoleon in 1798. Most European states have invoked it at some time, incl. Britain (1947-62). Introduced in US during Civil War.

conservation laws, in physics, laws stating that total value of some quantity does not change during physical processes, eg total electrical charge of a system remains constant. Laws of conservation of mass and of energy have been combined into single mass-energy law following Einstein's demonstration of equivalence of mass and energy.

conservatism, tendency to preserve and to oppose changes in estab. institutions or practices. In politics, manifested in parties advocating policies founded on belief in free enterprise, distrust of state intervention, and conservation in particular of sovereign and religious institutions. In UK, Conservative Party replaced TORY Party after Reform Bill of 1832. Survived splits in 1846 and 1905, became champion of propertied democracy and imperialism. Shared major party status with Liberals until 1922, after which alternated with Labour Party in govt. Prominent figures incl. Peel, Disraeli, the Chamberlains, Baldwin, Churchill. Most important Commonwealth counterpart is Canada's Progressive Conservative Party (named 1942), founded 1854 as Conservatives. In European democracies, conservative policies often promoted by Christian Democrat parties.

Constable, John (1776-1837), English painter. With Turner, leading English landscape painter of 19th cent.; his direct observations of nature, capturing effects of changing light, influenced French Romantic painters, incl. Delacroix, and later Barbizon school. *The Hay Wain* and *View on the Stour* won gold medals at Paris Salon of 1824.

Constance (*Konstanz*), town of S West Germany, on R. Rhine at exit from L. Constance. Pop. 61,000. Port; produces textiles, chemicals.

Held by Austria 1548-1805. Hist. buildings incl. minster (11th cent.). Dominican monastery. Scene of Council of Constance (1414-18) where Hus was condemned.

Constance, Lake (Ger. *Bodensee*), on Swiss-Austro-German border. Rhine enters at SE, leaves NW. Area 531 sq km (205 sq mi). Tourism, fishing. Ancient lake dwellings.

Constanța, city of SE Romania, on Black Sea. Pop. 186,000. Resort; main Romanian port, exports grain, timber, petroleum (pipeline from Ploești). Founded by Greeks: rebuilt by Emperor Constantine 4th cent. Ceded by Turkey to Romania (1878).

Constant [de Rebecque], [Henri] Benjamin (1767-1830), French author, politician, b. Switzerland. Known for short introspective novel, *Adolphe* (1816), prob. based on liaison with Mme de Staël.

Constantine [I] the Great (*c* 288-337), Roman emperor (306-37). Proclaimed emperor by troops in Britain on death of his father Constantius (306). Defeated rival Maxentius (312) in battle before which he is said to have had vision of Christ's cross. Legally recognized Christianity in empire with Edict of Milan (313). Gained control of E part of empire by 324 with defeat of rival Licinius. Consolidated and rebuilt empire; moved capital to Constantinople on Bosporus (330). Became a Christian 337.

Constantine II (1940-), king of Greece (1964-8). Formally cooperated with military junta that took power (1967), exiled 1968. Monarchy abolished by junta (1973); decision confirmed by popular vote (1974) after overthrow of junta.

Constantine (anc. *Cirta*), city of NE Algeria. Pop. 254,000. Grain, leather, wool trade. Ancient cap. of Numidia; destroyed AD 311, rebuilt AD 313 by Constantine I.

Constantinople, *see* ISTANBUL.

Constantius II (317-61), Roman emperor (337-61). Son of Constantine I, shared rule with his 2 brothers, being given control of E part of empire. United empire with defeat of usurper Magnentius (351) and ruled alone.

constellation, in astronomy, name given to groups of stars. In N hemisphere, names largely mythological, *eg* Orion; in S hemisphere (mapped 16th - 18th cent.) named after animals or scientific equipment, *eg* Telescopium. Greeks recognized 48 constellations; now 88 are recognized.

constitution, whole system of govt. of a country. In wide sense, applied to both laws and customs which estab. and regulate govt.; more narrowly, to selection of these which are codified in document. Most nations have written constitutions, UK being notable exception.

Constitution of the United States (1789), codification of system of federal govt. Consists of 7 articles, preamble, 26 amendments. Basis estab. (1787) by Federal Constitutional Convention, held in Philadelphia. Provided separation of powers into executive, judicial, legislative branches. First 10 amendments (Bill of Rights) guarantee individual liberties.

constructivism, artistic movement in Russia during years 1917-22, characterized by abstract and geometric design, massive structural form and use of modern materials. Principal exponents were brothers Antoine Pevsner and Naum Gabo.

consul, title of two chief magistrates of ancient Rome. Most powerful office of republic, controlling army, treasury, civil affairs. Became nominal under empire. Term also used (1799-1804) for one of three highest officials of French republic; Napoleon Bonaparte was first consul.

consumption, see TUBERCULOSIS.

contact lens, thin lens of glass or plastic used to correct defective vision. Usually covers only cornea and floats on tears of wearer.

continent, large continuous land mass on Earth's surface. Seven usually distinguished: Africa, Asia, Australia, North America, South America, Europe and Asia (sometimes taken as one, *ie* Eurasia). Upper level of Earth's crust, forming continents, consists of SIAL; lower level, underlying continents and ocean floors, of SIMA. Prob. formed at time crust first solidified, each continent has Precambrian shield at centre. Over ⅔ area of continents lies in N hemisphere.

Continental Congress (1774-89), legislature of Thirteen Colonies of America. First Congress sent petition of grievances to king, abolished trade with Britain. Second issued Declaration of Independence (4 July, 1776), created Continental Army, conducted American Revolution. Estab. Articles of Confederation, governed under them until Constitution adopted (1789).

continental drift, theoretical process by which continents on Earth's surface have changed their position through time. Alfred Wegener

suggested (1912) that in Palaeozoic era all land masses were joined as 1 continent (called 'Pangaea'), later splitting into 2 ('Laurasia' and 'Gondwanaland') which slowly split and drifted into present positions. Also *see* SIAL, SIMA.

continental shelf, submarine ledge bordering most continents. Covered by shallow water, usually less than *c* 180 m/600 ft deep. May show continental features, *eg* cliffs, river valleys. Commercially important, *eg* most fishing grounds, petroleum found there.

Continental System, policy devised (1806) by Napoleon I to curtail British power by economic boycott and unify European states under his rule. All trade with Britain forbidden. Its failure was result of British naval superiority. Russia's withdrawal (1810) from System provoked Napoleon's disastrous Russian campaign (1812).

contour, line on a map joining all points at same height above sea level. Set of contours thus shows relief of the mapped area.

contrabassoon, see BASSOON.

contraception or **birth control,** prevention of conception. Methods used incl. sterilization, abstinence during certain phases of female ovulation, hormone preparations (the 'Pill'), prevention of sperm entry into uterus, or intra-uterine devices. Modern movements for birth control began in 19th cent. following predictions of overpopulation by Malthus. Widely opposed on religious grounds, (*eg* by RC church) and in certain under-populated countries, it has greatly reduced birth rate in many countries.

contralto, in singing, lowest female voice, also called ALTO.

convection, transference of heat in liquids or gases by actual motion of fluid. Fluid in contact with heat source expands, becoming less dense; it rises and its place is taken by colder, denser fluid. Resulting circulation of fluid is called convection current.

convolvulus, *see* BINDWEED.

Conway (*Aberconway*), mun. bor. of Gwynedd, N Wales, at mouth of R. Conway. Pop. 12,000. Seaside resort. Has remains of 13th cent. castle and town walls; bridges by Telford (1826), Stephenson (1848).

cony, name given to mammals of order Hyracoidea, incl. damans, dassies and hyraxes.

Cook, James (1728–79), English naval officer, explorer. Commanded *Endeavour* on scientific expeditions to S Pacific (1768–71), mainly to observe transit of planet Venus; reached Tahiti, explored coasts of New Zealand and E Australia, claiming latter for UK. Landed at Botany Bay (1770). On 2nd voyage (1772–5) crossed Antarctic Circle, explored S Pacific, discovering Norfolk Isl. (1774). On 3rd voyage (1777–9) failed to find passage to Atlantic from N Pacific; killed by natives on Hawaii.

Cook, Thomas (1808–92), English travel agent. Organized railway excursions, starting 1841. Later conducted tours around Europe (1856) and arranged tours in America (1866). Founded travel agency bearing his name.

Cook, Mount, or *Aorangi*, highest mountain of New Zealand; in Southern Alps, South. Isl. Height

3762 m (12,349 ft); part of Mt. Cook National Park.

Cooke, [Alfred] Alistair (1908–), American journalist, b. England. Known in Britain for radio broadcasts 'Letter from America' (1938–), TV series 'America' (1972–3, pub. 1973).

Cook Islands, isl. group of SC Pacific Ocean. Area 240 sq km (93 sq mi); pop. 18,000; main isl. Rarotonga. Produce fruit, copra. Admin. by New Zealand from 1901, self-governing from 1965; formerly called Hervey Isls.

Coolidge, [John] Calvin (1872–1933), American statesman, president (1923–9). Gained prominence by using militia to end 1919 Boston police strike as governor of Massachusetts. Vice-president (1921–3), took office on death of Harding and pursued conservative policies.

Cooper, Alfred Duff, Viscount Norwich of Aldwick (1890–1954), British statesman. Conservative first lord of the Admiralty (1937–8), resigned over Munich Pact. Member of Churchill's war cabinet before becoming ambassador to France (1944–7). Wrote biographies of Talleyrand and Haig.

Cooper, Gary, pseud. of Frank J. Cooper (1901–61), American film actor. Famous for roles as reticent man of conscience, often cowboy, in such films as *A Farewell to Arms* (1932), *Mr Deeds Goes to Town* (1936), *Sergeant York* (1941), *High Noon* (1952).

Cooper, James Fenimore (1789–1851), American novelist. First American novelist to acquire international fame, known for 'Leatherstocking' series about frontiersmen, creating characters incl. Natty Bumppo. Novels, greatly influenced by Scott, incl. *The Deerslayer* (1841), *The Last of the Mohicans* (1826), *The Pathfinder* (1840).

Cooperative Commonwealth Federation, see NEW DEMOCRATIC PARTY.

cooperative movement, term covering variety of socio-economic organizations. Main type is consumer cooperative, which people join for purchase of goods in retail stores owned by cooperative, or to organize wholesale trade. Producers' cooperatives are rarer, comprise workers joined for common ownership and management of production. Movement began in 19th cent. Britain, developed variously throughout Europe. Consumers' cooperatives important in Britain, estab. (1844) permanently by followers of Robert Owen at Rochdale. Producers' cooperatives esp. important in Scandinavia, France.

Cooper's hawk, *Accipiter cooperi,* small North American hawk with long rounded tail and short wings.

coot, freshwater bird of Rallidae family, genus *Fulica*. Black with white forehead; unwebbed feet. Species incl. common European *F. atra*, American *F. americana*.

Coote, Sir Eyre (1726-83), Irish soldier. Active in Clive's occupation of Calcutta and victory at Plassey. Won battle of Wandiwash (1760) and captured Pondicherry, ending French attempt to dominate India. Returned to India (1779), defeated Hyder Ali several times.

Copenhagen (*Köbenhavn*), cap. of Denmark, on E Zealand and N Amagar Isls.; port on Oresund. Pop. 1,380,000. Admin., commercial, cultural centre. Shipbuilding, fishing, brewing, porcelain mfg. Exports dairy produce. Cap. from 1443; British defeated Danes in naval battle (1801). Univ. (1479); Christiansborg Palace (18th cent.), museums.

Copernicus, Nicolas (1473-1543), Polish astronomer. Set down in *De revolutionibus orbium coelestium* (pub. 1543) principles of Earth's axial rotation and position of Sun at centre of solar system, with planets in orbit around it. Provided foundation for work of Kepler and Newton.

Copland, Aaron (1900-), American composer. Some of his work is abstract, but much displays American idioms grafted on to European tradition, eg the ballets *Rodeo* and *Appalachian Spring*.

copper (Cu), reddish-brown malleable ductile metallic element; at. no. 29, at. wt. 63.54. Occurs free and as sulphide and oxide ores. Excellent conductor of electricity and heat; resists corrosion. Used in electrical wire, boilers, numerous alloys (bronze, brass, *etc*). Compounds used as fungicides and pesticides.

copperhead, *Ancistrodon contortrix,* poisonous snake of pit viper group of E North America and Canada. Name also applied to poisonous Australian *Denisonia superba*.

copra, see COCONUT.

Coptic, non-Semitic language of Afro-Asiatic family. With Ancient Egyptian formed Egyptian branch of family. Both languages now dead.

Coptic. *fl* during early Christian era, still used in Coptic church ritual.

Copts, native Christian minority (c 10%) of Egypt. Culturally rather than ethnically distinct, they belong to the Coptic Church which was isolated when declared heretical in 451. *See* MONOPHYSITISM.

copyright, exclusive right granted by law to authors, composers, artists, *etc*, to print, publish and sell their works for specified time. Agreement reached (Bern Convention, 1887) by many countries (excluding US) to safeguard rights internationally. Universal Copyright Convention came into force in US (1955), UK (1957).

coral, small marine coelenterate usually living in colonies in warm seas. Individuals (polyps) consist of jelly-like body surrounded by calcareous skeleton. With death of polyp, skeletons accumulate to build reefs.

coral reef, chain of calcareous rocks found in warm, shallow seas. Consists of skeletal material, mainly coral polyps, accumulated *in situ* over long period, together with transported and chemically precipitated organic debris. Forms incl. fringing reefs, barrier reefs, ATOLLS.

Coral Sea, arm of SW Pacific Ocean, between E Papua New Guinea and NE Australia. Incl. Great Barrier Reef. Scene of US-Australian victory (1942) over Japanese.

coral snake, one of various highly poisonous burrowing snakes of S US, subtropical America; related to cobra. Red, yellow and black bands around body.

cor anglais, *see* OBOE.

Corbusier, Le, pseud. of Charles Edouard Jeanneret (1887-1965), French architect, b. Switzerland. Influential innovator, he employed pure geometrical forms in his work, and industrial methods to mass-produce housing, *eg* Citrohan project (1921). Designed chapel at Ronchamp, Villa Savoye at Poissy, typical of later anti-rational style, and UN building. Devised town-planning schemes and wrote important *Towards a New Architecture* (1923).

Corday, Charlotte (1768-93), French political assassin. A Girondist sympathizer, she stabbed Marat in his bath, and was guillotined 4 days later.

Cordeliers, radical political club during French Revolution. Estab. 1790, active in overthrow of GIRONDISTS (1792-3). At first led by DANTON, Desmoulins, later by Marat, Hébert. Fell apart after Hébert's execution (1794).

Córdoba, city of C Argentina, cap. of Córdoba prov. Pop. 799,000. Railway jct., commercial and cultural centre; cars, tractors, textiles, glass mfg. Supplied with h.e.p. from Rio Primero. Founded 1573. Old buildings incl. cathedral, univ. (1613).

Córdoba or Cordova, city of S Spain, on R. Guadalquivir, cap. of Córdoba prov. Pop. 236,000. Tourism; industs. incl. textile mfg., engineering. Cap. of independent Moorish emirate, later caliphate, from 756; famous gold, silver, leather crafts. Taken by Castile 1236. Much Moorish architecture, esp. mosque (8th cent.) now a cathedral.

corduroy, *see* VELVET.

Corelli, Arcangelo (1653-1713), Italian composer, violinist. In his sonatas and *concerti grossi*, he developed characteristic style of writing for violin, both as solo and orchestral instrument.

Corfu (*Kérkira*), isl. of W Greece, in Ionian Sea. Area 637 sq km (246 sq mi). Olives, wine; tourism. Ancient *Corcyra*; settled by Corinth *c* 734 BC. Under Venetian rule 1386-1797, British 1815-64. Cap. is Corfu, pop. 27,000. Port, resort.

corgi, small Welsh dog of 2 varieties: Pembrokeshire, short-tailed and red or red and white; Cardiganshire, long-tailed and any colour except white. Stands *c* 30 cm/12 in. at shoulder.

coriander, *Coriandrum sativum*, annual herb of parsley family native to Mediterranean countries. Grown in Europe and US. Seeds used as flavouring, oil formerly used medicinally.

Corinth (*Kórinthos*), town of SC Greece, on Gulf of Corinth. Pop. 16,000. Port; raisin, wine trade. Founded *c* 1350 BC; traditional rival of Athens. Colonized Syracuse, Corfu; joined Achaean League. Remains incl. citadel (Acrocorinthus). Refounded (1858) after earthquake.

Corinth, Gulf of, Greece. Inlet of Ionian Sea between mainland and Peloponnese. Joined to Saronic Gulf by canal (1881-93) across Isthmus of Corinth.

Corinthian order, most elaborate of the Greek orders of architecture, similar to Ionic, but distinguished by its bell-shaped capital decorated with design of acanthus leaves and volutes. Oldest known example is at Bassae, *c* 420 BC; order was little used.

Corinthians 1 and **2,** epistles of NT, written by St Paul (*c* AD 55) prob. from Ephesus (1) and Macedonia (2). Admonish the people of Corinth for their notorious immorality.

Coriolanus, Gnaeus Marcius (*c* 500-450 BC), Roman general, named after capture of town of Corioli from Volscians. Exiled from Rome for tyrannical aspirations, joined Volscians. Prepared to attack Rome, but dissuaded by mother and wife. Put to death by Volscians. Hero of Shakespeare's play, *Coriolanus*.

Cork (*Corcaigh*), county of Munster prov., S Irish Republic. Area 7462 sq km (2881 sq mi); pop. 358,000. Crossed E-W by mountains; fertile valleys; indented coast incl. Bantry Bay. Agric., dairying; fishing. Co. town **Cork**, co. bor. with *Cóbh*, on R. Lee. Pop. 128,000. Exports agric. produce. Woollen mfg.; distilling. Protestant, RC cathedrals.

cork, outer tissue produced by evergreen cork oak, *Quercus suber*, of the Mediterranean region to replace epidermis as a protective layer. Impervious, compressible and elastic, used for stoppers, floorcoverings, floats, *etc*. Trees can be stripped about every 10 years for *c* 150 years.

corkwood, *see* BALSA.

corm, *see* BULB.

cormorant, diving seabird of Phalacrocoracidae family. Long neck and body, hooked bill, mainly black plumage; breeds in colonies. Tamed and used to catch fish in Japan, China. Species incl. widespread

Phalacrocorax carbo common on N Atlantic coast.

corn, *see* MAIZE; WHEAT; OATS.

corncrake, *Crex crex*, brown short-billed European game bird of rail family. Timid, frequents long grass.

cornea, *see* EYE.

Corneille, Pierre (1606-84), French dramatist. Principal formulator of French Classical theatre. Portrayed tragedy within man rather than in external events. Major works incl. *Le Cid* (1637), *Polyeucte* (1641). Finally eclipsed by Racine.

cornet, brass wind instrument created in France (*c* 1825) by adding valves to post horn, although a modern cornet resembles a squat trumpet. Sound more mellow than trumpet; used mainly in brass bands.

cornflower, *Centaurea cyanus*, hardy annual of daisy family native to Mediterranean regions. Formerly weed in European grainfields, now popular garden flower, esp. blue variety.

Cornish, *see* CELTIC.

Corn Laws, in Britain, restrictions placed on exports or imports of grain. Acts (1791, 1813) forced up price of grain by protective tariffs on imports, serving interests of land-owners. Opposition, esp. among new industrial classes over high food prices, culminated in formation of Anti-Corn Law League (1839), leaders of which incl. Bright, Cobden. Laws repealed 1846 by Peel under mounting public pressure during Irish famine (1845-6).

Cornwall, county of SW England. Area 3546 sq km (1369 sq mi); pop. 377,000; co. town Truro. Interior moorland, *eg* Bodmin Moor in E; rocky, rugged coastline; mild cli-mate. Tourism; dairy farming, fruit, vegetable growing; kaolin¹ indust. has replaced tin, copper mining.

Cornwallis, Charles Cornwallis, 1st Marquess (1738-1805), British general. During American Revolution, led retreat from Carolinas to Virginia; his surrender at Yorktown (1781) marked end of fighting. As governor-general of India, quelled Tippoo Sahib.

Coromandel Coast, *see* TAMIL NADU.

corona, *see* SUN.

Corot, Jean Baptiste Camille (1796-1875), French landscape painter. Sketches from nature noted for their simplicity of form and clarity of light. Later misty land-scapes, grey-green in tone, were popular successes.

corporate state, system in which state controls economy, comprised mainly of privately-owned businesses. Political and economic power vested in organization controlling corporations of employers and workers; dates from medieval guild system. Modified form under virtual dictatorships operated in Fascist Italy from 1920s and in Portugal until 1974. Collectivist in principle, use of private capital justified in capitalist context on grounds of national priorities. Post-war Western indust. states have taken on some corporate state characteristics.

Corpus Christi, port of S Texas, US; on Corpus Christi Bay, channel access to Gulf of Mexico. Pop. 205,000. Exports cotton, petroleum, fish. Natural gas, oil refining, shipping. Tourist resort.

Correggio, Antonio Allegri da (*c*

1494-1534), Italian painter. Known for his soft painterly style and use of extreme illusionism in his decorations; late works foreshadow Italian Baroque. Works incl. fresco *Assumption of the Virgin* in dome of Parma Cathedral.

Corsica (*Corse*), isl. dept. of France, in Mediterranean Sea, N of Sardinia. Area 8721 sq km (3367 sq mi); cap. Ajaccio. Plains along E coast, mountainous elsewhere, highest peak Monte Cinto (2709 m/8891 ft); extensive scrubland (*maquis*). Tourism, limited agric. (olives), fishing. Settled from Etruscan times, ceded (1768) to France by Genoa. Banditry and blood feuds rife until early 20th cent. Napoleon born in Ajaccio.

Cortés, Hernán or **Hernando Cortez** (1485-1547), Spanish conquistador. Led force of 600 men in conquest of Mexico. Entered Tenochtitlán (Mexico City) in 1519, where he was received by emperor Montezuma as god Quetzalcoatl. Recaptured Tenochtitlán (1521) after Spaniards had been expelled by Aztec revolt during his absence; victory marked fall of Aztec empire. Gradually lost political power in Mexico, failing to be appointed viceroy.

cortisone, crystalline steroid hormone produced by cortex of adrenal gland. Used to treat inflammatory diseases and allergies, eg arthritis, asthma; dangerous side-effects incl. muscle weakness, kidney damage.

Cortona, Pietro Berrettini da (1596-1669), Italian painter, architect. Major exponent of Roman high baroque style, painted huge illusionistic fresco *Allegory of Divine Providence and Barberini* •

Power (1633-9) on ceiling of Barberini Palace, Rome.

Coruña, La, or **Corunna**, city of NW Spain, on Atlantic Ocean, cap. of La Coruña prov. Pop. 190,000. Sardine fishing, cigar mfg. Armada sailed from here (1588). Scene of Peninsular War battle (1809) in which Sir John Moore was killed.

corundum, very hard mineral, form of aluminium oxide. Found chiefly among metamorphosed limestones, shales. Coarser varieties used as abrasives, eg EMERY; finer as gems, eg RUBY, SAPPHIRE. Major sources in Burma, Thailand, Australia, US.

corvette, originally, a full-rigged sloop of war, below a frigate in size, carrying up to 20 guns on upper deck. In WWII a small antisubmarine escort vessel.

Cos (*Kos*), isl. of Greece, in the Dodecanese off Turkey. Area 282 sq km (109 sq mi), main town Cos. Cereals, fruit, wine; Cos lettuce originated here. Ancient literary, medical centre (birthplace of Hippocrates).

Cosenza, city of Calabria, SW Italy, on R. Crati. Cap. of Cosenza prov. Pop. 103,000. Furniture, textiles; fruit market. Cathedral (12th cent.), castle (13th cent.).

Cosgrave, William Thomas (1880-1965), Irish statesman. After 1922 split of Sinn Fein, headed Irish Free State govt. (1922-32) until defeat by De Valéra. Resigned 1944 as opposition leader. His son, Liam Cosgrave (1920-), became PM in 1973 at head of Fine Gael govt. Introduced (1976) measures to prevent IRA activities in Republic supporting conflict in Northern Ireland. Defeated in 1977 election.

cosmetics, substances used to enhance personal appearance, eg by cleansing skin and covering blemishes. Use of cosmetics first recorded in ancient Egypt, and became common in imperial Rome. Oils and perfumes were brought to Europe from the East in 11th and 12th cents. In 20th cent. large-scale production of cosmetics on scientific basis began.

cosmic rays, high energy radiation reaching Earth from outer space. Primary cosmic rays consist largely of protons and alpha particles; these collide with particles in upper atmosphere to produce secondary cosmic rays containing mesons, neutrons, electrons, etc. Various subatomic particles, incl. positron, discovered in cosmic rays. Source unknown; some rays originate in solar flares, but most come from beyond Solar System.

cosmology, science of nature, origin and history of universe. Modern cosmology theories assume that universe looks same in all directions and from all positions. General theory of relativity provides framework for study of gravitation and its shaping effect on universe. Theories of origin of universe incl. BIG-BANG and STEADY-STATE theories.

Cossacks, people of S Russia and Siberia, famous as horsemen and cavalry. Settled in Don and Dnepr areas in 15th and 16th cents., held privileges of auton. govt. in return for military service. Participation in unsuccessful peasant revolts in 18th cent. led to loss of some auton. In 19th cent., organized by Russian govt. into 11 communities spread throughout country. Deprived of privileges after many fought against Bolsheviks (1918-20).

Costa del Sol, coastline of S Spain, between Almería and Tarifa. Popular resort region, eg Malaga, Torremolinos.

Costa Rica, republic of Central America, between Nicaragua and Panama. Area 50,700 sq km (19,575 sq mi); pop. 2,012,000; cap. San José. Language: Spanish. Religion: RC. Dormant volcanic mountains with jungle in N; plains on Caribbean, Pacific coasts. Mainly agric., coffee, bananas; timber exports. Part of Guatemala under Spanish rule until 1821; part of Central American Federation (1823-38).

Costermansville, see BUKAVU, Zaire.

cost of living index, measurement of cost of goods and services needed to maintain a specific standard of living. Originally used to indicate incidence of poverty, now used by govt. as guide to fiscal policy, and as basis for wage negotiations. In US, Consumer Price Index (1945) compiled by Bureau of Labor Statistics; in UK, Index of Retail Prices (1947) compiled by Cost of Living Advisory Committee.

Côte d'Azur, see RIVIERA.

Côte d'Or, range of hills in Burgundy, E France. Wine-producing region, main centres Dijon, Nuits St Georges, Beaune.

Cotman, John Sell (1782-1842), English painter. Leading member of Norwich School; his landscape watercolours are noted for simplicity of design and geometric composition.

cotoneaster, genus of shrubs of rose family native to Asia. Most species have glossy green leaves, small pink or white flowers and abundant crimson berries. *Cotoneaster horizontalis* is popular garden variety.

Cotopaxi, mountain of NC Ecuador; world's highest active volcano. Height 5897 m (19,347 ft). First climbed by Reiss (1872).

Cotswold Hills, W England, limestone range mainly in Gloucestershire. Form Severn-Thames watershed. Attractive stone villages. Wool centre until 17th cent.

Cotton, John (1584-1652), English Puritan clergyman. Fled (1633) from England to Massachusetts where Boston was named to honour his native English town. Responsible for banishment of ANNE HUTCHINSON and Roger Williams. Estab. Congregationalism in colony.

cotton, soft white seed hairs filling pods of various shrubs of genus *Gossypium* of mallow family, native to tropics. Cheapest and most widely used natural fibre. Has been spun, woven and dyed since prehistoric times. Cotton mfg. has been a major industry, esp. in Britain and US (18th and 19th cents.). USSR, India, China, Mexico are other major producers.

cottonmouth, see WATER MOCCASIN.

cottontail, one of several common non-burrowing American rabbits, genus *Sylvilagus,* with short fluffy tails, white underneath.

couch grass, *Agropyron repens,* perennial weed, troublesome on arable land, with creeping rhizomes of which each broken piece is capable of reproduction. Native to Europe, now common in North America.

cougar, see PUMA.

Coulomb, Charles Augustin de (1736-1806), French physicist. Used torsion balance to deduce Coulomb's law: force of attraction or repulsion between charged bodies is proportional to product of magnitude of charges and inversely proportional to square of distance between them. SI unit of charge named after him.

council, ecumenical, in Christianity, convocation of duly constituted authorities of whole church. Modern RC, canonists recognize 21 such councils incl. Nicaea (325), Ephesus (431), Basle (1431), Trent (1545), Vatican II (1962). Eastern Orthodox churches recognize the first 7 of these 21.

Council for Mutual Economic Assistance (COMECON), E European organization estab. (1949) to coordinate economic policy in Communist bloc. Its 1959 charter gave it same status as European Economic Community, expanded scope to regulate indust. production. Albania expelled (1961) from membership. Mongolian People's Republic joined (1962).

Council of Europe, organization of European states. Estab. (1949) to secure greater unity between its members; to safeguard common political, cultural heritage; facilitate economic, social progress. Members mainly from W and N Europe. European Commission investigates alleged violations of European Convention on Human Rights (signed 1950), submits findings to European Court of Human Rights (estab. 1958).

counterpoint, in music, art of

combining two or more independent melodies so that they form a harmonious whole. Dominant feature of much Renaissance and Baroque music; esp. developed in 16th cent. choral work by such masters as Palestrina.

Counter-Reformation, see REFORMATION, CATHOLIC.

countertenor or **male alto,** adult male singer with unusually high voice, produced by developing falsetto or head voice. Most often to be heard in early classical music.

Country Party, Australian political party. Origins in 19th cent.; arose out of rural discontent. In 20th cent., has often held 3rd party balance of power in alliance with Liberal party, esp. during and after WWI.

county, in England and Wales, main political, social and admin. division. As 'shire', unit of govt. before Norman Conquest (1066); form for most of 20th cent. estab. by Local Government Act (1888). Restructured by new act (1972) resulting in county and district councils. Now 45 counties in England, 6 in Wales. Scottish counties, by extension of legislation (1973), replaced by 9 regions, 3 island areas. In US, county is principal geographic and political subdivision of all states except Alaska.

coup d'état, in politics, sudden (usually forcible) overthrow of govt. by faction contending for power. Differs from revolution, involving radical restructuring of society, in that top level only of govt. or admin. is replaced. Hist. precedents range from Napoleon's rise to power in France to Amin in Uganda (1971) and Pinochet in Chile (1973).

Couperin, François (1668-1733), French composer, harpsichordist. Noted organist; wrote 4 books of harpsichord suites, also *L'Art de toucher le clavecin* on keyboard technique. Best known of distinguished musical family.

Courbet, Gustave (1819-77), French painter. Leader of realist school of French painting, his unidealized scenes from daily life incl. *Funeral at Ornans* (1850). Imprisoned after destruction of Vendôme Column during Paris Commune, he lived in Switzerland from 1873.

courgette or **zucchini,** *Cucurbita pepo,* small marrow, 5-20 cm/2-8 in. long. Ridged outer skin; used as vegetable, baked, fried or stuffed.

coursing, hunting of game, usually hares, by hounds trained to follow by sight rather than scent. In competitions, 2 dogs chase a hare and are tested for qualities of speed and agility.

court, in law, person or persons appointed to try cases, make investigation, render judgment. Secular, complex system developed in ancient Rome. In UK, High Court of Justice (estab. by Judicature Act, 1873) comprises chancery; King's (or Queen's) Bench; probate, divorce and admiralty; court of appeal. Two systems in US are federal and state. Supreme Court is at head of federal system.

Cousteau, Jacques Yves (1910-), French naval officer, underwater explorer. Invented aqualung (1943); helped develop bathyscaphe, underwater filming. Founder of French naval underwater research;

has produced many books, films on sea life.

Covenanters, in Scottish history, members of groups bound by oath to defend Presbyterianism Covenant of 1581 sought to combat RC church in Scotland; National Covenant of 1638 opposed Archbishop Laud's attempts to introduce Book of Common Prayer into Scotland. Supported Puritan Revolution only after English Parliament's acceptance of Solemn League and Covenant (1643), promising estab. of Presbyterianism in England. Resisted coercion after Restoration; movement ended with Glorious Revolution (1688).

Covent Garden, Royal Opera House, originally site of London Theatre; later of Royal Italian Opera House (opened 1732). Present house (opened 1858) home of Royal Opera Co. and Royal Ballet Co.

Coventry, city of West Midlands met. county, WC England. Pop. 335,000. Cars, aircraft, hosiery, rayon industs. Medieval weaving town. Centre destroyed in WWII bombing. New cathedral, incorporating old, completed 1962.

Coverdale, Miles (1488-1569), English translator of Bible. Pub. English translation of entire Bible (1535). Collaborated in Great Bible (1539); edited 'Cranmer's Bible' (1540).

cow, mature female of domestic cattle. Name also applied to mature female of other animals, *eg* buffalo, moose, whale.

Coward, Sir Noël (1899-1973), English actor, playwright, composer, film director. Best known for witty comedies incl. *Private Lives* (1930), *Blithe Spirit* (1941), *Present*

Laughter (1943), also wrote revues, songs incl. 'Mad Dogs and Englishmen', film scripts *eg In Which We Serve* (1942), *Brief Encounter* (1945).

Cowes, urban dist. of Isle of Wight, England, on R. Medina. Pop. 19,000. Yachting centre, has famous annual regatta. Osborne House nearby.

Cowley, Abraham (1618-67), English poet. Metaphysical works incl. Biblical epic *Davideis* (1656). Introduced Pindaric ode to England.

Cowper, William (1731-1800), English poet. Known for religious *Olney Hymns* (1779) incl. 'God moves in a mysterious way'; *John Gilpin's Ride* (1782), *The Castaway* (1803). Subject of Cecil's biog., *The Stricken Deer* (1928).

cowrie, gastropod mollusc of Cypraeidae family, abundant in tropical seas. Shells, shiny and brightly coloured, sometimes used as money or decoration.

cowslip, *Primula veris,* European plant of primrose family. Has yellow bell flowers.

Cox, David (1783-1859), English painter. Best known for his watercolours of N Wales, painted in broad manner.

coyote or prairie wolf, *Canis latrans,* small wolf of plains of W North America. Thick fur, bushy tail; largely nocturnal. Omnivorous, hunts singly or in packs.

coypu, *Myocastor coypus,* large herbivorous aquatic rodent of South America, *c* 90 cm/3 ft in length. Introduced into other countries for cultivation of fur (nutria).

Cozens, Alexander (*c* 1717-86), English painter, b. Russia. Best known for his 'blot drawings', means of building landscapes from haphazard arrangement of ink blots. His son, **John Robert Cozens** (1752-96), painted poetic watercolour landscapes in subdued tones of blue, grey and green; influenced Turner, Girtin.

crab, one of various crustaceans of suborder Brachyura with 4 pairs of legs, pair of pincers and flattened. shell; abdomen reduced and folded under thorax. Many species edible, incl. European *Cancer pagurus*.

crab apple, *Malus pumila,* tree of apple family of Europe and W Asia. Small reddish-yellow fruit with bitter flavour used in preserves. Parent of all cultivated apples.

Crabbe, George (1754-1832), English poet. Known for realistic, antipastoral heroic verse, *eg The Village* (1783), *The Borough* (1810) incl. 'Peter Grimes', used by Benjamin Britten as theme of opera. Marks transition from 18th cent. Classicism to Romanticism.

Crab nebula, gaseous nebula in constellation Taurus, remnant of supernova explosion seen in 1054. Emits radio waves and X-rays; at its centre is a PULSAR.

Cracow, *see* KRAKÓW, Poland.

Craig, [Edward] Gordon (1872-1966), English actor, producer, set designer. Illegitimate son of Ellen Terry. Staged productions in Europe, incl. *Hamlet* in Moscow. Pub. *On the Art of the Theatre* (1911).

Craigavon, James Craig, 1st Viscount (1871-1940), Irish statesman. Helped organize (1914) Ulster Volunteers to resist Irish Home Rule. First PM of Northern Ireland (1921-40).

Craigie, Sir William Alexander (1867-1957), British lexicographer, b. Scotland. Joint editor (1901-33) of *New English Dictionary* ('Oxford English Dictionary'). Chief editor of *A Dictionary of American English on Historical Principles* (1938-43).

Craiova, city of SW Romania, on R. Jiu. Pop. 188,000. Textiles; food processing; leather goods. Roman *Castra Nova*; hist. cap. of Lesser Walachia.

cramp, painful spasm of the muscles. May be caused by excessive loss of salt, effect of cold on nervous system, or by continual pressure on particular nerves.

Cranach, Lucas, real name Müller (1472-1553), German artist; known as 'The Elder'. Early works of religious subjects noted for their handling of landscape. Later associated with Luther, he was prolific producer of woodcuts, portraits and mythological figures, developing own style in painting erotic female nudes. Portraits incl. Luther, Charles V.

cranberry, *Vaccinium oxycoccus,* vine-like shrub with bitter, crimson berries, native to Europe and US. Traditional sauce with venison and turkey.

Crane, [Harold] Hart (1899-1932), American poet. Known for *White Buildings* (1926), influenced by Rimbaud, and *The Bridge* (1930). Rejected cultural pessimism of T.S. Eliot. Major influence on post-1946 American poetry.

Crane, Stephen Townley (1871-1900), American author. Best known for Civil War novel, *The Red Badge of Courage* (1895). Other works incl. *Maggie: A Girl of the Streets* (1893), classic short story 'The Open Boat' (1898), poetry.

crane, any of Gruidae family of long-necked, long-legged wading birds, found everywhere except South America. Species incl. grey European common crane, *Grus grus*, American whooping crane, *G. americana*, and only Australian crane (brolga), *G. rubicunda*.

crane fly or **daddy-long-legs**, slender harmless long-legged fly of Tipulidae family. Larvae, known as leatherjackets, live in ground and are pests of crops.

cranesbill, see GERANIUM.

Craniata, subphylum of chordates having definite head. Incl. vertebrates, but not hemichordates or protochordates.

Cranmer, Thomas (1489-1556), English churchman, archbishop of Canterbury (1533-56). Annulled Henry VIII's marriage to Catherine of Aragon despite papal opposition (1533). Encouraged translation of Bible into English and its circulation throughout churches. Under Edward VI, compiled 2 Anglican Prayer Books (1549, 1552). Under Mary I, condemned as traitor and heretic, burned at stake.

crannog, in archaeology, lake dwelling built on artificial island of stones, earth, timber. Often surrounded by wooden stockade. Most date from late Bronze Age in Ireland, Scotland.

craps, see DICE.

Crashaw, Richard (c 1612-49), English poet. Known for extreme metaphysical conceits, often regarded as tasteless, esp. in 'St Mary Magdalene, or The Weeper'. Best works incl. 'Hymn to St Teresa', in *Steps to the Temple* (1646).

Crassus, Marcus Licinius (c 108-53 BC), Roman soldier and political leader. Amassed fortune by buying confiscated estates. Crushed revolt of slaves under Spartacus (71). Formed 1st Triumvirate with Caesar and Pompey. Given charge of prov. of Syria, killed after defeat by Parthians in Mesopotamia.

crater, bowl-shaped depression in Earth's surface. May be formed by explosion, eg at summit of volcanic cone, or impact, eg by meteor striking Earth's surface, as at Meteor Crater, Arizona, US. Craters may be lake-filled.

Crawford, Joan, orig. Lucille le Sueur (1906-77), American film actress. Films incl. *Rain* (1932), *A Woman's Face* (1941), *Whatever Happened to Baby Jane?* (1962).

crayfish or **crawfish**, freshwater crustacean, esp. of genus *Astacus*, resembling small lobster; many edible species. Term also applied to crustaceans of Palinuridae family, eg Australian spiny crayfish, *Palinurus cygnus*.

Crécy (-en-Ponthieu), village of Picardy, NE France, near Abbeville. Scene of victory (1346) of Edward III of England over Philip VI of France.

credit card, card allowing user to charge bills to credit account. May be issued by retailer, eg department store, oil company, or by bank. Some systems allow payment to be delayed at cost of monthly interest charge.

Cree, North American Indian tribe of Algonquian linguistic stock, formerly inhabiting Manitoba. Plains Cree were buffalo hunters of prairies. Woodland Cree (related to OJIBWA) although warlike were friendly to early French and British fur traders around Hudson Bay.

creed, brief statement of religious belief. Examples incl. Nicene, a revised form of that adopted by 1st Council of Nicaea (325) to combat Arianism, used in RC and Eastern Orthodox churches; Apostles', dating from 650 and similar to Nicene, used in RC and Protestant churches; Augsburg Confession (1530) is official Lutheran statement; THIRTY-NINE ARTICLES, basic creed of Church of England, dates from reign of Elizabeth I; Westminster Confession (1645-7) is creed of Calvinist Presbyterian churches.

Crefeld, see KREFELD, West Germany.

cremation, ceremonial burning of the dead. Practice in ancient world was prob. based on belief in purifying power of fire. Discontinued in Europe because of Christian belief in resurrection of the body. Subsequently revived with problems of disposal in large cities. First crematorium in US opened 1876; legalized in UK 1884.

Cremona, town of Lombardy, N Italy, on R. Po. Cap. of Cremona prov. Pop. 84,000. Indust., commercial centre; foodstuffs, textiles. Famous for violin mfg. by Amati, Guarneri, Stradivari. Cathedral (12th cent.), tallest campanile in Italy.

creole, person of European parentage born in West Indies, Central America, tropical South America, or descendant of such a person. In linguistics, creolized language is a PIDGIN which develops into a native language when speakers of mutually unintelligible languages live in close and long-term contact with each other, with one of the contributing languages typically dominant. Examples incl. Haitian creole, Gullah of South Carolina and Georgia.

crepe or **crêpe,** thin fabric with crinkled texture, originally woven from raw silk. Black crepe is used for mourning, softer crêpe de Chine is used for blouses, lingerie, etc.

cress, Lepidium sativum, tiny plant of mustard family, native to Persia. Used as a garnish. Different genus from WATERCRESS.

Cretaceous period, final geological period of Mesozoic era; began c 135 million years ago, lasted c 70 million years. Widespread inundation; extensive chalk formation esp. in latter (upper) half of period. Echinoderms, lamellibranchs, last ammonites; mammals still small and rare, dinosaurs extinct by end of period. Also see GEOLOGICAL TABLE.

Crete (Kriti), largest isl. of Greece, in E Mediterranean. Area 8332 sq km (3217 sq mi); cap. Iráklion. Mostly mountainous, highest point Mt Ida. Olives, fruit, wine; tourism. Home of Minoan civilization (fl 2000-1400 BC); remains incl. KNOSSOS. Turkish from 1669, passed to Greece 1912.

cretinism, congenital deficiency of thyroid hormone secretion, with resulting retardation of physical and mental growth.

Crewe, mun. bor. of Cheshire, NW England. Pop. 51,000. Major railway jct.; railway engineering.

cribbage, old English card game for two players. Scores are marked with pegs on a board. Invention credited to Sir John Suckling (1609-42).

Crichton, James (1560-c 1582), Scottish scholar and adventurer, known as the 'Admirable Crichton'. Travelled in France and Italy, admired for his charm, learning. Died in street fight.

Crick, Francis Harry Compton (1916-), English biochemist. Shared Nobel Prize for Physiology and Medicine (1962) with Maurice Wilkins and James Watson for work establishing double helix structure of DNA molecule.

cricket, insect of Gryllidae family, related to grasshopper and locust, but with long antennae. Often lives in human habitations, being active at night. Male produces chirping sound by rubbing forewings.

cricket, eleven-a-side game played with bat, ball and wickets. Marylebone Cricket Club (MCC), founded 1787, was governing body of game in England until formation of Cricket Council in 1969. Organized county cricket dates from 1873. Test matches, dating from 1877, played between England, Australia, New Zealand, West Indies, India, Pakistan and, formerly, South Africa.

Crimea, penin. of USSR, in S Ukrainian SSR; extending into N Black Sea. Taken from Turks by Russia (1783); scene of Crimean War (1853-6). Coast is tourist centre.

Crimean War (1853-6), conflict between Russia and Britain, France and Turkey. General cause was Anglo-Russian dispute, esp. over control of Dardanelles. Pretext was Russian-French quarrel over guardianship of Palestinian holy places.

Turkey's rejection of Russian territ. demands prompted latter's occupation of Moldavia and Walachia. Turkey declared war (1853), France and Britain joined (1854), Sardinia (1855). Main campaign, centring on siege of SEVASTOPOL in Crimea, was marked by futile gallantry (eg charge of the Light Brigade at battle of BALAKLAVA) and heavy casualties; hospital work by FLORENCE NIGHTINGALE. Settlement at Congress of Paris checked Russian influence in SE Europe.

criminal law, body of law dealing with crimes punishable by state. In Britain developed out of COMMON LAW; in US, each state has own body of criminal law, based on English customs brought by colonists. Usually, test of criminal liability is intention to commit, so that children (ie under 14 years), insane persons, etc, are not liable.

criminology, scientific study of crime, criminal(s), subfield of sociology; 19th cent. attempts at definition of criminal 'type' gave way to work of, eg William Healy (early 20th cent.), Gluecks (1940s), showing environmental factors. Others have studied crime as business, or as normal learned behaviour.

Crippen, Hawley Harvey (1861-1910), English murderer, b. US. Known as 1st criminal captured through use of radio. Was arrested on board ship attempting to escape to US with mistress after murdering wife.

Cripps, Sir [Richard] Stafford (1889-1952), British politician. Expelled by Labour Party (1939) for urging 'Popular Front' with Communists against Chamberlain's 'appeasement' policy; readmitted 1945. Served in Churchill's war cabinet from 1942 and in Labour cabinet (1945-50); chancellor of exchequer from 1947.

critical mass, in nuclear physics, minimum mass of fissile material, *eg* uranium, that can sustain a chain reaction. If less than critical mass of material is present, reaction dies away.

critical pressure, minimum pressure required to liquefy a gas at its critical temperature.

critical temperature, temperature above which gas cannot be liquefied, regardless of the pressure applied.

Croaghpatrick, mountain of Co. Mayo, NW Irish Republic. Height 765 m (2510 ft). Traditionally where St Patrick first preached.

Croatia (*Hrvatska*), autonomous republic of NW Yugoslavia. Area 56,524 sq km (21,824 sq mi); cap. Zagreb. Incl. Dalmatia, Istria, Slavonia. Dinaric Alps in W, fertile plain in NE drained by Drava, Sava. Timber, coal, bauxite, most developed region of Yugoslavia; coastal tourism. United with Hungary 1091-1918, part of Yugoslavia from 1918. Strong nationalist sentiment.

Croce, Benedetto (1866-1952), Italian philosopher, historian. Believed ideas are reality, not merely representations. Idealism reflected in *The Philosophy of the Spirit* (1902-17). Minister of education (1920-1) before rise of Fascism.

Crockett, David ('Davy') (1786-1836), American frontiersman. Democrat Congressman from Tennessee. Died at the Alamo fighting for independence of Texas.

Crockett, Samuel Rutherford (1860-1914), Scottish novelist. Wrote sentimental novels of provincial life, *eg The Lilac Sunbonnet* (1894).

crocodile, large carnivorous reptile of order Crocodilia, found throughout tropics. Lives in rivers, swamps and on river banks. Species incl. Nile crocodile, *Crocodylus niloticus*, Australian *C. johnstoni* and American *C. acutus*.

Crocodilia (crocodilians), order of large reptiles with powerful jaws, elongated snout. Four-chambered heart, unique among reptiles. Body covered with scales, bony plates. Order incl. crocodile, gavial, alligator.

crocus, genus of spring-flowering plants of iris family with fleshy corms and yellow, purple or white flowers. Over 80 species, native to S Europe. Saffron crocus, *Crocus sativus*, cultivated for use as flavouring and for saffron yellow dye.

Croesus (d. *c* 546 BC), king of Lydia. Completed conquest of Ionian cities of Asia Minor. Allied himself with Babylonia and Egypt to resist Persia, but was defeated and captured by Cyrus the Great. Proverbial figure of great wealth.

crofting, system used esp. in highlands and islands of Scotland, where tenant rents and cultivates small holding or croft, producing food and raising animals for his own needs.

Cro-Magnon man, prehist. human being of Upper Palaeolithic period (*c* 30,000 years ago). Remains found (1868) in rock shelter of Cro-Magnon in Dordogne area of France.

Of same species as modern *Homo sapiens*, but taller.

Cromarty, see ROSS AND CROMARTY, Scotland.

Crome, John (1768-1821), English landscape painter, called 'Old Crome'. A leader of the Norwich school. Influenced by Gainsborough and Dutch 17th cent. painters, esp. Hobbema, he painted Norfolk scenes with fidelity to nature.

Cromer, Evelyn Baring, 1st Earl of (1841-1917), British colonial administrator. As consul-general of Egypt (1883-1907) acted as real ruler, reformed finances, administration.

Crompton, Samuel (1753-1827), English inventor. Devised (1779) spinning mule, an improvement of Hargreaves's spinning jenny, which spun fine yarn suitable for muslin.

Cromwell, Oliver (1599-1658), English soldier and statesman. Leading Puritan in Parliament before Civil War, assumed command of anti-royalist forces after victories at Edgehill (1642), Marston Moor (1644). Demanded execution of Charles I after Naseby (1645). Cromwell declared republic after king's execution (1649) and crushed Irish resistance; defeated royalist Scots under Charles II (1651). Dissolved 'Rump' Parliament (1653) and estab. Protectorate, which he ruled as lord protector (1653-8). Refused crown (1657), introduced constitution to strengthen his powers. Warred with Dutch (1652-4) after 1651 Navigation Act, and Spain (1655-8). Military genius but his govt. was marked by cruelty and intolerance. Succeeded by his son, **Richard Cromwell** (1626-1712), as lord protector; he resigned 1659 when Commonwealth was re-estab.

Cromwell, Thomas, Earl of Essex (c 1485-1540), English statesman. Secretary to Cardinal Wolsey, whom he succeeded as Henry VIII's chief adviser and lord chamberlain (1539). Instrumental in split with papacy, carried out suppression of monasteries. Failure of Henry's marriage to Anne of Cleves, which he had negotiated to secure German alliance, resulted in his execution for treason.

Cronin, A[rchibald] J[oseph] (1896-), Scottish novelist. Gave up career as doctor after success of *Hatter's Castle* (1931); other novels incl. *The Citadel* (1937). Works usually involve problems of social responsibility. Creator of Dr Finlay.

Cronus, in Greek myth, youngest of the TITANS. Led revolt against Uranus, became ruler of the world. Married his sister Rhea, fathered the OLYMPIAN GODS. Despite attempt to avoid fate by destroying his own children, was overthrown by ZEUS. Identified with Roman Saturn.

croquet, outdoor game in which players use mallets to drive wooden balls through a series of hoops placed in the ground. Believed to have originated in France, where it had become popular by 17th cent.

Crosby, Harry Lillis ('Bing') (1904-77), American singer, actor. World's most successful singer in terms of record sales, made 1st recording in 1926; famous for relaxed style. Also appeared in many films, esp. with Bob Hope.

cross, symbol found in many societies, eg in ancient India, among American Indians, but esp.

important in Christianity in remembrance of Jesus' crucifixion. May take several forms, eg Latin, St Andrew's, Iona. Crucifix is cross with a representation of the dying Jesus used in RC church.

crossbill, bird of finch family. European crossbill, *Loxia curvirostra,* inhabits coniferous forests, as does white-winged crossbill, *L. leucoptera.* Crossed bill used to extract seeds from fruit, cones.

crossbow, a bow fixed to a wooden butt and fired like a musket, the string being pulled back by a lever or winding gear and released by a trigger. Used mainly in the 12th-13th cent.

Crow, North American Indian tribe of Hokan-Siouan linguistic stock. Nomadic hunters in Yellowstone R. area. Allied with whites v Sioux in 1870s.

crow, any of Corvidae family of perching birds. Often intelligent, with thick beak, mainly black plumage; worldwide distribution. Species incl. carrion crow, *Corvus corone,* hooded crow, *C. corone cornix,* of Europe, and RAVEN, ROOK, MAGPIE.

crowberry, *Empetrum nigrum,* small prostrate trailing shrub. Found on moorland in N temperate regions. Black edible berries.

crowfoot, name loosely applied to many species of plants of genus *Ranunculus* of buttercup family. Deeply divided leaves resembling crow's foot. Water crowfoot, *R. aquatalis,* has white flowers.

Crown, the, in UK govt., monarch as head of state. Formal powers incl. royal assent, needed for all parliamentary legislation, and royal prerogative. Latter incl. domestic duties, eg appointment of ministers, creation of peers, summoning and dissolution of Parliament, pardoning criminals; foreign duties, eg right to make war, treaties, receive and send ambassadors etc. Royal prerogative extends to other Commonwealth countries, and to colonial governors in certain areas. Most Crown powers, in practice, delegated to ministers.

crown jewels or regalia, symbols of British royal authority, kept in Tower of London. Present set dates from Restoration; incl. replica of crown of St Edward the Confessor (used at coronation), imperial state crown (worn on state occasions), swords of state, orb and sceptre.

Croydon, bor. of S Greater London, England. Pop. 332,000. Created 1965 from former co. bor. and residential areas of N Surrey.

Crozet Islands, archipelago of c 20 isls. in SW Indian Ocean, forming part of French Southern and Antarctic Territs. Area 300 sq km (116 sq mi). Site of meteorological station.

Cruciferae, family of flowering plants, with c 220 genera incl. the mustards, cabbages, cresses. Cross-like arrangement of 4 petals. Annuals or biennials.

crucifixion, death imposed by hanging from wooden cross, used widely in Near East, adopted by Romans for slaves and most despised criminals. Romans used T-shaped cross until abolition when Christianity became a lawful religion in empire under Constantine I. JESUS CHRIST died by crucifixion.

Cruden, Alexander (1701-70), Scottish scholar. A London bookseller, he compiled the *Complete Concordance to the Holy Scriptures* (1737), on which later concordances were based.

Cruikshank, George (1792-1878), English caricaturist and illustrator. Popular political cartoonist, he satirized politicians, Prince Regent, *etc.* Illustrated Grimm's *German Popular Stories* (1823) and works of Dickens.

cruiser, originally a ship of war larger than a frigate. In modern navies, a fast, lightly armoured but heavily armed vessel used mainly for engaging enemy raiders and escorting convoys.

Crusades, series of wars by W European Christians (11th-14th cent.) to recover Holy Land from Moslems, so called from cross worn as badge by crusaders. First Crusade (1095-9) followed speech by Pope Urban II urging Christians to fight to recover Holy Sepulchre. Preached by wandering preachers, incl. Peter the Hermit and Walter the Penniless, who led disorderly bands of followers to Holy Land. Organized campaign, led by great nobles, monarchs of Europe, culminated in capture of Jerusalem (1099); followed by estab. of Latin Kingdom of Jerusalem, and orders of Knights Hospitallers and Knights Templars. These orders were mainstay of later crusades. Turkish reconquests of Christian territ. occasioned later Crusades, beginning with unsuccessful **Second Crusade** (1147-9). Capture of Jerusalem by Saladin (1187) provoked **Third Crusade** (1189-92), led by Richard I of England, Philip II of France and Emperor Frederick I. Ended without recapture of Jerusalem, but trucial rights. **Fourth Crusade** (1202-4), proclaimed by Innocent III, was diverted from purpose by political ambitions of Venetians and ended in sacking of Constantinople by Crusaders and estab. of Latin Kingdom thereof. **Children's Crusade** (1212) followed, ending in children being enslaved, or dying of hunger, disease. Innocent III preached **Fifth Crusade** (1217-21), directed at Egypt, with no positive conclusion. **Sixth Crusade** (1228-9) led by Emperor Frederick II, gained truce, partial surrender of Jerusalem, crowning of emperor as king thereof. Moslems soon reoccupied Jerusalem, and wars broke out again. **Seventh, Eighth and Ninth Crusades** were abortive attempts to stem decline of Christian power in Holy Land, ending with fall of last Christian stronghold, Acre (1291). There were also crusades, proclaimed by pope, against pagans, heretics, *eg* Wends, Hussites, Albigenses.

Crustacea (crustaceans), class of arthropods, incl. crabs, lobsters, barnacles, shrimps, water fleas. Mainly aquatic; 2 pairs of antennae, pair of mandibles, other appendages for walking, swimming, *etc.* Body sometimes covered with chitinous carapace.

Cruyff, Johann (1947-), Dutch footballer. Skilful goalscorer for Ajax team which won 3 successive European Cup finals (1971-3). Later joined Barcelona. Captained Dutch team defeated in 1974 World Cup final.

cryogenics, study of production of

very low temperatures and of their effect on properties of matter.

crypt, subterranean chamber or vault, esp. under a church floor. Crypts developed when early Christians built churches over tombs of martyrs or saints.

crystal, solidified form of a substance in which atoms or molecules are arranged in ordered geometrical patterns repeated regularly in space. Structure can be studied by examining diffraction patterns produced by passing beams of X-rays through specimens.

Crystal Palace, building of glass and iron, designed by Joseph Paxton to house Great Exhibition of 1851. Erected in Hyde Park, London, it was moved to Sydenham (1852-3); destroyed by fire (1936).

Cuba, isl. republic, largest of West Indies; incl. Isle of Pines. Area 114,524 sq km (44,218 sq mi); pop. 9,405,000; cap. Havana. Language: Spanish. Religion: RC. Mainly low-lying; mountainous in interior and SE. Sugar is main crop and export; tobacco growing (cigar mfg.), fruit growing; timber from inland forested mountains. Settled by Spanish in 16th cent. after Columbus' discovery (1492). Spanish-American War (1898) led to independence in 1902. Castro estab. Communist govt. after 1958 revolt; US-Soviet confrontation over missile installation in Cuba (1962).

cubism, art movement of early 20th cent., derived from work of Cézanne; subjects were portrayed, not as they appear, but by analysis into series of planes. Traditional perspective was abandoned and several different views of subject were often combined. Originated by Picasso and Braque, its formative period was 1907-14.

Cuchulain, hero of Celtic myth. Central to cycle based on exploits, in association with uncle, Conchobar, king of Ulster. Most famous deeds told in *Táin Bó Cúainge* (the cattle-raid of Cooley).

cuckoo, any of Cuculidae family of mainly insectivorous birds. Long slender body, greyish-brown on top, curved beak. Some species parasitic, laying eggs in other birds' nests, *eg* common European cuckoo, *Cuculus canorus*. American cuckoos, *eg* yellow-billed *Coccyzus americanus*, not parasitic.

cuckoo flower, *Cardamine pratensis*, bitter cress bearing white or purple flowers. Common in N temperate marshes.

cuckoo-spit, *see* FROGHOPPER.

cucumber, *Cucumis sativus*, creeping plant of gourd family, native to NW India. Widely grown in temperate regions for elongated, edible fruit. Gherkin is one of 30 related species.

cucumber tree, name for MAGNOLIA.

Cudworth, Ralph (1617-88), English philosopher. Leading Cambridge Platonist. Attempted to reconcile rational and mystical, opposed Hobbes' materialism. Known for *The True Intellectual System of the Universe* (1678).

Cuernavaca, town of C Mexico, cap. of Morelos state. Pop. 160,000. Health, tourist resort. Has beautiful churches, monasteries and mural decoration by Diego Rivera.

cuirass, originally a leather jerkin. From medieval times, metal armour protecting the body above the waist, esp. in the 'cuirassiers' or heavy cavalry of the 17th cent.

Cukor, George (1899-), American film director. Directed many intelligent, stylish films eg *Camille* (1936), *A Star is Born* (1954), *My Fair Lady* (1964).

Culdees, ancient order of monks of Ireland and Scotland. Renowned for extreme laxness. Last community, at Armagh, disbanded in 1541.

Culiacán, town of NW Mexico, cap. of Sinaloa state. Pop. 359,000. In irrigated agric. region producing maize, beans, sugar cane. Founded 1531.

Culloden Moor, near Inverness, Highland region, N Scotland. Scene of defeat (1746) of Bonnie Prince Charlie's Jacobite forces by Duke of Cumberland's Hanoverian army.

Cultural Revolution (1966-9), period of ferment in China initiated under Mao Tse-tung, resulting in purge of leadership within Communist Party and state bureaucracies in effort to recreate revolutionary spirit. Top officials removed incl. Chu Teh, Teng Hsiao-ping; radicals in army and youth (*see* RED GUARD), led by Lin Piao, Chiang Ching (Mao's wife), sparked open conflict, mass rallies. Continuing chaos led Chou En-lai to restore order under army.

cultured pearl, semi-precious pearl formed within certain molluscs, eg oyster, after introduction of irritant. Mainly produced in Japan.

Cumae, ancient city of Campania, W Italy, near Naples. Strabo calls it earliest Greek colony in Italy (founded *c* 750 BC). Taken 5th cent. BC by Samnites. Many remains, incl. **cavern** of Cumaean Sybil.

Cumans, Turkic people, known in Russia as the Polovtsi, who settled in steppes N of Black Sea in 11th cent. Made continued war against Kiev, Byzantine Empire and Hungary. Defeated and dispersed, mainly into Bulgaria and Hungary, by Mongols in mid-13th cent.

Cumberland, William Augustus, Duke of (1721-65), British army officer, son of George II. Commanded the allied forces in the War of the Austrian Succession, and crushed the 1745 rebellion at Culloden with notorious severity, earning himself the title 'Butcher'.

Cumberland, former county of NW England, now in Cumbria; co. town Carlisle. Lake Dist. in S, incl. Scafell Pike; drained by Derwent, Esk. Plain of Carlisle in N. Dairying, livestock farming; granite, slate quarries. Scene of border warfare until 1603.

Cumberland, river of EC US. Flows from E Kentucky 1106 km (687 mi) SW into Tennessee then NW through Kentucky to Ohio R. at Smithland. Rises in mountains of Cumberland Plateau (incl. Cumberland Gap, strategic frontier and Civil War position).

Cumbernauld, town of Strathclyde, C Scotland. Pop. 32,000. Created as 'new town' 1955; well-designed layout.

Cumbria, county of NW England. Area 6808 sq km (2628 sq mi); pop. 476,000; co. town Carlisle. Created 1974, incl. Cumberland, Westmorland, N Lancashire.

cumin, *Cuminum cyminum,* small annual plant of parsley family grown in Egypt and Syria. Umbels of small white or pink flowers. Aromatic seeds used to flavour pickles, curries esp. in Oriental cooking.

Cummings, E[dward] E[stlin] (1894-1962), American poet, painter. Known for poems of typographical experiment, novel *The Enormous Room* (1922) on his imprisonment in French prison camp.

cumulus cloud, *see* CLOUD.

Cunard, Sir Samuel (1787-1865), Canadian shipping magnate. With others, founded (1840) steamship company (later to become Cunard Line) to carry mail from Liverpool to North America.

cuneiform, from Latin meaning 'wedge-shaped', writing developed in Tigris-Euphrates basin, consisting of wedge-like marks impressed on clay tablets. Used by Babylonians and Assyrians, key finds have been made at Nineveh, Lagash and Susa.

Cunningham-Graham, Robert Bontine (1852-1936), Scottish writer. Known for travel books, eg *A Vanished Arcadia* (1907) on Latin America. Involved in politics as liberal, socialist; first president Scottish Nationalist Party (1928).

Cupid, Roman god of love, identified with Greek Eros and Roman Amor. Represented as irresponsible cherub with bow and arrow.

-cupro-nickel, alloy of copper and nickel; ductile, resists corrosion. Used in coinage.

Curaçao, largest isl. of Netherlands Antilles, in S Caribbean. Area 461 sq km (178 sq mi); pop. 144,000. Has cap. of isl. group, Willemstad. Agric., incl. sisal, citrus fruit growing; famous liqueur mfg.; refining of oil from Venezuela. Discovered by Spanish (1499); Dutch occupation from 1634.

curare, alkaloid from bark of plants of genus *Strychnos*. Used by Amazon Indians as arrow poison. Causes paralysis. Limited medicinal use to relax muscles.

curassow, any of Cracidae family of arboreal birds of tropical America. Black or brown plumage, erect crest; resembles chicken. Species incl. great curassow, *Crax rubra*.

Curie, Pierre (1859-1906), and **Marie Curie,** née Sklodowska (1867-1934), French scientists. Pierre studied effect of heat on magnetic substances, showing that magnetic properties are lost above certain temperature (Curie point); investigated PIEZOELECTRIC effect. Marie worked on uranium, radioactive element in pitchblende. Together they discovered radium and polonium and shared Nobel Prize for Physics (1903) with Becquerel. Later Marie pioneered medicinal use of radioactivity; isolated metallic radium, winning Nobel Prize for Chemistry (1911).

Curitiba, city of SC Brazil, cap. of Paraná state. Pop.. 608,000. Agric. market (coffee, timber, maté); centre of immigration influx from 19th cent.

curium (Cm), transuranic element of actinide series; at. no. 96, mass no. of most stable isotope 247. Prepared 1944 at Univ. of California by bombarding plutonium with alpha particles.

curlew, large wading bird with downward-curved bill, brownish-grey plumage. *Numenius arquata* is largest European wader.

curling, game played on ice, usually by two teams of four players, in which heavy stones are slid towards a target circle at far end of rink. Rules controlled by Royal Caledonian Curling Club (founded 1838). Played in Scotland, North America and parts of Europe.

Curran, John Philpot (1750-1817), Irish politician, lawyer. Opponent of British policy in Ireland, defended Irish rebels, incl. Wolfe Tone, against repressive British regime.

currant, shrub of genus *Ribes* of saxifrage family, native to W Europe. Fruit of black currant, *R. nigrum*, and red currant, *R. rubrum*, eaten fresh or made into conserves.

currency, *see* MONEY.

current, *see* ELECTRICITY.

curry, condiment originating in India made from turmeric, coriander, black and cayenne pepper, *etc.* Usually eaten with rice, meat, vegetables.

Curtin, John Joseph (1885-1945) Australian statesman, PM (1941-5). Leader of Labor Party from 1935. As head of wartime govt., organized Australian defence forces to oppose Japanese advances in Pacific.

Curzon, George Nathaniel, 1st Marquess Curzon of Kedleston (1859-1925), British statesman. Reform viceroy of India (1899-1905), pacified North West. Conservative foreign secretary, presided at Lausanne Conference (1922-3), resolving Turkey's objections to post-WWI settlement.

Cushitic, non-Semitic language group of Afro-Asiatic family. Spoken mainly in Ethiopia, Sudan, Somalia, Kenya and Tanzania. Most important language of group is Somali.

Custer, George Armstrong (1839-76), American army officer.

Fought with distinction in the Civil War. Commanded a cavalry unit against the Indians and was killed with all his men by the Sioux at Little Bighorn.

customs, *see* TARIFFS.

Cuthbert, St (c 634-87), English bishop. Preached in Northumberland and Scottish borders. Bishop of Lindisfarne (685-7).

cuttlefish, any cephalopod mollusc of Sepioidea family. Ten tentacles around head, parrot-like beak. Flattened shell, or cuttlebone, is internal. Protects itself by ejecting cloud of brown 'ink'.

Cutty Sark, most famous of tea clippers that sailed between China and England in 19th cent. Achieved record of 363 mi in one day in races to get new tea crop to London. By 1872 races died out owing to opening of Suez Canal and use of steam boats.

Cuvier, Georges Léopold Chrétien Frédéric Dagobert, Baron (1769-1832), French zoologist, geologist. Regarded as founder of comparative anatomy and palaeontology. Proposed 4-phylum system of animal classification based on inner structure. Identified and named pterodactyl.

Cuyp, Aelbert (1620-91), Dutch painter. Son of Jacob Cuyp and leading member of family of painters. Did landscapes, still lifes, town and river scenes; noted for his handling of light and atmosphere. Works incl. *View of Dordrecht*.

Cuzco, town of SC Peru, alt. 3400 m (11,200 ft). Pop. 105,000. Sugar cane, rice products from irrigated region; woollen textiles mfg. Cap. of Inca empire, its numerous palaces and temples, incl. Temple of the Sun, were destroyed by Spaniards under Pizarro. Many ruins remain.

Cwmbran, urban dist. of Gwent, SE Wales. Pop. 41,000. Designated 'new town' in 1949. Steel, metal working industs.; bricks, tiles mfg.

cyanide, salt of hydrocyanic acid (hydrogen cyanide or prussic acid, HCN). Potassium and sodium cyanide are intensely poisonous white crystalline solids, with odour of bitter almonds; used in extracting gold from low-grade ores, electroplating, steel hardening.

Cybele, in Greek and Roman myth, 'mother of the gods'. Nature goddess, often associated with ATTIS.

cybernetics, science dealing with comparative study of operations of electronic computers and human nervous system. Defined by Norbert Wiener (1948) as 'the study of control and communication in the animal and the machine'.

Cyclades, rocky isl. group of SE Greece, in Aegean Sea. Area 2576 sq km (995 sq mi). Incl. Delos, Naxos, Syros (has chief port Hermoupolis). Wine, tobacco. Turkish from 1566; passed to Greece 1829.

cyclamate, salt of organic cyclamic acid, esp. calcium or sodium salt, which has very sweet taste. Formerly used as artificial sweetener; use discouraged because of possible carcinogenic properties.

cyclamen, genus of plants of primrose family, native to Mediterranean region. Heart-shaped leaves, flowers white to deep red with reflexed petals. Species *Cyclamen persicum* is popular houseplant.

cycling, sport of bicycle riding. Various competitive events incl.

road racing, time trialling, pursuit racing and sprints. Esp. popular in France, Belgium, Netherlands, where professional long-distance races such as Tour de France are held. Olympic event since 1896.

cyclone, area of relatively low atmospheric pressure together with surrounding wind system. Tropical cyclone is violent storm, *eg* hurricane, typhoon; temperate latitude cyclone now referred to as a DEPRESSION. Wind circulation is clockwise in S hemisphere, anticlockwise in N hemisphere.

Cyclopes, in Greek myth, gigantic one-eyed beings. In Homer, race of shepherds, one of whom Odysseus blinds (*see* POLYPHEMUS). In Hesiod, they are craftsmen, sons of Uranus and Gaea.

cyclops, small freshwater crustacean of subclass Copepoda. Enlarged antennae used as oars; single median eye.

Cyclostomata (cyclostomes), class of marine chordates with eel-like body, jawless sucking mouth; no bone or scales. Attach themselves by mouth to fish, rasping flesh and sucking blood. Incl. LAMPREY and HAGFISH.

cyclotron, in physics, a kind of ACCELERATOR.

cymbals, orchestral untuned percussion instrument, of oriental origin; made of 2 concave metal discs which are clashed together or struck with a stick.

Cynewulf (*fl* late 8th-9th cent.), Old English poet. Large body of religious verse attributed to him, but only 4 poems certainly his, incl. masterpiece *Elene*.

Cynics, Greek school of philosophy

founded (4th cent. BC) by Antisthenes. Held desires to be impediment to happiness, hence self-sufficient ascetic life of followers, *eg* DIOGENES. Basis of STOICISM.

cypress, family of coniferous trees, Cupressaceae, native to Mediterranean region, Asia and North America. Dark green needle leaves in overlapping pairs, woody cones. Distinctive symmetrical form. Lawson cypress, *Chamaecyparis lawsoniana*, grows to c 60 m/200 ft.

Cyprus (Gk. *Kypros*), isl. republic of British Commonwealth, in E Mediterranean. Area 9270 sq km (3572 sq mi); pop. 639,000, 80% being Greek Cypriots; cap. Nicosia. Languages: Greek, Turkish. Religions: Eastern Orthodox, Islam. Irrigated plain between 2 mountain ranges. Pastoral economy; grain, wine, olives grown. Minerals incl. iron, copper. Ancient Bronze Age culture; subsequently ruled by Assyria, Persia, Rome, Turkey, Britain (1878-independence in 1960). Bitter conflict (1950-64, 1974) between Greek, Turkish Cypriots; Turkish invasion 1974.

Cyrano de Bergerac, Savinien (1619-55), French author. Satirized society in *Histoire comique des états et empires de la lune* (1657-62). Inspiration for Rostand's dramatic hero, as longnosed poet-soldier, skilled dueller.

Cyrenaica, region of E Libya. Incl. fertile coastal strip, Libyan Desert, Kufra oasis. First settled 7th cent. BC by Greeks, who founded Cyrene. Under Romans, Arabs prior to Turkish rule from 16th cent.; colonized by Italy 1911-42. Federal prov. (cap. Benghazi) 1951-63.

Cyrenaics, *see* ARISTIPPUS.

Cyril, St (*c* 827-69), Greek Christian missionary. With his brother, **St Methodius** (*c* 815-84), sent (863) to convert Moravians despite opposition of German rulers. Cyrillic alphabet, used in Bulgaria, Russia, Serbia, possibly invented by Cyril.

Cyrus the Great (d. 529 BC), founder of Persian empire. Overthrew Astyages of Media (551) and gained control of Asia Minor with defeat of Croesus (546). Captured Babylon (539). Ruled with toleration, respecting local customs; allowed exiled Jews to return to Palestine.

czar, *see* TSAR.

Czechoslovakia (*Ceskoslovensko*), republic of EC Europe. Area 127,842 sq km (49,360 sq mi); pop. 14,918,000; cap. Prague. Languages: Czech, Slovak. Religion: RC. Comprises plateau of Bohemia (W); lowland of Moravia (C); highlands of Slovakia (E) incl. W Carpathians, High Tatra. Agric. in fertile valleys (esp. cereals, sugar beet, hops); timber, coal, iron industs.; textiles, engineering. Formed (1918) from parts of Austria-Hungary. Occupied in stages by Germans (1938-45). Coup estab. Communist state (1948); liberalization movement suppressed by Russian invasion (1968).

Czerny, Karl (1791-1857), Austrian pianist, composer. Pupil of Beethoven; best known for technical studies, still in use. A famous teacher, Liszt was among his pupils.

Czestochowa, city of S Poland, on R. Warta. Pop. 189,000. Railway junction. Iron and steel works, chemicals indust., textile, paper mfg.

Monastery on Jasna Góra hill is pilgrimage centre (has image of Virgin said to have been painted by St Luke; reputed to shed tears). Under Prussian rule 1793-1918.

D

dab, *Limanda limanda*, food fish of flounder family, found in N Atlantic.

dabchick, bird of grebe family. Name applied to pied-billed grebe, *Podylimbus podiceps*, of North America. European species, *Podiceps ruficollis*, is diving bird.

Dacca, cap. of Bangladesh. Pop. 1,311,000. Commercial, indust. centre on R. Dhaleswari. Textiles, jute products, chemicals; muslin mfg. centre until late 19th cent. Mogul cap. of Bengal in 17th cent.; cap. of East Pakistan.

dace, *Leuciscus vulgaris*, small freshwater fish of carp family with silver colouring.

Dachau, town of S West Germany, near Munich. Pop. 30,000. Paper, textiles, machinery mfg. Site of concentration camp under Nazi regime.

dachshund, small German dog, with long body, drooping ears and short legs. Short-haired coat; stands 20-25 cm/8-10 in. at shoulder.

dada or **dadaism**, literary, artistic movement of period 1916-22. Dada review proclaimed intention to replace rationality with deliberate madness, chaos in art. Dadaists incl. poet Breton, artists Arp, Duchamp. Developed into SURREALISM.

daddy-long-legs, see CRANE FLY.

Daedalus, in Greek myth, craftsman and inventor. Built Labyrinth for Minotaur in Crete (see MINOS). Made wings of feathers and wax to escape from Crete with son Icarus. Icarus flew too near the sun, the wax melted and he was drowned in the sea.

daffodil, various plants of genus *Narcissus* of amaryllis family with trumpet-like flower. Name usually restricted to common yellow daffodil or lent lily, *N. pseudonarcissus*, found growing wild in woods and fields of temperate countries.

Dafydd ap Gwilym (*fl* 1340-70), Welsh poet. Regarded as the master of Welsh poetry, particularly of *cywydd* metre. Poems mostly deal with love and nature.

Dagenham, part of Barking, E Greater London, England. Former mun. bor. of Essex. Has Ford motor plant, clothing, chemical mfg.

Dagestan, auton. republic of S European RSFSR, USSR; between E Great Caucasus and Caspian Sea. Area *c* 50,250 sq km (19,400 sq mi); pop. 1,430,000; cap. Makhachkala. Mainly mountainous, with coastal plain along Caspian. Stock raising; grain, cotton, fruit cultivated. Minerals largely undeveloped; some oil, natural gas.

Daguerre, Louis Jacques Mandé (1789-1851). French scene painter, physicist. Invented daguerrotype, photograph produced on copper plate treated with silver iodide; 1st practical method of photography. Also invented diorama, series of pictorial views seen in changing light.

Dahl, Roald (1916-), American writer, b. England. Known for macabre short stories, eg *Kiss Kiss* (1960), also children's books.

dahlia, genus of perennial, tuberous-rooted late-flowering plants of daisy family. Native to Mexico and Central America. Widely cultivated for brightly coloured showy flowers. Well-known species incl. *Dahlia coccinea*, *D. pinnata* and *D. juarezii*.

Dahomey, see BENIN.

Dáil Eireann, legislative, popularly-elected assembly of Republic of Ireland. First assembled (1919) in Dublin. After creation of Irish Free State (1921), upper house, Seanad Eireann, created, which, with Dáil (lower house) constitutes state legislature.

Daimler, Gottlieb (1834-1900), German engineer, inventor. Improved internal combustion engine, furthering car indust. Founded (1890) Daimler Motor Company.

Dairen, Japanese form of Talien, now LU-TA.

dairying, business of producing and distributing milk and milk products. In most countries, milk is consumed in liquid form. In others, eg Denmark, New Zealand, transportable milk products such as butter, cheese and dried milk dominate dairy indust.

daisy, *Bellis perennis*, small perennial herb of COMPOSITAE family, native to Europe and W Asia. Other species incl. *Chrysanthemum leucanthemum*, ox-eye daisy.

Dakar, cap. of Senegal, on Cape Verde penin. Pop. 581,000. Admin.,

commercial centre; port, exports groundnuts, animal products; univ. (1949), Pasteur Institute. Former centre of slave trade. Cap. of French West Africa from 1902, of Senegal from 1958.

Daladier, Edouard (1884-1970), French statesman. Premier (1933, 1933-4, 1938-40), forced to resign (1934) after Stavisky affair; signed Munich Pact (1938) enabling Germany to occupy Sudetenland. Interned by Vichy govt. (1940), deported to Germany (1943-5).

Dalai Lama, head of Lamaist religion of Tibet and Mongolia. Considered divine, reincarnation of his predecessor; 5th Dalai Lama was given (1640) temporal rule over all Tibet and built monastery near Lhasa. During 1959 Tibetan revolt against Chinese Communists 14th Dalai Lama went into exile in India.

Dale, Sir Henry Hallett (1875-1968), English scientist. Shared Nobel Prize for Physiology and Medicine (1930) for studying acetylcholine's role in chemical transmission of nerve impulses.

Daley, Richard Joseph (1902-76), American politician. Mayor of Chicago from 1955, headed Democratic party machine which dominated Chicago politics. Notorious for Chicago police's use of violent methods to disperse demonstrators at Democratic National Convention (1968).

Dalhousie, James Andrew Broun Ramsay, 1st Marquess of (1812-60), British statesman. Governor-general of India (1847-56), annexed (1849) Punjab after 2nd Sikh War. Promoted public works, education and social reform. Annexation of Oudh (1856) contributed to INDIAN MUTINY.

Dali, Salvador (1904-), Spanish surrealist painter. Influenced by Freudian psychology, he painted irrational dream world in a detailed academic style; later work, in more traditional style, incl. religious subjects. Collaborated with Luis Buñuel on surrealist films *Un Chien Andalou* and *L'Age d'Or.*

Dallas, city of NE Texas, US; on Trinity R. Pop. 844,000. Commercial, indust. centre. Oil refining; important cotton market; aircraft, electronic equipment, chemical mfg. Settled 1841; grew up as cotton market. President J. F. Kennedy assassinated here (1963).

Dalmatia, region of Yugoslavia, in Croatia, on Adriatic coast. Mountainous, incl. Dinaric Alps. Resorts incl. Dubrovnik, Split, Zadar. Passed from Austria to Yugoslavia (1919); Zadar and isls. ceded by Italy (1947).

dalmatian, breed of dog developed in Dalmatia (Yugoslavia). Shorthaired, black spots on white coat; stands 48-55 cm/ 19-23 in. at shoulder.

Dalton, John (1766-1844), English chemist. Proposed theory that all matter is composed of indestructible atoms; atoms of same element were identical and differed from those of other elements only in weight. Prepared table of atomic weights and devised law of partial pressures of gases (Dalton's law).

Dam, Henrik (1895-1976), Danish biochemist. Discovered and studied vitamin K, important in clotting of blood, for which he shared Nobel Prize in Physiology and Medicine (1943).

dam, barrier built across river to store water or regulate its flow for irrigation or to supply power. (See HYDRO-ELECTRIC POWER.) Notable dams incl. Aswan Dam across R. Nile, Fort Peck Dam (largest capacity in US) in Montana, Indus barrage in Pakistan.

Daman (*Damao*), former Portuguese enclave in W India. Pop. 69,000. Captured by Portuguese (1559), seized by India in 1961. Part of union territ. of Goa, Daman and Diu.

Damascus (Arab. *Esh-Sham*), cap. of Syria. Pop. 837,000. Famous for silks and metalware. Early Christian centre under Romans; taken by Arabs (635), seat of caliph (661-750). Cap. of independent republic from 1941.

damask, reversible fabric of silk, cotton, wool, *etc*, with figured pattern formed by weaving. Name derives from city of Damascus where mfg. of fine coloured silk fabrics reached high point in *c* 12th cent.

Damocles, in classical legend, courtier of Syracuse who, to show him the perils of a ruler's life, was seated at a banquet by Dionysius I under a sword suspended by a single hair.

Dampier, William (*c* 1651-1715), English buccaneer, explorer. Took part in several buccaneering expeditions to Africa, Spanish America (1679-91). Commanded naval expedition to W and N Australia, New Guinea, New Britain (1699-1701). Later piloted voyage round world (1708-11).

damson, see PLUM.

Dana, Richard Henry (1815-82),

American author, lawyer. Known for classic *Two Years before the Mast* (1840) based on experience as sailor. Subsequently campaigned for seamen's rights.

Danaë, in Greek myth, daughter of Acrisius, king of Argos. Imprisoned by her father because of an oracle that she would bear a son who would kill him. Zeus entered the prison as a shower of gold and fathered PERSEUS.

Danang, port of N South Vietnam on S China Sea. Pop. 438,000. Major US military base during Vietnam war.

Danby, Thomas Osborne, Earl of (1631-1712), English statesman. Impeached for treasonable negotiations with France (on Charles II's behalf); imprisoned (1679-84). Joined Whigs in inviting William of Orange to replace James II; served as king's chief minister (1690-5).

dance, the art of rhythmical, expressive movement of the body, often to music. Developed from early ritual, eg fertility dances and mimetic dances illustrating movements of planets, events in battle, etc. Dancing is still part of the ritual of several ecstatic religious groups, eg dervishes, Hasidic Jews. In Greece, became part of drama, eg choral dances in honour of Dionysus. Allegorical forms developed in medieval Europe, eg dance of death (possibly inspired by outbreaks of hysterical mass dancing during plague epidemics). Division into court and folk dances stemmed from late Middle Ages with the *volta* becoming source of modern ballroom dances. BALLET first appeared in 16th cent. Italian

courts. In 20th cent. many dance crazes have been associated with jazz and rock music.

dandelion, several plants of genus *Taraxacum*, esp. *T. officinale*, wild, European plant, cultivated in Asia and North America. Leaves used in salads and as diuretic.

Daniel, apocalyptic book of OT, prob. written *c* 168 BC. Story of Daniel, a Jew living in 6th cent. BC. Captured and taken to Nebuchadnezzar's court, where he was famous for his wisdom. Written to encourage the Jews to keep the faith under persecutions of Antiochus IV of Syria.

Daninos, Pierre (1913-), French novelist. Known for humorous caricature of English officer in *Les Carnets du Major Thompson* (1954).

Danish, language of N Germanic group of Indo-European family. Official language of Denmark, spoken also in Greenland, Faeroes, Iceland, Virgin Isls. Developed from Old Norse. Literature in existence since *c* 850.

D'Annunzio, Gabriele (1863-1938), Italian author, soldier. Belief that sensual pleasure alone gives meaning to life reflected in works, eg play *La Gioconda* (1898), novel *Il Fuoco* (1900), poetry. Hero of nationalism, held Fiume for 15 months (1919-20), later pro-Fascist.

Dante [Alighieri] (1265-1321), Italian poet. Best known for *Divine Comedy*, long epic poem giving comprehensive view of human destiny, temporal and eternal; divided into journeys through Hell and Purgatory (guided by Vergil) and Paradise (guided by Beatrice). Other works incl. *La Vita Nuova* (1292), prose-linked lyrics addressed to idealized love, Beatrice.

Danton, Georges Jacques (1759-94), French revolutionary. Influential orator, took part in overthrow of Louis XVI (1792). Leader of revolutionaries in new National Convention, advocated spread of Revolution's ideas throughout Europe by war. Member of Committee of Public Safety (1793), eventually opposed REIGN OF TERROR. Guillotined after power struggle with extremists led by Robespierre.

Danube, river of C and SE Europe. Flows 2815 km (1750 mi) from Black Forest (West Germany) to Black Sea (Romania). Tributaries incl. Inn, Sava, Tisza, Prut. Ports incl. Vienna, Belgrade. Navigable below Ulm, passage controlled by commission based in Budapest.

Danzig, see GDAŃSK, Poland.

Daphne, in Greek myth, nymph loved by Apollo. In trying to flee from him, she was changed into a laurel tree.

daphne, genus of small evergreen flowering shrubs, native to Europe and Asia. *Daphne mezereum* and *D. laureola* or spurge laurel are found in Britain and Europe. Chinese *D. odora* and *D. retusa* are widely cultivated for fragrant flowers.

Daphnia, see WATER FLEA.

Dardanelles (anc. *Hellespont*), narrow str. separating European and Asiatic Turkey; 64 km (40 mi) long, connects Aegean Sea and Sea of Marmara. Of great strategic and commercial importance; Troy stood nearby. Crossed by Xerxes I in 480 BC and Alexander The Great in 334 BC. In Turkish hands by 1402, it controlled entrance to Constantinople. Focus of conflict in decay of Ottoman Empire in 19th cent. and also in WWI (*see* GALLIPOLI).

Dar-es-Salaam, cap. of Tanzania, on Indian Ocean. Pop. 344,000. Admin., commercial centre; port, exports sisal, cotton, diamonds; oil refining. Railway links to Kigoma and Zambia; univ. (1961). Founded 1862; cap. of German East Africa 1891-1916.

Darién, Gulf of, inlet of Caribbean, between Panama and Colombia. Scots settlers failed in attempts to colonize Darién isthmus in E Panama (*c* 1700).

Darién scheme, Scottish plan to set up a colony on Darién Isthmus, Panama, and gain access to trade in Pacific. Suggested by WILLIAM PATERSON. Two expeditions (1698, 1699) to Darién failed through illness and Spanish opposition; great losses suffered by Scottish investors hastened Act of Union (1707).

Darío, Rubén, orig. Félix Rubén García Sarmiento (1867-1916), Nicaraguan poet. Coined term 'modernism' for aesthetic values standing outside society. Known for *Azul* (1888), Parnassian-inspired *Prosas profanas* (1896); immense influence on Spanish prose and poetry.

Darius [I] the Great (d. 486 BC), Persian king (521-486). Estab. authority by suppressing revolts of usurpers in early years of reign, then organized personal representatives (satraps) to administer vast empire. Sent unsuccessful expedition to punish Greeks for supporting revolt of Ionian city states (492). Second expedition defeated at Marathon (490).

Darjeeling, resort town of West Bengal, NE India. Pop. 43,000. In Himalayan foothills at alt. of over 1830 m (6000 ft). Nearby tea plantations. Fine views of Kanchenjunga.

Darling, river of E Australia. Flows *c* 2750 km (1700 mi) SW from W Great Dividing Range to Murray R. at Wentworth. Flow variable; Menindee Lakes storage scheme controls water supply, irrigation, h.e.p.

Darlington, co. bor. of Durham, NE England. Pop. 86,000. Woollens, engineering industs. Stockton-Darlington was 1st passenger railway line (1825).

Darmstadt, city of WC West Germany. Pop. 142,000. Indust. centre, esp. railway engineering, chemicals. Former cap. of Hesse-Darmstadt duchy.

Darnley, Henry Stuart, Lord (1545-67), English nobleman, 2nd husband of Mary Queen of Scots, father of James VI of Scotland. Joined in murder (1566) of David Rizzio, Mary's favourite. Murdered, prob. at instigation of Earl of Bothwell, Mary's next husband.

darter, any of Anhingidae family of swimming and diving birds, related to cormorant. Inhabits tropical lakes and swamps. Species incl. *Anhinga anhinga* of S US. Name also applied to various brightly coloured fish of perch family of North America.

Dartford, mun. bor. of Kent, SE England, on R. Darent. Pop. 50,000. Has first English paper mill. Cement, chemical mfg. Tunnel under Thames to Purfleet (1963). Peasants' Revolt (1381) began here.

Dartmoor, moorland area of Devon, SW England; features large granite masses ('tors'). Mostly in national park; livestock rearing; wild ponies. Prison estab. 1806 for French captives, used for convicts from 1850.

Dartmouth, indust. town of S Nova Scotia, Canada. Pop. 65,000. Naval base across harbour from Halifax. Shipbuilding, sugar refining. Linked by suspension bridge with Halifax. Settled 1750.

Dartmouth, mun. bor. of Devon, SW England. Pop. 6000. Port; Royal Naval Coll. (1905).

Darwin, Erasmus (1731-1802), English physician, naturalist. Author of *Zoonomia* (1794-6), anticipating Lamarck's evolutionary theories. His grandson, **Charles Robert Darwin** (1809-82), was a naturalist. His observations and explorations during the *Beagle's* voyages in the Pacific led to theory of evolution known as Darwinism, recorded in *On the Origin of Species* (1859) and *The Descent of Man* (1871). Theories on man's ancestry and principle of natural selection bitterly contested by contemporaries on theological grounds.

Darwin, cap. of Northern Territ., Australia, on N shore of Port Darwin. Pop. 35,000. Port, exports uranium, iron ore; major airport. Settled (1869) as Palmerston; renamed 1911, when passed under federal control. Severely damaged in 1942 Japanese air raids, again by storms (1974).

date palm, *Phoenix dactylifera*, tree grown widely in N Africa and W

Asia. Now cultivated in S California and Mexico. Nutritious brown fruit eaten raw.

dating, in archaeology, assessment of age of remains. Methods incl. RADIOACTIVE DATING, dendrochronology.

Daubigny, Charles François (1817-78), French landscape painter. Associated with Barbizon school, was early exponent of painting in open air; influenced Monet and Sisley. Best known for scenes of Seine and Oise.

Daudet, Alphonse (1840-97), French author. Portrayed Provençal life in humorous, naturalistic short stories, *eg Lettres de mon Moulin* (1866), 'Tartarin' series. Also wrote novels of Parisian society, *eg Le Nabob* (1877).

Daumier, Honoré (1808-79), French artist. Caricatured bureaucrats, politicians, bourgeoisie; imprisoned for representing Louis Philippe as 'Gargantua'. Paintings, describing contemporary life or on Don Quixote theme, incl. *Third Class Carriage*.

dauphin, title of eldest son of kings of France. Prob. derives from dolphin device adopted (12th cent.) by counts of Vienne, first to bear the title. Title passed to French royal family in 1350.

Dauphiné, region and former prov. of SE France, cap. Grenoble. Mountainous in E; main rivers Drôme, Isère. Tourism, h.e.p., vines, silk mfg. Part of kingdom of Arles (10th-13th cent.), annexed by France (1456). Rulers took title *dauphin*, adopted by sons of French kings.

Davao, seaport of Philippines, on Davao Gulf, SE Mindanao isl. Pop. 464,000. Centre of region producing hemp, timber, coffee. Underwent great indust. growth in 1960s.

Davenant, Sir William (1606-68), English dramatist, poet. Possibly illegitimate son of Shakespeare. Wrote first English opera *The Siege of Rhodes* (1659). Better known as reviver of English theatre after Cromwell's Commonwealth.

David or **Dewi, St** (d. c 588), patron saint of Wales. First abbot of Menevia (now St David's). Founded several monasteries in Wales. Feast day is 1 March.

David (c 1060-c 970 BC), king of Israel; Hebrew national hero. Traditionally, harpist to King Saul and slayer of Philistine giant Goliath. Anointed king after death of Saul and Jonathan (c 1012). Captured Jerusalem, making it his cap. in place of Hebron.

David I (1084-1153), king of Scotland (1124-53). Supported his niece, Matilda, in her struggle with Stephen for the English crown. Invaded England in 1138, defeated by Stephen. Promoted Anglo-Norman aristocracy in Scotland, encouraged trade, church.

David II (1324-71), king of Scotland (1329-71), son of Robert the Bruce. Lived in France from 1333 after English victory, returned to Scotland 1341. Invaded England for French (1346), defeated and imprisoned till 1357. Unable to pay ransom, agreed with Edward to English successor, but succeeded by nephew, Robert II.

David, Gerard (d. 1523), Flemish painter of Bruges school. Influenced by earlier Flemish masters, he painted religious scenes in a style which became obsolete in his lifetime. Works incl. *The Judgment of Cambyses*.

David, Jacques Louis (1748-1825), French painter. Treated heroic and republican themes in austere neo-Classical manner; ardent supporter of Napoleon, he painted pictures glorifying his exploits. Works incl. *Oath of the Horatii* (1785), *Death of Marat*, *Napoleon crossing the Alps*.

Davies, Peter Maxwell (1934-), English composer. Music employs mediaeval and Renaissance techniques set in modern context, often using parody. Works incl. opera *Taverner*, *Eight Songs for a Mad King* for voice and chamber orchestra.

Davies, W[illiam] H[enry] (1871-1940), Welsh poet. Best known for prose *Autobiography of a Super-Tramp* (1907), reflecting life as a tramp in US and UK. *Complete Poems* (1943) are simple descriptions of nature.

da Vinci, see LEONARDO DA VINCI.

Davis, Bette, orig. Ruth Elizabeth Davis (1908-), American film actress. Known for intense, dramatic roles in, eg *Dark Victory* (1939), *Now Voyager* (1942), *All About Eve* (1950), *Whatever Happened to Baby Jane?* (1962).

Davis, Jefferson (1808-89), American statesman. Secretary of war (1853-7); withdrew as senator for Mississippi at state's secession (1861). President of Confederacy (1861-5), criticized for centralizing policies which contradicted Southern cause of states' rights. Captured and confined by Federal troops (1865-7), never prosecuted.

Davis or **Davys, John** (1550-1605), English navigator. Made 3 voyages (1585-7) in search of Northwest Passage, reached Baffin Bay via strait named after him. Killed while fighting Japanese pirates in East Indies.

Davis, Miles (1926-), American jazz musician. Noted for cool style in playing trumpet and flugelhorn, working with small groups in 1950s and 1960s. Compositions incl. *Sketches of Spain*.

Davis Strait, arm of N Atlantic between Baffin Isl. and W Greenland. Length 640 km (*c* 400 mi); width at narrowest point 290 km (*c* 180 mi). Named after explorer John Davis.

Davitt, Michael (1846-1906), Irish revolutionary. Joined FENIANS in 1865; imprisoned for treason-felony (1870). Released 1877, founded Land League with Parnell (1879). Imprisoned several times for involvement in land agitation. MP 1895-9.

Davos, town of E Switzerland, in Graubünden canton. Pop. 10,000. Health resort; winter sports.

Davy, Sir Humphrey (1778-1829), English chemist. Studied electrolysis, isolating sodium, potassium, boron, calcium, magnesium and barium. Discovered use of nitrous oxide as anaesthetic and identified chlorine as an element. Invented miner's safety lamp and electric arc.

Dawes, Charles Gates (1865-1951), American statesman. Author of Dawes plan (1924) to facilitate German payment of reparations after WWI; shared Nobel Peace Prize (1925). Vice-president under Coolidge (1925-9).

Dawson, town of W Yukon Territ.

Canada; on Yukon R. Pop. 760. Tourist centre. Founded 1896 during Klondike gold rush, when pop. rose to c 20,000. Territ. cap. until 1951.

Dayan, Moshe (1915-), Israeli military leader. Army chief of staff (1953-8). As defence minister (1967-74), largely responsible for Israeli victory over Arab states (1967). Blamed for early reverses in 1973 October War. Resigned. Made foreign minister (1977); involved in peace negotiations with Egypt.

Day-Lewis, C[ecil] (1904-72), English poet, b. Ireland. Member of left-wing literary movement of 1930s. Collections incl. *The Magnetic Mountain* (1933), *Overtures to Death* (1938). Wrote detective novels under pseud. Nicholas Blake. Created poet laureate 1968.

daylight saving time, time reckoned (usually 1 hour) later than standard time. Adopted in many countries as wartime measure; continued after WWII as 'summer' time by turning clocks ahead in spring and back in autumn.

Dayton, city of SW Ohio; on Great Miami R. Pop. 247,000. Machine tools, refrigerators, aircraft mfg. Wright brothers estab. aircraft research centre (1911). Centre of US military aviation development.

D-Day, term for the day in WWII on which the Allied invasion of Europe began; 6th June, 1944.

DDT, dichloro-diphenyl-trichloroethane, white powder used as insecticide, effective on contact. Developed during 1940s, it helps control insect-borne diseases, eg malaria, typhus, yellow fever. Use has been restricted because of harm-ful effects on animals caused by its accumulation in plants.

deadly nightshade, see NIGHT-SHADE.

Dead Sea, salt lake on Jordan-Israel border, c 70 km (45 mi) long. Lies in Ghor depression with surface 394 m (1292 ft) below sea level. Evaporation yields potash, bromide. Dead Sea biblical scrolls found nearby at Qumran.

Dead Sea Scrolls, collection of ancient Jewish religious writings, found in caves NW of Dead Sea (1947 and later). Written during 1st cents. BC and AD, possibly by a community of ESSENES, they are of importance in study of origins of Christianity.

deafness, total or partial inability to hear. May be caused by accumulated wax, growth of bone in middle ear, diseases affecting foetus in early pregnancy, injury. Electronic hearing aids are used to amplify sound and alleviate deafness.

Deakin, Alfred (1856-1919), Australian statesman, PM (1903-4, 1905-8, 1909-10). Liberal leader, advocated social reform, imperial trade preference and federation of Australian states.

Dean, Forest of, Gloucestershire, W England. Ancient royal forest. Early indust. region (wood, coal, iron ore exploitation); largely deforested by 17th cent.

death, end of life and cessation of all vital functions in animal or plant. Heart may beat after cessation of breathing and resuscitation is sometimes possible through stimulation of nervous system shortly after cessation of heartbeat. In humans there is danger of brain dámage if delay exceeds 20 mins.

death cap or death cup, *Amanita phalloides,* toadstool with pale yellow cap, white gills. Appears in autumn in deciduous woods. Deadly poisonous with no known antidote.

death penalty, see CAPITAL PUNISHMENT.

death's head hawk moth, *Acherontia atropos,* brown and yellow moth with skull-like mark on abdomen. Found in Europe, Africa; largest British moth with wingspan 13-15 cm/5-6 in. Larvae eat potato leaves.

Death Valley, arid basin of SE California, US; part of Great Basin region. Very high temperature in summer. Badwater is W hemisphere's lowest point (c 86 m/282 ft below sea level).

death watch beetle, *Xestobium rufovillosum,* small brown beetle of Anobiidae family which attacks seasoned wood. Noted for sound made by head knocking against hard surface.

Deauville, town of Normandy, N France, at mouth of R. Touques. Pop. 6000. Fashionable resort with casino, racecourse.

Debrecen, city of E Hungary. Pop. 168,000. Railway jct.; agric. market, machinery. Calvinist coll. (1550), now univ. Seat of revolutionary govt. (1849).

Debrett, John (1753-1822), English publisher. Compiled and pub. *Peerage of England, Scotland and Ireland* (1802). Revised editions bearing his name still appear.

Debs, Eugene V[ictor] (1855-1926), American trade unionist, socialist leader. President of American Railway Union, imprisoned (1894) for disobeying court order in Pullman strike. Pacifist. Imprisoned (1918) under Espionage Act.

Debussy, Claude (1862-1918), French composer. Works incl. piano music, *eg Clair de Lune,* orchestral pieces, *eg La Mer, L'Après-midi d'un faune, Nocturnes* and opera *Pelléas et Mélisande.* Although impressionistic, his works are innovative harmonically.

Decalogue, see TEN COMMANDMENTS.

decathlon, ten-event athlètic contest, comprising 100, 400, 1500 m runs, 110 m hurdles, javelin and discus throws, shot put, high jump, long jump and pole vault. Olympic event since 1912.

Deccan, triangular plateau of SC India, enclosed by Eastern and Western Ghats.

Decembrist Revolt, uprising in St Petersburg, Russia, on accession of Nicholas I in Dec. 1825. Group mainly of army officers plotted to replace Nicholas by his brother Constantine and obtain a constitution. Its failure ended with hanging of some leaders, but revolutionary ideas intensified despite repression.

decibel, in acoustics, numerical expression of relative loudness of a sound: difference in decibels of 2 sounds is 10 times the common logarithm of the ratio of their power levels.

decimal system, system of computation based on powers of 10. Decimal fractions are fractions having some power of 10 as denominator; denominator is not usually written but is expressed by decimal point. Thus 25.03 is 2503/100. Used in metric system of weights and measures, most national currencies.

Declaration of Independence, see INDEPENDENCE, DECLARATION OF.

decorated style, name given to second period of English Gothic architecture, which followed Early English in late 13th and 14th cents. Characterized by use of bar tracery in window design, and complicated vaulting. Wells Cathedral, near Bristol, exemplifies style.

decorations, civil or military reward for service. Originated in medieval practice of conferring KNIGHTHOOD. British civilian orders incl. GARTER, Thistle, Bath. Others incl. Red and Black Eagle (Prussia), Legion of Honour (France). Military orders incl. Iron Cross (Germany), Croix de Guerre (France), VICTORIA CROSS (UK), PURPLE HEART (US), Red Star (USSR).

deductive method, see INDUCTIVE METHOD.

Dee, several rivers of UK. 1, NE Scotland, flows 140 km (87 mi) from Cairngorms to North Sea at Aberdeen. 2, In Wales and England, flows 113 km (70 mi) from Gwynedd to Irish Sea via Cheshire.

deer, any of Cervidae family of ruminant mammals, incl. deer, elks, reindeer, moose. Worldwide distribution except Australia. Antlers, confined to males except for reindeer and caribou, usually branched and shed annually.

defence mechanism, in psychiatry, unconscious behaviour pattern designed to avert painful or anxiety-provoking feelings. Forms incl. repression of distress or its

sublimation into useful forms, regression to infantile behaviour, etc. **deflation,** see INFLATION.

Defoe, Daniel (1660-1731), English author. Best known as author of novels *Robinson Crusoe* (1719), *Moll Flanders* (1722) among 500 works, mainly non-fiction. Also wrote prolifically on politics, economics in his thrice-weekly *Review* (1704-13).

Degas, [Hilaire Germain] Edgar (1834-1917), French painter, sculptor. Associated with the impressionists, he sought to unite Classical art with immediacy of impressionism. Influenced by photography and Japanese prints, work achieves spontaneity by asymmetric composition and cut-off views. Themes incl. racecourses, ballet scenes, women washing.

De Gaulle, Charles André Joseph Marie (1890-1970), French military and political leader, president (1958-69). Opposed armistice with Germany (1940) and formed Free French forces in Britain. Served as interim president (1945-6). Recalled (1958) as premier, elected 1st president of newly-created Fifth Republic. Ended French colonial power in Algeria; withdrew French forces from NATO (1966); vetoed British attempts to join EEC. Policies marked by nationalism and desire for European economic and military independence from US. Resigned after referendum defeat.

De Havilland, Sir Geoffrey (1882-1965), English aircraft designer. Designed WWI fighters, WWII *Mosquito* fighter-bomber and the post-war *Comet*, 1st jet airliner.

De Havilland, Olivia (1916-), American film actress, b. Japan.

Known for comic or romantic roles in 1930s-40s, as in *Gone with the Wind* (1939), later developed range to appear in, eg, *Hush Hush Sweet Charlotte* (1964).

Deirdre, in Irish myth, beautiful woman whom Conchobar, King of Ulster, desired for his wife. She eloped with Naoise and had many adventures before being allowed to return. On return Naoise and his 2 brothers were treacherously killed, and Deirdre took her own life. Story forms basis of plays by G.W. Russell, Synge, Yeats.

deists, those who believe in the existence of God on purely rational grounds without reliance on revelation or authority. Term esp. used for 17th and 18th cent. rationalists, eg Voltaire, Rousseau, Ben Franklin, who held that proof of existence of God was to be found in nature. Also known as freethinkers.

Dekker or **Decker, Thomas** (c 1572-1632), English dramatist. Known for comedies of London life, esp. *The Shoemaker's Holiday* (1600), *The Roaring Girl* (c 1610) in collaboration with Middleton. Collaborated with John Ford on *The Witch of Edmonton*. Also wrote pamphlets on London low life.

Delacroix, [Ferdinand · Victor] Eugène (1798-1863), French painter. Major painter of Romantic movement in France, he was a noted colourist. Painted historical subjects, scenes of Arab life, themes from Shakespeare, Byron, etc. Works incl. *Massacre at Chios, Liberty Leading the People, Women of Algiers*.

De La Mare, Walter (1873-1956), English author. Known for fantasy

and children's verse, eg *The Listeners* (1912), *Peacock Pie* (1913), and novels, esp. *Memoirs of a Midget* (1921).

Delane, John Thaddeus (1817-79), English journalist. Edited *The Times* (1841-77), giving it international status.

Delaunay, Robert (1885-1941), French painter. Founder of orphism, attempt to introduce more colour into austere forms of cubism; painted abstract colour discs, suggestive of movement. Influenced many artists, incl. Marc and Klee.

Delaware, group of closely-related North American Indian tribes of Algonquian linguistic stock. Called Lenape until 18th cent. Migrated to Atlantic from NW. Made treaty with William Penn (1682), but Iroquois attacks drove them into Ohio. Survivors of massacre (1782) in Pennsylvania fled to Ontario, where their descendants now live.

Delaware, state of E US, on Atlantic. Area 5328 sq km (2057 sq mi); pop. 548,000; cap. Dover; largest city Wilmington. Mainly lowlying, hilly in N. Agric. incl. fruit, vegetable growing; poultry rearing, fishing important. Chemical indust. English settlement (1664); one of original 13 colonies of US. Remained in Union during Civil War (1861-5) despite being slave state.

De la Warr, Thomas West, Baron (1577-1618), English colonial governor. Became 1st governor of Virginia colony (1609); on arrival, persuaded desperate colonists not to leave. State of Delaware named after him.

Delcassé, Théophile (1852-1923), French statesman. As foreign minister (1898-1905), negotiated ami-. cable settlements of colonial differences with Britain, eg in FASHODA INCIDENT. Paved way for Entente Cordiale with Britain; also strengthened alliance with Russia.

Deledda, Grazia (1875-1936), Italian novelist. Wrote novels, short stories about peasants of native Sardinia, eg Elias Portoliu (1903), Ashes (1904), The Mother (1920). Nobel Prize for Literature (1926).

Delescluze, Charles (1809-71), French journalist. Leader of Paris Commune in 1871, allowed himself to be shot on barricades after realizing that defeat was at hand.

Delft, town of W Netherlands, on Schie canal. Pop. 81,000. Ceramics ('delftware') mfg. begun 16th cent. Prinsenhof museum; Gothic churches, tomb of William the Silent. Birthplace of Vermeer.

Delhi, union territ. of N India. Area 1484 sq km (573 sq. mi); pop. 3,630,000. Old Delhi, on R. Jumna, important railway centre; textile mfg., gold and silver filigree work. Reconstructed in 17th cent. by Shah Jehan; fort contains Imperial Palace (1638-48) and Jama Masjid mosque. Interim cap. of India (1912-31), succeeded by neighbour New Delhi, which became cap. of republic (1947). Pop. 293,000. Univ. (1922).

Delian League, union of Greek states founded at Delos (478 BC) under Athenian leadership; later developed into an Athenian empire. Disbanded at end of Peloponnesian War (404 BC). Confederation revived to resist Spartan aggression (378 BC); lasted until defeat by Philip of Macedon (338 BC).

Delibes, [Clément Philibert]

Léo (1836-91), French composer. Wrote ballet music and operas known for lyricism. Works include Coppélia, Silvia and Lakmé.

delirium, brain disturbance marked by extreme excitement, hallucinations, confused speech. May result from disease, high fever, etc. Delirium tremens is form of delirium associated with chronic alcoholism; symptoms incl. sweating, trembling, vivid hallucinations.

Delisle, Guillaume (1675-1726), French geographer, cartographer. Pioneer of modern cartography, used astronomical observations to improve accuracy of maps. His world map in 2 hemispheres was pub. 1700.

Delius, Frederick (1862-1934), English composer. Work is both romantic and impressionist with an individual harmonic quality. Best-known pieces incl. orchestral works On Hearing the First Cuckoo in Spring and Brigg Fair, and choral work Sea Drift.

della Robbia, see ROBBIA, LUCA DELLA.

De Long, George Washington (1844-81), American explorer. Attempted, with George Melville, to reach North Pole (1879-81); caught in pack ice and forced to abandon ship, he died on return journey. Expedition added much to geographical knowledge of area N of Siberia.

Delorme or de l'Orme, Philibert (c 1510-70), French architect. Court architect to Francis I and Henry II, he designed Renaissance château of Diane de Poitiers at Anet and the Tuileries in Paris. Little of his work remains.

Delos (Dhílos), small isl. of SE

Greece, in Cyclades. Traditional birthplace of Apollo, Artemis, important religious remains. Treasury of Delian League 478-454 BC.

Delphi (*Delphoi*), ancient city of C Greece, in Phocis, at foot of Mt. Parnassus. Site of Delphic oracle and Pythian games. Excavated 19th cent., many remains found, esp. temple to Apollo.

delphinium, genus of hardy plants of buttercup family. Spikes of spurred, irregular flowers, usually blue, on tall stalk. Widely distributed in N hemisphere. Also called larkspur.

delta, roughly triangular area of alluvial deposits formed at mouth of a river. Consists of complex of distributary channels, lagoons, marshes. Usually very fertile, many support large agric. pop. Name derived from Greek letter *delta* (Δ); applied originally to Nile delta, now to any similar feature, eg Hwang-Ho, Mississippi.

Delvaux, Paul (1897-), Belgian painter. Known for his meticulous surrealist works, in which nude or semi-clothed women wander dreamily through architectural settings.

Demerara, river of Guyana. Rises in Guiana Highlands, flows N c 320 km (200 mi) to enter Atlantic at Georgetown. Used to transport bauxite.

Demeter, in Greek myth, earth goddess of corn, harvest, fruitfulness. Daughter of Cronus and Rhea; mother by Zeus of PERSEPHONE. She and her daughter were leading figures in Eleusinian mystery cults, representing seasonal cycle. Identified with Roman Ceres.

De Mille, Cecil B[lount] (1881-1959), American film producer-director. Pioneer, later grand old man of Hollywood, known for adventure films in 1930s-40s, eg *The Plainsman* (1936), and later for biblical epics, eg *The Ten Commandments* (1956).

democracy, govt. in which the people hold power either directly or through elected representatives, rather than by class, group or individual. In Greek city states, democracy took direct form of plebiscite or popular assembly, with exclusion of slaves. Modern democracy evolved out of demands for political and legal equality; later economic and social equality; such demands provoked American and French revolutions. Locke, Montesquieu, Rousseau were chief theorists in 17th and 18th cents. Modern Western democracy is based on competing party system, with emphasis on rule of law and freedom of expression.

Democratic Party, in US, one of the two major political parties. Origins in Democratic Republican Party founded by Jefferson (1800) in opposition to Hamilton's Federalists. Name changed to present one under Jackson (1828). Splits, created by slavery issue and Civil War, led to eclipse of party; revived with support of South after RECONSTRUCTION (1876). Radical ascendancy under Bryan brought wider base, support from rural and urban working classes, although irreconcilable factions caused electoral defeat; in 20th cent., attracted Negro and ethnic minorities. Identified with reform, esp. after F.D. Roosevelt's NEW DEAL (1932), thereafter dominated Republicans except for periods 1953-61, 1969-77.

Democritus (*c* 460-*c* 370 BC), Greek philosopher. Developed atomistic theory of matter originally suggested by Leucippus. Held that truth could be discovered by thought and that perceptions lead to confusion.

demography, science of statistics dealing with distribution, density, data of birth, marriage, death of populations. Used to determine rates of birth, death, *etc*, in analysis of social systems.

Demosthenes (*c* 384-322 BC), Greek statesman, orator. Advocated resistance to growing power of Philip of Macedon in series of orations, *Philippics* and *Olynthiacs*, but Philip triumphed at battle of Chaeronea (338). After death of Alexander the Great, organized unsuccessful revolt against Antipater; took poison to avoid capture.

demotic writing, Egyptian flowing (cursive) script, derived from HIERATIC in 7th cent. BC and lasting until 5th cent. AD. Written from right to left.

Dempsey, William Harrison ('Jack'), (1895-), American boxer. World heavyweight champion (1919-26). Fight with Carpentier (1921) was first to produce gate of million dollars. Lost title to Gene Tunney (1926); controversial re-match (1927) again won by Tunney.

Denbighshire, former county of N Wales, now in Clwyd. Mountainous in S; scenic, fertile valleys. Coalmining (centred on Wrexham); slate quarrying; agric. Co. town was

Denbigh, mun. bor. in Vale of Clwyd. Pop. 8000.

denim, strong coarse twill-weave cotton fabric, first made in Nimes, France. Name derives from *serge de Nîmes*. Important feature of 20th cent. 'casual' clothing.

Denis or **Dionysius of Paris, St** (d. *c* 258), patron saint of France. First bishop of Paris. Traditionally a missionary sent into Gaul *c* 250 and martyred at Montmartre ('Martyr's Hill').

Denmark (*Danmark*), kingdom of NC Europe. Area 43,022 sq km (16,611 sq mi); pop. 5,073,000; cap. Copenhagen. Language: Danish. Religion: Lutheranism. Comprises Jutland penin., Baltic isls. incl. Zealand, Laaland, Fyn, Bornholm. Overseas territs. incl. Greenland, Faeroes. Agric., esp. dairying, livestock; fishing. United with Sweden (1397-1523), with Norway (1397-1814); lost Norway in Napoleonic wars, Schleswig-Holstein to Prussia (1864). Under German occupation (1940-5). Joined EEC in 1973.

density, in physics, mass per unit volume of a substance; usually measured in grams per cubic cm. Density of water is 1 gram per cc at 4°C.

dentistry, care and treatment of teeth and gums. Egyptian writings of *c* 16th cent. BC describe dental care, but professional dentistry dates from 19th cent. Important developments incl. use of X-rays, high speed drills, local anaesthetics and taking of fluoride to reduce dental caries.

dentition, number and kind of teeth and their arrangement in mouths of vertebrates. Most lower vertebrates are homodonts (teeth are all similar); in heterodonts, several different types of teeth are present (incisors, canines, premolars and molars).

Dent(s) du Midi, mountain group of SW Switzerland, in the Alps. Rise to 3259 m (10,696 ft) at Haute Cime.

Denver, cap. of Colorado, US; on South Platte R. Alt. 1609 m (5280 ft). Pop. 515,000. Transport jct.; mining machinery, meat produce, air defence indust. Has many parks; health and recreation centre. Founded 1859. Cap. from 1867; grew during gold, silver strikes in 1870s.

deodar, *Cedrus deodara,* species of cedar native to Himalayas with fragrant, durable, light-red wood. Cultivated as ornamental because of graceful drooping branches and soft green foliage.

depreciation, in accounting, reduction in value of CAPITAL through wear, deterioration or obsolescence. Allowance is made for this in bookkeeping so that income is not overestimated.

depression, in economics, period of crisis characterized by falling prices, contraction of production, restricted credit, unemployment, bankruptcies. Usually interpreted as overproduction of goods linked with decreased demand; the resulting fall in consumer purchasing power tends to give cumulative effect. Before 18th cent. usually had non-economic causes, eg crop failure. Subsequently, causes mainly indust. or commercial. The Great Depression followed 1929 crash of New York stock market.

depression, in meteorology, area of relatively low atmospheric pressure, characteristic of temperate latitudes. Formed by warm tropical air meeting and rising above cold polar air, with associated formation of fronts. May be very extensive; brings unsettled, rainy weather. Also *see* CYCLONE.

depression, in psychiatry, emotional condition characterized by feeling of hopelessness, inadequacy, loss of vigour. May be neurotic or psychotic, eg manic-depressive psychosis. Some forms are treated by drugs or electric shock therapy.

De Quincey, Thomas (1785-1859), English essayist. Known for *Confessions of an English Opium Eater* (1822). Pieces for journals, eg *Murder Considered as One of the Fine Arts* (1827), *The English Mail Coach* (1849), reflect ability to create dream experiences.

Derain, André (1880-1954), French painter. Prominent member of fauve group, his early work is characterized by use of patches of vibrant pure colour. Later influenced by Cézanne and cubism, reverted to sombre neo-Classical style.

Derby, Edward George Geoffrey Smith Stanley, 14th Earl of (1799-1869), British statesman, PM (1852, 1858-9, 1866-8). As Whig colonial secretary, sponsored bill abolishing slavery in British Empire (1833). Joined Tories under Peel; later headed protectionist Tories after split over Peel's free trade policies (1846).

Derby, English horse race, founded (1780) by Earl of Derby, run over course 1.5 mi (2.4 km) long at Epsom, Surrey, in May or June. Also *see* KENTUCKY DERBY.

Derbyshire, county of NC England. Area 2631 sq km (1015 sq mi); pop.

886,000; co. town Matlock. Peak Dist. in NW; lowland in S, E. Mineral springs (eg Buxton); stock rearing; coalmining. Co. bor. **Derby**, former co. town, on R. Derwent. Pop. 219,000. Railway jct; aircraft engines; famous porcelain mfg.

Derg, Lough, lake of C Irish Republic. In Shannon basin, separates Galway, Clare, Tipperary. Isl. has ecclesiastical ruins. Also small lake of Co. Donegal, with isl. cave, scene of St Patrick's purgatory.

dermatitis, inflammation of skin. Atopic dermatitis or eczema, characterized by an itchy rash, is often associated with allergies such as hay fever. Contact dermatitis is allergic reaction to substances touching skin.

Derry, see LONDONDERRY, Northern Ireland.

dervish, mendicant monk of ISLAM. Various sects are characterized by extreme methods of producing ecstatic states, *eg* whirling and howling dervishes. Strongly antinomian, claiming special favour with God. Theology based on SUFISM.

Derwent, several rivers of England. 1, in Cumbria, flows 56 km (35 mi) from Lake Dist. via Derwentwater to Irish Sea. 2, in Derbyshire, flows 96 km (60 mi) from Peak Dist. to R. Trent; supplies N Midlands reservoirs. 3, in North Yorkshire, flows 112 km (70 mi) from N York Moors to R. Ouse.

Derwentwater, lake of Cumbria, NW England. In Lake Dist.; length 5 km (3 mi). Lodore Falls at S end. Tourism.

Desai, [Shri] Morarji Ranchhodji (1896–), Indian political leader, PM (1977–). Member of Gandhi's civil disobedience move-

ment (1930s), imprisoned several times. Acted as minister in govts. (1956-69). Leader of opposition to Mrs Gandhi (1969-77), imprisoned under emergency powers. Led Janata coalition to 1977 election win.

Descartes, René (1596-1650), French philosopher, mathematician. Started from position of universal doubt, tempered only by dictum 'I think, therefore I am'. Created system known as Cartesian dualism, based on distinction between spirit and matter, in *Discours de la Méthode* (1637). Also regarded as founder of analytical geometry, developed algebraic notation. Contributed much to science of optics.

desert, any barren, unproductive region where rainfall is less than 25 cm/10 in. per year. Surface may be sandy or stony, sometimes with poor scrub vegetation; pop. is scant, specially adapted. Deserts may be hot (eg Sahara, Arabian), cool mid-latitude (eg Gobi) or cold and perpetually ice-covered (as in N Canada, Siberia).

De Sica, Vittorio (1901-74), Italian film director, actor. Achieved world fame with compassionate, realistic films in 1940s, eg *Shoeshine* (1946), *Bicycle Thieves* (1948), continued skilful, intelligent work with *Two Women* (1961).

Des Moines, cap. of Iowa, US; at confluence of Des Moines and Raccoon rivers. Pop. 201,000. Commercial, transport centre in Corn Belt. Coal mining, printing and publishing industs., agric. machinery mfg. Became cap. 1857.

Despenser, Hugh le (1262-1326), English courtier. Chief adviser to Edward II, joined at court by his son,

Hugh le Despenser (d. 1326). Both were banished by the barons (1321-2), but on return held real power over England, dominating Edward until his overthrow (1326) by ISABELLA and MORTIMER. Despensers then executed.

Des Prés or **Desprez, Josquin** (c 1440-1521), Flemish composer. He developed counterpoint to great expressive ends in his works, which incl. Masses, motets and secular songs.

Dessau, town of C East Germany, on R. Mulde. Pop. 96,000. Produces machinery (Junkers aircraft until 1945). Former cap. of Anhalt state.

destroyer, a warship originally built (1893) as a defence against fast boats carrying the newly-invented torpedo. Used in WWII for anti-submarine work, escort and reconnaissance, it has now been largely superseded by the smaller frigate.

detective fiction, story in which clues systematically examined lead to solving a crime, usually murder. First true detective story was Poe's 'The Murders in the Rue Morgue' (1841), with W. Collins' *The Moonstone* (1868) first in England. Genre estab. in 1880s by Conan DOYLE and his hero Sherlock Holmes. Subsequent exponents incl. Chesterton, Agatha Christie, Simenon. Hammett, Chandler initiated tough 'private eye' school in US in 1930s.

détente, relaxation of international tensions and hostilities, manifested in treaties or trade agreements. Détente was estab. as policy between US and USSR in mid-1970s, esp. in fields of strategic arms and influence in Third World.

detergent, substance used to improve cleansing power of water, eg soap. Acts by emulsifying oil on dirty surfaces, thus allowing oil to dislodge exposed dirt particles. Synthetic detergents produce no scum, but phosphate present in some is source of pollution.

determinant, in mathematics, number obtained from square MATRIX by specified sequence of additions and multiplications. Usually represented by square array of numbers. Wide use, particularly in solution of systems of linear equations.

determinism, in philosophy, doctrine that phenomena are conditioned by preceding data, eg denial of moral choice in ethics. Also finds support in psychoanalysis, which denies existence of causeless acts. *See* FREE WILL.

detonator, explosive compound, eg mercuric fulminate, capable of rapid decomposition. Shock waves created used to set off more inert explosives.

Detroit, port of SE Michigan, US: on Detroit R. between L. St Clair and L. Erie. Pop. 1,511,000. Major shipping, rail centre. World's leading automobile producer (Ford, General Motors, Chrysler). Other industs. incl. food processing, chemicals, steel mfg., shipyards, oil refining. Settled by French (1701).

Dettingen, village of Bavaria, SC West Germany, on R. Main. Scene of Allies' victory (1743) over French in War of Austrian Succession.

deuterium (D), isotope of hydrogen; mass no. 2. Constituent of HEAVY WATER (D_2O). Deuteron is name given to deuterium nucleus.

Deuteronomy (Gk.,=second law),

in OT, fifth book of **Pentateuch**. Contains core of Jewish law, ascribed traditionally to Moses.

De Valéra, Eamon (1882-1975), Irish statesman, b. US. Participant in Easter Rebellion, imprisoned (1916). Became head of Sinn Féin (1917) and of revolutionary **Dáil**. Left Dáil (1922) over exclusion of Northern Ireland after creation of Irish Free State; returned (1927) at head of Fianna Fáil party. PM (1937-48, 1951-4, 1957-9), kept Ireland neutral in WWII; president (1959-73).

devaluation, lowering of value of currency in terms of gold or other currencies, so that its exchange rate falls. Resulting increase in cost of imports and fall in price of exports may check deficit in BALANCE OF PAYMENTS through sale of more goods abroad.

Devil, the, see SATAN.

devil fish, name given to manta ray and type of American octopus.

devil's coach horse, *Staphylinus olens,* large carnivorous beetle of W Europe. Holds abdomen erect; emits offensive odour when threatened.

Devil's Island, see SALUT, ÎLES DU.

devil's paintbrush, *Hieracium aurantiacum,* C European weed of daisy family with flame-coloured flowers. Now a common weed in N US and Canada.

devolution, delegation of specific powers or authority by nation's central govt. to local governing units. Devolved powers restricted to education, health, transport, *etc.* Often adopted as constitutional response to national self-determination movements. Differs from FEDERALISM in that sovereignty

in all areas remains with central govt. and legislature.

Devolution, War of (1667-8), war arising out of Louis XIV's claim to Spanish Netherlands. France opposed by Triple Alliance of United Provinces, Sweden, England. Peace concluded with Treaty of Aix-la-Chapelle.

Devon, county of SW England. Area 6715 sq km (2592 sq mi); pop. 921,000; co. town Exeter. Hilly, over 610 m (2000 ft) on Dartmoor; rich agric. lowlands. Livestock rearing, dairy farming (esp. cream); fishing; mining; tourism. Sea ports were hist. important (esp. Plymouth).

Devonian period, fourth geological period of Palaeozoic era; began c 395 million years ago, lasted c 50 million years. Formation of Old Red Sandstone, shales; climax of Caledonian mountain · building period. Fauna incl. ammonoid cephalopods, jawed fish, crinoids, last graptolites; flora incl. treefern forests. Also see GEOLOGICAL TABLE.

Devon Island, E Franklin Dist., Northwest Territs., Canada; between Ellesmere and Baffin Isls. Area 54,100 sq km (20,900 sq mi). Most E of Parry Isls.

Devonshire, Spencer Compton Cavendish, 8th Duke of (1833-1908), British statesman. Held several posts in Liberal cabinets until 1885. Split with Gladstone over Irish Home Rule bill (1886), leading new Liberal Unionist party.

dew, water deposited on surfaces when decreasing temperature causes saturation of water vapour in air. Dew point is temperature at which dew forms; if below freezing point, dew freezes and hoar frost results.

Dewar, Sir James (1842-1923), Scottish chemist. Researched in low temperature physics; first to liquefy and solidify hydrogen. Developed vacuum flask for insulating fluids, forerunner of Thermos.

dewberry, trailing shrub of genus *Rubus*. Similar to blackberry but with earlier and larger fruit.

De Wet, Christian Rudolf (1854-1922), Boer general, statesman. Led short-lived revolt in opposition to entry into WWI in support of Britain; suppressed by Botha.

Dewey, John (1859-1952), American philosopher and educator. His philosophy, 'instrumentalism', held truth to be evolutionary and human activities to be instruments for resolving human problems. In education, advocated 'learning by doing' over authoritarian methods. Works incl. *The School and Society* (1899).

Dewey, Melvil (1851-1931), American librarian. Known for Dewey decimal system, by which books can be classified according to subject. Estab. 1st school of librarianship, was one of the founders of American Library Association.

De Wint, Peter (1784-1849), English landscape painter. Noted for watercolours, painted in broad washes of colour and conveying an atmosphere of calm.

diabetes, disease characterized by excessive secretion of urine. *Diabetes mellitus*, caused by insulin deficiency, leads to excess glucose in blood and urine. Marked by loss of weight; acidosis and coma may follow. Treatment by controlled diet and insulin injections.

Diadochi (Gk., = successors), Macedonian generals, incl. Antigonus, Antipater, Seleucus and Lysimachus, who fought series of civil wars for control of Alexander's empire after his death (323 BC). Empire broke up at finish of wars (281 BC).

Diaghilev, Serge Pavlovich (1872-1929), Russian ballet impresario. Revived Russian ballet, making it serious art involving leading dancers, musicians, artists of day, incl. Pavlova, Nijinsky, Stravinsky, Fokine, Bakst; put on new ballets, *eg Les Sylphides, L'Après-midi d'un faune, Sacré du Printemps*. Founded Ballets Russes (1909) which toured in W Europe, Americas, profoundly influencing ballet everywhere except Russia.

dialect, form of speech peculiar to a locality, community, or social group which is considered to deviate in a characteristic way from the postulated standard speech of users' native language. While contiguous dialects of same language are usually mutually intelligible, with increasing distance differences accumulate so that the dialects of same language become mutually unintelligible.

dialectical materialism, method of hist. analysis, formulated by Marx and Engels, which applies Hegel's dialectic method to observable social processes and natural phenomena. Following FEUERBACH, they substituted materialism for ideas as the basis of the thesis-antithesis-synthesis process. In society, control of means of production determines social structure of classes; conflict between them results in hist. change.

dialysis, in chemistry, separation of colloidal particles from substances in true solution. Technique involves dissolved molecules passing through a membrane more rapidly than larger colloid molecules. Artificial kidney purifies blood by dialysis.

diamagnetism, property of certain substances, eg bismuth, of being repelled by magnetic fields. Results from substance being weakly magnetized in direction opposite to external field.

diamond, hardest known mineral, a crystalline form of carbon. Occurs in alluvial deposits and ultrabasic igneous rocks. Gem forms are transparent, brilliant and colourless; others may be yellow, blue, black, etc. Flawless crystals used in jewellery; largest is 'Cullinan' in British crown; indust. diamonds used in cutting tools, abrasives, record player styli. Major source of gem diamonds is South Africa; indust. diamonds mainly from Zaire, Brazil, Ghana.

Diana, in early Roman myth, goddess of the moon, hunting, women in childbirth. Identified with Greek Artemis. Worshipped in Rome as Virgin goddess; her temple at Aricia associated with fertility cult.

diarrhoea, frequent discharge of watery faeces. Often caused by inflammation of intestine by bacteria, viruses, etc, or by nervous stress. May be treated by drugs or absorbents such as kaolin.

diastase, enzyme which converts starch into maltose and later into dextrose. Occurs in seeds of grain and in malt.

diatom, microscopic plant of ALGAE group with silica-containing shell, found in fresh or salt water in Arctic and other cold regions. Diatomaceous earth and diatomite, formed from shells of dead diatoms, are used industrially, esp. for insulating against heat.

Diaz or **Dias, Bartolomeu** (d. 1500), Portuguese navigator. First European to voyage around Cape of Good Hope (1488), opening up sea route to India.

Diaz, Porfirio (1830-1915), Mexican statesman. President (1877-80, 1884-1911) in period of growing prosperity based upon foreign investment. Neglected welfare and education of poor. Lost power during revolt under Madero, went into exile.

Diaz de Vivar, Rodrigo (c1040-99), Spanish soldier, national hero, called 'El Cid Campeador' (Lord Champion). Banished from Castile (1081) by Alfonso VI; became soldier of fortune, fighting both Moors and Christians. Captured Valencia (1094), ruling it until his death. Subsequently celebrated in literature, folklore; adopted as heroic leader of *reconquista* of Spain from Moors.

dice, small cubes usually of ivory or bone, sides of which are marked by different numbers of dots (so that opposite faces total 7). Several games of chance, incl. craps, poker dice and backgammon, are played with dice.

Dickens, Charles [John Huffam] (1812-70), English novelist. Began as journalist, soon started serial works attacking social abuses, often blending sentiment with humorous caricature, eg *Pickwick Papers* (1836-7), *Oliver Twist* (1838), *Nicholas Nickleby* (1838-9). Major works incl. *David Copperfield* (1849-50), *Great Expectations* (1860-1), *Our Mutual Friend* (1864-5). Other works incl. 'A Christmas Carol' (1853), hist. *A Tale of Two Cities* (1859). Known for detailed, realistic creation of world and inhabitants.

Dickinson, Emily [Elizabeth] (1830-86), American poet. Lived in seclusion, dominated by Calvinist father. Poetry (first pub. 1890) noted for intense, idiosyncratic style, often deals with problems of faith.

dictator, in ancient Rome, magistrate appointed in times of emergency to rule with absolute power. In modern usage denotes ruler with absolute power, authority, esp. one exercising it tyrannically. Characteristically, rule tends to TOTALITARIANISM. Examples incl. MUSSOLINI, STALIN, HITLER, military juntas, esp. in Latin America.

dictionary, book of alphabetically listed words in a language, with definitions, derivations, pronunciations, *etc.* Bilingual dictionaries provide equivalents of words in another language. Early English dictionaries incl. Nathan Bailey's *Dictionarium Britannicum* (1730), Samuel Johnson's *Dictionary of the English Language* (1755). In America, Noah Webster's *Dictionary of the English Language* (1806) is 1st example. French Academy has published a dictionary which attempts to be prescriptive since 17th cent.

Diderot, Denis (1713-84), French philosopher. Chief editor of *Encyclopédie* (1747-72), also wrote 1st French 'bourgeois drama', eg *Le Neveu de Rameau.* Forerunner of modern art criticism in *Salons* (1759-71). Anti-clerical, imprisoned for some works, eg *Lettres sur les aveugles* (1749), revealing scepticism and materialism.

Dido, founder-queen of Carthage in Roman legend. Best known through Vergil's use of legend in *Aeneid,* in which love between her and AENEAS almost causes him to betray his duty to found Rome. When he leaves, she kills herself.

Didot, François Ambroise (1730-1804), French printer. Acclaimed as best printer of his age, he designed a number of modern types. His sons, Pierre Didot (1761-1853) and Firmin Didot (1764-1836), pub. carefully edited, inexpensive books for students. Firmin invented stereotyping process.

Diefenbaker, John George (1895-1979), Canadian statesman, PM (1957-63). Leader of Progressive Conservatives (1956-67), won large victory at 1958 election.

dielectric, substance which does not conduct electricity but can sustain an electric field. Used to separate plates in capacitors.

Diem, Ngo Dinh (1901-63), Vietnamese political leader. Premier (1954), became president (1955) of South Vietnam when it was declared a republic. Favoured Catholics over Buddhists. Killed during military coup.

Diemen, Anton van (1593-1645), Dutch naval officer. As governor-general of Dutch East Indian

Company, sent TASMAN on expedition (1642) which discovered Van Diemen's Land (now Tasmania).

Dienbienphu, town of W North Vietnam. Vietminh victory (1954) marked end of French Indo-China.

Dieppe, town of Normandy, N France, on English Channel. Pop. 30,000. Port, ferry service to Newhaven (England); resort, fishing, shipbuilding. Scene of Allied commando raid (1942).

diesel engine, type of INTERNAL COMBUSTION ENGINE invented by German engineer Rudolf Diesel (1858-1913). Air drawn into cylinder is heated by compression, then ignites fuel oil injected into cylinder; resulting explosion provides power stroke. Though initially more expensive than equivalent petrol (gasoline) engine, uses cheaper fuel. Patented 1892.

Dietrich, Marlene, orig. Maria Magdalene von Losch (c 1904-), German film actress, cabaret singer. Moved to US in 1920s. Achieved fame in *The Blue Angel* (1930), developing stereotype as husky-voiced, arrogant *femme fatale*, esp. with director von Sternberg, as in *The Scarlet Empress* (1934).

differential, in automobile, arrangement of gears in driven axle allowing driving force to be distributed to both wheels, yet allowing wheels to turn at different speeds relative to each other (eg when vehicle rounds corner, outer wheel must travel further).

differential calculus, mathematical study of rates of change of continuously varying functions. Devised independently by Newton and Leibnitz to study problems in dynamics and geometry. Important applications in physics where many phenomena are described by laws dealing with rate of change; leads to study of differential equations.

diffraction, breaking up of ray of light into bright and dark bands or coloured bands, observable after ray has passed through narrow slit or over sharp edge of opaque object. Caused by INTERFERENCE. Effect used in diffraction grating to produce spectra; grating usually consists of glass plate or polished metal surface ruled with equidistant parallel lines.

diffusion, in chemistry, intermingling of liquids or gases by continuous thermal motion of their molecules or ions. Gases spread out and mix by diffusion.

digestion, process by which food is broken down by enzymes into forms which can be used in METABOLISM. In man, carbohydrates are broken down by ptyalin in saliva and by amylase in intestine; protein by pepsin in stomach; fats by action of lipase and bile salts.

Diggers, members of 17th cent. English socio-religious sect, offshoot of LEVELLERS; fl 1649-50. Led by Gerrard Winstanley, combined communistic and egalitarian principles; estab. colony on common land in Surrey, destroyed (1650) by a mob.

digital computer, see COMPUTER.

digitalis, genus of Old World plants of figwort family. Incl. FOXGLOVE.

Dijon, city of Burgundy, E France, cap. of Côte-d'Or dept. Pop. 145,000. Road and railway jct., engineering, food processing, wine trade; univ. (1722). Hist. cap. of Burgundy, passed to France (1477). Medieval cultural centre. Gothic cathedral (13th cent.), ducal palace (14th cent.).

dill, *Anethum graveolens,* European annual or biennial herb of parsley family. Aromatic seeds used in flavouring.

diminishing returns, law of, in economics, prediction that, after a certain point, an increase in one factor of production (other factors being constant) will yield relatively decreasing returns. Applied to indust. production and exploitation of land.

Dimitrov, Georgi (1882-1949), Bulgarian political leader. Arrested in Berlin on charge of setting fire to REICHSTAG (1933). Acquitted, went to Soviet Union; secretary-general of Comintern (1934-43). Returned to Bulgaria (1944) to lead Communist Party; premier (1946-9).

Dinaric Alps (*Dinara Planina*), mountain range of W Yugoslavia. Separates Dalmatia from Bosnia and Hercegovina. Name also applied to all limestone ranges between Julian Alps (NW) and Balkan system (SE).

dingo, *Canis dingo,* wolf-like wild dog, only indigenous carnivore of Australia. Erect ears, bushy tail; preys on sheep herds. Probably descended from domestic dogs introduced to Australia in prehist. times.

dinosaur, any of large group of extinct, mainly terrestrial reptiles of Mesozoic era. Reached lengths of 27.5 m/90 ft. Mainly herbivorous; later species of Cretaceous period carnivorous, with larger brains, *eg* tyrannosaur.

Diocletian, full name Gaius Valerius Diocletianus (245-313), Roman emperor (284-305), b. Dalmatia. Appointed Maximian joint emperor (286) and Galerius and Constantius sub-emperors (292) to help defend empire. Persecuted Christians severely. Abdicated in favour of Galerius.

diode, in electronics, thermionic valve consisting of evacuated tube containing 2 electrodes. Electrons are emitted by heated cathode and migrate to positively charged plate (anode). Used in conversion of alternating current to direct current, *eg* in radio and television receivers.

Diogenes (*c* 412-323 BC), Greek philosopher. Cynic and ascetic, pupil of Antisthenes. Said to have searched Athens for an honest man and to have lived in a tub.

Diomedes, in Greek myth, Thracian king, son of Ares. Fed his horses on human flesh. Killed by Heracles (8th Labour), who then took horses to Mycenae.

Diomedes, in Greek myth, son of Tydeus; one of principal Greek heroes in Trojan War. In some stories, helped Odysseus remove the Palladium (statue of Pallas Athena) from Troy; settled in Italy after Trojan War.

Dionysius the Areopagite, St (*fl* 1st cent), Athenian churchman. Converted by St Paul. Traditionally 1st bishop of Athens; martyred. Several theological writings falsely attributed to him in Middle Ages; now attributed to 'Pseudo-Dionysius'.

Dionysius the Elder (*c* 430-367 BC), Greek political leader in Sicily. Became tyrant of Syracuse (405) and carried out 2 successful wars against Carthage. Defeated disastrously in

3rd war. Succeeded by his son **Dionysius the Younger** (fl 350 BC), who was driven out of Syracuse by Dion. Returned after latter's murder (354) but expelled 344.

Dionysus (Roman name Bacchus), Greek god of wine, fertility, son of Zeus and Semele. His worship originated in Thrace and Asia Minor, accompanied by ecstasy in worshippers (esp. women) called Maenads or Bacchantes. Worshipped with Apollo at Delphi, and in countryside as god of vegetation.

Dior, Christian (1905-57), French fashion designer. Estab. fashion houses in Paris (1946) and New York (1948). Introduced 'New Look' (1947), extravagant style contrasting sharply with wartime fashions. Major influence in world fashion.

Dioscuri, in Greek and Roman myth, joint name for Castor and Polydeuces (Lat. Pollux), according to Homer, twin sons of LEDA by Zeus. Placed by him among stars as constellation Gemini.

diphtheria, acute infectious disease of throat and other mucous membranes caused by bacteria. Characterized by formation of membranous crust in air passages; toxin produced by bacteria can produce local paralysis.

diplodocus, genus of extinct semi-aquatic herbivorous dinosaurs, division Sauropoda. Similar in size and appearance to BRONTOSAURUS. Fossils have been found in Jurassic rocks of US.

diplomatic service, body of representatives of a govt. responsible for conduct of relations with foreign govts. Estab. systematically by Italians in 15th cent., esp. by Venice.

Soon imitated by leading European states. By 1815 classes, ie ambassadors, envoys, ministers resident and chargés d'affaires, recognized. Diplomatic immunity, ie diplomat being placed outside law of land, estab. 16th-17th cent. Diplomat is responsible to his own foreign minister, negotiates with foreign ministry of country to which he is accredited.

dipper or **water ouzel,** any of Cinclidae family of aquatic perching birds. Lives near mountain streams; able to walk under water in pursuit of insects, larvae. Species incl. European *Cinclus cinclus.*

Diptera, order of 2-winged flies. Mouthparts lengthened into proboscis for piercing, sucking. *See* FLY.

Dirac, Paul Adrien Maurice (1902-), English physicist. Introduced relativity theory into study of wave mechanics, extending de Broglie's ideas of wave nature of electron. Predicted existence of positron (discovered 1932). Shared Nobel Prize for Physics (1933) with Schrödinger.

direct current (DC), electric current flowing always in same direction. Produced by batteries.

Directory, executive body of five men, appointed by the two legislative chambers, which governed France (1795-9). Overthrown by coup of 18 Brumaire by which Bonaparte became first consul.

dirigible balloon, *see* AIRSHIP.

Dis Pater, Roman god of the underworld, identified with Greek Pluto.

disarmament, reduction of armed forces and armaments, *eg* to limit set by treaty. Since WWI international attempts have been made to restrict weapons, eg Disarmament Conference (1932-7). After 1945, nuclear weapons made problem more serious. Charter of United Nations provided for disarmament planning in Security Council. Commission set up (1946), reached impasse (1948). Geneva Conference (1955) led to conferences on test-ban treaty and moratorium on testing until 1961. Moscow Agreement (1963) banned tests in atmosphere, under water, outer space. USSR and US drafted non-proliferation treaty (1968), approved by UN. *See* also STRATEGIC ARMS LIMITATION TALKS (SALT).

Disciples, Twelve, see TWELVE DISCIPLES.

discount rate, *see* BANK RATE.

discrimination, accordance of differential or prejudicial treatment, esp. actions or policies directed against welfare of certain groups, minorities. Can be on racial, religious, sexual or class grounds. Racial discrimination provoked CIVIL RIGHTS movement in US, clashes in Africa (esp. in Rhodesia, South Africa in 1970s), passing of Race Relations Act in UK. Sexual discrimination, *eg* against women, homosexuals, became object of protest in 1960s and 1970s.

disinfectant, substance used to destroy harmful microbes. First used was phenol (carbolic acid), introduced by Lister (1867). Disinfectant applied to living things usually called an antiseptic.

Disney, Walt[er Elias] (1901-66), American film producer, famous for animated cartoons. Created character Mickey Mouse in 1928, Donald Duck in 1936. First full-

length cartoon was *Snow White and the Seven Dwarfs* (1938). Studio (estab. 1923) made innovations in animation techniques. Also produced documentaries on animals, *eg The Living Desert* (1953), and children's films with human casts, *eg Treasure Island* (1950).

dispersion of light, breaking up of light into its component colours, *eg* by a prism. Spectrum produced by shining white light through prism results from refractive index of glass differing for light of different wavelengths (different colours).

Disraeli, Benjamin, 1st Earl of Beaconsfield (1804-81), British statesman, PM (1868, 1874-80). Member of Young England Tories, opposed repeal of Corn Laws and helped defeat Peel's ministry after their repeal (1846). Chief figure in revitalized Conservatives after passage of 1867 Reform Bill extending franchise; succeeded Derby as PM (1868). Second term (1874-80) marked by aggressive imperial and military policy, esp. in S Africa, Balkans and Mediterranean; secured controlling interest in Suez Canal for Britain (1875). Had Victoria crowned empress of India (1876). Also known for novels, *eg Coningsby* (1844), *Sybil* (1845).

dissenter or **nonconformist, in** UK, one who adheres to the form of a religion other than that of the Established Church. Applied esp. to those who failed to accept Act of Uniformity (1662). Denotes more popularly the Protestant dissenter, *eg* Presbyterians, Baptists, Methodists, referred to in Toleration Act (1689).

distemper, in veterinary medicine,

any of several infectious catarrhal diseases of animals, esp. canine distemper, virus disease of young dogs. Controlled by vaccination.

distillation, vaporization of a liquid followed by condensation back into liquid form. Used to separate mixtures of liquids of different boiling points or to purify liquid contaminated by non-volatile impurities.

distribution, in economics, proportion of goods and services which each economic group receives from total production. Group may be social, geographical, etc. Redistribution of wealth often used by radicals as basis of argument for political change.

District of Columbia (DC), federal admin. dist. of E US; on Potomac R. Area 180 sq km (c 70 sq mi); pop. 757,000. Co-extensive with cap. Washington.

Diu, former Portuguese enclave in W India. Pop. 20,000. Taken by Portuguese (1534), seized by India (1961). Part of union territ. of Goa, Daman and Diu.

diver, fish-eating bird of N hemisphere of Gavidae family. Short legs, webbed feet; inhabitant of lakes, bays. Great Northern diver, *Gavia immer,* called loon in North America, found also in N Europe.

divine right, doctrine supporting hereditary kingship on grounds that it is according to divine and natural law, and cannot be set aside without breaking such law. Claimed by James I and Charles I of England, lost importance with 1688 Revolution and Parliament's growing power.

diving, sport in which competitor

projects himself into water from an elevated position, possibly executing somersaults before entering water. Divided into springboard and platform or high diving. Olympic event for men since 1904, for women since 1912.

division of labour, in economics, organization of workers so that different groups have specialized roles in production. May be geographical, *eg* region concentrates on one product, or occupational, *eg* on modern production line. First examined as concept by Adam Smith.

divorce, decree of dissolution of marriage granted by court. Distinct from nullity, decree that marriage was originally illegal. In UK, irretrievable breakdown of marriage is only ground; in US, grounds vary from state to state, but main ones are adultery, desertion, cruelty. Also *see* ALIMONY.

Diyarbakir, city of EC Turkey, on R. Tigris. Pop. 180,000. Commercial centre; trade in wool, grain. Became Roman colony AD 230, then under Persian and Arab rule. Taken by Turks (1515). Devastated by earth-.quake (1966).

Djailolo, *see* HALMAHERA.

Djajapura, cap. of Irian Jaya (West Irian), Indonesia. Pop. 16,000. Formerly known as Hollandia, Kotabaru and Sukarnapura.

Djakarta or **Jakarta,** cap. of Indonesia, on coast of NW Java. Pop. 4,576,000. Commercial, transport and cultural centre. Major export port area nearby Tanjungpriok. Founded (1619) as Batavia by Dutch, renamed 1949.

Djerba or **Jerba,** isl. of SE Tunisia,

on Gulf of Gabès. Area 510 sq km (197 sq mi). Tourist resort; olive, date growing; sponge fishing. Traditionally Homer's isl. of the lotus-eaters.

Djibouti, republic of E Africa, on Str. of Bab-el-Mandeb. Area 22,000 sq km (8500 sq mi); pop. 108,000; cap. 'Djibouti. Official language: Arabic. Religion: Islam. Mainly stony desert; nomadic pastoralism, exports cattle, hides, salt. Colony from 1896 as French Somaliland; later known as French Territory of the Afars and the Issas; voted in referendum (1977) in favour of independence. Became independent as Djibouti (1977).

Djibouti or **Jibuti**, cap. of Djibouti, on Gulf of Tadjoura. Pop. 62,000. Port, railway to Addis Ababa (Ethiopia); transit trade, exports cattle, hides, salt. Cap. of French Somaliland from 1892.

Dmitri (1582-91), Russian prince, son of Ivan the Terrible. Heir to his brother Feodor I, he was murdered prob. at instigation of regent, Boris Godunov. Claims to succession were made by Polish-backed impostors (false Dmitris), who invaded Russia but all were eventually killed.

DNA or **deoxyribonucleic acid**, fundamental genetic material found in the chromosomes of cell nuclei. Molecule consists of 2 interwound helical strands, each strand composed of long chain of nucleotides (derived from a nitrogenous base, a sugar and phosphate group). Sequence of bases in molecule constitutes genetic code which determines proteins and enzymes to be synthesized by cell. At cell division, DNA replicates itself, thus ensuring that hereditary information is passed to new cells.

Dnepr or **Dnieper**, river of USSR. Rises in Smolensk region, flows c 2250 km (1400 mi) generally S through Byelorussian and Ukrainian SSR into N Black Sea. Navigable above Zaporozhye (Dneproges dam).

Dneproges, see ZAPOROZHYE.

Dnepropetrovsk, city of USSR, EC Ukrainian SSR; on R. Dnepr. Pop. 903,000. Indust. centre, producing iron, steel and manganese. Grew with completion of Dneproges dam (1932).

Dnestr or **Dniester**, river of USSR. Rises in Carpathian Mts. of W Ukrainian SSR; follows winding course SE through Moldavian SSR to Black Sea. Length c 1350 km (850 mi).

Dnieper, see DNEPR.

Dobell, Sir William (1899-1970), Australian painter. Noted for his portraits, which convey keen sense of character perception; works incl. portrait *Joshua Smith*.

Doberman pinscher, breed of large dog, used as police or guard dog. Short-haired, smooth coated; stands 61-71 cm/24-28 in. at shoulder.

Dobruja (*Dobrogea*), region of SE Romania and NE Bulgaria. Forests; agric. Part of Roman Moesia, Byzantine, Ottoman empires. Divided after Congress of Berlin (1878); N to Romania, S to Bulgaria. S part became Romanian (1913-40), returned to Bulgaria.

dock or **sorrel**, any of genus *Rumex* of perennial herbs native to temperate regions. Large leaves, stout taproots, small green or brown flowers; popular antidote to nettle stings. Common sorrel, *R. acetosa*, is used in salads.

docks, berthing spaces in ports for ships. Two basic types: dry docks, which may be floating or fixed, used for building or cleaning and repairing ships; wet docks, usually equipped with wharves and quays, used for loading and unloading cargo. Floodgates may be necessary to maintain water levels in docks if there is a wide range in tides.

dodder, several species of *Cuscuta*, a parasitic genus of morning glory family. Native to tropical and temperate regions. Lack leaves, roots and chlorophyll; draw nourishment from host through suckers.

Dodecanese (*Dhodhekánisos*), isl. group of Greece, in SE Aegean Sea. Area 2720 sq km (1050 sq mi); cap. Rhodes. Incl. Rhodes, Cos, Kárpathos. Olives, fruit, sponges. Turkish from 1522, taken by Italy 1912; passed to Greece 1947.

Dodge City, SW Kansas, US; on Arkansas R. Pop. 15,000. Hist. trading post on Santa Fé trail and wild cattle town (Wyatt Earp). Wheat, livestock distribution centre.

Dodgson, C. L., *see* CARROLL, LEWIS.

dodo, *Raphus cucullatus*, flightless bird of Mauritius, resembling turkey. Became extinct in 17th cent. through persecution by man.

Dodoma, town of EC Tanzania. Pop. 15,000. Agric. centre; designated (1975) future national cap.

dog, *Canis familiaris*, domestic carnivore of Canidae family, to which wolf, jackal belong. Numerous varieties developed from wolf by selective breeding since *c* 8000 BC. Dogs classified as sporting, non-

sporting, hounds, terriers, working or toys.

doge, chief màgistrate in medieval and Renaissance Venice and Genoa. In 14th cent. held office for life; later office made elective for 2 year terms.

dogfish, small shark of several families of warm and temperate seas. Lesser spotted dogfish, *Scyliorhinus canicula*, found in European waters. Spiny dogfish, *Squalus acanthias*, is commonest.

Dogger Bank, large sand bank in North Sea, off Northumberland, England. Cod fisheries; scene of WWI naval battle (1915).

dogtooth violet, any plant of genus *Erythronium* of lily family. Species incl. American *E. americanum* and European *E. denscanis*.

dogwood, any of genus *Cornus* of trees and shrubs. Esp. *C. sanguinea*, a European flowering shrub and *C. florida*, a small tree of E US.

Dohnányi, Erno (1877-1960), Hungarian composer. Best known for his *Variations on a Nursery Song* for piano and orchestra. Wrote in more traditional style than his nationalist contemporaries Bartók and Kodály.

Dolet, Etienne (1509-46), French scholar, printer. Wrote and printed many works on grammar, history, philosophy, esp. *Commentaries on the Latin Language*. Often accused of heresy, was eventually convicted and burned in Paris.

Dollard des Ormeaux, Adam (1635-60), French adventurer in Canada. Heavily outnumbered, he and a small band of companions withstood an Iroquois attack at Long Sault rapids (1660); all were eventually killed. May have delayed

Iroquois attack on Montréal. Ensuing legend was later questioned.

Dollfuss, Engelbert (1892-1934), Austrian statesman. Christian Socialist chancellor (1932-4), in conflict with German-backed National Socialists over maintenance of Austrian independence. Assumed dictatorial powers (1933), estab. corporate state (1934). Assassinated by group of Austrian Nazis.

dolmen, Neolithic burial chamber, usually consisting of 2 or more upright standing stones, topped by capstone, probably covered originally by round or oval cairn. Many examples in Wales and Ireland.

Dolmetsch, Arnold (1858-1940), Swiss musicologist, resident in Britain from 1914. Revived interest in old and neglected instruments, esp. the recorder.

dolomite, greyish-white mineral, carbonate of calcium and magnesium. Also a rock, consisting of over 20% mineral dolomite; formed by replacement of calcium by magnesium in limestone. Rock may be metamorphosed into dolomitic marble. Used as building stone. Widespread; major sources in N Italy, US, Brazil.

Dolomites, range of NE Italy, in the Alps. Highest point Marmolada (3340 m/10,965 ft). Named from rock which forms them. Tourist area, chief resort Cortina d'Ampezzo.

dolphin, any of Delphinidae family of toothed whales, of worldwide distribution. Incl. common dolphin, *Delphinus delphis*, and KILLER WHALE. Bottle-nosed dolphin, genus *Tursiops*, highly intelligent; capable of communicating by sound.

Domagk, Gerhard (1895-1964), German chemist and pathologist. Discovered effect of dye Prontosil in treating streptococcal infections; its active constituent, sulphanilamide, was 1st sulphonamide drug. Awarded Nobel Prize for Physiology and Medicine (1939).

dome, vaulted roof, usually hemispherical in shape and circular in plan. Ancient domes incl. Mycenaean 'Treasury of Atreus' of 14th cent. BC, constructed in concentric rings of stones. Romans developed concrete dome, eg Pantheon in Rome. Other famous domes incl. those of St Peter's, Rome, and St Paul's, London.

Domenichino, orig. Domenico Zampieri (1581-1641), Italian artist of Bolognese school. A leading pupil of the Carracci, he maintained their Classical doctrines and was an influential landscapist. Executed numerous decorations in palaces, villas and chapels of Rome and Naples.

Domesday Book (1085-6), record of intensive survey of England made by order of William I (the Conqueror). Main aim was to aid taxation through knowledge of economic resources. Covered ownership of land and its value, and pop. Outstanding for speed with which it was compiled and thoroughness, and as basic source in medieval history.

Dominic, St, orig. Dominigo de Guzmán (c 1170-1221), Spanish churchman, founder of DOMINICANS. He and his bishop were sent by Innocent III to S France to preach to the Albigenses, 1st RC missionaries to be successful there.

Dominica, largest isl. of SE West Indies, in Windward Isls. Area 750 sq km (290 sq mi); pop. 76,000; cap. Roseau. Mainly mountainous with much volcanic activity (hot springs, gases). Fruit growing; rum, copra exports. Successive French, British occupation, then British colony; became associate state 1967. Independent in 1978.

Dominican Republic, republic of West Indies, occupying E Hispaniola. Area 48,734 sq km (18,816 sq mi); pop. 4,835,000; cap. Santo Domingo. Language: Spanish. Religion: RC. Mountains in interior; agric. land in E; sugar, coffee, cacao, tobacco produce. Bauxite, rock salt mining. Discovered by Columbus (1492); settled by Spanish; independence gained 1844; US military rule 1916-24; dictatorship under Trujillo (1930-61).

Dominicans, in RC church, order of preaching friars founded (1216) by St Dominic. Emphasize study; prominent in medieval universities. Officially the Order of Preachers, popularly called Black Friars because of black mantle and scapular worn over white habit. Aquinas was most notable Dominican theologian.

Domitian, full name Titus Flavius Domitianus (AD 51-96), Roman emperor (81-96). Son of Vespasian, succeeded brother Titus. After crushing revolt of Roman troops in Upper Germany (89), ruled despotically until stabbed to death.

Don, rivers of UK. **1,** in Yorkshire, flows 112 km (70 mi) from Pennines via Sheffield to R. Ouse. **2,** in Scotland, flows 129 km (80 mi) from Grampians to North Sea; famous for salmon fishing.

Don, river of USSR. Rises in C European RSFSR, flows SE and then SW, c 1900 km (1200 mi) to Sea of Azov. Joined by canal to R. Volga near Volgograd.

Donald Bane or **Ban,** king of Scotland (1093, 1095-7). Succeeded brother Malcolm III; initiated Celtic reaction to anglicizing influences of Malcolm's wife Margaret. Usurped by nephew Duncan II (1093), restored to throne (1095).

Donatello, orig. Donato di Niccolò di Betto Bardi (c 1386-1466), Italian painter and sculptor. Most influential sculptor of 15th cent., early work was in Gothic style. Sculptures *St Mark* and *St George* show new humanist expression. Pioneer in use of perspective, he introduced shallow relief technique into sculpture. Other masterpieces incl. bronze *David* and equestrian statue *Gattamelata*.

Donbas or **Donets Basin,** region of USSR in plain of R. Donets, E Ukrainian SSR. Largest coalfields of USSR support major indust., incl. iron and steel mfg.

Doncaster, bor. of West Yorkshire met. county, N England, on R. Don. Pop. 83,000. Coalmining; railway engineering; has famous racecourse. On Roman site (*Danum*).

Donegal, county of Ulster prov., N Irish Republic. Area 4830 sq km (1865 sq mi); pop. 108,000; co. town Lifford. Rocky, indented coast incl. Malin Head, most N point of Ireland; hilly interior. Fishing; livestock; woollen, tweed mfg.; h.e.p. **Donegal,** town on Donegal Bay. Pop. 2000. Ruined 15th cent. monastery.

Donets, river of USSR. Flows c 1050 km (650 mi) from S European RSFSR, through Ukrainian SSR, to join R. Don. *See* DONBAS.

Donetsk, city of USSR, E Ukranian SSR. Pop. 905,000. Indust. centre of Donbas; coal mining, iron and steel industs. Named Yuzovka then Stalino before 1961.

Dönitz, Karl (1891–), German naval officer. In WWII, commanded submarine activity; chief of naval staff (1943). Named to succeed Hitler, ordered German surrender to Allies (May, 1945). Imprisoned (1946-56) after Nuremberg trials.

Donizetti, Gaetano (1797-1848), Italian composer. Wrote tuneful operas, incl. *Lucia di Lammermoor*, *La Fille du régiment* and *Don Pasquale*.

donkey, see ASS.

Donleavy, J[ames] P[atrick] (1926–), American author, living mainly in Ireland. Novels, *eg The Ginger Man* (1955), *The Beastly Beatitudes of Balthazar B* (1969), combine bawdy humour with self-pity.

Donne, John (c 1572-1631), English poet, divine. Greatest of metaphysical school. Work, characterized by irony, intellectual 'conceits', incl. early love poetry, *eg Songs and Sonnets,* later religious verse, *eg* 'Death be not proud', 'Batter my heart three-person'd God', 'At the round earth's imagined corners'. Noted for sermons preached as Dean of St Paul's from 1621.

Donnybrook, suburb of Dublin, Irish Republic. Formerly village, site of riotous fairs, suppressed (1855).

Doolittle, Hilda, pseud. H.D. (1886-1961), American poet. Known as

IMAGIST for verse, wife of Richard Aldington. Attained new reputation with *Helen in Egypt* (1961).

Doppler, Christian Johann (1803-53), Austrian physicist. Predicted Doppler effect: apparent change in frequency of sound or electromagnetic radiation caused by relative motion of source and observer. Observed frequency is higher than emitted frequency as observer and source approach, lower as they recede. Effect used by astronomers to determine relative velocity of heavenly body and Earth.

Dorchester, mun. bor. and co. town of Dorset, S England, on R. Frome. Pop. 14,000. Maiden Castle prehist. hill fort nearby. Roman *Durnovaria,* many remains. 'Casterbridge' of Hardy's novels.

Dordogne, river of WC France. Flows c 465 km (290 mi) from Auvergne Mts. to R. Garonne, forming the Gironde estuary. Tourism, vineyards (incl. St Emilion), h.e.p.

Doré, Gustave (1832-83), French book illustrator. Illustrated Dante's *Inferno, Don Quixote,* the Bible; drew pictures of poor quarters of London (1869-71). Work is noted for his love of the grotesque.

Dorians, people of ancient Greece. Entered Greece from N and overthrew MYCENEAN CIVILIZATION c 1150-1000 BC.

Doric order, earliest and most used of the Greek orders of architecture. Characterized by its lack of base, massive tapering shaft with 20 flutes, simple capital. Parthenon in Athens shows the perfected order.

dormouse, small squirrel-like arboreal rodent of Gliridae family, widely distributed in Old World. Diet of seed, berries, *etc.* European species undergo long hibernation. Species incl. edible dormouse, *Glis glis*, garden dormouse, *Eliomys quercinus*, and common dormouse, *Muscardinus avellanarius*, only British variety.

Dorpat, *see* TARTU.

Dorset, county of S England. Area 2654 sq km (1024 sq mi); pop. 566,000; co. town Dorchester. Chalk downs (sheep); lowlands (dairying); Portland stone quarried. Coastal resorts *eg* Weymouth. Ancient remains incl. Maiden Castle hill fort. Setting of Hardy's Wessex novels.

Dortmund, city of W West Germany, in Ruhr. Pop. 642,000. Port, connected by Dortmund-Ems canal to North Sea; brewing, coal, steel, engineering industs. Member of Hanseatic League. Badly damaged in WWII.

dory, marine fish of Zeidae family. John dory, *Zeus faber*, yellow or golden with spiny dorsal fin, is common in Mediterranean.

Dos Passos, John Roderigo (1896-1970), American novelist. Works incl. *Manhattan Transfer* (1925), trilogy *U.S.A.* (1930-7); mixed 'newsreel', biog. techniques to form composite picture of society. Also wrote reportage, plays.

Dostoyevski, Feodor Mikhailovich (1821-81), Russian novelist. Combined vivid realistic narrative with psychological insight. Major works, incl. *Crime and Punishment* (1866), *The Idiot* (1868), *The Brothers Karamazov* (1879-80), reflect concern with guilt, religious faith.

Dou or **Douw, Gerard** or **Gerrit**

(1613-75), Dutch portrait and genre painter. Pupil of Rembrandt, he developed a minute detailed technique. His works incl. *Dropsical Woman.*

Douala, city of Cameroon, on Bight of Biafra. Pop. 250,000. Railway terminus and port, exports tropical hardwoods, cocoa, bananas. Former cap. of German colony of Kamerun.

Douay Bible, English version of the Bible translated from the Latin Vulgate edition for the use of RCs. NT pub. at Rheims (1582); OT at the RC college for English priests in Douai (1610).

double bass, four-stringed low-pitched instrument, considered either a survivor of VIOL family or lowest member of violin family. Played with bow in orchestra and plucked to supply bass line in popular music.

Doughty, C[harles] M[ontagu] (1843-1926), English traveller, author. Known for *Travels in Arabia Deserta* (1888) revealing passion for Arab culture. Poetry incl. *Mansoul, or The Riddle of the World* (1920).

Douglas, Lord Alfred Bruce (1870-1945), English poet. Friendship with Oscar Wilde precipitated latter's eventual prosecution for homosexual practices.

Douglas, Clifford Hugh (1879-1952), Scottish economist, engineer. Early theorist of SOCIAL CREDIT. Chief reconstruction adviser to Social Credit govt. of Alberta (1935-6).

Douglas, Gavin (*c* 1474-1522), Scottish poet. Known for version of *Aeneid* (1513), most sustained poetic achievement in Scots language.

Douglas, Sir James de Douglas,

Lord of (c 1286-1330), Scottish nobleman, called Black Douglas. After losing estates by order of Edward I, terrorized borders. Later joined Robert the Bruce, with whom he fought at Bannockburn. Died in Spain on way to Palestine to bury Robert's heart.

Douglas, Lloyd Cassell (1877-1951), American novelist. Known for best-selling sentimental novels on religious themes, esp. *The Robe* (1942).

Douglas, [George] Norman (1868-1952), Scottish novelist. Known for *South Wind* (1917), a celebration of Mediterranean hedonism. *Old Calabria* (1915) combines travel, philosophy, autobiog.

Douglas, Stephen Arnold (1813-61), American politician. Democratic senator from Illinois (1847-61), introduced KANSAS-NEBRASKA BILL (1854) in attempt to settle slavery issue. Later asserted doctrine of territ. rights to exclude slavery during famous election campaign debates (1858) with Lincoln.

Douglas, cap. of Isle of Man, UK. Pop. 20,000. Seaport, resort on E coast. Admin. and legislative buildings.

Douglas fir, *Pseudotsuga taxifolia*, evergreen tree of W North America. Timber exported in large quantities as lumber and plywood.

Douglas-Home, Alexander Frederick, Baron Home of the Hirsel (1903-), British statesman, PM (1963-4). Conservative foreign secretary (1960-3), renounced titles (originally 14th earl of Home) to become PM in succession to Macmillan. Lost ensuing election. Again

foreign secretary (1970-4), made life peer (1974).

Doukhobors, *see* DUKHOBORS.

Dounreay, village of Highland region, N Scotland. Site of UK's first large-scale nuclear reactor.

Douro (Span. *Duero*), river of Spain and Portugal. Flows c 770 km (480 mi) from NC Spain, W to Atlantic Ocean near Oporto. Used for irrigation, h.e.p.

Douw, Gerrit, *see* DOU, GERARD.

dove, medium-sized bird of same family (Columbidae) as pigeon. Short neck and legs, cooing cry; seed eater. Species incl. rock dove, *Columba livia*, ancestor of domestic pigeons; turtle dove, *Streptopelia turtur*, of S Europe, Africa.

Dover, mun. bor. of Kent, SE England. Pop. 34,000. Ferry port, shortest cross-Channel route (to Calais, 35 km/22 mi). Has Roman lighthouse; Norman castle; one of Cinque Ports.

Dover, cap. of Delaware, US. Pop. 17,000. Fruit canning indust. Settled 1683; became cap. 1777.

Dover, Strait of (Fr. *Pas de Calais*), between SE England and NE France, links English Channel with North Sea. At narrowest only 34 km (21 mi) wide.

Dowding, Hugh Caswall Tremenheere Dowding, 1st Baron (1882-1970), British air marshal. During Battle of Britain, he was chief of Fighter Command (1939-42).

Dowland, John (1563-1626), English composer and lutanist. Remembered for his plaintively beautiful lute songs and solos. Lutanist to Christian IV of Denmark and to James I and Charles I of England.

Down, former county of SE Northern Ireland. Hilly, incl. Mourne Mts. in SE; Ards Penin., Strangford Lough in E. Agric., linen mfg., tourism. Co. town was Downpatrick. Down, district; area 646 sq km (249 sq mi); pop. 49,000. Created 1973, formerly part of Co. Down.

Downing Street, London street off Whitehall, in which are located official residences of British PM (number 10) and chancellor of exchequer (number 11).

Downpatrick, town of SE Northern Ireland. Pop. 8000. Former co. town of Down. Its cathedral is reputed to have remains of Irish saints Patrick, Columba, Bridget.

Downs, S England. Chalk ranges running W-E. North Downs (up to 294 m/965 ft) of Surrey and Kent end at white cliffs of Dover. South Downs (up to 264 m/865 ft) of Sussex end at Beachy Head. Sheep pasture land. Hampshire, Berkshire, Marlborough downs further W.

Dowson, Ernest Christopher (1867-1900), English poet. Lived mainly in France, influenced by 'decadent' poets esp. Verlaine. Known for 'Cynara' (1896).

Doyle, Sir Arthur Conan (1859-1930), English author, b. Scotland. Created detective Sherlock Holmes in *A Study in Scarlet* (1887). Along with many Holmes stories, also wrote historical romances, *eg The White Company* (1891). Knighted for defence of British policy in Boer War.

D'Oyly Carte, Richard (1844-1901), English theatrical impresario. Known for productions of Gilbert and Sullivan operettas. Built Savoy Theatre, London (1881).

Drabble, Margaret (1939-), English author. Novels, *eg A Summer Birdcage* (1963), *The Millstone* (1966), deal with the problem of conflicting female roles.

Draco (*fl c* 623 BC), Athenian statesman. Devised code of laws noted for their severity, as almost all crimes carried death penalty.

Dracula, see STOKER, BRAM.

dragon, fabulous monster of Christian, Chinese, Japanese and other folklore. Usually represented as huge, fire-breathing, winged reptilian quadruped. Sometimes used in Christian art, literature to symbolize forces of evil.

dragon fish, any of Pegasidae family of small flying fish of Indian, Pacific oceans. Long snout, body covered with bony plates.

dragonfly, any of Odonata order of insects with 2 pairs of membranous wings, large eyes and long, thin brightly-coloured body. Feeds on small insects seized in flight. Wingspan of some fossil varieties *c* 60 cm/2 ft.

dragoon, cavalry soldier trained to fight on foot. The name comes from the short musket, called a dragon, carried by the French cavalry of Marshal Bussac (1600).

Drake, Sir Francis (*c* 1540-96), English naval officer. In 1570-3 took part in raiding expeditions to the Spanish Main and in the *Golden Hind* was 1st English mariner to circumnavigate the globe (1577-80), for which he was knighted by Elizabeth I. In 1585 he commanded a marauding fleet off Spanish America, and in 1587 destroyed the

Spanish fleet at Cádiz. In 1588 helped defeat Spanish Armada.

Drakensberg Mountains or **Quathlamba**, range of South Africa. Extends *c* 1125 km (700 mi) SW-NE from Cape Prov. to Transvaal; rises to 3481 m (11,425 ft) in Lesotho. Forms SE escarpment of C plateau.

drama, artistic form traditionally combining speech and action to tell story, but also incl. monologue, mime. Western drama originated in Greek Dionysiac festivals, leading to classical TRAGEDY. Popular COMEDY developed alongside using stock characters. Renaissance revived classical theories while in Italy popular COMMEDIA DELL'ARTE flourished. Fusion of classical and popular traditions led to Elizabethan and Jacobean drama in England. Classical models were more rigidly observed in France. Restoration drama was largely artificial and gave way to sentimental and then romantic drama. Realism introduced in 19th cent. leading to deeper psychological interest. *See* NO PLAY, JAPANESE LITERATURE.

Draper, John William (1811-82), American scientist, b. England. Contributed to fields of photochemistry and radiant energy, anticipating development of spectrum analysis. Author of *Human Physiology* (1856), which contained 1st photographs reproducing what is seen under microscope.

draughts or **checkers**, game of skill for 2 persons played with 24 round pieces on a board divided into 64 alternate light and dark squares. Played in Europe from 16th cent.

Drava, river of EC Europe. Flows *c*

725 km (450 mi) from S Austria through Yugoslavia to Danube near Osijek. Forms part of Yugoslav-Hungarian border.

Dravidian, major group of inhabitants of India, before Aryan invasion, therefore name for S India group possibly descended from pre-Aryan stock. Also name for family of languages mainly in S India and Sri Lanka, incl. Telugu, Tamil, Kannada and Malayalam.

Drayton, Michael (1563-1631), English poet. Remembered for *Polyolbion* (1612), a patriotic description of British countryside. Also wrote shorter poems, incl. sonnet beginning, 'Since there's no help, come let us kiss and part'.

dreams, sequences of sensations, images, thoughts, *etc*, occurring during SLEEP. Shown to be necessary in restorative process of sleep. Considered important in ancient times and among primitive peoples. Interest revived by Freud (who distinguished latent content and manifest content) and Jung.

Dred Scott Case (1856-7), test case brought before US Supreme Court. Decision rejected Negro slave's plea for freedom on ground that he had lived several years in free territ., decreed that Negro 'whose ancestors . . . were sold as slaves' was not entitled to rights of Federal citizen. Declared MISSOURI COMPROMISE unconstitutional, further aggravated North-South dispute.

Dreiser, Theodore (1871-1945), American naturalistic novelist. Known for naturalistic *Sister Carrie* (1900), *An American Tragedy* (1925) attacking the 20th cent. American dream. Also wrote plays, essays, autobiog. *A Hoosier Holiday* (1916).

Drenthe, prov. of NE Netherlands. Area 2644 sq km (1021 sq mi); cap. Assen. Infertile heathland, reclamation in W. Rye, potatoes, cattle; oil, natural gas.

Dresden, city of SE East Germany, on R. Elbe. Pop. 504,000. River port, railway jct.; produces machine tools, optical instruments. 'Dresden' pottery made at Meissen. Cap. of Saxony 1485-1918. Cultural centre with noted art collections, Baroque buildings; many destroyed in WWII.

Dreyfus affair (1894-1906), scandal arising out of trial of French army officer, Alfred Dreyfus (1859-1935), for treason. Accused of selling military secrets to Germany, he became centre of case arousing anti-Semitic tirades in press and dividing France into groups of royalists, militarists, Catholics on one side, and republicans, socialists, anti-clerics on the other. Dreyfus, a Jew, was imprisoned on Devils Isl.; pardoned (1899) after long struggle by supporters, incl. Zola, to show evidence against him was based on forgery. Affair discredited monarchists and army, united left wing.

drift, in geomorphology, transported material deposited during glaciation of a region. Consists of clay, sand, gravel, boulders. Fluvio-glacial drift is laid down by water run-off from glacier's edge; BOULDER CLAY is laid down directly from ice.

drill, see MANDRILL.

drive, in psychology, see LIBIDO.

Drogheda, town of Co. Louth, NE Irish Republic, on R. Boyne. Pop. 20,000: Exports cattle; linen, cotton mfg. Captured (1649) by Cromwell, massacre followed.

dromedary, see CAMEL.

drongo, any of Dicruridae family of insectivorous birds, with black iridescent plumage, arched bill. Commonest in S Asia, also found in Australia, Africa. Species incl. king crow, *Dicrurus macrocerus*, of India.

dropsy, see OEDEMA.

drugs, chemical substances taken for prevention or alleviation of disease. Types in use incl. antibiotics, sulphonamides, barbiturates, amphetamines. Name also applies to habit-forming narcotics, eg heroin, opium.

Druids, ancient religious body of priests, soothsayers, poets in Celtic Gaul and Britain. Taught immortality of soul; held oak and mistletoe sacred: Important in education of young; exercised political power through federation extending across tribal divisions. Druidism declined in Gaul by 1st cent. and soon after in Britain. Prehist. remains, eg Stonehenge, once attributed to Druids.

drum, percussion instrument; consists of a skin stretched over a hollow cylinder, which resonates when the skin is struck. Timpani or kettledrums produce notes of definite pitch and can be tuned, but other drums are of indefinite pitch.

drumlin, elongated, oval ridge consisting of BOULDER CLAY. Formed by deposition and moulding of material by ice-sheet flowing over area. Aligned parallel to direction of ice flow. Commonly occurs in swarms, eg Down, Northern Ireland and Wisconsin, US.

Drummond, William Henry (1854-1907), Canadian poet, b. Ireland. Known for poems in French-Canadian dialect on rural Québec life.

Drummond of Hawthornden, William (1585-1649), Scottish poet. Wrote melancholic sonnets, prose work *The Cypress Grove, or Philosophical Reflections against the Fear of Death* (1630).

Drury Lane, street in London, site of several theatres. First, built in 1663, destroyed by fire (1672). Present theatre dates from 1812.

Druses, secret religious sect in S Syria and Lebanon. Basically Moslem, but believe in the divinity of the Caliph Hakim (11th cent.). Fiercely resisted Ottoman rule. Perpetrated several massacres of Christians, esp. in 1860s.

Dryads, in Greek myth, NYMPHS who lived in trees. Died together with trees which had been their home.

dry cell, *see* CELL, VOLTAIC.

Dryden, John (1631-1700), English poet. Literary arbiter of Restoration. Known for *Absalom and Achitophel* (1681) written in heroic couplets, plays esp. *All for Love* (1678), prose criticism, translations of Vergil. Poet laureate (1668-89).

dry farming, system of farming without irrigation in an almost rainless region. Involves conserving natural moisture in soil and planting drought-resistant crops. Widely used in arid regions of, *eg* US, USSR, India.

drypoint, method of engraving by drawing on metal printing plate with sharp hard needle. Quality of drypoint lies in 'burr' of metal shavings turned up at side of furrow made by needle; ink collects in burr

and gives richness to the print. Technique was used by Dürer, Whistler, Rembrandt.

dry rot, fungous disease of seasoned timber resulting in its softening and eventual crumbling to powder; often occurs in humid unventilated conditions. Prevented by application of creosote or fungicides.

Drysdale, George Russell (1912-), Australian artist. Known for his paintings of the harsh Australian outback and loneliness and isolation of its people.

Dual Monarchy, *see* AUSTRO-HUNGARIAN MONARCHY.

Dubai, seaport of Dubai sheikdom, United Arab Emirates, on Persian Gulf. Pop. 70,000.

Dubček, Alexander (1921-), Czechoslovakian political leader. First secretary of Communist Party (1968-9), chief figure in 'liberalizing' movement in Czech politics, soon crushed by Soviet military intervention (1968). Later deprived of political office, succeeded by pro-Soviet govt. under Gustav Husák (1969).

Dublin, county of Leinster prov., E Irish Republic. Area 922 sq km (356 sq mi); pop. 850,000; co. town DUBLIN. Mountainous in S; elsewhere lowland. Agric., livestock.

Dublin (*Baile Atha Cliath*), cap. of Irish Republic, co. town of Dublin, on R. Liffey and Irish Sea. Pop. 566,000. Admin. and commercial centre, seaport; brewing, distilling, textile mfg. Trinity Coll. (1591), Univ. Coll. Has RC pro-cathedral, 2 Protestant cathedrals, Abbey Theatre (1904). Hist. focus of Irish political unrest, culminated in Easter Rising (1916).

Dubrovnik (Ital. *Ragusa*), town of Dalmatia, SE Yugoslavia, on Adriatic Sea. Pop. 23,000. Port, resort. Founded 7th cent. by Greeks; rich medieval republic rivalling Venice until 16th cent. Cathedral (17th cent.), ancient walls.

Duchamp, Marcel (1887-1968), French painter. Pioneer of the DADA group, he is known for his 'ready-mades', *eg* bottle rack, mounted bicycle wheel. Most famous work is *Nude Descending a Staircase*, which combines cubism and futurism.

duck, aquatic bird of Anatidae family with webbed feet, long neck and long flat bill. Plumage waterproofed by oil from gland near tail.

duckbilled platypus, *Ornithorhynchus anatinus*, semi-aquatic, egg-laying mammal of Australia, Tasmania. Thick fur, webbed feet, duck-like bill; poison spur on heel. Most reptile-like of mammals.

ductless glands, *see* ENDOCRINE GLANDS.

Dudintzev, Vladimir Dmitrievich (1918-), Russian novelist. Created sensation with *Not by Bread Alone* (1956) attacking Soviet bureaucracy. Exonerated by Khrushchev (1959).

Dudley, John, *see* NORTHUMBERLAND, JOHN DUDLEY, DUKE OF.

Dudley, Robert, *see* LEICESTER, ROBERT DUDLEY, EARL OF.

Dudley, co. bor. of West Midlands met. county, WC England. Pop. 186,000. Wrought iron indust.; metal goods.

duel, combat with swords or pistols, arranged by challenge and fought under conventional rules, usually to resolve personal quarrel or decide point of honour. Duelling is illegal in most countries and killing an opponent considered murder.

due process of law, in law, principle protecting individuals from state power. Common to modern democratic states, demands that no one may be deprived of life, liberty, property except by estab. practices of law. In US, guaranteed by 14th Amendment.

Duero, *see* DOURO.

Dufay, Guillaume (*c* 1400-74), Flemish composer. Travelled widely, serving in papal choir (1428-33, 1435-7) and at court of Burgundy. Leading composer of *chansons* and church music; works incl. Mass based on his song 'Se la face ay pale'.

Dufy, Raoul (1877-1953), French artist. Influenced by fauvism, he adopted style of simplified form and bright colour. Later work marked by calligraphic style and brilliant colour; also designed textiles.

dugong, *Dugong dugong*, whale-like herbivorous mammal of Red Sea and Indian Ocean. Brownish or greyish, reaches lengths of *c* 3 m/10 ft. Slow-moving and defenceless; much hunted, now rare. Also called sea cow.

Duhamel, Georges (1884-1966), French author. Leader of Abbaye (community of writers, artists). Subsequently wrote plays, *eg The Light* (1911), novel cycles *Salavin* (1920-32), *Pasquier Chronicles* (1933-45), and essay *The Heart's Domain* (1919) urging cultivation of inner life.

duiker, any of several small antelopes of African bush S of Sahara. Species incl. common grey duiker, *Sylvicapra grimmia*, with short horns on both sexes.

Duisburg, city of W West Germany, at confluence of Rhine and Ruhr. Pop. 449,000. Major port; steel, engineering, textile industs. Member of Hanseatic League. Heavy bombing in WWII.

Dukas, Paul (1865-1935), French composer. Best known for scherzo *The Sorcerer's Apprentice* (1897), opera *Ariane et Barbe-Bleue.*

Dukhobors or **Doukhobors,** Russian religious sect widespread 17th-19th cent., officially called Christians of the Universal Brotherhood. Believed in complete equality of man, denied authority of state and church. Persecuted, they emigrated (1890s) and settled in W Canada. Clashes with govt. and neighbours over social unorthodoxies of sect have continued.

dulcimer, a musical instrument in which strings stretched over a wooden frame are struck by mallets held in the hands. Originated in East in medieval times, lives on in E European folk music.

Dulles, John Foster (1888-1959), American statesman. Eisenhower's secretary of state (1953-9), pursued foreign policy based on collective security of US and Allies and development of nuclear weapons to retaliate in event of attack. His brother, **Allen Welsh Dulles** (1893-1969), was director of Central Intelligence Agency (1953-61).

Dulong, Pierre Louis (1785-1838), French scientist. Discovered explosive nitrogen trichloride. With A. T. Petit, formulated Dulong-Petit law: product of specific heat and atomic weight is approximately same for all solid elements.

dulse, *Rhodymenia palmata,* edible seaweed. Solitary or tufted red fronds grow on rocks, shellfish or other seaweeds.

Duluth, indust. town and port of NE Minnesota; at W end of L. Superior. Pop. 101,000. Shipping route esp. iron ore, coal, grain. Flour milling, sawmilling industs.

duma, Russian house of representatives, granted by Nicholas II after Revolution of 1905. Legislative powers restricted by tsar's prerogative. Last duma (1912-17) ended by March revolution.

Dumas, Alexandre, (père) (1802-70), French author. Known for c 300 vols. of swashbuckling romance, esp. *The Three Musketeers* (1844), *Count of Monte Cristo* (1845), plays, eg *La Tour de Nesle* (1832). His son, **Alexandre Dumas (fils)** (1824-95) known for plays esp. *La Dame aux Camélias* (1852), basis of Verdi's opera *La Traviata,* film *Camille.*

Du Maurier, George Louis Palmella Busson (1834-96), English novelist, illustrator, b. Paris. Remembered for cartoons in *Punch,* novels *Peter Ibbetson* (1892), *Trilby* (1894). His granddaughter, **Daphne Du Maurier** (1907-   ), known for romantic novels often set in Cornwall, eg *Jamaica Inn* (1936).

Dumbarton, town of Strathclyde region, W Scotland, on R. Clyde. Pop. 26,000. Former royal burgh and co. town of Dunbartonshire. Shipbuilding, engineering industs.; whisky distilling. Cap. of ancient Strathclyde kingdom.

Dumfries and Galloway, region of SW Scotland. Area 6369 sq km (2459 sq mi); pop. 144,000. Created 1975, incl. former Dumfriesshire, Kirkcudbrightshire, Wigtownshire.

Dumfriesshire, former county of S Scotland. Southern Uplands in N; plain of R. Solway in S; Annan, Nith valleys run N-S. Sheep, cattle rearing, root crops; coalmining. Co. town was Dumfries, former royal burgh on R. Nith. Pop. 29,000. Tweed mfg. Old Bridge (1280); Burns' Mausoleum (1815).

dun (Gaelic, = 'fort'), dry-stone fortification of Scottish and Irish Iron Age, often situated on hill-tops. Circular, oval or D-shaped, had very thick walls (often containing cells and galleries), and enclosed smaller area than great hill forts. Word has become element in many place names eg Dunkeld, Dumbarton.

Dunant, Jean Henri (1828-1910), Swiss philanthropist. Horrified by experience of tending wounded at battle of Solferino, promoted estab. of International Red Cross (1863). Shared 1st Nobel Peace Prize (1901).

Dunbar, William (c 1460-c 1520), Scottish poet. Influenced by Chaucer and Scottish traditions, but with vigorous personal voice expressed in technically innovative verse. Poems incl. 'Lament for the Makaris'.

Dunbar, town of Lothian region, E Scotland. Pop. 5000. Fishing port, resort. Scene of battle (1650) in which Cromwell defeated Scots.

Dunbartonshire, former county of W Scotland, now in Strathclyde region. Mountainous in N; incl. Loch Lomond (tourism); industs. along Clyde estuary and Vale of Leven, incl. shipbuilding, bleaching, dyeing.

Duncan I, king of Scotland (1034-1040), succeeded maternal grandfather, Malcolm II; father of Malcolm III and Donald Bane. Murdered by Macbeth.

Duncan II, king of Scotland (1093-4). Son of Malcolm III, lived as hostage in England. With English aid took throne from uncle Donald Bane (1093). Killed following year, Donald Bane restored.

Duncan, Isadora (1878-1927), American dancer. Toured Europe, US, performing own concept of dance, inspired by ancient Greek art, with long loose robes and bare feet, free and expressive movements.

Dundalk, co. town of Louth, E Irish Republic, on Dundalk Bay. Pop. 22,000. Exports agric. produce. Railway engineering; linen, hosiery mfg.

Dundee, John Graham of Claverhouse, 1st Viscount (c 1649-89), Scottish nobleman, known as 'Bonnie Dundee'. Hated by Covenanters, whom he attempted to suppress (1678-88), earning name 'Bloody Clavers'. Raised force to restore James II, killed in victory of Jacobites at Killiecrankie.

Dundee, city of Tayside region, E Scotland, on Firth of Tay. Pop. 182,000. Seaport; jute indust., clocks, cash registers, jam, confectionery mfg., publishing. Bridges (railway 1888, road 1966).

Dunedin, city of SE South Isl., New Zealand, on Otago Harbour. Pop. 82,000. Port, exports wool, meat; engineering, woollen mills. Founded 1848 by Scottish settlers; grew rapidly in 1861 gold rush. Has Anglican, RC cathedrals; Univ. of Otago (1869).

Dunfermline, town of Fife, E Scotland. Pop. 50,000. Silk, rayon mfg.; engineering. Has palace of

Scottish kings; royal tombs in 11th cent. abbey. Park, library donated by Carnegie, who was born here.

dung beetle, insect of scarab beetle family that rolls ball of dung in which to lay eggs and provide food for larvae. Important agent in disposal of animal dung.

Dunkirk (*Dunkerque*), town of Nord, N France, on Str. of Dover. Pop. 28,000. Port, shipbuilding, major iron and steel indust. Under English rule (1658-62). Scene of evacuation (1940) of *c* 300,000 Allied troops.

Dún Laoghaire, bor. of Co. Dublin, E Irish Republic, on Dublin Bay. Pop. 53,000. Resort; port, ferry service to Holyhead (Wales). Formerly called Kingstown.

Dunlop, John Boyd (1840-1921), Scottish veterinary surgeon. Patented (1888) Dunlop version of pneumatic tyre, producing it commercially in Belfast.

Dunoon, town of Strathclyde region, W Scotland, on Firth of Clyde. Pop. 10,000. Resort; nearby is US nuclear submarine base at Holy Loch.

Dunsany, Lord Edward John Moreton Drax Plunkett (1878-1957), Irish author. Known for short stories, eg in *The Gods of Pegana* (1905), plays *The Glittering Gate* (1909) produced by Yeats at Abbey Theatre.

Duns Scotus, John (*c* 1265-1308), Scottish philosopher. A Franciscan, opposed theories of Aquinas. Challenged harmony of reason and faith by showing limits of human reason. Known as 'Doctor Subtilis'.

Dunstable, John (d. 1453), English composer. Travelled abroad in service of English regent of France. Compositions, mainly for the Church, influenced composers of Burgundian school, eg Dufay. Works incl. song 'O rosa bella'.

Dunstan, St (*c* 924-88), English prelate, statesman. Became abbot of Glastonbury, where he began revival of regularized monasticism in England. As archbishop of Canterbury from 961, drew up national code for monasteries based on Benedictine rule. Principal adviser to all contemporary Wessex kings, virtual ruler of England under Edred and Edgar.

duodenal ulcer, see PEPTIC ULCER.

Dupleix, Joseph François (1697-1763), French colonial administrator. Governor of French possessions in India (1742-54), planned to estab. French supremacy through military and political measures. Initially successful until thwarted by CLIVE. Recall to France marked collapse of French colonial ambitions in India.

Du Pont, Eleuthère Irénée (1772-1834), American chemicals manufacturer, b. France. Founded (1802) powder mill near Wilmington, Delaware, expanding Du Pont firm into one of largest explosives makers. Firm developed numerous chemical manufactures, incl. nylon, and acquired other indusrs. under **Pierre Samuel Du Pont** (1870-1954), long-time president of business.

Duras, Marguerite (1914-), French novelist. Works incl. *Sea Wall* (1950), film scenario *Hiroshima mon amour* (1959).

Durazzo (*Durrës*), town of W Albania, on Adriatic. Pop. 53,000. Country's main seaport, exports olive oil, tobacco. Founded 7th cent.

BC; important Roman port (*Dyrrachium*).

Durban, city of Natal, South Africa, on Indian Ocean. Pop. 721,000, incl. large Asian community. Major port, exports minerals, grain, fruit; indust. centre, resort. Has part of Univ. of Natal (1909). Founded 1835. Scene of African-Indian riots (1949).

Dürer, Albrecht (1471-1528), German artist. Prolific master of woodcuts, copper engravings and drawings; following visits to Italy, he was largely instrumental in introducing discoveries of Italian Renaissance into North. Works incl. series of woodcuts for *Apocalypse*, watercolours of alpine scenery; few paintings incl. *Four Apostles*. Influenced by writings of Luther.

Durham, John George Lambton, 1st Earl of (1792-1840), British statesman. Promoted liberal measures, *eg* 1832 Reform Bill, earning nickname 'Radical Jack'. Governor-general of Canada, prepared *Report on the Affairs of British North America* (1839) advocating responsible self-govt.

Durham, county of NE England. Area 2435 sq km (940 sq mi); pop. 608,000. Pennines in W (sheep), fertile valleys; coastal plain in E, coalfield. Coalmining, iron and steel, shipbuilding industs., chemicals mfg. Co. town **Durham**, city on R. Wear. Pop. 25,000. Castle (1072) now site of univ. (1832). Cathedral (1093) has Bede's remains.

Durham, town of NC North Carolina, US. Pop. 95,000. Tobacco market, cigarette mfg. Seat of Duke Univ. (1924).

Durkheim, Emile (1858-1917), French sociologist. Stressed impor-tance of collective mind of society in creating personal morality, with loss of social controls leading to deep unhappiness (*anomie*). Works incl. *Suicide* (1897), *The Elementary Forms of Religious Life* (1912).

Durrell, Lawrence George (1912-), English author, b. India. Best known for 'The Alexandria Quartet' of *Justine* (1957), *Balthazar* (1958), *Mountolive* (1958), *Clea* (1960), using multiple viewpoints. Also wrote poetry celebrating Mediterranean.

Dürrenmatt, Friedrich (1921-), Swiss playwright. Known for ironic tragicomedies *The Marriage of Mr Mississippi* (1952), *The Visit of the Old Lady* (1956). Stage technique similar to Brecht's in disruption of illusion.

Durrës, *see* DURAZZO, Albania.

Duse, Eleonora (1859-1924), Italian actress. Known for tragic roles, *eg* Hedda Gabler, Magda in *The Seagull*. Appeared in Europe, America. Had intimate relationship with D'Annunzio.

Dushanbe, city of USSR, cap. of Tadzhik SSR. Pop. 400,000. Cotton and silk mfg.; meat packing. Called Stalinabad (1929-61).

Düsseldorf, city of W West Germany, on R. Rhine, cap. of North Rhine-Westphalia. Pop. 650,000. Has international airport. Iron, steel, vehicles, textiles mfg. Cultural centre, art academy (18th cent.). Chartered 1288, residence (14th-16th cent.) of dukes of Berg.

dust bowl, area where exposed top soil is raised by strong winds into dust storms and blown away. Occurs after removal of protective vegetation cover by ploughing. Term applied in particular to W prairies of US, severely affected in late 1930s.

Dutch, language of W Germanic group of Indo-European family. Written and spoken language diverge greatly, since former developed from sophisticated Flemish of 15th cent. Flanders, Brabant, latter from vernacular of Holland.

Dutch East Indies, see INDONESIA.

Dutch elm disease, virulent and widespread disease of elms caused by a fungus, *Ceratocystis ulmi*, carried by the ambrosia beetle. Produces wilting and drying of the leaves and ultimately death of the tree. First appeared in Netherlands.

Dutch Guiana, see SURINAM.

Dutch Reformed Church, see REFORMED CHURCH IN AMERICA.

Dutch Wars, three naval wars, arising from commercial rivalry, fought between England and Netherlands. First war (1652-4) was precipitated by seizure of Dutch merchant fleet and passage of Navigation Act (1651). English blockaded Dutch coast, defeated fleet under Tromp (1653). Second conflict (1664-7) sparked by continued threat to English sea power and trade. English raided Dutch colonies in Africa and North America. Dutch inflicted heavy losses on English fleet in raid on Thames (1667). Settlement of Treaty of Breda incl. favourable change in trade laws for Dutch. Third war (1672-4) formed part of Louis XIV's campaign against Netherlands (1672-8). England allied with France by terms of Treaty of Dover (1670); made peace 1674.

Duvalier, François ('Papa Doc') (1907-71), dictator of Haiti (1957-

71). Estab. dictatorship after becoming president (1957); used personal police force (Tonton Macoutes) to enforce brutal repression of opponents. Succeeded by his son, Jean-Claude Duvalier (1951-), as president for life.

Dvina, two rivers of W USSR. Northern Dvina flows *c* 750 km (470 mi) NW through N European RSFSR to Dvina Bay at Archangel. Western Dvina flows *c* 1020 km (640 mi) from Valdai Hills to Gulf of Riga in Latvian SSR.

Dvořák, Antonin (1841-1904), Czech composer. Encouraged by Brahms, much of his work was influenced by Czech folksong. Taught in America (1892-5). Compositions incl. 9 symphonies (best known is 9th, *From the New World*), string quartets, choral works, 2 cello concertos, violin concerto, piano concerto.

dwarf, in plants and animals, term applied to specimens which do not attain normal height. In humans, dwarfism may result from deficiency of pituitary hormone or from achondroplasia, hereditary disorder resulting in defective growth of limbs.

Dyak, non-Moslem peoples of Borneo. Divided into Sea Dyaks of coasts and rivers, and Land Dyaks of interior. Fishers, hunters (with poison darts) hardly influenced by modern civilization, retaining stringent taboos and custom of head hunting. Society organized around 'long houses' which contain whole village.

dyestuffs, materials used to impart colour to textiles or other substances. Originally obtained from natural materials, *eg* plant roots, best known being indigo and alizarin. Synthetic dyes manufactured from distillation products of coal tar and known as aniline colours.

Dyfed, county of SW Wales. Area 5765 sq km (2226 sq mi); pop. 319,000; co. town Carmarthen. Created 1974, incl. former Pembrokeshire, Cardiganshire, Carmarthenshire.

Dylan, Bob, orig. Robert Zimmerman (1941–), American singer, composer. Leading exponent in 1960s of 'folk rock' fusing folk and rock idioms, *eg Highway 61 Revisited.* Songs, often social commentaries, influenced many young singers and musicians.

dynamics, branch of physics dealing with the motion of bodies under the action of given forces. Also *see* STATICS.

dynamite, powerful explosive discovered by Alfred Nobel (1866). Consists of NITROGLYCERINE absorbed in porous substance, *eg* kieselguhr or wood pulp; varying amounts of ammonium or sodium nitrate added. Activated by detonator.

dynamo, device for converting mechanical energy into electrical energy. Simplest type consists of powerful magnet between whose poles an armature (laminated iron core with wire wound around it) is rotated. *See* ELECTROMAGNETIC INDUCTION.

dyne, unit of force in C.G.S. SYSTEM; 1 dyne acting on mass of 1 gram will produce acceleration of 1 cm/sec².

dysentery, any of various intestinal inflammations, characterized by intense diarrhoea, usually accompanied by blood and mucus. Amoebic dysentery is caused by parasitic protozoon *Entamoeba histolytica;* bacterial by a bacillus of *Shigella* group.

dyslexia, inability to read properly due to brain disorder which causes letters, or order of letters, to be confused. Sufferers may be of normal intelligence and can be helped by special teaching.

Dyson, Sir Frank Watson (1868–1939), English astronomer. Director of Greenwich Observatory (1910–33). Studied stellar motions and solar eclipses. Inaugurated radio transmission of Greenwich time.

dysprosium (Dy), soft metallic element of lanthanide group; at. no. 66, at. wt. 162.5. Discovered (1886) by Lecoq de Boisbaudran.

Dzungaria, region of Sinkiang prov., NW China. Area *c* 777,000 sq km (300,000 sq mi). Semi-desert plateau; agric. where irrigated. oilfields, mineral deposits.

E

eagle, carnivorous bird of Accipitridae family with long talons, feathered neck and head. Powerful flier, with keen eyesight; usually nests in inaccessible places (cliffs, mountains).

eagle ray, any of Myliobatidae family of large, flat cartilaginous fish. Long whip-like tail, large wing-like pectoral fins. Species incl. *Myliobatus aquila* of Mediterranean and African coasts.

Ealing, bor. of W Greater London, England. Pop. 299,000. Created 1965 from Ealing, Acton, Southall mun. bors. (all formerly in Middlesex). Film studios famous for 'Ealing Comedies' of 1950s.

ear, organ of hearing. Human ear consists of: external ear and auditory canal, ending at ear drum; middle ear, cavity containing 3 small bones which communicate vibrations of ear drum to inner ear, a labyrinthine structure in temporal bone; cochlea, containing auditory nerve endings, and 3 fluid-containing semicircular canals, important for balance, are found in inner ear.

Earhart, Amelia (1897-1937), American aviator. First woman to make solo flight of Atlantic (1932). Lost in Pacific during attempt to fly around the world.

Early English, name given to first period of English Gothic architecture (13th cent.). Characterized by pointed arches, long narrow windows without mullions. Salisbury Cathedral exemplifies the style.

Earth, the, fifth largest planet of solar system, third in distance from Sun; mean distance from Sun *c* 150,000,000 km (93,000,000 mi). Revolves in elliptical orbit about Sun, taking 365¼ days to complete orbit, its inclination producing change of seasons. Earth is slightly flattened at poles; equatorial radius *c* 6378 km (3963 mi), polar radius *c* 6357 km (3950 mi). Believed to have central core of iron and nickel, surrounded by mantle of silicate rocks which support thin outer crust.

earthquake, shaking or trembling of the Earth's crust originating naturally below the surface. Consists of series of shock waves generated at focus or foci, which may cause changes in level, cracking or distortion of surface. Often accompanied by volcanic activity, landslides, giant sea waves (*tsunamis*). Associated with younger fold-mountain regions of Earth, esp. fault lines; prob. the result of stresses caused by movement of crustal plates (*see* PLATE TECTONICS). Severity measured by various scales, eg Richter, Mercalli. Main zones of activity: (1) Pacific area incl. W coast of America, Alaska,

Japan, Philippines, New Zealand; (2) S Europe, NE Africa, Iran, Himalayas, East Indies; (3) mid-oceanic ridges. Recent severe earthquakes incl. Skopje, Yugoslavia (1963), Managua, Nicaragua (1972), Tangshan, China (1976).

earthworm, any of number of round, segmented worms that burrow in soil, class Oligochaeta. Common species of N hemisphere is *Lumbricus terrestris,* important for aerating and fertilizing soil. Giant earthworm of Australia, *Megascolides australis,* reaches lengths of 3.3 m/11 ft.

earwig, any of Dermaptera order of widely distributed insects. Short stiff forewings, conspicuous forceps at end of abdomen; omnivorous. European earwig, *Forficula auricularia,* introduced into America, Australia.

East Anglia, E England. Rich agric. area incl. Norfolk, Suffolk; flat, artificially drained. Crops incl. wheat, barley, sugar beet. Ancient kingdom (6th cent.) of Angles. Earldom from 10th cent.

East Bengal, see BENGAL.

Eastbourne, co. bor. of East Sussex, S England. Pop. 70,000. Coastal resort.

East China Sea, arm of Pacific Ocean, bordering on China and extending from Taiwan to Japan.

Easter, annual Christian festival commemorating resurrection of Jesus. Instituted *c* AD 68, named after Anglo-Saxon goddess of spring. In the West, falls on 1st Sunday after full moon after vernal equinox, between 22nd March and 25th April. In Eastern Orthodox Church, calculated from Julian calendar.

Easter Island (Span. *Isla de Pascua*), pastoral isl. off Chile, in E Pacific. Area 199 sq km (46 sq mi); pop. 1600. Agric. incl. livestock rearing, tobacco, sugar cane growing. Has mysterious statues, undeciphered wooden tablets. Discovered 1722; annexed by Chile 1888.

Eastern Orthodox Church, collective name for independent Christian churches of E Europe and W Asia. Rejected authority of Roman See under Pope Leo IX in 1054. Originally made up of 4 patriarchates (Constantinople, Alexandria, Antioch, Jerusalem), now also incl. certain autonomous churches of USSR, Greece, Romania.

Easter Rebellion, uprising in Dublin (24-29 April, 1916) against British rule in Ireland. Forcibly suppressed, leaders executed. Hardened split between loyalist and nationalist factions.

East Germany, see GERMANY.

East India Company, English company chartered (1600) by Elizabeth I for trade with East. Activities largely confined to India after 1623, where it thrived on export of textiles. After Clive's victories over French rivals, became virtual ruler of India. Trade monopoly withdrawn by govt. acts of 1813, 1833. British govt. assumed direct control after Indian Mutiny (1858); company dissolved 1874.

East Indies, vague term which once referred to SE Asia, incl. India, Malay and Indo-Chinese archipelagos; later referred to Netherlands East Indies (now Indonesia).

East Kilbride, town of Strathclyde region, WC Scotland. Pop. 64,000. Created 'new town' in 1947. Aircraft equipment, electronics, printing industs.

East London, city of SE Cape Prov., South Africa, on Indian Ocean. Pop. 123,000. Port, exports grain; fruit; fishing; indust. centre, resort. Founded 1847, formerly called Port Rex.

East Lothian, former county of E Scotland, now in Lothian region. Formerly known as Haddingtonshire. Low-lying in N; Lammermuir Hills in S. Agric., mainly sheep rearing; coalmining. Coastal regions incl. North Berwick. Co. town was Haddington.

Eastman, George (1854-1932), American inventor, founder of Eastman Kodak. Invented a dry-plate film process, Kodak camera, roll film and form of colour photography. Amassed large fortune from production of these; spent est. 100 million dollars on philanthropic projects.

East Pakistan, see BANGLADESH.

East Riding, see YORKSHIRE, England.

East Sussex, see SUSSEX, England.

Eastwood, Clint (1930-), American actor. After TV success, became famous in Italian 'spaghetti' westerns (esp. 'Dollars' series) as amoral gunfighter hero; later acted, directed in US, as in *Play Misty for Me* (1971).

eau de Cologne, perfume made from alcohol and aromatic oils. Believed to have been invented by F.M. Farina, who began production in Cologne c 1709.

Ebbw Vale, urban dist. of Gwent, SE Wales, on R. Ebbw. Pop. 26,000. Coalmining; iron, steel industs.

Ebert, Friedrich (1871-1925), German statesman. Social Democrat, headed provisional govt. after kaiser's abdication (1918). Elected 1st president of republic (1919), put down Spartacist uprising (1919) and Kapp putsch (1920).

ebony, trees or shrubs of genus *Diospyros* of Ebenaceae family. Grows in tropical and subtropical climates. Black hardwood used for cabinet work is derived largely from *D. ebenum* of S India and Sri Lanka. *D. kaki* (E Asia) and *D. virginiana* (W US) are other well-known species with edible plum-like fruit known as persimmons.

Ebro, river of NE Spain. Flows c 925 km (575 mi) from Cantabrian Mts., N Spain, via Saragossa to Mediterranean Sea near Tortosa. Used for irrigation, h.e.p. Ancient *Iberus*, gave name to Iberian penin.

Eccles, Sir John Carew (1903-), Australian physiologist. Shared Nobel Prize for Physiology and Medicine (1963) for explaining communication in body's nervous system.

Ecclesiastes, book of OT, written (prob. 3rd cent. BC) by a man of high station in Jerusalem (formerly ascribed to Solomon). Finds philosophical consolation in futility of the world.

Ecclesiasticus or **The Wisdom of Jesus,** apocryphal book of OT written (c 200-175 BC) by Jesus, son of Sirach. Celebrates value of wisdom.

Echegaray [y Eizaguirre], José (1832-1916), Spanish dramatist, mathematician. Works deal with theme of melancholic passion *eg El Gran Galeoto* (1881). Awarded Nobel Prize for Literature (1904).

echidna or **spiny anteater,** spiny-backed burrowing monotreme of Australasia. Long, toothless snout; extensile tongue used to catch ants, termites. Eggs hatched in pouch. Species incl. *Tachyglossus setosus* of Tasmania.

echo, in physics, repetition of sound by reflection of sound waves from a surface. Ships measure depth of water with an echo sounder which indicates time taken for sound pulse to echo off sea bed. *See* SONAR.

Eckhart, Johannes (c 1260–c 1328), German Dominican theologian, mystic; known as 'Meister'. Evolved popular mystical system with Aristotelian, scholastic elements. Theories condemned as heretical.

eclecticism, method or system of thought gathered from various doctrines. Differs from syncretism in that no attempt is made to resolve possible conflicts in the source doctrines, *eg* the medieval attempts to combine Christianity and Aristotelian philosophy.

eclipse, in astronomy, partial or complete obscuring of one celestial body by another as viewed from a fixed point. Solar eclipses occur when shadow of Moon falls on Earth; *c* 2 or 3 seen per year. Lunar eclipses occur when shadow of Earth falls on Moon; at most 2 seen per year.

ecology, interdisciplinary study of plants and animals in relation to their environment. Examines all sequences in development of these relationships up to final, stable or *climax* community. Term first used by Haeckel (1869).

econometrics, use of mathematical and statistical methods in field of economics to verify and develop economic theories, forecasting and planning.

economics, study of production, distribution and consumption of commodities. First attempts at analysis were by ancient Greeks, *eg* Plato (*Republic*) and Aristotle. Development of modern economics began with advocacy of LAISSER-FAIRE by physiocrats, and was elaborated by classical economists, *eg* Adam Smith (*Wealth of Nations*, 1776), Ricardo and J.S. Mill; founded on belief in inflexible natural laws governing exchange and production of goods. Challenged in 19th cent. by socialists, esp. Karl Marx (*Das Kapital*, 1867), who believed in societal change on moral and social grounds as well as economic, and threw light on weaknesses of classical market economy such as crisis recurrence. Classical form re-estab. (1870s) and applied mathematically by Alfred Marshall. KEYNES' theories on planning and spending increased govt. interventionist role in West's national economies; resisted in 1970s by monetarists who believed in controlling money supply.

Ecuador, republic of NW South America, incl. offshore Galápagos Isls. Area 283,561 sq km (109,483 sq mi); pop. 7,305,000; cap. Quito, chief port Guayaquil. Language: Spanish. Religion: RC. Pacific coast plain rises to volcanic Andes. Bananas, coffee are main crops; subsistence agric. in mountains. Spanish colony from 16th cent.; part of viceroyalty of Peru until liberated 1822; independence 1830 at dissolution of Greater Columbia.

ecumenism, term for movement aimed at unification of Christian churches. Early attempts incl. the Evangelical Alliance (UK 1846, US 1867). World Council of Churches (1948) brought together more than 200 Protestant, Orthodox and Old Catholic churches. Since 2nd Vatican Council (1962), RC Church has been increasingly involved in quest for Christian unity.

eczema, see DERMATITIS.

Edam, town of NW Netherlands. Pop. 8000. Market for Edam cheese; earthenware mfg.

Edda, title given to two distinct Icelandic works in Old Norse. *Poetic* or *Elder Edda* (late 13th cent.) is a collection of 34 anon. mythological heroic lays, most valuable set of texts in OLD NORSE LITERATURE. *Prose* or *Younger Edda*, by SNORRI STURLUSON,. sets down rules for scaldic poetry and gives account of Scandinavian mythology.

Eddy, Mary Baker (1821-1910), American religious leader. Founder and 1st pastor of Church of Christ, Scientist, in Boston. CHRISTIAN SCIENCE doctrine, inspired by belief in divine healing, formulated in her *Science and Health* (1875).

edelweiss, *Leontopodium alpinum*, small perennial flowering plant of daisy family. Native to high mountains of Europe and C Asia. Dense woolly white flowers.

Eden, [Robert] Anthony, 1st Earl of Avon (1897-1977), British statesman, PM (1955-7). Conservative foreign secretary (1935-8), resigned over Chamberlain's 'appeasement' policy of Germany. Again foreign secretary (1940-5, 1951-5). Resigned as PM after SUEZ CRISIS.

Eden, Garden of, in OT, first home of man. Created by God as home for ADAM and Eve; contained trees of life and knowledge. They were banished after tasting the forbidden fruit of the tree of knowledge (Genesis 2 : 3).

Edessa (*Edhessa*), town of Macedonia, N Greece. Pop. 16,000. Agric. market, textiles. Ancient *Aegeae*; earliest seat of Macedonian kings.

Edgar (c 943-75), king of all England (959-75). Called the Peaceful, allowed Danes limited autonomy in Danelaw. Restored monasticism with Dunstan. Danish-English peace ended with his death.

Edgar, king of Scotland (1097-1107). Son of Malcolm III; after his death fled to England in face of Celtic reaction to father's anglicization policies. On return, moved court from Dunfermline to Edinburgh, continued father's policies. Succeeded by brother Alexander I.

Edgeworth, Maria (1767-1849), Irish novelist, b. England. Known for Irish regional novels of manners *eg Castle Rackrent* (1800), *Ormond* (1817). Influenced Scott.

Edinburgh, Philip [Mountbatten], Duke of (1921-), consort of Elizabeth II of Great Britain, b. Greece. Son of Prince George of Greece and Princess Alice, daughter of George I of Greece. Married Elizabeth in 1947.

Edinburgh, cap. city of Scotland, in Lothian region, on S side of Firth of Forth. Pop. 453,000. Admin., commercial centre; printing, publishing; brewing, distilling. Has univ. (1583). Seaport at Leith. Annual arts festival from 1947. Buildings incl. castle (with Norman chapel), St. Giles Church (12th cent.), Holyrood Palace (royal residence from time of James IV); Royal Scottish Academy; National Gallery. Georgian architecture (esp. Adam) in 18th-19th cent. New Town.

Edirne, town of Turkey, in Thrace; formerly Adrianople. Pop. 46,000. Silk, cotton mfg. Founded by Hadrian in AD 125; scene of decisive defeat of Romans by Visigoths (378). Twice fell to Russians in 19th cent; taken by Turks in 1913. Has 16th cent. mosque of Sultan Selim II.

Edison, Thomas Alva (1847-1931), American inventor. Contributed to wireless telegraphy, telephony and generation of electricity. Invented phonograph (1878) and 1st practicable electric light. Developed 1st distribution system for electric lighting (built in New York, 1881-2). His companies, holding *c* 1300 patents, were consolidated as General Electric Company.

Edmonton, prov. cap. of Alberta, Canada; on N Saskatchewan R. Pop. 438,000. Transport, indust. centre in agric. and oil producing region; furs, oil refining, meat packing. Major airport. Has Univ. of Alberta (1906).

Edmund Ironside (d. 1016), king of England (1016). Led English opposition to Canute, coming to terms, after battle of Assandun, and partitioning England. Canute gained whole kingdom on Edmund's death.

education, process of training and developing knowledge, skill, mind, character, *etc,* esp. by formal schooling or study. Formal education began in Greece, with training in mathematics, music, Homer, philosophy. During Dark Ages, learning preserved by monks; became more general with estab. of monastic schools and univs. (11th-13th cents.). Education limited to clergy, nobility (training in chivalry), and future craftsmen. Renaissance brought widening of whom and what was taught, introducing classics to curriculum. After Reformation many more schools were estab. Important extension of popular education was a feature of late 19th cent. By late 20th cent., most countries in world provided universal, free education, often with private or religious organizations paralleling state-run schools. Also *see* COMPREHENSIVE EDUCATION.

Education Act (1944), legislation governing education in England and Wales; estab. Ministry of Education with centralized control and funding of state education. Divided school system into 2 levels, primary and secondary, making secondary education compulsory, and allowed for great expansion of education provided by state. Act sponsored by R.A. Butler.

Edward I (1239-1307), king of England (1272-1307). Fought for father Henry III against rebel barons 1264-7, was chief agent in their defeat. Conquered Wales, but failed in long campaigns to subdue Scots. Noted for legal reforms, esp. Statutes of Westminster. His Model Parliament (1295) gave greater representation to barons, clergy, merchants, estab. their right to approve king's collection of taxes.

Edward II (1284-1327), king of England (1307-27). Continued father Edward I's attempts to subjugate Scotland, but defeated by Robert the Bruce (1314). Favours to Piers Gaveston led to barons' revolt, and alienated his wife, Isabella. Later favourites, the Despensers, were virtual rulers until Isabella and lover Mortimer invaded from France. They defeated, deposed and later murdered Edward, executed the Despensers.

Edward III (1312-77), king of England (1327-77). Son of Edward II, overthrew (1330) rule of his mother Isabella and her lover Mortimer, who had been . regents. Reign dominated by Hundred Years War, beginning 1337, in which he and son Edward the Black Prince were prominent. Expenses of war allowed Parliament to win concessions from king by withholding money. Reign also marked by Black Death (1347), consequent social changes, and religious unrest, esp. through teachings of Wycliffe.

Edward IV (1442-83), king of England (1461-70, 1471-83). Son of Richard, duke of York, became king on defeat of Lancastrians at Mortimer's Cross. Fled to Holland after quarrel with Warwick, who briefly restored Henry VI. Recovered throne with victories at Barnet and Tewkesbury (1471).

Edward V (1470-83), king of England (1483). Son of Edward IV, imprisoned with brother Richard, duke of York, in the Tower of London by their uncle, Gloucester. Gloucester took throne as Richard III when they were declared illegitimate; he is believed to have had them murdered.

Edward VI (1537-53), king of England (1547-53). Son of Henry VIII and Jane Seymour. Succeeded father under council of regents controlled by uncle, EDWARD SEYMOUR. Reign saw growth of Protestantism and introduction of Book of Common Prayer. Seymour was overthrown by NORTHUMBERLAND who gained right of succession for Lady JANE GREY, a Protestant.

Edward VII (1841-1910), king of Great Britain and Ireland (1901-10). Eldest son of Queen Victoria, known for his involvement in fashionable society, love affairs and sporting activities. Promoted Entente Cordiale with France.

Edward VIII (1894-1972), king of Great Britain and Ireland (1936). Son of George V, created prince of Wales (1910). Following opposition of Baldwin's cabinet, forced to abdicate to avoid constitutional crisis over proposed marriage to American divorcée, Wallis Warfield Simpson. Married her (1937) after becoming duke of Windsor.

Edward Nyanza or **Lake Edward**, lake on border of Uganda and Zaïre. Area 2150 sq km (830 sq mi); part of Great Rift Valley. Drained by R. Semliki into Albert Nyanza. Discovered 1889, named after Prince of Wales.

Edward the Black Prince (1330-76), eldest son of Edward III of England. Notable as protagonist in Hundred Years War, esp. in victory at Poitiers (1356) when he captured John II of France. Held large parts of France under father. Opposed brother, John of Gaunt, who held power at end of Edward's reign. Died before father, who was succeeded by Black Prince's son, Richard II.

Edward the Confessor (d. 1066), king of England (1042-66). Grew up in Normandy until he succeeded Harthacanute. Showed favours to Normans, thereby increasing strife with Earl Godwin of Wessex, whose son, Harold, he recognized as heir after Godwin and family returned from exile. During their exile, prob. promised William of Normandy succession. Succession crisis resolved by Norman Conquest.

Edward the Elder (d. 924), king of S Wessex (899-924). Son of Alfred, with whom he ruled and fought in wars with Danes. Extended kingdom to reach Humber.

Edwin (c 585-632), king of Northumbria. Seized throne (616) from Ethelfrith and extended kingdom over all of England except Kent. Converted to Christianity 627. Encouraged conversion of his people by Paulinus.

EEC, see EUROPEAN COMMUNITIES.

eel, any of order Anguilliformes of snake-like bony fish. Naked skin or minute scales; no pelvic fins. Species incl. common eel, *Anguilla anguilla*, born in Sargasso Sea; crosses Atlantic in larval state to mature in European rivers.

eel grass, *Zostera marina*, flowering plant of the pondweed family. Grows underwater with long grass-like leaves. Found in Europe and North America in shallow salt water.

Egbert (d. 839), king of Wessex (802-39). United most of England under his rule by 829 with his victories in Cornwall and Mercia and by forcing Kent and Northumbria to submit to him.

Egerton, Thomas, Baron Ellesmere (1540-1617), English statesman. Adviser to Elizabeth I. Testified against former friend Essex (1601). Lord chancellor (1603-17), supported James I's use of royal prerogative; obtained dismissal of his opponent, Sir THOMAS COKE.

egg, in biology, see OVUM.

eggplant, see AUBERGINE.

eglantine, see BRIAR.

Egmont, Lamoral, Count of (1522-68), Flemish statesman. Supported overlord Philip II of Spain against France (1557-8). Stadholder of Flanders and Artois (1559-67), he protested against governorship of Netherlands by Cardinal Granvelle. Arrest and execution by duke of Alva aroused Netherlands to revolt, and was subject of Goethe's tragedy *Egmont*, for which Beethoven wrote overture, incidental music.

ego, in psychoanalysis, term used to denote personal consciousness, which mediates between impulses of the ID, standards of the SUPEREGO and the outside world.

egret, slender heron-like wading bird with white plumage. Species incl. great white egret, *Egretta alba*, and little egret, *E. garzetta*.

Egypt (*Misr*), republic of NE Africa. Area 1,001,000 sq km (386,500 sq mi); pop. 38,067,000; cap. Cairo; chief port Alexandria. Language: Arabic. Religion: Islam. Largely desert (incl. Eastern, Libyan); Qattara Depression in NW, Sinai penin. in NE. Pop. concentrated in fertile Nile valley (Upper Egypt), delta (Lower Egypt). Produces cotton, rice, cereals; petroleum, phosphates.

Ancient Egypt ruled by 30 dynasties grouped into 3 'kingdoms' 3100-332 BC. Conquered by Alexander the Great; ruled successively by Ptolemys, Rome, Arabs, Mamelukes, Ottoman Turks. Home of early Christian leaders 1st-6th cent.; Islam introduced 7th cent. by Arabs. Dominated by British, French in 19th cent.; made British protect. (1914). Constitutional monarchy from 1923, sovereign state from 1936. Republic proclaimed 1953; formed United Arab Republic 1958 with Syria, Yemen, disintegrated 1961; called Arab Republic of Egypt after 1971. Has led 4 Arab wars against Israel (1948, 1956, 1967, 1973) without success, leaving most of Sinai penin. under Israeli occupation. Initiated peace negotiations, 1977.

Egyptian, see COPTIC.

Ehrlich, Paul (1854-1915), German bacteriologist. Discovered means of staining and identifying tuberculosis bacilli; also discovered drug arsphenamine, 1st effective treatment against syphilis. Shared Nobel Prize for Physiology and Medicine (1908) for theory of antibodies' role in immunity.

Eichendorff, Joseph, Freiherr von (1788-1857), German poet. Known for lyrical poetry celebrating Silesian countryside, much of it set to music by Schumann, Brahms. Friend of late romantics, incl. Brentano. Also wrote novels.

Eichmann, [Karl] Adolf (1902-62), German Nazi official. Chief of Gestapo's Jewish section (from 1939); promoted use of gas chambers. Escaped after WWII. Abducted (1960) from Argentina by Israeli agents, executed in Israel.

eider duck, *Somateria mollissima,* large sea duck of N regions. Eiderdown used for stuffing quilts, pillows.

Eiffel, Alexandre Gustave (1832-1923), French engineer. Built bridges and viaducts. Contributed to aerodynamics. Designed Eiffel Tower, 400 m (984 ft) high, built for 1889 Paris Exhibition.

Elger, mountain of SC Switzerland, height 3973 m (13,042 ft). Notorious North Face, where many climbers have died.

Eight, The, see ASHCAN SCHOOL.

Eilat, port of S Israel, at head of Gulf of Aqaba. Pop. 12,800. Oil pipeline (opened 1957) bypasses Suez Canal. Biblical Elath.

Eindhoven, town of S Netherlands. Pop. 190,000. Rapid 20th cent. growth from radio, television indust.; also produces vehicles, plastics.

Einstein, Albert (1879-1955), American physicist, b. Germany. In 1905, enunciated special theory of relativity and gave theoretical explanation of Brownian motion and photoelectric effect. Published (1916) general theory of RELATIVITY, a geometric theory of gravitation superseding that of Newton. Awarded Nobel Prize for Physics (1921). Attempted to find unified theory of gravitation and electromagnetism.

einsteinium (Es), transuranic element of actinide group; at. no. 99, mass no. of most stable isotope 254. Discovered (1952) in debris of thermonuclear explosion.

Eire, see IRELAND, REPUBLIC OF.

Eisenhower, Dwight David (1890-1969), American general and statesman, president (1953-61). During WWII, chief of Allied forces in N Africa (1942-3), supreme commander of Allied invasion of Europe (1944). Army chief of staff (1945-8); commanded NATO forces (1950-2). Elected Republican president, defeating Adlai Stevenson. Fostered anti-Communist alliances in SE Asia, Latin America.

Eisenstein, Sergei Mikhailovich (1898-1948), Russian film director. Outstanding in history of film, pioneering cinematic techniques, eg montage. Won fame with *Battleship Potemkin* (1925), later made impressive epics on Russian history, eg *Alexander Nevsky* (1938), *Ivan the Terrible* (1942-6).

Eisteddfod, traditional Welsh festival for the encouragement of bardic arts, esp. music, poetry, by competition. Dates from before 12th cent. but discontinued 17th-19th cents. Now meets annually in August.

El-Aaiún, see SPANISH SAHARA.

eland, either of 2 large antelopes. Giant eland, *Taurotragus derbianus*, of C and S Africa, is largest species of antelope. Cape eland, *T. oryx*, found in grassland of S Africa.

elasticity, in physics, property in materials of returning to their original shape and dimensions after being deformed by external forces. Material is permanently distorted if applied forces exceed elastic limit.

Elath, see ELAT.

Elba, isl. of W Italy, separated from Tuscany by Str. of Piombino. Area 223 sq km (86 sq mi). Fishing, tourism; iron ore mining from Etruscan times. Principality (1814-15) under exiled Napoleon.

Elbe (Czech. *Labe*), river of C Europe. Flows 1167 km (725 mi) from NW Czechoslovakia via East and West Germany to North Sea at Hamburg. Navigable for c 800 km (500 mi); canal links with Rhine, Weser rivers.

Elberfeld, see WUPPERTAL, West Germany.

Elbert, Mount, peak of C Colorado, US; highest of US Rocky Mts. Height 4399 m (14,433 ft).

Elbrus or Elbruz, Mount, massif in Caucasus Mts., USSR, W Georgian SSR. Comprises 2 peaks of volcanic origin, one of which, at height of 5633 m (18,481 ft) is highest in Europe.

Elburz Mountains, mountain range in N Iran, running parallel to S Caspian Sea. Rise to 5771 m (18,934 ft) at Mt. Demavend. N slopes rainy and forested, S slopes arid.

Elche, city of Valencia, SE Spain. Pop. 123,000. Noted for date palms; also footwear mfg. Held by Moors 8th-13th cent.

elder, any of genus *Sambucus* of deciduous bushy trees of honeysuckle family. Esp. *S. nigra*, common in Europe, with small, strong-smelling white flower and red or black berries, used to make wine.

Eldon, John Scott, 1st Earl of (1751-1838), English statesman. Tory lord chancellor (1801-6, 1807-27), often dominating cabinet. Introduced repressive legislation, opposing liberal reform, Catholic Emancipation.

Eleanor of Aquitaine (c 1122-1204), queen of Henry II of England. Married Henry after annulment of marriage to Louis VII of France. Her sons, Richard I, John, became kings of England. Estab. own court at Poitiers and aided sons in unsuccessful revolt (1173) against Henry. After many years' confinement by Henry, she helped Richard secure throne (1189).

Eleanor of Castile (d. 1290), queen of Edward I of England. Remembered for 12 crosses Edward reputedly erected to mark stages of her funeral procession, eg at Lincoln, St Albans, Charing Cross.

elecampane, *Inula helenium,* tall perennial plant of daisy family with toothed leaves and clusters of yellow flower heads.

election, selection of persons for office by vote. Used occasionally in ancient Greece, regularly in Rome to appoint tribunes. Elections regularized in England (1688) although Commons elected in some manner since 14th cent. SUFFRAGE extended by REFORM BILL (1832). Ballot Act (1872) introduced secret ballot. In UK, general (ie national) election always follows dissolution of Parliament, at least every 5 years. In US, elections take place every 2, 4, 6 years.

electoral college, in US politics, body of electors from each state with formal duty of choosing president and vice-president. Electors of each state, equal in number to its members in Congress, expected to vote for candidates selected by popular vote in state. President need not obtain majority of popular vote in country.

electors, number of princes within Holy Roman Empire who had theoretical right to elect head of empire; in reality, in all elections after 1438 except one, a Habsburg became emperor. In 1356 number set at 7, usually archbishops of Mainz, Trier, Cologne, king of Bohemia, duke of Saxony, margrave of Bradenburg and electors of the Palatinate. Dismissed on dissolution of Empire (1806).

Electra, in Greek myth, daughter of AGAMEMNON and Clytemnestra. Helped brother ORESTES avenge Agamemnon's death in tragedies of Aeschylus, Sophocles, Euripides.

Electra complex, see OEDIPUS COMPLEX.

electrical engineering, branch of ENGINEERING dealing with generation and transmission of electrical power and with the devices that use it. *See* ELECTRONICS.

electric eel, *Electrophorus electricus,* large eel-like fish of pools, streams of NE South America. Capable of generating shock of c 500 volts, which will kill other fish and severely injure man.

electric fish, one of various fish capable of generating electricity by muscular contraction. Uses shocks for navigation, defence or killing prey. Incl. electric eel, electric ray, stargazer.

electricity, general term for physical phenomena associated with electric CHARGE. Flow of electric charge in conductors constitutes electric current. Charge can be generated by friction, by chemical means (eg in a cell) or by electromagnetic induction.

electric light, light produced by electrical means. Electric light bulb contains inert gas (eg nitrogen) and wire filament; current passing through filament heats it to white heat. First practical form developed by Edison (1879).

electric motor, device for converting electrical energy into mechanical energy. Simplest type consists of current-carrying coil or armature placed between poles of powerful magnet; mechanical force acting on armature causes it to rotate.

electrocardiograph, instrument used to diagnose heart disorders by tracing changes in electric current and voltage produced by contractions of heart. Invented by Dutch physiologist Willem Einthoven (1860-1927) who was awarded Nobel Prize for Physiology and Medicine (1924).

electrochemistry, science dealing with effect of electrical energy on chemical reactions or with production of electrical energy by chemical means.

electrode, terminal by which electric current enters or leaves conducting substances, eg liquid in electrolytic cell or gas in electrical discharge tube. Positive electrode is the anode, negative is the cathode.

electroencephalograph, instrument used to record electrical activity of nerve cells in the brain. Used to diagnose brain disorders, esp. epilepsy. Recorded results called EEGs.

electrolysis, decomposition of chemical compound (electrolytes) by passage of electric current through compound in solution or in molten state. Electrolyte dissociates into positive and negative ions; ions move to electrodes of opposite charge and give up their charge.

Technique used in electroplating of metals.

electromagnetic induction, production of electromotive force in a circuit by variation of a magnetic field. Effect observed independently by Faraday and Henry. Phenomenon forms basis of DYNAMO.

electromagnetic radiation, radiation propagated through space by variation in electric and magnetic fields. Such radiation consists of waves travelling at speed of light, nature of which depends on frequency. Incl. heat rays, radio waves, light, gamma rays and X-rays.

electromotive force, force of electric pressure that causes electric current to flow in circuits. Equivalent to difference in potential between points in circuit.

electron, elementary particle of matter which by convention carries one negative unit of charge. Electrons are constituents of atoms, assumed to move in orbits about the atomic nucleus; number of protons in nucleus equals number of circulating electrons. Movement of free (ie detached from their atomic orbit) electrons constitutes electric current.

electronic music, see MUSIC, ELECTRONIC.

electronics, branch of electrical engineering dealing with controlled movement of electrons through thermionic valves and semiconductors and with the devices that use them. Incl. technology of computers, radio circuitry, etc.

electron microscope, microscope using beam of electrons to obtain greatly enlarged images of objects. Electron beam passes through thin film of material under investigation and is focused by magnetic or electrostatic fields to form image on fluorescent screen.

electron tube, US term for THERMIONIC VALVE.

electron-volt, unit of energy used in nuclear physics; equals work done on an electron to pass it through potential difference of 1 volt. 1 GeV (BeV in US) = 10⁹ electron-volts.

electroscope, device used to detect electric charge. Gold leaf electroscope consists of 2 thin strips of gold leaf attached to metallic conducting rod. Leaves diverge under repelling action of like charges when rod acquires electric charge.

elegy, lyrical poem in contemplative tone lamenting the dead. Examples incl. Milton's 'Lycidas', Gray's 'Elegy Written in a Country Churchyard', Arnold's 'Thyrsis'.

element, in chemistry, substance which cannot be decomposed by chemical means into simpler substances. Elements consist of atoms of same atomic number; traditionally 92 occur in nature and 11 more have been made in the laboratory.

elementary particles, in physics, subatomic particles which are basic components of matter. Incl. electron, proton, neutrino which are stable, and neutron, various mesons and many other particles which are unstable. Each elementary particle has corresponding anti-particle, with same mass but opposite charge, spin, *etc.* Recent theories suggest that all elementary particles are composed of QUARKS and LEPTONS.

elementary school, *see* PRIMARY SCHOOL.

elephant, thick-skinned mammal of order Proboscidea, with flexible, strong trunk. Indian elephant, *Elephas maximus,* often domesticated, is used for heavy work in India, Burma, Sri Lanka; female without tusks. African elephant, *Loxodonta africana,* larger than Indian, with larger ears. Both species live in itinerant herds.

elephantiasis, chronic disease characterized by gross thickening of skin and connective tissue, esp. of legs and genitals. Caused by blockage of lymphatic vessels, usually by infestation with filaria worms.

Eleusis, ancient city near Athens with shrine of DEMETER. Home of Eleusinian mystery cults celebrating cycle of fertility and death through worship of Demeter, Persephone.

El Ferrol, *see* FERROL, EL, Spain.

Elgar, Sir Edward (1857-1934), English composer. First major figure in British music since Purcell. *Enigma Variations* estab. him in 1899. Other works incl. oratorio *The Dream of Gerontius* and marches *Pomp and Circumstance,* a tune from which was used for song *Land of Hope and Glory.*

Elgin, Thomas Bruce, 7th Earl of (1766-1841), British soldier, diplomat. Brought Elgin Marbles from Athens to England. His son, James Bruce, 8th Earl of Elgin (1811-63), was governor-general of Canada (1847-54). Carried out Earl of Durham's plan for govt. reform.

Elgin, town of Grampian region, N Scotland, on R. Lossie. Pop. 16,000. Former royal burgh and co. town of Morayshire. Market town, distilling; port at Lossiemouth. Has ruined cathedral (13th cent.).

Elgin Marbles, ancient sculptures removed from the Parthenon, Athens and acquired by Lord Elgin from the Turks. Brought to England (1803-12), bought by govt. and deposited in British Museum (1816).

Elgon, Mount, peak of Kenya-Uganda border, NE of L. Victoria. Extinct volcano; height 4319 m (14,176 ft). Former cave dwellings on slopes.

El Greco, see GRECO, EL.

Elijah, Hebrew prophet of 9th cent. BC. Violently censured the spread of idolatrous worship during reign of King Ahab. Major prophet of Jewish tradition.

Eliot, George, pseud. of Mary Ann or Marian Evans (1819-80), English novelist. Works deal with moral, social problems of her day, eg *The Mill on the Floss* (1860), *Silas Marner* (1861), *Middlemarch* (1872). Influenced by rationalist theology, sociology of Herbert Spencer.

Eliot, Sir John (1592-1632), English parliamentary leader. Led impeachment proceedings against duke of Buckingham (1626). Pressed Charles I to accept Petition of Right (1628). His further opposition to king led to his imprisonment; died in prison.

Eliot, T[homas] S[tearns] (1888-1965), English poet, b. US. Poetry, eg *Prufrock and Other Observations* (1917), *The Waste Land* (1922), *The Four Quartets* (1936-43), reflect classical, intellectually conservative attitude to culture. Verse dramas incl. *Murder in the Cathedral* (1935), *The Cocktail Party* (1949), on religious themes. Wrote influential criticism esp. on metaphysical poets, Dante. Awarded Nobel Prize for Literature (1948).

Elisabethville, see LUBUMBASHI, Zaïre.

Elisha, Hebrew prophet, disciple of ELIJAH. Sent messenger to anoint Jehu when he was in rebellion against house of Ahab.

elixir, hypothetical substance capable of turning base metals into gold, sought by alchemists. Elixir of life to prolong life was also thought to exist.

Elizabeth I (1533-1603), queen of England (1558-1603). Daughter of Henry VIII and Anne Boleyn, succeeded to throne after perilous early life. Re-estab. Protestantism by acts of Supremacy and Uniformity (1559). Persecuted Catholics in later years of reign after series of plots which aimed to replace her by MARY QUEEN OF SCOTS; signed Mary's death warrant (1587). Reign marked by growth of commerce, beginning of colonization of North America, defeat of Spanish Armada (1588), flourishing of drama, literature, music.

Elizabeth II (1926-), queen of Great Britain and Northern Ireland (1952-). Daughter of George VI, married (1947) Philip Mountbatten, Duke of EDINBURGH. Eldest son and heir apparent is CHARLES. Other children are Anne (1950-), Andrew (1960-) and Edward (1964-).

Elizabeth, town of NE New Jersey, US; on Newark Bay. Pop. 113,000. Shipbuilding, Singer sewing machine mfg. First settled 1664. American Revolution battleground.

Elizabethan drama, name given to plays written between c 1570 and

1600 combining traditions of English comedies, chronicle plays with Renaissance classicism. Examples incl. blank verse plays of Shakespeare, Marlow, Jonson, ranging from tragedy to comedy of sophisticated construction and wit.

Elizabethan style, in architecture, transitional style of English Renaissance; combined aspects of perpendicular Gothic with Italian Renaissance ideas and Flemish decoration. Exemplified by many country houses, *eg* .Longleat and Hardwick Hall.

elk, *Alces alces*, largest deer of Europe and Asia. Inhabitant of marshland. American variety is MOOSE. In America elk is alternative name for WAPITI.

Ellesmere, most N isl. of Canada, in NE Franklin Dist., Northwest Territs; largest of Queen Elizabeth Isls. Area 213,000 sq km (82,000 sq mi). Ice-cap in S and E; mountainous. Eskimo pop. Discovered by William Baffin (1616).

Ellice Islands, group of 9 atolls, colony of UK. Area 23 sq km (9 sq mi); cap. Funafuti. Produce copra. Sovereignty over 4 of group disputed by US. Formerly called Lagoon Isls. Withdrew from Gilbert and Ellice isls. colony (1976), formed separate colony of Tuvalu.

Ellington, Edward Kennedy ('Duke') (1899-1974), American pianist, composer. Major composer in jazz music, he also wrote many famous songs, incl. *Mood Indigo*, *Solitude*.

ellipse, in geometry, curve traced by point which moves so that sum of its distances from 2 fixed points (its

foci) is constant. One of the CONIC SECTIONS.

Ellis, [Henry] Havelock (1859-1939), English writer, psychologist. Known for *Studies in the Psychology of Sex* (7 vols., 1898-1928), one of 1st scientific examinations of sexuality.

Ellsworth Highlands, region of Antarctica, in unallocated area between Ross Dependency and British Antarctic Territ. Named after American explorer Lincoln Ellsworth (1880-1951).

elm, family (Ulmaceae) of deciduous trees with rough oval leaves, native to N temperate regions. Esp. denotes genus *Ulmus*, incl. wych elm, *U. glabra*, which reaches 35 m/120 ft in height, and English elm, *U. procera*. North American species incl. smooth-leaved elm, *U. carpinifolia*, and slippery elm, *U. rubra*. See DUTCH ELM DISEASE.

El Paso, border city of SW Texas, US; opposite Juárez (Mexico) on Rio Grande. Pop. 322,000. Travel jct., tourist and commercial centre. Copper smelting, oil refining. Settled 1827.

El Salvador, republic of Central America. Area 21,393 sq km (8260 sq mi); pop. 4,123,000; cap. San Salvador. Language: Spanish. Religion: RC. Pacific coastline rises to fertile plain (coffee, cotton growing; cattle rearing); volcanic mountains. World's main source of balsam. Spanish rule (1524-1821); member of Central American Federation until independence in 1838.

Elsinore, see HELSINGÖR, Denmark.

Eluard, Paul, pseud. of Eugène Grindel (1895-1952), French poet. After interest in dada, became a founder of SURREALISM. Works incl. *Les Nécessités d'une vie et les conséquences des rêves* (1921), *Les Yeux fertiles* (1936). Later poetry reflects political interests.

Ely, Isle of, region of Cambridgeshire, EC England, former admin. county. Fen drained to yield agric. land. City of Ely, on R. Ouse. Pop. 10,000. Agric. market. Cathedral (11th cent.) has Norman nave.

Elysée, palace in Paris, built 1718; once home of Madame de Pompadour, it became official residence of French president in 1873.

Elysium or **Elysian Fields,** in Greek myth, paradise for heroes favoured by the gods. In Homer, it lies on the most W edge of the world. Later tradition held it as part of underworld for all blessed dead.

Elzevir, Louis (*c* 1540-1617), Dutch publisher. Founded firm at Leiden (1583), which was continued by his descendants until 1712. Produced good inexpensive editions of Latin, French and Greek classics. Special type, known as 'old style' or Elzevir, was designed for firm by Christopher van Dyck.

Emancipation, Edict of (1861), proclamation freeing all Russian serfs (*c* ⅓ of pop.) issued by Alexander II. Complex procedures for land purchases by peasants and abuse of edict by landlords helped provoke Russian Revolution.

Emancipation Proclamation, in US history, edict freeing slaves in rebellious Confederate states. Issued by Lincoln (Sept. 1862), became law 1 Jan. 1863. Intended to deplete Confederacy's reserves of slave labour and improve Union cause in Europe.

embroidery, art of decorating cloth with varied stitches of coloured or metallic thread. Use is recorded in ancient Egypt, Babylon and China. From 12th to 14th cents., England was famous for its embroidered church vestments and altar-cloths.

embryo, in zoology, animal in earliest stages of its development, before it emerges from egg membranes, or in viviparous animals, from uterus of mother. Name foetus is often applied to later stages of embryo's development. Also *see* SEED.

emerald, gem form of BERYL. Green colour is due to presence of chromium compounds. Major sources in Colombia, Brazil, US.

Emerson, Ralph Waldo (1803-82), American philosopher, poet. Influenced by Puritanism. Founded transcendentalism, *ie* belief that man has intuitive knowledge of 'world soul'. Ideas formulated in *Nature* (1836). Wrote essays, lyrics, often in free verse form.

emery, finely granular form of CORUNDUM, containing some magnetite. Used as an abrasive. Major sources in Greece, Asia Minor.

Emilia-Romagna, region of N Italy, cap. Bologna. Apennines in S; fertile Po valley in C and N. Agric., food processing. Adriatic resorts, *eg* Rimini.

Eminence Grise, *see* JOSEPH, FATHER.

Emmet, Robert (1778-1803), Irish nationalist. Went to France (1800) to enlist support for an Irish uprising. Led small group of followers in insurrection (July, 1803). Captured and hanged.

emotion, in psychology, complex

response to stimulus, with both physiological and psychological effects, eg changes in rate of breathing, gland secretion, strong feelings of excitement, which usually involve impulse to definite action.

Empedocles (c 495–c 435 BC), Greek philosopher. Held matter to be composed of 4 elements: earth, water, fire, air. Explained motion as resolution of opposed forces of harmony and discord.

emperor moth, Saturnia pavonia, large European moth with 4 eye-like spots on wing; branched antennae.

emphysema, disease involving abnormal distention of air sacs of lungs. Occurs with old age or at an advanced stage of chronic bronchitis. Symptoms incl. difficulty in breathing, coughing with sputum.

Empire State Building, New York City, formerly tallest building in world, 380 m (1250 ft) high. Built 1930-1, it has 102 storeys and is a tourist attraction in Manhattan. See SKYSCRAPER.

Empire style, mode of furniture design and interior decoration popular in France c 1804-30. Originated by architects Percier and Fontaine who decorated state apartments for Napoleon; combined neo-Classical designs with Egyptian motifs. In women's costume, term refers to high-waisted gowns with flowing skirt and short, puffed sleeves.

empiricism, philosophical belief, opposed to RATIONALISM, that all knowledge is derived from experience. Denies innate ideas and a priori truth. Dominant tradition in British philosophy since Locke.

Empson, William (1906-), English critic, poet. Known for influential Seven Types of Ambiguity (1930), arguing that effects of poetry come from multiple meanings. Also wrote criticism on Milton, Joyce; poetry eg The Gathering Storm (1940).

Empty Quarter (Ar Rub Al Khālī), desert of S Saudi Arabia.

Ems, river of NW Germany. Flows c 370 km (230 mi) from Westphalia to North Sea near Emden. Linked to Ruhr by Dortmund-Ems canal. Oil, natural gas in surrounding area.

Ems dispatch (July, 1870), communication between William I of Prussia and his premier Bismarck which led to Franco-Prussian War. William refused to assure French ambassador Benedetti that no Hohenzollern would seek Spanish throne. Bismarck successfully provoked French govt. to declare war by publishing version of William's reply.

emu, Dromaius novaehollandiae, second largest living bird; flightless, capable of running fast. Found in Australian inland areas. Brown body; reaches height of 1.5 m/5 ft.

emulsion, colloidal suspension of 2 immiscible fluids, eg milk. Emulsions may be stabilized by emulsifying agents; milk is stabilized by casein.

enamel, vitreous glaze, coloured by metallic oxides, which can be fused to surfaces of metals, glass or pottery. Of ancient origin, art of enamelling, esp. cloisonné technique, was perfected by Byzantines in 10th cent. Limoges, France, was main centre of European enamelling from 12th to 16th cents.

encephalitis, name for viral inflammation of the brain, *eg* rabies, poliomyelitis. *Encephalitis lethargica* or sleepy sickness was widespread epidemic during WWI but vanished in 1920s.

enclosure, in English history, practice of fencing off land formerly subject to common rights (open field system). Arose out of demand at end of 14th cent. for wool to supply Flemish trade. Caused serious hardship, leading to rebellions in Tudor period. New wave of enclosures from 1750 to 1800 forced landless workers to move to cities, where they were to supply the labour for the Industrial Revolution.

encyclopedia, a book, or set of books, containing articles, usually arranged alphabetically, covering a general or specific area of knowledge. Earliest extant example is Pliny the Elder's *Historia Naturalis* (1st cent. AD). John Harris's *Lexicon Technicum* (1704) is first alphabetical example in English. The *Encyclopaedia Britannica* dates from 1768.

Encyclopedists, 18th cent. contributors to Diderot's *Encyclopédie*, incl. Voltaire, Montesquieu, Rousseau.

Enderbury Island, *see* CANTON AND ENDERBURY ISLANDS.

Enders, John Franklin (1897-), American microbiologist. With T. H. Weller and F. C. Robbins, shared Nobel Prize for Physiology and Medicine (1954) for growing poliomyelitis virus on embryonic tissue.

endive, *Cichorium endiva*, plant of daisy family, similar to dandelion. Native to Europe but widely cultivated in US, where it is known as chicory. Leaves used in salads.

endocrine glands or **ductless glands**, organs in body which secrete hormones directly into bloodstream; concerned with metabolism, growth and sexual functions. Principal glands are thyroid, pituitary, parathyroid, adrenals, testicles and ovaries, parts of pancreas.

endorphins, class of pain-killers, incl. enkephalin, found naturally in the brain and pituitary gland. May play a role in mental disorders, acupuncture and behaviour associated with addiction to opiates.

Endymion, in Greek myth, handsome shepherd of Mt. Latmos. Loved by the moon goddess Selene, she imposed eternal sleep on him so that she might visit him each night.

energy, in physics, the ability to do WORK. A body may have potential energy because of its position or kinetic energy because of its motion. It was believed that energy can neither be created nor destroyed, but can be converted from one form into another, *eg* electrical energy into heat energy. Einstein's law $E = mc^2$ (where $c =$ speed of light) now shows that mass and energy are equivalent; energy obtained from annihilation of mass accounts for nuclear energy and power of stars.

Enfield, bor. of N Greater London, England. Pop. 267,000. Created 1965 from mun. bor. of Middlesex. Small arms; cables mfg.

Engels, Friedrich (1820-95), German philosopher. Collaborated with Marx in evolving Communist doctrine, notably in *The Communist Manifesto* (1848). Lived in England after 1850, edited much of Marx's *Das Kapital*. His own works incl.

The Origin of the Family, Private Property and the State (1884).

engineering, science of putting scientific knowledge to practical use esp. in design and construction of engines, machines and public works. Field divided into civil, mechanical, chemical.

England, constituent country of UK, in S part of GREAT BRITAIN. Area 130,357 sq km (50,331 sq mi); pop. 45,870,000; cap. London. Major cities Birmingham, Liverpool, Manchester. Comprises 39 counties, 6 met. counties, Greater London. Main rivers Thames, Severn, Humber, Tees, Tyne. Pastoral uplands in NW (Pennines, Lake Dist.); lowland (agric., dairying) in SE. Indust. centred in Midlands (coal, iron), Lancashire, Yorkshire (textiles), NE (shipbuilding, engineering). Roman occupation (AD 43-5th cent.) followed by Saxon, Viking, Norman invasions. Successive royal dynasties Plantagenet, Lancaster, York, Tudor, Stuart, Orange, Hanover, Windsor. Church of England split from Rome under Henry VIII. Indust. Revolution began here (18th cent.), made England world's leading indust. nation in 19th cent. Estab. large overseas Empire (Commonwealth after 1931). United with Wales 1536, with Scotland 1707, with Ireland 1801 (partition 1921) to form UNITED KINGDOM.

England, Church of, established church in England. Henry VIII withdrew allegiance to Pope and declared sovereign to be head of English church; confirmed by Act of Supremacy (1543). Under Mary, England was again RC, but Elizabeth I restored Protestantism, Thirty-nine Articles adopted as basic doctrine. Act of Supremacy (1559) restored ecclesiastical jurisdiction to the crown. Presbyterianism substituted for episcopacy by Long Parliament (1646); episcopacy restored (1660). High Church tradition emphasizes ritualism and apostolic succession, Low Church stresses Bible and preaching. Archbishop of Canterbury is chief primate of Church of England and of unestablished Episcopal Church in Scotland, Church of Ireland, Church in Wales, Anglican Church of Canada, Church of England in Australia and Church of the Province of New Zealand.

English, language of W Germanic group of Indo-European family. Second only to Mandarin Chinese in number of speakers in world. First language in Britain, US, Australia, New Zealand. One of two working languages of United Nations. Incl. many dialects, *eg* American, Scots, Standard (received pronunciation) English. Developed from languages of 5th cent. Germanic invaders of Britain, which became regional dialects. West Saxon (of Wessex) became dominant in 9th cent. (*see* ANGLO-SAXON LITERATURE). Language of this period termed Old English. Norman Conquest (1066) brought change, Norman French being used as official, polite language. Development continued, Middle English (c 1150-c 1500) becoming standard in 14th cent. Important literature incl. *Gawayne and the Greene Knight, Piers Plowman.* Modern English developed from London dialect pre-1500, language of CHAUCER. Subsequent change mainly loss of inflections, gain of loan-words from French.

English Channel (Fr. *La Manche*), arm of Atlantic between England and France; length 563 km (350 mi), width varies from 160 km (100 mi) to 34 km (21 mi) at STRAIT OF DOVER. Many resorts on both coasts; ferry services. First balloon crossing 1785, first swum 1875, first aircraft crossing 1909.

engraving, process of cutting, etching or drawing marks on metal plates, wooden blocks, *etc*, for purpose of reproducing prints. Three main types: relief, incl. woodcutting; intaglio, incl. ETCHING, DRYPOINT; surface printing, incl. LITHOGRAPHY.

Enlightenment or **Age of Reason,** European movement of 18th cent., characterized by rationalism, learning, 'scientific' (*ie* sceptical), empirical approach. Based on work of Newton, Descartes, Locke in 17th cent. and expressed esp. in Diderot's *Encyclopédie*, and writings of Voltaire, Rousseau, Hume, Kant. Manifested by social reforms of 'enlightened despots', *eg* Frederick II of Prussia, Catherine II of Russia, and revolutionary movements in France, America.

Ennis, co. town of Clare, W Irish Republic. Pop. 6000. Agric. market, food processing, whiskey distilling. RC pro-cathedral; abbey ruins.

Enniskillen, town of SW Northern Ireland. Pop. 7000. Former co. town of Fermanagh. Agric. market. Hist. Protestant stronghold.

Ennius, Quintus (239–c 169 BC), Roman author. First major Latin classical poet, admired and imitated by later writers. Works incl. epic *Annales*.

Enosis, name given to Greek Cypriot movement for union of Cyprus with Greece. Esp. favoured by EOKA organization led by George Grivas both before and after independence from Britain.

Enschede, town of EC Netherlands. Pop. 143,000. Centre of cotton indust.; canal links to Ijssel, Rhine rivers. Rebuilt after 1862 fire.

Ensor, James Ensor, Baron (1860-1949), Belgian painter. Work has fantastic and macabre quality; used masks, skeletons, ghosts to depict everyday life. Precursor of expressionism. Works incl. *Entry of Christ into Brussels* (1888).

entablature, in classical architecture, horizontal superstructure supported by columns. Consists of architrave, surmounted by frieze, with cornice on top.

Entebbe, town of S Uganda, on N shore of Victoria Nyanza. Pop. 11,000. Commercial centre, international airport. Cap. of British Uganda (1894-1962).

Entente Cordiale, *see* TRIPLE ALLIANCE and TRIPLE ENTENTE.

enteritis, inflammation of the intestine, esp. small intestine. Common form is gastro-enteritis, characterized by abdominal pains, diarrhoea, vomiting; caused by bacterial food poisoning, viruses.

entomology, branch of zoology dealing with insects. Important aspect of entomology is need to control insects which spread disease to man and animals or destroy crops, and stored produce. Other aspects incl. taxonomy (classification of insects), ecology (place of insects in food webs).

entrepreneur, in economics, person who assumes risk and management of a business organization. Fully differentiated from ordinary capitalist by 19th cent. economists who saw him as coordinator and innovator necessary for corporate indust. Entrepreneurial class achieved prominence during Industrial Revolution.

entropy, in thermodynamics, term introduced to describe degree of disorder of a system. Entropy never decreases in an isolated system. When it increases the ability of the total energy in system to do useful work diminishes.

Enugu, city of SE Nigeria. Pop. 167,000. Indust. centre on railway to Port Harcourt; coalmining, engineering, sawmilling. Former cap. of Eastern Region; cap. of Biafra (1967-70) in civil war.

Enver Pasha (1881-1922), Turkish general, political leader. Leader in Young Turks' revolution (1908); became virtual dictator after coup (1913). Instrumental in bringing Turkey into WWI. Killed leading anti-Soviet forces in Bukhara.

enzymes, large group of proteins, produced by plant and animal cells, which act as catalysts in specific chemical reactions vital to life. A few are found in natural secretions, such as digestive juices pepsin and trypsin.

Eocene epoch, second geological epoch of Tertiary period. Alpine mountain building continued. Further evolution of primitive mammals which began in Palaeocene epoch. Increase in temperature, causing widespread subtropical conditions. Also *see* GEOLOGICAL TABLE.

Eos (Gk., = dawn), in Greek myth,

goddess of dawn. Daughter of Hyperion, sister of Helios (sun) and Selene (moon). Identified by Romans with Aurora.

Epernay, town of NE France, on R. Marne. Pop. 28,000. Centre of Champagne wine indust., has large underground cellars; cask mfg., bottling.

ephedrine, alkaloid drug extracted from certain Chinese plants or synthesized. Used to relieve nasal congestion and asthma.

Ephesians, epistle of NT, traditionally written to Christians at Ephesus by St Paul (c AD 60) during his Roman imprisonment, but possibly by a later writer. Uses metaphor of mystical body of Christ as a plea for Christian unity.

Ephesus, ancient Ionian city, on W coast of Asia Minor. Taken by Romans (133 BC), became cap. of Roman Asia. Had famous temple of Diana (Artemis); site of St Paul's epistle. Destroyed (262) by Goths, never recovered its importance.

epic, long narrative poem dealing with exploits of one or more heroic individuals, historical or legendary, usually in exalted style and moral tone. Examples incl. Iliad, Odyssey, Aeneid (classical); BEOWULF (Old English); *Chanson de Roland* (French); *Gerusalemme Liberate* (Italian); *The Lusiads* (Portuguese); *Paradise Lost* (English).

Epictetus, (fl c AD 100), Greek Stoic philosopher. An emancipated slave, taught in Rome before being banished. Advocated life free of desires, trust in providence.

Epicurus (c 340-c 270 BC), Greek philosopher. Founder of the Epicurean school of philosophy.

Advocated reliance on the senses. Saw freedom from pain or anxiety as greatest good, achieved by simple living.

Epidaurus, ancient city of Greece, in NE Peloponnese. Site of temple of Asclepius. Has best preserved ancient Greek theatre. Greek independence proclaimed (1822) at nearby Nea Epidhavros.

epiglottis, triangular flap of cartilage behind the tongue. Folds back over windpipe during swallowing, thus preventing food from entering lungs.

epigram, short poem, developed from Greek by Roman writers who estab. distinct satirical character, *eg* Martial. In English, Pope is most noted exponent.

epilepsy, group of chronic disorders of the brain characterized by fits. Classified as *petit mal,* in which there is momentary loss of consciousness, or *grand mal,* in which there is loss of consciousness and muscle stiffening for a few minutes. Treatment by sedatives and drugs.

Epiphany (Gk.,= showing), Christian feast, celebrated on 6th Jan. Commemorates baptism of Jesus, visit of wise men to Bethlehem, miracle of changing water to wine at Cana. More ancient and technically more important than Christmas. Eve of feast is Twelfth Night.

epiphyte or air plant, general name for plant which grows on another plant but is not a parasite and produces its own food by photosynthesis, drawing water from atmosphere. Incl. orchids, Spanish moss.

Epirus (*Ipiros*), region of NW Greece and SW Albania, between Pindus Mts. and Ionian Sea. Famed for cattle, horses. *Fl* 3rd cent. BC under Pyrrhus. Turkish from 15th cent., later divided between Greece and Albania.

episcopacy, system of church govt. by bishops, used in all pre-Reformation and some post-Reformation churches. Estab. by end of 1st cent. and not challenged until Luther's rejection of the supernatural powers of bishops in ordaining priests and ruling clergy. Calvin rejected system as major abuse. Degrees of authority are pope, patriarch, archbishop, bishop.

Episcopal Church (Protestant), see ANGLICAN COMMUNION.

epistles, in NT, 21 letters, traditionally ascribed to the Apostles, addressed to some of the new churches and individual members of them.

Epsom and Ewell, mun. bor. of Surrey, SE England. Pop. 72,000. Epsom Downs racecourse nearby (Derby). Has 17th cent. spa (Epsom salts).

Epsom salts, hydrated magnesium sulphate ($MgSO_4.7H_2O$), used as a purgative.

Epstein, Sir Jacob (1880-1959), British sculptor of Russo-Polish descent, b. New York. Works frequently aroused violent criticism; influenced by African art and vorticist movement. Sculpture incl. *The Rock Drill* and *Christ in Majesty* for Llandaff Cathedral (S Wales).

equation, in chemistry, expression of chemical reaction by means of formulae and symbols. The equation $2H_2 + O_2 = 2H_2O$ states that 2 molecules of hydrogen combine with 1 oxygen molecule to form 2 of water.

Equator, imaginary line around the Earth, equidistant from both poles and perpendicular to axis. Forms a GREAT CIRCLE; divides globe into N and S hemispheres.

Equatorial Guinea, republic of WC Africa, on Gulf of Guinea. Area 28,000 sq km (10,800 sq mi); pop. 316,000; cap. Malabo. Languages: Bantu, Spanish. Religions: native, RC. Comprises Rio Muni (mainland), Macias Nguema Biyoga isl. Hot, wet climate: exports coffee, cocoa, hardwoods. Colony as Spanish Guinea from 18th cent.; independent from 1968.

equestrianism, competitive sport for horse and rider. Divided into 3 events: dressage, which tests horse's training; show jumping; 3-day event, consisting of show jumping, dressage and cross-country phases. Olympic event since 1912.

equinox, time of year when Sun appears directly overhead at the Equator at noon. Night and day are thus of equal length throughout the world. Occurs twice a year: around 21 March (vernal equinox), 22 Sept. (autumnal equinox).

equity, in law, resort to general principles of fairness and justice when existing law is inadequate. In UK, developed to supplement COMMON LAW. In US, system of rules and doctrines supplementing common and statute law. Distinction between common law and equity removed by their amalgamation.

equivalent weight, in chemistry, number of grams of an element which will combine with or replace 1 gram of hydrogen or 8 grams of oxygen. Product of equivalent weight and valency of element equals its atomic weight. Equivalent weight of an acid is weight of acid containing 1 gram of hydrogen replaceable by a metal.

Erasmus, Desiderius (c 1466-1536), Dutch philosopher, humanist. Wrote Latin translation of New Testament (1516), satire *The Praise of Folly*. Believed in rational piety, took critical attitude to superstition. Opponent of religious bigotry, supported Luther's aims but hostile to results of Reformation which caused war. Influenced English humanists, esp. Thomas More.

Erastus, Thomas, orig. Lüber or Liebler (1524-83), Swiss Protestant theologian, physician. In *Explicatio* (pub. 1589) he opposed punitive powers of church, held that punishment of sin should be left to civil authorities; doctrine known as Erastianism.

erbium (Er), metallic element of lanthanide group; at. no. 68, at. wt. 167.26. Discovered (1843) by C.G. Mosander.

Erebus, in Greek myth, son of Chaos and father by his sister Nyx of Aether (clear air) and Hemera (day). Personification of darkness, esp. represents gloom around Hades.

Erebus, Mount, active volcano on Ross Isl., in Ross Sea, Antarctica. Height 4024m (13,202 ft). Discovered (1841) by James Ross.

Erfurt, city of SW East Germany, on R. Gera. Pop. 198,000. Machinery, electrical goods, agric. market. Founded by St Boniface 741; former univ. (1392-1816), cathedral (15th cent.).

erg, unit of work or energy in c.g.s. system: 1 erg represents work done when force of 1 dyne acts through distance of 1 cm.

ergonomics, the study of relationship between people and their environment, esp. the science that seeks to adapt work or working conditions to the worker.

ergot, parasitic fungus, *Claviceps purpurea*, of cereal grains, esp. rye. Contains toxic alkaloids which cause hallucinations but can be used medicinally to limit bloodflow.

Erhard, Ludwig (1897-1977), West German statesman. As minister of economics, laid foundation of German 'economic miracle' with currency reforms of 1948. Succeeded Adenauer as Christian Democrat chancellor (1963-6).

Ericaceae, family of flowering plants. Mostly evergreen, with woody, creeping stems. Incl. heaths and rhododendrons.

Ericsson, Leif, see LEIF ERICSSON.

Eric the Red (*fl* 10th cent.), Norse chieftain. Discovered and colonized Greenland. Unsuccessful in resistance to son Leif Ericsson's conversion of Greenland to Christianity.

Erie, North American Indian tribe of Hokan-Siouan linguistic stock. Sedentary farmers of area SE of L. Erie in 17th cent. Traditional enemies of Iroquois Confederacy, were almost exterminated in 1656 after one of the most destructive Indian wars. A few descendants live on reservations in Oklahoma.

Erie, port of NW Pennsylvania, US; on L. Erie. Pop. 264,000. Coal, timber, grain, petroleum shipping; paper, electrical equipment mfg. Estab. by French as Fort Presque (1753); passed to US (1785).

Erie, Lake, shallowest of Great Lakes, C Canada-US. Area 25,745 sq km (9940 sq mi). Trade route connecting L. Huron and L. Ontario. Chief ports Cleveland, Buffalo, Toledo. Discovered by French in 17th cent. Ice-bound from December-March.

Erigena, Johannes Scotus (*c* 810-*c* 877), Irish philosopher. Identified philosophy with theology. Attempted to combine Christianity with neoplatonism. Taught at Carolingian court of Emperor Charles II.

Erin, poetic name for Ireland.

Erinyes, see EUMENIDES.

Eritrea, prov. of N Ethiopia, on Red Sea. Area 118,500 sq km (45,750 sq mi); cap. Asmara, chief port Massawa. Arid, rugged region with narrow coastal strip. Nomadic pastoralism, hides, coffee, cereal products. Colonized 1890 by Italy, base for Italian invasions of Ethiopia 1896, 1935. Under British military rule from 1941; united federally with Ethiopia 1952, fully integrated 1962. Guerilla separation movement in 1970s.

Erivan, see YEREVAN.

Erlander, Tage Fritiof (1901-), Swedish political leader, Social Democrat premier (1946-69). Expert on social welfare and education, he extended scope of welfare state and maintained Sweden's neutrality in cold war.

Erlangen, town of SC West Germany, at confluence of Regnitz and Schwabach. Pop. 84,000. Indust. centre, esp. textiles, beer; univ. (1743). Rebuilt after fire (1706).

ermine, see STOAT.

Ernst, Max (1891-1976), German painter. A founder of DADA in

Cologne (1919) and surrealist movement in Paris (1924). Developed *frottage* technique (similar to brass rubbing) and used collage and photomontage. Works incl. 'collage novel' *Une Semaine de Bonté*.

Eros, in Greek myth, god of love, son of Aphrodite. Represented as beautiful but irresponsible in his infliction of passion. Also worshipped as fertility god. Identified by Romans with CUPID.

erosion, process by which features of Earth's surface are worn away. With weathering and transportation, forms one of constituent processes of denudation, although erosion is often used loosely as synonymous with latter. Results from mechanical action of transported debris, eg windblown particles may erode a cliff. Types incl. wind, river, marine, glacial erosion.

Erse, see GAELIC.

Ervine, St John Greer (1883–1971), Irish dramatist. Manager of ABBEY THEATRE (1915). Plays incl. *Mixed Marriage* (1911) on RC, Protestant bitterness, comedies eg *The First Mrs Fraser* (1928). Also wrote novels, lives of Wilde, Shaw.

Erzerum, see ERZURUM.

Erzgebirge or Ore Mountains, range on NW Czechoslovakia-SE East Germany border, rising to 1243 m (4081 ft). Silver, copper, lead ores now virtually exhausted; uranium mined from WWII. Spas, winter sports.

Erzurum or Erzerum, city of NE Turkey, in Armenia, at an alt. of 1920 m (6300 ft). Pop. 152,000. Of strategic importance, held by Armenians, Byzantines and Persians; taken by Turks (1515).

Esau, in OT, son of Isaac, older twin brother of JACOB, who tricked him into selling his birthright. Represented as man of the open air and skilful hunter. Ancestor of Edomites.

Esbjerg, town of W Jutland, Denmark, on North Sea. Pop. 68,000. Chief Danish fishing port; exports dairy produce. Ferry services to England.

escape velocity, minimum velocity required by a body to escape gravitational influence of a planet. Depends on mass and diameter of planet. For Earth, escape velocity is c 11.2 km/sec.

Eschenbach, Wolfram von, see WOLFRAM VON ESCHENBACH.

Escorial or Escurial, town of C Spain, near Madrid. Site of building complex incl. monastery, palace and mausoleum built 1563-84 by Philip II; contains many art treasures.

Esdras 1 and 2, apocryphal books of OT dating from c 100 BC-c AD 100. Mainly transcripts of EZRA. Esdras 2 is apocalyptic account of Ezra's revelation. In some canons, term is used for books of Ezra and Nehemiah, the apocryphal books then being Esdras 3 and 4.

Esenin, Sergei Aleksandrovich, see YESENIN, SERGEI ALEKSANDROVICH.

Esfahan, see ISFAHAN.

Eshkol, Levi, orig. Shkolnik (1895-1969), Israeli statesman, premier (1963-9). b. Ukraine. Emigrated to Palestine (1931). Minister of finance (1952-63), succeeded Ben-Gurion as premier.

Eskilstuna, town of SE Sweden. Pop. 69,000. Iron and steel centre;

cutlery, hardware, precision engineering. Chartered 17th cent.

Eskimo, people of Arctic and Labrador coasts, of Eskimo-Aleut linguistic stock. Pop. (1963) c 55,000, incl. c 1600 Chukchi Eskimos of NE Siberia. Six main cultural groups: MacKenzie; Copper or Blond Eskimos, thought to be of mixed descent from Norse colonists of Greenland; Caribou; Central; Labrador; East and West Greenlanders. Culture varies, but most build stone or earth winter huts (igloos are comparatively rare) and have skin summer tents. Economy depends on hunting (seal, bear, walrus, caribou). Live in loose, voluntary association under most skilled hunter. Origins thought to be Asian via Aleutian Isls.

Eskişehir (anc. *Dorylaeum*), city of WC Turkey, in Asia Minor. Pop. 243,000. Railway jct.; agric. trade, textile mfg. Has meerschaum deposits and sulphur springs nearby.

esparto, two kinds of tall, coarse grass, *Stipa tenacissima* and *Lygeum spartum*, native to S Spain and N Africa. Used to make cordage and paper.

Esperanto, artificial language for international (chiefly European) use. Invented (1887) by Polish oculist, Dr L. L. Zamenhof (1859-1917). Uses word bases common to main European languages. Has self-evident parts of speech (eg all nouns end in -o, all adjectives in -a), single and regular conjugation of verbs and simplified inflections.

espionage, clandestine procuring of information, esp. military intelligence. Not illegal under international law. Origins of modern military intelligence attributed to Frederick II of Prussia; by WWI, European powers had developed espionage systems. Recent trends incl. increased use of diplomatic officials, reconnaissance from satellites.

essay, short literary composition dealing in discursive way with its subject from a personal point of view. Genre estab. by Montaigne (1580), Bacon (1597), developed in periodicals of Addison, Steele (18th cent.). Now generally adopted as vehicle for literary criticism or political, economic reflection.

Essen, city of W West Germany, in Ruhr. Pop. 692,000. Major indust. centre from estab. of Krupp steelworks (early 19th cent.); coal, chemicals, engineering, h.e.p. Grew around 9th cent. convent. Badly damaged in WWII.

Essenes, Jewish community (2nd cent. BC-2nd cent. AD). Condemned slavery, trading; emphasized ceremonial purity. Subsisted by simple agric., handicrafts. Possibly referred to in Dead Sea Scrolls.

essential oils, volatile substances of vegetable origin, which impart characteristic flavour or odour to plant of origin. Mostly benzene derivatives or terpenes. Used as perfumes and flavouring agents.

Essex, Robert Devereux, 2nd Earl of (1567-1601), English nobleman. Distinguished himself as cavalry officer at battle of Zutphen (1586). Favourite of Elizabeth I; incurred royal displeasure through secret marriage (1590). Politically ambitious but failed to take power from Burghley; lord lieutenant of Ireland (1599), unable to quell Irish revolt under Tyrone. Excluded from court after unauthorized return to England. Executed for intriguing against govt. His son, Robert Devereux, 3rd Earl of Essex (1591-1646), was restored to father's estates by James I. Fought in Civil War, resigning (1645) after disastrous command of parliamentary forces in Cornwall.

Essex, county of SE England. Area 3673 sq km (1418 sq mi); pop. 1,398,000; co. town Chelmsford. Mainly lowland, low hills in N. Agric. (N), dairying (S), fishing, oysters. Coastal resorts eg Southend-on-Sea; seaports eg Tilbury. Oil refineries. Ancient Saxon kingdom, later English earldom.

estate, in law, degree, nature, extent and quality of interest or ownership person has in land. Real estate is interest in freehold land, personal estate any other kind of property. Since feudal times, term also used to refer to each of 3 social classes having specific political powers: 1st estate was Lords Spiritual (clergy); 2nd estate was Lords Temporal (nobility); 3rd estate was Commons (bourgeoisie).

Estates-General or **States-General,** French national assembly (1302-1789). Three ESTATES were represented as separate bodies in it. Summoned first by Philip IV, powers were never clearly defined; merely approved monarch's legislation. Did not meet (1614-1789) until Louis XVI called it to resolve govt. financial crisis. Commons and radicals in other 2 estates dominated it in move to make it legislative body. In June, 1789, declared themselves National Assembly, defying king. See FRENCH REVOLUTION.

Este, Alfonso d' (1476-1534), Italian nobleman, duke of Ferrara and Modena. Married Lucrezia Borgia (1501); upheld family tradition of art patronage. In Italian wars, fought against papacy.

ester, organic compound formed by replacing hydrogen of an acid by an organic radical. Many fats and oils are esters; others used as artificial fruit flavours.

Esther, historical book of OT. Story of Esther, Jewish wife of Ahasuerus (Xerxes I), king of Persia (486-465 BC), who prevented massacre of Jews.

Estienne or **Etienne,** family of printers in Paris and Geneva. Firm was founded in Paris by Henri Estienne (d. 1520). His son, Robert Estienne (d. 1559) was the royal printer; produced classics, dictionaries and lexicons, eg his own Latin thesaurus (1531). Forced to move business to Geneva (1550) on becoming a Protestant. His brother, Charles Estienne (c 1504-64), a scholar, wrote and printed many works, incl. a French encyclopedia. Robert's son, Henri Estienne (c 1531-98), also a scholar, pub. linguistically accurate critical editions of classical texts, also own Thesaurus graecae linguae (1572). Advocated use of French as literary language.

Estonian Soviet Socialist Republic (Eesti), constituent republic of W USSR. Area c 45,000 sq km (17,400 sq mi); pop. 1,357,000; cap. Tallinn. Bounded by Gulf of Finland to N; generally low-lying, with extensive forests. Agric., dairying. Under Swedish control in 17th cent., Estonia passed to Russia in 1721.

Independent 1920-40; occupied by Germany (1941-4).

etching, process of engraving a metal plate, usually of copper. Plate is covered with acid-resistant resin and design is drawn on this with a needle, exposing underlying metal. Plate is bathed in acid so that its exposed parts are eaten away, thus transferring design to plate.

ethane (C_2H_6), gaseous hydrocarbon of paraffin series. Found in natural gas; used as fuel and in organic synthesis.

ethanol or **ethyl alcohol** (C_2H_5OH), colourless inflammable liquid, the active ingredient of alcoholic drinks. Prepared by fermentation of sugar or by various indust. processes. Used as fuel and in organic synthesis. *See* PROOF SPIRIT.

Ethelbert or **Aethelbert** (c 552-616), Anglo-Saxon ruler. Became king of Kent (560). Married Christian princess, Berta, and was converted to Christianity by St Augustine. Made Canterbury a great Christian centre.

Ethelred or **Aethelred the Unready** (956-1016), king of England (978-1016). Rule constantly threatened by Danes after 991, when he began levies of Danegeld. Fled country after defeat (1013) by Sweyn. Restored on Sweyn's death (1014), succeeded by his son Edmund Ironside.

ether, in chemistry, organic compound in which two hydrocarbon radicals are linked by an oxygen atom. Name usually refers to diethyl ether ($C_2H_5OC_2H_5$), prepared by action of concentrated sulphuric acid on ethanol; used as anaesthetic and solvent.

ether, in physics, hypothetical medium, pervading all space, once believed necessary for transmission of electromagnetic radiation, *eg* light. Following failure of Michelson-Morley experiment to detect its existence, Einstein's relativity theory showed ether was unnecessary concept.

Etherege, Sir George (c 1635-91), English playwright, poet. Known for complex Restoration comedies, *eg Love in a Tub* (1664); masterpiece *The Man of Mode, or Sir Fopling Flatter* (1676).

Ethical Culture, movement originated in New York by Felix Adler (1870-1937). Members accept as supreme the ethical factor in all relations of life (personal, social, international) apart from any theological or metaphysical considerations. Stresses importance of education.

ethics, in philosophy, the study of standards of conduct and moral judgment. Classical works incl. Plato's *Republic*, Aristotle's *Nicomachean Ethics*. Christian ethics draw mainly on New Testament and Aristotle. Subsequently, debate has centred on extent to which morality is imposed from outside individual, with 'intuitionists' (*eg* Rousseau) holding that conscience is innate and 'empiricists' (*eg* Locke) holding that it is acquired.

Ethiopia or **Abyssinia,** republic of NE Africa. Area 1,222,000 sq km (472,000 sq mi); pop. 28,668,000; cap. Addis Ababa. Language: Amharic. Religions: Coptic Christianity, Islam. High plateau, bisected from

NE-SW by Great Rift Valley, incl. L. Tana, source of Blue Nile. Subsistence agric.; exports coffee, hides; gold mining, salt indust. Aksumite empire fl 1st-7th cent.; declined after Moslem incursions, dissolved into rival principalities. Reunited 19th cent., defeated invading Italians 1896. Occupied by Italy 1936; taken by British 1941, regained independence. United federally with ERITREA 1952, fully integrated 1962. Emperor Haile Selassie I deposed 1974 by military coup. Wars with Somalia and Eritrean rebels in late 1970s.

Ethiopic, minor Semitic language group of Afro-Asiatic family. Incl. classical Ethiopic (now dead), AMHARIC.

ethnology, branch of anthropology which deals comparatively with cultures, their distribution, social systems, *etc.*

ethyl alcohol, *see* ETHANOL.

ethylene (C₂H₄), colourless inflammable gas of olefine series. Obtained by catalytic cracking of petroleum. Used as an anaesthetic, in manufacture of polythene and to speed ripening of fruit.

Etienne, family of printers, *see* ESTIENNE.

Etna, volcano of E Sicily, Italy. Height 3261 m (10,705 ft); isolated peak with *c* 200 minor cones. Lower slopes densely pop., used for growing fruit, olives, almonds. Encircled by railway, road. Major eruptions 1669, 1928, 1971; Catania twice destroyed.

Eton, urban dist. of Buckinghamshire, SC England. Pop. 4000. On Thames opposite Windsor. Has Eton Coll. public school (1440).

Etruria, ancient region of NW Italy, incl. Tuscany, part of Umbria. Home of ancient Etruscans.

Etruscans, ancient people of NC Italy, believed to have emigrated from Asia Minor in 12th cent. BC. Distinctive culture emerged in 8th cent. BC; at height of civilization in 6th cent. BC. Wealth partly based on knowledge of metalworking; noted for sculpture, tomb paintings and architecture. Declined in 5th and 4th cents. BC in face of Gallic invasion from N and Roman conquests. Spoke non-Indo-European language, which has not been interpreted.

Etsch, *see* ADIGE, Italy.

etymology, branch of LINGUISTICS that deals with the origin and development of words. Concerned with changes in both meaning and sound. In 19th cent. study of sound changes in Indo-European languages revealed laws (*eg* Grimm's law) governing phonetic development. Subsequent linguists have tended to study language at a given time (synchronistically) without reference to development (diachronistically).

Euboea (*Evvoia*), isl. of E Greece, in Aegean Sea. Area 3800 sq km (1467 sq mi); cap. Chalcis. Mountainous, highest point Mt. Delphi (1742 m/5718 ft). Cereals, vines, livestock. Road bridge to mainland. Greek from 1830.

eucalyptus, genus of evergreen trees of myrtle family, native to W Australia. Pendent leaves, pink or white flowers. Yields timber, gums and aromatic oils. Common species is blue gum, *Eucalyptus globulus*.

Eucharist, Christian SACRAMENT in which bread and wine are consecrated and received as body and blood of Jesus. In RC and Orthodox churches, the elements are regarded as miraculously becoming the substance of God (transubstantiation); in most Protestant churches, the rite is regarded as symbolic and is known as the Lord's Supper. Also known as Holy Communion.

Eucken, Rudolf Christoph (1846-1926), German philosopher. Developed system (activism) which stressed ethical effort rather than intellectual idealism. Awarded Nobel Prize for Literature (1908).

Euclid (fl c 300 BC), Greek mathematician. Compiler of Elements, collection of all geometric knowledge of his time. Esp. noted for its emphasis on deductive reasoning; definitions are given, axioms stated and theorems deduced logically. Also contains important results in number theory. Taught at Alexandria; little else known of his life.

Eugène de Savoie-Carignan, Prince [François] (1663-1736), Austrian general, b. France. Joined Marlborough in War of Spanish Succession, defeating the French at Blenheim (1704), Oudenarde (1708), Malplaquet (1709). He fought with further success against the Turks in 1716-17, winning decisive victory at Belgrade.

Eugénie, née Eugenia María de Montijo de Guzmán (1826-1920), empress of the French, consort of Napoleon III; b. Spain. Married Napoleon III (1853); acted as regent when he was at war. Supported war against Prussia. Fled to England on husband's fall (1870).

Euler, Leonhard (1707-83), Swiss mathematician. Made numerous contributions to all branches of mathematics, esp. calculus of variations, number theory, hydrodynamics, mechanics and lunar motion. Many theorems bear his name.

Eumenides (Gk., = kindly ones), in Greek religion, the Furies who tortured conscience of evil-doers, esp. those who killed their own kindred. Born by Earth after Uranus' blood fell on her, named Alecto, Tisiphone, Megaera. 'Eumenides' is a propitiatory euphemism for Erinyes (Terrible Ones).

euphonium, low-pitched brass instrument with 4 valves, used in brass bands.

Euphrates, river of SW Asia. Length c 2740 km (1700 mi). Rises in E Turkey, flows SE through Syria, Iraq; merges with R. Tigris to form Shatt-al-Arab. Irrigated ancient Mesopotamia. Dam at Tabqa, Syria, irrigates large agric. area.

Euratom, see EUROPEAN COMMUNITIES.

Eureka Stockade (1854), armed rebellion of miners on Ballarat goldfield, Australia. Causes were resentment of high cost of mining licences, lack of political representation, Chinese competition on field. Rebellion put down swiftly, but legislation followed to satisfy miners' main grievances. Incident since acclaimed as beginning of democracy in Australia, but also seen as birth of 'White Australia' policy, as consequences incl. poll-tax on Chinese immigrants.

eurhythmics, method of training response to music through harmonious movement of the body.

Developed by Jaques-Dalcroze, influenced ballet, acting.

Euripides (c 484-406 BC), Greek tragic poet. Noted for innovations, incl. sympathetic portrayal of common people and women, social criticism, religious unorthodoxy, realistic characterization and language. Wrote over 80 plays, 18 extant, incl. *Alcestis, Medea, Hippolytus, Trojan Women, Electra* and *Bacchae.*

Europa, in Greek myth, daughter of Phoenician King Agenor. Zeus, in the shape of a bull, abducted her to Crete, where she bore him Minos, Rhadamanthus and Sarpedon.

Europe, smallest mainland continent. Area c 10,360,000 sq km (4,000,000 sq mi); pop. c 690,000,000. Forms penin. of Eurasia projecting into Atlantic, separated from Asia by Ural and Caucasus Mts., Black and Caspian Seas. Crossed W-E by ranges incl. Pyrenees, Alps, Carpathians, Balkans, Caucasus (highest peak Mt. Elbrus 5631 m/18,481 ft). Main rivers Don, Dnepr, Danube, Oder, Elbe, Rhine, Rhône, Loire, Tagus, Volga. Many isls. incl. Iceland, Great Britain, Ireland, Corsica, Sicily, Sardinia. Main penins. incl. Balkan, Italian, Iberian. Fertile N European plain extends France-Poland. Major focus of civilization from c 1500 BC. Greek, Roman empires followed by spread of Christianity, agric., commerce in Middle Ages, Renaissance (centred in N Italy), rise of nation states. Rapid indust. progress in 18th-19th cents. spurred colonialism, spreading European culture to America, Africa, India. Scene of many wars throughout hist.; focus

of 2 WWs in 20th cent. Basic political division from 1945 into communist (E), capitalist (W) blocs.

European Communities, international organization with aims of economic integration, political unity. Originally 6 W European countries (Belgium, France, West Germany, Italy, Luxembourg, Netherlands) under Treaty of Rome (1957) estab. 3 communities: European Coal and Steel Community (ECSC), European Economic Community (EEC or Common Market), European Atomic Energy Community (Euratom). Merged executives in 1967 to form one Commission. U.K, Denmark, Irish Republic joined 1973. Governed by Commission, Council of Ministers, European Parliament. Court of Justice regulates treaties' application, advisory committees monitor social, labour conditions, consumer affairs, *etc.* EEC estab. (1958) with goals of customs union (achieved 1968), common policies on trade, agric.; talks on foreign policy initiated 1970. ECSC estab. 1952 to achieve common market for coal, iron ore, scrap, steel. Harmonized external tariff, regulated internal competition, aided workers in contracting coal indust.; has eventual goal (with Euratom) of Common Energy Policy. Euratom estab. 1958 to promote peaceful uses of nuclear energy; coordinates and promotes research, pools information, promotes training of scientists, technicians.

European Economic Community, *see* EUROPEAN COMMUNITIES.
European Free Trade Association (EFTA), customs union and

trading group estab. 1960 by Austria, Denmark, Norway, Portugal, Sweden, Switzerland, UK. Finland became associate member (1961), Iceland joined 1970. UK and Denmark left 1972 to join EEC.

europium, metallic element of lanthanide series; at. no. 63, at. wt. 151.96. Occurs in monazite. Discovered (1896) by spectroscopic analysis.

Europoort, see ROTTERDAM, Netherlands.

Eurydice, see ORPHEUS.

Eustachio, Bartolommeo (d. 1574), Italian anatomist. His descriptions and drawings of various organs were completed in 1552 but not published until 1714. Discovered Eustachian tube, narrow canal connecting middle ear and throat.

Evans, Sir Arthur John (1851-1941), English archaeologist. Began excavations at Knossos, Crete, in 1899; in course of 30 years' work, he revealed an ancient culture which he named MINOAN CIVILIZATION.

Evans, Dame Edith (1888-1976), English actress. Estab. reputation as Millamant in *The Way of the World*. Known in many major roles incl. Nurse in *Romeo and Juliet*.

evaporation, conversion of a liquid into vapour, without boiling point of liquid necessarily being reached. Rate of evaporation increased by application of heat and by lowering pressure above liquid.

Evatt, Herbert Vere (1894-1965), Australian statesman. Justice of high court of Australia (1930-40); foreign minister (1941-9). Promoted interests of smaller nations as president of UN General Assembly (1948-9).

Eve, see ADAM.

Evelyn, John (1620-1706), English diarist. Known for *Diary* of 1641-1706 (pub. 1818) containing sketches of contemporaries. Also wrote on various topics, incl. gardening, pollution.

Everest, Mount, highest mountain in world, on Nepal-Tibet border; height 8848 m (29,028 ft). First climbed in 1953, by Hillary and Tensing.

Everglades, subtropical swampy region of S Florida US. Area 12,950 sq km (c 5000 sq mi). Notable plants, wildlife, esp. water birds, in National Park.

evergreen, tree or plant which remains in foliage throughout the year. In the tropics many broad-leaved angiosperms are evergreen, whereas in colder areas evergreens are mainly conifers.

everlasting flowers, blossoms which keep colour and shape when dried by hanging upside down. Often of Compositae family. Incl. flowers of *Xeranthemum, Helipterum, Waitzia* genera.

Everyman (c 1500), anon. English morality play. Dramatizes late medieval Christian view of human nature and destiny. Protagonist Everyman, summoned to last journey by Death, seeks help from friends, incl. Kindred, Worldly Goods, Beauty, but only Good Deeds stays with him to end.

Evesham, mun. bor. of Hereford and Worcester, WC England, on R. Avon. Pop. 14,000. In fertile Vale of Evesham; fruit, vegetable growing. Agric. market, canning. Simon de Montfort killed in battle here (1265).

evolution, in biology, theory that all

species of animals and plants developed from earlier forms by hereditary transmission of slight variations in genetic composition to successive generations. Theory of evolution by natural selection is due to Darwin (1859); earlier theories incl. Lamarck's inheritance of acquired characteristics. Opposed by theory of special creation, which supposes that each organism is created in its final form and has not undergone successive evolutionary changes.

Excalibur, see ARTHURIAN LEGEND.

exchange, foreign, rate at which currency of one country is exchanged for that of another. Varies with supply and demand of foreign currency (see BALANCE OF PAYMENTS). Apart from speculation, foreign currency is bought by importers and investors in foreign stocks.

excise, tax or duty on the manufacture, sale or consumption of various commodities within a country. Distinct from customs, paid on goods entering country from abroad. Developed in 17th cent. by Holland. Usual goods subject to such tax are tobacco, alcoholic beverages, luxury goods, etc.

excommunication, act of formally excluding a person from the sacraments, rights and privileges of a religious body, usually to punish the person expelled and to protect remaining members from his influence. Retained esp. in RC church which teaches that the offender separates himself on commission of the offence (eg heresy). Excommunicates are free to return to the church on repentance.

excretion, elimination of useless or harmful metabolic products; **organs** mainly concerned being kidneys and large intestines of vertebrates, Malpighian tubes of insects, nephridia of invertebrates and stomata of plants.

Exe, river of SW England, flows c 88 km (55 mi) from Exmoor to English Channel at Exmouth.

executive, in politics, that part of govt. concerned with admin. of laws, incl. bureaucracy and officials who direct it. In US, theory distinguishes between making of policy decisions and carrying them out. Also see SEPARATION OF POWERS.

executor, in law, person appointed by testator to carry out provisions and directions of will. May be appointed by court if deceased died intestate to collect assets, settle debts.

Exeter, city and co. town of Devon, SW England, on R. Exe. Pop. 96,000. Railway jct.; agric. market. Has 11th cent. cathedral, guildhall, univ. (1955).

existentialism, philosophical movement which holds that there is no fixed human nature, that man is free to act as he will and that this is the source of his anguish. Derived from Kierkegaard, exponents incl. SARTRE, JASPERS.

Exmoor, moorland of SW England, national park in Devon, Somerset. Formerly forested; sheep, wild deer, ponies. Scene of Blackmore's Lorna Doone.

Exmouth, urban dist. of Devon, SW England, on R. Exe. Pop. 26,000. Resort, fishing port.

Exodus (Gk., = going out), in OT, 2nd book of Pentateuch. Covers period of Jewish history during which Israelites, under Moses, escaped from bondage in Egypt. Deals with founding of the Jewish nation, incl. Moses receiving the TEN COMMANDMENTS and other laws.

exorcism, ritual act of driving evil spirits from person, places or things in which they are believed to dwell. Occurs in primitive societies and in sophisticated religious practice. Scriptural justification is found in the instances of Christ's driving out of devils in NT. Officially recognized in RC church.

expansion, thermal, increase in size of body due to increase in temperature. Caused by increased activity of component molecules. Gases expand by c 1/273 of their volume at O˚C for each degree rise in temperature.

explosive, substance which, when heated or otherwise excited, undergoes rapid decomposition with production of large volume of gas; rapid increase of pressure in confined space caused by gas produces explosion. High explosives, incl. TNT, dynamite and nitroglycerine, require detonators to set them off.

expressionism, term for art which tries to give objective expression to inner experience. In 20th cent. painting, associated with artists such as Soutine, Kokoschka, Rouault and the Blaue Reiter, Brücke movements; characterized by distortion of form, violent nonnaturalistic colour. Precursors of style incl. van Gogh, Munch. In literature, Strindberg was important forerunner; movement (esp. strong in Germany) incl. plays of Toller, poetry of Benn, novels of Kafka. In cinema, Weine's *Cabinet of Dr*

Caligari is masterpiece. Term also embraces early music of Schoenberg, Berg.

extrasensory perception (ESP), faculty of perception other than by known sense organs. Belief in existence of ESP is not widely accepted.

extreme unction, sacrament in RC and Orthodox churches of anointing and giving absolution of sins to the dying.

extroversion and **introversion,** in psychology, terms coined by JUNG to denote opposite types of personality. Extrovert personality directs his interest and activity outwards, depends on environment, other people, while an introvert directs his activity inwards to self, and is less affected by surroundings.

extrusive rock, any rock formed by solidification of molten material forced out at Earth's surface. All extrusive rocks are thus IGNEOUS ROCKS; they incl. volcanic lava and pyroclastic material.

Eyck, Hubert van (c 1370-1426) and **Jan van Eyck** (c 1390-1441), Dutch painters, brothers, who founded Flemish school. Little is known of Hubert; altarpiece of Ghent Cathedral *Adoration of the Lamb* was completed after his death by Jan. Work is characterized by descriptive realism conveyed in minute detail. Jan was court painter to Philip the Good of Burgundy; he is famous for his portraits, incl. *Arnolfini and his Wife.*

eye, organ of sight. Human eyeball has opaque white outer layer (sclera) with transparent bulge (cornea) in front. IRIS is located behind cornea and lens behind this;

watery aqueous humour fills space between these and jelly-like vitreous humour rest of eye. Light-sensitive RETINA lines inner surface of sclera and transmits sensation of light through optic nerves to brain.

Eyre, Lake, salt lake of NE South Australia. Area c 9100 sq km (3500 sq mi); falls to 12m (39 ft) below sea level. Much of it is perennially dry.

Eyre Peninsula, peninsula of S South Australia, between Spencer Gulf and Great Australian Bight.

Eysenck, Hans Jurgen (1916-), British psychologist, b. Germany. Known for advocacy of behaviour therapy rather than Freudian psychoanalysis, and for belief in absolute measurability of intelligence. Works incl. *Race Intelligence and Education* (1971).

Ezekiel, prophetical book of OT. Recounts visions of priest, Ezekiel (fl 592 BC). Focuses on fall of Jerusalem, but foretells restoration of its glory.

Ezra, historical book of OT, opening with return of Jews from exile in Babylon to Jerusalem (538 BC) and covering 80 years of life and teachings of Ezra, Hebrew prophet and scribe; incl. rebuilding of Temple.

Ezzelino da Romano (1194-1259), Italian Ghibelline leader. Supported Emperor Frederick II against pope; became greatest power in N Italy. Eventually defeated by strong alliance, died in prison.

F

Fabergé, Peter Carl (1846-1920), Russian goldsmith. His workshops were famous for exquisite masterpieces, incl. flowers, animals and series of imperial Easter eggs, commissioned by Alexander III for his wife.

Fabian Society, British socialist organization, founded 1884. Aimed to achieve socialism through gradual reformist strategy rather than revolutionary action. Instrumental in estab. British Labour Party. Prominent members have incl. G.B. Shaw, Sidney and Beatrice Webb. Continues political research and publication.

Fabius Maximus, Quintus (d. 203 BC), Roman soldier. Called *Cunctator* ('Delayer') for his successful delaying tactics employed against Hannibal after defeat at L. Trasimene. Romans were routed at Cannae (216 BC) after his recall to Rome.

fable, short moral tale, with animals, inanimate objects as characters. Best-known exponents incl. Aesop, La Fontaine.

fabliau, popular comic tale, usually bawdy or scurrilous, burlesquing human foolishness. Chaucer's *Miller's Tale* has many elements of fabliau.

Fabricius, Hieronymus (c 1537-1619), Italian anatomist and embryologist. Described embryonic development of mammals, birds, *etc*. His discovery of valves in veins influenced his pupil William Harvey.

Factory Acts, legislation enacted by British Parliament to regulate conditions and hours of work, safety and sanitary provisions in factories and workshops. First was Health and Morals of Apprentices Act (1802); Cotton Mills Act (1819) forbade employment of children under 9 and reduced hours of labour for under-16s. Act of 1845 banned night-work for women, and that of 1847 introduced 10 hour working day. Factory inspectors appointed 1833. Offices, shops, *etc*, covered 1963.

faeces, waste matter expelled from intestines. Consists of undigested food, bacteria, water and mucus. Colour is due to bile pigment, smell due to nitrogen compounds produced by bacteria.

Faeroes, isl. group of Denmark, in N Atlantic. Area 1399 sq km (540 sq mi); pop. 40,000; cap. Thorshavn. Rugged, treeless. Sheep; fishing. Passed from Norway to Denmark (1380); auton. legislature from 1948.

Fahrenheit, Gabriel Daniel (1686-1736), German meteorological instrument maker. Pioneered use of mercury in thermometers and devised Fahrenheit scale of temperature.

fainting, temporary unconsciousness caused by inadequate flow of blood to brain. May be treated by stretching out victim or lowering his head.

Fairbanks, Douglas (1889-1939), American film actor. Famous for roles as gallant swashbuckler, as in *The Mark of Zorro* (1920), *The Thief of Baghdad* (1923), and for marriage to Mary PICKFORD. Their son, Douglas Fairbanks, Jnr (1907-), also became a film star, known for debonair roles. Films incl. *The Prisoner of Zenda* (1937).

Fairbanks, town of C Alaska, US; on Tanana R. Pop. 15,000. Terminus of Alaska Highway. Founded after 1902 gold strike.

Fairfax, Thomas, 3rd Baron Fairfax of Cameron (1612-71), English general. Commanded New Model Army which defeated Charles I at Naseby (1645). Refused to preside over trial of Charles as he doubted the judges' impartiality. Resigned command rather than invade Scotland (1650).

Fair Isle, small isl. in Shetlands, N Scotland. Famous knitwear mfg. Has bird observatory.

fairy, in folklore, supernatural being with magical powers. Concept has existed from earliest times but has greatly varied: described as demonic, mischievous, loving, bountiful. National variations incl. Arab djinns, SW English pixies, German elves, Scandinavian trolls.

Faisal, *see* FEISAL.

Falange, orig. *Falange Española*, fascist movement and party in Spain. Founded (1933) by José Antonio Primo de Rivera; became only legal party in Spain under leadership of Franco (1937). Power

waned, esp. after Franco enacted new constitution (1966).

falcon, bird of prey of Falconidae family. Long pointed wings, powerful hooked beak; diet of birds, insects, small mammals. Some falcons trained for hunting small game. Species incl. peregrine, kestrel, merlin, South American caracara.

falconry, *see* HAWKING.

Falkirk, town of Central region, C Scotland. Pop. 38,000. Large iron foundries. Scene of Edward I of England's victory over Wallace (1298).

Falkland Islands (Span. *Islas Malvinas*), crown colony of UK, in S Atlantic Ocean. Comprise East and West Falkland, c 200 small isls. Area 12,100 sq km (4700 sq mi); pop. 2500; cap. Stanley. Sheep rearing. Dependencies incl. South Georgia, South Orkney, South Shetland, South Sandwich Isls., Graham Land. Entire area claimed by Argentina.

Falla, Manuel de (1876-1946), Spanish composer. Influenced by Spanish folk music. His few compositions incl. opera *La Vida breve*, *Nights in the Gardens of Spain* for piano and orchestra, ballets *El Amor brujo* and *The Three-cornered Hat*.

fall line, line joining waterfalls or rapids on a number of rivers flowing roughly parallel to each other. Marks sudden increase in slope, *eg* at edge of plateau; forms head of navigation, source of h.e.p. Applied in particular to boundary between piedmont plateau and coastal plain of E US, fall line cities incl. Trenton, Philadelphia, Richmond.

Fallopius or Gabriele Fallopio

(1523–62), Italian anatomist. Noted member of Paduan school of anatomists. Discovered Fallopian tubes, leading from ovaries to the uterus, in which fertilization takes place.

fall-out, radioactive material deposited on Earth's surface following nuclear explosions. May cause genetic damage or various diseases, eg leukaemia. Strontium 90 present in fall-out is very dangerous as it may replace calcium in body.

fallow deer, Dama dama, European deer of Mediterranean region, rare in wild state. Usually reddish-brown with white spots; also dark varieties. Introduced into many parts of N Europe, North America as park animal.

Falmouth, mun. bor. of Cornwall, SW England. Pop. 18,000. Ship repairs, fishing port, resort.

Famagusta, port of E Cyprus. Pop. c 40,000. Exports citrus fruits, potatoes; holiday resort. Near ancient Salamis on site of Arsinoë.

family, social unit consisting of parental couple and children ('nuclear family'). Other close relatives may be included, eg grandparents, aunts, uncles, etc ('extended family'). Depends on stability of parental relationship, obligations and bonds between blood relations, satisfaction of personal and social needs.

Fangio [y Cia], Juan Manuel (1911–), Argentinian racing driver. World champion 5 times (1951, 1954-7). Retired 1958.

Fanon, Frantz Omar (1925-61), Algerian revolutionary, b. Martinique. Involved in revolt against French rule in 1950s. Leading exponent of peasant revolution in Africa. Works incl. Black Skin, White Masks (1952), Wretched of the Earth (1961).

Fantin-Latour, [Ignace] Henri (1836-1904), French painter. Painted still lifes, flower pieces and romantic figure subjects. Best known for his portrait groups of famous contemporaries, eg Hommage à Delacroix.

FAO, see FOOD AND AGRICULTURE ORGANIZATION.

Faraday, Michael (1791-1867), English chemist and physicist. Studies in electrochemistry led to discovery of 2 quantitative laws of electrolysis (Faraday's laws). Discovered principle of electromagnetic induction, effect utilized in dynamo. His concept of electric and magnetic fields of force became basis of Maxwell's electromagnetic theory. Discovered benzene (1825).

Far East, vague term for countries of E Asia, incl. China, Japan, Korea and Mongolia. Sometimes also taken to incl. countries of SE Asia and Malay Archipelago.

Farewell, Cape, headland, most S point of Greenland on Egger Isl.

Fargo, William George (1818-81), American expressman. A founder of American Express Co. (1850). Joined Henry Wells to form (1852) Wells-Fargo to handle New York-San Francisco express traffic.

Farne Islands, c 30 isls. off Northumberland, NE England. Chapel to St Cuthbert (d. 687). Scene of Grace Darling's rescue of survivors from the Forfarshire (1838).

Farnese, Alessandro (1545-92), Italian general, duke of Parma and Piacenza. Nephew of John of Austria, whom he succeeded as

Spanish governor of Netherlands (1578). Recovered S Netherlands from rebels. Sent to France to support Catholics against Henry IV.

Faro, town of S Portugal, cap. of Algarve prov. Pop. 19,000. Port, exports wine, figs, cork; sardine, tuna fishing; tourism.

Faroe Islands, see FAEROES, Denmark.

Farouk I (1920-65), king of Egypt (1936-52). Exiled after military coup under Naguib and Nasser (1952). Succeeded by son Fuad, who was deposed in 1953.

Farquhar, George (1678-1707), English dramatist, b. Ireland. Developed Restoration comedy into more sentimental mode. Works incl. *The Recruiting Officer* (1706), *The Beaux' Stratagem* (1707). Former adapted by Brecht as *Trumpets and Drums* (1956).

Farrell, James T[homas] (1904-79), American novelist. Known for naturalistic novels esp. 'Studs Lonigan' trilogy (1932-5). Also wrote short stories, and criticism, *A Note on Literary Criticism* (1936) being statement of proletarian aesthetics.

fascism, political ideology of totalitarian, militarist and nationalistic character. Advocates govt. by one-party dictatorship and centralized control of private economic enterprise (see CORPORATE STATE). Nationalism most extreme in racist suppression of minorities, eg anti-Semitism; strong police measures used to maintain law and order, oppose democracy, Communism. Originated with Mussolini's Fascist party which held power in Italy (1922-43). Fascism had spread by

1936 to Germany (Nazis), Japan, Spain (Falange), most of E Europe.

Fashoda, see KODOK, Sudan.

Fashoda Incident (1898-9), Anglo-French dispute over control of upper Nile region. French forces took Fashoda (now Kodok) in S Sudan, but, fearing war, withdrew upon British insistence. Peaceful settlement marked end of French claims in area.

Fates (Gk. *Moirai*), in Greek myth, three goddesses who controlled course of human life; Clotho spun the thread of life, Lachesis measured it, Atropos cut it. The Roman Fates (*Parcae*) were Nona, Decuma, Morta.

Fathers of the Church, term for Christian teachers and writers of the early Church whose work is considered orthodox. In West, incl. those up to and incl. St Gregory the Great, and to St John of Damascus in East.

Fatimites or **Fatimids,** Moslem dynasty, claiming descent from Mohammed's daughter, Fatima, which ruled in N Africa and Egypt (909-1171). Founded by Obaidallah, whose cap. was in Tunisia. Successors conquered Sicily; W Arabia, Palestine and Syria. Cairo became Fatimite cap. (969). Rule ended with Saladin's conquest of Egypt.

fats, group of naturally occurring substances found in plants and animals. Consist of mixtures of esters of glycerol with higher fatty acids, eg stearic, palmitic, oleic acids. Excellent source of energy in food.

Faulkner or **Falkner, William** (1897-1962), American novelist, short story writer. Created imaginary county in Deep South, populated with vivid characters in complex, decaying society. Novels incl. *The Sound and the Fury* (1929), *Sanctuary* (1931), *Light in August* (1932). Awarded Nobel Prize for Literature (1949).

fault, in geology, fracture in rock strata along which movement has occurred to displace sides relative to each other. Movement may be upward, sideways, or both; uplift on one side of fault can result in steep cliff or 'fault scarp'.

Fauré, Gabriel (1845-1924), French composer. Wrote delicate and sensitive music. Works incl. nocturnes for piano, chamber music, operas, a Requiem, songs. A great teacher (of Ravel among others); director of Paris Conservatoire (1905-20).

Faust, hero of several medieval legends. Based on historical figure (d. *c* 1540), a philosopher who was said to have sold his soul to the Devil in exchange for knowledge and power. Story, first pub. in the *Faustbuch* of 1587, inspired Marlowe, Goethe, Thomas Mann, Gounod and many others.

fauvism, short-lived modern art movement (*c* 1905-8). Used bold distortion of form and brilliant pure colour. Exponents incl. Matisse, Derain, Vlaminck, Marquet; given name ('Les Fauves' = wild beasts) by critic at controversial 1st showing.

Fawkes, Guy (1570-1606), English conspirator. Catholic convert, served with Spanish armies in Netherlands. Involved in Gunpowder Plot (5 Nov. 1605) to blow up Houses of Parliament during opening of new session by James I.

Plot exposed, Fawkes and other leaders executed.

FBI, see FEDERAL BUREAU OF INVESTIGATION.

February Revolution (1848), revolution in France which overthrew Louis Philippe and estab. Second Republic; provoked REVOLUTION OF 1848 in much of Europe. After uprising, moderate provisional govt. granted demands for indust. reforms, but sabotage caused failure of policies and further revolt. Louis Napoleon elected president after formulation of new constitution.

Federal Bureau of Investigation (FBI), branch of US Dept. of Justice. Estab. (1908) to investigate all violations of Federal laws except those, as of currency, tax, postal laws, dealt with by other Federal agencies. Drew criticism during WATERGATE AFFAIR.

federalism, system of govt. dividing nation's sovereign powers between central (federal) authority and constituent subdivisions (states, provinces). Central govt. powers usually incl. foreign relations, defence, commerce, coinage; states usually control their internal affairs. Arbitration of disputes often delegated to courts with reference to written constitution and precedents. US, West Germany, USSR, Canada, Australia have federal govt. structures.

Federalist Papers, series of 85 essays written (1787-8) by Alexander Hamilton, James Madison and John Jay analysing Federal Constitution and urging its adoption by American states.

Federalist Party, in US history, political party (estab. *c* 1791) under leadership of Alexander Hamilton and John Adams. Advocated strong central govt., expansion of commerce, anti-French foreign policy. Lost power to Jeffersonians after 1800. National significance lost by 1817.

Federal Reserve System, central banking system of US (estab. 1913). Each of 12 regional reserve banks serves each Federal Reserve district. National banks maintain reserves on deposit with regional banks. Money supply and credit conditions regulated by Federal Reserve Board.

feedback, see AUTOMATION.

Feisal I or **Faisal I** (1885-1933), king of Iraq (1921-33). Joined with T.E. Lawrence in revolt against Turkey (1916). Proclaimed king of Syria (1920), deposed by French mandatory powers. British, who held mandate in Iraq, supported him in fight for Iraqi throne.

Feisal II or **Faisal II** (1935-58), king of Iraq (1939-58). Succeeded his father, Ghazi I; ruled through regent until 1953. Killed in military coup which estab. republic.

Feisal, Ibn Al-Saud (1905-75), king of Saudi Arabia (1964-75). Succeeded brother Saud as king. Reign marked by pro-Western policies, increasing wealth and technological advances, based on vast oil exports. Assassinated by a nephew.

feldspars or **felspars**, group of rock-forming aluminium silicate minerals. Distinct types contain calcium, potassium, sodium or, very rarely, barium. Comprise c 50% of Earth's crust; found in igneous rocks, eg granite, basalt. Clay is product of weathering of feldspars.

Felixstowe, urban dist. of Suffolk, E England. Pop. 19,000. Resort, major container port.

Fellini, Federico (1920-), Italian film director. Noted for sympathy for victims of violence, greed or apathy. Films incl. *La Strada* (1954), *Notte di Cabiria* (1957) (both won Oscars), *8½* (1963), *Satyricon* (1969).

felony, serious crime, as distinct from MISDEMEANOUR. In UK law, distinction only historically valid. In US, both federal and state law maintain it, usually trying felony by jury, with serious penalty.

femur, in man, same as thigh bone.

fencing, sport of combat with swords. Three types of sword used: foil, a light weapon; épée, derived from duelling sword; sabre, a cut-and-thrust weapon. Olympic event for men since 1896, for women since 1924.

Fénelon, François de Salignac de la Mothe (1651-1715), French theologian. Archbishop of Cambrai from 1695. Defended quietism in *Maximes des saints* (1697). Wrote utopian novel, *Télémaque* (1699), to instruct young prince.

Fenians, secret revolutionary society formed (c 1858) to secure Irish independence from Britain. Promoted risings and terrorism suppressed by British, thus drawing attention to Irish problems. Group of Irish emigrants in US attempted invasion of Canada (1866); invasion ended in failure but encouraged Canadian confederation. See also SINN FEIN.

fennec, *Fennecus zerda*, small fawn-coloured fox of desert areas of N Africa, Arabia. Large ears and eyes; diet of insects, rodents.

fennel, name for several herbs, esp. those of genus *Foeniculum* in parsley family, used to flavour fish sauces and salad dressings. Wild fennel, *F. vulgare*, is used in stuffing.

Fens, The, flat low-lying area of E England, W and S of The Wash, within Cambridgeshire, Lincolnshire, Norfolk. Formerly bay of North Sea, silting created marsh. Draining begun 1621 by Vermuyden (Dutch). Now fertile, rich agric. incl. cereals, sugar beet, fruit.

fer-de-lance, *Bothrops atrox*, highly venomous snake of pit viper group of tropical America, West Indies. Reaches lengths of *c* 1.8 m/ 6 ft.

Ferdinand (1793-1875), emperor of Austria (1835-48). Subject to fits of insanity; dominated by foreign minister METTERNICH. Fled country during Revolution of 1848; abdicated in favour of nephew Francis Joseph.

Ferdinand I (1503-64), Holy Roman emperor (1558-64). Claimed kingdoms of Bohemia and Hungary on death of brother-in-law, Louis II (1526). Claim to Hungary opposed by John Zapolya and Turkish allies, leading to war until 1538. Negotiated Peace of Augsburg (1555) before succeeding his brother, Charles V, as emperor.

Ferdinand II (1578-1637), Holy Roman emperor (1619-37). A fervent Catholic, his deposition as king of Bohemia (1619) by Bohemian Protestants marked beginning of THIRTY YEARS WAR. Reimposed Catholicism in Bohemia by force after victory at White Mountain (1620). Failed to sustain early successes of Tilly and Wallenstein.

Ferdinand (1861-1948), king of Bulgaria (1908-18). German prince, elected prince of Bulgaria (1887), although not recognized by European powers until 1896. Proclaimed Bulgarian independence from Ottoman Empire (1908), taking title 'tsar' of Bulgaria. Defeated in 2nd Balkan War (1913); joined Central Powers in WWI. Abdicated in favour of his son, Boris III.

Ferdinand (1865-1927), king of Romania (1914-27). Joined Allies in WWI; acquired territ. from Hungary and Russia after war. Reign marked by agrarian reform and introduction of universal suffrage.

Ferdinand I [the Great] (d. 1065), king of Castile (1035-65) and León (1037-65). Began reconquest of Spain, making Moorish emirs of Saragossa, Seville, Toledo, Badajoz his vassals.

Ferdinand V [the Catholic] (1452-1516), king of Aragón and Castile. Married his cousin Isabella of Castile (1469); they ruled Castile jointly (1474-1504) until her death. Became Ferdinand II of Aragón (1479), thus uniting all of Spain except Granada. In 1492, reconquered Granada and expelled Jews from Spain. Rivalled Portuguese colonial expansion, notably by financing Columbus.

Ferdinand VII (1784-1833), king of Spain (1808-33). Imprisoned in France (1808-14) by Napoleon. Restored (1814), precipitated revolt (1820) by revoking liberal constitution. Restored to absolute power by French military intervention. Reign saw loss of Spanish colonies in North and South America.

Ferdinand I (1751-1825), king of the Two Sicilies (1816-25). Became king of Naples and Sicily (1759). Influenced by wife Marie Caroline, opposed French in Revolutionary Wars. Lost Naples to France (1806-15). On restoration, he ruled despotically.

Fergusson, Robert (1750-74), Scottish poet. Known for lively, humane satires of urban life, written in Scots, incl. 'Auld Reikie', 'Leith Races', 'Hallow Fair'. Lived in poverty and died in lunatic asylum.

Fermanagh, former county of SW Northern Ireland. Hilly in NE, SW; bisected by Upper and Lower Lough Erne. Agric.; cattle rearing. Co. town was Enniskillen. Fermanagh, district; area 1876 sq km (724 sq mi); pop. 51,000. Created 1973, formerly Co. Fermanagh.

Fermat, Pierre de (1601-65), French mathematician. Anticipated Descartes' discovery of analytical geometry and certain features of differential calculus. Famed for work on number theory; his famous 'last theorem' remains unproved, despite his claims. Enunciated principle that path taken by light ray between 2 points is that taking least time.

fermentation, chemical change caused by enzyme action. Yeast enzyme system causes alcoholic fermentation of sugar, with production of ethyl alcohol and carbon dioxide.

Fermi, Enrico (1901-54), American physicist, b. Italy. Awarded Nobel Prize for Physics (1938) for work on neutron bombardment, esp. use of absorbing materials to slow down neutrons. Headed Univ. of Chicago group which achieved first controlled nuclear reaction (1942).

fermions, in physics, elementary particles, incl. electron, proton, which conform to Fermi-Dirac statistics and obey Pauli exclusion principle. Divided into baryons and leptons. Number of fermions taking part in nuclear interactions appears to be conserved.

fermium (Fm), transuranic element; at. no. 100, mass no. of most stable isotope 257. Discovered in debris of nuclear explosion (1953) and named after E. Fermi.

fern, any of a class, Filicineae, of flowerless perennial plants. Distinctive frond-shaped leaves. Reproduces by spores rather than seeds. More than 6000 species, widely distributed esp. in tropics. Fossils indicate many early varieties.

Fernandel, stage name of Fernand Constantin (1903-1971), French comedian. Known for role as priest in film of *The Little World of Don Camillo* (1953), as quins (playing all five) in *The Sheep has Five Legs* (1953).

Fernando Póo, see MACIAS NGUEMA BIYOGA.

Ferrara, city of Emilia-Romagna, NC Italy, cap. of Ferrara prov. Pop. 155,000. Agric. market, food processing; univ. (1391). Cultural centre 13th-16th cent. under Este family; incorporated 1598 into Papal States. Moated castle (14th cent.).

ferret, domesticated albino variety of polecat, genus *Mustela*. Tamed to hunt rabbits and rats.

Ferrier, Kathleen (1912-53), British contralto. Her rich, full voice rapidly brought her international fame after WWII; career cut short by cancer. Title role of Britten's *The Rape of Lucretia* written for her.

Ferrol (del Caudillo), El, town of

Galicia, NW Spain, on Atlantic Ocean. Pop. 88,000. Chief Atlantic naval base; fish processing. Birthplace of Franco ('El Caudillo').

ferromagnetism, property of certain metals, esp. iron, cobalt and nickel, of having high susceptibility to acquiring magnetism. Such materials exhibit HYSTERESIS and may be used as permanent magnets.

fertility drugs, substances used to increase possibility of conception. Male infertility sometimes treated by thyroid and pituitary hormones. Failure to ovulate in female can be treated by drug clomiphene, but this may cause multiple births.

fertility rites, ceremonies to ensure abundance of food and birth of children. Usually rituals involving personification of natural phenomena, eg seed, Sun, Earth, and invoking sympathetic magic.

fertilization, union of male sperm cell with female egg cell (ovum) to form a zygote, which develops to form new individual. See also POLLINATION.

fertilizer, substance put on soil to improve quantity and quality of plant growth, usually by supplying necessary nitrogen, phosphorus and potassium. Organic fertilizers incl. animal manure and bone meal; inorganic incl. nitrates and ammonium compounds, superphosphates and basic slag.

fescue, any of genus *Festuca* of perennial grasses. Many used in temperate regions for lawns or pasture, eg meadow fescue, *F. elatior.*

Festival of Lights, see HANUKKAH.

fetishism, worship of inanimate object believed to have supernatural power. See TABOO, TOTEMISM.

feudalism, economic, political, social system of medieval Europe. In ideal system, ownership of all land was vested in king, who granted it to highest nobles in return for military, personal service; they in turn granted land to lesser nobles, and so on, until lowest level (serf) reached. Local unit was manor, whose lord (seigneur) granted land to and protected peasants, villeins, serfs, in return for service. Church ownership of land worked in parallel. System declined with growth of money economy, rise of mercantile classes.

Feuerbach, Ludwig Andreas von (1804-72), German philosopher. Abandoned Hegelian idealism for naturalistic materialism. In *The Essence of Christianity* (1841) analysed religion anthropologically, asserting God to be man's projection of his own nature.

fever, abnormally high body temperature, usually a symptom of infection or disease. Believed to be caused by stimulation of temperature-control centre of brain during destruction of bacteria.

feverfew, *Chrysanthemum parthenium,* perennial herb of daisy family. Dried leaves and flowers used to make medicinal tea.

Feydeau, Georges (1862-1921), French playwright. Known for ingeniously contrived farces, incl. *La dame de chez Maxim* (1899), *Un fil à la patte* (1899).

Fez (Fr. *Fès*), city of N Morocco. Pop. 321,000. Route centre; carpet mfg., leather goods. Founded 808; sacred city of Islam with *c* 100 mosques; has ancient Moslem univ.

Fezzan, region of SW Libya. Mainly desert, some oases; produces dates. Formerly crossed by many caravan routes. Taken by Turks 1842; by Italy 1911; under French military govt. 1943-51. Federal prov. (cap. Sebha) 1951-63.

Fianna Fáil, Irish political party, estab. 1926 by opponents of Irish Free State. Under leadership of DE VALÉRA, controlled govt. from 1932, demanding separation from Britain. Opposed by FINE GAEL.

fiat money, see FIDUCIARY ISSUE.

fibre, thread-like tissue capable of being spun into yarn. Animal fibres, composed mainly of protein, incl. silk, wool, hair of goats, rabbits, *etc*; vegetable fibres, composed mostly of cellulose, incl. cotton, kapok, hemp. Modern synthetic fibres are usually polymers, *eg* nylon and various polyesters.

fibre optics, branch of optics dealing with transmission of light along very narrow flexible glass cables. Technique used to locate faults in machinery, investigate human body.

Fichte, Johann Gottlieb (1762-1814), German philosopher. Wrote *Critique of Religious Revelation* (1792), developing Kantian ethics. *Addresses to the German People* (1808) stirred national feeling against Napoleon's domination.

fiddler crab, small burrowing crab, genus *Uca*, of salt marshes and sandy beaches. Male has one claw much larger than other.

fiduciary issue or **fiat money**, in banking, the portion of an issue of currency notes which is not backed by gold or other tangible assets available on demand. Normally backed by bills of exchange or govt. securities.

Field, John (1782-1837), Irish composer, pianist. Worked mainly in Russia as teacher and performer. Devised *nocturne* form, later developed by Chopin. Compositions influenced several Romantic composers.

fieldfare, *Turdus pilaris*, European bird of thrush family, with grey head, brown back. Breeds in colonies in N Europe.

field hockey, see HOCKEY.

Fielding, Henry (1707-54), English author. Important in development of English novel. First novels, *eg Joseph Andrews* (1742), burlesqued trials of virginity of Richardson's *Pamela*, as well as using powerful social satire. Best known for *Tom Jones* (1749), complex comic masterpiece. Also wrote plays, political satire, criticism.

field mouse, see MOUSE.

Fields, Gracie, orig. Grace Stansfield (1898-1979), English comedienne, music-hall singer. Songs associated with her incl. 'The Biggest Aspidistra in the World', 'Sally'.

Fields, W. C., orig. Claude William Dukenfield (1880-1946), American film actor. Famous as gravel-voiced, alcoholic, intolerant comedian, who improvised many of his films. Starred in films from 1915, incl. *The Bank Dick* (1940), *Never Give a Sucker an Even Break* (1941).

field theory, in physics, means of representing effect of physical phenomena throughout space. Magnetic, electric and gravitational forces may all be represented by fields.

Fife, region of E Scotland, between firths of Tay and Forth. Area 1305 sq km (504 sq mi); pop. 328,000. Created 1975 from former Fife county. Lomond Hills in W. Rich agric. (esp. cereals); coalmining; fishing. Ancient Pictish kingdom.

fifth column, collaborationist group, native to one country but working for another. Term first used by Spanish Nationalist General Mola (1936) who, besieging Madrid with 4 columns, boasted of having a 'fifth column' already within.

fig, any of genus *Ficus* of mulberry family, esp. *F. carica*, broad-leaved cultivated tree bearing soft, many-seeded, edible fruit. Prob. grown first in Arabia; spread to Mediterranean countries and US.

fighting fish, *Betta splendens*, small brightly coloured freshwater fish of S Asia. Males, very aggressive to each other, bred in Siam for fighting.

figwort, perennial plant of genus *Scrophularia* with square stem. Species incl. common figwort, *S. nodosa*, with tuberous roots and water figwort, *S. aquatica*.

Fiji Islands, country of SW Pacific Ocean, comprising c 320 isls of which c 100 inhabited. Area 18,350 sq km (7080 sq mi); pop. 580,000; cap. Suva. Main isls. Viti Levu, Vanua Levu. Produces sugar cane, rice, fruit and gold; tourist centre. Discovered (1643) by Abel Tasman; British colony from 1874 until independence 1970. Large Indian pop., descendants of plantation workers imported 19th cent. Member of British Commonwealth.

filbert, two deciduous HAZEL trees, *Corylus maxima* and *C. avellana*. Native to W Asia, widely cultivated for nut crop.

Fillmore, Millard (1800-74), American statesman, president (1850-3). Whig vice-president, succeeded Zachary Taylor as president. Supported 'compromise' view on slavery issue. Presidential candidate (1856) for Know-Nothing party.

filtration, separation of suspended undissolved solids from liquids. Filters incl. absorbent paper, fabrics, sands and charcoal.

finch, any of Fringillidae family of small short-beaked, seed-eating birds. Incl. canary, sparrow, goldfinch.

Fine Gael, Irish political party, estab. 1933. Has held power three times, only in coalition with Labour Party. Opposed by FIANNA FÁIL.

Fingal's Cave, cavern in Staffa, (isl. of Inner Hebrides), W Scotland. Associated with legends.

fingerprint, impression of lines, whorls on inner surface of end joint of finger. Used by police for identification, impression being thought unique and permanent for each individual.

Finisterre, Cape, headland of La Coruña prov., most W point of Spanish mainland. Scene of two English naval victories (1747, 1805) over French.

Finland (*Suomi*), republic of NE Europe. Area 337,010 sq km (130,120 sq mi); pop. 4,727,000; cap. Helsinki. Languages: Finnish, Swedish. Religion: Lutheran. Tundra in N (Lapland), mainly within Arctic Circle; lakes, forests in S. Mostly low-lying; main rivers Torne, Kemi,

Oulu. Forestry (pulp, paper), h.e.p., some agric. Conquered (12th cent.) by Eric IX of Sweden, Swedish culture estab. in Middle Ages. Ceded to Russia 1809. Independence followed Russian Revolution (1917), republic estab. 1919. Lost territ. (incl. Karelia) after war with USSR (1939-40).

Finland, Gulf of, arm of Baltic Sea, between Finland and USSR. Frozen in winter. Main ports Helsinki, Leningrad, Tallinn, Vyborg.

Finn Maccumhaill, hero of Gaelic mythology. Leader of the Fiann, band of warriors with whom he had many adventures defending Ireland. Most famous story is of his pursuit and destruction of his lieutenant Diarmait, who had eloped with his betrothed, Gráinne. His son was OSSIAN.

Finno-Ugric or **Finno-Ugrian,** language group within URALIC family. Incl. Estonian, Finnish, Lapp, Hungarian (Magyar).

Finsteraarhorn, peak of WC Switzerland, highest in Bernese Oberland, 4273 m (14,026 ft).

fir, general name for any of the tall, widely distributed, coniferous, evergreen trees of genus *Abies,* and for other similar trees, *eg* Douglas fir.

Firbank, [Arthur Annesley] Ronald (1886-1926), English novelist. Known for artificial, fantastic novels of delicate wit *eg Vainglory* (1915), *Caprice* (1917).

firearms, weapons discharging projectiles by use of explosives. Primitive cannon were first used *c* 1300; hand-guns followed half a century later. The most rapid improvements came with the invention of the percussion cap, breech loading and the magazine in the 19th cent. Automatic weapons appeared *c* 1900.

fireclay, clay composed mainly of alumina and silica, capable of resisting intense heat. Used to make firebrick for lining kilns and metallurgical furnaces. Often found under coal seams.

firefly, any of Lampyridae family of luminescent beetles, most numerous in tropics. Light, produced by chemical action in special organs on abdomen, used as communication between sexes. Larvae, wingless females called glow-worms.

Firenze, *see* FLORENCE, Italy.

Fire of London (1666), fire which swept through city, devastating almost all of medieval London. In 4 days, it destroyed *c* 13,000 buildings, incl. St Paul's Cathedral. Rebuilding undertaken by Christopher Wren.

fireworks, preparations of explosives used for display purposes. Thought to have originated in China, introduced to Europe (13th cent.). Potassium nitrate and potassium chlorate commonly used with various metal salts to give range of colours.

First World War, *see* WORLD WAR I.

Fischer, Emil (1852-1919), German organic chemist. Awarded Nobel Prize for Chemistry (1902) for research on structure of sugars and purines. Analysed way in which amino- acids combine to form proteins and devised methods of synthesizing proteins.

Fischer, Robert James ('Bobby') (1943-), American chess player. First American world champion, he defeated Russian

Boris Spassky amidst worldwide publicity in Reykjavik (1972). Resigned title 1974.

Fischer-Dieskau, Dietrich (1925-), German baritone. Known particularly for his interpretation of *lieder*. Also sings in opera.

Fish, Hamilton (1808-93), American statesman. Secretary of state (1869-77), negotiated settlement of *Alabama* claim with Britain (1871). Negotiated settlement with Spain after seizure of American ship *Virginius* in Cuba, thus averting potential war.

fish (Pisces), cold-blooded aquatic vertebrate. Gill-breathing, finned; body usually covered with scales. Diet of plankton, plants and aquatic animals. Divided into cartilaginous fish (shark, ray, *etc*) and bony fish (with bone in skeleton). Largest is whale shark, c 17.2 m/50 ft. long. *See* ICHTHYOLOGY.

Fisher, Andrew (1862-1928), Australian statesman, b. Scotland. Labor Party leader; PM (1908-9, 1910-13, 1914-15). Terms marked by reforms in taxation and land policy.

Fisher, Geoffrey Francis, Baron Fisher of Lambeth (1887-1972), English churchman. Archbishop of Canterbury (1945-61). Promoted ecumenical movement, visiting pope in 1960; president of World Council of Churches (1946-54).

Fisher, St John (1459-1535), English churchman, scholar. Imprisoned (1534) for opposing Henry VIII's divorce from Catherine of Aragon; Pope Paul III consequently made him cardinal (1535). Henry had him beheaded.

Fisher, John Arbuthnot, 1st Baron (1841-1920), British ad-

miral. As first sea lord (1904-10) introduced the *Dreadnought* class of battleships. Recalled to the same office in 1914, but resigned because of differences with Churchill over the Dardanelles campaign (1915).

fisher or **pekan**, *Martes pennanti*, large North American carnivore of marten family. Nocturnal; forest dweller.

fisheries, pursuit and capture of aquatic animals. Most fish are caught by trawling, seining, drifting or by baited lines. Most highly developed fisheries are those of N Atlantic, esp. around Iceland, Newfoundland and Labrador. Modern intensive methods of fishing incl. use of factory ships which quickly freeze or can their catch. Major fishing nations are Japan, USSR, China, Peru, Norway and US.

Fishguard and Goodwick, urban dist. of Dyfed, SW Wales. Pop. 5000. Railway terminus; ferry services to Cork, Rosslare (Ireland).

Fisk, James, *see* GOULD, JAY.

fission, in biology, form of asexual reproduction occurring in various plants, protozoa, bacteria, *etc*, in which parent organism splits into 2 or more approximately equal parts, each becoming an independent individual.

fission, nuclear, splitting of heavy atomic nuclei (eg uranium or plutonium) into 2 fragments of approximately equal mass, accompanied by release of nuclear energy and neutrons. May occur spontaneously or be caused by impact of neutrons. *See* CHAIN REACTION.

Fitzgerald, Edward (1809-83), English author. Best known for creative verse translation, *The Rubaiyat of Omar Khayyam* (1859).

Fitzgerald, F[rancis] Scott [Key] (1896-1940), American author. Works reflect despair of 'lost generation' in 1920s America, eg novels *The Beautiful and the Damned* (1922), *The Great Gatsby* (1925), *Tender is the Night* (1934). Short stories incl., 'The Diamond as Big as the Ritz', collected in *Tales of the Jazz Age* (1922).

Fitzherbert, Maria Anne, née Smythe (1756-1837), wife of George, Prince of Wales. Married George (1785); marriage deemed illegal as she was a Catholic and he a minor. Relationship continued until 1803, despite his marriage to Caroline of Brunswick (1795).

Fiume, see RIJEKA-SUSAK, Yugoslavia.

Five, the, group of Russian composers, founders of nationalist school of music that drew on Russian history and literature as well as folk music. Comprised BALAKIREV, BORODIN, César Cui (1835-1918), MUSSORGSKY and RIMSKY-KORSAKOV. Also known as 'the Mighty Handful'.

fives, handball game played by 2 or 4 competitors in a special court. Chiefly confined to Britain, esp. to public schools. Three main forms: Rugby, Eton and Winchester.

Five Year Plan, Soviet economic programme, first introduced in USSR by Stalin (1928) to impose collectivization of agric. and enhance industrialization. Ruthlessly enforced, caused much suffering. Other programmes followed; practice has been adopted elsewhere, *eg* Cuba, China.

flagellants, term applied to severely ascetic Christian groups who practised public flagellation as a penance. Widespread in 12th cent. Europe. Prohibited (1349) by Pope Clement VI, but heretical groups persisted. Still survive in South America.

flame, region where chemical interaction between gases heated above kindling temperature takes place, with accompaniment of heat and light.

flamenco, Spanish style of singing and guitar-playing, often danced to. It is vigorous and may be extemporized along set patterns. Practised mainly in Andalusia; reflects Moorish influence.

flamingo, any of Phoenicopteridae family of large gregarious wading birds. Long thin legs, webbed feet, sinuous neck; red or pink plumage. Found in tropical and temperate zones.

Flaminius, Titus Quinctius (c 228-174 BC), Roman soldier. Defeated Philip V of Macedon at Cynoscephalae (197) and declared independence of Greek cities (196).

Flanders (Flem. *Vlaanderen*), region of SW Belgium and NE France. Former county of Low Countries. Medieval cloth centre (Bruges, Ghent); now indust. area based on coalfields. Battleground in many wars. In Belgium, divided into East, West Flanders provs.; in France, part of Nord region. Distinct Flemish language.

flatfish, any of order Pleuronectiformes of fish with compressed, asymmetric bodies. Larvae normal, but during growth, eyes migrate to same side of head. Eyed side of fish

flat foot, condition in which entire sole of human foot rests upon ground. Caused by weakness of muscles of the arches and consequent stretching of ligaments.

Flaubert, Gustave (1821-80), French novelist. Famous works, esp. *Madame Bovary* (1857), *L'Education sentimentale* (1869), *Three Tales* (1877), reveal perfection of form, extreme impersonality of style, despite tragic material.

flax, any plant of genus Linum, esp. *L. usitatissimum* with slender leaves and small blue flowers, of worldwide distribution. Stems are source of LINEN and seeds of LINSEED oil.

flea, any of Aphaniptera order of wingless, flattened insects. Long hind legs adapted for jumping. Adult sucks blood of mammals, birds; transmits disease, esp. bubonic plague and endemic typhus.

fleabane, any plant of genus Erigeron, of Compositae · family. Formerly thought to drive away flies.

Flecker, [Herman] James Elroy (1884-1915), English poet. Work reflects Eastern travels as diplomat. Best known for exotically lyrical *The Golden Journey to Samarkand* (1913).

Fleet Street, term for British national newspapers, since most are located in or around street of that name in London.

Fleming, Sir Alexander (1881-1955), Scottish bacteriologist. Discovered penicillin in a mould contaminating bacterial culture, but did not develop its large-scale antibiotic use. Shared Nobel Prize for Physiology and Medicine (1945) with Chain and Florey for work on penicillin.

Fleming, Ian Lancaster (1908-65), English novelist. Known for 'James Bond' 'spy' novels, eg *Casino Royale* (1953), *From Russia with Love* (1957), *Goldfinger* (1959).

Flemish, language of W Germanic group of Indo-European family. Usually thought to be Belgian variant of DUTCH, not distinct language. Spoken in N Belgium, France.

Fletcher, John (1579-1625), English dramatist. Wrote majority of 52 plays pub. with BEAUMONT. True collaborations incl. tragi-comedies *Philaster*, *A King and No King*. Wrote comedies, eg *The Wild Goose Chase*, alone. Also collaborated with Massinger, Shakespeare.

Flinders, Matthew (1774-1814), English naval officer, hydrographer. Surveyed and charted Australian coasts. First to circumnavigate Tasmania (1798), also circumnavigated Australia (1801-3). Wrote *Voyage to Terra Australis* (1814).

Flinders Island, see FURNEAUX ISLANDS.

flint, hard, fine-grained rock, a variety of quartz. Dark grey or black in colour. Often found in chalk and limestone, dates from upper Cretaceous and Tertiary periods. May be shaped by flaking; widely used in Stone Age for making tools, weapons.

Flintshire, former county of NE Wales, now in Clwyd. Clwydian Hills in ,W, Dee estuary to E. Coalmining; agric.; coastal resorts. Main indust. centre Flint, mun. bor.

on R. Dee. Pop. 15,000. Artificial silk mfg.

FLN, *see* NATIONAL LIBERATION FRONT.

Flodden, hill of Northumberland, NE England. Scene of battle in which James IV of Scotland defeated, killed by English under Earl of Surrey (1513).

flood, inundation of land by overflow of a body of water, usually a river. Often caused by melting of snow and ice into headwaters, but brief 'flash floods' may follow short, torrential downpours of rain. Natural flood plains of rivers, normally inundated annually, are rich in alluvium. Flood control performed by dams, locks, levées, *eg* Tennessee Valley Authority, US; seawater controlled by dykes, behind which reclamation is possible, *eg* Zuider Zee, Netherlands.

Flora, Roman goddess of flowers and fertility. Her festival (28th April - 3rd May) was celebrated with licentious farces.

Florence (*Firenze*), city of NC Italy, on R. Arno, cap. of Tuscany. Pop. 482,000. Indust., tourist centre; railway jct. Etruscan, then Roman settlement. Scene of Guelph-Ghibelline conflict (12th-13th cent.). Under Medici family became centre of Renaissance art, architecture; its famous artists incl. da Vinci, Donatello, Giotto, Michelangelo, Raphael. Birthplace of Dante. Buildings incl. Pitti palace, Ponte Vecchio, Uffizi gallery, domed cathedral. Cap. of Italy 1865-70. Damaged in WWII, 1966 floods.

Flores, isl. of Indonesia, in Lesser Sundas. Area *c* 17,000 sq km (6600 sq mi). Mountainous with many active volcanoes; interior forested.

Florey, Howard Walter, Baron Florey (1898-1968), British pathologist, b. Australia. With E. B. CHAIN, developed methods of purifying penicillin and producing it on a large scale for use during WWII. Shared Nobel Prize for Physiology and Medicine (1945).

Florida, state of SE US; mainly on penin. separating Atlantic and Gulf of Mexico. Area 151,670 sq km (58,560 sq mi); pop. 6,789,000; cap. Tallahassee; chief cities Jacksonville, Miami. Generally low-lying, swampy (Everglades); subtropical climate. Agric. esp. citrus fruits; fishing; aero-space industs. Major tourist region, resorts incl. Miami, Palm Beach. Spanish colonized area in 16th cent.; purchased by US 1821. Admitted to Union as 27th state (1845).

Florida Keys, chain of small isls., S of Florida, US. Largest are Key West and Key Largo. Linked by highway. Resort for game fishing.

flounder, *see* FLATFISH.

flour, finely ground and sifted meal of cereal, esp. wheat and rye, consisting mainly of starch and gluten. Different grades of flour make bread, pastry, macaroni, *etc*.

flower, part of seed plant containing reproductive organs, *ie* the male stamens bearing pollen in anthers, and the ovary or gynaecium, the whole surrounded by petals and sepals.

flugelhorn, brass instrument similar in shape to bugle, with 3 valves like a trumpet, but producing a fuller, more mellow sound. Played in brass bands but most characteristically in jazz.

fluidics, technology of building equivalents of electronic circuits using flow of fluid instead of electrons. Systems use valves which take place of transistors in logic circuits. Used when conditions (eg heat, ionizing radiation) make electronics unreliable.

fluke, any of order Trematoda of parasitic flatworms, with 2 suckers used for adhesion. Life cycle involves several larval forms and one or more hosts. Species incl. liver fluke of sheep, *Fasciola hepatica*, and Chinese liver fluke, *Clonorchis sinensis*, parasitic in humans.

fluorescence, property of certain materials of absorbing light of short wavelength (eg violet or ultra violet) and emitting light of longer wavelength (such as visible light). In fluorescent lamp, ultraviolet light, produced by passing current through mercury vapour, is converted to visible light by fluorescent substance on walls of glass tube.

fluoridation, addition of metallic fluorides, esp. sodium fluoride, to drinking water to reduce incidence of dental decay.

fluorine (F), pale yellow gaseous element of halogen family; at. no. 9, at. wt. 18.998. Very chemically active, not found free; occurs in cryolite and fluorspar. First prepared by Moissan (1886) by electrolysis. Used in manufacture of FLUOROCARBONS.

fluorite or **fluorspar**, crystalline mineral, composed of calcium fluoride. Transparent, sometimes fluorescent; colourless but tinted by impurities. Used in glassmaking, as flux in metallurgy; source of fluorine; 'Blue John' is blue, ornamental form. Major sources in US, Mexico, Germany, England.

fluorocarbons, group of synthetic organic compounds obtained by replacing some or all of the hydrogen atoms of hydrocarbons by fluoride atoms. Chemically stable, used in manufacture of oils, plastics (eg Teflon), refrigerants and aerosol propellants.

fluorspar, see FLUORITE.

Flushing (Vlissingen), town of SW Netherlands, on Walcheren Isl. at mouth of Western Scheldt. Pop. 39,000. Oil refining, fishing, shipbuilding. First Dutch city to rebel against Spain (1572). Strategic site, scene of Allied invasion (1944).

flute, woodwind instrument of metal or wood with range of 3 octaves, played by blowing across small aperture near one end. Alto flute sounds a fourth lower than concert flute and bass flute an octave lower. The piccolo sounds an octave higher.

fly, any of order Diptera of insects with 1 pair of functional membranous wings. Many flies transmit disease by blood-sucking or carrying germs on body. Species incl. MOSQUITO, HORSEFLY, TSETSE FLY. Name applied esp. to HOUSE FLY and also to other orders of insect.

flycatcher, any of Muscicapidae family of small birds with thin curved beak. Catches insects while in flight. Species incl. spotted flycatcher, *Muscicapa striata*, widespread in Europe.

Flying Dutchman, legendary spectral ship, believed to haunt Cape of Good Hope. Captain is doomed to sail forever. Subject of opera by Wagner.

flying fish, any fish capable of leaping from water, using enlarged pectoral fins to glide through air; mainly tropical. Species incl. Atlantic flying fish, *Exocoetus volitans*.

flying fox, one of several fruit-eating bats, found in tropics from Asia to Australia, genus *Pteropus*. Malayan kalong, *P. vampyrus*, has wingspan of c 1.5 m/5 ft, largest of all bats.

flying lemur, any of order Dermoptera of arboreal nocturnal mammals of SE Asia. Membrane stretched between legs enables it to make gliding leaps. Also called colugo.

flying squirrel, any of several nocturnal species of squirrel. Uses fold of skin stretched from foreleg to hind legs to glide from tree to tree. Species incl. American *Glaucomys volans*, European *Pteromys volans*.

Flynn, Errol (1909-59), Australian film actor. Known for roles as adventurous womanizer, as in *Captain Blood* (1935), *The Sea Hawk* (1940), *Too Much Too Soon* (1958).

FM (frequency modulation), *see* MODULATION.

Foch, Ferdinand (1851-1929), French general. Forestalled the initial German advance at the Marne (1914) and distinguished himself at the battles of Ypres (1915) and the Somme (1916). His appointment as Allied supreme commander in 1918 marked the beginning of the German decline.

focus, in optics, point at which rays of light reflected by a mirror or refracted by a lens meet (real focus), or would meet if continued back through lens or mirror (virtual focus). Focal length of thin lens is distance from its optical centre to point at which rays of light parallel to its principal axis are focused.

foetus, mammalian embryo in later stages of its development when main features of fully developed animal are recognizable; in man, embryo is considered as foetus after 2 months of gestation.

fog, mass of water droplets suspended in air, obscuring vision for any distance up to 1 km/0.62 mi. Formed by water vapour condensing on minute dust particles. Mixture of smoke and fog, common in indust. areas, results in smog.

Foggia, city of Apulia, SE Italy, cap. of Foggia prov. Pop. 139,000. Major wheat market; flour, cheese. Cathedral (12th cent.); palace gateway (13th cent.).

Fokine, Michel (1880-1942), American choreographer, dancer, b. Russia. One of founders of modern ballet, working with Diaghilev in most brilliant period of Ballets Russes (1909-14). Created *The Firebird*, *Le Spectre de la rose*, *Petrouchka*.

Fokker, Anton Herman Gerard (1890-1939), Dutch aircraft manufacturer, b. Java. Built WWI biplanes and tri-planes in German factories. Developed device to allow machine gun to be fired through moving propeller. Settled in US in 1922.

Folkestone, mun. bor. of Kent, SE England. Pop. 44,000. Cross-Channel ferry services. One of Cinque Ports.

folklore, term coined (1846) by W. T. Thoms to denote traditional beliefs, legends, customs, *etc*, of a people. Regarded as important by anthropologists as the imaginative expression of a society's cultural values.

Fonda, Henry (1905-), American actor. Appeared in films as gauche young rustic, eg *Young Mr Lincoln* (1939), *The Grapes of Wrath* (1940), later expressing likeable wisdom in *Twelve Angry Men* (1957). His daughter, **Jane Fonda** (1937-), is a film actress. Appeared in *Klute* (1971) and in political films, eg *Tout va bien* (1972). His son, **Peter Fonda** (1939-), is best known as actor-producer of *Easy Rider* (1969), expressing mood of late 1960s American youth.

Fontainebleau, town of Ile-de-France, N France, in forest of Fontainebleau. Pop. 20,000. Resort; NATO hq. (1945-67). Château, built by Francis I, was former residence of French kings; scene of revocation of Edict of Nantes (1685), of 1st abdication of Napoleon (1814).

Fontana, Domenico (1543-1607), Italian architect. Under patronage of Sixtus V, completed dome of St Peter's, built Lateran Palace and Vatican library.

Fontane, Theodor (1819-98), German author. Turned from poetry to novel late in life. Known for masterpiece, *Effi Briest* (1895) on theme of stifling of individual by social conventions.

Fontenoy, village of Hainaut prov., Belgium. Scene of French victory (1745) over British, Dutch, and Austrian forces.

Fonteyn, Dame Margot, orig. Margaret Hookham (1919-), English ballerina. Long-time *prima ballerina assoluta* of the Royal Ballet. Acclaimed for roles in such ballets as *The Sleeping Beauty*, *Giselle*. Famed for partnership with Rudolf Nureyev.

Foochow, cap. of Fukien prov., SE China on R. Min. Pop. 900,000. Fishing port; steel, chemical mfg. One of 5 original treaty ports, formerly major tea exports. Educational centre, summer resort.

food, any substance taken into and assimilated by a plant or animal, which enables it to grow and repair tissue and provides source of energy. Human food should contain: protein, necessary for building and repairing tissue; carbohydrates and fats, which provide energy; minerals, eg iron, calcium and phosphorus; vitamins.

Food and Agriculture Organization (FAO), specialized agency of UN, estab. 1945; hq. in Rome. Aims to help nations increase efficiency of farming, forestry and fisheries. Operations incl. research and development, financial and technical assistance, information services.

food poisoning, sickness caused by eating food contaminated by bacteria, eg salmonellae, or by toxin produced by bacteria, eg staphylococci, present in food before cooking. Also caused by inorganic compounds, eg those of lead, or organic compounds present in certain animals and plants, eg toadstools.

foot, end part of leg on which person or animal stands or moves. Human foot has 26 bones: 14 phalanges in toes, 7 tarsal bones forming the heel and 5 metatarsals in the ball of foot.

foot, in measurement, British unit of length: 1 ft = 0.3048 m.

foot-and-mouth disease, contagious virus disease of cloven-footed animals eg cattle, deer. Characterized by fever and blisters in mouth and around hoofs. Controlled by slaughter and strict quarantine.

football, see AMERICAN FOOTBALL; ASSOCIATION FOOTBALL; AUSTRALIAN RULES FOOTBALL; GAELIC FOOTBALL; RUGBY FOOTBALL.

Forbes-Robertson, Sir Johnston (1853-1937), English actor-manager. Known as Hamlet and the Stranger in *The Passing of the Third-Floor Back* (1908).

force, in mechanics, agency which alters state of rest or motion of a body, producing acceleration in it. SI unit of force is the newton. By Newton's law of motion, force is proportional to rate of change of momentum of body.

Ford, Ford Madox, pseud. of Ford Madox Hueffer (1873-1939), English novelist, editor. Known for *The Good Soldier* (1915), *Parade's End* tetralogy (1924-8). Founded *English Review* (1908).

Ford, Gerald Rudolph, orig. Leslie Lynch King (1913-), American statesman, president (1974-7). Republican leader in House of Representatives (1965-73). Vice-president (1973-4) after Agnew's resignation, president after Nixon's. Pardoned Nixon of any criminal acts committed during his presidency. Defeated by Carter in 1976 election.

Ford, Henry (1863-1947), American industrialist. Pioneer automobile manufacturer, developed mass-production techniques. Ford Motor Company by c 1915 was world's largest automobile producer. Controversial in his anti-union policy. Founded (1936) philanthropic Ford Foundation with his son, Edsel.

Ford, John (1586-c 1640), English dramatist. Collaborated with Dekker in early plays. Best known for *'Tis Pity She's a Whore* (c 1627), *The Broken Heart* (c 1629), reflecting typical Jacobean concern with sexual corruption.

Ford, John, orig. Sean O'Fearna (1895-1973), American film director. From 1917 made over 125 feature films; known for human dramas in 1930s, *eg The Informer* (1935), but famous for westerns, from 1940s onwards, incl. *She Wore a Yellow Ribbon* (1949).

foreign aid, financial, technical and military assistance, usually given to another country at govt. level. Aims incl. reconstructing economies of countries after war, strengthening defences of allies, promoting economic growth of underdeveloped countries. US aid began with Lend-Lease (WWII), and European Recovery Program (Marshall Plan, 1948). UN, US, French and UK programmes aid underdeveloped nations.

foreign exchange, see EXCHANGE, FOREIGN.

Foreign Legion, French force of foreign mercenaries under French officers and senior NCOs. Formed by Louis Philippe mainly to keep the peace in Algeria, with hq. at Sidi-bel-Abbès. It withdrew after Algeria became independent.

Foreland, North and South, two chalk headlands of Kent, SE England. Former N of Broadstairs; latter NE of Dover. Both have lighthouses.

Forester, C[ecil] S[cott] (1899-1966), English novelist. Best known for "Horatio Hornblower' novels about British naval officer in Napoleonic wars. Other novels incl. *The African Queen* (1935), *The Ship* (1943).

forestry, science of planting, tending and managing timber as a crop. Trees are classified as coniferous, often called softwoods, and broadleaved, called hardwoods. Major producers of coniferous wood, used for construction, pulp and paper, are USSR, US, Canada, Sweden and Finland. Broad-leaved woods are important in Brazil, Indonesia, India, China.

Forfar, town of Tayside region, E Scotland. Pop. 11,000. Former royal burgh and co. town of Angus. Jute, linen mfg.

forgery, act of imitating documents, signatures, works of art, *etc*, with intent to deceive. In law, crime limited to written documents.

forget-me-not, any annual or perennial plant of widely-distributed genus *Myosotis*. Oval leaves with blue, white, or yellow flowers. Species incl. common forget-me-not, *M. arvensis* and water forget-me-not, *M. scorpioides*.

Forlì, city of Emilia-Romagna, NC Italy, cap. of Forlì prov. Pop. 106,000. Textiles, furniture. Roman *Forum Livii*; part of Papal States from 1504. Medieval cathedral, citadel.

formaldehyde (HCHO), pungent gas, produced by oxidation of methanol. Dissolves readily in water, 40% solution being known as formalin. Used as disinfectant and preservative, and in manufacture of plastics.

Forman, Milos (1932-), Czech film director. Known for acutely observed comedies, eg *The Firemen's Ball* (1968). Became famous for *One Flew Over the Cuckoo's Nest* (1976).

formic acid (HCOOH), colourless liquid, found in nettles and ant and bee stings. Manufactured from steam and carbon monoxide by catalysis. Used in dyeing.

Formosa, see TAIWAN.

formula, in chemistry, representation of nature and number of atoms which constitute single molecule of chemical compound by means of letters and figures. Structural formula indicates arrangement of atoms and nature of chemical bonds linking them. Empirical formula indicates only relative proportions of atoms and not necessarily their actual numbers.

Forrest, John Forrest, 1st Baron (1847-1918), Australian explorer, politician. Led expedition from Perth to Adelaide (1870). Served as surveyor-general, then as premier (1890-1901) of Western Australia.

Forster, E[dward] M[organ] (1879-1970), English author. Novels, eg *Where Angels Fear to Tread* (1905), *Howard's End* (1910), *A Passage to India* (1924), contrast spontaneity of paganism with deficiencies of British middle class sensibility. Later abandoned novels for essays on politics and criticism.

forsythia, *Forsythia suspensa*, deciduous shrub with olive-brown twigs and yellow flowers which appear before leaves. Hybrids widely cultivated.

Fortaleza, Atlantic port of NE Brazil, cap. of Ceará state. Pop. 859,000. Important sugar refining, flour milling; carnauba wax, cotton exports; textile, soap mfg. Founded 1609.

Fort-de-France, cap. of MARTINIQUE.

Fort George, river of WC Québec, Canada. Flows W 770 km (c 480 mi) into James Bay at Fort George trading post.

Forth, river of C Scotland. Flows 105 km (65 mi) from Central region into Firth of Forth. Ports incl. Grangemouth, Leith. Estuary crossed by rail bridge (1890), 2 road bridges (1936, 1964). Linked to W coast by disused Forth and Clyde Canal.

Fort Lamy, see NDJAMENA, Chad.

Fortuna, Roman goddess of fortune. Originally associated with fertility, later identified with Greek Tyche (chance). Represented with cornucopia and ship's rudder.

Fortunate Isles, in classical and Celtic legend, isls. in far west where the souls of favoured dead lived in paradise. Sometimes identified with Madeira or Canaries.

Fort William, see THUNDER BAY, Canada.

Fort William, town of Highland region, - NW Scotland, on Loch Linnhe. Pop. 4000. Near Ben Nevis; tourist centre. Aluminium works, distilling. Pulp mill nearby. Fort dismantled 1866.

Fort Worth, city of NE Texas, US; on Trinity R. tributary. Pop. 393,000. Railway jct.; grain, livestock market; meat packing, aircraft mfg., oil and gas industs, Army fort estab. 1847.

forum, market and meeting place of Roman towns, usually surrounded by public buildings and colonnades. Forum in Rome extended from Capitoline Hill almost to Colosseum and contained various triumphal arches, basilicas, temples.

fossil, remains or impressions of animal or plant life preserved in rocks of Earth's crust. Study of fossils is called palaeontology. Can aid dating and correlating of geological strata, and study of evolution. Common fossils incl. amber, ammonite, coal.

Foster, Stephen Collins (1826-64), American composer. Wrote many famous songs, principally about life in the American South, incl. 'Oh! Susannah', 'My Old Kentucky Home', 'Camptown Races', 'Swannee River', 'Jeannie with the Light Brown Hair'.

Foucault, Jean Bernard Léon (1819-68), French physicist. Calculated speed of light through air and other media by arrangement of stationary and rotating mirrors. Demonstrated rotation of Earth by turning of plane of oscillation of long pendulum.

Fouché, Joseph (1759-1820), French political leader. As Consulate's and Napoleon's police minister (1799-1802, 1804-10), ran spy network; discovered Cadoudal plot (royalist conspiracy, 1804) against Napoleon. Organized ruthless political and police system. Created duke of Otranto (1809); eventually exiled from France.

Fouquet, Nicolas, Marquis de Belle-Isle (1615-80), French statesman. Superintendent of finance (1653-61) during Louis XIV's minority, acquired great personal wealth by embezzlement. Imprisoned for life (1664) after trial beginning in 1661. Patron of La Fontaine, Molière.

Four-H or **4-H Clubs,** service of US Dept. of Agriculture for rural youth between ages of 9 and 19. Estab. (1914), derives name from aim to improve use of 'head, heart, hands and health'.

Fourier, [François Marie] Charles (1772-1837), French social philosopher. Evolved system of utopian communism in *Théorie des quatre mouvements* (1808). Aimed to reorganize society into small, self-sufficient cooperative units (phalansteries). Influenced American communities, eg Brook Farm.

Fourier, Jean Baptiste Joseph, Baron (1768-1830), French mathematician. Famed for *Théorie analytique de la chaleur*, in which he developed Fourier series (representation of functions by infinite series of sines and cosines). This method is of fundamental mathematical importance.

Fournier, Henri Alban, *see* ALAIN-FOURNIER.

four o'clock, *Mirabilis jalapa*, perennial plant of tropical America. Red, yellow or striped tubular flowers, up to 5 cm/2 in. long, which open in late afternoon. Cultivated as temperate garden plant. Also called marvel of Peru.

four stroke (cycle) engine, *see* INTERNAL COMBUSTION ENGINE.

Fourteen Points, *see* WILSON, THOMAS WOODROW.

Fourteenth Amendment, US con-

stitutional amendment (1868). Estab. basis of US citizenship and forbade states to curtail individual privileges, to deprive person of rights of life, liberty or property without 'due process of law', or to deny equal protection of law. Used extensively and broadly interpreted by Supreme Court, eg on issue of racial discrimination (1954).

fowl, domestic bird used for food, esp. chicken, turkey, goose, duck, pheasant.

Fowler, H[enry] W[atson] (1858-1933), English lexicographer. Compiler of *A Dictionary of Modern English Usage* (1926). Collaborated with his brother, F[rancis] G[eorge] **Fowler** (1870-1918), on *The King's English* (1906) and *The Concise Oxford Dictionary of Current English* (1911).

Fowles, John (1926-), English novelist. Works, eg *The Collector* (1963), *The French Lieutenant's Woman* (1969), combine erudition and experiment with form of novel.

Fox, Charles James (1749-1806), English statesman, orator. Disliked by George III, who secured his dismissal as lord of the treasury (1774). Opposed Lord North's policy in America. Demanded British abstention during French Revolution. Advocated political rights for dissenters and Catholics; as foreign secretary (1806), urged abolition of slave trade (achieved 1807).

Fox, George (1624-91), English religious leader. Founded SOCIETY OF FRIENDS (Quakers), spreading doctrine in journeys to Scotland, North America, Holland. *Journal* (pub. 1694) was edited by William Penn.

fox, wild carnivore of dog family, common in N hemisphere. Nocturnal predator, diet of small animals, fruit; lives in burrows. European red fox, *Vulpes vulpes*, red-brown above, white below; hunted for fur and sport. American red fox, *V. fulva*, is related species.

Foxe, John (1516-87), English Protestant clergyman. Famous for *Actes and Monuments* (1563), known as *Book of Martyrs*, celebrating piety and heroism of Protestants martyred under Mary Tudor.

foxglove, *Digitalis purpurea*, perennial of figwort family, native to W and C Europe. Tapering spikes with purple, pink or white, bell-shaped flowers. Popular garden varieties developed. Leaves yield poisonous alkaloid, digitalin, used in medicine.

fox terrier, small terrier with smooth or wire-haired coat, originally bred for chasing foxes from hiding. Stands 38 cm/15 in. at shoulder.

Foyle, river of Northern Ireland. Flows through former Co. Tyrone to Atlantic via Lough Foyle (navigable inlet *c* 24 km/15 mi long), below Londonderry. Fishing.

f.p.s. system of units, British system of physical units based on fundamental units of foot, pound and second.

fractions, in mathematics, *see* RATIONAL NUMBER.

Fragonard, Jean Honoré (1732-1806), French painter. Painted frivolous, gallant and sentimental subjects which typified court life of Louis XV; career was ruined by the Revolution. Works incl. *The Swing*.

France, Anatole, pseud. of Jacques Anatole François Thibault (1844-1924), French author. Arbiter of French taste as literary editor of *Le Temps* in late 19th cent. Novels incl. *Le Crime de Sylvestre Bonnard* (1881), political satires *L'Ile des pingouins* (1908), *La Révolte des anges* (1914). Awarded Nobel Prize for Literature (1921).

France, republic of W Europe. Area *c* 547,000 sq km (211,000 sq mi); pop. 52,915,000; cap. Paris. Language: French. Religion: RC. Comprises 95 admin. depts., incl. Corsica. Mountainous regions incl. Vosges, Jura (E), Alps (SE), Massif Central (SC), Pyrenees (SW); fertile lowlands in Aquitaine, Paris Basin. Main rivers Seine, Loire, Rhône. Mainly agric. until recently, esp. cereals, livestock, vineyards. Indust. centred on NE coal and iron ore deposits (Nord, Lorraine). Tourism, esp. along S coast. Exports wines, luxury goods, motor cars. Roman prov. of Gaul until 5th cent.; Frankish kingdom estab. 9th cent. under Charlemagne, consolidated 10th-14th cent. by Capet dynasty. Regained much territ. from England in Hundred Years War; Louis XIV defeated in War of Spanish Succession. Revolution (1789) and Napoleonic Wars followed by brief restorations of monarchy, succession of republics. Fifth Republic created 1958 by De Gaulle. Suffered heavy losses in WWI, German occupation (Vichy regime) in WWII. Retains close ties with former overseas possessions, formed French Community (1958). Member of EEC.

Francesca, Piero della, *see* PIERO DELLA FRANCESCA.

Franche-Comté, region and former prov. of E France, hist. cap. Besançon (Dôle until 1678). Incl. parts of Jura, Vosges; forests, agric. esp. dairying. United in 9th cent. as Free County of Burgundy, part of Holy Roman Empire from 1034; under Spanish Habsburgs in 16th-17th cent. Ceded to France (1678).

Francis I (1768-1835), emperor of Austria (1804-35). Succeeded father Leopold II as Holy Roman emperor (1792). Unsuccessful in wars with France (1792-1809). After assuming Austrian title, forced to dissolve Holy Roman Empire (1806). Daughter, Marie Louise, married (1810) Napoleon. Joined Allies against Napoleon (1813); presided over Congress of Vienna.

Francis I (1708-65), Holy Roman emperor (1745-65). Married MARIA THERESA (1736), to whom he left exercise of power. Ceded duchy of Lorraine to STANISLAUS Leszczynski (1735) after War of Polish Succession. Father of Joseph II, Leopold II, Marie Antoinette.

Francis I (1494-1547), king of France (1515-47). Succeeded father-in-law, Louis XII. Continually at war in Italy with Emperor Charles V, who had won imperial election over Francis (1519). Campaigns largely unsuccessful; captured at Pavia (1525). Renaissance patron, invited Leonardo da Vinci, Benvenuto Cellini to France.

Francis, Duc d'Alençon (c 1554-84), French prince, youngest son of Henry II. Suitor of Elizabeth I of England. Invited to rule Low Countries by William the Silent (1580), forced to leave (1583). His death led to Henry IV's succession.

Francis Borgia, St (1510-72),

Spanish Jesuit leader. Member of Borgia family. Renounced his duchy (Candia) and joined Jesuits under St Ignatius Loyola. General of Order (1565-72); endowed Roman College, promoted foreign missions and edited Jesuit rule.

Francis Ferdinand (1863-1914), Austrian archduke. Heir apparent to Francis-Joseph; assassinated with wife in Sarajevo by Gavrilo Princip, Serbian nationalist. Death led to Austrian ultimatum to Serbia and outbreak of WWI.

Franciscans or **Grey Friars, in** RC church, members of several orders following the rule of ST FRANCIS OF ASSISI, incl. Capuchins and Conventuals. Noted missionaries, educators and preachers. Famous members incl. St Anthony of Padua.

Francis Joseph or **Franz Josef** (1830-1916), emperor of Austria (1848-1916). Succeeded on abdication of his uncle, Ferdinand. Subdued independence movements in Hungary, Sardinia (1849). Lost Lombardy (1859), Venetia (1866) to Italy. Reorganized empire into Austro-Hungarian Monarchy to placate Hungarian nationalists, becoming king of Hungary (1867). Reign saw growth of Slav nationalism in empire.

Francis of Assisi, St, orig. Giovanni di Bernardone (c 1182-1226), Italian friar. Attracted following by preaching, founded Franciscan order of friars in Rome (1209); its rule based on brotherhood, absolute poverty and concern for poor and sick. Many stories told of his simple life, gentleness with animals.

Francis of Sales, St (1567-1622), French Jesuit preacher. Bishop of Geneva (1602); converted many Huguenots. With St Jane Frances of Chantal, founded Order of the Visitation for women unable to undergo the austerity of the established orders.

Francis Xavier, St (1506-52), Basque Jesuit missionary, called 'Apostle to the Indies'. With ST IGNATIUS OF LOYOLA, founded Society of Jesus (Jesuits). Estab. missions in India, Japan and China, where he died.

francium (Fr), extremely unstable radioactive element of alkali metal group; at. no. 87, mass no. of most stable isotope 223. Discovered (1939) as decay product of actinium.

Franck, César Auguste (1822-90), Belgian composer. Lived mostly in Paris as teacher and organist. Leader of 19th cent. French Romantic school. Best known for *Symphony in D minor* and organ works.

Franco [Bahamonde], Francisco (1892-1975), Spanish military and political leader. Rose to power before SPANISH CIVIL WAR, led Fascist revolt with German and Italian support, becoming head of insurgent govt. (1936). Dissolved all political parties but FALANGE and began authoritarian rule. Despite agreements with Hitler, Mussolini, kept Spain neutral in WWII. Restored monarchy by law of succession (1947), retaining post of regent until his death. Chose JUAN CARLOS as successor and king.

Franconia (Franken), hist. region of SC West Germany, extending E from Rhine along Main valley. Cities incl. Frankfurt, Speyer, Würzburg. Medieval duchy, divided (939) into W (Rhenish), E. Name revived 1837, applied to 3 divisions of Bavaria. Homeland of Franconian (Salian) dynasty.

Franco-Prussian War (1870-1), conflict between German states and France. Napoleon III provoked into declaring war by Bismarck's EMS DISPATCH. France lost decisive battle of Sedan, Napoleon captured. French resistance continued briefly, peace concluded with Treaty of Versailles (1871); Paris Commune held out against Prussian siege until suppressed by French army. Results of war incl. German unification under Prussia, French loss of Alsace-Lorraine, estab. of Third Republic in France.

Frank, Anne (1929-c 1945), Dutch author of *The Diary of a Young Girl* (1947), recording experiences while hiding from Nazis in Amsterdam warehouse 1942-44. Died in Belsen concentration camp.

Frankfort, cap. of Kentucky, US; on Kentucky R. Pop. 22,000. Whisky distilling, trade.

Frankfurt (-am-Main), city of W West Germany, on R. Main. Pop. 658,000. Transport, commercial centre; publishing, chemicals, vehicles. Trade fairs held from c 1240. Founded 1st cent. by Romans; free imperial city 1372-1806. Seat of German Confederation (1815-66); treaty ending Franco-Prussian War signed here (1871). Cathedral, 15th cent. town hall (*Römer*). Birthplace of Goethe.

frankincense, aromatic resin from NE African trees of genus *Boswellia*. Used by ancient Egyptians and Jews as incense in religious rites.

Franklin, Benjamin (1706-90), American statesman, scientist, writer. His common sense and wit were popularized in his *Poor Richard's Almanack* (1732-57). Colonial leader, presented plan for union at Albany Congress (1754), helped draft Declaration of Independence (1776). Ambassador in Europe (1776-85), negotiated French recognition of new republic (1778) and peace with Britain (1781-3). Active in Federal Constitutional Congress (1787). Among many scientific experiments, flew kite in thunderstorm, proving presence of electricity in lightning; invented lightning rod.

Franklin, Sir John (1786-1847), English naval officer, explorer. Led 2 expeditions to Canadian Arctic (1819-22, 1825-7). Searched for Northwest Passage (1845), but entire expedition was lost; rescue parties found evidence that ships had become ice-bound.

Franklin, admin. dist. of N Northwest Territs., Canada. Area 1,422,565 sq km (549,253 sq mi); pop. 8000. Comprises Arctic archipelago (c 80 isls.); Melville and Boothia penins. Has Baffin Isl. National Park. Fur trapping; Eskimo pop. Named after British explorer, Sir John Franklin.

Franks, group of Germanic tribes who settled along lower Rhine in 3rd cent. Salian Franks invaded Gaul in 4th-5th cents. under their leader Clovis, who accepted Christianity and united all the Franks. Frankish empire expanded to incl. much of France, W Germany, Switzerland, Austria and parts of Italy by 9th cent.

Franz Ferdinand, see FRANCIS FERDINAND.

Franz Josef, see FRANCIS JOSEPH.

Franz Josef Land, Arctic archipelago of USSR, N of Novaya Zemlya. Comprises c 80 uninhabited isls., largely ice covered; site of meteorological stations. Discovered (1873) by Austrian expedition, annexed by USSR (1926).

Frasch process, method of mining sulphur by pumping superheated steam into underground deposits; molten sulphur is forced to surface by compressed air.

Fraser, Dawn (1937-), Australian swimmer. Won 100m freestyle at 3 successive Olympics (1956, 1960, 1964). Held 27 individual world records during career (1956-64).

Fraser, [John] Malcolm (1930-), Australian politician, PM (1975-). Became leader of Liberal Party (1975). Appointed PM of interim govt. (Nov. 1975) by governor-general, Sir John Kerr, replacing Whitlam's Labor admin. Won ensuing election.

Fraser, Simon (1776-1862), Canadian explorer and fur trader, b. US. Entered service of North West Co. (1792); explored S Canadian Rockies from 1805, estab. trading posts. Reached Pacific (1808) via Fraser R.

Fraser, chief river of British Columbia, Canada. Rises in E Rocky Mts.; flows NW, then SW 1370 km (c 850 mi) to Str. of Georgia, S of Vancouver. Salmon; scenic canyon in lower course. Navigable to Yale c 130 km (c 80 mi) from mouth. Named after Canadian explorer, Simon Fraser.

Fraserburgh, town of Grampian

region, NE Scotland. Pop. 11,000. Major herring fishing port; offshore oil service industs.

fraud, in law, intentional deception to cause person to give up property or other legal right. If contract is based on fraud, injured party may void it and claim damages.

Fray Bentos, port of SW Uruguay, on Uruguay R. Pop. 21,000. Commercial, indust. centre; has important meat packing, canning industs.

Frazer, Sir James George (1854-1941), Scottish classicist, anthropologist. Best known for *The Golden Bough* (1890), an exhaustive study of magic, superstition, primitive religion.

Frederick I [Barbarossa] (*c* 1122-90), German king (1152-90), Holy Roman emperor (1155-90). As king, pacified Germany. When emperor, conducted 4 Italian campaigns against Lombard League and papacy. At first successful, was defeated at Legnano (1176), conceded Lombard League's demands at Peace of Constance (1183); excommunicated by Pope Alexander III. Drowned in Cilicia on Third Crusade.

Frederick II (1194-1250), Holy Roman emperor (1220-50). Received (1197) Sicily from Pope Innocent III. Crusade, really state visit, resulted in cession of Jerusalem, Nazareth, Bethlehem to Christians, and his crowning (1229) as king of Jerusalem. Latter gave rise to long conflict with papacy, and his excommunication (1245).

Frederick IX (1899-1972), king of Denmark (1947-72). Married Princess Ingrid of Sweden (1935).

Succeeded by his daughter Margarethe.

Frederick VI (1768-1839), king of Norway (1808-14), of Denmark (1808-39). Allied himself with Napoleon after British attack on Copenhagen (1807). As result of peace settlement, lost kingdom of Norway to Sweden.

Frederick I (1657-1713), king of Prussia (1701-13). Succeeded father Frederick William as elector of Brandenburg (1688). Became 1st king of Prussia.

Frederick [II] the Great (1712-86), king of Prussia (1740-86). Initiated (1740) War of Austrian Succession against Maria Theresa, securing Silesia. His leadership and military genius in wars during rule made Prussia a leading European power. Further enlarged kingdom through 1st partition of Poland (1772). Prolific writer, composer, patron of arts, had noted association with Voltaire. Became symbol of German nationalism.

Frederick III (1831-88), emperor of Germany (1888). Son of William I. A liberal, often disagreed with Bismarck's aggressive policies. Died 3 months after accession.

Frederick Barbarossa, see FREDERICK I.

Fredericksburg, town of E Virginia, US; on Rappahannock R. Pop. 14,000. Settled 1671; Civil War battleground (Chancellorsville nearby). Has many hist. buildings.

Frederick the Winter King (1596-1632), king of Bohemia (1619-20). Elector palatine (1610-20), chosen by Bohemian Protestants to replace Ferdinand II as king of Bohemia.

Defeated at White Mountain (1620), lost Bohemia.

Frederick William (1620-88), elector of Brandenburg (1640-88), known as the 'Great Elector'. Rebuilt army and territ. after Thirty Years War, enlarging possessions at Peace of Westphalia (1648). Laid foundation of powerful Prussian state.

Frederick William I (1688-1740), king of Prussia (1713-40). Laid foundations of efficient admin. and army; avoided wars, built up treasury by careful economy. Father of Frederick the Great, whose talent he did not appreciate.

Frederick William III (1770-1840), king of Prussia (1797-1840). Tried to remain neutral in Napoleonic Wars. Defeated by Napoleon at Jena (1806); forced to accept Treaty of Tilsit (1807), which greatly reduced his territ. Later advised by Hardenberg, Scharnhorst, rebelled against Napoleon's domination (1813-14).

Frederick William IV (1795-1861), king of Prussia (1840-61). At first, gave in to 1848 revolutionaries' demands, later crushed them. Belief in divine right to rule led him to refuse offer of imperial crown from Frankfurt parliament (1849). Mental disturbance (1857) led to regency of his brother William I.

Fredericton, cap. of New Brunswick, Canada; on St John R. Pop. 25,000. Timber, leather products. Founded by United Empire Loyalists (1783); became cap. 1788.

free enterprise, economic practice in which relationship of supply and demand is allowed to regulate economy without govt. control. See LAISSER-FAIRE.

Freemasonry, principles and rituals of Free and Accepted Masons, international secret society practising brotherliness, charity and mutual aid. Masons claim roots in ancient times but order prob. derives from English and Scottish fraternities of stonemasons and cathedral builders in Middle Ages. Organized in self-governing national authorities known as grand lodges; first opened in London (1717), others in all European countries by 1800. Members must be male and believe in a higher being.

free port, port or zone within port free of customs regulation (see TARIFF). Estab. in late Middle Ages, eg by Hanseatic League. Present ones incl. Hong Kong, Singapore, parts of most international airports.

freesia, genus of bulbous plants of iris family, native to South Africa. Fragrant, usually white or yellow, funnel-shaped flowers.

freethinkers, see DEISTS.

Freetown, cap. of Sierra Leone, on Sierra Leone Penin. Pop. 179,000. Admin., commercial centre; good natural harbour, exports diamonds, iron ore, palm products. Settled (1787-92) by freed slaves. Cap. of British colony of Sierra Leone from 1808.

free trade, international trade conducted without restrictions, eg quotas on imports, protective tariffs, export bounties. Advocates hold that system allows each country to specialize in goods it can produce most cheaply. European Economic Community aims to abolish protective tariffs between members.

free will, in theology, doctrine that man can choose between good and evil independently of the will of God. Problematic when held alongside belief in God's omniscience. Aquinas argued that foreknowledge did not imply intervention. Calvin held the opposite belief, ie predestination. In philosophy, concept of free will is denied by DETERMINISM.

freeze drying, technique of drying food, vaccines, etc, by rapid freezing, followed by removal of frozen water by evaporation at low temperature and pressure.

freezing, conversion of liquid into solid form. For given pressure, freezing occurs at fixed temperature; this temperature may be lowered by dissolving substances in fluid.

Frege, Gottlob (1848-1925), German philosopher, mathematician. Founder of modern symbolic logic. Held all mathematics to be derivable from logical principles, and all verbal concepts expressible as symbolic functions.

Freiburg, see FRIBOURG, Switzerland.

Frèiburg (-im-Breisgau), city of SW West Germany, on W edge of Black Forest. Pop. 168,000. Textiles, paper mfg. Held by Austria 1368-1805. Scene of battle (1644) between French and Bavarians. Gothic cathedral, univ. (1457).

Fremantle, city of SW Western Australia, at mouth of Swan R. Pop. 25,000. Outport for Perth, exports oil, wheat, wool, minerals. Founded 1829.

Frémont, John Charles (1813-90), American explorer, politician. Explored Rocky Mts., Oregon, Nevada, California. Helped free California from Mexico (1846); governor of Arizona Territ. (1878-83).

French, John Denton Pinkstone, Earl of Ypres (1852-1925), British general. During Boer War, captured Bloemfontein. Chief of Imperial General Staff (1911-14), he commanded the British Expeditionary Force to France (1915). Lord-lieutenant of Ireland (1918-21).

French, Romance language belonging to Italic branch of Indo-European family. One of official languages of United Nations. Developed from vernacular Latin, with Celtic and Germanic elements in vocabulary. Historically divided into Old French (9th-13th cent.), Middle French (14th-16th cent.), Modern French (17th cent.-). French Academy aims to preserve language against foreign influences, slang.

French and Indian War (1754-60), North - American conflict between Britain and France, part of SEVEN YEARS WAR. Aided by Iroquois Indians, British attacked French forts and cities, finally taking Québec by victory on Plains of Abraham (1759). Treaty of Paris (1763) ended French claims to Canada.

French Community, political union (estab. 1958) comprising France, its overseas depts. and territs., and 6 independent African states: Central African Empire, Chad, Congo (Brazzaville), Gabon, Malagasy Republic, Senegal. Promotes economic, defensive and cultural cooperation. Originally incl. all former French colonies in Africa; most withdrew in 1962.

French Equatorial Africa, former French overseas territ. Comprised

present-day CENTRAL AFRICAN EM-
PIRE, CHAD, People's Republic of the
CONGO, GABON. Estab. 1910, cap.
Brazzaville; dissolved 1958.

French Guiana, overseas dept. of
France, NE South America. Area
91,000 sq km (35,135 sq mi); pop.
62,000; cap. Cayenne. Rises from
Atlantic coast to tropical forests and
mountains of Inini territ. Largely
undeveloped; main exports gold,
timber, rum. Site of former penal
colonies incl. Devil's Isl. Became
French dept. 1946.

French Guinea, see GUINEA.

French horn, brass instrument of
coiled tubing, whose bore widens
into a flared bell-shape. Well-known
concertos have been written for it by
Mozart and R. Strauss.

French India, group of 5 former
French settlements in India, incl.
Pondicherry on E coast, Mahe on W
coast. All transferred to India by
1954.

French Polynesia, overseas territ.
of France, in S Pacific Ocean.
Comprises Gambier, Marquesas,
Society, Tuamotu, Tubuai isl.
groups. Area 4000 sq km (1550 sq
mi); pop. 132,000; cap. Papeete
(Tahiti). Produce fruit, copra, pearl
shell; tourist indust. Acquired by
France during 19th cent.

French Revolution, political uprising, begun 1789. Product of 18th
cent. liberalism and assertion of
capitalist class against outdated
feudal system. Immediate cause was
state's vast debt. To raise money,
LOUIS XVI convened ESTATES-
GENERAL (May, 1789), which demanded sweeping political, social
and fiscal reforms and declared itself
National Assembly. Louis yielded,
but dismissal of NECKER led to mob's
storming of Bastille. National Guard
organized, feudal privileges abolished, and commune estab. as govt.
of Paris. Louis imprisoned (1791)
after attempt to flee country, forced
to accept new constitution. Republican GIRONDISTS and extremists
controlled legislative assembly; their
desire to spread revolutionary ideas
and Austrian threats to restore
Louis to absolute power served as
pretext for FRENCH REVOLUTIONARY
WARS. After abortive insurrections,
National Convention (estab. 1792)
abolished monarchy, set up First
Republic (Sept. 1792), convicted and
executed Louis for treason (Jan.
1793). Royalist backlash led to
REIGN OF TERROR. DIRECTORY estab.
1795; corrupt admin. led to
Napoleon's coup d'état of 18
Brumaire and Consulate (1799).

**French Revolutionary Calen-
dar,** official calendar of France
(1793-1805), dividing year into 12
months of 30 days, with 5 or 6 leap
days. Month was divided into 3
weeks of 10 days, day into 10 hours.
Computed from 22 Sept. 1792, date
of overthrow of monarchy.

French Revolutionary Wars,
general European conflict (1792-
1802), precipitated by French Revolution. Austrian and Prussian
intention to restore Louis XVI to
former power, and French desire to
spread revolution throughout
Europe, led France to declare war on
Austria. After early reverses, France
invaded Germany, Netherlands and
Italy (where Napoleon came to
prominence). By beginning of 19th
cent., Austria and its Russian allies
had withdrawn from war, leaving

21

Britain alone against France. Short-lived peace (1802) followed by Napoleonic Wars (1803-15). *See* NAPOLEON I.

French Southern and Antarctic Territories, French overseas territ. Area 410,000 sq km (158,000 sq mi). Formed 1955 from Adélie Land (Antarctica) and Kerguelen, Amsterdam, St Paul and Crozet isls. (Indian Ocean).

French Sudan, *see* MALI.

French West Africa, former French overseas territ. Comprised present-day BENIN, GUINEA, IVORY COAST, MALI, MAURITANIA, NIGER, SENEGAL, UPPER VOLTA. Estab. 1895, cap. Dakar; dissolved 1958.

Freneau, Philip Morin (1752-1832), American poet, journalist. Known for anti-British verse, *eg* The British Prison Ship (1781), nature lyrics incl. 'The Wild Honeysuckle', 'The Indian Burying Ground'.

frequency, in physics, number of periodic oscillations, vibrations or waves per unit of time; usually measured in cycles per second. For wave motion, frequency equals wave velocity divided by wavelength.

fresco, method of wall-painting with watercolours on ground of wet plaster. Technique was perfected in Italy in 16th cent.; Raphael's frescoes in Stanze of Vatican are esp. fine.

Fresnel, Augustin Jean (1788-1827), French physicist. His investigations on diffraction of light and double refraction gave support to transverse wave theory of light. Designed lenses to replace mirrors in lighthouses.

Fresno, town of SC California, US.

Pop. 166,000. Agric. produce esp. raisins; fruit drying, packing.

Freud, Sigmund (1856-1939), Austrian psychiatrist, founder of PSYCHO-ANALYSIS. His work on hysteria led him to believe that symptoms were caused by early trauma, and were expressions of repressed sexual energy. Devised 'free association' technique and dream interpretation to discover repressed experiences. Emphasized importance of infantile sexuality in personality's development in later life. Influenced Jung and Adler, who later opposed him. Works incl. *The Interpretation of Dreams* (1900), *The Psychopathology of Everyday Life* (1904), *The Ego and the Id* (1923).

Freya, in Norse myth, goddess of love, marriage and fertility. Wife of Odin, her worship became merged with that of FRIGG.

Fribourg (Ger. *Freiburg*), town of W Switzerland, cap. of Fribourg canton. Pop. 40,000. Chocolate mfg. Cathedral (13th cent.); univ. (1889).

friction, force opposing motion of one surface over another; heat produced by friction accounts for inefficiency of machinery.

Friedman, Milton (1912-), American economist. A leading monetarist, he rejected Keynesian thesis that govt. spending leads to economic improvement; advocated strict control of money supply. Awarded Nobel Prize for Economics (1976).

Friedrich, Caspar David (1774-1840), German romantic painter. Specialized in melancholy forest and mountain scenes, portrayed in strange light of dusk or moonlight.

Works incl. *Cross in the Mountains* (1807).

Friedrichshafen, town of SW West Germany, on L. Constance. Pop. 39,000. Port, resort; tanning. Former site of Zeppelin plant, heavily bombed in WWII.

Friendly Islands, see TONGA.

Friesland (anc. *Frisia*), prov. of N Netherlands. Area 3432 sq km (1325 sq mi); cap. Leeuwarden. Incl. W Frisian Isls. Noted for Friesian cattle. Distinct dialect, still widely spoken. Medieval region under counts of Holland, joined United Provs. 1579. East Friesland (N West Germany) separate from 1454.

frigate, originally a narrow-hulled oared sailing vessel in the Mediterranean. In the 18th cent. a full-rigged warship of up to 50 guns. In WWII a ship specially designed for convoy and anti-submarine work, superseding the destroyer.

frigate bird, any of Fregatidae family of large tropical seabirds with webbed feet, large hooked beak. Frequently robs other birds of their food.

Frigg or **Frigga**, in Germanic myth, mother goddess, wife of Odin, mother of Balder. Worshipped as deity of household and love. See FREYA.

Frisian Islands, offshore group of *c* 30 isls. in North Sea, stretching from Wadden Zee to Jutland. Comprise W Frisians (Netherlands), E Frisians (West Germany), N Frisians (Denmark, West Germany). Low-lying, sandy; cattle, fishing.

Friuli-Venezia Giulia, region of NE Italy. Alps in N, fertile plain in S; chief city Venice, cap. Trieste. Part (Istria) ceded to Yugoslavia 1947.

Frobisher, Sir Martin (*c* 1535-94), English navigator. Made 3 unsuccessful attempts (1567-8) to find Northwest Passage; discovered Frobisher Bay. Joined Drake in West Indies expedition (1585). Knighted for part in defeating Spanish Armada (1588).

Froebel, Friedrich Wilhelm August (1782-1852), German educator. Founded kindergarten system, estab. 1st kindergarten in 1837, 1st kindergarten training school in 1849. His theories had strong spiritual element; stressed pleasurable environment. Works incl. *The Education of Man* (1826).

frog, tailless amphibian of order Anura. Mainly aquatic or semi-aquatic, with webbed feet; arboreal forms have enlarged webbed hands, feet. Sticky tongue used to seize prey. Young, known as tadpoles, have fish-like form. Species incl. common frog, *Rana temporaria*; hind legs of edible frog, *R. esculenta*, eaten in France, S US.

frogbit, *Hydrocharis morsus-ranae*, floating pond weed with kidney-shaped leaves, white flowers. Sinks to bottom during winter. Common in N Europe.

froghopper, any of Cercopidae family of leaping insects. Larvae enveloped in froth (cuckoo-spit) secreted from anus; often seen on plants. Also called spittle bug.

Froissart, Jean (*c* 1338-*c* 1410), French chronicler, poet, traveller. Wrote *Chronicles*, lively and invaluable, though sometimes inaccurate, record of Europe 1325-1400, covering 1st half of Hundred Years War.

Fromm, Erich (1900-), American

psychoanalyst, writer, b. Germany. Works, dealing with alienation of people in indust. society, incl. *Escape from Freedom* (1941), *The Sane Society* (1955).

Fronde, name given to French civil wars during Louis XIV's minority (1648-53). First, caused by quarrels between Parlement of Paris and royal authority over taxation, was suppressed by MAZARIN and CONDÉ. Second, caused by attempt of nobles to limit power of Mazarin, was led by Condé. Condé, allied with Spain, continued fighting until 1659 although Fronde had collapsed by 1653.

front, in meteorology, line at Earth's surface marking boundary between cold and warm air masses. As warm air is lighter, it ascends the frontal plane or surface above cold air. Cold front results from advancing cold air mass; warm front from advancing warm air mass. Associated with DEPRESSIONS.

Frontenac, Louis de Buade, Comte de (*c* 1622-98), French governor of New France in Canada (1672-82, 1689-98). Helped promote fur trade, exploration. Authority disputed by Jesuits; recalled to France (1682). Reappointed 1689 to counter Iroquois aggression.

Frost, Robert Lee (1874-1963), American poet. Lyrics dealing with New England life incl. 'Mending Wall', 'The Death of the Hired Man', 'Stopping by Woods on a Snowy Evening'. Most famous verse in *North of Boston* (1914), *West-running Brook* (1928). Known for clear, simple, moral poetry, close to rural life and nature, which can also express irony, bitterness, despair.

frost, weather condition occurring when air temperature falls to 0 °C or below. Exists in 2 main forms: (1) hoarfrost, produced when water vapour crystallizes directly as white coating on ground; (2) ground or black frost, produced when sub-zero temperatures cause water to freeze. Latter type important in growing season available to crops, and in weathering tool.

frostbite, damage to skin and tissues resulting from exposure to intense cold. Caused by lack of blood circulation and formation of ice crystals; nose, hands, feet, and ears most often affected.

fructose or **fruit sugar**, crystalline sugar found in ripe fruit and honey.

fruit, mature, fertilized ovary of flower, varying in form from dandelion tufted seed. to cultivated apple. Edible fruit classified as tree, *eg* apple, orange; bush, *eg* strawberry, blackcurrant; stone, *eg* plum; pip, *eg* grape; berry, *eg* raspberry; and nut, *eg* walnut.

fruit bat, any of suborder Megachiroptera of large fruit-eating bats of Old World tropics. Species incl. FLYING FOX.

fruit fly, insect of Trypetidae family, whose larvae bore into fruit, other plants. Mediterranean fruit fly, *Ceratitis capitata*, is serious pest of citrus fruit.

Frunze, city of USSR, cap. of Kirghiz SSR. Pop. 452,000. Centre of fertile agric. region; produces machinery, textiles. Renamed (1925) in honour of revolutionary hero M. V. Frunze.

Fry, Christopher (1907-), English dramatist. Known for witty verse plays, *eg The Lady's Not for*

Burning (1949), *A Phoenix Too Frequent* (1949), *Venus Observed* (1950).

Fry, Elizabeth, née Gurney (1780-1845), English prison reformer, philanthropist. A Quaker, she improved conditions for women in Newgate and other prisons.

Fry, Roger Eliot (1866-1934), English art critic, painter. Arranged influential 'Manet and the Post-Impressionists' exhibition (1910) which introduced post-impressionist art into Britain. Writings on art incl. *Vision and Design* (1920) and *Cézanne* (1927).

Frye, Northrop (1912-), Canadian literary critic. Best known for *Anatomy of Criticism* (1957), advocating a scientific theory of criticism.

Fuad I, orig. Ahmed Fuad Pasha (1868-1936), king of Egypt (1922-36). Ruled as sultan (1917-22) before becoming king when British protect. in Egypt ended. Autocracy opposed in parliament by anti-colonialist Wafd party.

Fuchs, Sir Vivian Ernest (1908-), English geologist, explorer. Directed Falkland Isls. Dependencies Survey (1950-5). Led, with Sir Edmund Hillary, Commonwealth Trans-Antarctic Expedition (1957-8), 1st overland crossing of Antarctic.

fuchsia, genus of colourful shrubs of willow herb family with red or purple flowers. Most species native to tropical America. Widely cultivated ornamental.

fuel cell, cell which produces electricity by oxidation of fuel. Simplest type uses hydrogen and oxygen, with catalytic electrodes. Used in space flights.

Fugger, Jacob (1459-1525), German merchant, member of great Augsburg trading family. Brought family fortune to height through near monopolies in mining and trading of copper, mercury, silver. Owned fleets, vast land holdings, great houses. Helped finance Maximilian I, and to secure election of Charles V. Family patronized arts, learning. Fortune drained after his death by support for Habsburg wars.

fugue, piece of music in a set number of parts or voices, each of which follows separate yet interrelated melodic line. A fugue begins with each voice stating a theme in turn but thereafter is not confined to a set pattern. J.S. Bach achieved highest development of fugue composition.

Fujiyama or **Fuji-san,** highest mountain of Japan, in C Honshu isl.; alt. 3776 m (12,390 ft). A dormant volcano, last active in 1707. Place of pilgrimage, sacred to Japanese.

Fukien, prov. of SE China on Formosa Str. Area 119,000 sq km (46,000 sq mi); pop. (est.) 17,000,000; cap. Foochow. Mountainous, forested; lumber resources. Formerly great tea exports, famous preserved fruit. Troop bases because of strategic proximity of Taiwan.

Fukuoka, seaport of Japan, on Kyushu isl. Pop. 853,000. Shipbuilding, textile mfg. Scene of attempted invasions by Kublai Khan (1274, 1281).

Fulani, pastoralists of W Africa, found throughout area between Upper Nile and Senegal. Moslem; reached height of power in 19th cent., during which they conquered Hausa states of Nigeria.

Fulda, town of EC West Germany, on R. Fulda. Pop. 45,000. Agric. market, textiles. Christianity spread throughout C Germany from abbey (744); St Boniface buried in cathedral.

Fuller, Richard Buckminster (1895–), American architect, engineer. Constructor of geodesic dome, spherical structure of light but extremely strong triangular members. Exponent of *Dymaxion* principle of maximum effectiveness with minimum outlay of materials.

Fuller, Roy Broadbent (1912–), English poet. Works, eg *Counterparts* (1954), *Brutus's Orchard* (1957), often reflect discontent with English society. Also wrote novels, eg *The Ruined Boys* (1959).

fulmar, *Fulmarus glacialis*, large grey seabird of petrel family of Arctic and subarctic regions. Visits land only to breed.

Fulton, Robert (1765–1815), American engineer, inventor. Built *Clermont* (1807), 1st successful steamship in American waters.

fumitory, any plant of Fumariaceae family, esp. widely distributed species *Fumaria officinalis* with fernlike leaves and pink, spurred flowers. Formerly used in medicine.

Funchal, cap. of Madeira Isls., Portugal. Pop. 100,000. Commercial centre; port, exports Madeira wines; tourism.

function, in modern mathematics, rule which associates to each member of a set a member of another set. More familiarly, functions are expressed by formulae which express variation of 1 quantity (dependent variable) in terms of variation of other quantities (independent variables).

functionalism, in art and architecture, 20th cent. principle emphasizing unity of form and purpose, and rejecting all inessential ornament. Prominent exponents of the style were members of Bauhaus school and Le Corbusier.

fundamentalism, conservative, mainly Protestant, religious movement of 20th cent. Upholds traditional interpretations of Bible against modern textual criticism and scientific theory (eg Darwinism). Movement organized in 1909, esp. influential in US.

Fundy, Bay of, arm of N Atlantic, SE Canada; 270 km (c 170 mi) long; separates New Brunswick from Nova Scotia penin. Has tides up to 12-15 m (40-50 ft) high.

Fünen, see FYN, Denmark.

fungus, any of many plants of division Thallophyta. Lacking CHLOROPHYLL, they depend on organic matter for growth. Saprophytes feed on dead organisms, parasites on living. Reproduction by SPORE rather than seed. Incl. mushrooms, toadstools, yeasts.

fur, soft thick hair covering the skin of many mammals, eg sable, mink, ermine, chinchilla. Valued for both warm and luxurious clothing. Fur trade encouraged exploration of Asia and North America (17th-19th cents.). In Canada, Hudson's Bay Co. was largely instrumental in opening up country during the pursuit of beaver pelts.

Furies, see EUMENIDES.

Furneaux Islands, isl. group in Bass Str., off Tasmania, SE Australia. Largest is Flinders Isl. (area 2072 sq km/800 sq mi). Intensive cattle and sheep raising.

Furtwängler, Wilhelm (1886-1954), German conductor. Conductor of Berlin Philharmonic Orchestra (1922-45). Known for interpretation of Wagner's operas and orchestral work of Beethoven, Brahms, Bruckner.

furze, see GORSE.

Fuseli, Henry, orig. Johann Heinrich Füssli (1741-1825), Anglo-Swiss painter, b. Zurich. He produced highly imaginative works, depicting horrific and fantastic scenes. Works incl. *The Nightmare* and illustrations of Milton and Shakespeare. Influenced William Blake.

Fushun, city of Liaoning prov., NE China. Pop. 1,700,000. Major indust. centre; extensive open cast coal mines, oil shale refining; engineering, automobile mfg.

Fusin, city of Liaoning prov., NE China. Pop. 500,000. Indust. centre, coal mining.

fusion, nuclear, nuclear reaction in which two light atomic nuclei fuse to form heavier nucleus, with release of enormous energy, *eg* deuterium and tritium nuclei fuse to form helium nucleus. Nuclei must have sufficient kinetic energy to overcome repulsive forces; extremely high temperatures provide this energy. Potential source of useful energy; basis of stellar energy and hydrogen bomb.

Futuna Island, see WALLIS AND FUTUNA ISLANDS.

futurism, artistic and literary movement inaugurated by publication of Futurist Manifesto in Paris (1909) by Italian poet Marinetti. 'Manifesto of Futurist Painting' (1910) was signed by group of Italian painters incl. Boccioni, Balla, Carra. They sought to eliminate conventional form and to express vital dynamism of machine age. Influenced constructivism, dada, vorticism. Later became assimilated in fascist ideology.

Fyn (Ger. *Fünen*), isl. of Denmark. Area 2976 sq km (1149 sq mi); main town Odense. Dairying. Separated by Little Belt from Jutland (W), by Great Belt from Zealand (E).

Fyne, Loch, sea loch of Strathclyde region, W Scotland. Length 64 km (40 mi). Noted for herring, kippers.

G

gabbro, coarse-grained, plutonic igneous rock. Consists of plagioclase feldspar plus one or more varieties of pyroxene, eg augite. Dark coloured and heavy; formed by slow cooling of large underground masses. Common in Europe, US, South America.

Gaberones, see GABORONE, Botswana.

Gabès, town of SE Tunisia, on Gulf of Gabès. Pop. 77,000. Fishing port, railway to Tunis; exports dates, fruit from surrounding oasis.

Gable, Clark (1901-60), American film actor. Star for nearly 30 years, known as 'king' of Hollywood. Best-known for *Gone With the Wind* (1939).

Gabo, Naum (1890-1977), American sculptor, b. Russia. Uses modern synthetic materials in space-constructions; pioneer of kinetic art. With brother, Antoine Pevsner, wrote *Realistic Manifesto* of *Constructivism* (1920).

Gabon, republic of WC Africa. Area 268,000 sq km (103,500 sq mi); pop. 530,000; cap. Libreville. Languages: Bantu, French. Religions: native, RC. Coastal plain, interior plateau; largely tropical rain-forest. Exports petroleum, manganese, hardwoods. Reached c 1485 by Portuguese; slave trade 17th-19th cent. Part of French Congo from 1886; territ. of French Equatorial Africa from 1908; in-dependent republic from 1960. Member of French Community.

gaboon viper, *Bitis gabonica*, short, thick, brightly patterned snake of W African forests. Sluggish, it bites swiftly when disturbed.

Gabor, Dennis (1900-79), British physicist, b. Hungary. Awarded Nobel Prize for Physics (1971) for invention of principle of holography (1948), a 3-dimensional lensless system of photography, used in many fields. Practical applications began following invention of laser in 1960s.

Gaborone, cap. of Botswana. Pop. 26,000. Admin. centre. Small village until chosen (1964) as cap. of new republic from 1966; formerly Gaberones, renamed 1969.

Gabriel, archangel, messenger of God. Appears several times in Bible, notably to tell Virgin Mary she will bear child to be called Jesus. In Islam, revealed Koran to Mohammed. Christian tradition regards him as trumpeter of Last Judgment.

Gabrieli, Giovanni (?1557-1612), Italian composer. Numerous compositions incl. complex motets with instrumental accompaniment, colourful ensembles for up to 22 instruments, works for organ.

Gadafy, Muammar al-, see QADDHAFI, MUAMMAR AL-.

Gaddi, Taddeo (d. 1366), Florentine painter. Follower of Giotto, became leader of Florentine painting after Giotto's death. Works incl. fresco cycle *Life of the Virgin*. His son, **Agnolo Gaddi** (c 1350-96), also painted frescoes incl. *Legend of True Cross* cycle.

gadfly, name used for various blood-sucking flies, *eg* horsefly, that attack livestock.

gadolinium (Gd), metallic element of lanthanide series; at. no. 64, at. wt. 157.25. Some isotopes used in nuclear reactors to absorb neutrons.

Gadsden, James (1788-1858), American railway promoter, diplomat. Advocate of railway link between South and Pacific. Minister to Mexico (1853-6), negotiated Gadsden Purchase of land to build line along Mexican border.

Gaea, in Greek myth, goddess of earth. In Hesiod's *Theogony*, she emerged from primeval chaos and gave birth to Uranus, the sky. Her children by Uranus were the TITANS.

Gaelic or **Goidelic**, subgroup of CELTIC branch of Indo-European language family. Incl. Irish Gaelic (Erse), Scottish Gaelic, extinct Manx. Irish Gaelic divided into Old (7th-9th cent.), Middle (10th-16th cent.) and Modern periods. Revived in 20th cent. as national language of Eire. Scottish Gaelic identical with Irish until 17th cent.

Gaelic football, fifteen-a-side team game played with a round ball, combining aspects of soccer and rugby. Mainly confined to Ireland. Rules drawn up by Gaelic Athletic Association, founded 1884.

Gaelic literature, literature of Gaelic-speaking Ireland and Scotland. Not separated nationally until 17th cent., therefore divided into Old

Irish (before 900), Middle Irish (until 1350), Late Middle or Early Modern Irish (until 1650) and Modern Irish and Scottish Gaelic (from 1650). Old Irish works incl. Book of Leinster. Middle Irish works divided into 2 cycles of heroic tales, *ie* Red Branch or Ulster cycle (pagan), and Fenian (later, more complex, Christian), incl. work by poet OSSIAN. Modern Irish period saw rise of prose, less formal poetry. Scottish Gaelic poetry stimulated by events of 1745, as in poetry of Alexander MacDonald, and by *Ossian* of James MACPHERSON. Gaelic revival in late 19th cent. Ireland.

Gagarin, Yuri Alekseyevich (1934-68), Russian cosmonaut. First man to orbit Earth (April, 1961). His flight in satellite, *Vostok*, lasted c 89 mins. Killed in aeroplane accident.

Gainsborough, Thomas (1727-88), English painter. Influenced by Van Dyck, painted elegant portraits, *eg Blue Boy, Mrs Siddons*, members of Royal Family; also first authentically English landscapes; *Mr and Mrs Andrews in a Landscape* combines genres.

Gaitskell, Hugh Todd Naylor (1906-63), British politician. Labour chancellor of exchequer (1950-1). Leader of parliamentary Labour Party (1955-63), adopted moderate stance on nationalization and disarmament issues.

Galahad, *see* ARTHURIAN LEGEND.

Galápagos Islands or **Colón Archipelago**, isl. group of Ecuador, in E Pacific Ocean. Area *c* 7800 sq km (3000 sq mi); chief isls. San Cristóbal (Eng. Chatham) and Isabela (Albemarle). Unique flora and fauna (isls. named after giant tortoise, Span. *galápago*); visited (1835) by Darwin; now nature reserve.

Galatea, see PYGMALION.

Galati or **Galatz,** city of E Romania, on R. Danube. Pop. 191,000. Naval base; port, exports grain, timber.

Galatia, ancient region of C Asia Minor, around modern Ankara. Invaded by Gauls in 3rd cent. BC (hence name). Came under Roman rule in 2nd cent. BC; Roman prov. 25 BC.

Galatians, St Paul's Epistle to the, book of NT, possibly written *c* AD 48 at Ephesus. Exposition of how Christianity superseded law of Moses.

Galatz, see GALATI, Romania.

galaxy, large grouping of stars, gas and dust held together by mutual gravitational attraction. Milky Way is galaxy containing solar system. Most galaxies are elliptical or spiral shaped, a few being irregular in shape; *c* 10^9 are thought to exist.

Galbraith, J[ohn] K[enneth] (1908-), American economist, b. Canada. Adviser to J.F. Kennedy; US ambassador to India (1961-3). Advocate of using nation's wealth for public projects rather than consumer goods; early critic of dependence on economic growth. Works incl. *The Affluent Society* (1958), *The New Industrial State* (1967).

Galen (*c* 130-*c* 200), Greek physician. Wrote extensively on human anatomy, basing his work on dissection of animals. Systematized contemporary medical knowledge in series of treatises; authority remained unchallenged until 16th cent.

Galerius (d. AD 310), Roman

emperor (305-10). Created Caesar (sub-emperor) by Diocletian (293). Defeated Persians 297. Became joint emperor with Constantius I. Ruled Eastern empire until his death.

Galicia (Pol. *Galicja,* Ukr. *Halychyna*), region of SE Poland and W Ukraine. Incl. plains in N, N Carpathians in S; main rivers Dnestr, Vistula. Chief cities Kraków, Lvov. Hist. duchy, part of Poland from 14th cent.; ceded to Austria by 1772 partition.

Galicia, region and former kingdom of NW Spain. Mountainous with deep valleys, indented coast; drained by R. Miño. Stock raising, fishing. Main towns La Coruña, Vigo, Santiago de Compostela. Taken from Moors by Asturias (9th cent.).

Galilee, Sea of, lake of NE Israel. Length 23 km (14 mi), area *c* 166 sq km (64 sq mi). Lies below sea level, fed by hot mineral springs. Fisheries since Biblical times. Also known as L. Tiberias.

Galileo Galilei (1564-1642), Italian astronomer and physicist. Constructed first astronomical telescope (1609) and discovered 4 brightest satellites of Jupiter. Investigated motion of falling bodies, his findings contradicting Aristotle's teaching. Supported Copernican theory; later forced by Inquisition to renounce this belief. His use of observation, experiment and mathematics helped lay foundation of modern science.

gall, growths on plants caused by insects, esp. of Cynipidae family. The common oak apple gall is produced by a chemical irritant deposited by the gall wasp (*Diplolepis* or *Rhodites*) when it lays its eggs on the underside of a leaf. Each gall contains a wasp larva.

Gallatin, Albert (1761-1849), American politician, financier, b. Switzerland. Secretary of the treasury (1801-14), curtailed US military expenditure and reshaped federal financial policies. Led negotiations concluding War of 1812 between US and Britain.

gall bladder, membranous sac which stores and concentrates bile from liver in most vertebrates. In humans, attached to underside of liver; contracts to eject bile into duodenum to aid digestion.

galleon, a square-rigged warship of the 16th cent. with narrow hull, beaked bow and rectangular forecastle, carrying usually 2 tiers of guns. Used by Spanish to bring treasure from Americas.

galley, long, low-built vessel propelled by oars and sail. Used in ancient and medieval times, esp. in Mediterranean. Rowers were generally slaves or prisoners.

Gallicanism, term for movement in French RC church claiming limited autonomy from pope; opposed to ULTRAMONTANISM. Important principles enunciated in the 4 Gallican Articles of 1682, ie kings, general councils not subject to pope. Lost legitimacy with Vatican Council's enunciation of papal infallibility (1869).

Gallico, Paul William (1897-1976), American author. Known for popular novels, eg The Adventures of Hiram Holliday (1939), The Snow Goose (1941), Love of Seven Dolls (1954).

Gallic Wars, campaigns of Julius Caesar during his proconsulship in Gaul (58-51 BC). Defeated the Helvetii and the German king Ariovistus (58), then the Belgae (57). Invaded Britain twice (55, 54). Quelled revolt of Ambiorix (53). Conquest of Gaul was completed when Caesar crushed rebellion led by Vercingetorix (52).

Gallienus (d. AD 268), Roman emperor (253-68). Shared power with his father, Valerian, until Valerian was captured by the Persians (260). Rebellions occurred in most of the provs. during his reign. Murdered by his troops.

Gallipoli (Gelibolu), penin. of European Turkey, between Gulf of Saros and Dardanelles. Scene of unsuccessful landings by Allies to capture Constantinople via Dardanelles (1915-16).

gallium (Ga), soft metallic element; at. no. 31, at. wt. 69.72. Used to make high temperature thermometers and alloys of low melting point. Existence predicted by Mendeleev; discovered spectroscopically in 1875.

gallon, unit of liquid measure. British Imperial gallon is volume occupied by 10 pounds of water under specified conditions; equals c 4.546 litres. US gallon is c 5/6 of Imperial gallon.

Galloway, area of SW Scotland, in Dumfries and Galloway region. Rhinns of Galloway penin. in SW, with Mull of Galloway at S end (most S point in Scotland). Dairying; black Galloway cattle.

Gallup, George Horace (1901-   ), American statistician. Founded Gallup Poll and American Institute of Public Opinion (1935).

Galois, Evariste (1811-32), French mathematician. Pioneer in use of modern techniques in algebra, he showed impossibility of solving general polynomial of 5th degree by algebraic means.

Galsworthy, John (1867-1933), English author. Known for the 'Forsyte Saga' (1906-22) portraying Edwardian moneyed class. Also wrote Ibsenesque plays of ideas dealing with social injustice, eg Strife (1909), The Skin Game (1920). Awarded Nobel Prize for Literature (1932).

Galt, John (1779-1839), Scottish novelist. Known for chronicle novel of Scots provincial life Annals of the Parish (1821). Other works incl. The Provost (1822), The Entail (1823).

Galton, Sir Francis (1822-1911), English scientist. Founded and coined term for eugenics, movement to improve species through control of hereditary factors. Developed statistical correlation and questionnaire techniques.

Galvani, Luigi (1737-98), Italian physician. Discovered contraction of frog's muscles produced by contact with 2 different metals. Ascribed source of electricity to animal tissue; theory discredited by Volta.

galvanization, plating of iron or steel sheets with zinc to protect them from atmospheric corrosion. Sheets usually immersed in molten zinc; zinc can also be deposited by electrolysis.

galvanometer, device used to measure or detect small electric currents. Usually consists of current-carrying coil suspended between poles of permanent magnet; magnetic field produced by current interacts with field of magnet, causing coil to move.

Galveston, port and tourist resort of SE Texas, US; on Galveston Isl. in Gulf of Mexico inlet. Pop. 62,000. Shipyards; exports sulphur, cotton, wheat. Oil, cotton processing; chemical, hardware mfg. Damaged by hurricanes (1900, 1961).

Galway, county of Connacht prov., W Irish Republic. Area 5939 sq km (2293 sq mi); pop. 148,000. Indented coast, mountains in W; incl. scenic Connemara, Aran Isls. Agric., fishing; marble quarrying. Co. town Galway, on Galway Bay. Pop. 27,000. Fishing port, esp. salmon; univ. coll. (1849).

Gama, Vasco da (c 1469-1524), Portuguese navigator. Discovered sea route to India via Cape of Good Hope (1497-9), opening up East Indian trade and leading to development of Portuguese empire. Made 2 further voyages (1502, briefly viceroy (1524).

Gambetta, Léon Michel (1838-82), French statesman, premier (1881-2). Organized resistance in Franco-Prussian War; escaped from siege of Paris by balloon. Played important part in estab. of Third Republic.

Gambia, republic of W Africa. Area 10,360 sq km (4000 sq mi); pop. 538,000; cap. Banjul. Official language: English. Religions: native, Islam. Smallest country in Africa, surrounded by Senegal; extends c 320 km (200 mi) along R. Gambia. Exports groundnuts, hides. First discovered in 15th cent. by Portuguese. British colony from 1843; independent (1965). Member of British Commonwealth.

Gambier Islands, archipelago of S Pacific Ocean, part of French

Polynesia. Main isl. Mangareva. Produce copra, coffee, pearl shell. Acquired by France (1881).

Gamelin, Maurice Gustave (1872-1958), French general. As commander of the Allied armies in France at the outset of WWII, bore responsibility for the disastrous defeat of June 1940, and was replaced by Weygand. Imprisoned for treason in 1943, he was released by the Allies (1945).

gamete, in biology, reproductive cell, haploid and usually sexually differentiated. Male gamete (spermatozoon) unites with female gamete (ovum) to form the cell (zygote) which develops into new individual.

game theory, use of mathematical analysis to select best available strategy in order to maximize one's winnings or minimize opponent's winnings in a game, war, business, *etc.* Important in mathematical economics. Founded by VON NEUMANN.

gamma globulin, fraction of protein in human blood plasma containing most antibodies. Can be separated from blood and used to provide temporary immunity against disease, *eg* hepatitis.

gamma rays, high frequency electromagnetic radiation, similar to X-rays. Emitted by atomic nuclei during radioactive decay; great penetrating power.

Gander, town of NE Newfoundland, Canada; N of Gander L. Pop. 8000. Grew up round airport from 1935; important air base in WWII.

Gandhi, Indira (1917-), Indian stateswoman, PM (1966-77). Daughter of Nehru, succeeded Shastri as leader of Congress Party and PM. Declared war on Pakistan (1971) in support of Bangladesh independence (estab. 1971). Proclaimed state of emergency (1975-7); retained premiership, suspending most democratic processes, imprisoning opponents. Lost ensuing election; subsequently faced corruption charges.

Gandhi, Mohandas Karamchand (1869-1948), Indian political and religious leader. Known as *Mahatma* (great souled). Studied law in England; went to Africa (1893), where he championed rights of Indians. Returned to India (1915), began campaign for independence. Asserted Hindu ethics by abstaining from Western ways, practising asceticism. Imprisoned (1930) by British for civil disobedience campaigns, employing passive resistance and fasting as political weapons. Prominent in conferences leading to independence (1947), disappointed by partition into Hindu and Moslem states. Shot by Hindu nationalist fanatic.

Ganesa, in Hindu religion, god of wisdom and patron of literature. Son of Siva and Parvati; usually represented with head of an elephant.

Ganges, river of N India and Bangladesh. Rises in Himalayan Uttar Pradesh, flows *c* 2500 km (1560 mi) through Allahabad, Varanasi and Patna to form delta at Bay of Bengal. Major irrigation source. Sacred to Hindus.

ganglion, mass of nerve cells serving as centre from which nerve impulses are transmitted. Name also applies to small cystic tumour growing on tendon sheath.

gangrene, decay of tissue in injured part of body caused by loss of blood supply to that part. Gas gangrene occurs when certain bacteria invade wounds, destroying nearby healthy tissue and forming gas. Damaged tissue must be removed surgically.

Gangtok, cap. of SIKKIM.

gannet, marine bird of Sulidae family, found on all coasts except Antarctica. Nests in colonies on cliffs. Commonest species is northern gannet or solan goose, *Sula bassana.*

Ganymede, in Greek myth, son of Tros, king of Troy. Because of his great beauty, Zeus, in the form of an eagle, carried him to Mt. Olympus to be cup-bearer of the gods.

gar, see GARPIKE.

Garbo, Greta, orig. Greta Gustafsson (1905-), Swedish film actress. Spent most of her career in US. Became symbol of aloof allurement, enhancing this by early retirement. Films incl. *Queen Christina* (1933), *Camille* (1936), *Ninotchka* (1939).

García Lorca, Federico (1898-1936), Spanish poet. Major poet of his generation, murdered by Falangists in Civil War. Revived Spanish ballad form with *Romancero gitano* (1929), expressing preoccupation with death in intensely sensual imagery. Also known for plays, esp. tragedy *Blood Wedding* (1933).

Garda, Lake, N Italy, mainly in Lombardy. Largest lake in Italy, area 370 sq km (149 sq mi). Fishing; resorts, fruit growing on shores.

garden city, planned residential and indust. town designed to combine advantages of town and country. Features incl. encircling rural belt, predetermined max. pop.,

community ownership of land. Term first used (1869) by A.T. Stewart in US; adopted and greatly modified by Sir Ebenezer Howard (1898) in England. Led to development of Letchworth and Welwyn Garden City.

gardenia, genus of evergreen trees and shrubs of madder family. Native to subtropical S Africa and Asia. Glossy leaves, highly fragrant white or yellow, waxy flowers.

Gardiner, Stephen (c 1493-1555), English churchman. Secretary to Wolsey before gaining royal favour through attempts to obtain Henry VIII's divorce from Catherine of Aragon. Appointed bishop of Winchester (1531), supported royal supremacy in Church of England. Lord high chancellor under Mary I.

Gardner, Erle Stanley (1889-1970), American author. Known for over 100 crime novels, creating detective Perry Mason.

Gardner, Dame Helen Louise (1908-), British scholar. Known for influential criticism on metaphysical poets, *eg The Divine Poems of John Donne* (1952).

Garfield, James [Abram] (1831-81), American statesman, president (1881). Republican congressman from Ohio (1863-80), nominated as compromise candidate for presidency (1880). Fatally shot by disappointed office-seeker.

gargoyle, water spout in form of grotesque figure, human or animal, projecting from the gutter of a building. Many examples found on Gothic cathedrals.

Garibaldi, Giuseppe (1807-82), Italian soldier and patriot. Fought in South American wars (1836-48) after involvement in unsuccessful republican plot. Returned to Italy, fought for Sardinia against Austria (1848) and for Roman Republic against France (1849). With 1000 volunteer 'Red Shirts', conquered Sicily and Naples (1860), making Victor Emmanuel king of Italy. Twice attempted (1862, 1867) to unite Papal States with new kingdom.

Garland, Judy, orig. Frances Gumm (1922-69), American film actress, singer. Started as juvenile star, as in *The Wizard of Oz* (1939), later films incl. *Easter Parade* (1948), *A Star is Born* (1954).

garlic, *Allium sativum,* perennial plant of lily family, native to Asia. Pungent, bulbous root is used to flavour meat and salad dishes.

garnet, crystalline silicate mineral. Hard, colours incl. red, white, green, brown, yellow. Found in metamorphic rocks, esp. gneiss, mica, hornblende schists. Red, transparent variety is semi-precious gemstone; others used as abrasives. Major sources in India, Brazil, US.

Garonne, river of SW France. Flows *c* 645 km (400 mi) from SW Pyrenees via Toulouse to join R. Dordogne near Bordeaux, forming Gironde estuary.

garpike, any of Lepisosteidae family of primitive long, thin fish. Long snout, diamond-shaped scales; found in fresh water of North and Central America. Species incl. longnose gar, *Lepisosteus osseus,* a voracious predator.

Garrick, David (1717-79), English actor-manager. Manager of Drury Lane Theatre (1747-76). Did much to revive Shakespeare's popularity. Also wrote comedies. Most popular actor of day.

Garter, [Most Noble] Order of the, oldest British order of knighthood, estab. *c* 1344. Limited to 25 knights and members of royal family. Has motto, *Honi soit qui mal y pense.*

garter snake, small, harmless, striped snake of genus *Thamnophis,* common in North America.

gas, state of matter in which molecules move freely, causing matter to expand indefinitely to fill its container.

Gascony (*Gascogne*), region and former prov. of SW France, hist. cap. Auch. Incl. sandy Landes, hilly Armagnac, part of Pyrenees; agric., vineyards, brandy. Duchy created 7th cent., incorporated (11th cent.) into Aquitaine. Under English rule (1154-1453). Basque language and customs survive in some areas.

Gaskell, Elizabeth Cleghorn, née Stevenson (1810-65), English novelist. Works, incl. *Mary Barton* (1848), *Cranford* (1853), *Sylvia's Lovers* (1863), deal with social, moral problems of Victorian age. Wrote life of Charlotte Brontë (1857).

gas mask, protective face covering with absorption system to remove toxic gases from inhaled air. Filters usually made of activated charcoal and soda lime. Used against poison gas in warfare and in industry.

gasoline, *see* PETROLEUM.

Gaspé, penin. of E Québec, Canada, extending into Gulf of St Lawrence. Mountainous interior; wooded. Coastal fishing, lumbering, pulp milling; tourism.

Gasperi, Alcide de (1881-1954),

Italian statesman, premier (1945-53). Helped found Christian Democrat party, representing centre-right. As premier, worked for European unity.

Gastein, valley of C Austria, in Hohe Tauern. Resort area; spas incl. Bad Gastein, which has thermal radium springs.

gastric ulcer, *see* PEPTIC ULCER.

Gastropoda (gastropods), class of molluscs with distinct head, eyes and tentacles. Large flattened foot used for motion. Incl. snail, limpet, with one-piece spiral shell, and slug, with reduced shell.

Gates, Horatio (1727-1806), American army officer, b. England. During American Revolution, defeated British under Burgoyne at Saratoga (1779). Rival of Washington but plan to replace him with Gates failed. Commander in Carolina campaign.

Gateshead, co. bor. of Tyne and Wear met. county, NE England, on R. Tyne. Pop. 94,000. Opposite Newcastle, linked by tunnel, bridges. Shipbuilding, engineering industs., chemicals mfg. Rebuilt after 1854 fire.

Gatling, Richard Jordan (1818-1903), American inventor. Developed the Gatling revolving battery gun (1861-2), precursor of MACHINE GUN.

Gaudier-Brzeska, Henri (1891-1915), French sculptor. Member of vorticist group, he worked in London from 1911. Work incl. fluid drawings of animals and sculpture influenced by African art.

Gaudi y Cornet, Antoni (1852-1926), Spanish architect. His art nouveau buildings are known for their undulating façades and decorations of ceramics. Designed church of Sagrada Familia in Barcelona, which remains unfinished.

Gauguin, [Eugène Henri] Paul (1848-1903), French painter. Began painting in impressionist manner, became leading artist of synthetist style, his work is characterized by use of pure unnaturalistic colours applied in flat areas. Rejecting Western civilization, he sought simplicity of primitive life in Tahiti. Works incl. *The Yellow Christ.* Great influence on 20th cent. art.

Gaul (anc. *Gallia*), hist. region of W Europe, mainly coextensive with modern France. Originally comprised Cisalpine Gaul (Italy N of Apennines) conquered 3rd cent. BC by Romans, and Transalpine Gaul (modern France) conquered by Julius Caesar in Gallic Wars (58-51 BC).

gaur, *Bibos gaurus,* wild ox of forested hills of India, Burma. Largest of wild cattle. Gayal, *B. frontalis,* considered a domesticated form of gaur.

Gauss, Karl Friedrich (1777-1855), German mathematician. Made numerous contributions to mathematics, incl. number theory, algebra, geometry; discovered a form of non-Euclidean geometry. Calculated orbit of asteroid Ceres (1801). Worked on terrestrial magnetism, electromagnetism; invented an electric telegraph with Weber (1833). Works incl. *Disquisitiones arithmeticae* (1801).

Gautier, Théophile (1811-72), French author. Poetry, with its emphasis on form, provided model for Parnassians, esp. *Emaux et*

Camées (1852). Novels incl. *Mlle de Maupin* (1835), *Le Capitaine Fracasse* (1863).

Gaveston, Piers (d. 1312), courtier, favourite of Edward II of England. The king allowed him great power, incl. regency in own absence, which roused anger of barons. They banished Gaveston twice, and finally had him beheaded.

gavial, *Gavialis gangeticus*, animal of crocodile group, distinguished by long, narrow snout. Diet of fish; not dangerous to man. Found in large rivers of India, Burma.

Gävle, town of E Sweden, on Gulf of Bothnia. Pop. 65,000. Port, exports iron ore, timber; fish canning. Formerly called Gefle.

Gawain or **Gawaine,** *see* ARTHURIAN LEGEND.

Gay, John (1685-1732), English poet, playwright. Remembered as author of *The Beggar's Opera* (1728) satirizing literary conventions, political figures, and as friend of Pope, Arbuthnot. Also wrote miscellaneous satirical verse, essays.

gayal, *see* GAUR.

Gay-Lussac, Joseph Louis (1778-1850), French chemist, physicist. Discovered independently Charles' law of expansion of gases. Stated law of combining gas volumes: volumes of gases which combine to give gaseous product are in ratio of small whole numbers to each other and to volume of product. First to make ascent by balloon to collect scientific data.

Gaza, city of NE Egypt, on Mediterranean Sea. Pop. 118,000. Port; admin., commercial centre of Gaza Strip coastal region. Formerly one of chief cities of Philistines,

taken by Alexander the Great 332 BC. Battlefield in WWI (1917). Under Egypt from 1949; occupied by Israel from 1967 war.

gazelle, small swift-running antelope of Africa, Asia, genus *Gazella*. Usually fawn coloured, with backward-pointing horns. Species incl. Dorcas gazelle.

Gaziantep, city of S Turkey, near Syrian border. Pop. 275,000. Agric. centre; textile mfg. Strategically important, taken by Saladin in 1183. Fell to French (1921) after siege during their Syrian mandate; returned (1922). Formerly called Aintab.

Gdańsk, city of N Poland, on Gulf of Gdańsk, cap. of Gdańsk prov. Pop. 370,000. Port, exports coal, timber, grain; shipbuilding, food processing. Hist. known as Danzig. Hanseatic League member; under Prussian rule 1793-1919. Free city under League of Nations from 1919; annexed by Germany 1939, returned 1945.

Gdynia, city of N Poland, on Gulf of Gdańsk. Pop. 192,000. Port, exports coal, timber, grain; naval base, shipbuilding. Developed after 1924 from fishing village to replace free city of Danzig (Gdańsk) as major Polish port.

gearbox, box containing system of toothed wheels which are used to transmit motion from one part of a machine to another. Different ratios of diameters of driving and driven wheels can be used to vary speed and torque. In automobile, ratios may be changed while in motion to allow engine to operate near its most efficient speed for a wide range of road speeds.

gecko, any of Gekkonidae family of harmless lizards of tropical and subtropical regions. Many can walk vertically on smooth surfaces, using adhesive pads on feet. Catches insects with extensile tongue. Tail can break off when seized; new one grows.

Geddes, Sir Patrick (1854-1932), Scottish biologist, sociologist. Pioneered human geography; applied biological training to civic welfare, planning. Replanned many cities, incl. Edinburgh and several in India. Writings incl. *City Development* (1904).

Geelong, city of S Victoria, Australia, on Corio Bay. Pop. 115,000. Port, exports wheat, wool, meat products; textile mfg., oil refining. Founded 1838, grew after 1851 gold rush.

Geiger counter, device used to detect and measure ionizing radiation, esp. alpha, beta and gamma rays. Consists of positively charged wire inside negatively charged metal cylinder. Ions, formed by incoming radiation, migrate to electrodes and produce electrical pulse.

Geisel, Ernesto (1907-), Brazilian general, political leader, president (1974-). Estab. as president by chiefs of armed services after managing state oil monopoly for 4 years. Term marked by economic difficulties, suppression of dissidents.

gel, in chemistry, solid, jelly-like material formed by coagulation of colloidal solution.

gelatin, colourless, clear, water-soluble animal protein obtained from animal tendons, ligaments, *etc.* Used in food preparation and preservation, photography, as culture medium for bacteria, *etc.* Glue is impure form.

Gelderland, prov. of EC Netherlands. Area 5017 sq km (1937 sq mi); cap. Arnhem. Drained by Ijssel, Waal, Lower Rhine. Fertile Betuwe in SW. Medieval duchy. E part incl. Geldern, ducal cap., ceded to Prussia (1715).

Geliboiu, see GALLIPOLI.

gelignite, blasting explosive consisting of nitroglycerine, nitrocellulose, wood pulp and potassium nitrate.

Gell-Mann, Murray (1929-), American physicist. Awarded Nobel Prize for Physics (1969) for contributions and discoveries concerning elementary particles and their interactions. Worked on theory of 'strange' particles; devised system of particle classification ('eight-fold way'). Introduced concept of QUARK as building block for elementary particles.

Gelsenkirchen, city of W West Germany, on Rhine-Herne canal. Pop. 345,000. Major coalmining centre of Ruhr coalfield; grew rapidly after 1850. Heavily bombed in WWII.

Gemini, see ZODIAC.

gemstone, mineral which when cut and polished may be used as a gem. Hard, normally transparent and crystalline. Precious varieties incl. diamond, emerald, ruby, sapphire; semi-precious incl. amethyst, aquamarine, garnet.

gene, unit of hereditary material. Genes are arranged into linear sequence to form chromosomes, each gene occurring at a specific point. Composed of DNA; changes in structure of DNA cause mutation of genes, leading to changes in inheritable characteristics.

General Agreement in Trades and Tariffs (GATT), United Nations agency estab. (1948) as interim arrangement in advance of International Trade Organization. Since latter never effected, GATT remained only international body laying down code of conduct for trade and acting as forum for solving related problems. Aims to reduce tariffs *etc*, assist trade of developing countries. Notable GATT negotiations incl. Kennedy Round (1964-7), Tokyo conference from 1973.

general strike, withdrawal of labour by workers in an entire indust. or throughout a region or country. Often politically motivated in that it seeks govt. concessions or overthrow of govt. Examples incl. that in Russia (Oct. 1905), resulting in granting of democratically-elected DUMA, and in Northern Ireland (May, 1974) which brought down power-sharing executive. In Britain, the General Strike (May, 1926) was called by TUC in response to national lockout of coalminers. Less than half the workers responded and govt. was able to keep most services running. TUC capitulated, miners remained on strike until Nov.

Genesis, in OT, 1st book giving an account of the creation of the world and of man. Traces Hebrew history from Abraham to Joseph. Generally thought to have been compiled after the Exile, but contains much Babylonian and Egyptian folklore, *eg* Flood, Creation myths.

Genet, Jean (1910-), French dramatist. Convicted criminal, became leading exponent of ABSURD drama. Plays incl. *The Maids* (1948), *The Balcony* (1956). Other works incl. novel *Our Lady of the Flowers* (1949).

genet, cat-like carnivore of Viverridae family, related to civet. Preys nocturnally on rodents, birds; most abundant in Africa. Common genet, *Genetta genetta,* found in S Europe.

genetics, branch of biology dealing with heredity and variation in similar or related animals and plants. Documented studies on sweet pea by Mendel were foundation of genetics. Modern developments are based on genetic code, which describes various arrangements of nitrogenous bases that constitute DNA, the fundamental genetic material.

Geneva (Fr *Genève,* Ger. *Genf*), city of SW Switzerland, on R. Rhône and L. Geneva, cap. of Geneva canton. Pop. 174,000. Cultural, commercial centre; watches, optical instruments; confectionery. Prehist. then Roman site; part of Holy Roman Empire during Middle Ages. Joined Swiss Confederation 1815. Centre of Reformation; Calvin's Academy (1559) became univ. (1873). Palais des Nations was seat of League of Nations 1920-46, now used by UN agencies. Red Cross hq.

Geneva, Lake (Fr. *Lac Léman,* Ger. *Genfersee*), on Swiss-French border. Rhône enters at E, leaves SW. Area 578 sq km (223 sq mi). Attractive scenery, tourism.

Geneva or 'Breeches' Bible, version produced (1560) as Protestant propaganda against Queen Mary. Annotated and financed by English Calvinist exiles at Geneva.

Gained its popular name from the account of Adam and Eve in Genesis 3:7, *ie* 'made themselves breeches'.

Geneva Conference, name given to two meetings held in Geneva (April-July, 1954, July, 1955) to discuss peace solutions for Indo-Chinese and Korean wars. In Vietnam, set up international commission to supervise ceasefire and partition of country. Failed to achieve permanent solution to armistice position in Korea. Second meeting became 'summit conference' between leaders of US, Britain, France and USSR. Resulted in suggestions for supervision of military installations, armaments. Name also given to DISARMAMENT talks, *etc*, held at various times in Geneva.

Geneva Convention, an international agreement (1864) regulating the treatment of wounded in war. Later extended to cover treatment of sick and prisoners and protection of civilians in war-time. Revised (1906, 1929, 1949).

Genghis Khan or **Jenghiz Khan** (*c* 1167-1227), Mongol chieftain. Conquered Mongolia (1206), most of Chin empire in China (1213-15), Turkestan, Transoxania, and Afghanistan (1218-24), and invaded SE Europe. He ruled finally over all lands between the Yellow and the Black seas. His grandson Kublai Khan conquered the rest of China.

Genoa (*Genova*), town of NW Italy, on Ligurian Sea, cap. of Liguria and of Genoa prov. Pop. 822,000. Port, shipbuilding; engineering; univ. (1243). Medieval maritime republic, *fl* during Crusading era. Birthplace

of Columbus, John Cabot. Has fine palaces and churches.

genre, style of painting in which subjects or scenes from everyday life are treated realistically. Genre painting was prominent in 17th cent. Dutch art; its exponents incl. Steen, Vermeer, de Hooch.

Gent, *see* GHENT, Belgium.

gentian, family, Gentianaceae, of low-growing plants of worldwide distribution, esp. those of genus *Gentiana* with many species popular in rock gardens. *G. lutea* contains a bitter component used as a tonic.

Gentile da Fabriano (*c* 1370-1427), Italian painter. A leading exponent of International Gothic style, his masterpiece is *Adoration of the Magi* (Florence). Painted frescoes in Lateran Basilica, Rome (now destroyed).

genus, in biology, *see* CLASSIFICATION.

geodesy, science of measuring shape and size of the Earth, and of locating points on its surface. Geodetic Survey deals with such large areas that curvature of Earth's surface must be taken into account.

Geoffrey of Monmouth (*c* 1100-54), British chronicler. Wrote *Historia Regum Britanniae* (modern edition, 1929), which provided basis for the Arthurian cycles, and was treated as history well into 17th cent.

geography, study of the similarities, differences, and relationships between regions of the Earth's surface. Falls into 2 sections: physical geography (incl. study of climate, landforms, soils) and human geography (incl. economic, political, urban, historical geography). First developed by Greeks,

GEOLOGICAL TABLE: TIME SCALE

Estimated ages in millions of years

	ERA	PERIOD	EPOCH	TIME BEGAN
PHANEROZOIC EON	CENOZOIC	**Quaternary**	Holocene	*c* 10,000 yrs
			Pleistocene	*c* 2
		Tertiary	Pliocene Miocene Oligocene Eocene Palaeocene	*c* 13 *c* 25 *c* 36 *c* 58 *c* 65
	MESOZOIC	**Cretaceous**		*c* 135
		Jurassic		*c* 195
		Triassic		*c* 225

MAJOR EVENTS	ANIMAL AND PLANT LIFE
Retreat of ice; present landscape formed. Major Ice Ages; pluvials	Rise of man; beginning of extinction of mammals eg mammoths, sabre-tooth carnivores.
Alpine-Himalayan mountain building. Shallow seas in Europe; extensive clay plains formed.	Proliferation of mammals; ancestors of modern fauna. Vegetation of modern types.
Extensive inundation; chalk formation.	Echinoderms, lamelli-branchs, last ammonites. Dinosaurs become extinct.
Widespread limestone formation.	Ammonites, brachio-pods, lamellibranchs, insects. 1st birds. Dinosaurs reach max.size.
Extensive arid, semi-arid areas. Red sands in North America.	Ammonites, crinoids, lamellibranchs. 1st mammals, dinosaurs.

	ERA	PERIOD	EPOCH	TIME BEGAN
PHANEROZOIC EON	PALAEOZOIC	**Permian**		*c* 280
		Carboniferous Pennsylvanian Mississippian		*c* 345
		Devonian		*c* 395
		Silurian		*c* 435
		Ordovician		*c* 500
		Cambrian		*c* 570
PRECAMBRIAN ERA				*c* 4500

MAJOR EVENTS	ANIMAL AND PLANT LIFE
Increasing aridity; salt beds formed. Marls, sandstones, evaporites developed.	Last trilobites. Increasing ammonites, reptiles. More advanced conifers.
Formation of coal measures. Shallow seas over continents, vast swamps.	Crinoids, brachiopods; increasing fish, amphibians, insects. 1st reptiles. Club mosses, horsetails.
Climax of Caledonian mountain building; formation of Old Red Sandstone.	Cephalopods, jawed fish, crinoids, last graptolites. Treefern forests.
Extensive seas; Caledonian mountain building continues.	Graptolites, trilobites, brachiopods, cephalopods. Jawless fish. 1st land plants.
Extensive seas; beginning of Caledonian mountain building.	Graptolites dominant; also trilobites, crinoids, corals. 1st vertebrates (fish) in North America.
Europe largely submerged. Large shallow seas covered North America.	Trilobites dominant; also graptolites, brachiopods. Some algae, lichens.
Formation, consolidation of continental shields eg Canadian, African, Australian.	Rare traces of rudimentary life, found only in Late Precambrian. Forerunners of trilobites, worms, sponges, jellyfish. Some algae, fungi.

eg Thales, Eratosthenes, Ptolemy; regional description advanced by Strabo in Roman times. Arabs, eg Idrisi, Ibn Khaldun, maintained study through Middle Ages until new impetus came from Spanish, Portuguese exploration of 15th–16th cents. Modern systematic (ie topical) and regional approaches to geography estab. by Humboldt and Ritter respectively. In 19th cent., regional tradition dominated through work of Vidal de la Blache and French school; 20th cent. has seen ascendancy of systematic approach and quantitative techniques in analysing geographical data.

geology, study of the composition, structure and history of the Earth, and the processes resulting in its present state. Study of composition incl: crystallography, mineralogy, petrology and geochemistry; study of structure incl. structural geology and geophysics; study of history incl. historical geology, stratigraphy and palaeontology. Physical geology studies processes of change. Term first used in 18th cent. by Swiss geologists, although study of Earth dates back to Greek times. Georgius Agricola studied minerals in 16th cent.; modern geology pioneered by Hutton's theory of uniformitarianism (1795); 20th cent. research in atomic structure, radioactivity, etc, has greatly advanced geology.

geometry, branch of mathematics that deals with points, lines, surfaces and solids. Elementary geometry is based on exposition given by EUCLID. Analytic geometry uses algebraic methods to study geometry. Later developments incl.

differential geometry, which uses calculus to study surfaces, projective geometry and non-Euclidean geometry.

geomorphology, study of landforms, esp. their character, origin and evolution. Employs both geographical and geological knowledge. Current ideas rest on 'cycles of erosion' theory of W.M. Davis (1850-1934).

George, St (c 4th cent.), patron saint of England. Traditionally, Palestinian soldier martyred in Asia Minor. In art, literature, represented as slayer of a dragon. Cult brought to England in Crusades. His red cross is on the Union Jack. No longer considered saint by RC church.

George I (1660-1727), king of Great Britain and Ireland (1714-27). Elector of Hanover (1698-1727), became king under terms of ACT OF SETTLEMENT. Left admin. of govt. to ministers, practice which initiated cabinet govt. in Britain.

George II (1683-1760), king of Great Britain and Ireland (1727-60). Son of George I, whose policy of ministerial govt. he continued. Last British king to lead troops in battle (Dettingen, 1743).

George III (1738-1820), king of Great Britain and Ireland (1760-1820). Ruled through sympathetic ministers (Bute, North) in attempt to assert authority until younger Pitt's ministry curbed ambitions. Chief event of reign was AMERICAN REVOLUTION, result of North's coercive policies. Intermittent insanity led to regency of his son (later George IV).

George IV (1762-1830), king of Great Britain and Ireland (1820-30).

Served as prince regent during insanity of his father, George III (1811-20); leader of dissolute social set. Personally unpopular, esp. through attempts to divorce his wife, Caroline of Brunswick.

George V (1865-1936), king of Great Britain and Ireland (1910-36). Second son of Edward VII. Played role as moderator in constitutional crisis over Parliament Act of 1911. His wife, Mary of Teck (1867-1953), bore him 5 sons and a daughter. During WWI, changed name of royal house from Saxe-Coburg-Gotha to Windsor.

George VI (1895-1952), king of Great Britain and Northern Ireland (1936-52). Became king when his brother, Edward VIII, abdicated. Married Elizabeth Bowes-Lyon (1900-   ), now known as the Queen Mother. Elder daughter succeeded him as Elizabeth II.

George II (1890-1947), king of Greece (1922-3, 1935-47). Deposed, went into exile. After restoration, allowed METAXAS to take dictatorial powers. Exiled during German occupation, returned after plebiscite (1946) in favour of monarchy.

George, Stefan (1868-1933), German poet. Influenced by Nietzsche and French symbolists, saw poet as priest with duty to people as well as self. Collections incl. *The Year of the Soul* (1897), *The New Kingdom* (1928).

George Cross, highest British civilian award for acts of courage. Instituted 1940.

George Town, Malaysia, *see* PENANG.

Georgetown, cap. of ·CAYMAN ISLANDS.

Georgetown, cap. of Guyana, Atlantic port at mouth of Demerara R. Pop. 166,000. Sugar, rice, bauxite exports. Famous botanical gardens (palms, orchids). Devastated by fire (1945, 1951).

Georgia, state of SE US. Area 152,489 sq km (58,876 sq mi); pop. 4,590,000; cap. Atlanta. Large areas of swamp and forest; Atlantic coastal plain rises gradually to Appalachians. Subtropical climate. Agric. produce incl. peanuts, cotton, maize, tobacco. Minerals esp. kaolin clay. Cotton milling, wood processing. British colony estab. after struggle with Spanish (1754). One of original 13 colonies of US. Devastated by Union forces during Civil War (1864).

Georgian Bay, arm of NE L. Huron, E Ontario, Canada. Separated from L. Huron by Manitoulin Isl. Georgian Bay Isls. National Park estab. 1929; summer resort.

Georgian Soviet Socialist Republic, constituent republic of W USSR. Area *c* 69,876 sq km (26,900 sq mi); pop. 4,688,000; cap. Tbilisi. Bounded by Black Sea in W, Greater Caucasus in N and Lesser Caucasus in S. Tea, citrus fruit, tobacco grown on Black Sea coast; rich manganese deposits. Region contained ancient kingdom of Colchis, legendary home of Golden Fleece. As independent kingdom, *fl* in 12th and 13th cent., but accepted Russian protection in 18th cent. Joined USSR (1922), becoming constituent republic (1936).

Georgian style, name given to English architecture during reigns of George I, II and III (1714-1820). Revival of Palladianism, led by

Campbell, Earl of Burlington and W. Kent, dominated first half of period. Neo-Classicism of Adam, Soane, etc, dominated second half.

Gera, city of SC East Germany, on White Elster R. Pop. 111,000. Railway jct.; produces textiles, machinery. Town hall (16th cent.).

geranium, family, Geraniaceae, of widely distributed plants, esp. those of genera *Geranium* and *Pelargonium* native to S Africa. Cranesbill geranium grows wild in Americas. Many species yield extracts used in pharmacy.

Gérard, François Pascal, Baron (1770–1837), French painter, b. Rome. Pupil of David; leading portraitist, court painter to Napoleon, Louis XVIII. Historical scenes incl. *Battle of Austerlitz*.

gerbil, small burrowing rodent of desert regions of Africa, Asia. Large hind legs used for leaping. Mainly nocturnal, with large eyes and long tail; diet of seeds, grain. Popular as pet.

geriatrics, branch of medicine dealing with diseases and care of old people. Diseases associated with old age incl. degeneration of arteries (arteriosclerosis), osteoarthritis, and weakening of bone tissue (osteoporosis), which makes old people prone to bone fractures.

Géricault, [Jean Louis André] Théodore (1791–1824), French painter. Regarded as a founder of French Romantic school; painted many horse and racing subjects. Realistic treatment of *The Raft of the Medusa* (1819) provoked public protest.

German, W Germanic language of Indo-European family. Official language of Federal Republic of Germany, German Democratic Republic, Austria, and most common language in Switzerland. First language for many elsewhere, important as second esp. in commerce. Divided into High German (spoken in southern areas), Low German (northern lowlands). Latter can incl. Dutch, Flemish, English. Modern standard German descends from German used for Luther's translation of Bible, a High German dialect.

germander, any plant of genus *Teucrium* of mint family. Worldwide distribution; common North American forms, *T. canadense* and *T. occidentale,* and British, *T. scorodonia,* are known as wood sage.

Germanic languages, branch of Indo-European family of languages. Divided into East, North and West Germanic groups. East incl. Gothic, Burgundian, Vandalic, all dead. North, also called Scandinavian, incl. Danish, Norwegian, Swedish, Icelandic; all descend from Old Norse. West incl. English, Dutch, German.

Germanic religion, see TEUTONIC MYTHOLOGY.

germanium (Ge), soft metalloid element; at. no. 32, at. wt. 72.59. Semiconductor, used in transistors; also used as a rectifier.

German measles, see RUBELLA.

German shepherd, see ALSATIAN.

Germany (*Deutschland*), country of NC Europe, now divided into East and West Germany. Language: German. Religions: Protestant, RC. Low, sandy plain in N; block mountains, forests in C; Rhine valley in W; Bavarian Alps in S. Main rivers Rhine, Elbe, Oder, Danube; extensive canal system. Industs. centred in Ruhr (W), Saxony (E). Separated from France on death of Charlemagne (AD 814), principalities formed Holy Roman Empire (962-1806). Confederation from 1815 under Prussian hegemony, empire estab. 1871. Colonial expansion in late 19th cent. Nationalist, expansionist aims contributed to WWI, after which Weimar Republic proclaimed. Rise of Hitler led to WWII; much territ. lost (incl. E Prussia), occupation by 4 allied powers 1945 followed by partition 1949. **East Germany** (*Deutsche Demokratische Republik*), occupied by USSR after WWII; communist govt., member of Warsaw Treaty Organization, COMECON. Area *c* 108,000 sq km (42,000 sq mi); pop. 16,786,000; cap. East Berlin. **West Germany** (*Bundesrepublik Deutschland*), occupied by UK, USA, France after WWII; federal govt., member of NATO, EEC. Area *c* 249,000 sq km (96,000 sq mi); pop. 61,498,000; cap. Bonn.

germination, process whereby plant embryo within seed resumes growth after period of dormancy. This period varies from a few days (most grasses) to over 400 years (Indian lotus). Process requires water, oxygen and in many cases light. Temperature is also critical.

Germiston, city of S Transvaal, South Africa. Pop. 281,000. Railway jct., important goldmining and refining, indust. centre in Witwatersrand. Founded 1887, after discovery of gold.

germ warfare, the use of disease bacteria, biological poisons, hormones, *etc* as a weapon of war. Employed in crude forms (pollution of water supplies, deliberate planting of contaminated material, *etc*) for many years. It has been avoided in modern warfare despite much research.

gerrymander, in politics, rearranging of voting areas to advantage of one party. Derived from its practice in Massachusetts by state governor Elbridge Gerry (1744-1814), who was US vice-president (1813-14).

Gershwin, George (1898-1937), American composer. Treated jazz idiom in symphonic form: Works incl. *Rhapsody in Blue, An American in Paris* and Negro opera *Porgy and Bess.* Also composed many tuneful songs for Broadway musicals.

Gesenius, Wilhelm (1786-1842), German theologian, Hebrew scholar. Opened Hebrew to scientific study, esp. with his grammar and dictionary.

Gesner, Konrad von (1515-65), Swiss naturalist, philologist. Wrote plant dictionary *Historia plantarum* (1541). His *Historia animalium* (1551-8) is considered basis of modern zoology.

Gestalt, in psychology, affirmation that experience consists of organized wholes (*gestalten*) rather than of sum of distinct parts. Developed in Germany, exponents incl. Kurt Koffka.

Gestapo (*Geheime Staatspolizei*), secret police in Nazi Germany (1933-45). Combined with Hitler's SS after 1936 under Himmler. Carried out ruthless policy of investigation, torture and extermination. Infiltrated and destroyed organizations opposed to Nazism. Indicted as one body at Nuremberg war crimes trials (1945-6).

Gethsemane, traditional site of Jesus' betrayal in garden at foot of Mount of Olives near Jerusalem. In Jordanian territ. since 1948.

Getty, [Jean] Paul (1892-1976), American businessman. Long considered richest man in world. controlled empire of *c* 200 businesses.

Gettysburg, bor. of S Pennsylvania, US. Pop. 7000. Scene of Federal repulse of Confederate's advance into North during Civil War; also of Lincoln's famous Address (1863).

Gettysburg Address (19 Nov. 1863), brief speech delivered by President Lincoln at dedication of cemetery on site of Battle of Gettysburg. Contained famous statement of the principles of American govt. 'of the people, by the people, for the people'.

Gettysburg campaign (June-July, 1863), episode in American Civil War. After Confederate victory at Chancellorsville, R.E. Lee invaded S Pennsylvania. Met Union forces W of Gettysburg; driven to Cemetery Hill, where Confederates were decisively defeated. Marked turning point of war.

Geulincx, Arnold (1624-69), Flemish philosopher. Resolved problems of Cartesian dualism by positing doctrine of occasionalism, *ie* that although mind and matter cannot interact God intervenes in each instance where an act of mind seems coordinated with a movement of the body.

geyser, spring from which columns of superheated water and steam are intermittently ejected. Caused by hot lava heating water which has percolated into geyser's central tube; found in active or recently active volcanic areas. Famous geyser regions are Iceland, New Zealand, and Yellowstone Park, Wyoming, US.

Ghana, republic of W Africa, on Gulf of Guinea. Area 238,500 sq km (92,100 sq mi); pop. 10,309,000; cap. Accra. Official language: English. Religions: native, Christianity. Largely forest, with savannah in N; main river Volta. Cocoa, hardwoods, palm products; also gold, diamonds, manganese. Former centre of slave trade; British Gold Coast colony estab. 1874. Ghana formed as independent state (1957) from Gold Coast, Ashanti, Togoland, Northern territs. Republic from 1960; Nkrumah's rule ended by coup (1966). Member of British Commonwealth.

Ghats, two mountain ranges of S India: Eastern Ghats (E coast), av. height *c* 450 m (1500 ft); Western Ghats, av. height *c* 900 m (3000 ft). Together enclose Deccan plain. Joined at highest peak, Anai Mudi (2695 m/8840 ft).

Ghent (Flem. *Gent*, Fr. *Gand*), city of WC Belgium, on R. Scheldt, cap. of East Flanders prov. Pop. 153,000. Port, canal to Terneuzen; industs. incl. textiles, steel. Hist. cap., cultural centre of Flanders. Castle, cathedral 12th cent.; Cloth Hall (14th cent.), univ. (1816).

gherkin, *see* CUCUMBER.

ghetto, section of a city inhabited mainly by members of racial or religious minority group and characterized by poverty and social deprivation. Originally applied to early medieval European cities in which segregation of Jews into autonomous community was voluntary. First compulsory segregation began late 14th cent. in Spain and Portugal; others incl. Frankfurt (1460), Venice (1516). Nazis estab. Jewish ghettos, eg in Warsaw.

Ghibellines, see GUELPHS AND GHIBELLINES.

Ghiberti, Lorenzo (1378-1455), Florentine sculptor. Best known for bronze doors of Baptistery in Florence, which took him 23 years to complete. Commissioned to make 2nd pair of doors (1425-52). His workshop was centre of artistic activity.

Ghirlandaio or **Girlandaio, Domenico** (1449-94), Florentine fresco painter. Noted for his ability to portray contemporary life and manners, as in his *Calling of the Apostles* (Sistine Chapel, Rome). Michelangelo was apprenticed to him.

ghost dance, central ritual of North American Indian religion of 19th cent. Originated among PAIUTE (c 1870), rapidly spread through W tribes. Danced on the nights of 5 successive days, inducing hypnotic trances.

Giacometti, Alberto (1901-66), Swiss sculptor, painter. Member of surrealist group in 1930s; work from this period incl. *The Palace at 4 am*. Returned to realistic single figures, usually elongated and emaciated, in plaster of Paris on a wire foundation.

giant panda, see PANDA.

giants, in myth and folklore, man-like beings of more than human size and strength, but lacking super-natural status of gods, civilization of men. In Greek myth, attempted unsuccessfully to conquer Olympian gods in revenge for defeat of TITANS; in Scandinavian myth, regarded as first of world's inhabitants. Perpetuated in allegories and children's stories, eg 'Jack the Giant Killer'.

Giant's Causeway, headland of N Northern Ireland, in former Co. Antrim. Comprises many levels of hexagonal basalt columns. In legend, built as giant's route to Scotland.

Gibbon, Edward (1737-94), English historian. Author of panoramic *The History of the Decline and Fall of the Roman Empire* (6 vols., 1776-88), inspired by visit to Rome. Attacked for criticism of rise of early Christianity.

Gibbon, Lewis Grassic, pseud. of James Leslie Mitchell (1901-35), Scottish novelist. Known for trilogy *A Scots Quair* (1932-4) about Aberdeenshire life before and after WWI.

gibbon, smallest of anthropoid apes, genus *Hylobates*, found in SE Asia. Arboreal, uses long arms to swing through branches. Only monkey to walk upright.

Gibbons, Grinling (1648-1721), English woodcarver, sculptor, b. Rotterdam. Famous for carvings of fruit, flowers, and animals; employed by Wren to decorate choir stalls of St Paul's Cathedral, London. Royal master carver from reign of Charles II to George I.

Gibbons, Orlando (1583-1625), English organist, composer. Finest keyboard player of his day, organist at Westminster Abbey. Composed anthems, madrigals, *eg Silver Swan*, instrumental pieces.

Gibbons, Stella Dorothea (1902–   ), English novelist. Known for burlesque of genre of rural pessimism, *Cold Comfort Farm* (1932).

Gibraltar, British crown colony of S Iberian penin., on Str. of Gibraltar. Area 6.5 sq km (2.5 sq mi); pop. 30,000; rises to 425 m (1400 ft). Free port, heavily fortified naval base, tourist resort. Rock of Gibraltar was one of the ancient 'Pillars of Hercules'. Held by Moors from 8th cent., by Spain 1462–1704. British control long challenged by Spain.

Gibraltar, Strait of, channel connecting Mediterranean Sea and Atlantic Ocean. Narrowest width c 13 km (8 mi); separates S Spain from N Africa. Headlands at Rock of Gibraltar (N) and Ceuta (S) formerly called Pillars of Hercules.

Gibson, Charles Dana (1867–1944), American illustrator. Created 'Gibson Girl', idealized type of American young woman; illustrated Hope's *Prisoner of Zenda*.

Gide, André (1869–1951), French author. Works reflect own struggle for self-development balancing hedonism with asceticism. Novels incl. *La Porte étroite* (1909), *Les Faux-monnayeurs* (1926). Founded *La Nouvelle Revue Française* (1909). Nobel Prize for Literature (1947).

Gielgud, Sir [Arthur] John (1904–   ), English stage, film actor, producer. Played many leading roles in Sheridan and Shakespeare (esp. Hamlet).

Gijón, city of Asturias, NW Spain, on Bay of Biscay. Pop. 188,000. Port, exports coal and iron ore; iron and steel, glass industs.

gila monster, *Heloderma suspectum*, venomous lizard of deserts of SW US and Mexico. Body covered with bead-like scales arranged in bands of orange and black.

Gilbert, Sir W[illiam] S[chwenck] (1836–1911), English author. Known as librettist of SULLIVAN's light operas, *eg Trial by Jury* (1875), *H.M.S. Pinafore* (1878), *The Pirates of Penzance* (1879), *Iolanthe* (1882) *The Mikado* (1885).

Gilbert and Ellice Islands, two ex-colonies of UK, in WC Pacific Ocean. Incl. Gilbert Isls., Ellice Isls., some of Line, Phoenix Isls. Area 930 sq km (360 sq mi); pop. 64,000; cap. Tarawa (Gilbert Isl.). Produce copra, phosphates; fishing, tourist industs. Gilbert, Ellice groups became protectorate 1892; colony formed 1915. Line, Phoenix groups joined 20th cent. Ellice Isls. withdrew, formed separate territ. of Tuvalu (1976); independent (1978). Gilbert Isls. became independent as Kiribati (1978).

Gilgamesh, hero of Babylonian epic. Earliest known written epic (c 2000 BC) found on clay tablets in ruins of Nineveh. Gilgamesh story prob. much older, of Sumerian origin, tells of his search for immortality after friend Enkidu dies. Some parallels with OT, *eg* Noah figure, Flood.

Gill, [Arthur] Eric [Rowland] (1882–1940), English sculptor, engraver, type designer. Attempted to revive religious attitude to art; sculpture incl. *Stations of the Cross* in Westminster Cathedral. Illustrated books and designed 'Gill Sans-serif' alphabet.

gill, organ in aquatic animals for absorption of oxygen dissolved in water. Consists of membrane or outgrowth of body surface through which oxygen passes into blood and carbon dioxide into water. Fish have internal gills; external gills found on amphibian larvae, molluscs, *etc.*

Gillingham, mun. bor. of Kent, SE England on R. Medway. Pop. 87,000. Dockyards; fruit growing.

Gillray, James (1757-1815), English caricaturist. Satirized family of George III in *A New Way to Pay the National Debt* (1786); lampooned the French, politicians and social customs of his day.

gin, alcoholic spirit distilled from grain and flavoured with juniper berries. Major producers are Netherlands, where it originated in 17th cent., Britain and US.

ginger, *Zingiber officinale*, perennial plant. Originally from S China but known to ancient Greeks, Romans and Indians. Hot, spicy root is sliced and preserved in syrup as confection. Ground ginger is used as spice.

ginkgo or **maidenhair tree**, *Ginkgo biloba*, deciduous tree, native to China. Fan-shaped leaves, fleshy seeds in edible kernel. Survivor of prehistoric era. Widely cultivated as ornament.

Ginsberg, Allen (1926-), American poet. Leader of BEAT GENERATION. Best known for *Howl* (1956) lamenting sickness of American society. Other works incl. *Reality Sandwiches* (1965), *Ankor Wat* (1968).

ginseng, aromatic plant of genus *Panax*. Species incl. Chinese, *P. schinseng* and *P. quinquefolium* of North American woodlands. Aromatic root has sweetish taste and was valued medicinally in China.

Giorgione [da Castelfranco], orig. Giorgio Barbarelli (c 1477-1510), Venetian painter. His *Tempest* is considered 1st example of 'landscape of mood'; work has poetic, evocative quality, based on new effects of light and colour. Formative influence on work of Titian and other Venetian artists; little is known of his life.

Giotto [di Bondone] (c 1266-c 1337), Florentine artist. Regarded as founder of modern painting, he broke with formula of Byzantine art and introduced new naturalism into his figures. Works incl. fresco cycle in Arena Chapel, Padua, depicting life and passion of Christ. Probably painted fresco cycle of *Life of St Francis* in Upper Church at Assisi.

gipsy, see GYPSY.

gipsy moth, *Lymantria dispar*, European moth, extinct in Britain since c 1850. Introduced into North America, has become serious pest in forests; caterpillars eat so many leaves that trees die.

giraffe, hoofed long-legged mammal of African grasslands. Tallest of animals (reaches height of 5.5 m/18 ft), uses long neck to eat leaves of trees. Two species, genus *Giraffa*.

Giraudoux, [Hippolyte] Jean (1882-1944), French author, diplomat. Known for highly stylized, verbal plays, eg *Judith* (1931), *La Guerre de Troie n'aura pas lieu* (1935), often adapted from classical myth. Novels incl. *Suzanne et le Pacifique* (1921). Diplomatic career recalled in memoirs.

Girl Guides and **Girl Scouts**, *see*
Boy Scouts.

Gironde, estuary of W France, *c* 72
km (45 mi) long, formed by jct. of
Garonne and Dordogne rivers near
Bordeaux. Major artery of wine
trade.

Girondists, French political party
during Revolution. Moderate republicans, instrumental in estab. of
First Republic (1792-3). Favoured
European war to spread revolutionary ideas. Overthrown by
extremist Jacobins and Cordeliers.

Girtin, Thomas (1775-1802), English landscape painter. Revolutionized watercolour technique in
England, abandoning topographical
style of 18th cent.; introduced bold
style, using broad washes of strong
colour. Works incl. *White House at
Chelsea* (1800).

Giscard d'Estaing, Valéry (1926-
  ), French statesman, president
(1974-). Finance minister (1962-6,
1969-74). Leader of Independent
Republicans (allied with Gaullists),
defeated Mitterrand in presidential
election.

Gish, Dorothy, orig. Dorothy de
Guiche (1898–1968), American
silent film actress. Famous for roles
in D.W. Griffith's films from 1912.
Appeared with her sister, **Lillian
Gish**, orig. Lillian de Guiche (1896-
  ), in *Orphans of the Storm* (1922).

Gissing, George Robert (1857-
1903), English novelist. Works describe crushing effects of poverty,
esp. in *New Grub Street* (1891), on
writers. Also wrote *By the Ionian
Sea* (1901).

Giza, El, or **Gizeh**, city of N Egypt,
on R. Nile opposite Cairo. Pop.
712,000. Produces cotton textiles,

cigarettes, footwear. Nearby is
Great Pyramid of Khufu (Cheops),
one of Seven Wonders of the World,
and the Sphinx.

glacier, moving mass of snow and
ice formed in high mountains and
polar regions. Compaction turns
snow into névé then to granular ice.
Types incl. mountain or valley
glacier, piedmont glacier, ice sheet.

gladiators, the professional fighters
of ancient Rome, who engaged in
mortal combat as a public spectacle,
using sword and shield or sometimes
trident and net.

gladiolus, genus of corm-based
plants native to S Africa. Member of
Iridaceae family. Widely cultivated
as garden plant. Sword-like leaves in
flat vertical fans, spikes of funnel-
shaped flowers.

Gladstone, William Ewart (1809-
98), British statesman, PM (1868-74,
1880-5, 1886, 1892-4). Renowned
orator, policies based upon strong
religious and moral convictions. As
chancellor of the exchequer, promoted free trade and progressive
taxation policy. Headed Liberal
govts. which achieved Irish land
acts, civil service and army reforms,
development of education. Last
ministry, dominated by Irish problems, ended after defeat of Home
Rule bill.

Glamorgan, county of S Wales.
Area 2250 sq km (869 sq mi); pop.
1,299,000; co. town Cardiff. Mountainous in N; fertile Vale of
Glamorgan in S; Gower Penin. in
SW. Main rivers Taff, Neath. Major
indust. area; rich coal deposits
(Rhondda, Merthyr Tydfil); iron and
steel works (Swansea, Port Talbot).

Admin. divided (1974) into West, Mid, South Glamorgan.

gland, organ which builds up chemical compounds from the blood and secretes them. Most glands discharge through ducts either to outer surface of skin, eg sweat glands, or to an inner surface, eg digestive glands secreting into gut. Ductless or ENDOCRINE GLANDS secrete hormones directly into the blood.

Glasgow, Ellen Anderson Gholson (1874-1945), American novelist. Works, eg *Barren Ground* (1925), *In This Our Life* (1941), deal with development of the post-Reconstruction South.

Glasgow, largest city of Scotland, in Strathclyde region, on R. Clyde. Pop. 897,000. Major city; industs. incl. shipbuilding, engineering, textiles, brewing, whisky distilling. Founded 6th cent. by St Kentigern; royal burgh, grew mainly 18th-19th cents. through tobacco, cotton trade; R. Clyde first deepened 1768. Has 12th cent. cathedral; 2 univs. (1451, 1964); noted art gallery.

glass, hard brittle substance, usually made by fusing sand (silica) with lime and soda or potash; molten mass is rapidly cooled to prevent crystallization. Other metallic oxides, eg lead, barium or aluminium, are added to increase durability, impart colour or provide special optical properties.

glass fibre, fine filaments of glass which may be woven into a cloth and impregnated with hard-setting resins. The resulting material is extremely strong, lightweight and corrosion resistant. Used in boat and vehicle-body construction.

glass snake, lizard of genus *Ophisaurus* of slow-worm family. Legless and with vestigial limbs; diet of insects, small animals. Tail breaks easily, hence name. Species incl. *O. apodus* of Asia Minor and Balkans.

Glastonbury, mun. bor. of Somerset, SW England. Pop. 7000. In legend, site of 1st English Christian church estab. by Joseph of Arimathea; burial place of King Arthur. Has ruined 8th cent. abbey. Ancient lake villages nearby.

glaucoma, disease of the eye characterized by abnormally high pressure within eyeball; often results in impaired vision or blindness. Usually requires surgery or treatment by drugs.

Glazunov, Aleksandr Konstantinovich (1865-1936), Russian composer. Wrote in romantic rather than nationalist style of his teacher Rimsky-Korsakov. Composed 8 symphonies.

Gleiwitz, see GLIWICE, Poland.

Glencoe, valley of R. Coe, Strathclyde region, W Scotland. Scene of massacre (1692) of clan Macdonald by Campbells and English.

Glendower, Owen (c 1359-c 1416), Welsh chieftain. Led series of revolts in Wales against Henry IV, defeating king's forces in campaigns of 1400-2. Lost ground after 1405, the revolt being effectively over by 1409.

Glenn, John Herschel (1922-), American astronaut. First American to orbit Earth (Feb. 1962), achieved aboard *Mercury* space capsule.

gliding, sport of flying heavier-than-air machine without engine power, using air currents to gain height, and gravity to maintain forward motion. First gliders were developed by Otto

Lilienthal in 1890s and also by the Wright brothers. Sport first organized in 1920s.

Glinka, Mikhail Ivanovich (1804-57), Russian composer. One of founders of Romantic movement, he also created a characteristic 'Russian' style. Best-known works are operas *A Life for the Tsar* and *Russlan and Ludmilla*.

Gliwice (Ger. *Gleiwitz*), city of S Poland. Pop. 171,000. Coalmining, steel works, engineering. Under Prussian rule 1742-1945.

globe fish, any of several tropical fish that can inflate themselves into globular form as defence measure by swallowing air. Incl. PUFFER fish.

Globe Theatre, Elizabethan playhouse in London. Built in 1599, destroyed by fire (1613) during first night of Shakespeare's *Henry VIII*. Rebuilt but finally demolished in 1644 by Puritans. Most of Shakespeare's plays first staged here.

glockenspiel, tuned percussion instrument consisting of set of steel bars of different lengths, which player hits with hammers. Produces high but penetrating bell-like sound.

Glorious Revolution (1688-9), in English history, overthrow of Catholic James II by united Whig and Tory opposition. William of Orange was petitioned by Whig and Tory leaders to rule as William III jointly with Mary, James' Protestant daughter. Their acceptance of Bill of Rights assured Parliament's authority in place of 'divine right of kings'.

glottis, opening between vocal chords in larynx, which controls production of sound.

Gloucester, Gilbert de Clare, 8th Earl of (1243-95), English

nobleman. Joined de Montfort in defeat of Henry III at Lewes (1264). Took royalist side in defeat of de Montfort at Evesham (1265). Captured London (1267) and eventually became reconciled to Henry III.

Gloucester, Thomas of Woodstock, Duke of (1355-97), English nobleman. Led baronial opposition to Richard II. Forced dismissal of Richard's chancellor (1386) and defeated (1387) his adviser, de Vere, leaving the king powerless. Reconciled to Richard (1389), later arrested for further intrigues and prob. murdered.

Gloucestershire, county of W England. Area 2638 sq km (1018 sq mi); pop. 482,000. Cotswold Hills in E (sheep); lower Severn valley in C (dairying, fruit); Forest of Dean in W (coal). Co. town Gloucester, on R. Severn. Pop. 90,000. City, river port; timber trade. Hist. Roman town; has cathedral (15th cent.) on site of abbey (681).

glow-worm, larva or wingless female of various luminescent beetles of Lampyridae family, esp. *Lampyris noctiluca*. Organs on abdomen produce greenish light by enzyme action.

Glubb, Sir John Bagot (1897-), British soldier, known as 'Glubb Pasha'. Commander of Arab legion from 1939. Dismissed as result of anti-British public opinion (1956).

Gluck, Christoph Willibald von (1714-87), German composer, active in Paris, Vienna. Reformed opera by stressing importance of drama, simplicity. Works incl. *Orfeo ed Euridice*, *Alcestis*, *Iphigénie en Tauride*.

glucose, crystalline sugar, occurring in fruit and honey. Sugars and other carbohydrates are converted into glucose in body; its oxidation to carbon dioxide and water is major energy source. Produced commercially by hydrolysis of starch.

gluten, sticky protein substance, found in wheat and other grain; gives dough its elastic consistency.

glutton, see WOLVERINE.

glycerol or **glycerin[e],** colourless viscous alcohol, obtained by hydrolysis of fats during manufacture of soap. Glycerides, its esters with fatty acids, are chief constituents of fats and oils. Used in manufacture of explosives, resins, foodstuffs, toilet preparations and as antifreeze.

glycogen or **animal starch,** carbohydrate formed from glucose and stored in animal tissues, esp. liver and muscles. Can be reconverted into glucose to supply body's energy needs.

glycol or **ethylene glycol,** colourless viscous liquid, used in manufacture of polyester fibres (Dacron, Terylene) and as antifreeze.

gnat, two-winged fly of mosquito family with piercing mouthparts and long antennae. Name applied to mosquito in Britain, to smaller flies in US.

gnatcatcher, small insectivorous American warbler of genus *Polioptila.*

gneiss, coarse-grained, crystalline rock, resembling granite. Formed by metamorphism of igneous and sedimentary rock; displays alternate bands of constituents, *eg* feldspar, hornblende, mica. Major sources in Scotland, Scandinavia, Canada.

Gnosticism, system of belief combining ideas from Christian theology, Greek philosophy and diverse mystic cults. Arose during 1st cent. Followers believed in salvation through direct spiritual knowledge rather than faith. Influenced early Christianity by forcing it to define its doctrine in declaring Gnosticism heretical.

gnu or **wildebeest,** large antelope of E and S Africa, with buffalo-like head, hairy mane, beard and tail. Two species, genus *Connochaetes;* white-tailed gnu, *C. gnu,* nearly extinct but now protected.

Goa, former Portuguese enclave of W India. Area *c* 3500 sq km (1350 sq mi); pop. 537,000; cap. Panjim. Captured by Portuguese (1510), seized by India (1961). Has tomb of missionary St Francis Xavier. Part of union territ. of Goa, Daman and Diu.

goat, hollow-horned ruminant, genus *Capra,* related to sheep. Usually coarse-haired, males bearded. Domesticated varieties kept for nutritious milk, flesh, hair; wild goats incl. IBEX.

goatsucker, see NIGHTJAR.

Gobelins, Manufacture Nationale des, French tapestry manufactory. Founded in 15th cent. as dye works, purchased 1662 by Louis XIV. Now state-controlled.

Gobi Desert, sandy region of C Asia (China, Mongolia). Area *c* 1,295,000 sq km (500,000 sq mi); av. alt. 1200 m (4000 ft). Grassy fringes inhabited by pastoral Mongols. Several sites where dinosaur eggs have been found.

goby, any of Gobiidae family of spiny-finned carnivorous fish. Pelvic fins joined to form suction disc, used to cling to rocks. Freshwater and saltwater varieties. Species incl. giant goby, *Gobius cobitis*.

God, in the three major monotheistic religions (Judaism, Christianity, Islam), creator and ruler of the universe. Regarded as eternal, infinite, immanent, omniscient. Often given attributes of goodness, love, mercy. In Christianity, believed to have lived on earth in person of Jesus Christ. *See* TRINITY.

Godard, Jean-Luc (1930-), French film writer-director. After semi-surrealist *A Bout de Souffle* (1960), *Alphaville* (1965), made political films, eg *Tout va bien* (1972).

Godavari, river of SC India. Flows *c* 1440 km (900 mi) SE from Western Ghats (Maharashtra) across the Deccan to Bay of Bengal. Sacred to Hindus.

Gödel, Kurt (1906-1978), American mathematical logician, b. Czechoslovakia. Noted for work on foundations of mathematics. Showed that, beginning with any set of axioms, there will always be statements, within a system governed by these axioms, that are neither provable nor disprovable in the system; thus mathematics cannot be proved consistent.

Godesberg or **Bad Godesberg**, town of W West Germany, on R. Rhine. Mineral springs; embassies, diplomats' residences. Site of meeting (1938) between Chamberlain and Hitler prior to Munich Pact. Incorporated (1969) into Bonn.

Godfrey of Bouillon (*c* 1059-1100), duke of Lower Lorraine, leader of the 1st Crusade (1096). After conquest of Jerusalem (1099), was elected its ruler, but refused the title of king, preferring 'protector of the Holy Sepulchre'.

Godiva (*fl c* 1040-80), wife of Leofric, earl of Mercia. According to legend, she rode naked through the streets of Coventry so that her husband would grant her request to relieve the people of his heavy taxes.

Godolphin, Sidney Godolphin, 1st Earl of (1645-1712), English statesman. Noted for financial expertise, served as first lord of treasury (1684-9, 1700-1, 1702-10). Close associate of Marlborough. Dismissed (1710) by Queen Anne.

Godoy, Manuel de (1767-1851), Spanish statesman. Royal favourite, became (1792) chief minister to Charles IV. Opposed revolutionary France, but made peace (1795). Subsequent dependence on France and corrupt regime led to his overthrow (1808).

God Save the King/Queen, British national anthem. Of obscure origin, its 1st public performance was during Jacobite rebellion of 1745. Same tune is also used for songs 'God Save America' and 'My Country 'Tis Of Thee'.

Godthaab, cap. of Greenland, on Godthaab Fjord. Pop.6000. Port; founded 1721, first Danish colony on Greenland.

Godunov, Boris (*c* 1551-1605), tsar of Russia (1598-1605). Favourite of Ivan IV; ruled as regent during reign of Feodor I (1584-98) before succeeding him. Prob. had Dmitri, Feodor's brother and heir, murdered. Died while opposing pretender who claimed to be Dmitri.

Godwin (d. 1053), earl of Wessex, chief adviser to Canute and Edward the Confessor. Helped Edward to the throne (1042) and married his daughter Edith to him. Led opposition to king's French favourites, for which he and sons were exiled. Invaded England (1052), forced Edward to reinstate him. His son Harold succeeded Edward for 4 months.

Godwin, William (1756-1836), English writer. Best known for *An Enquiry Concerning Political Justice* (1793) arguing that best society would be one of rational individualists. Theories influenced Romantic poets. Wrote novel, *Caleb Williams, on Things as They Are* (1794). Husband of MARY WOLLSTONECRAFT.

Godwin-Austen, Mount, see K2.

godwit, migrant wading bird of sandpiper family, genus *Limosa*. European species incl. black-tailed godwit, *L. limosa*, with chestnut breast, and bar-tailed godwit, *L. lapponica*.

Goebbels, Paul Joseph (1897-1945), German political leader. Nazi propaganda minister (1933-45), took control of press, radio and cinema to further Nazi ideals; noted orator. Committed suicide during fall of Berlin.

Goering or **Göring, Hermann Wilhelm** (1893-1946), German political leader. Took part in Munich 'putsch' (1923). Air minister under Hitler (1933); controlled German economy (1937-43). Responsible for expansion of Luftwaffe and air war against Britain (1940-1). Committed suicide after being sentenced to death at Nuremberg trials.

Goes, Hugo van der (d. 1482), Flemish painter. Famous for *Portinari Altarpiece* (Florence), large work depicting the Adoration of the Shepherds. Other works incl. *Monforte Altarpiece* (Berlin).

Goethe, Johann Wolfgang von (1749-1832), German author. Leading figure in STURM UND DRANG movement, also held important cabinet post at Weimar and researched into plant biology and optics. Known for romantic novel *The Sorrows of Young Werther* (1774). Later classical works incl. plays *Iphigenia in Tauris* (1787), *Torquato Tasso* (1790), novel *Wilhelm Meister* (2 vols., 1796). Later works indicate regained sympathy with Romanticism. *Faust* (Part I, 1808; Part II, 1832) remains his masterpiece, a symbolic representation of the human search for knowledge and experience.

Gog and Magog, giant gods of ancient Britain. Gog was husband or son of mother goddess Magog, who was associated with a horse cult and worshipped throughout western Europe. They may be represented by certain hill figures in Britain.

Gogarty, Oliver St John (1878-1957), Irish poet. Known as Dublin wit at time of Irish renaissance, prototype of Buck Mulligan in Joyce's *Ulysses*. Works incl. autobiog. *As I Was Going Down Sackville Street* (1936).

Gogh, Vincent van (1853-90), Dutch painter. Early work, dark and heavy in form, replaced by lighter impressionist technique in Paris (1886). Settled at Arles (1888), where he was briefly joined by Gauguin. From 1888, subject to fits of insanity, he produced portraits and landscapes, painted in bold colour with swirling brushstrokes. Committed suicide in Auvers. Work, which influenced later expressionists, incl. *Sunflowers* and *Starry Night.*

Gogol, Nikolai Vasilyevich (1809-52), Russian author. Works mix stark realism with grotesque caricature and fantasy as in short story 'The Overcoat' (1842), satirical comedy *The Inspector General* (1836) about provincial bureaucracy. Novel *Dead Souls* (1842) is about trickster who mortgages dead serfs to make fortune.

Goiânia, town of C Brazil, cap. of Goiás state. Pop. 389,000. Commercial centre, livestock market, coffee exports. Modern planned city, built to replace Goiás City as state cap. (1937).

goitre, enlargement of thyroid gland producing swelling on front of neck. Simple goitre is caused by iodine deficiency; incidence is reduced by adding iodine to table salt. Exophthalmic goitre or Grave's disease, caused by over-activity of thyroid, is accompanied by protrusion of eyeballs.

Golan Heights, mountain ridge of SW Syria. Great strategic importance; taken by Israelis in 1967 war; after 1973 war occupied by UN forces.

gold (Au), ductile, malleable metallic element; at. no. 79, at. wt. 196.97. Chemically inert; resists corrosion; found free. Used in coinage, jewellery and dentistry (alloyed with silver or copper).

Gold Coast, see GHANA.

goldcrest, *Regulus regulus,* smallest European bird, with yellow crown, olive green upper-parts. Found in coniferous woods.

golden eagle, *Aquila chrysaetos,* large eagle of mountainous regions of N hemisphere. Dark plumage with golden tinge on head. Diet of birds, rodents.

Golden Fleece, in Greek myth, fleece of winged ram which carried Phrixus and Helle from the intrigues of their father's concubine. Phrixus sacrificed ram; fleece guarded by dragon at Colchis. Later recovered by JASON.

Golden Gate Bridge, suspension bridge over Golden Gate waterway, San Francisco, US. Opened 1937, its total length is 2824 m (9266 ft); main span 1280 m (4200 ft) is one of world's longest bridges.

Golden Hind, ship in which Sir Francis Drake circumnavigated the world (1577-1580), and on whose deck he was knighted by Elizabeth I on return.

Golden Horde, Mongol warriors of Batu Khan, so-called from the splendour of his camp. Their empire was estab. in mid-13th cent. and comprised most of Russia. They took part in Kublai Khan's Chinese conquests. Empire broke up into autonomous khanates after 1405, finally crushed by IVAN III (1487).

Golden Horn, see BOSPORUS.

goldenrod, any of genus *Solidago* of perennial plants of Compositae family, with spikes of yellow flowers. Native to Europe and North America. Species incl. *S. virgaurea* and *S. canadensis.* Formerly thought to have medicinal properties.

goldfinch, *Carduelis carduelis,* Eurasian finch with scarlet face, black and yellow wings. Sociable, found in gardens, orchards, etc.

goldfish, *Carassius auratus*, small freshwater fish of carp family, of Asiatic origin. Many domestic varieties obtained by controlled breeding; often kept in ponds, fishbowls.

Golding, William Gerald (1911–), English novelist. Best known for first novel, moral allegory *Lord of the Flies* (1954). Other novels incl. *Pincher Martin* (1956), *The Spire* (1964).

Goldsmith, Oliver (1730–74), English author, b. Ireland. Known for humorous pastoral novel *The Vicar of Wakefield* (1766). Also wrote poem *The Deserted Village*, regretting rural enclosures, and comedy *She Stoops to Conquer* (1773).

gold standard, system whereby a unit of currency is equal to and redeemable in a specified quantity of gold. Used as international reference for currencies in late 19th cent. International gold standard broke down in WWI. Many currencies now fixed to US dollar.

Goldwyn, Samuel, orig. Samuel Goldfish (1882–1974), American film producer, b. Poland. Leading producer since *The Squaw Man* (1913), other films incl. *Wuthering Heights* (1939), *The Best Years of Our Lives* (1946). With L.B. MAYER, formed Metro-Goldwyn-Mayer (MGM) (1924).

golem, in medieval Jewish legend, a robot servant artificially created by cabalistic rites. Often associated with rabbis in European countries, esp. Rabbi Löw in 16th cent. Prague.

golf, game played with ball and clubs over outdoor course. Origins can be traced back to 15th cent. in Scotland. Original 13 rules were drawn up by Royal and Ancient Club, St Andrews, Scotland (1754). Great growth as leisure activity and as professional sport, esp. in US, dates from 1920s. Standard golf course comprises 18 holes of varying length (total *c* 4500–5000 m/5000-.6000 yd).

Golgotha, Aramaic name for CALVARY.

Goliath, in OT, giant champion of Philistines, enemies of Israel. Killed by David with a stone from his sling (1 Samuel 17).

Gollancz, Sir Victor (1893–1967), English writer, publisher. Founded Left Book Club (1936).

Gompers, Samuel (1850–1924), American labour leader, b. England. Instrumental in founding American Federation of Labor (1886), serving as its president (1886–94, 1896–1924). Opposed to radical or socialist programmes, goals incl. less working hours and higher wages.

Gomułka, Władysław (1905–), Polish political leader. Became leader of Polish Communist Party (1943), expelled (1949) for 'nationalist deviations'. Reinstated after Poznań riots (1956). Resigned during 1970 riots over massive food price increases.

Goncharov, Ivan Aleksandrovich (1812–91), Russian novelist. Known for classic realist novel *Oblomov* (1859) creating prototype of rich, idle 'superfluous man'.

Goncourt, Edmond [Huot] de (1822–96) and **Jules de Goncourt** (1830–70), French writers, brothers. Novels *Renée Mauperin* (1864), *Germinie Lacerteux* (1869) anticipate Naturalism. Best known for *Journal*, kept from 1851-70, recording French literary life. Edmond left sum in will to found Académie Goncourt which awards annual Prix Goncourt for best piece of imaginative prose.

gong, percussion instrument of Oriental origin, consisting of free-hanging metal disc with turned-in edges; struck with mallet.

gonorrhoea, acute infectious inflammation of mucous membranes of genital passages; caused by a gonococcus transmitted during sexual intercourse. Symptoms are pain in passing water and discharge of pus from urethra. Treated by antibiotics, eg penicillin.

Good Friday, the Friday before Easter Sunday, observed by Christians as commemoration of Jesus' crucifixion.

Good Hope, Cape of, headland of SW Cape Prov., South Africa, on W side of False Bay. Rounded (1488) and named 'Cape of Storms' by Bartolomeu Dias; renamed by Henry the Navigator.

Goodman, Benjamin David ('Benny') (1909-), American band leader, clarinettist. Organized his own orchestra from 1933, and contributed to development of swing music. First American band leader to employ both black and white musicians.

Goodwin Sands, sandbars off Kent, SE England. Length 16 km (10 mi); marked by lightships, shipping hazard.

Goodyear, Charles (1800-60), American inventor. Developed vulcanization process for rubber (1839) which prevents it melting in hot weather.

goose, long-necked web-footed bird, related to duck and swan. Two genera, *Anser* being grey, *Branta* black. Domestic goose bred from greylag goose, *Anser anser*. Wild goose is migratory, breeding in tundra regions of N hemisphere. Species incl. Canada goose, *Branta canadensis*, of North America.

gooseberry, shrub of genus *Ribes* of saxifrage family. Esp. *R. uva-crispa*, native to cool, moist climates. Berry used in preserves.

gopher, small burrowing rodent of Geomyidae family of North America. Carries food in fur-lined cheek pouches. Also called pocket gopher.

Gordon, Charles George (1833-85), British soldier and administrator, known as 'Chinese' Gordon. Commanded 'ever victorious army' which suppressed TAIPING REBELLION in China. Governor of Sudan (1877-80); killed after 10-month siege of Khartoum, having been sent to evacuate it during MAHDI's revolt.

Gordon, Lord George (1751-93), English politician. Led mob which marched on Houses of Parliament to petition for repeal of Catholic Relief Act, which had lifted civil restrictions on Catholics. March degenerated into week-long destructive 'Gordon Riots' (1780). Tried for treason, acquitted.

Gorgons, in Greek myth, three sisters (Euryale, Medusa, Stheno) with snakes instead of hair. Their gaze turned people to stone. Medusa, only mortal one, slain by Perseus.

gorilla, *Gorilla gorilla*, largest of anthropoid apes, reaching height of

1.8 m/6 ft; found in forest of W equatorial Africa. Terrestrial, walks on all fours using knuckles; vegetarian diet.

Gorizia (Ger. *Görz*), town of Friuli-Venezia Giulia, NE Italy, on R. Isonzo. Pop. 42,000. Resort; textiles, machinery. Former duchy, passed (1508) to Habsburgs. Battleground in WWI.

Gorki, Maksim, pseud. of Aleksei Maksimovich Peshkov (1868-1936), Russian author. Early works, *eg* short stories *Twenty-six Men and a Girl* (1899), play *The Lower Depths* (1902), autobiog. *Childhood* (1913-14), draw on wide variety of experiences to express humanist ideals convincingly. After Revolution, formulated conceptual 'socialist realism'.

Gorky, Arshile (1904-48), American painter, b. Armenia. Influenced by cubism of Picasso and surrealism of Miró, he was pioneer of abstract expressionism, using flowing colour to achieve emotional effect.

Gorky or **Gorki**, city of USSR, C European RSFSR; major port at confluence of Volga and Oka. Pop. 1,213,000. Indust. centre, producing textiles, automobiles, chemicals. Founded as Nizhni Novgorod, famous for its fair in 19th cent.; renamed 1932 after novelist Gorki.

Görlitz, town of SE East Germany, on R. Neisse. Pop. 89,000. On Polish border; engineering, textiles. Church has 15th cent. replica of Holy Sepulchre.

gorse or **furze**, spiny evergreen bush of Leguminosae family. Fragrant yellow flowers followed by black, hairy seed pods. Species incl. common *Ulex europaeus*.

Gort, John Vereker Gort, 1st Viscount (1886-1946), British army officer. Commanded the British Expeditionary Force at the beginning of WWII and organized the Dunkirk evacuation. Governor of Gibraltar (1941) and of Malta (1942-4) where he organized its defences against constant air attack.

Gorton, John Grey (1911-), Australian statesman, PM (1968-71). Resigned to be succeeded as Liberal leader by W. McMahon.

goshawk, *Accipiter gentilis*, hawk of Eurasia, North America. Feeds on birds, small mammals; trained for falconry.

Gospels of Matthew, Mark, Luke and John, first 4 books of NT. First 3 (known as Synoptic Gospels) agree in subject matter and order of events of life, death and teachings of Jesus. Gospel according to John is a more philosophical book demonstrating Jesus as the vital force in the world.

Gosport, mun. bor. of Hampshire, S England. Pop. 76,000. Port on Portsmouth Harbour; yacht building; has naval barracks.

Gossaert, Jan, *see* MABUSE, JAN.

Gosse, Sir Edmund William (1849-1928), English author. Known for account of his fanatically religious upbringing, *Father and Son* (1907), biog., esp. of Donne, translations of Ibsen influential in bringing the 'new drama' to England.

Göta Canal, waterway of S Sweden. Length c 385 km (240 mi), from Göteborg via R. Göta, Lakes Vänern, Vättern to Baltic Sea near Söderköping. Opened 1832.

Göteborg or **Gothenburg**, city of SW Sweden, icefree port on Kattegat at mouth of R. Göta. Pop. 486,000. Fishing; marine engineering. Founded (1619) by Gustavus Adolphus; cathedral, 17th cent. town hall, univ. (1891).

Gotha, Almanach de, reference book on European royalty and nobility, pub. annually (1863-1944) at Gotha, Germany. Incl. details of admin. and statistics on most countries.

Gothenburg, see GÖTEBORG, Sweden.

Gothic, style of architecture which developed in France (12th cent.) and was dominant in W Europe until 16th cent. Characterized by use of flying buttresses, ribbed vaulting, pointed arches. Early examples of style incl. St Denis Abbey (1140) and Notre Dame in Paris (1163). English Gothic is divided into Early English (eg Salisbury Cathedral), decorated (eg Exeter Cathedral) and perpendicular (eg Gloucester Cathedral).

Gothic revival, in architecture, revival of Gothic style in late 18th and 19th cents., esp. in Britain and US. Horace Walpole's Strawberry Hill (1750-70) is early example of style. Influential writings of Pugin and Ruskin made it dominant in Victorian era, esp. for design of churches.

Goths, Germanic people, originally inhabiting the Vistula basin, who invaded E parts of Roman empire in 3rd and 4th cents. Divided into 2 branches: West Goths or VISIGOTHS; East Goths or OSTROGOTHS.

Gotland, Baltic isl. of SE Sweden. Area 3173 sq km (1225 sq mi); cap. Visby. Cereals, sugar beet; tourism. Trade centre from Stone Age. Taken by Sweden (1280); held by Danish (1570-1645).

Gottfried von Strassburg (fl 13th cent.), German poet. Wrote major epic, Tristan (c 1210), on which Wagner based opera Tristan und Isolde.

Göttingen, city of NE West Germany, on R. Leine. Pop. 111,000. Precision instruments, machinery mfg. Hanseatic League member from 1351. Univ. (1724), famous for expulsion (1837) of brothers Grimm; now noted for maths, physics.

Gottwald, Klement (1896-1953), Czechoslovak political leader. Premier in provisional govt. (1946-8), replaced (1948) Beneš as president after Communist coup. Supported Soviet Union and satellite status of country, purged party of liberal elements.

gouache, method of painting which mixes watercolours with gum arabic, thus rendering them opaque.

Gouda, town of W Netherlands. Pop. 46,000. Market for Gouda cheese; pottery. Gothic town hall.

Gould, Jay (1836-92), American financial speculator. With James Fisk (1834-72), gained control over Erie Railroad, defeating Cornelius Vanderbilt, and ruined it through stock manipulation. Also with Fisk, caused Black Friday stock speculation scandal (1868). Controlled Union Pacific and other railways.

Gounod, Charles (1818-93), French composer. Outstanding works are operas Faust and Romeo and Juliet; also wrote church music, eg La Rédemption.

gourami, Osphronemus goramy, freshwater, food fish of SE Asia.

Brightly coloured varieties popular as aquarium fish.

gourd, member of Cucurbitaceae family of trailing plants with succulent, usually edible fruit *eg* squash, melon, pumpkin; mostly of Asian and Mexican origin. Esp. *Cucurbita maxima,* a globular yellow gourd which weighs up to 110 kg/240 lb.

gout, metabolic disease confined mainly to males. Characterized by excess of uric acid in blood and deposition of sodium urate crystals in joints. Results in painful and tender inflammation of affected parts (often big toe). Treatment by drugs and dietary control.

Gow, Niel (1727-1807), Scottish violinist. Most famous exponent of traditional Scottish fiddle music. Added many collections of reels and strathspeys to published repertoire.

Gower, John (d. 1408), English poet. Friend of Chaucer, known for moral and didactic works, *eg Confessio Amantis* (1390), series of tales illustrating Seven Deadly Sins. Also wrote French, Latin, other English poems.

Gowon, Yakubu (1934-), Nigerian military, political leader. Emerged as head of federal military govt. after 1966 coups. Crushed Biafran attempt to secede (1967-70). Overthrown by coup (1975) after period of economic mismanagement.

Goya [y Lucientes], Francisco José de (1746-1828), Spanish painter. Court painter to the king (1786), his paintings of royal family show his contempt for their stupidity Produced series of etchings incl. 'Caprices', 'Bullfight', 'Disasters of War'. Macabre 'black paintings' of later years incl. *Saturn Devouring his Children.* Work influenced 19th cent. French painters, esp. Manet.

Gozo, see MALTA.

Gozon, Marquis de (1712-59), French general. Commanded French forces in Canada after 1756, capturing Fort William and defending Ticonderoga (1758). He was defeated and mortally wounded at Québec by British under Wolfe.

Grable, Betty (1916-73), American film actress. Most famous pin-up of WWII, films incl. *Million Dollar Legs* (1939), *Tin Pan Alley* (1940).

Gracchus, Tiberius Sempronius (163-133 BC), Roman politician. As tribune (133), introduced law to redistribute state land held by the rich among small land-holders. Attempt to be re-elected tribune was declared illegal by the senate and he was killed during subsequent riots. His brother, **Gaius Sempronius Gracchus** (153-121 BC), was elected tribune (123, 122), reintroduced Tiberius' agrarian reforms and reduced power of aristocracy. Failed in re-election bid (121) and was killed during election riots.

Grace, W[illiam] G[ilbert] (1848-1915), English cricketer. Greatest cricketer of his times, he scored over 54,000 runs, incl. 126 centuries, and took over 2800 wickets in his first-class career. Captained England 13 times.

grace, in Christian theology, the unmerited love and favour of God towards man, which redeems his original sin and allows him to enjoy eternal life. Most theologies retain man's freedom in accepting grace, but CALVINISM holds that grace is irresistible but only offered to those whose salvation is predestined.

Graces, see CHARITES.

grackle, any of several North American blackbirds, esp. purple grackle, *Quiscalus quiscula*, common in cities.

Graeae or **Graiae,** in Greek myth, Deino, Enyo and Pemphredo, sisters of the GORGONS. Personification of old age; born with grey hair and only one eye and one tooth between them.

graft, in surgery, see TRANSPLANTATION.

grafting, in horticulture, practice of uniting two plants and growing them as one. The stock may be a mature plant or a root, the scion (part to be grafted on) may be a bud or a cutting.

Graham, Martha (1895-), American choreographer, dancer. One of most important figures in modern dance, creating new forms and her own highly developed technique. Works incl. *Appalachian Spring* (1944).

Graham, Thomas (1805-69), Scottish chemist. Evolved Graham's law on relationship between diffusion rates and densities of gases. Pioneered study of colloid chemistry and developed dialysis process to separate crystalloids from colloids.

Graham, William Franklin ('Billy') (1918-), American evangelist. Has used revivalist techniques with success in US and abroad from 1949.

Grahame, Kenneth (1859-1932), British author. Remembered for children's classic *The Wind in the Willows* (1908).

Graham Land, mountainous penin. of Antarctica, lying between Bel-

lingshausen and Weddell seas. Part of British Antarctic Territ. from 1962.

Grail, Holy, in medieval legend and literature, variously depicted as chalice, dish, stone, or cup. Many pagan elements in legend, but best-known version is Christian one, identifying Grail as cup used in Last Supper, later used by Joseph of Arimathea to catch crucified Christ's blood. Carried by Joseph to England, handed down from generation to generation. Became subject of quest by Arthur's knights, would be revealed only to pure knight. See ARTHURIAN LEGEND.

Grainger, Percy Aldridge (1882-1961), Australian composer, pianist. Known for arrangements of folk music, eg *Shepherd's Hey, Country Gardens*. Settled in US (1914).

gram, unit of mass in c.g.s. system; 1000 grams = 1 kilogram = 2.20462 pounds.

grammar school, in England, state-financed secondary school, attended by pupils selected on academic ability. Also see COMPREHENSIVE EDUCATION. Elsewhere, formerly used to refer to some primary or elementary schools.

gramophone or **phonograph,** instrument for reproducing sound that has been mechanically transcribed in a spiral groove on a disc or cylinder. Needle following the groove in rotating disc or cylinder picks up and transmits the sound vibrations. First built (1878) by Thomas Edison; use of discs introduced (1887) by Emile Berliner. Subsequent developments incl. electronic reproduction, stereo.

Grampian, region of NE Scotland.

Area 8702 sq km (3360 sq mi); pop. 437,000. Created 1975, incl. former Morayshire, Banffshire, Aberdeenshire, Kincardineshire.

Grampians, mountain system of Scotland, N of line joining Helensburgh and Stonehaven, and S of Great Glen. Incl. .Ben Nevis, Cairngorms.

grampus, see KILLER WHALE.

Gramsci, Antonio (1891-1937), Italian political thinker. Developed Marxist concept of hegemony to show how dominant social class projects its economic, political and social attitudes, so that these are accepted as natural order; thus revolution involves creation of alternative hegemony as well as transfer of political and economic power.

Granada, city of S Spain, cap. of Granada prov. Pop. 190,000. Agric. market, tourist centre, univ. (1531). Cap. of Moorish Kingdom from 1238; last Moorish stronghold in Spain, fell to Castile 1492. Moorish architecture incl. Alhambra palace (13th cent.) and Generalife gardens; cathedral (16th cent.) contains tombs of Ferdinand and Isabella.

Granados [y Campiña], Enrique (1867-1916), Spanish composer. Known for piano pieces, *Goyescas* (1911), later made into opera (1916), inspired by work of Goya. Nationalist influence reflected in *Twelve Spanish Dances*.

Gran Chaco, see CHACO.

Grand Alliance, War of the (1688-97), conflict between France and European coalition known as League of Augsburg (Grand Alliance after 1689), begun when Louis XIV invaded Palatinate. England had sea victories, but Alliance was defeated

in land battles. Concluded by TREATY OF RYSWICK.

Grand Banks, see LABRADOR CURRENT.

Grand Canal (*Yun-ho*), waterway of E China. Extends from Peking to Hangchow, c 1600 km (1000 mi) long. Navigable throughout year by junks, small steamers. Begun in 6th cent. BC taking 2000 years to complete. Economic importance now reduced after silting.

Grand Canyon, gorge of NW Arizona, US; on Colorado R. Length 349 km (217 mi); width 6.4-29 km (4-18 mi); depth 1.6 km (c 1 mi). Has spectacular scenery. Popular tourist region of geological importance. Part of Grand Canyon National Park.

Grand National, annual English steeplechase, run since 1839 in March or April at Aintree, Liverpool, over course 4.5 mi (7.2 km) long. Considered world's greatest steeplechase.

Grand Rapids, town of WC Michigan, US; on Grand R. Pop. 198,000. Agric. market in fruitgrowing area; furniture, paper, electrical goods mfg. Estab. as lumber town in 1820s.

Grand Remonstrance, list of protests against autocratic rule of Charles I of England, drawn up by Long Parliament (1641). Demanded parliamentary control of appointment of royal ministers, church reform.

Grangemouth, town of Central region, C Scotland; on Firth of Forth at E end of Forth and Clyde Canal. Pop. 25,000. Port; oil refining, chemicals mfg.

Granger movement (1867-75), American agrarian grouping estab.

to further educational and social ideals. Organized in local units, called granges; became politicized in protest against economic abuses. Ceased political action after 1875.

granite, coarse-grained, crystalline, igneous rock. Whitish-grey in colour, hard; consists mainly of quartz, feldspar, mica. Formed at depth, occurs as dykes, sills, batholiths; often exposed by erosion of overlying rocks. Used in building. Commonest of plutonic rocks; major sources in US, Canada.

Gran Paradiso, mountain of NW Italy, in Graian Alps. Highest peak (4059 m/13,323 ft) in Italy.

Gran Sasso d'Italia, mountain group of C Italy. Highest part of Apennines, rising to 2913 m (9560 ft) at Monte Corno.

Grant, Cary, orig. Archibald Leach (1904-), British film actor. Star since early 1930s as suave, often humorous, hero of such films as *Bringing up Baby* (1938), *Arsenic and Old Lace* (1944), *Indiscreet* (1958), *Charade* (1963).

Grant, Duncan (1885-1978), British artist. Member of Bloomsbury group; work influenced by Cézanne, Matisse and African art. Output incl. portraits, landscapes, textile designs, stage scenes.

Grant, Ulysses Simpson (1822-85), American general and statesman, president (1869-77). Commanded Union army (1864-5) in Civil War after success of his Vicksburg campaign. Wore down Confederate army by sustained war of attrition, forcing Lee's surrender at Appomattox Courthouse (1865). Republican admin. characterized chiefly by

bitter partisan politics and corruption.

Granville, John Carteret, 1st Earl, *see* CARTERET, JOHN, 1ST EARL GRANVILLE.

Granville-Barker, Harley (1877-1946), English dramatist, director, critic, actor. Known for critical *Prefaces to Shakespeare* (1923-47), plays, eg *The Voysey Inheritance* (1905). Stagings of Shakespeare (1911-13) radically changed production techniques.

grape, smooth-skinned juicy berry of many vines of genus *Vitis*. Globular or oblong shaped, colours vary from green to white, black to purple; grows in clusters. Numerous hybrids and varieties of Old and New World types. Species incl. *V. vinifera* and *V. rotundifolia*. Since ancient times eaten both fresh and dried as fruit, and fermented to produce wine.

grapefruit, *Citrus paradisi*, edible fruit widely cultivated in tropical areas. Round in shape, growing in clusters, with bitter yellow rind and acid juicy pulp.

grape hyacinth, any plant of genus *Muscari* which is hardy bulbous perennial of lily family. Spikes of small blue flowers. Over 40 species native to Europe and Asia Minor.

graphite, soft crystalline form of carbon, known as plumbago or black lead. Occurs naturally. Used as lubricant, in electrical machinery and in making 'lead' pencils.

graptolites, extinct colonial animals, whose skeletons are found as fossils in Cambrian, Ordovician and Silurian rocks. Classified among Protochordata.

Grasmere, *see* AMBLESIDE, England.

Grass, Günter (1927-), German

author, sculptor. Novels incl. *The Tin Drum* (1959), *Dog Years* (1963), *Local Anaesthetic* (1969), reflect political concerns. Also wrote plays, poetry.

grass, any plant of Gramineae family. Long, narrow leaves, jointed stems, flowers in spikelets, seed-like fruit, *eg* wheat, sugar cane, bamboo. Also incl. hay and pasture grasses. Worldwide distribution.

Grasse, town of Provence, SE France. Pop. 32,000. Resort, flower growing; perfume mfg.

grasshopper, insect of order Orthoptera, with hind legs adapted for jumping, thickened forewings, membranous hind wings. Two families: short-horned grasshoppers (Acrididae) and long-horned grasshoppers (Tettigoniidae). Males make chirping noise by rubbing body parts.

grass of parnassus, *Parnassia palustris,* perennial plant with solitary, delicate, white buttercup-like flower. Found in European marshland.

grass snake, *Natrix natrix,* harmless snake common in Europe. Good swimmer, often found near water; diet of mice, fish, frogs. Normally greenish-brown with yellow collar.

Gratian (AD 359-83), Roman emperor (375-83). Ruled Western empire with his brother Valentinian II. Became eastern emperor (378) but appointed Theodosius in his place (379). Influenced by Ambrose, bishop of Milan, he vigorously attacked paganism in Rome. Assassinated by followers of rebel Maximus.

Grattan, Henry (1746-1820), Irish politician, patriot. Led opposition which secured (1782) right of Irish parliament to initiate legislation; gained vote for Catholics in Ireland. Supported Catholic Emancipation; opposed Act of Union (1800) ending Irish parliament.

Graubünden, *see* GRISONS, Switzerland.

gravel, coarse sediment, precisely defined in geology as having particle size between 2 mm and 4 mm. Commonest constituent is quartz. Term also used loosely for mixture of pebbles and rock fragments, used in roadbuilding *etc*.

Graves, Robert Ranke (1895-), English author. Known for autobiog. *Good-bye to All That* (1929) giving account of WWI experiences, historical novels of classical Rome, *eg I, Claudius* (1934), mythography, esp. *The White Goddess* (1948), and poetry in *Collected Poems* (1965).

Gravesend, mun. bor. of Kent, SE England, on R. Thames. Pop. 54,000. Yachting centre; customs and pilot station. Tomb of POCAHONTAS (d. 1617).

gravitation, universal force of attraction between bodies. Newton's law of gravitation states that any 2 particles attract each other with force proportional to product of their masses and inversely proportional to distance between them. Gravity is gravitational force between Earth and bodies near its surface; accounts for weight of a body and its tendency to fall to earth. Modern gravitational theories are based on Einstein's general theory of relativity, in which distribution of matter determines the structure of SPACE-TIME CONTINUUM.

gravitational collapse, in astronomy, tendency of a star to contract under influence of its own gravitation as its store of nuclear fuel becomes depleted. Depending on mass of star, may become white dwarf, supernova or neutron star; for sufficiently large mass, BLACK HOLE may be formed.

Gray, Thomas (1716-71), English poet. Famous for 'Ode on a Distant Prospect of Eton College' (1747), 'Elegy Written in a Country Churchyard' (1751). Other works, mainly Pindaric odes, incl. 'Ode on the Death of a Favourite Cat' (1748).

grayling, *Thymallus thymallus,* grey-coloured freshwater fish of salmon family, widely distributed in Europe.

Gray's Inn, *see* INNS OF COURT.

Graz, city of SE Austria, on R. Mur, cap. of Styria prov. Pop. 249,000. Produces iron, steel, textiles, paper. Built around Schlossberg, ruined hilltop fortress. Gothic cathedral, univ. (1586).

Great Artesian Basin, artesian water-bearing basin of E Australia. Largest in world, area c 1,735,000 sq km (670,000 sq mi); mainly in SW Queensland. Provides water for stock raising.

Great Australian Bight, large bay of S coast of South and Western Australia, part of Indian Ocean. Extends c 1125 km (700 mi) E-W.

Great Barrier Reef, coral reef off NE coast of Australia, extends c 2000 km (1250 mi) from Torres Str. to Tropic of Capricorn. Incl. c 350 types of coral colony; area of tourism.

Great Bear Lake, W Mackenzie Dist., Northwest Territs., Canada. Area 31,800 sq km (c 12,275 sq mi). Drained by Great Bear R. into

Mackenzie R. Navigable only 4 months of year.

Great Belt, *see* BELT, GREAT and LITTLE, Denmark.

Great Britain, largest isl. of British Isles, comprising ENGLAND, SCOTLAND, WALES. isls. governed with mainland (but not N Ireland, Isle of Man, Channel Isls.) Area 230,608 sq km (89,038 sq mi). Bounded by Atlantic, Irish Sea (N, W), English Channel (S), North Sea (E). Highland in N, W (Scottish Highlands, Lake Dist., Pennines, Wales); lowlands in SE. Maritime temperate climate. Political unit from 1707, extended to Ireland 1801. UNITED KINGDOM formed by partition of Ireland (1921).

great circle, circle described on surface of a sphere by a plane which passes through centre of sphere. Shortest distance between 2 points on a sphere lies on great circle passing through them.

Great Dane, breed of large powerful dog with short dense coat. Stands c 76 cm/30 in. at shoulder.

Great Dividing Range, mountain system of E Australia, running parallel to coast from Cape York Penin. to S Victoria. Comprises series of ranges, incl. Blue Mts., Snowy Mts. Forms major watershed.

Great Exhibition, first modern, international indust. exhibition. Held (May-Oct. 1851) under patronage of Prince Albert in CRYSTAL PALACE. Had aim of encouraging craftsmanship, indust. design. Incl. c 100,000 exhibits from c 14,000 exhibitors. Surplus funds were used to estab. Victoria and Albert Museum, Science Museum, Royal College of Art.

Great Glen, fault valley of N Scotland. Length *c* 97 km (60 mi) runs SW-NE from Loch Linnhe to Moray Firth.

Great Lakes, *c* 5 freshwater lakes between Canada and US. They are lakes Superior, Michigan, Huron, Erie, Ontario. Form important transport route with St Lawrence Seaway to E. Main cargoes iron ore, coal, grain. Also have important commercial fisheries, tourist resorts.

Great Plains, grassy plateau region of WC US-Canada. Extend from Rocky Mts. to prairies of Mississippi valley, S to Texas-Oklahoma. Mainly stock-grazing land.

Great Rift Valley, fault system of SW Asia and E Africa. Extends *c* 4800 km/3000 mi from R. Jordan valley (Syria) to C Mozambique; divides into W, E sections in E Africa, filled by many lakes. Ranges from 396 m/1300 ft below sea level (Dead Sea) to 1830 m/6000 ft above sea level (S Kenya).

Great Salt Lake, inland salt lake of N Utah, US. Area 2590 sq km (*c* 1000 sq mi). Salt extracts; size has varied greatly. Is remnant of hist. L. Bonneville.

Great Schism, see SCHISM, GREAT.

Great Slave Lake, S Mackenzie Dist., Northwest Territs., Canada. Area 28,400 sq km (*c* 10,980 sq mi). Drained by Mackenzie R. Gold deposits at Yellowknife. Named after Slave Indians who once lived on its shores.

great tit, *Parus major,* largest Eurasian tit, with blue-black head, yellow under-parts and black stripe on breast.

Great Trek, see TREK, GREAT.

Great Wall of China, fortification across N China running *c* 2400 km (1500 mi) along S edge of Mongolian plain from Kansu prov. to Hopeh prov. on Yellow Sea. First built in 3rd cent BC as protection against hostile nomadic tribes.

Great Yarmouth, co. bor. of Norfolk, E England. Pop. 50,000. Coastal resort; herring indust. ('bloaters' once famous). Large 12th cent. church rebuilt after WWII.

grebe, any of Podicipedidae family of freshwater diving birds with short tail, partially webbed feet; worldwide distribution. Nests in floating vegetation. Largest species is crested grebe.

Greco, El, pseud. of Domenicos Theotocopulos, (*c* 1541-1614), Greek-Spanish painter, b. Crete. Trained in Venice, was influenced by Titian, Michelangelo and Byzantine art. In Toledo, painted visionary religious works in highly mannerist style, characterized by vivid colour, harsh light, twisting of natural shapes. Works incl. *Burial of Count Orgaz, View of Toledo.*

Greece (*Ellas, Hellas*), republic of SE Europe, incl. S Balkan penin., Aegean and Ionian isls. Area 132,000 sq km (50,900 sq mi); pop. 9,165,000; cap. Athens. Language: Greek. Religion: Eastern Orthodox. Pindus Mts. run N-S; fertile valleys. Agric. backward (tobacco, currants, olives); tourist indust. Home of Minoan, Mycenaean civilizations; powerful city-states (eg Athens, Sparta, Corinth) from 6th cent. BC. Centre of literature, art, science. Weakened by city state rivalry (eg Peloponnesian War), conquered 338 BC by Philip II of Macedon. Fell to

Romans 146 BC. Turkish from 1453, revolts led to independence 1829, monarchy from 1832. Territ. gained in Balkan Wars (1913), WWI. Influx of refugees from Turkey in 1920s. Coup (1967) exiled king, estab. military govt. until 1974.

Greek, branch of Indo-European language family. Ancient Greek language associated with major civilization, literature. Its dialects incl. Aeolic, Arcadian, Attic, Ionic, Doric, Cyprian, of which Attic (dialect of Athens) was dominant. From Attic, *koinē* (common language) developed, used all over Mediterranean. NT written in *koinē*, and Modern Greek descended from it. Latter divided into *katharevousa* (written form), and *dēmotikē* (vernacular).

Greek Church, see EASTERN ORTHODOX CHURCH.

Greek myths, legends and literature revolving around themes in Greek religion. Taken from many sources, some indigenous, others Minoan, Mycenaean, Egyptian and Asian, so that the classical Greek pantheon drew deities from all the cultures involved. First consistent picture of resultant blend found in *Iliad*; fullest conscious attempt to connect myths in Hesiod's *Theogony*. As told by Homer, OLYMPIAN GODS were represented as being in charge of natural forces but were not omnipotent and were subject to fate. By time of the tragic dramatists and Plato (c 5th cent. BC) the importance of myth was declining in Greek thought.

Greeley, Horace (1811-72), American newspaper editor, political leader. Founded New York *Tribune*

(1841) as responsible, cheap paper for working class. Advocate of social reforms, coined phrase, 'Go West, young man'. Supported Liberal Republican Party, after earlier encouraging U.S. Grant. Unsuccessful presidential candidate (1872).

Green, Henry, pseud. of Henry Vincent Yorke (1905-73), English novelist. Works, eg *Living* (1929), *Loving* (1945), *Concluding* (1948), expose man's inadequacies in a gently comic light.

green algae, any of the division Chlorophyta of ALGAE in which the chlorophyll is not masked by any other pigment. Considered ancestral type from which higher green plants evolved. Aquatic, mainly freshwater, or terrestrial in moist areas.

Greenaway, Kate (1846-1901), English watercolour painter. Illustrated children's books, eg *Mother Goose, Birthday Book*; her depiction of children in quaint early 19th cent. costume influenced children's fashions.

Greenback Party, political party in US promoting currency expansion (1874-84). Members, mainly farmers, wanted inflated currency to wipe out farm debts from period of high prices. As Greenback Labor Party, enjoyed some success in 1878 congressional election.

green belt, tract of open land surrounding a town or city. Involves restrictions on development to preserve area for farming, woodland, recreational purposes.

Greene, [Henry] Graham (1904-), English author. Novels, concerned with individuals faced with moral dilemmas, incl. *Brighton Rock* (1938), *The Power and the Glory*

(1940). Also wrote 'literary thrillers', esp. *The Third Man* (1950), 'entertainments', eg *Our Man in Havana* (1958), essays and plays.

greenfinch, *Carduelis chloris*, common European songbird. Male is olive-green, with yellow on wings and tail.

greengage, small round variety of plum. Sweet and golden-green in colour. Native to France, introduced into England in 18th cent.

greenhouse effect, the retention of heat from sunlight at the Earth's surface, caused by atmospheric carbon dioxide that admits short-wave radiation but traps longwave radiation emitted by the Earth. Some posit that, because of enormous amounts of carbon dioxide released through man's activities, Earth will suffer continuous heating-up.

Greenland, isl. of Denmark, in N Atlantic, mostly N of Arctic Circle. Area 2,176,000 sq km (840,000 sq mi); pop. 50,000; cap. Godthaab. Ice-cap (incl. Humboldt Glacier of NW) covers most of interior, up to 2450 m (8000 ft) thick. Cryolite mining at Ivigtut; sheep in SW; cod, halibut industs. US air bases at Thule, Sondre Stromfjord. Discovered (*c* 982) by Eric the Red, from whom colonization begun *c* 1721. Danish colony until 1953.

Greenland Sea, arm of Arctic Ocean, connecting it with the Atlantic; lies between Greenland and Spitsbergen. Largely covered with drifting pack-ice.

Greenland shark, *Somniosus microcephalus*, large shark of colder N Atlantic; reaches length of 6.5 m/21 ft. Appears sluggish but is active predator.

Green Mountain Boys, see ALLEN, ETHAN.

Greenock, town of Strathclyde region, WC Scotland. Pop. 69,000. Container port, shipbuilding, sugar refining.

green turtle, *Chelonia mydas*, edible turtle, widely distributed in tropics; feeds on algae. Flesh and eggs highly prized, leading to rarity of species.

Greenwich, bor. of SE Greater London, England, on R. Thames. Pop. 216,000. Created 1965, incl. former Greenwich, Woolwich met. bors. Original site of Royal Observatory (1675) now in Herstmonceux; on prime meridian (long. 0°), source of Greenwich Mean Time. Has Royal Naval Coll.; maritime museum.

Greenwich Village, see NEW YORK CITY.

Greenwood, Walter (1903–), English novelist. Known for first novel *Love on the Dole* (1933), which publicized suffering of working classes during Depression.

Gregorian chant, see PLAINSONG.

Gregory [I] the Great, St (*c* 540–604), Roman monk, pope (590–604). Extended and defined papal authority, promoting monasticism, missions to England. Refusal to recognize patriarch of Constantinople furthered split with Eastern Church. Responsible for major doctrinal pronouncements, changes in liturgy and contribution to development of plainsong (Gregorian chant).

Gregory VII, St, orig. Hildebrand (d. 1085), pope (1073–85). First known as Benedictine monk for Hildebrandine reform, attacking simony, lay investiture, clerical unchastity. Carried on reforms as pope, causing strife with Henry IV of Germany, who sided with party which resented papacy's domination in temporal sphere. Henry, excommunicated twice, captured (1083) Rome, forcing Gregory into exile.

Gregory XI, orig. Pierre Roger de Beaufort (1330-78), French churchman, pope (1370-8). Encouraged by prophecies of Catherine of Siena, he removed the papacy, after much struggle, to Rome from Avignon (1376-7). He condemned Wycliffe's teachings. Elections following death led to Great SCHISM.

Gregory XII, orig. Angelo Corrario (c 1327-1417); Italian pope (1406-15). Attempted to end Great SCHISM by agreeing to resign if Avignon antipope Benedict XIII did so too. Agreement was broken, and later Council of Pisa (1409) deposed both him and antipope. After being pronounced canonical pope by Council of Constance (1415), Gregory resigned.

Gregory XIII, orig. Ugo Buoncompagni (1502-85), Italian churchman, pope (1572-85). Prominent in Council of Trent (1562-3), became cardinal 1565. Supported Jesuits. Introduced Gregorian calendar.

Gregory, Lady [Isabella] Augusta, née Persse (1852-1932), Irish author. A founder manager, director of Abbey Theatre, Dublin. Friend and patron of Yeats, and influential in awakening of self-consciously Irish literary movement.

Grenada, isl. state of SE West Indies, in Windward Isls. Area 311 sq km (120 sq mi); pop. 96,000; cap. St. George's. Cacao, limes, fruit, spice exports; cotton, rum mfg. British colony from 1783, became independent (1974).

grenade, a metal container filled with explosive, thrown by hand or special launcher and detonated by a short time-fuse.

Grenadines, isl. group of SE West Indies, in Windward Isls. Admin. by Grenada and St Vincent.

Grenoble, city of SE France, on R. Isère, cap. of Isère dept. Pop. 162,000. Tourist, winter sports centre; glove mfg., metals indust. based on h.e.p., nuclear research; univ. (1339). Hist. cap. of Dauphiné. Medieval cathedral, 16th cent. Palais de Justice.

Grenville, George (1712-70), British statesman, PM (1763-5). Began (1763) prosecution of JOHN WILKES. His policy of internally taxing America (Stamp Act, 1765) antagonized colonists. His son, **William Wyndham Grenville, Baron Grenville** (1759-1834), was also PM (1806-7). Served as foreign secretary (1791-1801) before forming coalition of 'all the talents' which secured abolition of slave trade.

Grenville, Sir Richard (c 1542-91), English admiral. Commanded (1585) fleet carrying 1st colonists to Virginia. As commander of the *Revenge* he continued to engage a large Spanish fleet off the Azores although mortally wounded and deserted by rest of squadron.

Gresham, Sir Thomas (c 1519-79), English financier. Founder of Royal Exchange; endowed Gresham College, London. Name given to Gresham's law, *ie* that 'bad' money tends to drive 'good' money from circulation.

Greville, Sir [Charles Cavendish] Fulke, 1st Baron Brooke (1554-1628), English author, courtier. Remembered for memoir of friend, *The Life of the Renowned Sir Philip Sidney* (1652). Also wrote love lyrics, philosophical treatises.

Grey, Charles Grey, 2nd Earl (1764-1845), British statesman, PM (1830-4). Foreign secretary (1806-7), resigned over George III's opposition to measure of Catholic Emancipation. His admin. was noted for REFORM BILL of 1832.

Grey, Edward, 1st Viscount Grey of Fallodon (1862-1933), British statesman. Liberal foreign secretary (1905-16), worked in vain to prevent war. Achieved accord with Russia (1907), completing TRIPLE ENTENTE.

Grey, Sir George (1812-98), British colonial administrator. Governor of South Australia (1841-5), then of New Zealand (1845-53, 1861-8), where he helped placate Maoris. Premier of New Zealand (1877-9).

Grey, Lady Jane (c 1537-54), English noblewoman. Married Lord Guildford Dudley, son of NORTHUMBERLAND, who persuaded Edward VI to make Jane his successor, rather than Mary Tudor. She was actually proclaimed queen (July, 1553), imprisoned after 9 days and beheaded.

Grey, Zane (1875-1939), American author. Known for best-selling 'Western' novels incl. *The Last of the Plainsmen* (1908), *Riders of the Purple Sage* (1912), doing much to estab. genre.

greyhound, breed of tall, slender hound, once used to hunt small game; racing of greyhounds popularized in 20th cent. Stands *c* 66 cm/26 in. at shoulder.

greyhound racing, sport in which greyhounds chase mechanically-propelled 'hare' around an oval track. Derived from coursing, it originated in US (1919-20); 1st English track opened 1926.

grey whale, *Eschritius glaucus*, migratory whalebone whale of Arctic; winters on N Pacific coast. Reaches lengths of 13.7 m/45 ft. Almost extinct in 19th cent., now protected.

Grieg, Edvard Hagerup (1843-1907), Norwegian composer. Work combines romantic with national idioms. His *Piano Concerto in A minor* is among the most popular of all concertos; also known for *Peer Gynt* suite.

griffin, mythical creature with body and hind legs of a lion and head and wings of an eagle. Originated in ancient Middle Eastern legend, possibly as protective device representing vigilance.

Griffith, Arthur (1872-1922), Irish statesman. Founder of journal *The United Irishman* (estab. 1899), which he used to campaign for a separate Irish parliament. Leader of SINN FÉIN separatist movement. Became 1st president of Irish Free State (1922).

Griffith, D[avid] W[ark] (1880-1948), American film director-producer. First major US director. Pioneered cinematic techniques, eg flashback, cross-cutting, close-up; best remembered for *Birth of a Nation* (1915), *Intolerance* (1916).

Grignard, François Auguste Victor (1871-1935), French chemist. Awarded Nobel Prize for

Chemistry (1912) for discovery of Grignard reagents, organic compounds of magnesium with alkyl halides; of great importance in organic synthesis.

Grillparzer, Franz (1791-1872), Austrian dramatist. Works, influenced by Shakespeare, incl. historical tragedy *King Ottocar's Success and Downfall* (1825). Also wrote sentimental novella *The Poor Minstrel* (1831).

Grimaldi, Francesco Maria (1618-63), Italian physicist. First to discover diffraction of light and evolve wave theory of light. Also studied and named Moon's dark areas.

Grimm, Jakob Ludwig (1785-1863) and his brother, **Wilhelm Karl Grimm** (1786-1859), German philologists and literary scholars. Famous for collection of folk tales *Grimm's Fairy Tales* (1812-15). Jakob considered founder of comparative philology, famous for Grimm's law, theory of sound changes in Indo-European languages, formulated in *Deutsche Grammatik* (1819-37).

Grimsby, co. bor. of Humberside, E England, at mouth of Humber. Pop. 96,000. Major fishing port; boat building.

Gris, Juan, pseud. of José Victoriano González (1887-1927), Spanish painter. Associated with Picasso, pioneered synthetic cubism, non-representational phase of cubism. Wrote *Les Possibilités de la peinture* (1924).

Grisons (Ger. *Graubünden*), canton of E Switzerland. Largest Swiss canton, area 7110 sq km (2745 sq mi); cap. Chur. Forested mountains; glaciers; headwaters of Inn; Rhine;

resorts. Joined Swiss Confederation 1803.

gritstone, durable, coarse variety of SANDSTONE.

Grivas, George (1898-1974), Greek Cypriot revolutionary. Under the name 'Dighenis' led the EOKA terrorist movement against British rule in Cyprus from 1954 until the settlement of 1959. Launched further terrorist campaign (1971).

grizzly bear, *Ursus horribilis,* brown bear of Alaska, W Canada and Rocky Mts. Most carnivorous of bears, nearly exterminated for attacking livestock.

Gromyko, Andrei Andreyevich (1909-), Soviet diplomat. Held several ambassadorial posts before becoming foreign minister (1957).

Groningen, prov. of NE Netherlands. Area 2328 sq km (899 sq mi). Dairying, large natural gas deposits. Cap. Groningen, pop. 171,000. Railway jct.; agric. market, chemicals. Hanseatic town; did not join Dutch revolt against Spain, taken by Dutch 1594. Univ. (1614).

Groote Eylandt, isl. of Northern Territ., Australia, in Gulf of Carpentaria. Area *c* 2460 sq km (950 sq mi). Part of ARNHEM LAND reserve; 2 mission stations. Manganese deposits.

Gropius, Walter (1883-1969), German architect. Leading functionalist architect, his early factory designs, constructed with industrial materials, were pioneering works in modern style. Founder-director of the Bauhaus (1919-28). Lived in UK, then US from 1930s.

Gros, Antoine Jean, Baron (1771-1835), French painter. Pupil of

David; travelled with Napoleonic armies as official war artist. Best known for his depiction of exploits of Napoleon, incl. *The Battle of Eylau* and *The Plague-stricken at Jaffa.*

Groseilliers, Médard Chouart, Sieur des (c 1618–c 1690), French trader. Explored Canada in search of furs with brother-in-law PIERRE RADISSON. His success influenced English to estab. Hudson's Bay Co.

Grossglockner, highest mountain of Austria, in Hohe Tauern. Height 3796 m (12,460 ft); Grossglocknerstrasse, mountainside road (1935), reaches 2346 m (7700 ft).

Grossmith, George (1847–1912) and his brother, **Weedon Grossmith** (1853–1919), English actors. Known for their collaboration in *Diary of a Nobody* (1892), affectionately satirizing lower middle class life.

Grosz, George (1893–1959), German artist. Associated with dadaism, satirized bourgeoisie, militarism. Later painted symbolic anti-war pieces. Lived in US after 1933.

ground beetle, any of Carabidae family of carnivorous beetles. Larvae and adults found in debris, under rocks, *etc*; feed on insects, slugs, snails. Some have bright metallic colouring, *eg Carabus nitens.* Violet ground beetle, *C. violaceus,* commonest species.

ground ivy, *Glechoma hederacea,* creeping aromatic perennial plant of mint family. Originally European, naturalized in North America.

groundnut, *see* PEANUT.

groundsel or **ragwort,** any plant of *Senecio* genus of Compositae family. Esp. *S. vulgaris* of temperate areas

of Europe, with small yellow flowers and deeply cut leaves.

ground squirrel, one of various burrowing mammals of temperate zones of N hemisphere, genus *Citellus.*

grouse, gamebird of moorlands of N hemisphere with mottled feathers, round body. Species incl. PTARMIGAN, CAPERCAILLIE, and red grouse, *Lagopus lagopus,* common in Scotland.

Grove, Sir George (1820–1900), English musicographer. His *Dictionary of Music and Musicians* (1879–89) is a standard reference work. First director of Royal College of Music (1882–94).

Grozny, city of USSR, cap. of Chechen Ingush auton. republic, S European RSFSR. Pop. 355,000. Major oil centre; connected by pipeline to Caspian and Black seas. Oil discovered here (1893).

Grundtvig, Nikolai Frederik Severin (1783–1872), Danish educator, minister, writer. Founded Danish folk high school system, emphasized teaching of national history and literature.

Grünewald, Matthias (c 1470–1528), German painter. Famous for *Isenheim Altarpiece,* a dramatic depiction of the Crucifixion painted in late Gothic style; work is noted for its portrayal of intense suffering of Christ.

Gruyères (Ger. *Greierz*), town of W Switzerland. Pop. 1000. Famous cheese first made here; cattle.

Guadalajara, city of WC Mexico, cap. of Jalisco state. Pop. 1,196,000. Commercial and route centre, famous glass, pottery industs. Settled 1542. Has 17th cent. colonial architecture; univ. (1792), 16th-17th cent. cathedral. Popular health resort on plateau *c* 1500 m (5000 ft) high.

Guadalajara, town of C Spain, cap. of Guadalajara prov. Pop. 32,000. Agric. market. Scene of Republican victory (1937) in Civil War. Infantado palace (15th cent.).

Guadalcanal, largest of Solomon Isls., in SW Pacific. Area *c* 6500 sq km (2500 sq mi); pop. 24,000; main town Honiara. Copra exports. Discovered 1788; occupied by Japan in WWII, retaken by US (1943) after intensive fighting.

Guadalquivir, river of Spain. Rises in Sierra de Segura, Jaén prov.; flows SW 580 km (360 mi) through Cordoba, Seville. Navigable below Seville. Used for irrigation, h.e.p.

Guadalupe Hidalgo, Treaty of (1848), settlement, signed in suburb of Mexico City, ending war between Mexico and US. Texas and much of SW US recognized as American territ. US paid compensation and settled claims against Mexico.

Guadeloupe, overseas isl. dept. of France, in Leeward Isls., West Indies. Area 1779 sq km (687 sq mi); pop. 360,000; cap. Basse-Terre (pop. 16,000). Comprises 2 islands (Guadeloupe, Grande-Terre), 3 dependencies and N half of ST MARTIN. Fruit, coffee, rum, cacao products. Settled by French in 17th cent.; dept. from 1946.

Guam, largest of Mariana Isls., W Pacific Ocean, territ. of US. Area 540 sq km (210 sq mi); pop. 102,000; cap. Agana. Subsistence farming; economy dominated by US military base. Discovered (1521) by Magel-

lan; taken from Spain by US (1898). Occupied by Japanese (1941-4).

guanaco, *Lama huanacos*, American mammal of camel family, found in arid regions of Andes. Thought by some to be ancestor of domesticated llama; woolly, resembles long-legged sheep.

guano, accumulated excrement of seabirds, found esp. on isls. off coast of Peru. Rich in phosphate and nitrogen, it was formerly an important fertilizer.

Guardi, Francesco (1712-93), Venetian painter. Specialized in Venetian scenes in manner of Canaletto, although his treatment of light is more impressionistic. Collaborated with his brother on religious subjects.

guards, the elite regiments of an army, generally originating from the sovereign's bodyguard. The British guards comprise 2 sections: the Household Cavalry (Life Guards and Horse Guards) and the Foot Guards (Grenadiers, Coldstream, Scots, Irish and Welsh).

Guareschi, Giovanni (1908-68), Italian journalist. Known for humorous stories, eg *The Little World of Don Camillo* (1950), about friendly feud between parish priest and communist mayor.

Guarini, Giovanni Battista (1538-1612), Italian poet. Best known for seminal pastoral play *Il Pastor Fido* (1590), imitating Tasso's *Aminta*, but combining tragedy, comedy.

Guarini, Guarino (1624-83), Italian architect, philosopher, mathematician. His Sindone Chapel and Church of San Lorenzo, Turin, with their complex domes, are major examples of later Baroque.

Guarneri or **Guarnerius,** family of Italian violin makers in Cremona. Founded by **Andrea Guarneri** (c 1626-98), a pupil of AMATI. Most famous member was **Giuseppe Guarneri** (1687-1744), known as 'del Gesu' from cross and letters IHS which appear on his labels.

Guatemala, republic of Central America. Area 108,889 sq km (42,042 sq mi); pop. 6,256,000, mostly Indian; cap. Guatemala City. Languages: Spanish, Indian dialects. Religion: RC. Volcanic mountains near Pacific coast; jungle in N (Péten). Agric. economy: coffee, cotton, banana growing. Hist. civilizations incl. Maya-Quiché; Spanish conquest 1524; gained independence 1821; basis of Central American Federation (1825-38). Frequent earthquakes, esp. 1976.

Guatemala City, cap. of Guatemala, alt. 1520 m (c 5000 ft). Pop. 731,000, largest city in Central America. Coffee exports, textiles, cement, soap mfg. Founded 1776 as cap., rebuilt after 1917-18 earthquakes, badly damaged in 1976 earthquake. Has Univ. of San Carlos (1676).

guava, *Psidium guajava,* small tree of tropical America. Yellowish, pear-shaped, edible fruit is used in preserves.

Guayaquil, port of W Ecuador, at mouth of Guayas R. Pop. 794,000. Bananas, cacao, coffee exports; iron founding, textile mfg. Linked by rail and road with Quito. Founded c 1535; site of hist. Bolívar-San Martin meeting (1822). Suffered from fire and earthquake damage.

gudgeon, *Gobio gobio,* small Euro-pean freshwater fish with 2 barbels; used for bait.

guelder rose or **snowball,** *Viburnum opulus,* bush of honeysuckle family. Native to N temperate regions. Grows to c 2 m/6 ft, with spherical clusters of white flowers.

Guelph, town of S Ontario, Canada; on Speed R. Pop. 60,000. In rich agric. region; electrical goods mfg. Founded 1827.

Guelphs and Ghibellines, rival political factions in late medieval Europe. Rivalry began with strife between Guelphs or Welfs and the Hohenstaufen emperors, to whom Ghibellines were loyal, in 12th cent. Germany. Continued in 13th-14th cent. Italy after Hohenstaufen line died out, with Guelphs at first loyal to papacy and Ghibellines to Holy Roman emperor; later broke up into petty feuds.

Guernica, town of Basque prov., N Spain. Pop. 15,000. Hist. meeting place of Basque parliament. Destruction (1937) by German bombing during Civil War inspired painting by Picasso.

Guernsey, second largest of Channel Isls., UK. Area 62 sq km (24 sq mi); pop. incl. dependencies 54,000; cap. St Peter Port. Fruit, vegetables, flower growing; Guernsey cattle; tourism.

guerrilla warfare, harassing action by small bands of men in enemy-occupied territ. Significant in Communist strategy in SE Asia from 1950s.

Guevara, Ernesto ('Che') (1928-67), Cuban revolutionary, b. Argentina. Guerrilla leader in Cuban invasion (1956), economic adviser in Castro govt. (1959-65). Went to

Bolivia to further Communist revolution; captured while leading guerrilla band, executed. Exploits inspired many left-wing revolutionary movements.

Guggenheim, Meyer (1828-1905), American industrialist, b. Switzerland. Amassed fortune in metal processing. His son, Daniel Guggenheim (1856-1930), was instrumental in merging (1901) smelting interests with American Smelting and Refining Co., of which he was made president. Another of Meyer's sons, Simon Guggenheim (1867-1941) estab., with his wife, the John Simon Guggenheim Memorial Foundation (1925). Another son, Solomon Guggenheim (1861-1949), estab. foundation which founded Solomon R. Guggenheim Museum for modern art (1937).

Guiana, region of NE South America, bounded by Negro, Orinoco, Amazon rivers and Atlantic in E. Mainly highlands, with humid coastal strip. Incl. Guyana, Surinam, French Guiana, parts of Venezuela, N Brazil.

guided missile, type of ROCKET or jet-propelled missile with explosive warhead, controlled in flight by radio or automated guidance system. Developed by Germans in WWII (esp. V-2, using gyroscopic control). Advances in electronics have led to great accuracy in control over thousands of miles. US Minuteman and Polaris missiles are key strategic weapons.

Guienne, see GUYENNE, France.

Guildford, mun. bor. of Surrey, SE England. Pop. 57,000. Has hospital, guildhall (both 17th cent.); cathedral (1936); Univ. of Surrey (1966) Medieval cloth trade.

guilds or **gilds,** associations of people within same craft or trade, powerful in medieval W Europe. They had local control over craft or trade, set standards for craftsmen to work to and prices of goods, protected trade from taxation and estab. status of members in society. Merchant guilds were oldest, craft guilds grew in importance in 12th cent. Disappeared with Industrial Revolution.

guillemot, long-billed diving bird, abundant on N Atlantic coasts. Nests in large colonies on cliffs. Species incl. common guillemot, *Uria aalge,* and black guillemot, *Cepphus grylle.*

Guinea, republic of W Africa. Area 246,000 sq km (95,000 sq mi); pop. 4,529,000; cap. Conakry. Language: French. Religion: Islam. Humid, marshy coastal plain rises to interior highlands, esp. Fouta Djallon dist. in N. Cattle raising important; exports bananas, iron ore, alumina. Former French Guinea estab. 1895; part of French West Africa from 1904; became independent 1958.

Guinea, Equatorial, see EQUATORIAL GUINEA.

Guinea, Gulf of, inlet of Atlantic Ocean off W Africa. Extends from Cape Palmas (Liberia) to Cape Lopez (Gabon). Incl. bights of Benin and Bonny.

Guinea-Bissau, republic of W Africa. Area 36,130 sq km (13,950 sq mi); pop. 534,000; cap. Bissau. Language: Portuguese. Religions: native, Islam. Coastal mangrove swamp, tropical forest; produces palm oil, hardwoods, copra, groundnuts. Centre of slave trade 17th-18th cent.; became Portuguese colony (1879), overseas prov. (1951). Independence gained 1974. Claims right to Cape Verde Isls.

guinea fowl, *Numida meleagris,* turkey-like domestic fowl of African origin. Flesh considered delicacy by Greeks and Romans.

guinea pig, domesticated form of South American cavy. Popular as pet, also used in laboratory experiments.

Guinness, Sir Alec (1914-), English stage, film actor. Best known for parts in films, *eg Kind Hearts and Coronets, The Lavender Hill Mob, The Bridge on the River Kwai.* On stage, remembered for modern-dress *Hamlet* (1958).

Guise, Claude de Lorraine, 1st Duc de (1496-1550), French nobleman. Given title by Francis I; founder of Guise family. His daughter, Mary of Guise, married James V of Scotland and was mother of Mary Queen of Scots. His sons, **François de Lorraine, 2nd Duc de Guise** (1519-63) and **Charles de Lorraine, Cardinal de Guise** (c 1525-74), shared control of France during reign of Francis II, husband of Mary Queen of Scots. Led militant Catholic party which provoked civil war with Huguenots. François was assassinated. His son, **Henri de Lorraine, 3rd Duc de Guise** (1550-88), was largely responsible for Saint Bartholomew's Day Massacre. Formed Catholic League (1576) to oppose Huguenots. Assassinated at king's instigation after leading revolt against HENRY III.

guitar, six-stringed, flat-backed instrument with frets on the finger-

board. Popular in 17th-18th cent., interest in guitar music renewed in 20th cent. Electric guitar, introduced to amplify the sound, has become an instrument in its own right in the hands of rock musicians.

Gujarat, state of W India. Area 190,000 sq km (72,000 sq mi); pop. 26,687,000; cap. Ahmedabad. Mainly fertile plain; incl. Kathiawar penin. and marshy Rann of Kutch. Cereals, cotton grown. Formed (1960) from N and W parts of former Bombay state.

Gujarati, Indic language in Indo-Iranian branch of Indo-European family. Leading West Indic tongue, spoken mainly in Gujarat, Maharashtra states.

Gulbenkian, Calouste Sarkis (1869-1955), British industrialist, diplomat, b. Turkey. He made a vast fortune in oil, becoming known as 'Mr Five Per Cent' through holding 5% of shares in each firm in which he was interested. He estab. the Calouste Gulbenkian Foundation, leaving it most of his fortune, incl. a valuable art collection.

Gulf Stream, warm ocean current of N Atlantic. Flows from Gulf of Mexico NE up US coast. Off Newfoundland merges with the North Atlantic Drift, tempering climate of W and N Europe.

gull, any of Laridae family of web-footed seabirds. White or grey in colour; usually nests on cliffs, rocky coasts. Black-headed gull, *Larus ridibundus,* breeds inland on marshes, moors. HERRING GULL is commonest coastal gull.

gullet, see OESOPHAGUS.

gumbo, see OKRA.

gum tree, see EUCALYPTUS.

gun, *see* ARTILLERY, FIREARMS, PISTOL, MACHINE GUN.

gunboat, originally a small, shallow-draught fighting ship built to operate on rivers. Since WWII a high-speed coastal patrol vessel.

Gunn, Thom (1929-), English poet. Poetry, expressing values of energy, will, intellect, incl. *Fighting Terms* (1954), *The Sense of Movement* (1957), *My Sad Captains* (1961).

gunpowder, an explosive made from potassium nitrate, sulphur and carbon. Believed to have been invented in 9th cent. China and introduced to Europe in 14th cent., its use as a propellant revolutionized warfare, but it is now seldom used except in fireworks.

Gunpowder Plot, *see* FAWKES, GUY.

guppy, *Lebistes reticulatus*, small tropical freshwater fish of South America and Caribbean. Many brightly-coloured varieties bred for aquaria.

Gurkha, certain predominantly Hindu tribes of Nepal. Famed for their fighting qualities, they provided the British army with 10 regiments in WWI, and in WWII fought with distinction in N Africa, Malaya and Burma.

Gustavus I (1496-1560), king of Sweden (1523-60). Elected king after leading peasant rebellion which achieved Swedish independence from Denmark. Estab. Lutheran National Church (1527), gained economic freedom from German-dominated Hanseatic League, made crown hereditary in Vasa family.

Gustavus [II] Adolphus (1594-1632), king of Sweden (1611-32).

Championed Protestant cause in THIRTY YEARS WAR. Brilliant commander, gained series of victories while campaigning in Germany (1630-2). Defeated WALLENSTEIN at Lützen, but was killed.

Gustavus V (1858-1950), king of Sweden (1907-50). Maintained Sweden's neutrality in WWI, WWII. Reign marked by further democratization and strong economy.

Gutenberg, Johann (c 1397-1468), German printer. Regarded as inventor of printing from movable type (c 1437). Entered partnership in Mainz with Johann Fust (1455) to finance publishing of *Mazarin Bible*. Lost press to Fust for defaulting in payment of debt; Fust may have completed printing of this bible (dated 1456).

Guthrie, Sir [William] Tyrone (1900-71), English actor, producer. Administrator of Old Vic and Sadler's Wells theatres (1939-45). Helped found Canada's Shakespeare Festival at Stratford, Ontario (1953).

gutta-percha, rubber-like gum produced from LATEX of several SE Asian trees of *Palaquium* and *Payena* genera. Used in electrical insulation, manufacture of golf balls.

Guyana, country of NE South America, member of British Commonwealth; formerly British Guiana. Area 215,000 sq km (83,000 sq mi); pop. 783,000; cap. Georgetown. Language: English. Religions: Hinduism, Islam, Christianity. Mainly jungle with cultivable coastal strip. Chief products sugar (demerara), rice, bauxite. Settled by Dutch in 17th cent.; British occupation (1796); independence (1966) as Guyana.

Guyenne or **Guienne,** hist. region of SW France, cap. Bordeaux. Formed, with Gascony, duchy of Aquitaine; under English rule (1154-1453).

Gwalior, city of Madhya Pradesh, NC India. Pop. 406,000. Indust. centre; flour milling, cotton goods. Overlooked by Hindu fort containing temples, palaces. Cap. of former princely state of Gwalior.

Gwelo, town of C Rhodesia. Pop. 55,000. Agric. market, footwear mfg., chrome and asbestos industs. Founded 1894.

Gwent, county of SE Wales. Area 1376 sq km (531 sq mi); pop. 442,000; co. town Newport. Created 1974, formerly known as Monmouthshire.

Gwyn or **Gwynne, Eleanor ('Nell')** (1650-87), English comic actress. Principally remembered as favourite and mistress of Charles II, by whom she had 2 sons.

Gwynedd, county of NW Wales. Area 3868 sq km (1493 sq mi); pop. 221,000; co. town Caernarfon. Created 1974, incl. former counties Anglesey, Caernarvonshire, Merionethshire.

gymnastics, performance of athletic exercises, whose competitive form can be traced to ancient Greek Olympics. Modern form was developed in early 19th cent. in Germany, esp. by Ludwig Jahn. First international competition held at 1896 Olympics. Events incl. vaulting and pommel horse, rings, parallel and asymmetric bars, beam and floor exercises.

Gymnophiona, order of limbless, worm-like amphibians. Functionless eyes hidden under skin. Found in Asia, Africa, Central America. Formerly called Caecilia.

gymnosperm, botanical term for seed plants in which ovules are not enclosed in an ovary. They incl. cycads and conifers.

gynaecology, branch of medicine concerned with ailments specific to women, esp. those of reproductive system.

Györ (Ger. **Raab**), city of NW Hungary, on R. Raba. Pop. 107,000. River port; indust. centre. Nearby is abbey founded by St Stephen.

gypsum, hydrous calcium sulphate mineral. Soft, white or grey; found among clays and limestones. Occurs in various forms, eg alabaster, selenite. Used in cement, fertilizers, plaster of Paris. Major sources in US, Mexico, France, Italy.

gypsy, gipsy or **Romany,** member of nomadic tribe, believed to have originated in NW India. Entered Europe in early 15th cent. Spread throughout Europe and North America but mostly found in Balkans, Spain, Italy. Have their own language (Romany) which belongs to Indo-Iranian group. Traditionally earned living by metalworking, fortune telling, horse trading. Est. numbers c 5 million.

gyroscope, wheel mounted so that it is free to rotate about any axis. When spun, its support may be turned in any direction without altering wheel's original plane of motion. Used in gyrocompass, as control device for guided missiles, and, in large form, as ship stabilizer.

H

Haag, Den, *see* HAGUE, THE, Netherlands.

Haakon VII (1872-1957), king of Norway (1905-57). Second son of Frederick VIII of Denmark. Elected king after Norway achieved independence from Sweden. Led resistance to German occupation (1940-5) from Britain.

Haarlem, city of W Netherlands, on R. Spaarne, cap. of North Holland prov. Pop. 173,000. Centre of bulb, flower indust.; printing, chocolate. Sacked by Spanish 1573; centre of painting 16th-17th cents. Church (15th cent.), town hall, Frans Hals museum.

Habakkuk, prophetic book of OT, possibly written c 600 BC. Consists of set of poems on triumph of divine justice and mercy over evil.

habeas corpus (Lat.,= you must have the body), in law, writ or order from judge to custodian of detained person requiring that person be brought before court at stated time, place, for decision on legality of his detention. In UK and US, serves as chief safeguard against illegal detention.

Haber, Fritz (1868-1934), German chemist. Known for Haber process by which ammonia is produced catalytically from hydrogen and nitrogen at high pressures; used in fertilizer manufacture. Awarded Nobel Prize for Chemistry (1918).

Habsburg or **Hapsburg,** ruling house of Austria (1282-1918), also of Hungary and Bohemia (1526-1918), Spain (1516-1700). Austria became hereditary possession under RUDOLPH, count of Habsburg. From 1438, all Holy Roman emperors but one belonged to Habsburg house. Acquired Low Countries through Maximilian I's marriage (1477) to Mary of Burgundy. Reached greatest height as world power under Emperor CHARLES V, who brought Spain into Habsburg dominions. Hungary and Bohemia incorporated (1526) through marriage of Charles' brother, FERDINAND I. Habsburgs lost some territ., *eg* Spain, through wars of succession in 18th cent. With FRANCIS II's assumption of title emperor of Austria (1804), family history became synonymous with that of Austria (AUSTRO-HUNGARIAN MONARCHY) after 1867. After death of Charles I, who abdicated 1918, claims to dynasty passed to his son, Archduke Otto.

Hackney, bor. of NC Greater London, England. Pop. 217,000. Created 1965, former met. bor. incl. Shoreditch, Stoke Newington. Hackney Marsh once highwaymen's haunt.

Haddington, town of Lothian region, SE Scotland. Pop. 7000. Former royal burgh and co. town of

East Lothian. Market town; woollens mfg.

haddock, *Melanogrammus aeglefinus*, marine fish of Gadidae family, similar to cod but smaller; conspicuous black lateral line. Found on N Atlantic coasts of Europe, North America. Eaten fresh or smoked.

Hades, in Greek myth, home of the dead, ruled by Pluto (or Hades) and Persephone. Separated from living world by rivers Styx (hateful), Lethe (forgetfulness), Phlegethon (fiery), Cocytus (wailing), Acheron (woeful). Dead ferried across Styx by CHARON. Entrance was guarded by CERBERUS.

Hadrian (AD 76–138), Roman emperor (117–38), b. Spain. Estab. Euphrates as E frontier of empire, abandoning Trajan's conquests in Mesopotamia. Adopted defensive policy, building walls in Germany and across Britain from Tyne to Solway Firth (126).

hadrons, class of ELEMENTARY PARTICLES which experience the STRONG NUCLEAR INTERACTION. Incl. protons, neutrons, mesons. Hadrons are held to be composed of QUARKS, unlike LEPTONS, the other basic class of elementary particles.

Haeckel, Ernst Heinrich (1834–1919), German biologist. Principal German exponent of Darwinism; his biogenetic law, that each organism in its development repeats stages through which its ancestors passed in course of evolution, was influential in 19th cent. First to construct genealogical trees of living organisms.

haematite or **hematite** (Fe₂O₃), iron ore mineral. Consists of ferric oxide; occurs as reddish-brown earthy masses or dark grey crystals. Found among all types of rocks, often causing reddish colour. Important source of iron. Major sources in US, Canada, Australia.

haemoglobin, red colouring matter of red blood cells of vertebrates. Consists of protein (globin) combined with iron-containing haem. Carries oxygen from lungs to tissues in form of easily decomposed oxyhaemoglobin and carries carbon dioxide back to lungs.

haemophilia, condition in which one of normal blood-clotting factors is absent. Characterized by prolonged bleeding from minor injuries and spontaneous internal bleeding. Inherited only by males through mother.

haemorrhage, escape of large quantities of blood from blood vessels. Blood from cut artery is bright red and comes in spurts; blood from veins is much darker and flows smoothly.

haemorrhoids or **piles**, painful swelling of veins in region of the anus. May occur during pregnancy, as a result of constipation, *etc*. Treated by suppositories or surgery.

Hafiz, Shams al-Din Mohammed (*c* 1326–90), Persian poet. Famed for *c* 500 short lyrics on themes of love and wine.

hafnium (Hf), metallic element; at. no. 72, at. wt. 178.49. Resembles zirconium; found in zirconium minerals. Used in manufacture of tungsten filaments. Discovered (1923) by X-ray spectroscopy.

Hagen, city of W West Germany, in Ruhr. Pop. 200,000. Indust. centre (iron, steel, chemicals, vehicles), formerly noted for textile mfg.

hagfish, any of Myxinidae family of saltwater CYCLOSTOMES, with worm-like body; reaches lengths of 60 cm/2 ft. Lives in mud on sea bottom, feeding on worms, crustaceans; parasitic on fish. Secretes mucus for protection.

Haggada, see TALMUD.

Haggai, prophetic book of OT, written c 520 BC in Jerusalem after return from the Exile. Consists of exhortations to rebuild the Temple; gives picture of conditions in Palestine.

Haggard, Sir [Henry] Rider (1856-1925), English novelist. Known for adventure stories in African setting, esp. *King Solomon's Mines* (1885), *Allan Quatermain* (1887).

Hagia Sophia, domed basilica in Istanbul, built (532-7) as Christian church for Justinian by Anthemius of Tralles and Isidore of Miletus. A masterpiece of Byzantine art, it was converted into a mosque following Turkish conquest (1453). Now a museum.

Hague, The (*Den Haag, 's-Gravenhage*), city of W Netherlands, cap. of South Holland prov., seat of Dutch govt. Pop. 525,000. Site of 1899, 1907 Peace Conferences; seat of International Court of Justice (1913). Residence of Stadholders 17th-18th cents. Buildings incl. Binnenhof (legislature), Mauritshuis (art gallery).

Hague Conferences, two international peace conferences held 1899, 1907. Failed to achieve aim of arms reduction, but set up arbitration procedures, conventions respecting rules of war. First conference estab. Hague Tribunal, Permanent Court of Arbitration on international disputes. Superseded (1945) by International Court of Justice.

Hahn, Kurt [Matthias Robert Martin] (1886-1974), British educator, b. Germany. Best known for association with Outward Bound schools, stressing training for leadership through physical hardship, danger. Estab. Gordonstoun School (1933).

Hahn, Otto (1879-1968), German physical chemist. Discovered several radioactive isotopes, incl. protactinium (with Lise Meitner). Awarded Nobel Prize for Chemistry (1944) for inducing nuclear fission in uranium by bombardment with neutrons.

Haifa, port of NW Israel, on Mediterranean. Pop. 335,000. Indust. centre; oil refining, chemicals, textiles. Rail jct. and international airport. Seat of Technion (Israel Institute of Technology).

Haig, Douglas Haig, 1st Earl (1861-1928), British army officer, b. Scotland. Commanded 1st Army Corps in France (1914); commander-in-chief of British forces (1915-17). His costly strategy of prolonged trench warfare provoked criticism, but he was architect of final victory.

hail, hard pellets of ice, often associated with thunderstorms. Nucleus, *eg* dust particle, is carried upward by air current until layer of ice coats it; gathers further layers on descent. Hailstones can cause damage, eg to crops, property, aircraft.

Halle Selassie, orig. Tafari Makonnen (1891-1975), emperor of

Ethiopia (1930-74). Led resistance to Italian invasion (1935), fled to England (1936). Regained throne (1941). Leader of pan-African movement. Deposed (1974) by military coup.

Hainan, isl. of Kwangtung prov., S China. Area c 33,670 sq km (13,000 sq mi); pop. 2,800,000; main port Hoihow. Produces timber, rubber, coffee, iron ore. Large naval base at Yulin.

Haiphong, chief seaport of NE North Vietnam. Pop. 390,000. Naval base near mouth of Red R. Commercial, indust. centre; cement, textile, chemical industs. Heavily bombed by US in Vietnam war.

hair, filamentous outgrowth of the skin, consisting mainly of keratin. Grows from small depression (follicle) at whose side is a sebaceous gland, providing oil for skin. Hair is characteristic of mammals.

Haiti, republic of West Indies, occupying W HISPANIOLA. Area 27,713 sq km (10,700 sq mi); pop. 4,668,000, mainly Negro; cap. Port-au-Prince. Languages: French, Creole dialect. Religion: RC. Consists of 2 penins. and 2 isls. Largely wooded mountains; tropical climate. Subsistence agric.; commercial crops incl. coffee, sugar, sisal; timber, bauxite. Spanish ceded possession in 17th cent. to French sugar planters. Independence 1804; hist. ruled by despots, esp. Duvalier (1957-71).

hake, marine food fish of Merlucciidae family, related to the cod; long-bodied, with projecting lower jaw. Species incl. European *Merluccius merluccius*, now scarce through overfishing.

Hakluyt, Richard (c 1552-1616), English geographer. Encouraged exploration, esp. in North America; translated foreign accounts of journeys, voyages. Best known as author of *The Principal Navigations, Voyages, Traffics and Discoveries of the English Nation* (1 vol. 1589, 3 vols. 1600).

Halakah, see TALMUD.

halberd, combined spear and battle-axe, of German origin, used by foot-soldiers in the 15th-17th cents.

Haldane, John Scott (1860-1936), British scientist, b. Scotland. Studied regulation of breathing by carbon dioxide in blood. Investigated physiological effects of working in mines and of deep-sea diving. His son, J[ohn] B[urdon] S[anderson] Haldane (1892-1964) worked in genetics and wrote popular scientific essays.

half-life, time taken for half the atoms of a radioactive substance to disintegrate. Uranium 238 has half-life of 4.5×10^9 years.

half-tone, see PHOTOENGRAVING.

halibut, *Hippoglossus hippoglossus*, largest flatfish, reaching lengths of 2.4 m/8 ft; found in N Atlantic. Popular food fish. Related species in N Pacific.

Halicarnassus, ancient city of SW Asia Minor (modern Turkey). Site of mausoleum, built (c 350 BC) in memory of King Mausolus of Caria by his wife. White marble structure, decorated with sculpture, it was one of Seven Wonders of the World.

Halifax, Charles Montagu, Earl of (1661-1715), English statesman. Instrumental in estab. national debt (1692), Bank of England (1694).

Chancellor of the exchequer (1694), first lord of the treasury (1697-9).

Halifax, Edward Frederick Lindley Wood, 1st Earl of (1881-1959), British statesman. Viceroy of India (1926-31). As foreign secretary (1938-40) instrumental in 'appeasement' policy which led to Munich Pact (1938).

Halifax, cap. of Nova Scotia, Canada; largest port in Maritimes; Canada's principal ice-free Atlantic port. Pop. 122,000. Railway terminus. Shipbuilding, oil refining, food processing (fish). Founded 1749 as naval base; important during both WWs. Has Citadel fortress, Dalhousie Univ. (1818).

Halifax, co. bor. of West Yorkshire met. county, N England. Pop. 91,000. Woollens, carpets mfg. Former centre of Flemish immigration.

Halle, town of SC East Germany, on R. Saale. Pop. 254,000. Railway jct.; salt (saline springs), lignite mining. Former Hanseatic League member; univ. (1694). Birthplace of Handel.

Halley, Edmund (1656-1742), English astronomer. Astronomer Royal after 1720. Studied motion of comets and predicted return of comet of 1682 (Halley's comet); it returns every 75 or 76 years (expected again in 1986). Indicated how transit of Venus could be used to determine solar parallax. Financed publication of Newton's *Principia*.

Halloween, eve of ALL SAINTS' DAY. Esp. celebrated in countries with strong Celtic influence; prob. derives from pre-Christian feasts to mark beginning of winter. Modern customs incl. bobbing for apples, telling tales of witches, ghosts, 'trick-or-treat' (US).

Hallstatt, village of C Austria. Salt mined from prehist. times. Site of late Bronze, early Iron Age remains; given name to Hallstatt culture in archaeology.

hallucination, false sensory impression which invents or misinterprets external phenomena. May occur during schizophrenia or be induced by certain drugs, *eg* mescaline, cannabis or LSD.

Halmahera or **Djailolo,** isl. of Indonesia, in N Moluccas. Area *c* 18,200 sq km (7000 sq mi). Mountainous, with active volcanoes. Produces nutmeg, sago.

halogens, in chemistry, the 5 elements fluorine, chlorine, bromine, iodine and astatine (unstable). Chemically similar, monovalent and highly reactive.

Hals, Frans (*c* 1580-1666), Dutch genre and portrait painter. His bold brushstrokes give impression of gaiety to individual portraits, *eg Laughing Cavalier*; captures fleeting expressions in his large groups of archers and musketeers.

Halsey, William Frederick (1882-1959), American naval officer. Commander of Third Fleet during WWII, defeated Japanese off the Solomons (Nov. 1942). Admiral of the fleet (1945-7).

Hälsingborg or **Helsingborg,** town of S Sweden, on Oresund. Pop. 82,000. Port, ferry service to Helsingör (Denmark). Copper refining; textiles. Contested by Denmark until 1710.

Hama, city of WC Syria, on R. Orontes. Pop. 137,000. Market centre; textile mfg. Noted for enormous wooden waterwheels used for irrigation. Ancient city of

Hittite origin, often mentioned in Bible as Hamath.

Hamburg, city of N West Germany, on R. Elbe, cap. of Hamburg state. Pop. 1,782,000. Major port (outport at Cuxhaven), transshipment trade, shipbuilding, chemicals industs.; cultural, broadcasting centre. Founded by Charlemagne, archbishopric from 834. Alliance (1241) with Lübeck formed basis of Hanseatic League. Rapid growth in 19th cent., incorporated Altona 1938. Severely damaged in 1842 fire, WWII. Birthplace of Brahms, Mendelssohn.

Hameln (Eng. *Hamelin*), town of NW West Germany, on R. Weser. Pop. 49,000. Food processing indust. Scene of the legend of the Pied Piper, depicted in 'Ratcatcher's House' (built 1603).

Hamersley Range, mountain range of NW Western Australia. Highest peak Mt. Bruce (1226 m/4024 ft). Extensive high-quality iron ore deposits..

Hamilcar Barca (d. 228 BC), Carthaginian soldier. Commander in Sicily during First Punic War (247-241), but was defeated and forced to withdraw. Virtual dictator of Carthage after 237. Led successful invasion of Spain (237-228) but was killed. Father of Hannibal.

Hamilton, Alexander (1755-1804), American statesman, b. West Indies. Instrumental in ratification of Constitution esp. through contribution to *Federalist Papers*. Dominated President Washington's cabinet as first secretary of the treasury (1789-95), pursued centralization of finances, stabilization of economy. Leader of FEDERALIST PARTY. Supported Jefferson in

presidential ballot (1800) against AARON BURR, who later killed him in duel.

Hamilton, Lady Emma, nee Lyon (1765-1815), English courtesan. Became mistress, later wife (1791), of Sir William Hamilton, British ambassador to Naples. Became mistress (1798) to Horatio Nelson, bearing (1801) him a daughter. Died in poverty.

Hamilton, Iain Ellis (1922-), Scottish composer. Has written abstract works in 12-note technique. Compositions incl. operas, concertos, *Sinfonia* for 2 orchestras.

Hamilton, James Hamilton, 1st Duke of (1606-49), Scottish nobleman. As adviser to Charles I on Scottish affairs, attempted to appease Covenanters; failed and led army (1639) against them. Fought for Charles at Preston (1648), captured and executed.

Hamilton, Sir William (1788-1856), Scottish philosopher. Influential in introducing Kant and Hegel into British thought.

Hamilton, Sir William Rowan (1805-65), Irish mathematician. Known for his development of quaternions, noncommutative algebra used in geometric problems. His work in dynamics was influential in later quantum mechanics.

Hamilton, cap. and chief port of Bermuda, on Bermuda isl. Pop. 2000. Tourist resort. Founded 1790; succeeded St George as cap. (1815).

Hamilton, port of S Ontario, Canada; at W end of L. Ontario. Pop. 309,000. Railway jct.; mfg. centre; steel works, auto and rail machinery. Founded 1813. Has McMaster Univ. (1930).

Hamilton, town of N North Isl., New Zealand, on Waikato R. Pop. 75,000. Agric. market, food processing; agric. research stations.

Hamilton, town of Strathclyde region, WC Scotland. Pop. 46,000. Coalmining area; engineering, textiles industs. Rudolf Hess landed nearby (1941).

Hamilton, river of E Canada, *see* CHURCHILL (2).

Hammarskjöld, Dag (1905-61), Swedish statesman. As secretary-general of the UN (1953-61) increased its influence. Influential in Suez Crisis (1956), active in attempts to solve Congo problem (1960-1) until his death in plane crash. Nobel Peace Prize (posthumously awarded, 1961).

Hammerfest, town of Kvaløy Isl., N Norway, most northerly in Europe. Pop. 7000. Ice-free port, whaling, sealing. German naval base in WWII, severely damaged.

hammerhead shark, any of genus *Sphyrna* of medium-sized sharks that have hammer-like lobes on head, with eyes and nostrils at extremities.

Hammersmith, bor. of W Greater London, England. Pop. 185,000. Created 1965, former met. bor. incl. Fulham. Olympia, White City stadium.

Hammerstein, Oscar (1895-1960), American librettist, lyricist. Famous for musicals created with composer Richard Rodgers, *eg Oklahoma, Carousel, South Pacific.*

Hammett, Dashiell (1894-1961), American author. Known for economically written 'tough guy' detective novels incl. *The Maltese Falcon, The Thin Man* (1932).

Hammurabi (*fl* 18th cent. BC), king of Babylon (*c* 1792-1750 BC). Founded ancient Babylonian empire. Best remembered for his legal code, found carved in cuneiform on a diorite column (1901).

Hampden, John (*c* 1594-1643), English statesman. Became focus of resentment against Charles I through imprisonment for refusal (1636) to pay 'ship money' tax. One of five MPs whose attempted arrest by Charles (1642) was a cause of Civil War.

Hampshire, county of S England. Area 3772 sq km (1456 sq mi); co. town Winchester. Incl. New Forest; downs in N, SE; fertile lowland. Crops incl. cereals, root crops; livestock rearing. Indust. in ports of Southampton, Portsmouth.

Hampstead, part of Camden, NC Greater London, England. Former met. bor. until 1965. Hampstead Heath park, Parliament Hill, famous inns. Long favoured by artists, authors.

Hampton Court, English palace on R. Thames, built by Cardinal Wolsey (1514) as his private residence. Later passed to Henry VIII and became royal residence. Partially rebuilt by Christopher Wren. Site of conference (1604) authorizing King James Bible.

hamster, rat-like burrowing rodent of Europe and W Asia, with internal cheek pouches to carry food. Common hamster, *Cricetus cricetus,* is grey or brown. Golden hamster, *Mesocricetus auratus,* is popular pet; also used for medical research.

Hamsun, Knut Pederson (1859-1952), Norwegian novelist. Work, * eg Hunger* (1899), *The Growth of the*

Soil (1917), affirms elemental values of nature, condemns modern life. Awarded Nobel Prize for Literature (1920).

Han, dynasty of China (202 BC-AD 220), broken by Hsin dynasty (AD 9-25). Noted for territ. expansion and artistic development; ink and paper came into use, making of porcelain began. Buddhism introduced.

Hancock, John (1737-93), American revolutionary statesman. First signer of Declaration of Independence (1776). President of Continental Congress (1775-7).

hand, prehensile extremity of arm. Human hand contains 27 bones: 8 carpal bones in wrist, 5 long metacarpals, and 14 phalanges forming the fingers and thumb (3 in each finger, 2 in thumb).

handball, eleven-a-side team game played by catching, passing and throwing an inflated round ball. Aim is to score by throwing ball into goal. First played in Germany, c 1890. Olympic event since 1932.

Handel, George Frideric (1685-1759), German composer. Settled in England under patronage of George I, having studied in Italy. Tried to introduce Italian opera to London, then turned to oratorio. Numerous works incl. *concerti grossi,* keyboard suites, oratorios *Messiah* (1742), *Judas Maccabaeus,* miscellaneous orchestral music, eg *Water Music.* Greatly influenced English choral tradition.

Hangchow, cap. of Chekiang prov., E China. Pop. 1,100,000. Port on R. Tsientang. Famous for silk weaving. Indust. centre, producing iron and steel, chemicals, etc. Cap. of S China during 12th and 13th cent., it was

centre of learning and trade. Destroyed (1861) by Taiping rebels.

Hanging Garden of Babylon, terraced building planted with gardens, constructed by Nebuchadnezzar II (d. 562 BC). One of the Seven Wonders of the World.

Hanko (Swed. *Hangö*), town of SW Finland, on Gulf of Bothnia. Pop. 10,000. Port, resort. Hanko penin. leased to USSR as naval base 1940-4.

Hankow, see WUHAN.

Hanna, Marcus Alonzo (Mark) (1837-1904), American capitalist, politician. Active in politics, urging economic policy favourable to big business. Supported McKinley for governor of Ohio (1891, 1893), ran his presidential campaign (1896). Dominated Republican party until death.

Hannibal (247-182 BC), Carthaginian soldier. Commander in Spain (221), his capture of Saguntum led Rome to declare war on Carthage (218). Crossed Alps to invade Italy; defeated Romans at L. Trasimene (217) and Cannae (216), but had insufficient support to capture Rome. Recalled (203) to defend Carthage, defeated by Scipio Africanus at Zama (202). After peace, became ruler of Carthage; Romans forced him to flee to Syria (196). Took poison in Bithynia to avoid being surrendered to the Romans.

Hanno (*fl* 500 BC), Carthaginian navigator. Founded colonies in Morocco and explored coast of NW Africa.

Hanoi, cap. of North Vietnam. Pop. 920,000. Port on Red R.; rail jct.; agric., indust., cultural centre. Hist. cap. of Annam and Indo-China.

Heavily damaged in US air raids during Vietnam war.

Hanover (*Hannover*), city of N West Germany, on R. Leine, cap. of Lower Saxony. Pop. 517,000. Indust., commercial centre; univ. (1879). Hanseatic League member from 1386; cap. of electorate of Hanover from 1692 (electors became kings of UK from 1714). Badly damaged in WWII.

Hanover, House of, British royal house. Succession claimed through Sophia, granddaughter of James I and wife of Elector Ernest Augustus of Hanover. ACT OF SETTLEMENT (1701) made their son, George, heir to Queen Anne, thus excluding Catholic Stuart line. Hanoverian monarchs were George I, II, III and IV and William IV. Lost right to British crown with Victoria (1837) because of Salic law of succession barring women from throne of Hanover.

Hansard, popular name for official report of British parliamentary proceedings. Luke Hansard began (1774) printing accounts of debates. Made official in 1803, remained in family to 1889. Now pub. by Her Majesty's Stationery Office.

Hanseatic League, medieval trading organization of N German towns. From groups of individual *hansa,* an association of merchants trading to foreign countries, league became a great confederation by 14th cent., with companies at most seaports on the Baltic and North seas. Provided trading privileges and protection of its own army. Declined steadily until dissolution in 17th cent.

Hanukkah or Festival of Lights, Jewish festival commemorating the rededication of the Temple by Judas Maccabaeus in 165 BC. Celebrated for 8 days in December with the lighting of special candles.

Hanyang, see WUHAN.

Hapsburg, see HABSBURG.

hara-kiri, traditional Japanese honourable suicide. Involves ritual self-disembowelment with dagger. Originally practised among warrior class to avoid dishonour of capture; *c* 1500 became privileged alternative to execution. Still occasionally practised, *eg* by officers at end of WWII. Also known as *seppuku.*

Harappa, one of the twin centres of the INDUS VALLEY CIVILIZATION.

Harbin, cap. of Heilungkiang prov., NE China. Pop. 2,750,000. Main port on R. Sungari; major jct. on Chinese Eastern and S Manchurian railways. Railway engineering; aircraft, tractor mfg. Developed by Russians (1896-1924).

Hardanger Fjord, inlet of North Sea, SW Norway. Length *c* 183 km (114 mi); many mountains, waterfalls. Tourist area.

Harden, Sir Arthur (1865-1940), English biochemist. Shared Nobel Prize for Chemistry (1929) for investigations into role of enzymes in sugar fermentation; showed that inorganic phosphates were involved in process.

Hardenberg, Friedrich von, see NOVALIS.

Hardie, [James] Keir (1856-1915), British socialist, b. Scotland. Founder, 1st president (1893-1900) of Independent Labour Party. Influential in formation (1906) of Labour Party, leading it in House of Commons (1906-7).

Harding, Warren Gamaliel (1865-1923), American statesman, president (1921-3). Admin. known for inefficiency, corruption. Died before exposure of TEAPOT DOME SCANDAL.

hardness, in mineralogy, resistance a substance offers to being scratched. Measured by Mohs scale ranging from softest (1) to hardest (10), each number being represented by a standard mineral, eg calcite (3), topaz (8), diamond (10).

hard water, water containing dissolved calcium and magnesium salts which interfere with lathering and cleansing properties of soap. Fatty acids in soap form insoluble precipitates (scum) with these salts. Temporary hardness, caused by dissolved bicarbonates, can be removed by heating; permanent hardness, caused by sulphates, is removed by addition of soda (sodium carbonate) or zeolite.

Hardy, Thomas (1840-1928), English novelist, poet. Novels, set in native 'Wessex' (SW England), eg *Far from the Madding Crowd* (1874), *The Mayor of Casterbridge* (1886), *Tess of the D'Urbervilles* (1891), *Jude the Obscure* (1896), reflect vision of human possibilities destroyed through malevolent destiny. Also wrote poetry, incl. *The Dynasts* (1903-8).

Hare, William, see BURKE, WILLIAM.

hare, swift rabbit-like mammal, but non-burrowing and with longer ears and hind legs than rabbit. Formerly classed as rodent, now put with rabbits in order Lagomorpha. Species incl. European brown hare, *Lepus europaeus*, and mountain hare, *L. timidus*, whose coat turns white in winter.

harebell, see BLUEBELL.

harelip, congenital cleft of one or both lips, but usually only the upper one; often occurs with associated cleft palate. May be corrected by early surgery.

Harfleur, town of Normandy, N France, at mouth of R. Seine. Pop. 16,000. Major French port until 16th cent., declined due to silting. Scene of successful siege (1415) by Henry V of England.

Hargreaves, James (c 1720-78), English engineer. Built 'spinning jenny' (1764) enabling one person to spin several threads simultaneously.

Haringey, bor. of N Greater London, England. Pop. 237,000. Created 1965 from mun. bors. of Middlesex. Incl. Highgate.

Harlech, village of Gwynedd, W Wales. Seaside resort. Former co. town of Merionethshire. Has ruined 13th cent. castle.

Harlem, see NEW YORK CITY.

Harlequin, stock character of COM- MEDIA DELL'ARTE, became buffoon of French, then English pantomime. Traditionally wears mask, particoloured tights.

Harley, Robert, 1st Earl of Oxford (1661-1724), British statesman. Tory lord treasurer (1711-14), became chief minister to Queen Anne. Instrumental in Peace of Utrecht (1713). Lost office to St John (Bolingbroke), imprisoned (1715) over dealings with Jacobites. Manuscript collection, Harleian Library, now in British Museum.

Harlow, Jean, orig. Harlean Carpentier (1911-37), American film actress. Famous as wise-cracking platinum blonde of 1930s, Hollywood's 1st great sex symbol. Films incl. *Public Enemy* (1931), *Red Dust* (1932), *Bombshell* (1933).

harmonica or **mouth organ**, simple musical instrument consisting of enclosed box containing tuned metal reeds with holes through which air is blown or sucked. Originated in China, not reaching the West until early 1800s.

harmonium, small organ in which the sound is produced by forcing air through reeds. Pressure is raised by pumping bellows with the feet.

harmony, in music, the combining of notes to form CHORDS in ways that are musically correct or interesting. It is a dominant feature of Western music, often of great emotional significance, but much less important in Eastern music.

Harmsworth, Alfred, *see* NORTHCLIFFE, ALFRED CHARLES WILLIAM HARMSWORTH, VISCOUNT.

harness racing or **trotting**, horse race in which horse pulls 2-wheeled sulky in which driver sits. Two forms of standard bred horse used: trotter, which raises alternately diagonally opposite hind and foreleg; pacer, which raises left legs together, then right. Popular in North America since 19th cent. and in Australia since 1920s.

Harold (c 1022-66), king of England (1066). Son of GODWIN, was recognized as heir to throne by Edward the Confessor, but had earlier been forced to swear to support William of Normandy's claim. On death of Edward, defeated and killed brother Tostig and Harold III of Norway, who invaded N England, but was defeated and killed himself by William at Hastings.

Harold Harefoot (d. 1040), king of England (1037-40). Bastard son of Canute, he claimed throne on father's death (1035), and was elected king after conflict with half-brother Harthacanute.

Harold [III] Hardrada (d. 1066), king of Norway (1046-66). Ruled jointly with Magnus I for a year, became sole ruler on Magnus's death. Joined with Tostig to invade England (1066), and was killed by Harold of England at Stamford Bridge.

harp, stringed musical instrument, with triangular frame; player plucks the strings. Modern orchestral harp has range of 6½ octaves and each string can play any of 3 notes at the touch of a pedal.

Harpers Ferry, small resort town of E West Virginia, US; at confluence of Potomac and Shenandoah rivers. Pop. 430. Site of John Brown's raid on military arsenal (1859). Captured by Confederate forces under Jackson (1862).

Harpies, in Greek myth, repellent birds with the faces of women. Associated with the powers of the underworld and believed to carry off people who disappeared without trace. Also said to devour everything in sight.

harpsichord, string keyboard musical instrument, in which the strings are plucked mechanically. Popular from about 1550 to 1800, but then replaced by the piano. Now revived for authentic performances of Baroque music.

harrier, hawk of genus *Circus*. Hen harrier, *C. cyaneus*, once common in

Europe but now rare, is also called marsh hawk.

Harris, Sir Arthur Travers (1892-), British airforce officer. Acquired the nickname 'Bomber Harris' as commander-in-chief of Bomber Command (1942-5), in which capacity he organized the saturation raids on German indust. centres.

Harris, Frank (1856-1931), Irish writer, journalist. Edited several reviews and magazines in Britain and US. Works incl. play *Mr and Mrs Daventry* (1900), biography *Oscar Wilde : His Life and Confessions* (1918), autobiography *My Life and Loves* (1923-7), banned till 1963.

Harris, Joel Chandler (1848-1908), American author. Known for 'Brer Rabbit' Negro folk collections in authentic dialect, eg *Uncle Remus: His Songs and His Sayings* (1880). Also wrote novels.

Harris, see LEWIS WITH HARRIS, Scotland.

Harrisburg, cap. of Pennsylvania, US; on Susquehanna R. Pop. 68,000. Railway jct.; in coal mining region. Steel, bricks, clothing mfg. Settled *c* 1715.

Harrogate, mun. bor. of North Yorkshire, N England. Pop. 62,000. Spa from 1596; holiday centre.

Harrow-on-the-Hill or **Harrow,** bor. of NW Greater London, England. Pop. 203,000. Created 1965 from former mun. bor. Has 11th cent. church on hill; public school (1571).

Hart, Basil Henry Liddell, see LIDDELL HART.

hartebeest, large red-brown African antelope with short curved horns. Cape hartebeest, *Alcelaphus caama,* found in S Africa.

Hartford, cap. of Connecticut, US; on Connecticut R. Pop. 158,000; state's largest city. Commercial, insurance centre. Industs. incl. firearms, typewriters etc. Settled 1635-6.

Harthacanute (d. 1042), king of Denmark (1035-42) and of England (1040-2). Son of Canute, gained English throne on death of Harold Harefoot, leaving it to Edward the Confessor.

Hartlepool, co. bor. of Cleveland, NE England, on Hartlepool Bay. Pop. 97,000. United with West Hartlepool 1967. Fishing, shipbuilding industs. Grew around 7th cent. convent.

Hartmann, [Karl Robert] Eduard von (1842-1906), German philosopher. Influenced by Hegel, Schopenhauer. Wrote *Philosophy of the Unconscious* (1869) on conflict between impulse and reason.

Harun al-Rashid (*c* 763-809), Abbasid caliph of Baghdad. Faced by many insurrections in the empire throughout his reign, he lost all but nominal control of N Africa. Made Baghdad centre of Arab culture; idealized in *Thousand and One Nights.*

Harvard University, Cambridge, Massachusetts, US. Oldest American coll. (founded 1636), became univ. 1780. Affiliated with Radcliffe Coll. for women; graduate and professional schools are coeducational. Noted for business studies, law, also has great library and Fogg Museum of Art.

harvest mouse, *Micromys minutus,* small red-brown European field mouse that builds its nest among stalks of plants, esp. growing grain.

Harvey, William (1578-1657), English anatomist, physiologist. Discovered circulation of. blood; demonstrated flow of blood from heart through arteries and back to heart through veins. Pub. findings in *Exercitatio anatomica de motu cordis et sanguinis in animalibus* (1628). Pioneer in description of embryology of chicks.

Harwich, mun. bor. of Essex, SE England. Pop. 15,000. Port; ferry services to N Europe.

Haryana, state of N India. Area c 44,000 sq km (17,000 sq mi); pop. 9,971,000; cap. Chandigarh. Mainly flat, dry and barren. Formed (1966) from Hindi-speaking parts of Punjab.

Harz Mountains, forested range of C Germany, in both German republics. Highest peak BROCKEN. Former silver, lead mining. Tourism (mineral springs).

Hasdrubal (d. 207 BC), Carthaginian soldier. Took command in Spain after his brother, Hannibal, invaded Italy. After long campaign against the Scipios, crossed Alps with reinforcements for Hannibal. Defeated and killed at Metaurus.

Hašek, Jaroslav (1883-1923), Czech author. Known for classic satire of military bureaucracy, *The Good Soldier Svejk* (1923).

hashish, see HEMP.

Hasidism, beliefs of Jewish mystical movement founded (18th cent.) in Poland by BAAL-SCHEM-TOV. Spread rapidly among uneducated; still exerts some influence in Jewish life and also in modern Christian theology through MARTIN BUBER.

Hassall, John (1868-1948), English artist. Famous for his posters, eg the 'Skegness is so bracing' poster which featured the Jolly Fisherman.

Hassan II (1929-), king of Morocco (1961-). Introduced constitutional monarchy (1963); survived coups, assassination attempts. Led civilian 'army' in march into N of Spanish Sahara (1975) to estab. Morocco's claims to territ.

Hastings, Warren (1732-1818), British colonial administrator. First governor-general of India (1773-1784). In spite of financial, admin., judicial reforms and strengthening British position in India, he met opposition in Britain. After return (1785), impeached (1787) on charges of malpractice. Acquitted (1795), made privy councillor (1814).

Hastings, co. bor. of East Sussex, SE England. Pop. 72,000. Seaside resort. Norman victory over Saxons nearby at Battle (1066). Chief of Cinque Ports.

Hastings, Battle of, confrontation between invading William, duke of Normandy (William the Conqueror), and Harold, king of England (14 Oct. 1066). Fought at Senlac Hill, near Hastings, England, until Harold was killed. First, most decisive and celebrated victory of Norman Conquest.

Hathaway, Ann (1556-1623), English farmer's daughter. Married Shakespeare in 1582.

Hatteras, Cape, promontory of E North Carolina, US; on isl. between Pamlico Sound and Atlantic. Hazard to shipping; lighthouse (1798).

Hauptmann, Gerhart (1862-1946), German author. Early plays, eg *Before Dawn* (1889), *The Weavers* (1892), estab. German naturalism. **Later works reflect** more mystical interest, esp. *The Sunken Bell* (1896); novel, *The Fool in Christ, Emanuel Quint* (1910). Awarded Nobel Prize for Literature (1912).

Hausa, people of N Nigeria, S Niger. Farmers and far-ranging traders. Hausa languages are basically Hamitic but people mainly Negroid. Predominantly Moslem.

Haussmann, Georges Eugène, Baron (1809-91), French politician, city planner. Prefect of the Seine (1853-70). Reshaped Paris; laid out boulevards and parks (*eg* Bois de Boulogne), improved water supply and sewage system.

Havana (*La Habana*), cap. of Cuba, on Gulf of Mexico. Pop. 1,131,000. Port with excellent harbour; exports sugar, cotton, tobacco. Commercial centre; textiles, cigars, chemicals, rum mfg. Founded 1514; cap. from 1552. Blowing up of battleship *Maine* in harbour resulted in war with US and American occupation (1898-1902). Tourism declined after Castro's coup (1959). Has 18th cent. cathedral.

Havering, bor. of NE Greater London, England. Pop. 247,000. Created 1965 from Romford, Hornchurch (both in Essex).

Havre, Le, see LE HAVRE, France.

Hawaii, volcanic isl. group and state of US; in C Pacific. Area 16,706 sq km (6450 sq mi); pop. 770,000; cap. Honolulu. Incl. Hawaii (area 10,456 sq km/4037 sq mi), Oahu, Maui, Kauai, Molokai isls. Coral reefs, several large active volcanoes. Extensive fishing. Agric. incl. sugar cane, pineapple production. Important tourist industs. International air and shipping base; naval base at Pearl Harbor, Oahu (attacked by Japanese in 1941 bringing US into WWII). Pop. of Japanese, Caucasian, Polynesian origin. Known as Sandwich Isls. after discovery by Cook in 1778; native rule until annexed by US (1898); was territ. (1900-59). Admitted to Union as 50th state (1959).

Haw-Haw, Lord, see JOYCE, WILLIAM.

Hawick, town of Borders region, SE Scotland, on R. Teviot. Pop. 16,000. Sheep market; woollen, tweed mfg.

hawk, name for several birds of prey with short, rounded wings, hooked beak and claws. Incl. kites, buzzards, harriers, falcons, caracaras.

Hawke, Edward Hawke, 1st Baron (1705-81), British admiral. Defeated French squadron off Cape Finisterre (1747) and by annihilation of French fleet at Quiberon Bay (1759) removed threat of invasion.

Hawke's Bay, region of E North Isl., New Zealand. Area 11,030 sq km (4260 sq mi); pop. 134,000; main town Napier. Mainly hilly; lowlands around Hawke Bay. Sheep, cattle rearing, dairying, fruit and vegetable growing.

hawking or **falconry,** sport of hunting game, using trained hawks or falcons. Practised in Arabia, Persia, India since ancient times, became popular in medieval Europe. Trained bird is carried on gloved wrist of falconer; unhooded and released on sight of prey.

Hawkins, Sir Anthony Hope, see HOPE, ANTHONY.

Hawkins or **Hawkyns, Sir John** (1532-95), English privateer. Made very profitable slaving expeditions

(1562-7) to Guinea. Treasurer and comptroller of navy (1573), rear admiral in defeat of Spanish Armada (1588). Died at sea in expedition under Drake.

hawk moth, any of Sphingidae family of moths with thick body and long pointed forewings. Long proboscis used to suck flower nectar. Species incl. DEATH'S HEAD HAWK MOTH.

Hawks, Howard (1896-1977), American film director. Known for comedies, action films, incl. *Scarface* (1932), *Bringing up Baby* (1938), *The Big Sleep* (1946), *Rio Bravo* (1958).

hawksbill turtle, *Eretmochelys imbricata*, tropical marine turtle, whose shell provides commercial tortoiseshell.

Hawksmoor, Nicholas (1661-1736), English architect. Collaborated with Wren on St Paul's and Greenwich Hospital, with Vanbrugh on Blenheim Palace. His own work in very personalized Baroque style incl. Christchurch, Spitalfields (1723-9).

Hawley-Smoot Tariff Act (1930), most highly protective tariff legislation in US history. Retaliatory action by foreign govts. led to sharp decline in US foreign trade. Policy reversed by Trade Agreements Act (1934).

hawthorn, any of genus *Crataegus* of thorny shrubs or small trees of rose family. Native to Eurasia and North America, unknown S of equator. Clusters of fragrant white or pink flowers, small red fruits called haws.

Hawthorne, Nathaniel (1804-64), American author. Known for novel,

The Scarlet Letter (1850), on themes of Puritanism, secret sin. Other works incl. *Twice-told Tales* (1837), *The House of Seven Gables* (1851) and *Tanglewood Tales* (1853), a collection of Greek myths re-told for children.

Haydn, [Franz] Joseph (1732-1809), Austrian composer. Estab. classical forms of the sonata and symphony. Prolific composer, wrote over 100 symphonies, 84 string quartets, piano sonatas, operas and choral works, *eg The Creation*, *The Seasons*. Musical director for the Esterházy family (1761-90).

Haydon, Benjamin Robert (1786-1846), English historical painter. Attempted to revive painting of historical and religious subjects in 'Grand Manner' of Reynolds. Largely responsible for purchase of Elgin Marbles. Wrote autobiog. memoirs.

Hayes, Rutherford Birchard (1822-93), American statesman, president (1877-81). Republican presidential candidate (1876) at time of Democratic revival; returns disputed, electoral commission gave Hayes victory by 1 electoral vote.

hay fever, inflammation of mucous membranes of eyes or nose. Usually caused by allergic reaction to plant pollen. Characterized by sneezing, watering of eyes.

Hayworth, Rita (1918-), American film actress and dancer, often in stormy roles. Films incl. *Only Angels Have Wings* (1939), *Cover Girl* (1944), *Miss Sadie Thompson* (1953).

hazel, any of genus *Corylus* of shrubs and trees of birch family. Native to Eurasia. Yields useful elastic wood. Twigs traditionally used in water divination. Edible fruit variously known, according to variety, as hazelnut, cob, filbert, Barcelona nut.

Hazlitt, William (1778-1830), English essayist. Known for perceptive criticism of Romantic poets, Elizabethan drama, eg *Characters of Shakespeare's Plays* (1817), *Lectures on the English Poets* (1818). Noted prose stylist. Also wrote on philosophy and politics.

head, part of body uppermost in humans, apes, etc and foremost in most other animals. Bony structure in higher animals containing brain and incl. eyes, mouth, nose, jaws.

Healey, Denis Winston (1917-), British politician. Labour chancellor of exchequer (1974-79). Attempted to reduce rate of inflation with 'social contract' between TUC and govt., restricting wage increases.

health insurance, plan by prior payment to provide services or cash for medical care in times of illness or disability. Can be part of voluntary or compulsory national insurance scheme connected with SOCIAL SECURITY scheme. Early forms were in Germany (1883), most comprehensive scheme coming in UK (*see* NATIONAL HEALTH INSURANCE ACT). In US, amendments (1965) to Social Security Act estab. schemes for old people (Medicare), and for people with low incomes (Medicaid).

hearing aid, device worn to compensate for hearing loss. Battery-operated electronic aids incorporate receiver and transistor amplifier. Two main types: those which transmit sounds through bone of skull and those which conduct sounds through air to stimulate ear drum.

Hearst, William Randolph (1863-1951), American journalist, publisher. Founded vast newspaper empire, was most sensational of all 'yellow press' publishers. Influential in politics, advocated extreme isolationism.

heart, muscular organ which maintains blood circulation in vertebrate animals. Human heart is divided into 2 halves by muscular wall; each half is divided into 2 chambers, upper atrium and lower ventricle. Oxygenated blood from lungs enters left atrium and is pumped into left ventricle by contraction of heart, then into arteries. Venous blood enters right atrium, is pumped into right ventricle and then into lungs to regain oxygen.

heart attack, sudden instance of heart failure, esp. that associated with coronary thrombosis.

heat, internal energy of substances produced by vibrations of constituent molecules and which passes from places of higher temperature to those of lower temperature. Transmitted by conduction, convection and radiation. SI unit of heat is joule; quantity of heat held by body is product of its mass, specific heat and temperature. Increase in heat of a body may result in increase in temperature or change of state. *See* LATENT HEAT.

Heath, Edward Richard George (1916-), British statesman, PM (1970-4). Elected leader of Conservative Party in 1965. Successfully pursued policy of British entry into EEC (achieved 1973). Admin. marked by bad relations with trade unions culminating in miners' strike. Replaced as party leader (1975) after leadership election.

heath or **heather**, any of genera *Erica* and *Calluna* of shrubs of Ericaceae family. Found on temperate moorlands throughout world. Plants have bell-shaped hanging flowers. Species incl. common or Scotch heather, *C. vulgaris*, and bell heather, *E. cinerea*.

Heathrow, Greater London (Hounslow), SE England. Site of London's main airport, one of world's busiest, 24 km (15 mi) from city centre.

heatstroke, illness caused by exposure to excessive heat. May cause cramp and collapse from salt loss, or fainting. Extreme rise in body temperature may result if body's temperature-regulating mechanism breaks down.

heaven, in Judaeo-Christian theology, dwelling place of God and his angels, where the blessed will live after death. Similar beliefs exist in Islam, Mahayana Buddhism and Hinduism.

Heaviside, Oliver (1850-1925), English physicist. His work on increasing inductance of telephone wires made long distance telephony practicable. Independently of Kennelly, predicted existence of gaseous ionized layer in upper atmosphere (Kennelly-Heaviside layer) from which electromagnetic waves are reflected.

heavy spar, *see* BARITE.

heavy water (D_2O), water composed of deuterium and oxygen, found in ordinary water at concentration of 1 part in 5000. Used as moderator in nuclear reactors. Name also applies to water containing substantial quantities of D_2O or HDO.

Hebbel, [Christian] Friedrich (1813-63), German dramatist. Known for realistic tragedies, esp. *Maria Magdalena* (1844), reflecting Hegelian view of historical turning points through depiction of conflict between individual and general order.

Hebe, in Greek myth, goddess of youth. Daughter of Zeus and Hera, wife of Heracles after his deification. Cupbearer of the gods before GANYMEDE. Identified with Roman Juventas.

Hébert, Jacques René, (1757-94), French revolutionary, journalist. Had nickname derived from paper *Le Père Duchesne*, in which he expressed radical republicanism. Led CORDELIERS, active in Paris Commune; enemy of Girondists. Earned enmity of Robespierre, arrested with followers, guillotined.

Hebrew, NW Semitic language of Afro-Asiatic family. From 586 BC to 19th cent., preserved by Jews in religion, learning, their vernacular languages being Aramaic, Yiddish. Rise of Zionism in 19th cent. caused adoption as national language, which it became with estab. of Israel (1948).

Hebrew literature, literature of Jews. Earliest works were OT, *Apocrypha*, parts of *Pseudepigraphia*, and Dead Sea Scrolls. *Talmud, Midrash* and *Targum* date from 2nd-4th cent. *Masora* developed in Palestine (6th-7th cent.), Babylonian Talmudic commentaries written 6th-11th cent. Post-11th cent. writing shifted to Spain, incl. poetry, philosophy. In 14th cent.

Zohar, principal text of CABALA, appeared. Medieval Hebrew writers incl. Ibn Gabirol, Rashi, Maimonides and Caro. Moses Mendelssohn began modern Hebrew literature, which incl. work of Sforim (pseud. of Abramovich), Bialik, Agnon and Moshe Shamir.

Hebrews, epistle of NT, traditionally ascribed to St Paul but not now accepted as his. Written before AD 90. Exhorts Christians not to return to Judaism under pressure of persecution.

Hebrides, c 500 isls. off NW Scotland. Formerly admin. by Argyllshire, Inverness-shire, Ross and Cromarty. Mild, wet climate; crofting, fishing, tourism, tweed mfg. Depopulation (c 100 isls. inhabited). Under Norwegian rule 6th-13th cents. **Inner Hebrides** incl. Coll, Colonsay, Iona, Islay, Jura, Mull, Rhum, Skye, Tiree. **Outer Hebrides** incl. Barra, Benbecula, Lewis with Harris, St Kilda, North and South Uist. Now admin. by WESTERN ISLES isl. authority. Outer Hebrides are separated from mainland and Skye by the Minch and Little Minch.

Hebron (Arab. *Al Khalil*), town of W Jordan. Pop. 43,000. Trade centre in vine, cereal region at alt. of 910 m (3000 ft). Sacred to Jews and Moslems; Cave of Machpelah is traditional site of tomb of Abraham and his family.

Hecate, in Greek myth, goddess of witchcraft, ghosts, with power to conjure phantoms and dreams. Worshipped at crossroads. Sometimes represented with three bodies.

Hecht, Ben (1894-1964), American journalist, dramatist, film script-

writer and critic. Scripts incl. *The Front Page* (1931), *Soak the Rich* (1936), *Spellbound* (1945). Plays incl. *The Scoundrel* (with Noël Coward).

hectare, metric unit of area, equal to 10,000 square metres; 1 hectare = *c* 2.47 acres.

Hector, in Greek legend, eldest son of King Priam and husband of Andromache. Greatest hero of Trojan troops under Trojan War. Killed by Achilles in revenge for his killing of Patroclus.

Hecuba, in Greek legend, wife of King Priam of Troy and mother of Hector, Paris, Troilus, Cassandra. To save him from the Greeks sent her youngest son, Polydorus, to King Polymestor of Thrace. As captive of Odysseus, she discovered that Polymestor had murdered Polydorus and in revenge blinded him.

hedgehog, any of Erinaceidae family of spiny-backed insectivores widely distributed in Old World. Protects itself by curling up into ball with spines standing outwards. Hibernates in winter.

hedge sparrow, *Prunella modularis,* small European bird with reddish-brown back, grey head and white-tipped wings. Also called dunnock.

hedonism, in ethics, theory that pleasure or happiness of self or society is object of actions. Exponents incl. Aristippus, Epicurus, J. S. Mill.

Hegel, Georg Wilhelm Friedrich (1770-1831), German philosopher. Formulated concept of historical dialectic: fusion (synthesis) of opposite concepts (thesis and antithesis). Activating principle is 'world spirit' (*Weltgeist*) in universe of continuous self-creation. Works incl. *Phenomenology of Mind* (1807), *Science of Logic* (1812-16). Greatly influenced subsequent philosophers of history, esp. Marx.

hegemony, leadership or dominance, esp. of one state or nation over another. Usage in 20th cent. extended by Gramsci through development of Marxist theory of superstructure to incl. cultural dimension.

hegira or **hejira**, the flight of Mohammed from Mecca to Medina in AD 622. The Mohammedan era is dated from 16 July of that year, with (in West) AH after year number, *ie* After Hegira.

Heidegger, Martin (1889-1976), German philosopher. Link between Kierkegaard and later existentialists. Concerned with 'problem of being' and Western man's lost sense of being. Major work, *Being and Time* (1927).

Heidelberg, city of WC West Germany, on R. Neckar. Pop. 122,000. Precision instruments, printing industs.; wine, fruit, tourism. Residence of Electors Palatine 13th-18th cent. Famous univ. (1386) centre of German Reformation (16th cent.); ruined 13th cent. castle. Remains of prehist. 'Heidelberg man' found nearby.

Heifetz, Jascha (1901-   ), American violinist, b. Russia. Exhibited prodigious ability, even as a child, and rose rapidly to international reputation.

Heike-monogatari ('Tales of the Heike'), Japanese historical romance. Composed in early 13th cent., tells of 12th cent. conflict between 2 great families, Minamoto (Genji), and Taira (Heike), leading to latter's downfall. Important influence on later literature, stories providing material for NO and later drama, and prose style looking forward to that of novel.

Heilbronn, city of SW West Germany, on R. Neckar. Pop. 102,000. River port, railway jct., indust. centre. Name derived from Holy Spring (*Heiligbronn*) near 11th cent. church.

Heilungkiang, prov. of NE China. Area *c* 705,000 sq km (272,000 sq mi); pop. (est.) 21,000,000; cap. Harbin. Wheat, soya beans grown; major timber indust. Indust. centres in S, minerals (oil, coal, gold). Contiguous with USSR.

Heine, Heinrich, pseud. of Chaim Harry Heine (1797-1856), German poet. Attracted by spirit of July Revolution (1830), settled in Paris (1831). Wrote in German, French. Known for travel sketches, *Trip in the Harz Mountains* (1826), romantic lyric poetry in *Book of Songs* (1827), incl. treatment of 'Lorelei' myth. Subsequently critical of Romanticism.

Heinkel, Ernst (1888-1958), German aircraft designer. Developed jet aircraft (*c* 1939) independently of Whitle. His company was Germany's largest producer of warplanes in WWII.

Heisenberg, Werner Karl (1901-76), German physicist. Developed form of quantum theory based on matrix methods. His uncertainty principle states that certain pairs of quantities (*eg* position and momentum of particle) cannot both be measured completely accurately.

Awarded Nobel Prize for Physics (1932).

Hekla, volcano of S Iceland. Height 1520 m (5000 ft). Many eruptions recorded from 12th cent., incl. disaster of 1766; most recent 1970.

Hel, in Norse myth, goddess of the underworld, daughter of Loki. Ruled the home of dead not killed in battle.

Helen, in Greek myth, beautiful wife of King Menelaus of Sparta; daughter of Zeus by Leda. Her abduction to Troy by Paris instigated Trojan War. Reconciled to Menelaus after fall of Troy.

Helena, cap. and tourist resort of Montana, US. Pop. 23,000. Ranching, mining region. Founded after gold strike (1864).

Helensburgh, town of Strathclyde. region, W Scotland, on Firth of Clyde. Pop. 10,000. Resort, at SW end of 'Highland line'.

helicopter, aircraft with horizontal rotating wings (rotors) which enable it to take off and land vertically, to move in any direction (by inclining axis of rotor) and to hover. Mainly used for short-range transportation, air-sea rescue, firefighting. *See* SIKORSKY.

Heligoland (*Helgoland*), isl. of West Germany, in North Sea, off W Schleswig-Holstein. Exchanged (1890) by UK for Zanzibar. Fortified by Germans in both WWs, submarine base in WWII.

Heliopolis, ancient ruined city of N Egypt. Centre of sun-worship; schools of philosophy, astronomy. Original site of 'Cleopatra's Needles', removed 19th cent. to London, New York.

Helios (Gk., = sun), in Greek myth, sun god, son of TITANS Hyperion and Theia. Crossed the sky daily from east to west in chariot drawn by 4 horses. Kept herd of sacred oxen on Thrinacia (Sicily). Later identified with Apollo.

heliotrope, any plant that turns to face the sun, esp. genus *Heliotropium* of plants of borage family with clusters of white or purple flowers.

helium (He), inert gaseous element; at. no. 2, at. wt. 4.003. Found in natural gas in Texas and in atmosphere. Used in balloons and airships because of lightness and non-flammability; low boiling point makes it useful in cryogenics. First discovered in Sun (1868), abundant in stars.

Hell, in Christian theology, dwelling place of devils to which sinners are doomed to eternal punishment after death. Often represented with images of fire. Similar concepts occur in Greek myths (Hades), Islam, Judaism.

hellebore, any of genus *Helleborus* of winter-blooming perennials of the buttercup family. Found in Europe and Asia, frequently cultivated as ornamental, esp. Christmas rose, *H. niger*.

Heller, Joseph (1923-), American author. Best known for *Catch-22* (1961), a novel using black humour to satirize bureaucracy in the army.

Hellespont, *see* DARDANELLES.

Hellman, Lillian (1905-), American dramatist. Works, incl. *The Children's Hour* (1934), *The Little Foxes* (1939), *Toys in the Attic* (1960), often reflect left-wing political interests.

Helmholtz, Hermann von (1821-94), German physician, scientist.

Developed concept of conservation of energy. Pioneer of physiological optics and acoustics; extended Young's theory of colour vision. Invented ophthalmoscope (1851).

Helpmann, Sir Robert [Murray] (1909-), Australian choreographer, dancer, actor. Principal dancer of Sadler's Wells Ballet, choreographed such ballets as *Miracle in the Gorbals*. Theatre work incl. leading Shakespearian roles, directing of plays; director of Australian Ballet.

Helsingborg, *see* HÄLSINGBORG, Sweden.

Helsingfors, *see* HELSINKI, Finland.

Helsingör or **Elsinore,** town of NE Zealand, Denmark, on Öresund. Pop. 42,000. Port, ferry service to Hälsingborg (Sweden). Kronborg Castle is scene of Shakespeare's *Hamlet.*

Helsinki (Swed. *Helsingfors*), cap. of Finland, on Gulf of Finland. Pop. 627,000. Admin., cultural centre; univ. (moved from Turku 1828). Chief port, kept open in winter by ice-breakers, exports timber, paper, wood products. Founded 1550, cap. from 1812. Largely rebuilt after fire (1808). Scene of 1952 Olympics.

Helvellyn, mountain of Lake Dist., Cumbria, NW England. Height 950 m (3118 ft).

Helvetia, region now within W Switzerland, formerly occupied by Celtic Helvetii (2nd cent. BC–5th cent. AD). Name still used poetically for Switzerland, and on Swiss postage stamps.

hematite, *see* HAEMATITE.

Hemel Hempstead, mun. bor. of Hertfordshire, EC England. Pop. 69,000. Designated new town 1946; light industs.

Hemingway, Ernest Miller (1899–1961), American author. Member of 'lost generation' of expatriates as described in *The Sun Also Rises* (1926). Works, eg *A Farewell to Arms* (1929), *For Whom the Bell Tolls* (1940), novella *The Old Man and the Sea* (1952), celebrate physical courage in terse, dramatic understatement. Nobel Prize for Literature (1954).

hemlock, *Conium maculatum,* biennial umbelliferous herb of N hemisphere. Source of alkaloid poison coniine used medicinally and by ancient Greeks as instrument of capital punishment, notably in case of Socrates. Also, any of genus *Tsuga* of North American and Asiatic evergreen trees of the pine family; bark is used in tanning.

Hémon, Louis (1880–1913), Canadian writer, b. France. Best known for popular novel of farm life in Québec, *Maria Chapdelaine* (1916).

hemp, *Cannabis sativa,* tall Asiatic herb of nettle family. Male and female flowers on separate plants. Stems yield fibre for rope, coarse cloth, paper. Seeds used as birdfood and oil extracted from them as base of paints and soaps. Resin from female flower yields intoxicating drug cannabis or marijuana, or whole flower may be processed as hashish. These, when smoked or eaten, may cause mild hallucinations and sense of euphoria.

henbane, *Hyoscyamus niger,* poisonous plant of nightshade family, native to Old World. Source of alkaloid drugs scopolamine and hyoscamine.

Henderson, Alexander (1583-1646), Scottish churchman. Leading Presbyterian. Prepared National Covenant (1638), Solemn League and Covenant (1643, *see* COVENANTERS). Intermediary between Church of Scotland and Charles I.

Henderson, Arthur (1863-1935), British statesman. As Labour foreign secretary (1929-31) worked for international peace, supporting League of Nations, attempting to ease Franco-German relations. President of World Disarmament Conference (1932-5). Nobel Peace Prize (1934).

Hendon, part of Barnet, W Greater London, England. Mun. bor. until 1965. Has Univ. of London observatory; site of former airfield.

henge, in archaeology, ritual monument of early British Bronze Age. Usually consisted of circular or oval earthen bank with one or two entrances surrounding pattern of posts, stones or pits. Examples at Stonehenge, Avebury.

Henley-on-Thames, mun. bor. of Oxfordshire, C England, on R. Thames. Pop. 11,000. Scene of annual rowing regatta from 1839.

henna, *Lawsonia inermis,* small Old World tropical shrub. Fragrant white or red flowers; leaves yield reddish-brown dye used as hair or body dye.

Henri, Robert (1865-1929), American painter, teacher. Leader of ashcan school, attempted to introduce contemporary French technique to portray American scene. Influential teacher, emphasized social role of art.

Henrietta Maria (1609-69), queen consort (1625-49) of Charles I of England. Daughter of Henry IV of France. Aroused popular resentment against Charles through attempts to aid Catholic cause.

Henry III (1017-56), Holy Roman emperor (1046-56). Son of Conrad II, with whom he was joint king of Germany from 1028, later sole king from 1039. The empire reached the peak of its power during his reign with Henry 3 times choosing who was to be pope.

Henry IV (1050-1106), Holy Roman emperor (1084-1105). Succeeded his father, Henry III, as king of Germany (1056). Conflict with Pope Gregory VII over his right to elect bishops led to his excommunication (1075); absolved at Canossa (1077). Again excommunicated (1080), he invaded Italy and deposed Gregory (1084). Crowned emperor by antipope, Clement III. Forced to abdicate.

Henry V (1081-1125), Holy Roman emperor (1111-25). Became king of Germany (1105) after forcing abdication of his father, Henry IV. Continued father's struggle with papacy over election of bishops until compromise reached in Concordat of Worms (1122).

Henry I (1068-1135), king of England (1100-35). Youngest son of William I, seized crown on death of brother, William II, excluding his elder brother Robert II, duke of Normandy. Later seized Normandy (1105) and imprisoned Robert for life. Attempted to secure throne for daughter MATILDA.

Henry II (1133-89), king of England (1154-89). By marriage with Eleanor of Aquitaine, gained huge tracts of land in France. Named as successor by mother Matilda, invaded England

and forced Stephen to name him as heir. Estab. power of throne by subduing barons, strengthening royal courts. Attempted to extend power over Church; entered long controversy with Thomas à Becket, ending in Becket's murder. Struggles with sons ended in defeat by son, Richard I. Reign saw beginning of English conquest of Ireland.

Henry III (1207-72), king of England (1216-72). Son of John, came to power (1227) after regency. Expensive, unsuccessful campaign in France and autocratic rule led to Barons' War (1263). Simon de MONTFORT, barons' leader, defeated Henry at Lewes and summoned Parliament. Order restored by Henry's son, later Edward I.

Henry IV (1367-1413), king of England (1399-1413). Son of John of Gaunt; exiled 1398-9 by Richard II. Returned and forced Richard to abdicate; claim to throne upheld by Parliament. Reign, marked by barons' uprisings and revolt in Wales, left crown in serious debt.

Henry V (1387-1422), king of England (1413-22). Son of Henry IV; claiming French throne, reopened Hundred Years War. Defeated French at Agincourt (1415) and seized Normandy. Married Catherine of Valois; recognized as heir to French throne by her father, Charles VI.

Henry VI (1421-71), king of England (1422-61, 1470-1). Succeeded father Henry V in infancy. His claims to French throne were unrecognized by the French, whose victories under Joan of Arc and Charles VII drove English from France. Dominated by his wife Margaret of Anjou. Subject

to insanity after 1453, became pawn in struggle between Houses of York and Lancaster. Deposed by Edward IV (1461). Briefly restored 1470. Imprisoned in the Tower, where he died.

Henry VII (1457-1509), king of England (1485-1509); until accession, Henry Tudor, Earl of Richmond. Head of house of Lancaster after death of Henry VI (1471), fled to France. Invaded England (1485), seized throne from Richard III after victory at Bosworth Field. United houses of York and Lancaster by marrying (1486) Elizabeth, daughter of Edward IV. Defeated Yorkist impostors Lambert Simnel, Perkin Warbeck. Centralized govt. and finances, estab. Tudor tradition of autocratic rule.

Henry VIII (1491-1547), king of England (1509-47). Son of Henry VII. Married (1509) brother's widow, Catherine of Aragon. Govt. dominated by WOLSEY until he failed to secure annulment of marriage from pope. This initiated split from Rome, culminating in estab. of Henry as 'supreme head' of Church of England (1534). With chief minister T. CROMWELL, carried out dissolution of monasteries, confiscating wealth. Executed 2nd wife, Anne Boleyn (1536) on charge of adultery, married Jane Seymour (1537) who bore him Edward VI. Successive marriages were to Anne of Cleves (1540), Catherine Howard (1542), Catherine Parr (1543). Wars with Scotland, Ireland, France left crown in debt.

Henry II (1519-59), king of France (1547-59). Son of Francis I,

Dominated by Montmorency, his mistress Diane de Poitiers and de Guise family. Continued wars against Emperor Charles V, England (winning Calais, 1558), Spain. Married (1533) Catherine de' Medici.

Henry III (1551-89), king of France (1574-89). Reign marked by continuing Catholic-Huguenot strife and conflict with Catholic League led by de Guise. Expelled from Paris (1588) by revolt inspired by de Guise. Made alliance with Huguenot leader, Henry of Navarre (later Henry IV), to regain city. Had de Guise murdered; assassinated by fanatic monk.

Henry IV, orig. Henry of Navarre (1553-1610), king of France (1589-1610), king of Navarre (1572-89). Became leader of Huguenots (1569) and legal heir to French throne (1584); fought 10 year war to estab. rule after death of Henry III. Became Catholic as political move (1593). Estab. religious tolerance with Edict of Nantes (1598). Married (1600) Marie de' Medici after marriage to Margaret of Valois annulled. In final years (1600-10), avoided war, encouraged agric., indust., reformed finances. Assassinated by fanatic.

Henry, Joseph (1797-1878), American physicist. Independently of Faraday, discovered principle of electromagnetic induction. Developed electromagnet and invented electromagnetic telegraph. Discovered self-inductance and invented an electric motor. First secretary of Smithsonian Institution.

Henry, O., pseud. of William Sidney Porter (1862-1910), American short-story writer. Known for sentimental tales with surprise endings. Collections incl. *Cabbages and Kings* (1904), *The Four Million* (1906).

Henry, Patrick (1736-99), American revolutionary. Renowned orator, led opposition to British rule; advocate of individual liberty. Prominent supporter of first 10 amendments to Constitution (Bill of Rights).

Henry the Navigator (1394-1460), Portuguese prince, son of John I. Patron of navigation and exploration of W Africa, laying basis for development of Portuguese overseas empire.

Henryson, Robert (c 1430-c 1505), Scottish poet. Best known for *Testament of Cresseid*, a severe moral treatment of 'Troilus' story.

Henslowe, Philip (d. 1616), English theatre manager. With 'Ned' Alleyn, owned Rose and Fortune theatres. Diary valuable to theatrical historians.

Henze, Hans Werner (1926-), German composer. Much of his early work was highly abstract and used 12-note technique; now concentrates on music concerned with social values. His operas incl. *The Bassarids*, *The Young Lord*.

hepatica, see LIVERWORT.

hepatitis, inflammation of liver. Two common forms, transmitted by viruses: serum hepatitis, conveyed by traces of blood on hypodermic needles used in transfusions, *etc*, and infectious hepatitis.

Hepburn, Katharine (1907-), American stage and film actress. Known for clipped voice, cool acting; long associated with Spencer Tracy. Films incl. *Morning Glory* (1933), *Bringing up Baby* (1938),

Adam's Rib (1949), *The African Queen* (1951).

Hephaestus, in Greek myth, god of fire, son of Zeus and Hero, patron of smiths and craftsmen. Represented as mighty, usually bearded and comic figure. Made Achilles' armour. Identified by Romans with Vulcan.

Hepplewhite, George (d. 1786), English cabinet maker, furniture designer. Known for designs appearing in *The Cabinet-maker and Upholsterer's Guide* (pub. 1788). Developed light elegant style, esp. in his chairs, often with shield or heart-shaped backs.

Hepworth, Dame Barbara (1903-75), English abstract sculptor. Early work was carved directly in stone and wood; experimented with piercing holes in sculpture. Later work in bronze shows attempt to achieve perfection of form.

Hera, in Greek myth, daughter of Cronus and Rhea; sister and wife of Zeus. Patron of sexual life of women and marriage. Jealous, she persecuted Zeus' mortal offspring. Sometimes identified with Roman Juno.

Heracles, in Greek myth, son of Zeus and Alcmene. Popular Greek hero famed for strength and courage. Driven mad by Hera, he killed his wife and children. To expiate this crime served King Eurystheus of Tiryns for 12 years, achieving 12 labours: (1) brought back skin of Nemean lion, (2) killed the Hydra, (3) captured the Ceryneian hind and (4) the Erymanthian boar, (5) cleaned the stables of Augeas, (6) destroyed the Stymphalian birds, (7) captured the Cretan bull and (8) the man-eating mares of Diomedes, (9) stole the girdle of Queen Hippolyte of the Amazons, (10) brought back the cattle of Geryon, (11) stole the apples of the Hesperides, (12) captured Cerberus from Hades. Also involved in many other adventures incl. Argonauts' quest. On death he obtained immortality, married Hebe. Known as Hercules by the Romans.

Heraclitus (c 535-c 475 BC), Greek philosopher. Believed that all things imply their opposites, that change is the only reality, permanence an illusion. Held fire to be underlying universal substance.

Herakleion, see IRÁKLION, Greece.

heraldry, system of inherited symbols (traditionally displayed on shield, surcoat) used for identification of individuals, families, institutions. Prob. originated in Germany (12th cent.); in Middle Ages, rules for personal devices such as coats of arms, badges, crests, were regularized.

herb, any seed plant whose stem withers back to the ground after each season's growth, as distinguished from a tree or shrub whose woody stem lives from year to year. Also any plant used as a medicine or seasoning; *eg* thyme, basil.

Herbert, Sir A[lan] P[atrick] (1890-1971), English writer, politician. Known for humorous *Misleading Cases in the Common Law* (1st series 1927) reflecting legal training. Secured reform of English divorce laws. Also wrote light verse, novel *The Water Gipsies* (1930).

Herbert, George (1593-1633), English poet. Best known for collection of metrically, typographically inventive metaphysical poems *The*

Temple (1633) covering all facets of the religious life. His brother, **Edward Herbert, 1st Baron Herbert of Cherbury** (1583-1648), was a philosopher, diplomat; sought rational basis for religion in *De Veritate* (1624).

herbivore, name applied to any animal, esp. mammal, which feeds entirely or mainly on vegetation.

Hercegovina, *see* BOSNIA AND HERCEGOVINA.

Herculaneum (Ital. *Ercolano*), ancient city of SW Italy, near Naples. Roman resort, buried (AD 79) with POMPEII in eruption of Vesuvius. Site discovered 1709.

Hercules, Roman name of HER-ACLES.

Herder, Johann Gottfried von (1744-1803), German philosopher, poet. Known for collection *Folk Songs* (1778-9) influencing STURM UND DRANG movement. Also wrote *Outlines of the Philosophy of Man* (1784-91) taking evolutionary approach to history.

heredity, process whereby characteristics of living organisms are transmitted from parents to offspring by means of genes carried in chromosomes. Mutation in chromosomes can result in changes in inherited characteristics. Studied scientifically as genetics.

Hereford and Worcester, county of W England. Area 3927 sq km (1516 sq mi); pop. 577,000; co. town Worcester. Created 1974, comprises former Herefordshire, Worcestershire.

Herefordshire, former county of W England. Malvern Hills in E; Wye Valley in C; Black Mts. in SW. Hereford beef cattle; fruit growing,

esp. apples, pears. Co. town was Hereford, city on R. Wye. Pop. 47,000. Agric. market. Has 11th cent. cathedral displaying many architectural styles.

Herero, nomadic BANTU people of South West Africa (Namibia). Noted for their large cattle herds. Majority of pop. massacred by Germans *c* 1908.

Hereward the Wake (fl 1070), English chieftain. Led Anglo-Saxon rebellion against William the Conqueror (1070-1). Took Isle of Ely as his stronghold but was defeated (1071).

hermaphrodite, animal or plant possessing both male and female reproduction systems, *eg* earthworms. Name sometimes applied to humans possessing physical characteristics of opposite sex due to hormone imbalance.

Hermes, in Greek myth, messenger of the gods; son of Zeus and Maia. Patron of merchants, travellers, roads and thieves. Represented with staff, winged shoes and broad hat. Associated with milestones and signposts (herms). Identified by Romans with Mercury.

Hermes Trismegistus, Greek name for Egyptian god THOTH, supposed author of the 17 treatises of *Corpus Hermeticum*. Prob. compiled in 3rd cent., they describe the mystical harmonies of the universe, *eg* astrology, alchemy. Influenced neoplatonists and became centre of cults in 17th cent. England.

Hermitage, museum and art gallery in Leningrad. Collection was built up by Catherine the Great; opened to public 1852. Its holdings of French art are esp. fine.

hermit crab, type of crab of Paguridae family that protects its soft abdomen by living in empty mollusc shell which it drags around when walking.

Hermon, Mount, scenic mountain, alt. 2814 m (9232 ft), in Anti-Lebanon range. On Syria-Lebanon border.

Hermosillo, town of NW Mexico, cap. of Sonora state, on Sonora R. Pop. 207,000. Commercial centre in agric. (maize, cotton, fruit), mining region (gold, silver). Winter resort.

hernia or **rupture**, abnormal protrusion of an organ through a tear in wall of surrounding structure, esp. loop of intestine into top of thigh. Usually treated by surgery.

Hero, in Greek myth, priestess of Aphrodite at Sestos. Her lover, Leander, used nightly to swim the Hellespont to visit her. She allowed the light with which she guided him to blow out and he drowned. In despair she threw herself into the sea.

hero, in Greek religion, man of proven strength and courage favoured by the gods, often having divine ancestor, and worshipped as quasi-divine. Also 'faded' gods who had been demoted to human status, or real or imaginary ancestors. Hero cults centred on reputed place of hero's tomb. Notable exception was HERACLES who was worshipped as a full god.

Hero or **Heron of Alexandria** (*fl* AD 2nd cent.), Greek mathematician, inventor. Developed double force pump, water organ and steam devices. Investigated operations of screws, wheels, levers and pulleys.

Herod Antipas (d. *c* AD 40), tetrarch of Galilee and Peraea. Married Herodias, mother of Salome; banished by Caligula (AD 39) after seeking title of king. Responsible for execution of John the Baptist; ruled at time of Jesus' death.

Herodotus (*c* 484–*c* 424 BC), Greek historian, called the 'Father of History'. Travelled widely through known world, observing and recording customs and beliefs. Major work, *History of Graeco-Persian Wars*, combines colourful anecdotes with critical style.

Herod the Great (*c* 74–4 BC), king of Judaea. Declared king of Judaea through Mark Antony's influence (40). Estab. his cap. at Jerusalem (37), where he rebuilt Great Temple. According to St Matthew, ordered massacre of male infants in Bethlehem to prevent survival of Jesus.

heroic couplet, English verse form with pair of rhymed lines, each with 5 iambic feet. Used esp. by Dryden, Pope.

heroin or **diacetyl morphine**, white crystalline powder derived from morphine. Introduced as supposed non-addictive painkilling substitute for morphine, it proved to be a powerful habit-forming narcotic.

heron, long-legged, long-necked wading bird of Ardeidae family. Breeds in colonies or heronries high in trees.

herpes, name given to 2 different virus diseases, characterized by eruption of small blisters on skin and mucous membranes. *Herpes simplex* is group of inflamed blisters (cold sores) often around mouth. H.

zoster or shingles is painful infection of sensory nerves around spinal cord.

Herrick, Robert (1591-1674), English poet. Known for collection, *Hesperides* (1648), incl. religious verse, love lyrics influenced by Classical poets and Jonson.

herring, *Clupea harengus,* common food fish of N Atlantic. Once fished in great numbers, stocks greatly depleted in some areas. Related species in N Pacific.

herring gull, *Larus argentatus,* common marine bird of N hemisphere. Scavenger around harbours; feeds on fish.

Herriot, Edouard (1872-1957), French statesman. Radical Socialist leader, premier (1924-5, 1932), president of National Assembly (1947-54). Imprisoned by Germans (1940-5). Advocated conciliatory foreign policy, payment of war debts to US.

Herschel, Sir Frederick William (1738-1822), British astronomer, b. Germany. Considered founder of modern astronomy, he discovered planet Uranus (1781), 2 of its satellites (1787), and 2 satellites of Saturn. Constructed powerful reflecting telescopes and discovered numerous nebulae and double stars. His son, **Sir John Frederick William Herschel** (1792-1871), extended his study of heavenly bodies and made observations in southern hemisphere.

Hertfordshire, county of EC England. Area 1634 sq km (630 sq mi); pop. 940,000. Low-lying; Chiltern Hills in NW. Cereals, market gardening, dairy farming. Co. town Hertford, mun. bor. on R. Lea. Pop. 20,000. Important hist. Saxon town.

Hertz, Heinrich Rudolf (1857-94), German physicist. Confirmed (1888) existence of electromagnetic waves predicted by Maxwell and showed that they obey same laws as light. Unit of frequency named after him, equal to one cycle per second.

Hertzog, James Barry Munnik (1866-1942), South African soldier, politician, PM (1924-39). Organized anti-British National party (1913). Advocated neutrality in WWI, WWII.

Hertzsprung-Russell diagram, in astronomy, graph obtained by plotting absolute luminosity of stars against their spectral type (determined by colour or temperature). Most stars lie in diagonal band stretching from top left hand corner (main sequence); white dwarfs and giant stars form separate groups. Has proved useful in theories of stellar evolution.

Herzegovina, alternative form of Hercegovina; *see* BOSNIA AND HERCEGOVINA.

Herzl, Theodor (1860-1904), Hungarian writer. Founded ZIONISM after Dreyfus affair. Wrote famous pamphlet *Der Judenstaat* (1896).

Hesiod (*fl c* 8th cent. BC), Greek poet. Earliest of Greek poets after Homer. Prob. Boeotian farmer, wrote didactic poem *Works and Days* on farming. May have written *Theogony*.

Hesperides (Gk.,=in the west), in Greek myth, daughters of Evening who, with the help of dragon Ladon, guarded the golden apples of the tree given by Gaea to Hera on her marriage to Zeus. Heracles killed Ladon, stole apples as his 11th labour.

Hess, Rudolf (1894–), German Nazi leader, b. Egypt. Hitler's deputy from 1933. In apparent peace bid, flew stolen plane to Scotland (1941); imprisoned. Sentenced to life imprisonment at Nuremberg trials (1946).

Hesse, Hermann (1877-1962), German author. Influenced by Romanticism, eg *Romantic Songs* (1899). Best-known novels incl. *Demian* (1919), *Steppenwolf* (1927), *The Glass-Bead Game* (1943), reflect interest in Indian mysticism, psychoanalysis. Swiss citizen from 1921. Nobel Prize for Literature (1946).

Hesse (Hessen), state of WC West Germany, cap. Wiesbaden. Mainly forested uplands; agric., vine growing, minerals. Resorts incl. several spas, eg Bad Homburg. Region incl. parts of former Hesse-Nassau prov. and Hesse-Darmstadt duchy.

Hestia, in Greek myth, goddess of the hearth; daughter of Cronus and Rhea. Regarded as kindest of the gods representing security of the home. Identified by the Romans with Vesta.

heterocyclic compounds, organic compounds with cyclic molecular structure in which atoms of carbon and at least one other element are joined in a ring, eg pyridine C_5H_5N.

Hevesy, Georg von (1885-1966), Hungarian biophysicist, chemist. Used radioactive isotopes to study chemical processes and in medical research; awarded Nobel Prize for Chemistry (1943). Co-discoverer of element hafnium (1923).

Heyerdahl, Thor (1914–), Norwegian ethnologist. Known for practical demonstrations of feasibility of early racial migrations. Works incl. *Kon Tiki* (1950) on voyage from Peru to Tuamotu Isls., *The Ra Expeditions* (1971) on crossing Atlantic by papyrus boat.

Heysham, see MORECAMBE AND HEYSHAM, England.

Heywood, Thomas (c 1574-1641), English actor, dramatist. Known for classic domestic tragedy *A Woman Killed with Kindness* (1603). Other works incl. defence of stage against Puritans, *The Apology for Actors* (1612).

hibernation, winter sleep of certain animals in temperate regions. Complete hibernation involves temperature drop, no food, spring awakening; practised by some mammals, most amphibians. Partial hibernation, practised by eg bats, involves periodic awakening for food.

hibiscus, genus of ornamental plants of mallow family, comprising c 150 herbs, shrubs and trees. Found in tropical and warm temperate areas. Some species cultivated for food and fibre products.

hiccup or **hiccough**, involuntary spasm of diaphragm followed by intake of air which is halted by sudden closing of glottis. Most hiccup attacks pass quickly but some may last for weeks.

hickory, any of genus *Carya* of timber and nut-producing trees of walnut family. Native to E Canada and US. Species incl. PECAN.

hieratic, Egyptian cursive script derived from hieroglyphics for purpose of writing on papyrus. Gave way to DEMOTIC from 7th cent. BC but survived longer as religious script.

hieroglyphics, ancient Egyptian pictographic writing developed in pre-dynastic times, ie before 3100 BC. Used 3 classes of symbol: ideograms or pictograms, representing words in pictorial form; phonograms, representing sounds of words; determinatives, to indicate sense. See ROSETTA STONE.

higher education, see COLLEGE; UNIVERSITY.

Highland games, sports meeting, often professional, originating in N Scotland in early 19th cent. Events incl. caber tossing, hammer throwing, Highland dancing and bagpipe playing.

Highlands, area of Scotland, N of line joining Helensburgh and Stonehaven. Mainly uplands, mountains rising to 1342 m (4406 ft) at Ben Nevis; many sea, freshwater lochs; bisected by Great Glen. Crofting, fishing, distilling, tourist industs. Oil discovered off N, E coasts; h.e.p. Highland, region of N Scotland. Area 25,141 sq km (9709 sq mi); pop. 175,000. Created 1975, incl. former Sutherland, Caithness, Ross and Cromarty, Inverness-shire, Nairnshire.

high school, see SECONDARY SCHOOL.

highway, in British law, any road over which right of way has been estab., as by 21 years' uninterrupted use. In US, any of national trunk roads, controlled and partly sponsored by federal govt. See also MOTORWAY.

highwayman, formerly, robber on horseback, who robbed travellers on highway. Esp. prevalent in UK in 17th-18th cents., leading to estab. of Bow Street Runners. Claude Duval, Dick Turpin among best known.

hijacker, originally, one who steals goods, esp. truck and contents, in transit. Term applied from late 1960s to one who forces pilot of aircraft to fly to non-scheduled landing point. Became tactic of international guerrilla warfare, esp. by Palestinian Liberation Front.

Hildebrand, see GREGORY VII, ST.

Hill, Archibald Vivian (1886-1977), English physiologist. Shared Nobel Prize for Physiology and Medicine (1922) for his discoveries in generation of heat in muscles. Showed that oxygen is used up after muscle's contraction.

Hill, David Octavius (1802-1870), Scottish portrait painter and pioneer photographer; worked with Robert Adamson (1821-1848), using calotype process. Commissioned to paint disruption meeting of Scottish churches (1843), used photographic portraits for studies. Went on to take numerous portraits of fellow Scots in everyday surroundings.

Hill, Sir Rowland (1795-1879), English educator. As school headmaster in Birmingham, estab. selfgovt. system. Also responsible for introduction of pre-paid post (1840).

Hillary, Sir Edmund Percival (1919-), New Zealand mountaineer, explorer. He and Tensing Norkay (1914-), were first to reach summit of Mt. Everest (May, 1953), as part of British Everest Expedition. Hillary journeyed to South Pole (1958) by overland route.

hill figure, large monumental figure, usually a horse or man, cut from turf to show underlying chalk. Found mainly in downs of S

England. Oldest is White Horse of Uffington, dating from Late Iron Age.

Hilliard, Nicholas (c 1547-1619), English painter, goldsmith. First true miniaturist in England, he was court painter to Elizabeth I and James I. Works incl. portraits of Queen Elizabeth, Raleigh, Drake, Sidney.

Hillingdon, bor. of W Greater London, England. Pop. 235,000. Created 1965 from Middlesex towns incl. Uxbridge.

Hilton, James (1900-54), English novelist. Known for *Lost Horizon* (1933), best-seller *Good-Bye, Mr Chips* (1934) on the life of an English schoolmaster.

Hilversum, town of WC Netherlands. Pop. 97,000. Summer resort; textiles, electrical goods. Chief Dutch radio, television broadcasting centre.

Himachal Pradesh, state of N India. Area c 56,000 sq km (21,600 sq mi); cap. Simla (in Punjab). Pop. 3,424,000. In W Himalayas, bordering on Tibet. Forests yield softwood timber. Formed (1948) from former Hill States; more areas from Punjab added in 1966.

Himalayas, world's highest mountain system, stretching c 2400 km (1500 mi) across C Asia; forms natural barrier between Tibet and India, Nepal, and Bhutan. Peaks incl. Mt. Everest, Kanchenjunga, Nanga Parbat.

Himmler, Heinrich (1900-45), German Nazi leader. Became head of SS (1929), commander of entire police force (1936), minister of interior (1943). Responsible for enforcement of extermination policies. Committed suicide.

Hindemith, Paul (1895-1963), German composer, violinist and viola player. Output large, varied, modern in style. Works incl. symphonies and operas, *eg Mathis der Maler*. Also a noted music theorist, basing much of his music on his theoretical work. Music banned by Nazis, after 1940 lived in US, Switzerland.

Hindenburg [und Beneckendorff], Paul von (1847-1934), German military, political leader. Became supreme commander of Central Forces (1916), directing German war effort until end of WWI. Elected president of Reich (1925-32) with Junkers' support. Re-elected (1932), appointed Hitler chancellor (1933).

Hindi, Indic language in Indo-Iranian branch of Indo-European family. Official language of India. Variant of Hindustani. Divided into Western and Eastern dialect groups, latter being vehicle of major literature.

Hinduism, Western term for the religion and social system of loosely-related sects which incl. most of India's pop. Has no single founder but grew over period of c 5000 years, assimilating many beliefs. All Hindus traditionally subscribe to CASTE system and the sacredness of VEDA scriptures.

Hindu Kush, mountain range, mainly in NE Afghanistan, separated from W Himalayas by Indus valley. Tirich Mir in Pakistan, height 7692 m (25,236 ft), is highest peak. Has passes used by Alexander the Great and Tamerlane.

Hindustani, group of Indic languages in Indo-Iranian branch of Indo-European family. Some use term only for spoken forms of Hindi and Urdu, others incl. N Indian vernaculars. Developed from PRAKRIT. Used as lingua franca in modern India. Has 3rd largest number of speakers in world after Chinese and English.

hinny, see ASS.

hinterland, area behind a coastal port which supplies most of its exports and provides a market for most of its imports. Often extended to mean area serving and served by an inland market town. First used by Germans in 1880s concerning region behind their occupied coastal territ. in N Africa.

hip, see BRIAR.

Hipparchus, tyrant of Athens. See HIPPIAS.

Hipparchus (2nd cent. BC), Greek astronomer. A founder of systematic astronomy, he made catalogue of hundreds of stars and discovered precession of equinoxes; first to use trigonometry. His findings influenced Ptolemy.

Hippias, tyrant of Athens (527-510 BC). Son of Pisistratus, shared rule of Athens with his brother Hipparchus, until latter's murder. Deposed by Alcmaeonidae family with aid of Sparta.

Hippocrates (c 460-c 370 BC), Greek physician, known as the 'Father of Medicine'. Leader of school of medicine on isl. of Cos, whose members emphasized scientific basis of medicine, distinguishing it from philosophy and religion. Corpus Hippocraticum (72 books) represents their teaching.

Hippocratic oath, taken by medical graduates, said to represent his ethical ideas.

Hippolyte, see AMAZONS.

Hippolytus, St (d. c 236), Roman theologian. After split with Church, became 1st antipope (c 217). Died in exile although reconciled with Church.

Hippolytus, see PHAEDRA.

hippopotamus, heavy thick-skinned herbivorous mammal common to rivers of Africa. Large tusks in lower jaw source of ivory. Two species: Hippopotamus amphibius, of C Africa, and pygmy hippopotamus, Choeropsis liberiensis, of Liberia.

hire purchase, system whereby goods are bought on payment, over a stated period, of equal instalments. Usually financed by specialist company. Buyer has use of, but does not own, goods until agreed terms have been fulfilled.

Hirohito (1901-), emperor of Japan (1926-). Reign marked by increase in militarism, with Sino-Japanese war (beginning 1937) and pact (1940) with Germany, Italy in WWII. Surrendered (1945). Allowed by Allies to remain as constitutional emperor, renounced (1946) claims to imperial divinity.

Hiroshima, seaport of Japan, SW Honshu isl. Pop. 542,000. Shipbuilding, car and textile mfg. Devastated by 1st atomic bomb (6 Aug. 1945), with loss of c 80,000 lives.

Hispaniola, isl. of Greater Antilles, West Indies, lying between Cuba and Puerto Rico. Area 76,483 sq km (29,530 sq mi). Comprises Haiti in W, Dominican Republic in E. Discovered by Columbus in 1492.

Hiss, Alger (1904-), American public official. Accused (1945) of conveying govt. secrets to agents of USSR, indicted on 2 counts of perjury. After 2 trials, found guilty (1950), imprisoned. Released 1954 still denying charges.

histamine, white crystalline substance found in animal tissue. Released when tissue is injured or during allergic reactions. Dilates blood vessels and stimulates gastric secretion.

history, branch of knowledge which deals systematically with the past, recording, analysing, correlating and · interpreting past events. Sources incl. buildings, artifacts as well as chronicles, contemporary written records. Herodotus considered 1st historian; Thucydides, in record of Peloponnesian War, was more limited in scope but began tradition of accuracy, continued by Tacitus in Roman period. Storytelling element stressed by Xenophon, Livy. Medieval historians preoccupied with theological interpretation of world's history, or with simply chronicling events (as by Saxo Grammaticus, Matthew of Paris), although Moslem chronicles maintained literary quality. Secular histories emerged in 12th cent., and Renaissance brought emphassis on textual criticism, esp. in 16th-17th cent. by, *eg,* Bodin. Accuracy was again combined with moral, social concern with 18th cent. writers, incl. Voltaire, Montesquieu. 19th cent. saw · emergence of archaeology, philology, and development of history into academic discipline. Philosophy of history influenced by HEGEL, MARX, TOYN-

BEE. Other linked disciplines incl. anthropology, sociology, economics, psychology.

Hitchcock, Alfred [Joseph] (1899-), British film director. Famous for suspense thrillers. Films incl. *Blackmail* (1929), *The Thirty-Nine Steps* (1935), *The Lady Vanishes* (1938), *Rebecca* (1940), *Psycho* (1960).

Hitler, Adolf (1889-1945), German dictator, b. Austria. Founded (1921) National Socialist (Nazi) Party. During imprisonment (1923) for attempted coup (beer hall 'putsch') in Munich, wrote *Mein Kampf* (my struggle), statement of ideology. Economic depression after 1929 brought mass support, making (1932) Nazis largest party in Reichstag. Hitler was appointed chancellor (Jan. 1933), estab. dictatorship (March, 1933) by attributing Reichstag fire to Communists. Estab. (1934) Third Reich, assuming title of Führer. Political opponents, Jews, socialists were persecuted or killed. Aggressive foreign policy and Anglo-French 'appeasement' led to MUNICH PACT (1938). Invaded Poland (1939) beginning WWII. Personal command of Russian campaign (1941) led to Stalingrad defeat. Survived assassination attempt (1944) by high-ranking officers. Faced with total defeat, committed suicide (April, 1945) with his wife, Eva Braun.

Hittites, people inhabiting Asia Minor and Syria from 3rd to 1st millennium BC. At peak of power 1450-1200, when they challenged Assyria and Egypt. Spoke one of earliest recorded Indo-European languages. Thought to be among 1st peoples to smelt iron.

hives, popular name for URTICARIA.

Hobart, cap. of Tasmania, Australia, on Derwent estuary. Pop. 153,000. Admin. centre; port with fine natural harbour, exports fruit, timber, metals; food processing, metal refining; univ. of Tasmania (1890). Founded 1804.

Hobbema, Meindert (1638-1709), Dutch painter. Considered last great 17th cent. Dutch landscape master. Influenced by Jacob van Ruisdael, he painted quiet landscapes, specializing in watermills and woodland scenes. Work incl. *Avenue at Middelharnis* (1689).

Hobbes, Thomas (1588-1679), English philosopher. Best-known work, *Leviathan* (1651), argued that humans are naturally violent, self-seeking, only to be controlled in totalitarian state, ruled by absolute monarch. Theories attacked by Locke.

hobby, *Falco subbuteo,* small European falcon with long wings, short tail. Preys on insects and birds such as swallow, lark.

Hobhouse, Leonard Trelawney (1864-1929), English philosopher, sociologist. Combining history, anthropology, held that development of mind is paralleled by development of societies. Works incl. *The Metaphysical Theory of the State* (1918).

Ho Chi Minh, orig. Nguyen That Thanh (1890-1969), Vietnamese political leader. Helped found French Communist Party (1920) and Vietnamese Communist Party (1930). Organized and led Viet Minh, fighting guerrilla war against Jap-anese in WWII; headed provisional govt. after war. Gained complete control of North Vietnam after Indo-Chinese War (1946-54) against French. Geneva settlement divided Vietnam, Ho given control N of 17th parallel. Pursued militant policy in effort to reunite Vietnam through guerrilla war (VIET CONG) with South in 1960s.

Ho Chi Minh City, cap. and chief city of South Vietnam; formerly Saigon. Pop. c 1,805,000. Indust. centre with neighbouring Cholon, with canal link to R. Mekong. French colonial cap. from 1887 until independence in 1954. Hq. of US and South Vietnamese forces in Vietnam war; seriously damaged in guerrilla fighting.

Ho Chi Minh Trail, supply route through E Laos used by North Vietnamese forces in Vietnam war, esp. after US-South Vietnamese invasion of Cambodia (1970) closed alternatives.

hockey, game played on field or ice. Field hockey, an eleven-a-side game played with ball and stick, developed in England, becoming popular in 1870s. Olympic event since 1908, now played widely in Commonwealth countries, Germany, Netherlands, *etc.* Ice hockey, six-a-side game played with stick and rubber puck, originated in Canada in 1870s. Professional National Hockey League teams (US and Canada) compete annually for Stanley Cup.

Hockney, David (1937-), English artist. Early work, using commercial imagery, is related to pop art. Later style is more realistic and colourful; excels in depiction of water. Works incl. *Mr and Mrs Clark and Percy.*

Hodgkin, Dorothy Mary Crowfoot (1910-), British biochemist, b. Egypt. Used X-rays to determine structure of vitamin B$_{12}$ and cholesterol iodide (antidote for pernicious anaemia). Won Nobel Prize for Chemistry (1964).

Hoek van Holland, see HOOK OF HOLLAND.

Hoffmann, E[rnst] T[heodor] A[madeus] (1776-1822), German author, composer. Influential during Romantic period through literary style; stories used by Offenbach for libretto of *Tales of Hoffmann*.

Hofmannsthal, Hugo von (1874-1929), Austrian writer. Abandoned lyric poetry for mythological drama eg *Death and the Fool* (1899), *Elektra* (1903), *The Tower* (1925). Wrote libretti for Richard Strauss's operas, incl. *Rosenkavalier* (1911).

hog, name applied to several members of pig family. Species incl. red river hog, *Potamochoerus porcus*, of C and S Africa, pygmy hog, *Sus salvanius,* of Nepal, and WART HOG.

Hogarth, William (1697-1764), English painter, engraver. Painted series of morality pictures, incl. *The Harlot's Progress, The Rake's Progress, Marriage à la Mode,* which satirized social abuses; engravings of these were popular successes. Portraits incl. *Captain Coram* and *The Shrimp Girl.*

Hogg, James (1770-1835), Scottish author. Known as 'The Ettrick Shepherd'. Wrote *The Private Memoirs and Confessions of a Justified Sinner* (1824) dealing with Calvinist doctrine of predestination. Also wrote poetry, eg *The Mountain Bard* (1807).

Hoggar Mountains, see AHAGGAR MOUNTAINS.

Hohenstaufen, German princely family, originating as dukes of Swabia. Holy Roman emperors (1138-1208, 1214-54); kings of Sicily (1194-1268).

Hohenzollern, German dynasty, founded by Frederick of Hohenzollern in Nuremberg (1192). His sons estab. 2 lines of family in Prussia and Bavaria, adding (1415) electorate of Brandenburg. Duchy of Prussia estab. by Albert of Brandenburg (1525). Territs. extended (1640-88) by Frederick William to become (1701) kingdom of Prussia under Frederick I. Emperors of Germany (1871-1918).

Hokkaido, isl. of N Japan, separated from Honshu isl. by Tsugaru Str. Area c 78,000 sq km (30,000 sq mi). Forested, with mountainous interior; harsh climate in winter. Fishing main indust.; produces coal, timber. Originally inhabited by aboriginal Ainus, settled by Japanese in 16th cent.; called Yezo until 1869.

Hokusai, Katsushika (1760-1849), Japanese painter and designer. Master of Japanese wood-block print (*ukiyo-e*), he is famous for his imaginative landscapes; his simplified design and dramatic composition influenced Western art. Works incl. series *36 Views of Mount Fuji.*

Holbein, Hans, ('the Younger') (c 1497-1543), German painter. Leading realist portrait painter of the N European Renaissance, he illustrated Luther's Bible and produced woodcut series *The Dance of Death.* Court painter to Henry VIII, his portraits incl. many of Erasmus, *Georg Gisze* and the *Ambassadors*.

Holborn, part of Camden, NC Greater London, England. Met. bor. until 1965. Has British Museum; 2 Inns of Court.

Hölderlin, [Johann Christian] Friedrich (1770-1843), German poet. Lyric poetry, *eg Bread and Wine* (1800-3), combines classical style with Romantic inspiration. Epistolary novel *Hyperion* (1797-9) reflects yearning for values of ancient Greece. Became insane in 1803.

Holguin, town of E Cuba. Pop. 193,000. Commercial centre in agric. region. Tobacco, coffee, maize, sugar cane exports; furniture, tile mfg.

Holiday, Billie, orig. Eleanora Fagan (1915-59), American jazz singer. Remembered for her subtle rendition of such songs as 'Strange fruit' and 'Am I blue?'. Autobiog. *Lady Sings the Blues* describes her difficult life.

Holinshed, Raphael (d. c 1580), English chronicler. Wrote *Chronicles of England, Scotland and Ireland* (1577), used as source for plots by Elizabethan dramatists, incl. Shakespeare.

Holland, Sir Sidney George (1893-1961), New Zealand statesman, PM (1949-57). Leader of National Party from 1946.

Holland, hist. region of W. Netherlands. County from 10th cent., held Zeeland, part of Friesland during Middle Ages. Prosperity at height 15th-16th cents. through commerce, cloth indust. Led Dutch independence struggle, chief of United Provs. 1579-1795. Divided 1840 into

North Holland, prov. incl. some Frisian Isls. Area 2631 sq km (1016 sq mi); cap. Haarlem, chief city Amsterdam. South Holland, prov., area 2810 sq km (1085 sq mi); cap. The Hague, chief towns Rotterdam, Leiden.

Holland, Parts of, former admin. region of Lincolnshire, E England. Co. town was Boston.

holly, any of genus *Ilex* of evergreen, smooth-leaved trees and shrubs. Species incl. American holly *I. opaca*, and European holly *I. aquifolium* with red berries. Traditional Christmas decoration.

hollyhock, *Althaea rosea*, biennial plant of mallow family. Native to China, now widely cultivated garden plant. Large showy flowers on long spikes. Grows up to c 3 m/10 ft.

Hollywood, suburb of Los Angeles, US. Centre of American film industry.

Holmes, Oliver Wendell (1809-94), American writer, physician. Best known for wide-ranging prose dialogues, *eg The Autocrat of the Breakfast Table* (1858). Also wrote novels, poetry, *eg The Chambered Nautilus* (1858). His son, Oliver Wendell Holmes (1841-1935), was associate chief justice of US Supreme Court (1902-32). Dissented from view that law has fixed universal power over society. Wrote *The Common Law* (1881).

holmium (Ho), metallic element of lanthanide group; at. no. 67, at. wt. 164.93. Discovered spectroscopically (1878).

Holocene or **Recent epoch,** second and current geological epoch of Quaternary period. Began c 11,000 years ago. When Pleistocene glaciers melted, climate was for a time warmer than now; present landscape formed, eg lakes, deserts. Man dominant; culture developed through Mesolithic and Neolithic, Bronze and Iron Ages to present level of civilization. Also *see* GEOLOGICAL TABLE.

holography, means of producing 3-dimensional images without use of lenses. Light from a laser is split into 2 beams, one of which falls directly onto photographic plate. Other beam illuminates subject to be reproduced and then recombines with reference beam to form interference pattern (hologram) on plate. A 3-dimensional virtual image can be seen by shining laser light through developed film.

Holst, Gustav (1874-1934), British composer. His music is often eclectic but contains original rhythmic and harmonic devices. Work incl. opera *The Perfect Fool,* choral work *Hymn of Jesus,* orchestral suite *War* *The Planets.*

Holt, Harold Edward (1908-67), Australian statesman, Liberal Party leader and PM (1966-7). Increased number of Australian troops in South Vietnam. Drowned.

Holy Alliance, treaty signed (1815) by emperors of Russia, Austria, Prussia, with all European sovereigns eventually signing except George IV of Britain, pope, and sultan of Turkey. Estab. to preserve 1815 status quo, suppressed revolutions until Revolution of 1848 rendered it ineffective.

Holy Communion, *see* EUCHARIST.

Holy Ghost, *see* TRINITY.

Holy Grail, *see* GRAIL, HOLY.

Holyhead, urban dist. of Gwynedd,

NW Wales, on Holy Isl. Pop. 11,000. Tourist resort; has ferry services to Irish Republic.

Holy Island, *see* LINDISFARNE, England.

Holy Land, *see* ISRAEL.

Holy Loch, *see* DUNOON, Scotland.

Holyoake, Sir Keith Jacka (1904-   ), New Zealand statesman, PM (1957, 1960-72). Succeeded Sidney Holland as National Party leader and PM.

Holy Roman Empire, revival of ancient Roman Empire of the West, founded by CHARLEMAGNE (800). After period of decline and disunity, empire was revived by coronation of OTTO I (962), who united Lombardy with Germany. Dominions incl. Germany, Austria, Bohemia, Belgium and, until 1648, Switzerland and Netherlands. Habsburgs became hereditary rulers after 1438. Opposed Protestant Reformation in 16th cent. Influence declined after Thirty Years War (1618-48), power thereafter being wielded by Spanish and Austrian branches. Dissolved (1806) after Napoleon's conquests.

Holyrood House, royal palace in Edinburgh, Scotland, built c 1500 by James IV on site of 12th cent. abbey. Almost destroyed by fire (1650) and rebuilt by Charles II in 1670s. Scene of Rizzio murder (1566).

Holy Week, in Christian calendar, week preceding Easter, commemorating Jesus' passion and death.

Home, Sir Alec Douglas-, *see* DOUGLAS-HOME, ALEXANDER FREDERICK.

Home Guard, in UK, originally the Local Defence Volunteers, formed (1940) as makeshift anti-invasion force, became efficient army of *c* 2 million by 1945.

homeopathy, system of therapeutics introduced by German physician Samuel Hahnemann (1755-1843). Based on belief that cure of disease is effected by minute doses of drugs capable of producing in a healthy individual symptoms of the disease being treated.

Homer (*fl c* 8th cent. BC), Greek epic poet. Traditionally regarded as author of ILIAD and ODYSSEY, although opinions differ over single authorship, with some doubt over his existence. Said to have been blind wanderer. Epics were models for all later European epics.

Homer, Winslow (1836-1910), American artist. After working as an illustrator, he devoted himself to painting pictures of outdoor life, expressing the American spirit. Best known for his depiction of the Maine coast; works incl. *The Gulf Stream*.

Home Rule, in Irish history, slogan used by Irish nationalists in 19th cent. who wished to obtain self-govt. for Ireland within British empire. Home Rule movement began in 1870s under leadership of PARNELL. Gladstone's 1st Home Rule Bill (1886) defeated; 2nd (1893) thwarted by House of Lords; 3rd (1912) never put into effect because of WWI and Irish pressure for independent republic.

Homestead Act (1862), law passed by US Congress permitting settlers to own up to 160 acres of previously unoccupied land after 5 year residence. Encouraged settlement of West.

Homo erectus, extinct species of man, incl. JAVA MAN and PEKING MAN. Skeletal remains *c* million years old have been found at OLDUVAI GORGE but more recent finds suggest that *Homo erectus* may have existed more than 2 million years ago in E Africa.

homosexuality, sexual attraction towards individuals of same sex. In women, commonly called lesbianism. Acceptance varies from culture to culture, male homosexual practices being illegal until recently in UK.

Homs (anc. *Emesa*), city of WC Syria. Pop. 215,000. Agric. centre; oil refining, textile mfg. Had ancient temple devoted to sun god.

Honan, prov. of EC China. Area 168,350 sq km (65,000 sq mi); pop. 50,000,000; cap. Chengchow. Sparsely pop. in mountainous W, agric.; indust. in E; cereals, cotton, coal mining. Crossed by Hwang Ho.

Honduras, republic of Central America, incl. off-shore Bay Isls. Area 112,088 sq km (43,277 sq mi); pop. 2,831,000; cap. Tegucigalpa. Language: Spanish. Religion: RC. Humid Caribbean coast (US-owned banana plantations); Mosquito Coast in NE; mainly forested mountains in interior with important silver mines. Visited by Columbus (1502), colonized by Spanish; gained independence 1821; member of Central American Federation 1825-38. Disastrous floods in 1974.

Honecker, Erich (1912-), East German political leader. Secretary of Communist Party (1971-), succeeding Ulbricht.

Honegger, Arthur (1892-1955), Swiss composer, one of 'les Six'. Works incl. chamber and orchestral music, operas *Judith*, *Le Roi David*, and music for films. His best-known piece is *Pacific 231*, an orchestral evocation of a locomotive.

honesty or **moonwort**, *Lunaria annua*, European flowering plant with distinctive silver moon-shaped seed pods. Purple or white flowers in spring.

honey, sweet sticky fluid manufactured by honey bees from nectar taken from flowers, and stored in honeycombs as food. Consists of various sugars produced by action of enzymes on sucrose in nectar. Colour and flavour depends on type of flower·from which nectar was collected.

honey bee, *Apis mellifera*, social bee of Old World origin. Builds nests of wax, storing honey in hexagonal cells; often kept in hives by man to supply honey.

honey eater, any of Meliphagidae family of brightly coloured Australasian birds. Tongue is brush-tipped for extracting nectar and insects from flowers. Species incl. wattlebird and bellbird.

honeymouse or **honey opossum**, *Tarsipes spenserae*, long-tailed mouse-like marsupial of SW Australia. Long pointed snout and bristly tongue used for sucking nectar.

honeysuckle, any of genus *Lonicera* of wild and cultivated, erect or climbing shrubs. *L. periclymenum*, best-known in Europe, has fragrant yellow or white flowers. Name often used for family Caprifoliaceae, incl. viburnums, elder, as well as true honeysuckle.

Hong Kong, British crown colony of SE Asia, connected to S China. Area 1034 sq km (398 sq mi); pop.

4,383,000; cap. Victoria. Incl. Hong Kong isl., Kowloon penin., joined by tunnel (1972), and New Territ. (leased from China for 99 years in 1898). Major textile, garment industs.; shipbuilding, electrical equipment mfg. Important link for Chinese trade. Free port, with fine harbour.

Honolulu, cap. and chief port of Hawaii, US; on SE Oahu isl. Pop. 325,000. Has international airport. Financial, tourist centre; sugar processing, pineapple canning. Cap. from 1845.

Honshu, chief isl. of Japan. Area *c* 230,000 sq km (89,000 sq mi). Mountainous (Fujiyama), little arable land; rivers short and rapid. Densely populated; indust. centres incl. Tokyo, Yokohama, Nagoya, Osaka.

Honthorst, Gerard van (1590-1656), Dutch artist. Influenced by Caravaggio, he painted biblical, mythological and genre scenes. Noted for his candlelight effects, as in *Christ before the High Priest*.

Hooch or **Hoogh, Pieter de** (1628-*c* 1684), Dutch genre painter. Remembered for his depiction of interiors and courtyards; his rendering of effects of light is esp. fine.

Hood, Samuel Hood, 1st Viscount (1724-1816), British naval officer. Outmanoeuvred French fleet off St Kitts (1782), shared with Rodney victory off Dominica (1782). Blockaded Toulon (1793) and captured Corsica (1794).

Hood, Thomas (1799-1845), English poet, humorist. Wrote sentimental, comic verse. Serious works incl. *The Dream of Eugene Aram*

chases (over obstacles). HARNESS RACING performed by horses trained to trot. In England, Jockey Club (founded 1750) controls horse racing. Famous events are Epsom Derby, St Leger Stakes, One and Two Thousand Guineas, Oaks and Grand National. American 'Triple Crown' comprises Kentucky Derby, Preakness and Belmont Stakes.

horseradish, *Armoracia rusticana,* perennial herb of mustard family, native to S Europe and naturalized in North America. Grated, pungent root is used as relish.

horseshoe bat, bat of Europe and Asia, of Rhinolophoidae family. Has horseshoe-shaped membranous outgrowths of skin (nose-leaves) around nose, used for navigation.

horsetail, any of genus *Equisetum* of rush-like plants related to fern and club moss. Survivor of primitive, once abundant group of vascular plants.

Horta, Victor, Baron (1861–1947), Belgian architect. Early exponent of art nouveau, he is known for flowing decorative ironwork. Works incl. Maison du Peuple, Brussels (1896–9), now destroyed.

Horthy [de Nagybánya], Nicholas (1868–1957), Hungarian statesman, admiral. Led counter-revolutionary 'white' forces against Béla Kun's Communist govt. (1919–20). Became regent of Hungary (1920). Forced to resign, deported by occupying Germans (1944).

horticulture, science of growing flowers, fruits, vegetables and shrubs, esp. in gardens and orchards.

Horus, in ancient Egyptian religion, god of the sun, light and goodness; son of Osiris and Isis. Represented with head of falcon. Known as Horus the child (Harpocrates) by Greeks and Romans, and represented as small boy with finger held to his lips and worshipped as god of silence.

Hosea, prophetic book of OT written by Hosea (8th cent. BC). Largely a sermon against moral decadence in N kingdom of Israel.

Hospitallers, see KNIGHTS HOSPITALLERS.

Hot Springs, resort town of C Arkansas, US; in Ouachita Mts. Pop. 36,000. In National Park which has many hot mineral springs.

Hotspur, see PERCY, HENRY.

Hottentot, people of South West Africa (Namibia) and NW Cape Prov. Pastoral nomads prob. related to Bushmen. Numbers diminished since Dutch settlement, pop. (est. 1963) 24,000.

Houdini, Harry, pseud. of Erich Weiss (1874–1926), American escapologist. Renowned for spectacular escapes from ropes, handcuffs, *etc.* Exposed fraudulent spiritualism by demonstrating how phenomena could be produced mechanically.

Hounslow, bor. of W Greater London, England. Pop. 206,000. Created 1965 from Middlesex towns. Has Heathrow airport.

house fly, *Musca domestica,* two-winged fly of worldwide distribution. Vomits digestive juice on food before eating it, spreading disease germs. Breeds in manure or decaying matter.

house mouse, see MOUSE.

House of Commons, lower chamber of British PARLIAMENT. Composed of members (MPs) popularly elected by single-ballot system, each representing specific constituency of UK; presided over by Speaker. More powerful of 2 Houses, govt. (*see* CABINET) depending on majority in it and answerable to it for all actions. Initiates all major legislation, controls national finance.

House of Lords, upper chamber of British PARLIAMENT. Composed largely of hereditary peers, with Anglican archbishops, bishops, number of life peers. Derived from medieval king's council. Presided over by Lord Chancellor. Powers curtailed by PARLIAMENT ACTS (1911, 1949). Also acts as UK's final court of appeal.

House of Representatives, lower house of US CONGRESS. Composed of members elected by populace for 2 year terms on proportional basis; presided over by Speaker. Originates revenue bills, has power to impeach president.

housing, living accommodation available to a community. Provision of housing of reasonable standard is one of the most pressing problems facing the world. It results mainly from rural-urban migration, lowering of death rate due to medical advances, and insufficient allocation of resources by govts. to housing. In developed countries this migration has now slowed, though much housing remains unfit; in developing nations it continues, leading to overcrowding, growth of ramshackle 'shanty towns' peripheral to cities, eg La Paz, Bolivia, and Caracas, Venezuela.

Housman, A[lfred] E[dward] (1859-1936), English poet, scholar. Known for collection of pessimistic lyric poems, *A Shropshire Lad* (1896).

Houston, Sam[uel] (1793-1863), American statesman, frontiersman. Led Texan defeat of Mexicans at San Jacinto (1836), capturing Santa Anna. First president of independent Texas (1836-8, 1841-4), state governor (1859-61) after Texas joined Union. Removed for refusal to join Confederacy.

Houston, port of SE Texas, US; on canal with access to Gulf of Mexico. Pop. 123,000. In important oil, sulphur mining region; exports cotton, chemicals, petroleum. Nearby victory at San Jacinto ended Texas independence (1836). Cap. of Texas republic (1837-9). Has NASA space centre; Rice Univ. (1912).

Hove, mun. bor. of East Sussex, SE England. Pop. 73,000. Resort, adjoins Brighton.

hovercraft or **air-cushion vehicle,** amphibious vehicle developed (1959) in UK by Sir Christopher Cockerell (1910-). Supports itself on cushion of air, usually generated by horizontal fan; forward motion provided by propellers or jets. First commercial service was Rhyl to Wallasey (UK) passenger ferry (1962).

hover fly, any of Syrphidae family of 2-winged insects. Resembles wasp with yellow and black bands on abdomen. Larvae feed on aphids, performing useful control.

Howard, Catherine, *see* HOWARD, THOMAS.

Howard, John (1726-90), English reformer. Tour of English prisons led to 2 acts of Parliament (1774) improving prison conditions. Howard League for Penal Reform (founded 1866) continues his work.

Howard, Leslie, orig. Leslie

Stainer (1890-1943), British film actor. Typically cast as romantic intellectual, eg *Intermezzo* (1939), other films incl. *The Scarlet Pimpernel* (1935), *Gone with the Wind* (1939).

Howard, Thomas, 2nd Duke of Norfolk (1443-1524), English nobleman. Defeated Scots at Flodden (1513). His son, **Thomas Howard, 3rd Duke of Norfolk** (1473-1554), a Catholic, had influence at Henry VIII's court through niece, Anne Boleyn, Henry's 2nd wife. Avoided execution for treason (1547) only by death of Henry; imprisoned throughout reign of Edward VI. His other niece, **Catherine Howard** (c 1521-42), was Henry's 5th wife; she was executed primarily to remove Howard family influence. His son, **Henry Howard, Earl of Surrey** (c 1517-47), was a poet, introducing sonnet forms, also iambic blank verse. Arrested with his father and executed. His son, **Thomas Howard, 4th Duke of Norfolk** (1536-72), favourite of Elizabeth I, was executed after failure of plot to free Mary Queen of Scots. His cousin, **Charles Howard, 1st Earl of Nottingham** (1536-1624), became lord high admiral (1585), commanding English fleet against Spanish Armada (1558). **Philip Howard, 13th earl of Arundel** (1557-95), eldest son of 4th Duke of Norfolk, was suspected of complicity in Throgmorton's Plot, became RC in 1584, and was condemned to death but died in prison; he was canonized in 1970.

Howard, Trevor Wallace (1916-), English actor. In films since 1944, has appeared in widely contrasted roles. Films incl. *Brief Encounter* (1946), *The Third Man* (1949), *Mutiny on the Bounty* (1962).

Howe, Geoffrey (1926-), British politician. Conservative chancellor of exchequer (1979-).

Howe, Joseph (1804-73), Canadian journalist, statesman. Opposed confederation with Canada. Premier of Nova Scotia (1860-3).

Howe, Richard Howe, 1st Earl (1726-99), English admiral. Commanded Channel fleet in Seven Years War, British fleet during American Revolution. Defeated French off Ushant ('Glorious First of June', 1794). His brother, **William Howe, 5th Viscount Howe** (1729-1814), became British commander-in-chief in America after victory at Bunker Hill (1775). Defeated Washington at Brandywine (1777). Resigned 1778.

Howells, William Dean (1837-1920), American author. Known for realistic novels, eg *A Modern Instance* (1881), *The Rise of Silas Lapham* (1885), *Indian Summer* (1886).

howler monkey, largest of New World monkeys, genus *Alouatta*, of forests of tropical America. Noted for howling noise; has prehensile tail.

Howrah, city of West Bengal, NE India. Pop. 740,000. On R. Hooghly, connected by bridge to Calcutta on opposite side. Indust. centre; textile, jute, glass mfg.

Hoxha, Enver (1908-), Albanian statesman. Led radical resistance against Italians (1939-44), founded Albanian Communist Party (1941). First secretary of party (1943-), premier of Albanian Republic (1944-

54). Supported China during and after Sino-Soviet split (1961).

Hoy, isl. of Orkney, N Scotland. Has 'Old Man of Hoy' rock stack (137 m/450 ft high).

Hoyle, Sir Fred (1915-), English astronomer, author. Developed mathematical form of steady-state theory of universe. Author of *The Nature of the Universe* (1950) and *Galaxies, Nuclei and Quasars* (1965).

Hsüan-tsang or **Hiouentang** (c 605-64), Chinese Buddhist scholar. Made extended pilgrimage to India collecting religious literature and writing accounts of his travels. Translated Buddhist scriptures.

Hua Kuo-feng (c 1921-), Chinese political leader. Deputy premier and minister of public security (1975-6), appointed premier (April, 1976) on death of Chou En-lai. Succeeded Mao Tse-tung as party chairman.

Huascarán, highest mountain of Peru; in W Andes. Height 6768 m (22,205 ft). Avalanche in 1962 killed 20,000 people in foothill villages.

Hubble, Edwin Powell (1889-1953), American astronomer. Discovered large galaxies beyond the Milky Way. Formulated law that distant galaxies are receding with velocities proportional to their distances following observations of red shift in their spectra; this expansion of universe is explained by big-bang theory.

huckleberry, any of genus *Gaylussacia* of North American shrubs of heath family. Dark-blue berries, resembling blueberries, but with 10 large seeds.

Huddersfield, co. bor. of West Yorkshire met. county, N England.

Pop. 131,000. Woollens, carpets mfg; textile machinery.

Hudson, Henry (c 1550-1611), English explorer. In search of Northwest Passage, explored (in Dutch service) Hudson R. and (in English service) Hudson Bay. Disappeared after being cast adrift by mutinous crew.

Hudson, river of E New York, US. Rises in Adirondack Mts. Flows S 510 km (c 315 mi) to New York City harbour. Chief tributary Mohawk R. Major commercial route linked to Great Lakes, St Lawrence Seaway.

Hudson Bay, inland sea of EC Canada, in SE Northwest Territs. Area 1,230,000 sq km (c 475,000 sq mi). James Bay in S. Discovered 1610 by Henry Hudson. Fur trade; exploration sponsored by Hudson's Bay Co. Churchill is main port. Hudson Strait provides access to the Atlantic.

Hudson's Bay Company, chartered 1670 for purpose of obtaining furs for the English market. Its vast territories, known as Rupert's Land, incl. all land drained by rivers flowing into Hudson Bay, were sold to Canadian govt. (1869). In 20th cent. its operations were diversified into retailing and mfg.

Hué, city of N South Vietnam. Pop. 200,000. Market centre; cement mfg. Cap. of hist. kingdom of Annam. Palaces and tombs of Annamese kings destroyed during North's Tet offensive of 1968.

Huelva, town of SW Spain, on penin. between mouths of Odiel and Tinto, cap. of Huelva prov. Pop. 97,000. Port, exports copper, iron ores; fishing, tourism. Nearby is monastery where Columbus planned his 1st voyage.

Huesca, town of NE Spain, cap. of Huesca prov. Pop. 33,000. Agric. market, pottery mfg. Site of Roman school (77 BC); cap. of Aragón 1096-1118. Cathedral (13th cent.), royal palace.

Huggins, Sir William (1824-1910), English astronomer. Pioneer of astronomical spectroscopy, he showed that certain nebulae are gaseous; developed photographic methods of recording spectra. First to apply Doppler principle to determine radial motion of stars.

Hughes, Ted (1950-), English poet. Poetry, powerfully conveying sense of brute, forces in man and nature, incl. *Lupercal* (1960), *Wodwo* (1968), *Crow* (1970).

Hughes, Thomas (1822-96), English author. Known for novel *Tom Brown's Schooldays* (1857) expounding doctrine of 'muscular' Christianity. Also wrote on religion, life of David Livingstone.

Hughes, William Morris (1864-1952), Australian statesman, b. England, PM (1915-22). Headed Labor, then National wartime govts.

Hugh of Lincoln or **of Avalon, St** (d. 1200), English churchman, b. France. Called to England (c 1176) by Henry II, he was created bishop of Lincoln (1186). Sided with barons in refusing money for Richard I. Famed for piety, championing the poor.

Hugo, Victor Marie (1802-85), French poet, dramatist, novelist, leader of Romanticism. Introduced flexibility, melody into French verse, *eg* in play *Hernani* (1830), verse collections *Odes et ballades* (1826),

Chants du crépuscule (1835), *Les Rayons et les ombres* (1840). Novels incl. *Notre Dame de Paris* (1831), *Les Misérables* (1862), *Les Travailleurs de la mer* reflect compassion for common man.

Huguenots, Calvinist Protestants of France, protagonists in Wars of Religion (1562-98), ending with Edict of Nantes. Many emigrated after its revocation (1685).

Huhehot, cap. of Inner Mongolia auton. region, N China. Pop. 700,000. Centre of caravan routes to Mongolian People's Republic; chemicals, motor vehicle mfg. Mongolian religious centre.

Hull, Cordell (1871-1955), American statesman. Secretary of state (1933-44). Awarded Nobel Peace Prize (1945) for work leading to UN's creation.

Hull, town of S Québec, Canada; opposite Ottawa at confluence of Gatineau and Ottawa rivers. Pop. 64,000. Pulp and paper centre (matches); h.e.p. Founded 1800.

Hull or **Kingston-upon-Hull**, city and co. town of Humberside, NE England, on Humber estuary. Pop. 285,000. Port; ferry services to Europe; fishing. Has 13th cent. church; univ. (1954).

Hulme, T[homas] E[rnest] (1883-1917), English philosopher, poet. Anti-romantic, influenced Pound, Eliot, IMAGISTS. Poetry pub. in Pound's *Ripostes* (1915), essays in *Speculations* (1924).

humanism, movement in thought and literature, originally applied to Italian Renaissance. Involved reaction against medieval religious authority, rediscovery of secular Classical ideals and attitudes. Notable humanists incl. **Sir Thomas More**, Colet, Irving Babbitt.

Humber, estuary of NE England, of rivers Trent, Ouse. Length *c* 60 km (37 mi); ports incl. Hull, Grimsby.

Humberside, county of NE England. Area 3512 sq km (1356 sq mi); pop. 847,000; co. town Hull. Created 1974, comprising former East Riding of Yorkshire, N Lincolnshire.

humble bee, *see* BUMBLE BEE.

Humboldt, [Friedrich Heinrich] Alexander von (1769-1859), German explorer, scientist, geographer. Expedition to Central and South America (1799-1804) resulted in greater understanding of scientific factors in geography. Explored Russia and C Asia (1829). Wrote *Kosmos* (1845-62), physical description of the Earth. His brother, **Wilhelm von Humboldt** (1767-1835), was govt. official and philologist. Prussian education minister (1809-10), reformed school system. Made pioneering study of Kawi language of Java.

Humboldt Glacier, glacier of NW Greenland, flowing into Kane Basin. Largest in N hemisphere, *c* 100 km (60 mi) wide at mouth.

Hume, David (1711-76), Scottish philosopher. Took ideas of Locke, Berkeley to logical extension of SCEPTICISM. Held that reason could only be subject to passions and rejected any rational theology. Works incl. *Treatise of Human Nature* (1739), *An Enquiry Concerning Human Understanding* (1748), *History of Great Britain* (1754).

humidity, *see* RELATIVE HUMIDITY.

hummingbird, any of Trochilidae family of small brightly coloured New World birds. Feeds on insects and nectar, hovering over flowers with rapidly-vibrating wings. Bee hummingbird, *Mellisuga helenae*, of Cuba is world's smallest bird.

Humperdinck, Engelbert (1854-1921), German composer and teacher. Friend of Wagner. His chief work was the opera *Hansel and Gretel* (1893).

Humphrey, Hubert Horatio (1911-78), American politician, vice-president (1965-9). First Democrat from Minnesota to be elected (1948) to Senate. Democratic presidential candidate (1968), narrowly lost to Nixon.

humus, amorphous, black organic matter in soil. Humification is process of decomposition of plants and animals into elements useful in maintaining soil fertility. Sometimes extended to incl. partially decomposed matter in soil.

Hunan, prov. of SC China. Area *c* 207,000 sq km (80,000 sq mi); pop. (est.) 38,000,000; cap. Changsha. Leading rice producer. Major lead, zinc, antimony mines.

Hundred Years War (1337-1453), conflict between England and France, resulting from commercial and territ. rivalries. Begun when EDWARD III claimed French throne (1337). English successes at Sluis, Crécy, Poitiers were countered by later French victories under du Guesclin; French recovered most of their lost territ. by 1377. War was renewed by HENRY V who conquered much of Normandy after victory at Agincourt (1415). JOAN OF ARC began French recovery after 1429; by 1453 Calais was only English possession in France.

Hungary (Magyar *Népköztár-*

sasag), republic of EC Europe. Area 93,012 sq km (35,912 sq mi); pop. 10,596,000; cap. Budapest. Language: Magyar. Religions: RC, Protestant. Danube runs N-S; to E is Alföld plain; to W is Bakony Forest (hilly), L. Balaton. Agric. (esp. cereals) on collective system; indust. developing (coal, petroleum, bauxite). Kingdom estab. by St Stephen (11th cent.); ruled by Ottoman Turks until 1683; part of Habsburg empire until 1848 revolt; part of 'dual monarchy' (Austria-Hungary) 1867-1918, then independent republic. Joined Axis in WWII. Communist govt. estab. 1948. Revolt (1956) suppressed by USSR.

Huns, nomadic pastoralists of NC Asia who invaded E Europe *c* 370, forcing the Ostrogoths and Visigoths to migrate westwards. Under their leader Attila, overran Balkans and forced Emperor Theodosius to pay tribute. When tributes ceased Huns invaded Gaul but were defeated at Châlons (451). Subsequent invasion of Italy was abandoned (452).

Hunt, Lord Henry Cecil John (1910-), English soldier, mountaineer, explorer. Led British Everest Expedition (1953) on which Hillary and Tensing became first to reach summit. Wrote *The Ascent of Everest* (1953).

Hunt, [James Henry] Leigh (1784-1859), English poet, essayist. Wrote essays on music, painting, Italian literature. Imprisoned for attacking Prince Regent in *The Examiner* (1813). Poetry incl. 'Abou Ben Adhem' (1834), 'Jenny Kissed Me' (1844).

Hunt, William Holman (1827-1910), English painter. Founder member of Pre-Raphaelite Brotherhood with Rossetti and Millais; work is noted for its detail, harsh colour and laboured symbolism. Travelled to Palestine and Egypt to paint biblical scenes with accurate local settings. Works incl. *Light of the World.*

Hunter, John (1728-93), Scottish surgeon, physiologist. Made studies in comparative anatomy and introduced new techniques in surgery. His collection of anatomical specimens was acquired by Royal College of Surgeons, London. His brother, **William Hunter** (1718-83), was an obstetrician, known as a lecturer in anatomy. His collections formed basis of Hunterian Museum in Glasgow Univ.

Huntingdonshire, former county of EC England, now part of Cambridgeshire. Low-lying, Fens in NE; pasture, market gardening, cereals. Co. town was Huntingdon (and Godmanchester), mun. bor. on R. Great Ouse. Pop. 17,000. On Roman Ermine St.; bridge (14th cent.). Birthplace of Oliver Cromwell.

Hupeh or **Hupei,** prov. of EC China. Area *c* 186,000 sq km (72,000 sq mi); pop. (est.) 34,000,000; cap. Wuhan at jct. of Yangtze and Han rivers. C part is low-lying, with many lakes and rivers. Grains, cotton, rice grown. Steel complexes.

hurling, fifteen-a-side team game played with sticks and ball, mainly in Ireland. Played for several cents. prior to formation of Gaelic Association standardized rules (1884).

Huron, confederation of 4 North American Indian tribes of Hokan-Siouan linguistic stock. Lived in

Ontario in 17th cent. Numbered *c* 20,000. Farmers, crops incl. tobacco. Defeated and dispersed by Iroquois in 1649. Remaining members settled near Detroit and in Ohio, and later in Oklahoma.

Huron, Lake, 2nd largest of Great Lakes, C Canada-US border. Area 59,596 sq km (23,010 sq mi). Bounded by Ontario (Canada), Michigan (US). Georgian Bay is NE extension; Saginaw Bay in S. Trade route connecting L. Superior, L. Michigan with L. Erie, used by oceangoing and lake vessels. Main cargoes iron ore, grain, limestone, coal. Ice-bound in winter.

hurricane, violent cyclonic storm occurring in tropical areas. Consists of high-speed wind system revolving around a calm, low pressure centre or 'eye'. Common in Caribbean, Gulf of Mexico areas; occur in Pacific as 'typhoons' or 'tropical cyclones'. Term also used to describe winds of velocity over 120 kmh (75 mph), *ie* force 12 on Beaufort Scale.

Hus or **Huss, Jan** (*c* 1370–1415), Bohemian religious reformer. Influenced by views of Wycliffe, his preaching against clerical privilege attracted popular support and led to his excommunication (1410). Granted safe conduct to explain views to Council of Constance (1414), he was tried and condemned for heresy. Death by burning led to HUSSITE WARS.

Husein (*c* 626-680), Shiite Moslem saint, grandson of prophet Mohammed. Led unsuccessful insurrection in support of claim to succeed as CALIPH. Died in attempt. His claim is upheld by the SHIITES.

hussars, originally Hungarian cavalry in the 15th cent., the name was later applied to light horse regiments in many European armies.

Hussein I (1935-), king of Jordan (1952-). Moderate pro-Westerner, but led Jordan against Israel in 1967 Arab-Israeli war. After loss of Jordan W of R. Jordan, conflict arose with Palestinian guerrillas, leading to 1970 war. Although victorious, ceded W Bank to PLO (1974).

Husserl, Edmund (1859-1938), Austrian philosopher. Founder of phenomenology, *ie* belief that external data have no priority over imagination. Works incl. *Logical Inquiries* (1901), *Thoughts toward a Pure Phenomenology* (1913). Influenced later existentialists.

Hussites, followers of Jan Hus in Bohemia and Moravia who demanded religious freedoms and ending of clerical privilege; radical Taborite group, drawn mainly from peasantry, also sought social equality. Moderate Utraquist group accepted compromise settlement with Church drawn up at Council of Basle. Civil war resulted when Taborites rejected settlement, but they were defeated by Utraquists at Lipany (1434).

Hussite Wars, conflicts in Bohemia and Moravia begun when HUSSITES opposed succession of SIGISMUND as king of Bohemia (1419). Under Zizka and Prokop, Hussites defeated crusading forces sent against them. Peace treaty (Compactata) drawn up at Council of Basle was accepted by moderate Hussites. Conflict broke out again during regency of George of Podebrad after Compactata was revoked (1462).

Huston, John (1906-), American film director. Films incl. *The Maltese Falcon* (1941), *Treasure of the Sierra Madre* (1947), *The African Queen* (1951), *Fat City* (1972).

Hutcheson, Francis (1694-1746), Scottish philosopher, b. Ireland. Equated 'moral sense' with other senses. Anticipated utilitarians' doctrine of 'greatest happiness of the greatest number.'

Hutchinson, Anne (c 1591-1643), English religious leader in New England. After banishment for antinomianism from Massachusetts Bay Colony (1637), helped found Portsmouth, Rhode Isl.

Hutton, James (1726-97), Scottish geologist. Originated several basic principles of modern geology, notably theory of UNIFORMITARIANISM. This belief that Earth's surface has been shaped since its origin by unchanging processes of denudation and deposition aroused much controversy; later simplified by Playfair. Wrote *Theory of the Earth* (1795).

Huxley, Thomas Henry (1825-95), English biologist. Foremost British exponent of Darwin's theory of evolution; his writings deal with conflict of traditional religion and science. Also studied physiology, anatomy, vertebrate skull and coelenterates. His grandson, Sir Julian Sorell Huxley (1887-1975), English biologist and author, was active in popularizing science. Works incl. *Heredity, East and West* (1949). First director-general of UNESCO (1946-8). His brother, **Aldous Leonard Huxley** (1894-1963), was a novelist and essayist. Known for novels of ideas, eg *Point Counter Point* (1928), anti-Utopian *Brave New World* (1932), *Eyeless in Gaza* (1936). Essays on religion, philosophy incl. *Heaven and Hell* (1956).

Huygens, Christiaan (1629-95), Dutch mathematician, physicist, astronomer. Invented pendulum clock. Discovered nature of Saturn's rings. Developed Huygens' principle in wave theory of light which explained polarization, reflection and refraction.

Huysmans, Joris-Karl (1848-1907), French novelist. Known for decadent novels, esp. *Against Nature* (1884), describing the restless quest for new sensation.

Hvar (Ital. *Lesina*), Adriatic isl. of Yugoslavia, off Dalmatian coast. Area 290 sq km (112 sq mi); main town Hvar. Fishing, fruit, tourism. Founded c 390 BC by Greeks as Pharos.

Hwang Ho or **Yellow**, river of N China. Flows c 4800 km (3000 mi) from Tsinghai prov. into Pohai gulf. Millennia of silting have resulted in North China Plain, which despite frequent flooding is agric. heart of country.

hyacinth, any of genus *Hyacinthus* of plants of lily family. Native to Mediterranean and S African regions. Narrow, channelled leaves, spikes of bell-shaped flowers.

hyaena, carnivorous wolf-like mammal of Africa and Asia, with bristly mane, short hind legs and powerful jaws. Feeds on carrion but will attack other animals. Species incl. spotted hyaena, *Crocuta crocuta*, of E and S Africa.

hybrid, offspring produced by crossing 2 individuals of unlike genetic constitution, eg those of different race or species. Hybrid may be fertile or infertile. Hybridization is used in agric. to achieve greater vigour, growth in offspring, eg mule, hybrid corn.

Hyde, Douglas, known in Irish as An Craoibhin Aoibhinn (1860-1949), Irish scholar, statesman, president of Irish Republic (1938-45). Instrumental in revival of Irish language; 1st president of Gaelic League (1893-1915).

Hyde, Edward, see CLARENDON, EDWARD HYDE, 1ST EARL OF.

Hyde Park, in Westminster, London; area 146 ha (361 acres). Incl. Serpentine lake and Rotten Row, famous riding track. Site of Great Exhibition (1851).

Hyderabad, cap. of Andhra Pradesh, SC India. Pop. 1,799,000. Transportation centre; textile mfg. Wall encloses old city containing Four Minarets (1591) and Great Mosque. Cap. of former princely state of Hyderabad (1724-1948).

Hyderabad, city of SE Pakistan. Pop. 624,000. Textile, machinery mfg. Cap. of Sind (1768-1843) until taken by British.

Hyder Ali (1722-82), Indian military leader, ruler of Mysore (1766-82). In Anglo-French conflict sided with French until defeat by British (1781). Succeeded by his son, Tippoo Sahib.

Hydra, in Greek myth, many-headed monster. When 1 head was cut off 2 grew in its place. The 2nd labour of Heracles was to kill the monster, which he did by burning the stump of neck after cutting off each head.

hydra, solitary freshwater coelenterate polyp, class Hydrozoa, which lacks free-swimming medusa stage. Tube-like body with tentacles around mouth; reproduces asexually by budding.

hydrangea, genus of flowering shrubs of saxifrage family, native to Americas. White, blue or pink flowers.

hydraulic press, device consisting of 2 liquid-filled cylinders of unequal diameter connected by a pipe and fitted with pistons. By Pascal's law, a force exerted on smaller piston will result in a greater force (proportional to quotient of the surface areas of pistons) on larger piston. Invented by J. Bramah (1795).

hydraulics, branch of ENGINEERING dealing with mechanical properties of water and other liquids. Divided into hydrostatics dealing with liquids at rest, eg in hydraulic presses, and hydrokinetics dealing with problems of friction and turbulence in moving liquids.

hydrocarbon, organic compound containing hydrogen and carbon only.

hydrocephalus, enlargement of an infant's head caused by accumulation of fluid in the cranium. Damage to the brain and mental retardation may result.

hydrochloric acid, strong corrosive acid formed by dissolving hydrogen chloride HCl in water. Used in ore extraction, metal cleaning and as chemical reagent.

hydrocyanic acid (HCN), weak, highly poisonous acid with smell of bitter almonds, formed by dissolving hydrogen cyanide in water. Used as fumigant and in organic synthesis. Also called prussic acid.

hydro-electric power, electrical energy obtained from generators driven by water-turbines. Source of water may be natural (waterfall) or artificial (river-damming). Amount of power is proportional to rate of water flow and vertical distance through which it falls. During periods of low demand excess electricity is used to pump water back to source.

hydrofoil, wing-like device which produces upward lift when moved through water. Watercraft which use such devices to lift hull above water are capable of high speeds because of low drag.

hydrogen (H), colourless gaseous element; at. no. 1, at. wt. 1.008. Lightest known substance, its molecule consists of 2 atoms. Burns in oxygen to form water. Occurs in water, organic compounds, petroleum, coal, *etc.* Obtained by electrolysis, decomposition of hydrocarbons, or from water gas. Used in manufacture of ammonia, margarine and synthetic oils. Deuterium and tritium are isotopes important in nuclear research.

hydrogen bomb, nuclear weapon operating on principle of nuclear FUSION. Consists of atomic bomb surrounded by layer of lithium deuteride; intense heat produced by atomic fission causes nuclei of hydrogen isotopes to fuse into helium nuclei, with resultant release of enormous quantity of energy.

hydrogen ion concentration, in chemistry, number of grams of hydrogen ions per litre in an aqueous solution. The pH-value of a solution is the common logarithm of the reciprocal of the hydrogen ion concentration and acts as a measure of acidity or alkalinity. Pure water

has pH-value of 7; acids have values from 0 to 7, alkalis from 7 to 14.

hydrogen peroxide (H_2O_2), viscous liquid, often used in aqueous solution as a bleach and disinfectant. Powerful oxidizing agent; in concentrated form, used as rocket propellant.

hydrology, study of water upon, under and above the Earth's surface. Evaporation, precipitation, and flow through and over the Earth's surface together constitute the 'hydrological cycle'.

hydrolysis, in chemistry, decomposition by water. Hydrolysis of organic compounds may be effected by aqueous alkalis or dilute acids, eg esters of higher fatty acids are hydrolyzed in presence of alkalis to form soap. Inorganic salts undergo hydrolysis into acids and bases through action of hydrogen and hydroxyl ions in water.

hydrometer, instrument for measuring specific gravity of a liquid. Liquid is placed in graduated tube, which is then immersed in water. Depth to which tube sinks shows the specific gravity.

hydrophobia, see RABIES.

hydroponics, science of growing plants in solutions of the necessary minerals instead of in soil. Developed by J. von Sachs and W. Knop *c* 1860. Increasingly used commercially since 1930s.

hydroxide, compound consisting of element or radical joined to hydroxyl (OH) radical, eg potassium hydroxide KOH.

Hygeia, in Greek myth, daughter of ASCLEPIUS; goddess of health.

hygrometer, instrument for

measuring RELATIVE HUMIDITY of atmosphere.

Hymen or **Hymenaeus**, in Greek myth, beautiful youth; personification of marriage.

Hymettus (*Imittos*), mountain group of Attica, SE Greece. Highest point Mt. Hymettus (1027 m/3370 ft). Famous honey; marble quarries.

hymn, song in praise or honour of a deity. Christian hymn developed as metrical form in 4th cent.; polyphonic settings evolved in 13th-16th cents. Lutheran CHORALE developed after Reformation. Dissenters of 18th cent. began English hymn tradition with collections such as those of Isaac Watts, John Wesley.

hyperbola, in geometry, curve traced by point which moves so ratio of its distance from a fixed point to distance from fixed line is a constant greater than 1. Curve has 2 branches; it is also a conic section.

Hyperboreans, in Greek myth, inhabitants of region of sunshine and everlasting spring in far north. Associated with cult of Apollo.

Hyperion, in Greek religion, one of the TITANS. Husband of his sister Theia, and by her, father of Helios, Selene and Eos. Sometimes appears as a sun god.

hypermetropia or long sight, defect of eye in which images are focused behind the retina, so that distant objects are seen more clearly than near objects. Caused because lens of eye is too short or its refractive power too weak. Corrected by glasses with convex lenses. Called far sight in US.

hyperons, in physics, elementary particles of baryon group with mass intermediate between that of neutron and deuteron. Decay rapidly into neutrons and protons.

hypertension, abnormally high blood pressure. May be symptom of disease, eg kidney disease, arteriosclerosis, but cause is sometimes unknown.

hypnosis, sleep-like condition induced in subject by monotonous repetition of words and gestures. Subject responds only to operator's voice and returns to normal consciousness when told to. Sometimes used to treat neurosis as repressed memories can be recalled under hypnosis.

hyrax, any of order Hyracoidea of rabbit-sized hoofed mammals of Africa and SW Asia. Two genera: rock-dwelling *Procavia* and arboreal *Dendrohyrax*.

hyssop, *Hyssopus officinalis*, small perennial aromatic plant, native to Mediterranean region. Blue flowers. Used in folk medicine as tonic.

hysterectomy, surgical removal of uterus, usually necessitated by presence of fibroid tumours or cancer.

hysteresis, in magnetism, lag in magnetization when ferromagnetic body is magnetized. Body retains residual magnetism when external field is removed. Graph of magnetizing field against magnetic induction in body is closed loop which indicates this lag.

hysteria, form of neurosis in which sustained anxiety expresses itself as bodily disturbance. May result in apparent paralysis of a limb or simulation of blindness.

Hythe, mun. bor. of Kent, SE England. Pop. 12,000. One of Cinque Ports, harbour now silted up.

I

iambus or **iamb,** metrical foot of 2 syllables, 1st unstressed, 2nd stressed. Term usually followed by word denoting number of feet in line, *eg* iambic pentameter (5 feet).

Iaşi (Ger. *Jassy*), city of NE Romania. Pop. 202,000. Industs. incl. textiles, metal goods. Cultural centre; univ. (1860). Scene of German massacre of Jews (1941).

Ibadan, city of SW Nigeria. Pop. 758,000. Admin., indust. centre on Lagos-Kano railway; trade in cacao, cotton, palm oil; univ. (1962). Centre of Yoruba culture.

Iberia, penin. of SW Europe, comprising Spain and Portugal, separated from rest of Europe by Pyrenees. Name derived from Greek for people living beside R. Iberus (mod. *Ebro*).

Ibert, Jacques (1890-1962), French composer. Style light and unpretentious. Wrote concertos, suites, *eg Escales,* also operas and ballets.

ibex, any of several species of mountain goats with backward-curving horns, found in Europe and Asia. Incl. Alpine ibex, *Capra ibex,* with short legs, powerful horns.

ibis, wading bird of Threskiornithidae family, related to stork, found mainly in tropical regions. Species incl. sacred ibis of ancient Egypt, *Threskiornis aethiopica.*

Ibiza, *see* IVIZA, Spain.

Ibn Gabirol, Solomon ben Judah (*c* 1020-1058), Jewish poet, also known as Avicebron. Wrote religious poetry and philosophical *The Well of Life,* a subsequent influence on Christian theology.

Ibn Saud (*c* 1880 - 1953), king of Saudi Arabia. Leader of WAHABI movement in Islam, captured Riyadh (1902) and took control of Nejd. Defeated rival Husein ibn Ali (1924) and annexed his kingdom of Hejaz. United Nejd and Hejaz (1932) to form kingdom of Saudi Arabia.

Ibn Sina, *see* AVICENNA.

Ibo, people of SE Nigeria. Number *c* 7 million. One of most advanced tribes in country, active in struggle for independence. Constitute most of pop. of BIAFRA.

Ibsen, Henrik Johan (1828-1906), Norwegian dramatist. Works stress importance of individuals' joy in living rather than conventional society's needs. Best-known plays incl. verse *Peer Gynt* (1867); social tragedies *A Doll's House* (1879), *Ghosts* (1881), *Hedda Gabler* (1890); symbolic dramas *The Wild Duck* (1884), *When We Dead Awaken* (1899) dealing with spiritual death through denial of love.

Icarus, *see* DAEDALUS.

ice, water in solid state, formed by cooling below freezing point. As water expands on freezing, ice is less dense than liquid water.

Ice ages, glaciations of PLEISTOCENE

EPOCH when ice sheets and glaciers periodically advanced to cover large areas of America, Asia and Europe. Four major advances normally distinguished, most recent ending *c* 11,000 years ago. Greatly affected landscape formation. Believed to have been caused by perturbations in Earth's orbit about Sun.

Iceberg, mass of ice broken off from a glacier or ice barrier and floating in the sea. Normally only *c* 1/9th total mass is visible above the surface. Hazard to shipping, *eg* sinking of *Titanic* (1912).

ice hockey, see HOCKEY.

Iceland (*Island*), isl. republic of Europe, in N Atlantic. Area 102,950 sq km (39,750 sq mi); pop. 220,000; cap. Reykjavik. Language: Icelandic. Religion: Lutheran. Uninhabited C plateau; over 100 volcanoes (many active), hot springs, icefields (incl. Vatnajökull). Rugged coastline; mild, wet climate, stunted vegetation. Fishing (esp. cod, herring), h.e.p., grazing. Colonized 9th cent. by Norwegians; first parliament in Europe (930); united with Denmark (1380-1918). Independent republic from 1944.

Icelandic, see GERMANIC LANGUAGES.

Icelandic literature, best known for early works (*c* 1000-1300), EDDAS and SAGAS closely linked to OLD NORSE. Chivalric romances written from *c* 1300 on; after Reformation strong religious influence seen in hymns, *etc*, poems of Einar Sigurdsson. Only with romantic revival of mid-19th cent. did literature reach peak of pre-1300, creating new classical Icelandic style. Notable figures of 19th-20th cent. incl. Thoroddsen, Sigurdsson, Brandes, Gunnarsson, Kamban, Gudmundsson, and Nobel laureate Laxness.

I Ching or **Book of Changes,** one of five Chinese Confucian classics, originally written *c* 1027-256 BC. Contains system of divination based on 64 hexagrams.

ichneumon, *Herpestes ichneumon,* riverside-dwelling mongoose found in S Spain and throughout Africa. Sacred in ancient Egypt, often mummified.

ichthyology, branch of zoology dealing with fish, their structure, classification and life history. Fish are divided into 3 main classes: jawless fish (Cyclostomata), incl. lampreys and hagfish; cartilaginous fish (Chondrichthyes), incl. sharks and rays; bony fish (Osteichthyes), comprising majority of fish. Over 20,000 living species exist.

ichthyosaur, large extinct aquatic reptile, known from fossils of Jurassic period. Dolphin-like, with 4 paddle-shaped flippers and long snout.

icon, image or picture of Christ, Virgin Mary or a saint, venerated in Eastern Orthodox church. In common use by end of 5th cent., few survived outbreak of iconoclasm in 8th and 9th cents. Following fall of Constantinople, icon-making fl in Russia until the Revolution.

Iconium, see KONYA.

Ictinus (*fl* 5th cent. BC), Greek architect. Leading Athenian architect of time of Pericles, collaborated with Callicrates on building of the Parthenon (447-432 BC). Temple of Apollo at Bassae attributed to him.

id, term used by Freud to denote that

part of personality which is unconscious, primitive, instinctual, dynamic, as opposed to the EGO and SUPEREGO.

Ida, Mount (*Psiloríti*), mountain of C Crete, Greece. Height 2455 m (8058 ft).

Idaho, state of NW US. Area 216,413 sq km (83,557 sq mi); pop. 713,000; cap. Boise. Dominated by Rocky Mts.; crossed by Snake, Salmon rivers. Timber, agric. in S (potato, wheat, sugar beet production); silver, lead, antimony mines. Settled in 1860s. Admitted to Union as 43rd state (1890).

idealism, in philosophy, theory that nothing outside ideas has any reality. The only reality of objects is in the impression they make on the mind. Normally implies the existence of absolutes, *eg* good, truth. Developed along separate lines by *eg* Plato, Berkeley, Kant, Hegel.

Idomeneus, in Greek legend, king of Crete. Led his subjects against Troy in Trojan War. During a storm on the return journey, he vowed to sacrifice to Poseidon the 1st living thing he met on landing. This turned out to be his son, whom he slew.

If, Château d', fortress, formerly used as prison, on isl. of If, off Marseilles, S France. Built 16th cent., scene of imprisonment in Dumas' *The Count of Monte Cristo*.

Ife, city of SW Nigeria. Pop. 157,000. Trade in cacao, palm and kernels; univ. (1961). Hist. religious centre of Yoruba tribe.

Ifni, region of SW Morocco. On edge of Sahara; fruit growing, coastal fishing. Overseas prov. of Spain from 1860, cap. Sidi Ifni; returned to Morocco 1969.

Ignatius of Loyola, St, (1491-1556), Spanish monk. Gave up military career after severe wounds, became religious (1521). Planned and organized Jesuit order, approved by pope (1540) on basis of *Formula* (revised as *Constitutions*, pub. at his death). Elected (1541) 1st general of order. Also wrote devotional *Spiritual Exercises*.

igneous rocks, rocks formed by cooling and solidification of molten magma. Consist of mass of interlocking crystals due to different rate of cooling of constituent minerals. Those formed after reaching Earth's surface, *ie* EXTRUSIVE ROCKS, are commonly finely crystalline; those formed at depth, *ie* INTRUSIVE ROCKS, are commonly coarsely crystalline.

Iguaçu or **Iguassú**, river of S Brazil. Flows W 1200 km (750 mi) to join Paraná at Argentina border. H.e.p. at Iguaçu Falls (joint Brazil-Argentina control).

iguana, any lizard of Iguanidae family of tropical America. Common species is *Iguana iguana* of Mexico and N South America; greenish, with row of spines from neck to tail. Many species can change colour.

iguanodon, two-legged herbivorous dinosaur, reaching lengths of 7.6 m/25 ft. Fossils found in Cretaceous rocks esp. in Belgium.

Ijsselmeer or **Ysselmeer**, freshwater lake of NW Netherlands, fed by R. Ijssel. Created from former ZUIDER ZEE by dam (31 km/19 mi long) completed 1932. Four polders reclaimed, giving rich agric. land; also fishing.

Ikhnaton or **Akhenaton**, orig. Amenhotep IV (d. *c* 1354 BC), Egyptian pharaoh (*c* 1372–*c*

1354 BC), husband of Nefertiti. Built Akhetaton (modern AMARNA) as centre of his new religion devoted to worship of sun god Aton, in whose honour he changed his name.

Ile-de-France, hist. region of France, in centre of Paris basin. Agric. area, providing Paris with food; drained by rivers Seine, Oise, Marne; forests at Fontainebleau, Compiègne. Power base of 1st kings of France.

Iliad, Greek epic in 24 books, attributed to Homer, prob. written *c* 6th cent. BC, composed *c* 8th cent. BC. Set in Trojan War (Ilium=Troy), theme is wrath of Achilles and course of war.

Ilium, *see* TROY.

Illich, Ivan (1926–), American educationalist, writer, b. Austria. Known for books attacking conventional education, health services *etc*, *eg Deschooling Society* (1971), *Medical Nemesis* (1975).

Illinois, state of NC US. Area 146,676 sq km (56,400 sq mi); pop. 11,114,000; cap. Springfield; major city Chicago. Mississippi R. forms W border. Mainly plains; agric. important esp. livestock, corn, maize, wheat. Large mineral resources in S *eg* coal, oil. Mfg. and indust. concentrated on L. Michigan shore around Chicago (meat packing, oil refining). French estab. missions in 17th cent.; passed to British 1763; taken by US in Revolution. Admitted to Union as 21st state (1818).

Illuminati (Lat.,=enlightened), mystic sects claiming special knowledge of God, esp. order founded (1776) in Germany by Adam Weishaupt. Aims were republican and anti-Catholic. With close affinities with Freemasonry, it was denounced and suppressed by Bavarian govt. (1785).

illumination of manuscripts, decoration of hand-written books with coloured pictures, esp. initial letters and marginal decorations. Early Christian examples incl. Irish *Book of Kells* (8th cent.); later ones incl. *Très Riches Heures du Duc de Berri* by Limbourg brothers (15th cent.).

Illyria, region on Adriatic coast of Yugoslavia and N Albania. Ancient tribal kingdom estab. 3rd cent. BC, partly conquered (34 BC) by Romans. Name revived by Napoleon (1809), Austria (1816-49).

image, in optics, visual likeness of object produced by reflection from a mirror or refraction by a lens. Real image is formed by light rays actually meeting at a point and entering observer's eye; may be shown on a screen. Virtual image is seen at point from which rays appear to come and cannot be shown on a screen.

imagists, group of poets incl. Richard Aldington, T.S. Eliot, Hilda Doolittle, Amy Lowell, who followed leadership of T.E. HULME, EZRA POUND in reacting against stultified Georgian romanticism. Works characterized by total precision in presentation of each image within short, free verse form. Active 1910-18 but had great influence.

imam (Arab.,=leader), in Islam, any recognized leader incl. successors of Mohammed. Esp. used by SHIITES for the unknown descendants of HUSEIN, *ie* the hidden imamate. *See* MAHDI. Imam also refers to leader of prayers in mosque.

Imhotep (*fl c* 2900 BC), Egyptian

statesman, architect, physician of the third dynasty. Designed Step Pyramid; later deified as god of healing.

immanence, in theology, the presence throughout natural universe of a spiritual principle. Opposed to transcendence, *ie* the existence of a spiritual principle outside the natural universe. Three main monotheistic religions believe that God is both immanent and transcendent.

immunity, natural resistance of an organism to specific infections. Presence of microbes in body stimulates formation of antibodies which provide temporary immunity for subsequent attacks of a particular disease. Can be induced by use of vaccines.

impala, *Aepyceros melampus,* medium-sized reddish antelope of S and E Africa. Male has long lyre-shaped horns. Noted for extraordinary leaping ability.

impeachment, bringing of public official before proper tribunal on charge of wrong-doing. In UK, trial is before House of Lords on Commons' accusation. Rare, although much used 1640-2. WARREN HASTINGS case (1788-95) was one of last in Britain. In US, House of Representatives has right of impeachment, Senate tries cases. Best-known case that of President A. Johnson (1868), who was acquitted. Impeachment procedure begun (1974) against Nixon, who resigned.

Imperial Conference, *see* COMMONWEALTH, BRITISH.

imperialism, extension of rule or influence by one country over another by diplomatic, military or economic means; manifested in empire. Esp. applied to European expansion (late 19th cent.) into Asia and Africa. Modern concept of neo-imperialism refers to economic or political domination of affairs of less developed countries.

impetigo, contagious disease of the skin caused by staphylococci. Characterized by eruption of isolated pus-filled blisters on hands, neck, face. Treated by antibiotics.

impressionism, school of painting, which originated in France in 1860s; name is derived from painting *Impression, Sunrise* by Monet shown at first Impressionist Exhibition (1874). Main exponents were Monet, Pissarro, Sisley, but Cézanne, Manet, Renoir and Degas were originally associated with movement. Their aim was to capture a momentary glimpse of a subject, reproducing changing effects of light in short strokes of pure colour.

impressment, practice of forcibly seizing recruits for military or naval duty. In UK, declared illegal in respect of soldiers (1641); legitimately used for naval recruitment down to early 19th cent. *See* PRESS-GANG.

incarnation, the assumption of human form by a god. Concept occurs in many religions, *eg* ancient Egyptian and Indian beliefs that certain kings were divine incarnations; also Greek belief that gods used human forms to communicate with men. Christians believe Jesus to be both wholly divine and human.

Incas, name ordinarily given to the pop. of Peru before conquest by Pizarro (1533), but properly restricted to ruling caste, ruler himself being the Inca. Civilization, centred at Cuzco, may go back to 1200. Achieved high level of culture as shown by social system, knowledge of agric., roadmaking, ceramics, textiles, buildings, eg Temple of the Sun at Machu Picchu.

incendiary bomb, canister containing highly inflammable substance such as thermite. Often dropped from aircraft in conjunction with explosive bombs.

incest, sexual relations between people of close kinship. Prohibited by law or custom in most societies although exceptions can be found in royal households of ancient Egypt and the Incas. Definitions of kinship, often complex, vary among societies.

Inchon, seaport of NW South Korea. Pop. 646,000. Ice-free harbour on Yellow Sea. Commercial and indust. centre; produces steel, textiles, chemicals, coke. Formerly called Chemulpo.

inclosure, alternative spelling of ENCLOSURE.

income tax, govt. tax on individual or corporate incomes. Modern form introduced in Britain by Pitt (1799) to raise funds for Napoleonic Wars; permanent tax adopted (1874). In US first levied during Civil War, present form adopted (1913). Now major source of revenue.

incubus, male demon which, in folklore, has intercourse with sleeping women, so fathering demons, witches, deformed children. Stories of them esp. common in Middle Ages. Female counterpart is succubus.

Independence, town of W Missouri. Pop. 112,000. Agric. machinery mfg. Hist. starting point on Santa Fé and Oregon trails.

Independence, American War of, see AMERICAN REVOLUTION.

Independence, Declaration of, formal statement adopted (4 July, 1776) by 2nd Continental Congress declaring the 13 American colonies free and independent of Britain. Almost entirely written by Thomas Jefferson, document sets out principle of govt. under theory of natural rights.

Independent Treasury System, estab. (1846) in US out of distrust of banks after President Jackson's refusal to recharter Bank of the US. Public revenues placed in Treasury, held independently of banking system in attempt to reduce Treasury's speculation in money market. Inconsistent govt. policy led to termination (1920) after enactment of FEDERAL RESERVE SYSTEM.

Index [librorum prohibitorum], list of publications that the RC church forbade its members to read, except by special permission, as dangerous to faith or morality. First pub. in 1559; put in care of Holy Office (1917). Abolished by 2nd Vatican Council (1962).

India (*Bharat*), republic of SC Asia. Area c 3,268,000 sq km (1,262,000 sq mi); pop. 610,077,000; cap. New Delhi. Official language: Hindi; religions: Hinduism, Islam. Indian penin. bounded by Himalayas, Pakistan and Bangladesh. Largely plains, cut by Ganges, Brahmaputra, Godavari. Climate mainly tropical monsoon; agric. economy (esp. rice, cotton, tea, timber). Divided into 22 states and 9 union territs. Major cities Bombay, Calcutta. Hinduism estab *c* 1500 BC, Buddhism and Jainism introduced in 6th cent. BC. Country united under Moguls (16th-18th cent.); East India Co. rule (1757-1858) transferred to Britain after Indian Mutiny. Independence struggle led by Gandhi; independence achieved (1947) with partition of Pakistan; republic estab. 1950. Member of British Commonwealth.

Indiana, state of NC US. Area 93,994 sq km (36,290 sq mi); pop. 5,194,000; cap. Indianapolis. Mainly rolling plains; agric. esp. maize, wheat, livestock, coal mining, limestone quarrying. Settled by French; ceded to British 1763; captured by US 1779; became territ. 1800 when Indians were dispossessed of their land. Admitted to Union as 19th state (1816).

Indianapolis, cap. of Indiana, US; on White R. Pop. 743,000. Transport jct.; grain, livestock market. Meat packing; produces motor car and aircraft parts. Annual speedway races ('500').

Indian corn, *see* MAIZE.

Indian literature, vernacular writings of Indian subcontinent. Only extensively produced after 1500, but ancient VEDA, PALI, and Prakrit (Jainist) religious literature existed previously. Hindu pietistic movements encouraged popularization of Sanskrit, leading language of great classics, eg *Ramayana, Bhagavad-Gita,* in popular verse form. Urdu verse written for Mogul court in Persian tradition. Modern literature incl. works in English and major languages of subcontinent. Writers incl. Tagore, Iqbal, Narayan, Ghose, Naidu.

Indian Mutiny or **Sepoy Rebellion** (1857-8), revolt of native soldiers (sepoys) in Bengal army of British East India Co. Troops resented annexation of Oudh (1856), homeland of many of them, and were angered by issue of cartridges coated with fat of cows (sacred to Hindus) and of pigs (forbidden to Moslems). Revolt, beginning Feb. 1857, spread over NC India; Delhi captured, Lucknow besieged, British garrison massacred at Kanpur. Mutiny subdued by March, 1858. Resulting reforms incl. transfer of rule from East India Co. to British Crown.

Indian National Congress, Indian political party, founded (1885) to increase Indian involvement in formation of British policy in India. Soon split into opposing groups seeking dominion status or complete independence. Became more militant after 1919, adopting policy, advocated by Gandhi, of civil disobedience and passive resistance to British rule. Under Nehru, became ruling party of India and maintained power until 1977 elections.

Indian Ocean, smallest of 3 world oceans, lying between Antarctica, Africa, Asia and Australia. Area *c* 73,430,000 sq km (28,350,000 sq mi). Reaches greatest depth in Java Trench (7725 m/ 25,344 ft). Main isls. Madagascar, Sri Lanka. Arms incl. Arabian Sea, Bay of Bengal. Seasonal winds (monsoons) yield rain in S and SE Asia.

Indian paintbrush, any of genus *Castilleja* of plants of figwort family. Brilliantly coloured orange flowers and red or yellow upper leaves.

Indians, American, *see* AMERICAN INDIANS.

India rubber tree, *see* RUBBER PLANT.

Indic, largest group of languages in Indo-Iranian branch of Indo-European family. Incl. ancient forms Vedic, Sanskrit, Prakrit; modern Punjabi, Sindhi, Hindi, Urdu, Assamese, Bengali, Gujarati, Singhalese, Marathi.

indicator, in chemistry, substance used to indicate completion of chemical reaction by sharp changes in colour. Indicators, *eg* litmus, often used to test for acidity or alkalinity, esp. during titration. Colour change indicates when neutralization has occurred. In ecology, species of plant or animal, or a community, whose occurrence serves as evidence that certain environmental conditions exist.

indictment, in law, formal written accusation charging specific persons with commission of a crime. In US, presented by grand jury to the court when jury has found, after examining presented evidence, that there is a valid case.

indigo, any plant of genus *Indigofera* of Leguminosae family. *I. tinctoria* is source of colourless indican which is oxidized to blue dye, indigo; it was used in ancient India and Egypt.

indium (In), soft metallic element; at. no. 49, at. wt. 114.82. Found in traces in zinc ores. Used in dental alloys and to protect bearings. Discovered spectroscopically (1863).

Indo-China, former federation of SE Asian states, comprising French colony of Cochin China and French protects. of Laos, Cambodia, Tonkin and Annam. Republic of Vietnam formed from Cochin China, Tonkin and Annam in 1949.

Indo-Chinese War, conflict fought (1946-54) between Viet Minh (coalition of nationalist and Communist groups under HO CHI MINH) and the French after failure of negotiations for Vietnamese independence. Decisive battle fought at Dienbienphu (1954) broke French resistance. Subsequent GENEVA CONFERENCE divided Indo-China into North and South Vietnam, Laos and Cambodia.

Indo-European, language family with more speakers than any other, *ie* c half of world's pop. Similarities in vocabulary and grammar point to ancient parent language, originating pre-2000 BC. Differences postulated to have arisen as migration separated groups speaking it. Major branches are Anatolian, Baltic, Celtic, Germanic, Greek, Indo-Iranian, Italic, Slavic, Thraco-Illyrian, Thraco-Phrygian, Tokharian.

Indonesia, republic of SE Asia. Area c 1,904,000 sq km (736,000 sq mi); pop. 139,616,000; cap. Djakarta. Official language: Bahasa Indonesian. Religion: Islam. Comprises former Dutch East Indies, consisting of c 3000 isls., incl. Java, Sumatra, Borneo, Lesser Sundas, Moluccas, Irian Jaya. Most isls. mountainous; equatorial climate with heavy rainfall. Rice main crop; exports rubber, spices, petroleum. Hinduism and Buddhism introduced under Indian influence; Islam dominant by end of 16th cent. Colonized by Dutch East India Co. (17th cent.). Independence proclaimed 1945, sovereignty transferred 1949.

Indore, city of Madhya Pradesh, C India. Pop. 573,000. Chemical, textile mfg. Cap. of former princely state of Indore.

Indra, in early Hindu religion, god of war and storms. Represented as an amoral, boisterous god. Ruler of Amaravati, an inferior heaven.

inductance, electrical, property of an electric circuit by which a changing electric current in it produces varying magnetic field. This magnetic field may induce voltages in same circuit (self-induction) or in neighbouring circuits (mutual induction).

induction, in physics, name given to 3 phenomena in electricity and magnetism. Electrostatic induction is production of charge on a body when another charged body is brought near. Magnetic induction is production of a magnetic field in ferromagnetic material by external magnetic field. *See also* ELECTROMAGNETIC INDUCTION.

inductive method, logical procedure formulated by Francis Bacon of arguing from particular observations to general principles. Opposite of deduction which argues from known principles to particular applications. Whereas deduction is infallible if original proposition is true, induction can only attain a high degree of probability. Both methods central to scientific research.

indulgence, in RC Church, total or partial remission of temporal or purgatorial punishment for sin. Granted by the Church providing the sin has already been forgiven and sinner is in a state of grace. System was once notoriously abused with sale of indulgences, and violently opposed by Luther. Council of Trent (1563) outlawed sale of indulgences but approved the system in moderation.

Indus, river of SC Asia. Rises in SW Tibet, flows c 2700 km (1700 mi) SW through Kashmir and Pakistan to Arabian Sea. Irrigates plains of Sind; little used for navigation. Centre of early civilization (Indus Valley) *fl* 2500 BC.

industrial democracy, sharing of power in an indust. organization among the workers. Involves their participation in making decisions affecting them, an area previously considered the prerogative of directors. May lead to estab. of WORKS COUNCIL or placing of a few workers' representatives on the board. Both are legal requirements in large companies in West Germany, Netherlands, Sweden. West Germany has 2-tier structure, with at least ⅓ of supervisory board being workers' representatives but with management board still appointed by shareholders. By mid-1970s EEC had plans for introduction of indust. democracy similar to West German model. Also *see* WORKERS' CONTROL.

Industrial Relations Act, in UK, legislation passed (1971) by Conservative govt., aimed to regulate labour relations by legal sanctions. Provisions incl. making collective agreements legally enforceable, registering trade unions, giving individual workers right not to join union in CLOSED SHOP. Repealed by Labour govt. (1974).

Industrial Revolution, social and economic change resulting from replacement of hand tools by machine and power tools and the development of large-scale indust. production; applied esp. to this change in Britain (from about 1760). Founded on widening overseas markets, development of banking, and invention of machines and new processing methods. Expansion of production took place, esp. in iron and steel, coal, textile and pottery industs. Accompanied by population increase and transport developments, it turned Britain from predominantly agric. country into leading indust. nation of world. Rapid change spread to Germany, US (after 1860), Japan, USSR, and others in 20th cent.

Industrial Workers of the World (IWW), revolutionary labour union estab. (1905) in Chicago, its leaders incl. Eugene Debs, Daniel De Leon. Aims based on SYNDICALISM. Effective mainly in US, leading 150 strikes. Declined during WWI, large numbers leaving to join Communist Party in 1917. Members known as 'Wobblies'.

Indus Valley civilization, ancient culture which fl c 2500-1500 BC in valley of R. Indus (area now in Pakistan). Two chief towns were Harappa, in Punjab, and Mohenjo-Daro in Sind; excavations carried out at these sites since 1920s have found evidence of organized agric., flourishing art and well-planned architecture.

inert gases, the elements helium, neon, argon, krypton, xenon, radon. As their external electron shells are complete, they are virtually chemically inert, but compounds with fluorine have been produced. Also called noble or rare gases.

inertia, in physics, the tendency of bodies to resist changes in motion.

infancy, stage of human development covering first 2 years of life. In law, term infant denotes person under age of 18 (21 in some countries), though girls from age 12 and boys from age of 14 more commonly known as minors.

infantile paralysis, *see* POLIOMYELITIS.

infantry, branch of the army trained, equipped and organized to fight on foot. Became dominant in European warfare after invention of firearms.

infection, in medicine, invasion of body by micro-organisms, *eg* bacteria, viruses, protozoa. After period of incubation, inflammation of tissue follows and more widespread effects may result from toxins released by bacteria.

inferiority complex, in psychiatry, neurotic state resulting from real or imagined physical or social inadequacy. Behavioural patterns may be dictated by attempts to compensate for it. Basis of ADLER'S psychiatric theories.

infinity, in mathematics, term used loosely to denote numerical value of a non-finite quantity. A sequence is said to 'tend to infinity' if it increases beyond all bounds.

inflammation, in medicine, defensive reaction of body to injury, infection or irritation. Heat, redness, swelling and pain are signs of inflammation, caused by increased flow of blood and lymph fluid. White blood cells engulf and destroy invading bacteria, forming pus when they die.

inflation, in economics, increase in

amount of money in circulation resulting in a sudden and relatively sharp fall in its value and hence rise in price of goods and services. Wars have been common cause; govt. borrows and issues paper money, domestic production is incapable of meeting consumer demand thus causing prices to rise. Other instances of inflation incl. hyperinflation in Germany in 1923, worldwide inflation in 1970s caused by limited supply of oil-related products. Its opposite is deflation, condition characterized by decline in prices, business and employment.

influenza, virus infection, usually of mucous membranes of air passages. Accompanied by muscular pains, weakness and fever. Sometimes occurs in worldwide epidemics; different strains of influenza virus minimize possibility of gaining immunity.

information theory, mathematical study of processes of communication and transmission of messages; deals esp. with information content of messages and probability of signal recognition in presence of electrical noise, etc. Formulated mainly by Claude E. Shannon (1948).

infrared radiation, electromagnetic radiation whose wavelength is longer than that of the red part of the visible spectrum but shorter than that of radio waves. Emitted by hot bodies; it has penetrating heating effect. Film sensitive to infrared radiation is used to photograph in total darkness or in haze.

Ingolstadt, town of SC West Germany, on R. Danube. Pop. 70,000. Textiles, machinery, vehicle mfg. Resisted siege (1632) by Gustavus Adolphus in Thirty Years' War. Univ. (1472-1800) now in Munich.

Ingres, Jean Auguste Dominique (1780-1867), French painter. Pupil of David, he upheld rigid classicism against the Romantic movement led by Delacroix. Works incl. portraits, nude and Oriental scenes, eg Vow of Louis XIII, Bain Turc, Madame Moitessier.

initiation, in anthropology, magical or religious ceremony among primitive peoples to mark transition from one status in society to another, eg from boy to man. Often involves ordeal to test subject's worthiness, or ritual representation of death and resurrection.

initiative, the right of a group of citizens to introduce a matter for legislation either to the legislature or to the voters. A **referendum** is a submission of that matter to direct vote of people; ensues automatically in latter case, and on legislature's so deciding in former. Laws passed by legislature may be submitted to referendum. Switzerland pioneered these techniques, now used in most states in US.

injection, method employed in medicine to introduce liquid into body. Usually administered by means of fine needle and syringe. May be subcutaneous (into skin), intravenous (into vein), intramuscular (into muscle), spinal (into spinal tissue).

injunction, in law, formal written order of court ordering or prohibiting some action. Courts have broadened interpretation from original prohibitive injunction to incl. positive commands.

ink, coloured liquid used in printing and writing. Blue and black writing inks usually consist of tannin extract with iron salts added; coloured writing inks use dissolved dyes. Printing ink consists of pigment mixed with linseed varnish, resins, *etc.*

Inkerman, suburb of Sevastopol, USSR, Ukrainian SSR; on Crimean penin. Scene of French and British victory over Russians in Crimean War (1854).

Inland Sea, sea between Japanese isls. of Honshu (on N) and Kyushu and Shikoku (on S). Notably scenic region, rich in fish.

Inner Hebrides, *see* HEBRIDES, Scotland.

Inner Mongolia, auton. region of N China. Area c 425,000 sq km (164,000 sq mi); pop. (est.) 13,000,000; cap. Huhehot. Mainly steppe, becoming increasingly arid towards Gobi Desert in W. Stock-raising; cereals grown in bend of Hwang Ho. Valuable mineral deposits.

Inner Temple, *see* INNS OF COURT.

Innocent III, orig. Giovanni Lotario di Segni (1161-1216), Italian church-man, pope (1198-1216). Estab. papal supremacy over temporal rulers by asserting will in political affairs. Named Stephen LANGTON as archbishop of Canterbury (1206) in defiance of King John; excom-municated John, and forced him to submit to papal authority. Proclaimed 4th Crusade (1202-4) and crusade against Albigensians (1208). Presided over Fourth Lateran Council (1215).

Innsbruck, city of W Austria, on R. Inn, cap. of Tyrol prov. Pop. 115,000.

Tourist centre, esp. winter sports. Castle (15th cent.), Hofkirche (1563), univ. (1677), Fürstenburg (Princes' Palace) with gilt-roofed royal box (15th cent.).

Inns of Court, four London legal societies having exclusive right to admit persons to practise at the bar in England (*see* BARRISTER). They are Lincoln's Inn, Gray's Inn, Inner Temple, Middle Temple. Date from before 14th cent.

inoculation, method of immuni-zation against disease. Active inoculation consists of injection of weak strain of infecting microbe and consequent formation of antibodies to provide immunity. Passive inoculation, used to gain short-term immunity when antibodies have not been built up, consists of injection of antitoxins from previously infected subjects.

Inonu, Ismet (1884-1973), Turkish statesman. Chief of staff in war against Greece (1919-22). Premier under Ataturk, succeeded him as president (1938-50). Returned to power as premier (1961-5) after military coup.

inquest, in law, any inquiry, but esp. coroner's investigation, into cause of a death. Only necessary in cases in which cause is in doubt, or is sudden or violent.

Inquisition, in RC Church, general tribunal estab. (1233) by Gregory IX for the discovery and suppression of heresy and punishment of heretics (at that time ALBIGENSIANS). Notori-ous for torture of the accused and other abuses esp. when secular rulers used system to their own gain. Continued until 19th cent. The Spanish Inquisition was an independent institution estab. (1478) by Ferdinand V and Isabella of Spain and controlled by the Spanish kings. Infamous for its rigour under TORQUEMADA.

insanity or **lunacy**, legal and colloquial terms, rather than medico-scientific, used for those forms of mental disorder which relieve individual of responsibility for certain acts, and which may lead to his being confined in an institution.

Insecta (insects), largest class of arthropods, with c 800,000 species. Adult has body divided into head, thorax and abdomen. Head bears pair of antennae; thorax has 3 segments with 3 pairs of legs and usually 2 pairs of wings. Usually 3-stage life history involving egg, larva and pupa before adulthood.

insecticide, chemical used to destroy insect pests. In 19th cent. inorganic compounds, esp. of arsenic and copper, used. Modern organic chemicals, incl. DDT, highly effective; use sometimes restricted because of cumulative toxic effect on animals and contamination of food.

Insectivora (insectivores), order of small insect-eating mammals, incl. shrews, hedgehogs and moles.

insectivorous plants, plants which supplement nitrogen supply by digesting small insects caught in cavities of plant, eg PITCHER PLANT, by viscidity of leaves, eg Portuguese fly catcher, or by movement, eg VENUS' FLYTRAP. Mainly found in bogs where nitrogen content of soil is low.

insemination, artificial, see ARTIFICIAL INSEMINATION.

instalment buying, see HIRE PURCHASE.

instinct, innate, often complex behaviour pattern of animals, developed without any learning process; common to all members of species. Example is nest-building behaviour of birds.

Institut de France, collection of learned academies, state controlled, founded in 1795. Incl. L'Académie Française, L'Académie des Inscriptions et Belles-Lettres, L'Académie des Sciences, L'Académie des Beaux Arts, and L'Académie des Sciences Morales et Politiques.

insulation, electrical, resistance to passage of electric current exhibited by certain substances, eg dry air, rubber, wax.

insulin, hormone formed in pancreas and secreted into bloodstream. Regulates amount of glucose in blood; lack of insulin causes glucose to accumulate and spill over into urine. See DIABETES.

insurance, system of compensating individuals or companies for loss arising, eg by accident, fire, theft, etc. Payment is made from fund to which those who are exposed to similar risks have made payments (premiums) in return for cover. System practised from ancient times, eg in Phoenician trade. Shipping insurance almost universal in Europe by 14th cent., dominated by LLOYD'S of London by 17th cent.; fire insurance arose in Germany (15th cent.); life insurance in England (16th cent.). Since late 19th cent. the state has been prominent in social insurance (see SOCIAL SECURITY).

intaglio, design or figure carved,

incised or engraved into a hard material so that it is below the surface. Commonest example is engraved seal-ring.

integer, in mathematics, any positive or negative whole number or zero; eg 3 or -5.

integral calculus, mathematical study inverse to differential calculus; involves reconstruction of a function given form of its derivative. Used in finding areas, volumes, etc, and solving differential equations.

integrated circuit, electronic circuit consisting of several circuit elements and amplifying devices formed on single unit, esp. chip of semiconducting material, esp. silicon. Used in calculators, computers, etc.

intelligence, ability of organisms to learn from experience and adapt responses to new situations; capacity to understand and relate concepts; measurement of general factor underlying individual's performance on varied specific mental tasks. Product of genetic potential and influence of environment, but relative importance of these factors is matter of controversy. BINET first developed intelligence tests enabling measurement over range of intellectual problems, with scales based on norms for specific age groups. Tests since adapted and used as predictive, diagnostic instrument in education, army, etc.

intelligence quotient (IQ), ratio of mental age, as measured by intelligence tests, to chronological age, expressed as a percentage.

interest, money paid for use of borrowed capital. Usually at fixed percentage rate paid yearly, half-yearly or quarterly. May be simple or compound (ie interest on accumulated interest). Usury, in legal terms, is interest charged on a loan above specified level, first legislated against in England (1545).

interference, in physics, interaction of 2 combining wave motions of same frequency. Waves reinforce or neutralize one another according to their relative phases on meeting. Two light beams can combine to give alternate light and dark bands (interference fringes); two sounds of nearly equal frequency can produce beats (alternate increases and decreases in loudness).

interior decoration, treatment of interior of buildings in style reflecting contemporary architecture. Thus French classical styles in 17th cent. were reflected in 'Louis XIV' interiors. In Britain, the Adam brothers pioneered the design of buildings as integrated wholes during 18th cent.

Interlaken, town of WC Switzerland, on R. Aare. Pop. 6000. Tourist centre of Bernese Oberland, between Lakes Thun (W), Brienz (E).

intermezzo (Ital., = in the middle), an instrumental interlude in the middle of an opera. Term also applied to free and short instrumental composition, and to comic opera developed from comic interlude in 17th cent. opera or ballet.

internal combustion engine, engine which derives its power from the explosion of a fuel-air mixture in a confined space. In typical 4 stroke automobile engine, fuel-air mixture is drawn into cylinder by downward movement of reciprocating piston (connected to a crank) and compressed as piston returns upwards. At top of stroke SPARKING PLUG ignites mixture and the rapid expansion drives piston downwards giving power stroke. The burnt gases are exhausted from cylinder by upward return of piston and the cycle begins again. Arrangement of valves, opened and closed by engine-driven cam shaft, allows mixture to be drawn in, compressed and exhausted. Two stroke engine has arrangement of valves allowing power stroke every two instead of four strokes. See DIESEL ENGINE, WANKEL ROTARY ENGINE.

International Atomic Energy Agency, agency of UN, estab. (1957) to promote peaceful use of atomic energy. Provides technical assistance, training and maintains research laboratories.

International Bank for Reconstruction and Development (World Bank), agency of UN, estab. 1945; hq. Washington. Funded by UN member states, serves as loan agency for member states and private investors. Aims to facilitate investments, foreign trade, discharge international debts.

International Brigade, volunteer force, largely drawn from Communist sympathizers, which fought for the Republicans during Spanish Civil War (1936-9).

International Civil Aviation Organization (ICAO), agency of UN estab. (1947) at Montréal. Promotes international safety codes and symbols and investigates accidents.

International Court of Justice, court estab. (1945) as advisory or arbitrational judicial organ of UN. Replaced Permanent Court of International Justice. Comprises 15 justices; normally sits at The Hague. Renders decisions binding on member states on matters of international law. Advises on request of General Assembly.

International Criminal Police Commission (INTERPOL), organization estab. (1923) to coordinate police activities of participating nations. Has Paris hq.

international date line, imaginary line drawn N and S through Pacific Ocean, roughly following 180° meridian of longitude. Used to mark start of calendar day; 24 hours are lost when crossing it W to E and gained E to W.

Internationale, international Communist anthem, used as national anthem of USSR until 1944. Words written by a French woodworker Eugène Pottier in 1871, music composed by Belgian composer Pierre Degeyter in 1888.

International Finance Corporation (IFC), agency of UN, estab. 1956 as an affiliate of INTERNATIONAL BANK FOR RECONSTRUCTION AND DEVELOPMENT to encourage growth of productive enterprise in member states, esp. in underdeveloped areas.

International Labour Organization (ILO), agency concerned with conditions of work in its member countries. Estab. by Treaty of Versailles, affiliated to League of Nations (1919-45), then to UN (1946).

international law, rules generally observed and regarded as binding in relations between nations. By late

19th cent., Hague conferences were frequently resorted to for arbitration of disputes. **Institute for International Law** set up (1875) at Ghent, Belgium, for research, recording such arbitration. Awarded Nobel Peace Prize (1904). Reorganized (1961).

International Monetary Fund (IMF), agency of UN, estab. 1945; hq. Washington. Facilitates discharge of international debt by enabling member states to buy foreign currencies.

International Red Cross Committee, see RED CROSS.

International [Workingmen's Association], called First International, organization estab. (1864) in London under leadership of Marx; aimed to unite workers and achieve political power according to principles of *Communist Manifesto*. Dissolved (1876) after conflict with anarchists. Second or Socialist International (estab. 1889) was dominated by German and Russian Social Democrat parties; broke up during WWI. Third International (*see* COMINTERN) created in 1919. Fourth International formed in 1938 by followers of Trotsky.

Interpol, see INTERNATIONAL CRIMINAL POLICE COMMISSION.

Interstate Commerce Commission (ICC), US govt. agency regulating commercial transport between states. Estab. (1887) after public outcry against railway malpractices. In 1906 and 1910 its range was extended from railways to incl. other means of communication, *eg* ferries, pipelines, wireless, cable. In 1950s and 1960s, enforced desegregation of passenger transport after Supreme Court decision.

intestine, lower part of alimentary canal extending from stomach to anus, where, latter stages of digestion and collection of waste products take place. Consists of convoluted upper part (small intestine), shorter but wider large intestine, and rectum.

Intolerable Acts, American revolutionaries' name for 5 acts (incl. QUEBEC ACT) passed 1774 by British Parliament. Limited geographical, political freedom. Four of acts retribution for BOSTON TEA PARTY.

introversion, *see* EXTROVERSION.

intrusive rock, any rock formed by solidification of molten material below the Earth's surface. All intrusive rocks are thus igneous rocks, forced into or between solid rocks while molten. May be formed at great depth, *ie* plutonic, or moderate depth, *ie* hypabyssal.

intuitionism, in philosophy, doctrine that man can perceive truth and ethical principles without assistance of intellect or experience. Common among medieval Christian mystics.

Inverary, town of Strathclyde region, W Scotland, on Loch Fyne. Pop. 1000. Former royal burgh and co. town of Argyllshire. Herring fishing. Has 18th cent. castle, seat of dukes of Argyll.

Invercargill, city of S South Isl., New Zealand, on inlet of Foveaux Str. Pop. 47,000. Fishing, food processing, sawmilling; outport at Bluff Harbour.

Inverness-shire, former county of N Scotland, now in Highland region. Mainly mountainous (Ben Nevis), crossed by Great Glen; incl. S Outer Hebrides, Skye. Livestock rearing, forestry, fishing, h.e.p., tourist industs. Co. town was Inverness, at NE end of Great Glen. Pop. 35,000. Distilling, woollens, tourism.

invertebrate, any animal without a vertebral column.

Io, in Greek myth, daughter of King Inachus of Argos. Loved by Zeus who changed her into a white heifer to conceal her from Hera. Hera tormented Io with a gadfly which drove her across Europe and Asia until she came to Egypt where Zeus restored her to human form.

iodine (I), non-metallic element of halogen family; at. no. 53, at. wt. 126.9. Consists of grey-black crystals which sublimate to form violet vapour. Compounds found in seaweed and Chile saltpetre. Essential to functioning of thyroid gland. Compounds used in medicine, photography and organic synthesis.

ion, electrically charged atom or group of atoms; positively charged ion (cation) results from loss of electrons, negatively charged ion (anion) from electron gain. Ions can be created by collisions with charged particles, high energy radiation (X-rays, gamma rays) or by dissolving suitable compounds (electrolytes) in water.

Iona, small isl. of Inner Hebrides, W Scotland, in Strathclyde region. Centre of Celtic Christianity after St Columba founded monastery (563). Has 13th cent. cathedral (restored 20th cent.), reputed royal burial ground.

Ionesco, Eugène (1912–), French playwright, b. Romania. Leading exponent of ABSURD in plays, eg The

Bald Prima Donna (1950), Rhinoceros (1959).

ion exchange, chemical process by which ions held on porous solid material (usually synthetic resin or zeolite) are exchanged for ions in a solution surrounding the solid. Used in water softening, desalination of sea water, extraction of metals from ores.

Ionia, region of W coast of Asia Minor, incl. Aegean Isls. Colonized by ancient Greeks (Ionians) c 1000 BC; based on a religious league of 12 cities, prospered commercially. Conquered by Persians (6th cent. BC), revolt of cities (500 BC) led to Persian Wars. Important part of Roman and Byzantine empires, declined under Turks.

Ionian Islands, isl. chain of W Greece, in Ionian Sea. Incl. Corfu, Cephalonia, Levkas, Zakinthos. Mainly mountainous; wine, fruit, olives. Venetian 15th-18th cent.; British protectorate until 1864. Devastated by earthquake 1953.

Ionian Sea, part of Mediterranean Sea, between SW Greece and SE Italy. Connected to Adriatic by Strait of Otranto.

Ionic order, one of the Greek orders of architecture, characterized by its slender column and 2 ornamental scrolls (spiral volutes) on the front of the capital and 2 on the back. Developed in Greek colonies of Asia Minor in 6th cent. BC.

ionization chamber, device used to measure intensity of ionizing radiation, eg gamma rays, or disintegration rate of radioactive substances. Usually consists of gas-filled chamber containing 2 electrodes between which electric potential is maintained; current flows when gas is ionized by incoming radiation.

Ionosphere, region of upper atmosphere, starting c 50 km above ground, in which an appreciable concentration of ions and electrons is produced by solar radiation. Divided into 3 layers, incl. Kennelly-Heaviside and Appleton. Important to radio transmission as it reflects radio waves back to Earth.

Iowa, state of NC US. Area 145,791 sq km (56,290 sq mi); pop. 2,825,000; cap. Des Moines. Mainly rolling plains; lying between Missouri, Mississippi rivers; hilly in NE. Major agric. region; wheat, dairy, livestock farming. Region explored by French fur traders in 17th cent.; purchased by US as part of Louisiana Purchase (1803). Admitted to Union as 29th state (1846).

Ipecac, *Cephaelis ipecacuanha*, tropical South American shrub. Roots contain the alkaloid emetine used as emetic and to relieve coughs.

Iphigenia, in Greek myth, daughter of Agamemnon and Clytemnestra. Sacrificed by her father in order to end the contrary winds which were delaying the Greek ships heading for the Trojan War. In Euripedes' *Iphigenia in Tauris*, she survives to save life of brother, Orestes.

Ipoh, cap. of Perak state, NW Malaysia. Pop. 248,000. Tin mining centre. Rubber plantations nearby.

Ipswich, co. town and co. bor. of Suffolk, E England, on R. Orwell. Pop. 123,000. Agric. machinery; food processing industs, brewing. Saxon *Gipeswic*; 16th cent. ecclesiastical centre.

IQ, see INTELLIGENCE QUOTIENT.

Iquitos, town of NE Peru, at head of navigation on Amazon R. Pop. 74,000. Coffee, cotton, timber exports. Fl during early 20th cent. rubber boom.

IRA, see IRISH REPUBLICAN ARMY.

Irák_lion (*Herakleion*) or **Candia**, town of NC Crete, Greece, cap. of Iráklion admin. dist. Pop. 64,000. Port, exports olive oil, wine. Museum of Minoan antiquities.

Iran, kingdom of SW Asia; formerly Persia. Area 1,648,000 sq km (636,000 sq mi); pop. 33,400,000; cap. Tehran. Language: Persian. Religion: Shia Islam. Consists of C plateau surrounded by Elburz Mts. in N, Zagros Mts. in S and W. Produces wool for carpet mfg., rice, cotton; economy based on rich oil resources. Divided into 13 provs. Centre of ancient Persian empire under Cyrus; conquered by Alexander the Great (c 330 BC). Object of British-Russian rivalry (19th-20th cent.), intensified by oil finds. Pahlevi dynasty founded (1925); name, changed to Iran 1935. Shah exiled (1979); Islamic republic estab. under Ayatollah Khomeini.

Iranian, group of languages belonging to Indo-Iranian branch of Indo-European family. Divided into East and West subgroups, incl. Baluchi, Pashtu, Kurdish, Persian. Spoken in Iran, Afghanistan, Pakistan, parts of USSR.

Iraq (Arab. *Iraqia*), republic of SW Asia. Area c 435,000 sq km (168,000 sq mi); pop. 11,505,000; cap. Baghdad. Language: Arabic. Religion: Islam. Drained by .R. Tigris, R. Euphrates. Mountainous N rich in oil; cotton and dates grown in irrigated SE. Borders correspond to ancient MESOPOTAMIA. Ottoman domination until WWI. Kingdom (1921-58); became republic after military coup.

Ireland, John (1879-1962), British composer. Works incl. varied orchestral and choral works, delicate music for piano, and attractive songs, eg 'Sea Fever'.

Ireland, isl. of British Isls., separated from Great Britain by Irish Sea. Area c 84,000 sq km (32,450 sq mi); pop. 4,576,000. Fertile C lowland with highland rim (Mourne, Wicklow, Kerry, Ox mountains). Main rivers Shannon, Erne, Foyle. Irregular W coast incl. many isls., inlets. Mild, damp climate favours vegetation, esp. grass; led to name 'Emerald Isle'. Partitioned (1921) into NORTHERN IRELAND, and Republic of Ireland (Eire). Area c 70,000 sq km (27,000 sq mi); pop. 3,162,000; cap. Dublin. Languages: Irish, English. Religion: RC. Comprises 26 counties in 4 provs. (Connacht, Leinster, Munster, Ulster). Main towns Cork, Limerick. Mainly agric., esp. dairying; fishing; tourism. Long struggle for independence from UK ended with estab. of Irish Free State (1921). Republic proclaimed (1949), left Commonwealth. Joined EEC (1973).

Irene, in Greek myth, goddess of peace, one of the HORAE. Identified by Romans with Pax.

Ireton, Henry (1611-51), English parliamentary army officer in Civil War. Fought at Edgehill (1642) and Naseby (1645). Married Cromwell's daughter (1646); as lord-deputy in Ireland (1650) assisted in Cromwell's repressive measures before dying there of plague.

Irian Jaya (West Irian), prov. of Indonesia, occupying W half of New Guinea. Area c 414,000 sq km (160,000 sq mi); cap. Djajapura. Exports timber, oil. Known as Netherlands New Guinea until transfer to Indonesia (1963), when named Irian Barat. Present name dates from 1973.

iridium (Ir), brittle metallic element; at. no. 77, at. wt. 192.2. Hard and chemically resistant; found in platinum ores. Alloys used in pen points, watch and compass bearings.

Iris, in Greek myth, goddess of the rainbow and a messenger of the gods.

iris, in anatomy, round pigmented membrane in front of eye, between cornea and lens. Its muscles adjust width of pupil, which it surrounds, and regulate amount of light entering eye.

iris, genus of perennial plants of Iridaceae family, native to temperate regions. Sword-shaped leaves, flowers composed of 3 petals and 3 drooping sepals. Many varieties grown as garden flowers.

Irish language, see GAELIC.

Irish Republican Army (IRA), para-military organization which developed after Dublin Easter Rebellion (1916), pressing for an Irish republic which would incl. Ulster. After being declared illegal by De Valéra (1936) became underground terrorist movement. Sectarian militancy and 'civil rights' disturbances in 1969 sparked off resurgence of activity by the IRA, now with 2 wings, 'official' and 'provisional', the latter for some years source of systematic terrorist campaign in Northern Ireland. See SINN FEIN.

Irish Sea, between Ireland and Great Britain. Connected to Atlantic Ocean by North Channel (N), St George's Channel (S).

Irish wolfhound, breed of large hound with rough grey coat. Tallest of dogs, stands c 86 cm/34 in. at shoulder.

Irkutsk, city of USSR, SC Siberian RSFSR; port at confluence of Angara and Irkut. Pop. 473,000. Indust.; produces aircraft, automobiles, machine tools. Founded 1652 as Cossack fortress.

iron (Fe), malleable ductile metallic element, easily magnetized; at. no. 26, at. wt. 55.85. Occurs in various ores, incl. magnetite, haematite and pyrites. Manufactured in blast furnace from oxide ores, limestone and coke. Usually converted (see BESSEMER) into wrought iron or steel, their properties depending on amount of carbon present. Compounds essential to higher forms of animal life.

Iron Age, archaeological period following Bronze Age, characterized by use of iron to make tools, weapons. Iron-working techniques were developed by Hittites in 2nd millennium BC but prob. kept secret. Knowledge spread to Middle East and Europe on collapse of Hittite empire (1200 BC). In Europe, iron-working is associated with HALL-STATT (c 800-500 BC) and LA TÈNE cultures.

Iron Gate, gorge of R. Danube on Romanian-Yugoslav border, between Orşova and Turnu-Severin; length c 3 km (2 mi).

iron lung, device used to maintain artificial respiration in a person who has difficulty in breathing, eg as a result of poliomyelitis. Effects expansion and contraction of lungs by mechanical changes in air pressure c 12 times per min.

iron pyrites, see PYRITE.

Ironside, William Edmund Ironside, 1st Baron (1880-1959), British general. Commanded anti-Bolshevik Archangel expedition (1918). Chief of Imperial General Staff at outbreak of WWII. Promoted to field-marshal in 1940, he was put in charge of home forces.

ironwood, any of various trees with extremely hard, heavy wood, esp. HORNBEAM.

Iroquois, five North American Indian tribes (Mohawk, Oneida, Onondaga, Cayuga, Seneca) of Hokan-Siouan linguistic stock. Iroquois Confederacy founded (c 1570) by Onondaga, led by Hiawatha and prophet Deganawidah. Estab. advanced culture in New York state. Settled hunters and farmers; lived in palisaded long houses. Dispersed Huron tribes in 1649. Strongly hostile to French but pro-British even during American Revolution. There were c 25,000 Iroquois left by 1970s.

Irrawaddy, chief river of Burma. Rises in NW and flows through Mandalay to Andaman Sea; c 2100 km (1300 mi) long. Of great economic importance; its delta is major rice growing area.

irredentism, policy of Italian nationalist movement, founded 1878, which sought to recover for Italy adjacent regions, eg Trentino, inhabited largely by Italians but under Austrian control. Main reason for Italy's entry into WWI. Term now refers to any similar nationalist policy.

Irrigation, artificial distribution of water to soil to sustain plant growth in areas of insufficient rainfall. Methods used incl. sprinkler systems, flooding areas from canals and ditches, and running of water between crop rows. Irrigation has been used extensively in China, India and Egypt since ancient times and is now important in other countries, incl. US, USSR.

Irtysh, river of C Asia. Rises in Altai Mts. of Sinkiang-Uighur (NW China), flows c 2900 km (1800 mi) NW to join R. Ob in NW Siberia.

Irving, Sir Henry, orig. John Henry Brodribb (1838-1905), English actor-manager. Estab. reputation with 1874 performance of Hamlet; played Mathias in melodrama, *The Bells*. Became manager of Lyceum Theatre, London (1878). First actor to be knighted (1895).

Irving, Washington (1783-1859), American author. Known for comic essays, tales, *eg History of New York* by 'Diedrich Knickerbocker' (1890), 'Rip Van Winkle', 'Sleepy Hollow'. Wrote lives of J.J. Astor, Washington.

Isaac, in OT, only son of ABRAHAM and Sarah. Offered by his father as sacrifice to God but saved by divine intervention. Father by Rebecca of Esau and Jacob.

Isabella (1296-1358), queen consort of England. Daughter of Philip IV of France, married Edward II. Badly treated by Edward, she raised an army in France with lover Roger de MORTIMER and invaded England. Deposed Edward and ruled as regent for son Edward III (1327-30) until deposed by him.

Isabella I (1451-1504), queen of Castile (1474-1504). Married (1469) Ferdinand II of Aragón, who ruled both Aragón and Castile with her as FERDINAND V.

Isabella II (1830-1904), queen of Spain (1833-68). Dispute with her uncle Don Carlos over succession led to civil war (1833-9), ending with defeat of CARLISTS. Her rule continued to be one of insurrections and political instability until she was deposed.

Isaiah, prophetic book of OT, attributed to Isaiah (*fl* 710 BC), possibly incl. other writings. Warns of the power of Assyria and foretells the destruction and redemption of Israel.

Ise, city of Japan, on Ise Bay, S Honshu isl. Pop. 105,000. Shinto religious centre; three shrines, one of which is sacred to imperial family.

Isfahan or **Esfahan** (anc. *Aspadana*), city of C Iran, cap. of Isfahan prov. Pop. 575,000. Carpet, textile mfg; notable silver filigree work. Cap. of Persia (17th cent.); magnificent architecture incl. Masjid-i-Shah (royal mosque).

Isherwood, Christopher [William Bradshaw] (1904-), English author. Known for novels depicting decadence of Weimar Republic, *eg Mr Norris Changes Trains* (1935), *Goodbye to Berlin* (1939) using filmic narrative techniques. Collaborated with Auden in expressionist plays, *eg The Ascent of F.6* (1937).

Iseult, *see* TRISTAN *and* ISOLDE.

Ishmael, in OT, son of Abraham and Hagar. Exiled in desert with mother through his wife Sarah's jealousy. Regarded by Moslems as ancestor of Arabs.

Ishtar, Babylonian and Assyrian goddess of fertility, love and war. Went to the underworld to recover her lover TAMMUZ, during which time all fertility ceased on earth. Cult was widely assimilated throughout W Asia.

Isis, ancient Egyptian nature goddess. Sister and wife of OSIRIS; mother of Horus. Represented with cow's head. Her cult (having spread throughout Mediterranean) persisted in Roman Empire and resisted early Christian teachings.

Islam or **Mohammedanism,** monotheistic religion in which supreme deity is Allah and chief prophet and founder is MOHAMMED. Based on revelations of Mohammed in *Koran.* Concepts of god, heaven and hell akin to Judaeo-Christian beliefs, with recognition of OT prophets and Jesus (as prophet). Religious duties incl. sincere profession of the creed, prayer 5 times daily, generous alms-giving, observance of Ramadan fast and pilgrimage to Mecca. Main sects are Sunnites and Shiites who are divided over caliphate. Faith spread rapidly after foundation (7th cent.) and today incl. N Africa, the Middle East, Iran, Pakistan, Indonesia and isolated pockets of SE Europe, USSR, China and S Pacific. There are *c* 350 million faithful, called Moslems or Muslims.

Islamabad, cap. of Pakistan, NW of Rawalpindi. Pop. 77,000. Built in 1960s as new cap.

island, land mass surrounded by water. Island-forming processes incl. upward movement of Earth's crust, lowering of sea level, volcanic action, deposition of sediments, coral formation. Sea isls. may be continental, *ie* formed by separation from mainland, or oceanic, *ie* formed in the ocean. Two isls., Australia and Antarctica, are continents; largest true isl. is Greenland.

Islay, isl. of Inner Hebrides, W Scotland, in Strathclyde region. Area 609 sq km (235 sq mi); main town Port Ellen. Agric., fishing, distilling.

Islington, bor. of N Greater London, England. Pop. 199,000. Met. bor. until 1965. Incl. Finsbury; has Holloway, Pentonville prisons.

Ismail Pasha (1830-95), khedive of Egypt (1863-79). Encouraged building of Suez Canal; after incurring serious debt, forced to sell his canal shares to Britain (1875). Placed country's finances under Anglo-French management (1876). Abdicated in favour of son, Tewfik Pasha.

isobar, line on a map connecting points of equal atmospheric pressure. Since pressure varies with altitude, pressure values used for weather charts are reduced to sea-level equivalents before isobars are drawn.

Isolde, see TRISTAN AND ISOLDE.

isomerism, in chemistry, existence of 2 or more compounds with same molecular formula whose physical and chemical properties differ through distinct arrangements of atoms in the molecule.

isostasy, theory of equilibrium between high and low parts of Earth's crust. Continental land masses, composed of thicker layers of lighter rocks, 'float' above heavier ocean floor. Flow of molten material at depth corresponds to land movement at surface to maintain equilibrium.

isotherm, line on a map connecting points of equal temperature. May represent value at one time or average readings over a period. Since temperature varies with altitude, values are normally reduced to sea-level equivalents before isotherms are drawn.

isotopes, atoms of same element which differ in mass number, possessing different numbers of neutrons in their nuclei. Have essentially similar chemical properties, but may differ in physical properties. Most elements consist of mixtures of various isotopes.

Israel, in OT, name given to JACOB as eponymous ancestor of the Israelites.

Israel, republic of SW Asia, on Mediterranean. Area, c 21,000 sq km (8100 sq mi); pop. 3,465,000; cap. Jerusalem. Language: Hebrew. Religion: Judaism. Fertile coastal plain (citrus fruit) rises in N to Galilee (grain) and in S to Negev desert (irrigation schemes, co-operative farms *kibbutzim*). Part of hist. PALESTINE, region disputed by neighbours after Hebrews consolidated it (c 1000 BC). Subsequent occupations incl. Roman (70 BC–AD 636), Ottoman (1516–1917). British mandate (1920–48) ended in estab. of Israel as Jewish home. Fought Arabs in wars of 1948, 1956, 1967, 1973; occupied Sinai from 1967; parts were returned to Egypt after 1973 war. More returned after peace treaty with Egypt (1979).

Issyk Kul, lake of USSR, Kirghiz SSR. Area c 6220 sq km (2400 sq mi).

Istanbul, city of NW Turkey, on both sides of Bosporus, at entrance to Sea of Marmara. Pop. 2,376,000. Major port; cultural, indust. and trade centre; starting point of Baghdad railway. Anc. *Byzantium* founded 658 BC by Greeks. Rebuilt as Constantinople by Constantine I (4th cent. AD) as new Roman imperial cap. Later cap. of Byzantine empire; often attacked, fell to soldiers of 4th Crusade (1204) and finally to Turks (1453). Ottoman and Turkish cap. until 1923; name changed 1930. Harbour is in Golden Horn. Notable architecture incl. Church of St Sophia, built by Justinian in 6th cent.; became a mosque after Turkish conquest. Uskūdar (Scutari) is indust. suburb; Florence Nightingale ran hospital here in Crimean War.

Istria (*Istra*), penin. of NW Yugoslavia, in Adriatic Sea. Main towns Pula, Opatija. Agric., fishing, tourism. Ceded to Italy after WWI; all except Trieste to Yugoslavia 1947.

Italian, Romance language in Italic branch of Indo-European family. Official language of Italy, and one of Switzerland's. Developed from Latin, Florentine dialect becoming dominant in 14th cent., giving rise to modern standard Italian.

Italic, branch of Indo-European family of languages. Subdivided into 2 groups: ancient Italian, incl. Latin; ROMANCE LANGUAGES, all developed from Latin.

italic, form of type in which characters slope upwards to the right. Introduced 1501 by ALDUS MANUTIUS. Used to distinguish certain sets of words, eg book titles, foreign language words.

Italy (*Italia*), republic of S Europe. Comprises penin., isls. incl. Sardinia, Sicily. Area 301,165 sq km (116,280 sq mi); pop. 56,189,000; cap. Rome. Language: Italian. Religion: RC. Chief cities Milan, Naples, Turin, Genoa. Member of EEC. Alps in N, fertile Po basin in NE, Apennines run NW-SE. Indust. based in N and Po basin, using h.e.p. from Alps. Barren S has some agric. (fruit, wine, olives), slow indust. growth. Major tourist indust. Settled by Etruscans, Greeks before rise of Imperial ROME 5th cent. BC; fell to Ostrogoths AD 5th cent. Part of Holy Roman Empire from 962; later medieval growth of city republics, eg Florence, Venice, fl in Renaissance period. United by Cavour, Garibaldi as kingdom (1861). Fascist rule under Mussolini led to expansion (Abyssinia, Albania) and alliance with Germany in WWII. Colonies lost, republic created 1946.

Ithaca (*Itháki*), isl. of W Greece, one of Ionian Isls. Area 85 sq km (33 sq mi); main town Ithaca. Home of Homer's Odysseus.

Ivan [III] the Great (1440-1505), Russian ruler, grand duke of Moscow (1462-1505). Conquered Novgorod (1478) and expanded territ. of Muscovy by conquest and treaty. Threw off domination of Tartars of the Golden Horde (1480). Married Zoe, niece of last Byzantine emperor, who introduced Byzantine customs to his court.

Ivan [IV] the Terrible (1530-84), Russian tsar (1547-84). In 1533, became grand duke of Moscow on death of his father Vasily III;

regency held by his mother until 1538, then by various boyars, until he was crowned tsar (1547). Began eastward expansion with conquest of Kazan (1552) and Astrakhan (1556). Unbalanced after 1560, became a harsh tyrant; in a rage, killed his son Ivan (1581). Broke political power of boyars in reign of terror.

Ivanov, Vsevolod Vyacheslavovich (1895-1963), Russian novelist. Best known for *Armoured Train No. 14-69* (1922) reflecting spirit of insurgent proletariat.

Ivanovo, city of USSR, C European RSFSR. Pop. 434,000. Hist. centre of cotton textile indust. Founded 14th cent.

Ives, Charles Edward (1874-1954), American composer. Anticipated many later developments in music, incl. complex combinations of rhythms and keys. Successful insurance broker, he gained little musical recognition in his lifetime. Works incl. orchestral piece *The Unanswered Question*.

Ivigtut, town of SW Greenland. Pop. c 200. World's largest cryolite mine.

Iviza (*Ibiza*), third largest of Balearic Isls., Spain. Area 572 sq km (221 sq mi); main town Iviza. Tourism, agric.

ivory, hard white substance, a form of dentine, making up tusks of elephants, walruses, etc. Used for piano keys, cutlery handles, decorative carvings.

Ivory Coast (Fr. *Côte d'Ivoire*), republic of W Africa, on Gulf of Guinea. Area 322,500 sq km (124,500 sq mi); pop. 5,017,000; cap. Abidjan. Official language: French. Religions: native, Islam. Savannah in N, tropical forest in C, coastal swamps in S. Railway link with Upper Volta. Produces coffee, cotton, bananas, tropical hardwoods. Former centre of slave, ivory trade. French colony from 1893, part of French West Africa from 1904; independent 1960.

ivy, *Hedera helix,* evergreen climbing shrub of Araliaceae family, native to Europe. Woody stem, greenish flowers in autumn, poisonous berries in spring. Climbs walls and trees by tiny roots. *See* POISON IVY.

Iwo, city of SW Nigeria. Pop. 192,000. Agric. centre, esp. cocoa, coffee, palm products; cotton mfg. Former cap. of Yoruba kingdom, *fl* 17th-19th cent. .

Iwo Jima, *see* VOLCANO ISLANDS.

Ixion, in Greek myth, king of Thessaly. Murdered his father-in-law; Zeus then took him to Olympus to purify him. Attempted to seduce Hera but Zeus created phantom of her, by which Ixion fathered Centaurs. Punished by being eternally chained to a fiery, revolving wheel in Hades.

Izhevsk, city of USSR, cap. of Udmurt auton. republic, E European RSFSR. Pop. 456,000. Metallurgical centre; steel mills and ammunition factories estab. early 19th cent.

Izmir, port of W Turkey, on Gulf of Izmir; formerly Smyrna. · Pop. 591,000. Naval base; exports tobacco, cotton. Colonized by Ionians, prosperous under Roman rule; early Christian centre. Taken by Turks in 1424. Held by Greeks (1919-22); Greek pop. expelled (1923).

Izmit (anc. *Nicomedia*), city of NW Turkey, on Sea of Marmara. Pop. 142,000. Situated in rich tobacco region. Built (264 BC) by Nicomedes of Bythinia as his cap.

Izvestia (Russ., = news), official daily newspaper of USSR. Founded (1917) after the February Revolution.

Izvolsky, Aleksandr Petrovich (1856-1919), Russian statesman. Negotiated Anglo-Russian agreement (1907) which estab. spheres of influence in Persia, Afghanistan. This agreement marked completion of TRIPLE ENTENTE.

J

Jabalpur, city of Madhya Pradesh state, C India. Pop. 534,000. Railway jct. and indust. centre; armaments mfg.

jaborandi, dried leaflets of various South American plants of genus *Pilocarpus* which yield the alkaloid pilocarpine, used to stimulate sweat or contract pupil of eye.

jacana, any of Jacanidae family of tropical and subtropical birds. Has long toes enabling it to walk on floating plants, eg lily leaves. Also called lilytrotter or lotus bird.

jacaranda, genus of tropical American trees of bignonia family. Finely divided foliage, large clusters of lavender flowers. Introduced into Australia.

jackal, wolf-like wild dog. Hunts nocturnally in packs, taking carrion or living prey. Species incl. oriental jackal, *Canis aureus,* of N Africa and S Asia.

jackdaw, *Corvus monedula,* black bird of crow family, found in Europe and W Asia.

jack rabbit, large North American hare, genus *Lepus.*

Jackson, Andrew (1767-1845), American general and statesman, president (1829-37). Gained victory over British at New Orleans (1815) after formal conclusion of War of 1812. Narrowly defeated as Democratic presidential candidate (1824), successful in 1828. Estranged South in conflict with South Carolina over taxation rights (NULLIFICATION crisis, 1832). Successfully opposed attempts to re-charter Bank of the United States. Jacksonian democracy brought SPOILS SYSTEM of political rewards and strengthened the executive.

Jackson, Thomas Jonathan ('Stonewall') (1824-63), American Confederate general. Fought in Civil War, victorious in Shenandoah Valley campaign (1862) and 2nd battle of Bull Run (1862). Mortally wounded at Chancellorsville.

Jackson, cap. of Mississippi, US; on Pearl R. Pop. 154,000. Railway jct., indust. and commercial centre; cotton, textiles mfg. Estab. as cap. 1821.

Jacksonville, deep-water port of NE Florida, US; on St John's R. Pop. 513,000; state's largest city. Commercial, transport centre; timber, fruit exports. Tourist resort.

Jack the Ripper, popular name for notorious murderer, never identified, of 6 women prostitutes in E London in 1888.

Jacob, in OT, twin brother of Esau. Gained Esau's birthright and their father's dying blessing by trickery. Fled to escape his brother's anger. During flight, had vision of angels ascending and descending ladder to heaven. On return, after marrying Leah and Rachel, wrestled with angel, received name Israel. The 12 tribes of Israel were descended from his sons.

Jacobean, term applied to English architecture and decoration characteristic of reign of James I. Classical features were used more widely and elaborate ornamental wood and plaster decoration employed.

Jacobean drama, term used for plays written in, and reflecting spirit of, reign of James I. Comedies were generally satires of human folly, eg Jonson's *Volpone*. Tragedies characterized by emphasis on human, esp. sexual, corruption, often with revenge theme, eg Webster's *The White Devil, The Duchess of Malfi,* Tourneur's *The Revenger's Tragedy.*

Jacobins, French society of radical democrats, formed 1789. Originally incl. GIRONDISTS, whose support of war throughout Europe later caused split. Became increasingly radical and, under Robespierre, instituted REIGN OF TERROR. Influence ended by Robespierre's fall and execution (1794).

Jacobite Church, Christian church of Iraq, Syria, parts of India. Founded (6th cent.) by Jacob Baradaeus. Regarded as heretical by RC and Orthodox churches (*see* MONOPHYSITISM).

Jacobites, supporters of claims of house of STUART to English throne after 1688. Sought restoration of James II and his descendants. Aided by France and Spain, raised rebellion of 1715 in support of James Edward Stuart. Charles Edward Stuart led last Jacobite rebellion from Scotland, defeated at Culloden (1746).

Jacob's ladder, any plant of genus *Polemonium* of phlox family. Blue-flowered perennial. Species found in Europe and North America.

Jacquard, Joseph Marie (1752-1834), French inventor. Developed (1801-6) Jacquard loom, first to weave figured patterns; used system of punched cards.

jade, either of 2 silicate minerals used as gem. Jadeite, a pyroxene, is rarer and more valuable than nephrite, an amphibole. Normally green in colour, may be white, yellow, pink. Used in ornamental carving, jewellery. Major sources in China, Japan, USSR, New Zealand.

jaeger, *see* SKUA.

Jaén, town of S Spain, cap. of Jaén prov. Pop. 79,000. Produces olive oil, wine, leather goods; lead mines nearby. Moorish kingdom until 1246. Cathedral (16th cent.).

Jaffa, *see* TEL AVIV.

jaguar, *Panthera onca,* large cat of Central and South America. Resembles leopard, with black spots and yellow coat; nocturnal hunter.

Jainism, Indian religion. Arose (6th cent. BC) with Buddhism as protest against formalism of Hinduism. Doctrine based on belief in eternity of all living things, stresses asceticism, respect for all forms of life. The soul retains identity through transmigration and eventually attains NIRVANA. Adhered to by c 2 million Indians.

Jaipur, cap. of Rajasthan state, NW India. Pop. 613,000. Commercial centre; famous for jewellery. Enclosed by wall, has maharajah's palace. Cap. of former princely state of Jaipur.

Jakarta, *see* DJAKARTA.

Jamaica, independent isl. state of

West Indies, member of British Commonwealth. Area 10,962 sq km (4232 sq mi); pop. 2,057,000, mainly Negro; cap. Kingston. Language: English. Religion: Protestant. Blue Mts. in E (coffee growing). Tropical climate. Agric. economy (sugar, fruit, spice, tobacco growing); bauxite exports. Important tourism. Discovered by Columbus (1494); captured from Spanish by English (1655); slavery abolished (1833). Gained independence after it seceded from Federation of West Indies (1962).

James [the Elder], St (d. *c* AD 44), one of the Twelve Disciples, son of Zebedee. In NT, put to death with brother John by Herod Agrippa. Traditionally, body moved to Santiago de Compostela, Spain, site of famous shrine.

James I (1208-76), king of Aragón (1213-76). Conquered Balearic Isls. (1229-35) and Valencia (1238). Fought long against Moors in Murcia. Called 'El Conquistador' (the conqueror).

James I (1566-1625), king of England, Scotland and Ireland (1603-25). Succeeded to Scottish throne (1567) as James VI on abdication of mother, Mary Queen of Scots, and to English throne on death of Elizabeth I. Reign marked by conflict with Parliament, influence of his favourites (eg BUCKINGHAM), exercise of royal prerogative, raising of revenue. Antagonized Puritans at Hampton Court Conference (1604), which commissioned translation of Bible (Authorized Version).

James II (1633-1701), king of England, Scotland and Ireland (1685-8). A convert to Catholicism, subject to Whig attempts to exclude him from succession, which were frustrated by his brother, Charles II. After succession, put down Monmouth's rebellion; alienated subjects by autocratic rule, pro-Catholic policies. Fled country after William of Orange had been invited to become king. His restoration bid was foiled by defeat at the Boyne in Ireland (1690).

James I (1394-1437), king of Scotland (1424-37). Sent by his father to France (1406), he was captured by English and held until 1424. Tried to suppress power of his nobles and maintain peace; murdered by group of nobles.

James II (1430-60), king of Scotland (1437-60). Succeeded father James I. During minority, central govt. estab. by father weakened. Took over govt. in 1449, and ended conflict with Douglas clan with victory at Arkinholm. Killed by misfire of own cannon while taking Roxburgh castle from English.

James III (1451-88), king of Scotland (1460-88). Succeeded father James II. Gained Orkney and Shetland by marriage with Margaret of Denmark. Defeated English-backed invasions of brother Albany and Earl of Douglas. Killed at battle of Sauchieburn fighting rebel nobles who held his young son, future James IV, as figure-head.

James IV (1473-1513), king of Scotland (1488-1513). Reign marked by stability and beginnings of prosperity. As part of alliance with France, invaded England but was defeated and killed at Flodden. Marriage to Margaret Tudor (1503) formed basis of Stuart claims to English throne.

James V (1512-42), king of Scotland (1513-42). Succeeded father James IV. Took real power in 1528. Resisted urgings of Henry VIII of England to break with France and Rome. Henry invaded Scotland and defeated Scots at Solway Moss; James died soon after. Succeeded by daughter, Mary Queen of Scots.

James VI, see JAMES I.

James, Jesse [Woodson] (1847-82), American outlaw. With brother, **[Alexander] Frank[lin] James** (1843-1915), led notorious outlaw gang which robbed banks and trains in midwest during 1870s. Jesse was killed by a gang member.

James, William (1842-1910), American philosopher, psychologist. Opposed 'pure' metaphysical philosophy, argued for practical philosophy, ie pragmatism, and relativity of truth. Works incl. *The Principles of Psychology* (1890). His brother, **Henry James** (1843-1916), was a novelist. Novels deal with social relationships between Old World and New, eg *The Europeans* (1878), *The Portrait of a Lady* (1881), *The Bostonians* (1886). Short stories incl. *The Turn of the Screw* (1898). Settled in England (1877), became British national (1915).

James, two rivers of US. 1, rises in C North Dakota, flows 1143 km (710 mi) across Dakotas to Missouri R. 2, formed in SW Virginia, flows E 547 km (340 mi). On its lower course was Jamestown, 1st permanent English settlement in America (1607).

James, in NT, epistle traditionally ascribed to St James the Less.

Propounds general points of practical morality.

James Bay, arm of SE Hudson Bay, Canada; between Ontario and Québec Has many isls., largest Akimiski. Trading posts; oil development. Explored (1631) by Thomas James.

Jameson, Sir Leander Starr (1853-1917), British colonial administrator. Led unauthorized Jameson raid (1895) into Boer colony of Transvaal to support 'Uitlanders' (largely British settlers); captured, briefly imprisoned by British. Premier of Cape Colony (1904-8).

Jamestown, Virginia, US, see JAMES, river (2).

Jammu and Kashmir, state of N India. Area c 142,000 sq km (55,000 sq mi); pop. 4,615,000; cap. Srinagar (summer), Jammu (winter). Almost entirely mountainous. Famous for goats' wool (cashmere). At 1947 partition this Hindu-ruled Moslem region disputed by Pakistan and India. Jammu and Kashmir declared part of India 1956; Pakistan retained Azad Kashmir.

Jamshedpur, city of Bihar state, NE India. Pop. 465,000. Major iron and steel works. Founded 1909 by industrialist Tata family.

Janáček, Leoš (1854-1928), Czech composer. Wrote music in national style. Works incl. rhapsody *Taras Bulba* and operas, eg *Jenufa*, *The Cunning Little Vixen*. Orchestral works incl. *Sinfonietta*.

Jane, Frederick (1870-1916), English naval officer, journalist. Founder, 1st editor of annuals *Jane's Fighting Ships* (1898), *All The World's Aircraft* (1910).

Janissaries, elite corps of the Turkish army formed in the 14th cent. from press-ganged Christians and prisoners of war. Liquidated by Mahmud II (1826) after a mutiny.

Jansen, Cornelis (1585-1638), Dutch theologian. Attempted to reform RC church by returning to teachings of St Augustine. Attacked orthodox Jesuit teaching in *Augustinus* (pub. 1642), advocating austerity, belief in predestination similar to Calvin's but within Catholicism. Leading followers (Jansenists) set up community at Port Royal, France. Condemned in papal bulls of 1705 and 1713. Noted Jansenists incl. Arnauld, Pascal.

Jansenism, *see* JANSEN, CORNELIS.

Janus, in Roman religion, god of doorways and hence of the beginnings of enterprises. One of principal gods, regarded as custodian of the universe. Represented with double-faced head so that he could look to front and back.

Japan (*Nippon*), country of E Asia, archipelago with 4 main isls. Honshu, Hokkaido, Kyushu and Shikoku, separated from mainland by Sea of Japan. Area c 372,000 sq km (142,000 sq mi); pop. 112,-768,000; cap. Tokyo. Language: Japanese. Religion: Shinto, Buddhism. Mountainous with active volcanoes, frequent earthquakes; monsoon climate, abundant rainfall. Intensive cultivation yields rice, cereals, soya beans; major fisheries. Buddhism, Chinese culture introduced 6th cent AD; was feudal society under warrior leaders (shoguns) until 19th cent. European contacts estab. in 16th cent. Became world power after defeating China (1894-5), Russia (1904-5); 2nd Chinese war merged with WWII

after Japanese attack on Pearl Harbor (1941). Surrendered 1945; imperial power curtailed (1947).

Japanese, language of Japan and Ryukyu Isls. Appears to be un-related to any other language, although grammar similar to Korean. Written language adapted from Chinese since 3rd-4th cent., with simplified phonetic characters added since WWII.

Japanese beetle, *Popillia japonica*, shiny green and brown beetle; accidentally brought from Japan to US, major pest of fruit and crops.

Japanese literature, in poetry, traditional verse forms are *tanka* (5-line stanzas of 5,7,5,7,7 syllables), *haiku* (3-line stanzas of 5,7,5 syllables). In drama, the NO PLAY developed (14th cent.) from religious ceremony. The *kabuki* theatre, dating from 17th cent., is more popular form allowing greater freedom of expression. In the novel, influences have been mainly European, esp. Russian. Also *see* HEIKE-MONOGATARI.

japonica or flowering quince, spiky Asiatic shrub of genus *Chaemoneles*. Pink or red flowers, hard yellow fruit used in preserves.

Jarry, Alfred (1873-1907), French writer, dramatist. Famous for play *Ubu Roi* (1896) whose 'hero' is grotesque caricature of bourgeois greed and violence. Regarded as predecessor of surrealists and ABSURD school.

jasmine, any of genus *Jasminum* of shrubs of olive family. Native to Asia, South America and Australia. Popular as garden plant for fragrant flowers of yellow, red or white. Used in perfumes or for scenting tea.

Jason, in Greek myth, leader of the ARGONAUTS. Promised his right to throne of Iolcus by the usurper Pelias if he could recover the GOLDEN FLEECE. Secured the fleece from King Aeëtes of Colchis, whose daughter MEDEA helped him in return for promise of marriage. On return to Iolcus, Medea tricked Pelias' daughters into murdering their father, but Jason failed to retain kingdom. Reigned with Medea over Corinth until he broke faith with her. For this, condemned to exile by gods. Died when prow of *Argo* crushed him as he was resting in its shade.

jasper, impure, cryptocrystalline QUARTZ used as gem. Opaque, usually red, yellow or brown in colour.

Jaspers, Karl (1883–1969), German philosopher. Influenced by Kierkegaard. Interpreter of German EXISTENTIALISM. Held man to be encompassed in continual struggle of love and hate. Works incl. *Man in the Modern Age* (1931), *Reason and Existence* (1935).

jaundice, condition characterized by yellow discoloration of skin, mucous membranes and urine. Caused by excess bile pigment in blood. May result from infectious hepatitis, blockage of bile ducts.

Jaurès, Jean Léon (1859–1914), French politician. Advocated democratic socialism and international pacifism. Founded socialist journal *L'Humanité* (1904). Assassinated while trying to prevent outbreak of WWI.

Java, most important isl. of Indonesia. Area c 132,000 sq km (51,000 sq mi). Narrow, crossed by volcanic mountains; humid, tropical vegetation. Produces rice, rubber, coffee. Densely populated; has ⅔ of Indonesian pop. and cap. Djakarta.

Java man, forerunner of modern man whose fossilized remains were found in Java by Eugène Dubois (1891). Originally classified as *Pithecanthropus erectus*, Java man now considered to be an example of *Homo erectus*.

jaw, either of 2 bones which hold the teeth and frame the mouth in most vertebrates. Upper jaw (maxilla), a component of skull, does not move; lower jaw (mandible), hinged to skull, is movable.

Jawlensky, Aleksei (1864–1941), Russian painter. Worked in Germany, where he was associated with Blaue Reiter group. Early work was in expressionist style, using simplified forms and flat areas of colour; later concentrated on representations of human head.

Jay, John (1745–1829), American statesman, first chief justice (1789–95). Signed Anglo-American settlement (Jay's Treaty, 1794), authorizing negotiation by joint commission of boundary disputes in North America.

jay, brightly coloured bird of crow family. Eurasian jay, *Garrulus glandarius*, has pinkish-brown body, blue-back wings. Blue jay, *Cyanocitta cristata*, of US has blue plumage.

jazz, music that originated in US at turn of 19th cent., deriving from American Negro music. Has now spread through much of world, esp. Europe and Japan. Key features are use of improvisation (eg Louis Armstrong) and rhythmic drive.

Several styles are still current, *eg* traditional or New Orleans jazz, but contemporary jazz is merging both, with rock and avant-garde music.

Jean Paul, *see* RICHTER, JOHANN PAUL.

Jedburgh, town of Borders region, SE Scotland. Pop. 4000. Former royal burgh and co. town of Roxburghshire. Tweed, woollen, rayon mfg. Has ruined 12th cent. abbey. Hist. notorious for 'Jeddart justice' (trial followed hanging).

Jeddah, *see* JIDDAH.

jeep, four-wheel drive military motor vehicle with ¼ ton carrying capacity; used for reconnaissance, passengers and light cargo. Developed by US in WWII.

Jefferson, Thomas (1743-1826), American statesman, president (1801-9). Wrote much of Declaration of Independence (1776). As secretary of state (1790-3) in Washington's cabinet, opposed centralizing Federalists led by ALEXANDER HAMILTON. Elected president by House of Representatives after tie with Aaron Burr. Admin. highlighted by Louisiana Purchase (1803). Much of subsequent Democratic Party doctrine derived from Jeffersonian Republicans.

Jefferson City, cap. of Missouri, US; on Missouri R. Pop. 32,000. Agric. processing. Lincoln Univ. founded (1866) for Negroes by 2 Negro regiments.

Jeffreys, George, 1st Baron Jeffreys of Wem (c 1645-89), English judge. Notorious for harshness at 'Bloody Assizes' after Monmouth's rebellion (1685), hanging c 200 and flogging, transporting many more. Lord chancellor under James II.

Jehovah, mistaken reconstruction of the ineffable name of God (YHWH) in OT. The form *Yahweh* is now regarded as more correct.

Jehovah's Witnesses, *see* RUSSELL, CHARLES TAZE.

Jellicoe, John Rushworth Jellicoe, 1st Earl (1859-1935), British admiral. Commanded Grand Fleet (1914-16), notably in battle of Jutland (1916); first sea lord (1916-17). Governor-general of New Zealand (1920-4).

jellyfish, free-swimming medusa form of certain coelenterates. True jellyfish, class Scyphozoa, have gelatinous bell-shaped bodies and tentacles with stinging cells for capturing prey.

Jena, town of SW East Germany, on R. Saale. Pop. 84,000. Precision engineering, incl. Zeiss optical instruments. Univ. (1558). Scene of Napoleon's victory (1806) over Prussians.

Jenghiz Khan, *see* GENGHIS KHAN.

Jenkins, Roy Harris (1920-), British politician. Chancellor of exchequer (1967-70), home secretary (1974-6) in Labour govts. Resigned to become (1977) president of European Commission (executive of European Community).

Jenkins' Ear, War of (1739-41), conflict between Britain and Spain, which merged into the WAR OF AUSTRIAN SUCCESSION. Robert Jenkins, a master mariner, claimed to have had his ear cut off by the Spanish; his story so aroused public opinion that Walpole was forced to declare war.

Jenner, Edward (1749-1823), English physician. Made 1st successful vaccination (1796) against smallpox by immunizing patient with cowpox virus. Described work in *Inquiry into the Cause and Effects of the Variolae Vaccinae* (1798).

Jensen, Johannes Vilhelm (1873-1950), Danish author. Known for prose epic, *The Long Journey* (1908-22), tracing Teutonic race from baboon stage to 16th cent. in Darwinian terms. Nobel Prize for Literature (1944).

Jerba, see DJERBA, Tunisia.

jerboa, fawn-coloured nocturnal rodent of Dipodidae family from desert regions of N Africa and Asia. Has very long back legs for jumping. Species incl. Egyptian jerboa, *Jaculus jaculus.*

Jeremiah, prophetic book of OT, taking place during reign of Josiah. Tells story of priest Jeremiah who was imprisoned for foretelling fall of Jerusalem. Went into Egypt with the remaining Jews when prophecy fulfilled (586 BC).

Jerez (de la Frontera), city of Andalusia, S Spain. Pop. 150,000. Produces wine, sherry (named after town); bottle and cask mfg., horse breeding. Held by Moors 711-1264.

Jericho, ancient city of NW Jordan, at N end of Dead Sea, near modern village of Ariha. Thought to date from c 8000 BC. Canaanite city captured by Joshua and Israelites; often destroyed, rebuilt.

Jerome, Jerome K[lapka] (1859-1927), English author. Known for comic novels, esp. *Three Men in a Boat* (1889). Also wrote modern morality play, *The Passing of the Third Floor Back* (1908).

Jerome, St, full name Sophronius

Eusebius Hieronymus (c 347-c 419), Dalmatian churchman, scholar. Served Pope Damasus I in Rome before retiring (386) to monastery in Bethlehem. Latin translations of Bible from Hebrew served as basis for the VULGATE.

Jersey, largest of Channel Isls., UK. Area 116 sq km (45 sq mi); pop. 73,000; cap. St Helier. Tourism; Jersey cattle; potato, tomato growing. Origin of woollen 'jerseys'.

Jersey City, in NE New Jersey, US; opposite New York City on Hudson R. Pop. 261,000. Shipping terminal; meat packing, oil refining; foundry and paper products, chemicals mfg. Settled by Dutch in 1620s.

Jerusalem, cap. of Israel, hist. cap. of Palestine. Pop. 305,000. Partitioned 1948 between Israel (new city) and Jordan (old city). Latter contains most of Jewish, Christian, Moslem holy sites. Enclosed by Turks (16th cent.). Sacred sites are Wailing Wall, Mosque of Omar, Church of Holy Sepulchre, monastries, Mt. of Olives. Old city occupied by Israelis after 1967.

Jerusalem artichoke, see ARTICHOKE.

Jervis, John, Earl of St Vincent (1735-1823), British naval officer. Commanded the Mediterranean fleet in victory (1797), aided by Nelson, over a larger Spanish fleet off Cape St Vincent. As first lord of the admiralty (1801-6) he instituted important reforms.

Jervis Bay, inlet of Tasman Sea, SE Australia. Shore area (73 sq km/28 sq mi) became federal territ. 1915; proposed as port for Australian Capital Territory. Naval base.

Jesse, in OT, father of David. Name

later symbolized royal line and its Messianic associations, eg Jesse's Rod (Jesus) and Jesse's Root (Virgin Mary).

Jesuits, see JESUS, SOCIETY OF.

Jesus, Society of, or **Jesuits**, RC religious order for men founded (c 1534) by IGNATIUS OF LOYOLA. Approved by pope (1540). Original aims were educational and missionary work (eg in Japan, India, North and South America). Characterized by disciplined organization and long, rigorous training. Political involvement (18th cent.) resulted in expulsion from France, Portugal, Spain and its dominions. Suppressed by Pope Clement XIV (1773). Revived (1814) as worldwide order.

Jesus Christ (c 4 BC-c AD 29), Jewish religious leader, central figure of Christianity. Born in Bethlehem to Mary, wife of Joseph of Nazareth. Lived at time when Jews were eager for deliverance from Roman domination. After baptism by his cousin, John the Baptist, Jesus became a wandering teacher accompanied by band of disciples. Attracted great crowds with preaching. Govt.'s fear of his power led to arrest in Jerusalem during Passover after betrayal by Judas Iscariot. Tried and convicted of blasphemy by the ecclesiastical court. Crucified by order of Pontius Pilate. According to Gospels, arose 3 days later. Book of Acts relates that, 40 days later, in sight of his disciples, he ascended to Heaven. See TRINITY.

Jet, hard, black variety of LIGNITE. May be highly polished and used in jewellery. Major sources in England, US, France.

Jet propulsion, forward movement achieved by reaction caused by expanding gases ejected rearwards. Usually air is compressed, mixed with fuel and burnt. This combustion provides rapid expansion of the gas which produces the rearward jet and also drives the intake compressor.

Jewish Autonomous Region, see BIROBIDZHAN.

Jews, people regarded as descended from the ancient Hebrews of Biblical times, whose religion is JUDAISM. In OT, lineage traced from Abraham and 12 tribes of Israel. Originally in Canaan, then Egypt; persecution resulted in Exodus led by Moses. Resettled in Canaan under Saul after period of wandering in desert. First Temple built by Solomon. Kingdom then split into Israel and Judah. Temple destroyed by Babylonians (586 BC), people exiled until their return was allowed by Cyrus the Great and Temple rebuilt (516 BC). Jerusalem destroyed by Romans (AD 70). After fall of Roman Empire, Jews appeared in W Europe but were widely persecuted from 12th-18th cent. Capitalism and 19th cent. revolutionary movements improved their conditions. Emancipation led to cultural assimilation and ZIONISM. New wave of persecution spread from Russia after assassination (1881) of Alexander II. Rise to power of Nazis in Germany resulted in extermination of 6 million Jews before and during WWII. Refuge sought in Palestine, resulting in formation of Jewish state of Israel (1948) by UN.

Jezebel (d. c 846 BC), wife of Ahab, king of Israel. Introduced worship of Baal into Israel and persecuted the prophets. Vigorously denounced by Elijah, who prophesied her death; executed after Jehu's defeat of Ahab.

Jibuti, *see* DJIBOUTI.

Jiddah or **Jeddah,** port of W Saudi Arabia, on Red Sea coast of Hejaz. Pop. 300,000. Provides sea access for Mecca for thousands of pilgrims.

Jiménez, Juan Ramón (1881–1958), Spanish poet. Works, eg *Sonetos Espirituales* (1917), prose-poem *Platero and I* (1917) noted for concentration of form. Nobel Prize for Literature (1956).

Jinnah, Mohammed Ali (1876–1948), Indian statesman. President of Moslem League after 1934, successfully advocated partition of India into separate Moslem and Moslem states at independence (1947). First governor-general of Pakistan.

jinni or **djinni,** in Moslem literature, Arab folklore, human-like being with powers to change size, shape, place. May be good or evil.

Joachim, Joseph (1831–1907), Hungarian violinist. Friend of Schumann, Mendelssohn, Brahms. He founded Joachim Quartet (1869) and was renowned for his interpretation of Beethoven and Brahms.

Joan of Arc, St (c 1412–31), French national heroine. Claimed to hear voices urging her to aid the dauphin in struggle against English. Led army which raised siege of Orléans (1429), then persuaded the dauphin to be crowned as Charles VII at Rheims. Captured at Compiègne (1430) by the Burgundians and delivered to the English. Tried and condemned by court of French ecclesiastics at Rouen as heretic and sorceress; burned at stake.

Job, poetical book of OT, of unknown authorship, prob. written 600–400 BC. Criticizes the association of sin with suffering by telling of the sufferings inflicted on the righteous Job by God.

Jodrell Bank, site of large radio telescope, near Macclesfield, Cheshire. Has steerable parabolic dish, 76m in diameter.

Joel, prophetic book of OT, predicting plague of locusts in Judah. Promises the forgiveness of God upon repentance of sin.

Joffre, Joseph Jacques Césaire (1852–1931), French marshal. Commanded French armies on Western Front (1914–16) until outmoded strategy (notably at Verdun, 1916) led to his replacement. Chairman of Allied War Council (1916–18).

Johannesburg, city of S Transvaal, South Africa, in Witwatersrand. Pop. 1,433,000, country's largest city. Major indust., commercial centre in world's richest goldmining region; engineering, chemical mfg., diamond cutting. Two univs., stock exchange. Founded (1886) as mining settlement.

John [the Divine] or **[the Evangelist], St** (AD 1st cent.), one of Twelve Disciples, son of Zebedee and brother of James the Elder. Traditionally regarded as the unnamed disciple 'whom Jesus loved' and to whom he entrusted the care of his mother on his death. Regarded as author of 4th Gospel and Revelations.

John XXIII, orig. Angelo Giuseppe Roncalli (1881–1963), Italian churchman, pope (1958–63). Promoted reform within Church, reconciliation with other Christian churches and world peace. Despite opposition to Communism, advocated socialist reforms. Summoned influential 2nd Vatican Council.

John (1167-1216), king of England (1199-1216). Tried to usurp his brother, Richard I, during his absence on 3rd Crusade. Lost most of his French dominions to king of France in dispute over right to succeed Richard. Had to yield to papal authority in dispute over Stephen LANGTON. Forced to sign MAGNA CARTA (1215).

John III [Sobieski] (1624-96), king of Poland (1674-96). Leader of Christian campaigns against Turks; acclaimed a hero after relieving Turkish siege of Vienna (1683). Last years of reign marked by opposition from nobles.

John II [the Perfect] (1455-95), king of Portugal (1481-95). Broke power of the feudal nobility, executing their leader, duke of Braganza. Concluded Treaty of Tordesillas (1494) with Spain, which estab. limits of each country's colonization of New World. Encouraged African exploration of Diaz.

John, Augustus Edwin (1878-1961), Welsh painter. Influenced by post-impressionism and Rembrandt, he painted portraits of many leading personalities of his day; later society portraits failed to realize his early promise. Works incl. *The Smiling Woman* and portraits of Shaw and Hardy.

John Balliol, *see* BALLIOL, JOHN.

John Bull, popular personification of England. Depicted as bold, honest but hot-tempered man. First appeared (1712) in *The History of*

John Bull, a collection of pamphlets by John ARBUTHNOT.

John, Gospel according to St, fourth of NT gospels, traditionally attributed to St John the Divine. Prob. written *c* AD 100. Most philosophical of gospels, propounding concept of LOGOS.

John, three epistles of NT, ascribed to apostle John the Divine; discourses setting forth the nature of Christian fellowship.

John Birch Society, extreme right-wing American anti-Communist organization (founded 1958). Named after John Birch, an intelligence officer killed by Chinese Communists (1945).

John Chrysostom, St (*c* 347-407), Greek churchman, theologian, patriarch of Constantinople (398-403). Deposed as result of court intrigues. Renowned preacher; author of influential commentaries, esp. on Paul's epistles.

John dory, *see* DORY.

John of Austria, Don (1545-78), Spanish soldier, illegitimate son of Emperor Charles V. Commanded Venetian and Spanish fleets which defeated Turks at Lepanto (1571). He conquered Tunis (1573), after which Philip II, suspicious of his intention to set up as ruler there, sent him to the Netherlands as viceroy.

John of Gaunt, Duke of Lancaster (1340-99), English nobleman. Fourth son of Edward III, became effective ruler of England during last years of Edward and minority of Richard II. Claimed throne of Castile through his wife Constance; withdrew claim after unsuccessful invasion of Castile (1386).

John of Leiden, orig. Jan Bockelson (c 1509-36), Dutch preacher. Anabaptist leader in Münster, overthrew religious and civil authorities and estab. (1534) theocracy, featuring polygamy and collective ownership of property. Tortured and executed after city was retaken.

John of the Cross, St, orig. Juan de Yepis y Alvarez (1542-91), Spanish mystic, poet. Friend of St Theresa of Avila. A founder of reformed order of Discalced Carmelites. Known for mystical poetry, eg *Spiritual Canticle*, written in prison, and treatises on mystical theology.

John O'Groats, in Highland region, N Scotland. Point of mainland Britain furthest from LAND'S END, England.

John Paul I, orig. Albino Luciani (1912-78), Italian churchman, pope (1978). Died one month after succeeding Paul VI.

John Paul II, orig. Karol Wojtyla (1920-), Polish churchman, pope (1978-). First non-Italian pope since 16th century.

Johns, Jasper (1930-), American artist. Precursor of pop art, he is known for his attempts to transform everyday objects into art. Work incl. series of targets, flags and bronze cast *Beer Cans* (1961).

Johns Hopkins University, Baltimore, US, privately funded univ. founded in 1867. Noted for medical school, graduate research.

Johnson, Andrew (1808-75), American statesman, president (1865-9). A Democrat, elected vice-president (1864); became president on Lincoln's assassination. Post-Civil War RECONSTRUCTION programme impeded by radical Republicans. Narrowly acquitted in Senate vote over impeachment charge arising from attempt to remove secretary of war, Edwin Stanton, from office (1868).

Johnson, John Arthur ('Jack') (1878-1946), American boxer. First black boxer to win world heavyweight title (1908), which he held until 1915. His controversial personality led to widespread desire for a 'white hope' to beat him.

Johnson, Lyndon Baines (1908-73), American statesman, president (1963-9). Achieved power in Senate as Democratic majority leader (1955-60). Elected vice-president (1960), became president on Kennedy's assassination. Legislative record of social reform offset by escalation of Vietnam war. Term also marked by race riots, anti-war movement.

Johnson, Samuel (1709-84), English writer. Known for *A Dictionary of the English Language* (1755), *Rasselas* (1759), *Lives of the Poets* (1783), many miscellaneous essays in the *Rambler* and the *Idler*. Edited Shakespeare with critical prefaces. In 1763 met Boswell who wrote his biog. Founded (1764) famous Literary Club. Tour of Hebrides produced *A Journey to the Western Islands of Scotland* (1775).

John the Baptist, St (d. c AD 29), Jewish prophet. In NT, son of priest of the Temple, Zacharias; cousin of Jesus. Called on people to repent in preparation for the Messiah whom he recognized in Jesus and baptized. Condemnation of Herod Antipas for his marriage to Herodias led to his beheading at her and her daughter Salome's instigation.

joint, in anatomy, place of union between 2 bones, usually one which admits of motion of one or both bones. Joints are particularly susceptible to diseases such as gout and arthritis.

Joinville, Jean, Sire de (1225-1317), French chronicler. Wrote biog. of St Louis (Louis IX) from viewpoint of friend, companion on his 1st crusade, giving valuable picture of character of king, contemporary France.

Joliot-Curie, Irène (1897-1956), and her husband **Jean Frédéric Joliot-Curie** (1900-58), French scientists. Discovered artificial radioactivity by producing radioactive phosphorus isotope by alpha particle bombardment of aluminium; shared Nobel Prize for Chemistry (1935).

Jolson, Al, pseud. of Asa Yoelson (1886-1950), American singer, entertainer, b. Russia. Long known on Broadway, famous for appearance in 1st 'talkie', *The Jazz Singer* (1927), and for singing, with blackened face, such songs as 'Mammy', 'Swannee River'.

Jonah, prophetic book of OT, relating story of Jonah's missionary journey. Incl. story of Jonah being swallowed by a fish. A parable to warn Jews of the dangers of being inward-looking.

Jones, Inigo (1573-1652), English architect. Influenced by Palladio, he brought Italian classicism to England. Designed Queen's House, Greenwich (1616-35) and Banqueting House, Whitehall (1619-22). Also designed scenery and costumes for court masques under James I and Charles I.

Jones, James (1921-), American novelist. Works incl. best-seller *From Here to Eternity* (1951) dealing with army life before Japanese attack on Pearl Harbor.

Jones, John Luther ('Casey') (1864-1900), American locomotive engineer, folk hero. Saved passengers in crash of Cannon Ball express (1900) in Mississippi, but was himself killed.

Jones, John Paul (1747-92), American naval officer, b. Scotland. During American Revolution, raided coast of Britain. Sailing in *Bon Homme Richard*, defeated British ship *Serapis* in famous engagement (1779). Later served as admiral in Russian navy.

Jones, LeRoi (1934-), American writer. Works incl. poetry, *eg The Dead Lecturer* (1964), plays, *eg The Slave* (1964). Autobiog. novel, *The System of Dante's Hell* (1965), explores stylistic innovation.

Jongkind, Johan Barthold (1819-91), Dutch landscape painter. Precursor of impressionism, his handling of light and atmosphere in his marine and port views strongly influenced the young Monet.

Jönköping, town of SC Sweden, at S end of Lake Vättern. Pop. 81,000. Match mfg.; paper mills; iron foundries. Chartered (1284).

jonquil, *see* NARCISSUS.

Jonson, Ben (1572-1637), English author. Known for 'comedies of humours', *eg Everyman in His Humour* (1599), *Volpone* (c 1605), *The Alchemist* (1610). Also wrote tragedy *Sejanus* (1603), court masques, classical verse.

Jordaens, Jacob (1593-1678), Flemish painter. Influenced by Rubens, he is remembered for elaborate genre scenes of drinking peasants, eg *The King Drinks*. Also painted portraits, religious and allegorical subjects.

Jordan, kingdom of SW Asia. Area c 98,400 sq km (38,000 sq mi); pop. 2,779,000; cap. Amman. Language: Arabic. Religion: Sunni Islam. Mountains, arid desert; limited cultivation (wheat, fruit). Part of Ottoman empire (16th cent.- 1918), mandated to Britain as Transjordan; full independence 1946. Defeated by Israelis (1967), who subsequently occupied territ. W of R. Jordan.

Jordan, river of Palestine. Length c 320 km (200 mi). Rises in Anti-Lebanon Mts., flows S to Sea of Galilee and Dead Sea. Not navigable but used in irrigation schemes. After 1967 Israeli victory formed part of *de facto* border with Jordan.

Joseph, St (*fl* 1st cent. BC - AD 1st cent.), Jewish carpenter, husband of Virgin Mary. Patron of RC church and of dying.

Joseph II (1741-90), Holy Roman emperor (1765-90). One of the 'benevolent despots', ruled solely after death (1780) of his mother, MARIA THERESA. Cut feudal power of nobles by abolishing serfdom, restricted Church's power, extended education. Attempt to annex Bavaria thwarted by Frederick II of Prussia.

Joseph (c 1840-1904), American Indian leader. Led Nez Percé Indians in attempt to reach Canada (1877) after they were about to be removed from land fraudulently ceded to US. Defeated US forces at Big Hole but forced to surrender before reaching Canada.

Joseph, in OT, favourite son of Jacob and Rachel. Sold into slavery in Egypt by his envious brothers where he rose to position of governor under the pharaoh. Saved his father and brothers when they were driven by famine into Egypt.

Joseph, Father, orig. François Leclerc du Tremblay (1577-1638), French Capuchin monk, known as 'Eminence Grise'. Confidant of Richelieu, advocated anti-Habsburg policy.

Josephine, full name Marie Josèphe Tascher de la Pagerie (1763-1814), empress of France, b. Martinique. First husband, Alexandre de Beauharnais, was guillotined (1794). Married Napoleon (1796), who had marriage annulled (1809) because of her alleged sterility.

Joseph of Arimathea, St (*fl* AD 1st cent.), wealthy member of Jewish Sanhedrin who, according to NT, provided tomb for Jesus. Traditionally visited Glastonbury, England.

Josephus, Flavius, orig. Joseph ben Matthias (AD 37-c 95), Jewish historian, soldier. Govenor of Galilee during war with Rome. When his stronghold fell he won Vespasian's favour, adopting name Flavius. Works incl. *The Jewish War, Antiquities of the Jews.*

Joshua, historical book of OT, describing invasion and occupation of Palestine by the Hebrews under Moses' successor as leader, Joshua. Incl. story of the fall of Jericho.

Joshua tree, see YUCCA.

Josiah, king of Judah (c 639-c 609 BC). Reformed religious worship after discovery of lost book of the law (possibly Deuteronomy) in the Temple. Forbade all provincial sanctuaries and concentrated worship of Yahweh alone in Jerusalem.

Jotunheim Mountains, range of WC Norway. Rises to Galdhöpiggen and Glittertind (both c 2465 m/8100 ft). Name from Norse 'Home of the Giants'.

Jouhaux, Léon (1879-1954), French trade union leader. Leader of Confederation générale du Travail (1909-47). A founder of anti-communist International Confederation of Free Trade Unions (1949). Awarded Nobel Peace Prize (1951).

Joule, James Prescott (1818-89), English physicist. Discovered law describing heating effect of electric current. Worked on interchangeability of mechanical energy and heat energy. Calculated mechanical equivalent of heat: 4.18×10^{9} ergs produce 1 calorie of heat.

joule, SI unit of work or energy, defined as work done on an object by force of 1 newton acting through distance of 1 metre. Also measured as work done per sec by current of 1 ampère flowing through resistance of 1 ohm. Named after James Prescott Joule.

journalism, gathering, writing, editing, and publishing of news, newspapers, magazines, radio, TV, film, *etc.* Developed first as offshoot of politics, business, at end of 18th cent. With technological advances, emphasis on quick reporting of events rather than polemic has encouraged growth of news agencies, wire services, *etc.*

Jove, see JUPITER.

Jowett, Benjamin (1817-93), Brit-

ish scholar, educator. As master of Balliol Coll., Oxford, vice-chancellor of Oxford, greatly influenced pupils. Wrote outstanding translation of Plato's dialogues (1871).

Joyce, James Augustine Aloysius (1882-1941), Irish novelist. Works incl. greatly influential *Portrait of the Artist as a Young Man* (1916), *Ulysses* (1922), *Finnegans Wake* (1939). Used complexly allusive language combining naturalism, symbolism. Leading prose innovator of 20th cent.

Joyce, William (1906-46), British Nazi propagandist, b. US. Went to Germany at outbreak of WWII and regularly broadcast German propaganda to Britain, gaining nickname Lord Haw-Haw. Hanged for treason.

Juan Carlos (1938-), king of Spain (1975-). Heir-designate from 1969, assumed monarchy on Franco's death.

Juan Fernández Islands, small isl. group of Chile, 640 km (c 400 mi) W of Valparaiso. Lobster fishing. Believed to be scene of Daniel Defoe's *Robinson Crusoe.*

Juárez, Benito Pablo (1806-72), Mexican statesman. After overthrow of Santa Anna (1855), revised law to restrict power of church and army. Became president in 1858. Thwarted Napoleon III's attempt to re-estab. empire under Maximilian (1864-7). Died while resisting revolution of Diaz.

Juárez, border town of N Mexico, on Rio Grande, opposite El Paso, Texas. Pop. 436,000. Commercial, agric. centre; cotton processing, tourism. Formerly El Paso del Norte, renamed 1888.

Judaea, see JUDAH.

Judah, hist. kingdom of S Israel ruled by house of David (931 BC-586 BC). At time of Jesus, it was Roman prov. of Judaea.

Judaism, religious beliefs and observances of the Jews; oldest of the monotheistic religions and fundamental to Christianity and Islam. Based primarily on OT, TALMUD and TORAH. Observances incl. male circumcision, daily services in Hebrew, observance of Sabbath (7th day of week) and the 3 principal festivals, Passover, Pentecost and Tabernacles. Movements in Judaism have incl. Pharisees, Sadducees and Essenes of NT times; Karaites (8th cent.), Hasidism (18th cent.). In West, the 3 modern branches (Orthodox, Conservative, Reform) evolved in Germany (19th cent.). Festivals celebrated in SYNAGOGUE or in home. Priest known as rabbi.

Judas Iscariot (*fl* 1st cent. AD), Disciple of Jesus. According to NT, in return for a bribe, betrayed Jesus by kissing him, thus identifying him to Romans. Hanged himself after the Crucifixion.

Judas tree, see REDBUD.

Jude, epistle of NT. Traditionally ascribed to Disciple St Jude, brother of James the Younger, between AD 65-80. Warns against false prophets and heresy.

judge, public official with authority to hear legal disputes, pronounce sentence in court of law. In UK, appointed by lord chancellor on govt. nomination; must be barrister of several years' standing. In US, usually chosen by popular election, can be appointed by state governor or legislature.

Judges, historical book of OT.

Describes govt. of the 'judges' (*ie* tribal leaders) who ruled Israel before union of the tribes. Recounts repeated apostasy of Israel from God, consequences at hands of alien nations and God's eventual creation of a deliverer in Saul.

judiciary, in politics, that part of govt. concerned with admin. of justice, comprising judges and law courts. Also *see* SEPARATION OF POWERS.

Judith, Apocryphal book of OT. Describes attack on Jewish city of Bethulia by Holofernes. Judith, a widow of beauty, enters enemy camp and kills Holofernes.

judo, combat sport developed (1882) in Japan by Jigoro Kano, based on practices of JU-JITSU. A coloured belt worn indicates level of proficiency (black being highest). Olympic event since 1964.

Juggernaut or **Jaganath**, in Hindu religion, an incarnation of VISHNU. Cult centres on Puri, India, where his image is annually hauled through the streets. Devotees reputedly threw themselves under wheels of the cart. Has come to denote any irresistible force.

Jugoslavia, see YUGOSLAVIA.

jugular vein, either of 2 large veins in the neck. Larger internal jugular vein carries most blood from brain back to heart; smaller external jugular vein receives blood from face and scalp.

Jugurtha (d. 104 BC), king of Numidia. Inherited joint rule of Numidia with his 2 cousins (118), whom he later usurped. His actions led to war with Rome (111-106). Captured (106), died in prison in Rome.

Juiz de Fora, town of SE Brazil, on Paraibuna R. Pop. 238,000. Textile mfg. esp. knitwear; sugar refining, brewing; coffee, tobacco exports.

ju-jitsu or **jiu-jitsu**, method of weaponless self-defence, from which JUDO is derived, developed in ancient Japan. Systematized forms date from 16th cent. Strength and weight of opponent are used against him.

jujube, edible, date-like fruit of several trees and shrubs of genus *Zizyphus*, esp. *Z. jujuba*; known when preserved in syrup as Chinese dates. Used to make confectionery.

Juliana (1909-), queen of Netherlands (1948-). Succeeded on abdication of mother, Queen Wilhelmina. Married Prince Bernhard of Lippe-Biesterfeld (1937). Her daughter Beatrix is heir apparent.

Julian calendar, *see* CALENDAR.

Julian the Apostate (*c* AD 331-63), Roman emperor (361-3). Influenced by the Athenian philosophy of his teachers, renounced Christianity in favour of paganism. Proclaimed sole ruler on death of Constantius II. Attempted to reintroduce paganism.

Julius II, orig. Giuliano della Rovere (1443-1513), Italian churchman, pope (1503-13). Restored Papal States to Church. Joined League of Cambrai in Italian Wars. Called 5th Lateran Council (1512) to counter French influence. Patronized Raphael, Michelangelo, Bramante.

Julius Caesar, *see* CAESAR, GAIUS JULIUS.

July Revolution or **Revolution of 1830**, French coup d'état which deposed Charles X. Liberal opposition to reactionary govt. led POLIGNAC to issue July Ordinances, dissolving chamber of deputies and restricting press freedom. Ensuing fighting led to Charles' abdication and Louis Philippe's succession.

Jumna, river of NC India. Rises in Himalayas of Uttar Pradesh, flows *c* 1370 km (850 mi) through Delhi and Agra to join Ganges near Allahabad.

Juneau, cap. of Alaska, US; in Alaskan Panhandle. Pop. 14,000. Icefree port; salmon canning indust., sawmilling. Settled in 1880s gold rush; became cap. 1906.

Jung, Carl Gustav (1875-1961), Swiss psychologist. One of founders of analytical psychology, worked with Freud until Jung's divergent view of libido as asexual, primal energy, forced split. Later diverged further from Freud in postulating 'collective unconscious', *ie* innate 'memory' common to all, revealed in dreams, myths, and containing archetypal features. Also formulated extrovert, introvert types.

Jungfrau, mountain of WC Switzerland, in Bernese Oberland. Height 4156 m (13,642 ft); first climbed 1811. Highest railway in Europe to Jungfraujoch.

juniper, any of genus *Juniperus* of small evergreen shrubs of cypress family. Native to temperate regions throughout world. Needle-like foliage, aromatic wood; small berry-like cones used to flavour gin.

Junkers, privileged land-owning class in Prussia, who formed large part of the military elite in Prussian army.

Juno, in Roman religion, wife and sister of Jupiter. Like Greek Hera, patron of women, esp. in their sexual life. Later became major goddess of the state, worshipped (with Jupiter and Minerva) on Capitol.

junta, name given to group of military men in power after coup d'état. Name was applied to military regimes in Greece (1967), Chile (1973).

Jupiter or **Jove,** in Roman religion, the supreme god in the pantheon, identified with Greek Zeus. Originally god of rain and agriculture, later became prime patron of state with temple on Capitol.

Jupiter, largest planet of solar system, *c* 778,340,000 km from Sun; diameter 142,800 km; circles Sun in 11 years 315 days; 12 known satellites. Surface temperature *c* -125°C; shrouded in clouds, only permanent feature is oval marking, 'Great Red Spot'. Largely or entirely composed of gases (hydrogen, helium, ammonia and methane).

Jura, limestone mountain range of E France, W Switzerland, SW West Germany. Part of Alpine system; source of Doubs, Ain rivers. Forests, pastures; tourism, h.e.p., watchmaking. Gives name to Jurassic period.

Jurassic period, second geological period of Mesozoic era; began *c* 195 million years ago, lasted 60 million years. Extensive limestone formation. Flora incl. conifers, ferns, cycads. Fauna incl. ammonites, brachiopods, lamellibranchs, insects; dinosaurs reached max. size, 1st birds evident. Also *see* GEOLOGICAL TABLE.

Juruá, river of NW South America. Rises in Peru, flows NE 2400 km (*c* 1500 mi) through Brazil to join Amazon.

jury, in law, group of people (usually 12) sworn to hear evidence, inquire into facts in a case, and give decision on basis of findings. Has origin in Germanic custom, introduced into England by Normans. By 18th cent., took form known today, was incl. in US Constitution. Jurors selected from voters' roll, with certain excepted classes.

Jussieu, Bernard de (1699-c 1777), French botanist. Devised system of plant classification based on natural affinities, which was elaborated by his nephew, Antoine Laurent de Jussieu (1748-1836), in *Genera plantarum* (1789). Antoine organized botanical collection of Museum of Natural History, Paris.

justice of the peace (JP), in England, local magistrate appointed by special commission to try minor cases, commit others to higher courts, grant licences to publicans, *etc.* In US, elected by people to try minor cases, conduct marriages.

Justinian I (483-565), Byzantine emperor (527-65). Recovered N Africa from the Vandals and Italy from Ostrogoths by victories of his generals Belisarius and Narses. Codified Roman law in *Corpus Juris Civilis*, basis of much European jurisprudence. Built many churches, incl. HAGIA SOPHIA in Constantinople.

jute, natural fibre from tropical annual plants of genus *Corchorus*. Main sources are 2 species grown in valleys of Ganges and Brahmaputra. Known in W since *c* 1830. Coarse fibre used for sacking, rope, carpet backing, *etc.*

Jutes, Teutonic people originally inhabiting areas around mouths of the Rhine. Settled in 5th cent. in S England, esp. Kent, Isle of Wight.

Jutland (*Jylland*), penin. of N Europe, incl. parts of Denmark, N Germany. Main towns Aarhus, Aalborg. Low-lying, sand dunes in W. Agric., esp. dairying, in E. Scene of WWI naval battle (1916).

Juvenal, full name Decimus Junius Juvenalis (AD *c* 60-*c* 130), Roman poet. Famous for *Satires* attacking degenerate Rome for criminality, sexual corruption and tyranny.

juvenile courts, law courts estab. in US (1899), UK (1908) to deal with cases involving children under certain age (ranges from 14-21 years).

K

K2 or **Mount Godwin-Austen**, N Kashmir, world's second highest mountain, height 8611 m (28,250 ft). Surveyed by Godwin-Austen, officer of British Army (1851-77). First climbed by Italian expedition (1954).

Kaaba, in Islam, the most sacred of all Moslem shrines, in the Great Mosque at Mecca. Small cubic building enclosing Black Stone said to have been given to Abraham by the angel Gabriel. Centre of Moslem world and prime goal of pilgrimage, towards which believers face when praying.

kabbala, see CABALA.

Kabul, cap. of Afghanistan, on R. Kabul. Pop. 315,000. Indust. and cultural centre; 1800 m (5900 ft) above sea level. Of strategic importance, many great invading forces have passed through. Became cap. 1773.

Kádár, János (1912-), Hungarian political leader. First secretary of Hungarian Socialist Workers' party from 1955, he was also twice premier (1956-8, 1961-5). Formed pro-Soviet govt. during 1956 revolt and later had revolt's leaders executed.

Kaffirs or **Kafirs**, name applied by Europeans to members of certain Bantu-speaking tribes of SE Africa. Name often used contemptuously by Europeans for all black Africans.

Kafka, Franz (1883-1924), German author, b. Czechoslovakia. Novels, eg The Trial (1925), The Castle (1926), short story Metamorphosis (1915), depict world, both real and dream-like, of threatening absurdity, futility.

Kairouan, town of NC Tunisia. Pop. 82,000. Rug and carpet indust., leather goods. Founded 670; seat of Arab governors of W Africa until 800, of Aghlabid dynasty until 909. Moslem holy city, has 9th cent. Sidi Okba mosque.

Kaiser, Georg (1878-1945), German dramatist. Wrote expressionist plays of ideas, eg From Morn till Midnight (1916), trilogy Gas (1917-20), indicting mechanization of society.

kakapo, Strigops habroptilus, flightless New Zealand parrot with green body, yellow markings. Climbs trees in search of food.

Kalahari, desert of Botswana and NE South Africa. Av. height over 920 m (3000 ft); mainly grass, scrubland. Peopled by nomadic hunters; cattle and sheep rearing, national park in SW.

kale or **cole**, Brassica oleracea acephala, hardy variety of CABBAGE with curly leaves which do not form a head. Grown as winter vegetable; also used as animal fodder.

kaleidoscope, optical device composed of tube containing 2 mirrors that meet each other at angle, reflecting coloured chips of glass enclosed in one end. Symmetric design seen through eyepiece can be changed by rotation.

Kalevala, Finnish national epic. Once thought to date from 1st millennium BC, prob. created in Middle Ages. Fragments first collected by Elias Lönnrot and pub. in 1835. Contains Creation myth, accounts of cosmic disaster and heroic wars.

Kalgan, see CHANGKIAKOW.

Kali, in Hindu myth, black goddess of death and destruction; as Parvati, she is consort of Siva. Personifies mother goddess devouring life she has produced. Represented as garlanded with skulls and bearing bloody sword. Patron of THUGS.

Kalimantan, Indonesian part of BORNEO. Area c 539,000 sq km (208,000 sq mi). Occupies C and S region of isl.

Kalinin, Mikhail Ivanovich (1875-1946), Russian revolutionary, 1st president of the USSR (1919-38). He founded (1912) the newspaper *Pravda*, prominent in the October Revolution.

Kalinin, city of USSR, WC European RSFSR; port on R. Volga. Pop. 367,000. Rolling stock, machinery, textile mfg. Founded in 12th cent. as Tver, rivalled Moscow in importance in 14th cent.; renamed (1931) after M. I. Kalinin.

Kaliningrad (Ger. *Königsberg*), city of USSR, in W European RSFSR enclave on Baltic. Pop. 315,000. Naval base; indust. centre. Founded 1255 as fortress of Teutonic Knights. Hist. cap. of East Prussia. Birthplace of Kant, who taught at univ. (founded 1544). Suffered heavy

damage in WWII. Transferred to USSR 1945.

Kama, river of USSR. Flows generally S c 1930 km (1200 mi) through E European RSFSR to join Volga below Kazan. Chief tributary of Volga; used to transport timber.

Kamchatka Peninsula, arm of extreme E USSR, between Bering Sea and Sea of Okhotsk. Mountainous, with active volcanoes; fishing and fur trapping main occupations.

Kamenev, Lev Borisovich, orig. Rosenfeld (1883-1936), Soviet political leader. Member of ruling triumvirate with Stalin and Zinoviev after Lenin's death (1924); supported his brother-in-law Trotsky against Stalin. Executed with Zinoviev in purges.

Kamet, Himalayan peak of NW Uttar Pradesh, N India; height 7756 m (25,447 ft). First climbed 1931.

kamikaze (Jap., = divine wind), name given to Japanese suicide pilots, who during WWII, intentionally crashed bomb-laden planes on their targets.

Kampala, cap. of Uganda, on N shore of Victoria Nyanza. Pop. 331,000. Admin., commercial, educational, communications centre (Entebbe airport nearby); food processing, clothing mfg.; Makerere Univ. (1961). Former seat of kings of Buganda; cap. of Uganda from 1962.

Kampuchea, new name for CAMBODIA.

Kananga, city of SC Zaïre, on R. Lulua, cap. of Kasai prov. Formerly called Luluabourg. Pop. 506,000. Cotton market, on Port Francqui-Lubumbashi railway. Stronghold of Luba tribe; rebel cap. (1960-1) during secession of Kasai prov.

Kanchenjunga, world's third highest mountain, in Himalayas on Nepal-Sikkim border; height 8579 m (28,146 ft). First climbed 1955 by British expedition.

Kandahar, city of S Afghanistan. Pop. 140,000. In fruit growing region; has fruit processing plants. Occupied by many forces throughout its history, incl. British (1879-81). National cap. in 18th cent.

Kandinsky, Wassily (1866-1944), Russian painter. Credited with painting 1st purely abstract work (1910). A founder of Blaue Reiter group (1911); expounded his ideas on analogy between painting and music in *On the Spiritual in Art* (1912). Later work was more geometric and explored basic elements of design; taught at Bauhaus (1922-33).

Kandy, city of C Sri Lanka. Pop. 93,600. Centre of tea trade. Has Temple of Tooth, said to contain a tooth of Buddha; original tooth possibly destroyed by Portuguese in 16th cent. Formerly called Candy.

kangaroo, large herbivorous marsupial of Australasia with short forelegs, large hind legs and thick tail. Great grey kangaroo, *Macropus major,* reaches heights of 1.8 m/6 ft. Young do not leave mother's pouch for first 6 months. Hunted relentlessly in some areas for hide and flesh.

kangaroo rat, *Dipodomys deserti,* small nocturnal jumping rodent of desert regions of SW US. Has cheek pouches, long hind legs.

Kannada, see DRAVIDIAN.

Kano, city of N Nigeria. Pop. 357,000. Indust. centre on railway to S, has international airport; agric.

market, esp. for groundnuts, cotton, hides. Ancient Hausa city state, hist. caravan route centre. Taken (1903) by British.

Kanpur or Cawnpore, city of Uttar Pradesh, NC India, on R. Ganges. Pop. 1,273,000. Important transport jct. Indust. centre; textile, chemical mfg. Ceded to British (1801), scene of massacre of British garrison (1857) during Indian Mutiny.

Kansas, state of C US. Area 213,064 sq km (82,264 sq mi); pop. 2,249,000; cap. Topeka; other major city Wichita. Mainly prairie; major wheat production, also sorghum, cattle. Oil, natural gas, coal resources; quarrying. Region disputed by French, Spanish until bought by US as part of Louisiana Purchase (1803). Admitted to Union as 34th state (1861).

Kansas City, two cities of C US, opposite each other in Kansas (pop. 168,000) and Missouri (pop. 507,000) at jct. of Kansas and Missouri rivers. Railway yards; grain, livestock market and distribution centre; meat packing, flour milling industs.

Kansas-Nebraska Bill, in US, legislation introduced by Stephen A. Douglas (1854), by which territs. of Kansas and Nebraska were created out of that part of Louisiana Purchase closed to slavery by MISSOURI COMPROMISE (1820). Territs. had right of self-determination on slavery which intensified conflict between North and South.

Kansu, prov. of NC China. Area c 777,000 sq km (300,000 sq mi); pop. 13,000,000; cap. Lanchow. Mountainous; fertile soil but little rain. Oil, coal, ores. Strategic importance in communications with USSR.

Kant, Immanuel (1724-1804), German philosopher. Wrote *Critique of Pure Reason* (1781), *Foundations of the Metaphysics of Ethics* (1785). Distinguished between the world of objects as we know them (phenomena) and world of objects in themselves (noumena). In ethics, posited 'categorical imperative' (*ie* that one should act as if the maxim on which one acts were to become a universal law) as basis of moral action. Profoundly influenced 19th cent. philosophy.

Kaohsiung, chief seaport of S Taiwan. Pop. 915,000. Exports sugar, rice, salt. Indust. centre; produces textiles, petroleum products. Developed rapidly from fishing village under Japanese rule.

kaolin, see CHINA CLAY.

kapok, silky fibres around seeds of several tropical trees of bombax family, esp. *Ceiba pentandra*. Used for stuffing sleeping bags, life jackets, *etc*.

Karachi, chief seaport of Pakistan, on Arabian Sea. Pop. 3,469,000. Exports cotton, hides. Commercial, transport and mfg. centre. Became British (1843) with capture of Sind. Cap. of Pakistan (1947-59).

Karafuto, see SAKHALIN.

Karaganda, city of USSR, C Kazakh SSR. Pop. 541,000. Coal-mining centre; iron and steel mfg. Developed after 1928 to supply coal to Urals indust. region.

Karageorge, orig. George Petrovich (*c* 1766-1817), Serbian nationalist, founder of Karageorgevich dynasty. Led independence movement against Turks from 1804,

gaining many victories. Ruled (1808-13) until defeated after loss of Russian support. Murdered on orders of MILOSH.

Karajan, Herbert von (1908-), Austrian conductor. Has conducted Berlin Philharmonic Orchestra from 1955. Known for opera performances at Salzburg Festival.

Karakoram Range, mountain system of Kashmir, N India. Separated from W Himalayas by R. Indus, extends *c* 480 km (300 mi) NW-SE. Its peaks incl. K2.

Karakorum, ruined city of C Mongolia. Founded *c* 1220 when Genghis Khan made it his capital. Abandoned 1267 by Kublai Khan. Discovered (1889) by N. M. Yadrintsev, who found 8th cent. Orkhon Inscriptions, earliest known examples of Turkic language.

Kara Kum, desert of S USSR, Turkmen SSR, between Caspian Sea and R. Amu Darya. Agric., esp. cotton growing, possible through irrigation by Kara Kum canal.

Karamanlis, Constantinos (1907-), Greek politician. Premier 3 times between 1955 and 1963. In exile after 1963, opposed military junta estab. in 1967. Returned as premier 1974 following restoration of democratic govt. following Turkish invasion of Cyprus.

Kara Sea, part of Arctic Ocean, lying N of Siberia. Bounded by Severnaya Zemlya in E, Novaya Zemlya in W. Receives R. Ob through Gulf of Ob.

karate, method of unarmed self-defence developed in Japan. Involves use of hands and feet to deliver sharp blows to vulnerable parts of body. Considered part of the discipline of Zen Buddhism, modern form introduced to Japan from Okinawa in 1922.

Karelia, auton. republic of NW European RSFSR, USSR. Area *c* 172,000 sq km (67,000 sq mi); pop. 714,000; cap. Petrozavodsk. Has numerous lakes, marshes; heavily forested. Lumbering, wood product mfg. and fishing main occupations. Iron ore mined; h.e.p. derived from rivers. Karelians, known since 9th cent., are of Finnish origin; region annexed by Russia (1721), increased by land ceded by Finland (1940).

Kariba, Lake, artificial lake on Rhodesia-Zambia border, along R. Zambezi. Length *c* 280 km (175 mi). Created by construction of Kariba Dam, built 1955-9, height 128 m (420 ft); provides h.e.p. for Rhodesia and Zambia.

Karl-Marx-Stadt, city of S East Germany, known as Chemnitz until 1954. Pop. 300,000. Textile centre; mining (coal, lignite). Badly damaged in WWII.

Karloff, Boris, pseud. of William Henry Pratt (1887-1969), British film actor. Famous as the monster in *Frankenstein* (1931), became stereotyped in horror parts, as in *Bride of Frankenstein* (1935), *The Body Snatcher* (1945).

Karlsruhe, city of SW West Germany. Pop. 258,000. Indust., admin. centre; has Federal Court of Justice, univ. (1825). Founded 1715, cap. of duchy of Baden from 1771.

Karlstad, town of WC Sweden, on Lake Vänern. Pop. 52,000. Timber indust., textiles. Union of Sweden and Norway ended by treaty (1905).

karma, in Indian religion and philosophy, sum of an individual's actions which are carried forward from one existence to next, determining incarnation for good or bad. Differing interpretations are found in Hinduism, Buddhism and Jainism.

Karnak, village of C Egypt, on R. Nile. Occupies part of site of ancient city of THEBES. Noted for temple of Amon (14th cent. BC).

Karnataka, maritime state of SW India. Area *c* 192,000 sq km (74,000 sq mi); pop. 29,260,000; cap. Bangalore. Formerly known as Mysore state, renamed 1973. Mainly on S Deccan plateau, with coastal plain on Arabian Sea. Largely agric. economy; coffee, rice, cotton. Forests provide sandalwood. Iron and manganese ore; major gold-mining region.

Karroo, semidesert plateau of Cape Prov., South Africa. Little Karroo (S) rises to 610 m/2000 ft; Great Karroo (C) rises to 915m/3000 ft; Northern Karroo (N), alternative name for High Veld, rises to 1830 m/6000 ft. Sheep, goat rearing; fruit, cereal growing.

Karsh, Yousuf (1908-), Canadian photographer, b. Armenia. Famous for portraits using high contrast, esp. 'bulldog' portrait of Churchill in WWII. Estab. (1933) studio in Ottawa.

Karst (*Kras*), arid limestone plateau of NW Yugoslavia, in Dinaric Alps. Area of ridges, potholes, caves (*eg* POSTOJNA), underground channels. Name also generally applied to all limestone areas with similar topography.

karting, sport of driving and racing low tubular-framed vehicle powered by a small-capacity engine. Speeds of 160 km/hr (100 mph) may be reached. Developed 1956 in US.

Kasai (Port. *Cassai*), river of Angola and Zaïre. Flows c 2090 km (1300 mi) from C Angola to R. Congo. Trade artery; rich in alluvial diamonds. Forms part of Angola-Zaïre border; main S tributary of R. Congo.

Kasavubu, Joseph (1917-69), Congolese political leader. First president of independent Congo (1960-5), he was involved in power struggle with LUMUMBA. Deposed in MOBUTU's 2nd coup.

Kashmir, see JAMMU AND KASHMIR.

Kassala, town of E Sudan. Pop. 81,000. Cotton market on Sennar-Port Sudan railway. Founded (1840) as Egyptian military post.

Kassel or **Cassel,** town of EC West Germany, on R. Fulda. Pop. 215,000. Railway engineering, optical instrument mfg. Formerly cap. of Hesse-Kassel electorate and of Hesse-Nassau prov. Aircraft, tank production in WWII, heavily bombed.

Kästner, Erich (1899-1974), German writer. Known for children's story *Emil and the Detectives* (1928). Also wrote satirical verse, novel *Fabian* (1931).

Katanga, region of SE Zaïre, main town Lubumbashi. Fertile plateau, rich in minerals (esp. cobalt, copper, uranium). Seceded (1960-3) after independence of Congo, rejoined after UN intervention. Prov. from 1967, renamed Shaba (1972).

Kathiawar, penin. of Gujarat state, W India, between Kutch and Gulf of Cambay.

Katmandu, cap. of Nepal. Pop. 210,000. Has 16th cent. wooden temple (Katmandu means 'wooden temple'). Captured (1768) by Gurkhas; became their cap.

Katowice (Ger. *Kattowitz*), city of SC Poland, cap. of Katowice prov. Pop. 306,000. Mines produce coal, iron, lead, zinc; engineering, metal industs. Chartered 1865; passed from Germany to Poland 1921.

Katrine, Loch, lake of Central region, C Scotland, on N edge of TROSSACHS. Source of Glasgow's water supply from 1859. Scene of Scott's *Lady of the Lake.*

Kattegat, str. between Denmark and Sweden. Connects with North Sea via Skagerrak (N), with Baltic Sea via Oresund (S).

Kauffmann, Angelica (1741-1807), Swiss decorative painter. In London from 1766-81, she designed small-scale history pieces which were often used to decorate houses designed by the Adam brothers.

Kaunda, Kenneth David (1924-), Zambian statesman. Founded (1960) United National Independence party; successfully opposed inclusion of Northern Rhodesia (Zambia) in Federation of Rhodesia and Nyasaland. Elected president (1964) at independence. Leader in African opposition to white rule in Rhodesia.

Kautsky, Karl Johann (1854-1938), German politician. Influential in adoption of Marxist principles in Erfurt Programme for German Social Democrat party (1891); opposed revisionist policies of EDUARD BERNSTEIN. Condemned Russian Revolution as bourgeois and non-Marxist.

Kaválla or **Kavala** (anc. *Neapolis*), town of NE Greece, on Aegean Sea, cap. of Kaválla admin. dist. Pop.

541

44,000. Port; centre of tobacco indust.

Kawabata, Yasunari (1899-1972), Japanese novelist. Known for *Snow Country* (1935), *Thousand Cranes* (1955). Nobel Prize for Literature (1968).

Kawasaki, city of Japan, on Tokyo Bay, SE Honshu isl. Pop. 973,000. Shipbuilding, engineering, steel and textile mfg. Has Heigenji temple.

kayak, an Eskimo canoe made of skins, esp. sealskins, stretched over a frame of wood to cover it completely except for opening where paddler sits. This allows vessel to capsize with less risk of sinking.

Kaye, Danny, pseud. of Daniel Kominski (1913-), American stage, film comedian. Known for films incl. *The Secret Life of Walter Mitty* (1946), *Hans Christian Andersen* (1952).

Kayseri, city of C Turkey. Pop. 183,000. Agric. centre; carpet, textile mfg. As *Caesarea Mazaca* was cap. of ancient kingdom of Cappadocia.

Kazakh Soviet Socialist Republic, constituent republic of SC USSR. Area 2,720,000 sq km (1,050,000 sq mi); pop. 12,850,000; cap. Alma-Ata. Mainly dry steppe land, rising to Altai Mts. in E and S. Wheat in N, sheep and cattle raising in C; mineral resources incl. coal, oil, copper. Came under Russian rule (1730-1820); constituent republic (1936).

Kazan, Elia (1909-), American stage and film writer-director, b. Turkey. On stage, directed *Death of a Salesman*. Films incl. *On the Waterfront* (1954), *East of Eden* (1955).

Kazan, city of USSR, cap. of Tatar auton. region, E European RSFSR; on Volga. Pop. 904,000. Indust. and cultural centre. Cap. of Tartar khanate in 15th cent.; taken by Ivan the Terrible in 1552. Suyumbeka tower of its kremlin and mosques reflect Moslem influences.

Kazantzakis, Nikos (c 1883-1957), Greek author. Works, incl. novel *Zorba the Greek* (1946), long epic poem *The Odyssey: A Modern Sequel* (1938), deal with duality of man as flesh and spirit.

kea, *Nestor notabilis*, yellowish-green parrot of mountainous regions of New Zealand. Feeds on carrion, insects, berries; can injure sheep while pecking at blowfly larvae living in wool.

Kean, Edmund (c 1788-1833), English tragic actor. Best-known roles incl. Shylock, Richard III, Othello, which he played with wild emotion.

Keaton, Buster, pseud. of Joseph Francis Keaton (1895-1966), American silent film comedian. Famous for unsmiling persistence in face of disaster. Acted in, directed classics *Our Hospitality* (1923), *The General* (1926); other films incl. *The Navigator* (1924).

Keats, John (1795-1821), English poet. Leading Romantic lyricist. Works incl. sonnets, *eg* 'On First Looking into Chapman's Homer', Horatian odes, *eg* 'Ode on a Grecian Urn', 'Ode to a Nightingale', 'Ode to Autumn', unfinished blank-verse epic *Hyperion*. 'La Belle Dame Sans Merci', 'The Eve of Saint Agnes' reflect medieval influence. Died of tuberculosis.

Keble, John (1792-1866), English

clergyman, poet, hymn writer. Inspired OXFORD MOVEMENT with his 'National Apostasy' sermon (1833), expressing alarm at suppression of 10 Irish bishoprics. Works incl. devotional verse, eg *The Christian Year* (1827), and hymns.

Kecskemét, town of C Hungary. Pop. 74,000. Agric., fruit, cattle market. Wine, preserves mfg.

Keeling Islands, see COCOS ISLANDS.

Keewatin, admin. dist. of SE Northwest Territs., Canada. Area 590,934 sq km (228,160 sq mi). Incl. E mainland, Hudson Bay isls., James Bay. Indian, Eskimo pop. Fur trapping.

Keflavik, town of SW Iceland, on Faxa Bay. Pop. 6000. Fishing port; international airport from WWII, US air force base.

Kekkonen, Urho Kaleva (1900-), Finnish statesman. Three times PM before becoming president (1956). Fourth term of office as president began 1974.

Kekulé [von Stradonitz], Friedrich August (1829-96), German chemist. His work on composition of carbon compounds was of basic importance to modern chemistry. Devised theory that structure of benzene is hexagonal ring.

Keller, Gottfried (1819-90), Swiss novelist. Known for autobiog. novel *Green Henry* (1854, radically revised 1879-80), novella cycle *The People of Seldwyla* (1856-71).

Keller, Helen [Adams] (1880-1968), American author, lecturer. Blind and deaf from age of two, she was taught to read, write and speak by companion, Anne Sullivan Macy. She graduated from Radcliffe Coll.

(1904), and became famous for work for handicapped.

Kellogg, Frank Billings (1856-1937), American statesman. Secretary of state (1925-9), advocated peaceful settlement of international disputes. Promoted Kellogg-Briand Pact against war, signed by 15 nations in 1928. Awarded Nobel Peace Prize (1929).

Kells (*Ceanannus Mór*), town of Co. Meath, E Irish Republic. Pop. 2000. Monastery founded in 6th cent. by St Columba, dissolved (1551). *Book of Kells*, illustrated 8th cent. manuscript, found here; now in Trinity Coll. library, Dublin.

Kelly, Edward ('Ned') (1854-80), Australian bushranger. Notorious for bank robberies in SE region, captured (1880) and hanged.

Kelly, Gene (1912-), American singer, dancer, actor, choreographer. Famous for 'Singin' in the Rain' sequence from film of same name (1952), other films incl. *On the Town* (1949), *An American in Paris* (1951).

Kelly, Grace [Patricia] (1928-), American film actress. Had star roles in 1950s as icy blonde, retired to marry Prince Rainier of Monaco. Films incl. *Rear Window* (1954), *High Society* (1956).

kelp or **tangle**, general terms for large seaweeds of the BROWN ALGAE. Used as source of alginates and formerly of iodine. Name also applies to ashes of seaweed from which potassium salts were once obtained.

kelpie, see COLLIE.

Kelvin, William Thomson, Baron (1824-1907), British physicist. Formulated 2nd law of thermodynamics; supported Joule's theories of interchangeability of heat and mechanical energy. Introduced absolute scale of temperature, named Kelvin scale in his honour. Estimated age of Earth by calculations involving rate of cooling. Later years spent in perfecting Atlantic submarine telegraph cable.

Kemal Pasha, Mustafa, *see* ·ATATURK, KEMAL.

Kemble, Roger (1722-1802), English actor-manager. Toured with wife, children as strolling company. Daughter was SARAH KEMBLE SIDDONS. His son, **John Philip Kemble** (1757-1823), was manager of Drury Lane and Covent Garden. Important roles incl. Hamlet, Brutus, Coriolanus. Another son, **Charles Kemble** (1775-1854), was known in Shakespearian supporting roles. His daughter, **Frances Anne ('Fanny') Kemble** (1809-93), was highly successful in tragedy, comedy, *eg* as Juliet. Toured America with father (1832).

Kemerovo, city of USSR, SC Siberian RSFSR. Pop. 404,000. Centre of coalmining region of Kuznetsk Basin; chemical, fertilizer mfg.

Kempis, *see* THOMAS À KEMPIS.

Kendall, Edward Calvin (1886-1972), American biochemist. Identified and isolated over 20 hormones secreted by adrenal cortex; prepared cortisone and investigated its effect on rheumatoid arthritis. Shared Nobel Prize for Physiology and Medicine (1950) with Hench and Reichstein.

Kennedy, John Fitzgerald (1917-63), American statesman, president (1961-3). Son of diplomat and industrialist, Joseph Kennedy, who was US ambassador to Great Britain (1937-40). Successful Democratic candidate in 1960 election. Formed Alliance for Progress with Latin America and Peace Corps. Criticized for allowing abortive invasion of Cuba by Cuban exiles (1961); forced Soviet withdrawal of nuclear weapons from Cuba (1962). Expanded American military role in Vietnam. Assassinated in Dallas (Nov. 1963), allegedly by Lee Harvey Oswald. His brother, **Robert Francis Kennedy** (1925-68), was attorney general (1961-4). Assassinated in Los Angeles while campaigning for Democratic presidential nomination. Another brother, **Edward Moore Kennedy** (1932-), was Democratic senator for Massachusetts after 1962 election.

Kennedy, Cape, *see* CANAVERAL, CAPE.

Kennelly, Arthur Edwin (1861-1939), American electrical engineer, b. India. Predicted existence of layer of ionized particles in upper atmosphere (1902), independently of Heaviside. This layer was discovered by Appleton.

Kennelly-Heaviside Layer, layer of IONOSPHERE, between 90 and 150 km above Earth's surface, from which radio waves can be reflected. Electron concentration decreases during night and reaches maximum at noon.

Kenneth MacAlpin, *see* MACALPIN, KENNETH.

Kensington and Chelsea, royal bor. of WC Greater London, England. Pop. 184,000. Created 1965 from met. bors. Has Kensington

Palace; Albert Hall; museums incl. Victoria and Albert.

Kent, William (1685-1748), English architect, painter and landscape gardener. Associated with Earl of Burlington in development of neo-Palladianism in England. His naturalistic gardens were designed to harmonize with the country house.

Kent, county of SE England. Area 3732 sq km (1440 sq mi); pop. 1,435,000; co. town Maidstone. N Downs in N, curving SE to Dover; Weald in SW; elsewhere low-lying. Orchards, hops, market gardening ('Garden of England'). Chalk, Dover; resorts incl. Margate, Broadstairs. Roman conquest 55 BC; Anglo-Saxon kingdom; Christianity estab. at Canterbury (AD 597).

Kentigern, St. see MUNGO, ST.

Kentucky, state of EC US. Area 104,623 sq km (40,395 sq mi); pop. 3,219,000; cap. Frankfort; major city Louisville. Ohio R. forms N border. Bluegrass region (horse breeding); hilly plains; tobacco, corn; coal mining; bourbon whisky distilling. British claimed region from French (1763); frontier explored by Daniel Boone. Admitted to Union as 15th state (1792); slave state, remained in Union in Civil War (1861-5).

Kentucky and Virginia Resolutions, in US history, resolutions passed by legislatures of Kentucky and Virginia (1798). Kentucky Resolution, written by Jefferson, denied to Federal govt. powers over states not delegated to it by the Constitution. Virginia Resolution, written by Madison, similar, though milder. Regarded as 1st clear statement of STATES' RIGHTS doctrine.

Kentucky Derby, American horse race held annually since 1875 at Churchill Downs, Louisville, Kentucky. Run in May over course 1¼ mi (2 km) long.

Kenya, republic of E Africa. Area 583,000 sq km (225,000 sq mi); pop. 13,847,000; cap. Nairobi. Languages: Swahili, English. Religions: native, Christian. Coastal strip; arid plains in N, highlands in W; incl. Great Rift Valley, part of Victoria Nyanza. Produces coffee, tea, sisal, grain, cattle; large game reserves (eg Tsavo); unexploited minerals. Coast controlled by Portuguese, then Arabs, until British trade exploration 19th cent.; leased by UK from Zanzibar 1887, became Kenya Protectorate 1920. Interior became crown colony 1920. Discontent among Kikuyu natives led to Mau Mau terrorism 1952-6. Coast and interior united at independence 1963; republic from 1964. Member of British Commonwealth.

Kenya, Mount, peak of C Kenya. Snow-capped extinct volcano with many glaciers; height 5197 . m (17,058 ft). First climbed 1899.

Kenyatta, Jomo (c 1893-1978), Kenyan statesman. Imprisoned (1953-9) for alleged involvement in Mau Mau revolt. Elected president of Kenya African National Union (1960). Became PM (1963) at Kenyan independence and president in 1964.

Kenyon, Kathleen Mary (1906-1978), British archaeologist. Expert on archaeology of Holy Land; excavated Jericho, showing double walls predated Joshua, and found traces of Neolithic settlement (c 6800 BC).

Kepler, Johannes (1571-1630), German astronomer. A founder of modern astronomy, he deduced 3 laws of planetary motion from Brahe's detailed observations. These laws were basis of Newton's law of universal gravitation and showed that the Sun controls motion of planets.

Kerala, maritime state of SW India on Malabar Coast. Area c 38,850 sq km (15,000 sq mi); pop. 21,280,000; cap. Trivandrum. Largely plains, with hills in E; grows rice, rubber, coconuts. Created (1956) out of Travancore-Cochin state.

keratin, tough protein forming principal matter of hair, nails, horns, wool, etc.

Kerensky, Aleksandr Feodorovich (1881-1970), Russian politician. A moderate socialist, he succeeded Prince Lvov as premier (July, 1917). His indecisive policies ended in overthrow by Bolsheviks in Nov. 1917. Lived in US after 1940.

Kerguelen Islands, group of isls. in S Indian Ocean, forming part of French Southern and Antarctic Territs. Area c 7000 sq km (2700 sq mi). Comprises one large volcanic isl. (Kerguelen or Desolation), which rises to 1865 m (6120 ft), and over 300 small isls.

Kerman, city of EC Iran, cap. of Kerman prov. Pop. 100,000. Shawl, carpet mfg. Surrounded by clay walls; has mosque dating from 11th cent.

Kermanshah, city of W Iran. Pop. 239,000. Market centre for rich

agric. area; oil refinery. Founded by Sassanids (4th cent.).

kerosene, see PARAFFINS.

Kerouac, Jack (1922-69), American author. Leading figure of BEAT GENERATION. Novels, eg On the Road (1957), came to represent contemporary youth. Big Sur (1963), set in California, used similar frenetic style.

Kerr, Sir John Robert (1914-), Australian lawyer, public official. Governor-general from 1974, precipitated constitutional crisis (1975) by dismissing Whitlam as PM after refusal by Senate to work with Labor govt. Replaced him with MALCOLM FRASER.

Kerr effect, phenomenon by which an applied electric field makes certain transparent media capable of double refraction. Effect utilized in Kerr cell, a high-speed shutter capable of opening or closing in 10^{-8} seconds.

Kerry, county of Munster prov., SW Irish Republic. Area 4701 sq km (1815 sq mi); pop. 113,000; co. town Tralee. Mountains incl. Macgillicuddy's Reeks; Lakes of Killarney inland; indented coast incl. Dingle Bay. Agric., fishing, tourism.

Kesey, Ken (1935-), American novelist. Best known for One Flew over the Cuckoo's Nest (1962), using experience as nurse in mental hospital to satirize the dehumanization of American society.

Kesselring, Albert (1885-1960), German army officer. Commanded the Luftwaffe (1939-40) and the German armies in Italy (1943-5). Sentenced to life imprisonment (1946), he was released in 1952.

Kesteven, Parts of, former admin.

county of Lincolnshire, EC England. Co. town was Sleaford.

kestrel, *Falco tinnunculus,* small brown and grey European hawk. Hovers against wind before swooping on prey of mice, insects.

Keswick, urban dist. of Cumbria, NW England. Pop. 5000. In Lake Dist.; tourism.

ketone, organic compound containing divalent carbonyl group (CO) and 2 hydrocarbon radicals. Formed by oxidation of secondary alcohols. Simplest ketone is ACETONE.

kettledrums, see DRUM.

Kew Gardens, site of Royal Botanic Gardens, S London, England. Area c 117 ha/288 acres. Founded 1761, opened to public 1841. Has botanical research centre.

key, see SCALE.

keyboard instruments, musical instruments which produce sound when player depresses levers set in a row at front. Group incl. pipe and reed organs, harpsichord (virginals and spinet), clavichord, pianoforte and celesta.

Keynes, John Maynard Keynes, 1st Baron (1883-1946), English economist. Outlined economic fallacies of Versailles treaty in *The Economic Consequences of the Peace* (1919). After Depression (1929), advocated govt. planned spending and intervention in market to stimulate employment and national purchasing power. *The General Theory of Employment, Interest, and Money* (1936) profoundly affected capitalist economic attitudes.

Key West, see FLORIDA KEYS.

KGB (Komitet Gosudarstvennoye Bezhopaznosti), security police or intelligence agency of USSR, estab. 1954 to replace notorious NKVD, known for terror tactics in carrying out security operations.

Khabarovsk, city of USSR, indust. centre of SE Siberian RSFSR; on R. Amur. Pop. 462,000. Fur trade; oil refining. Founded (1652) as fort by explorer Khabarov.

Khachaturian, Aram Ilich (1903-1978), Russian composer. Influenced by Armenian folk music. Works incl. ballets *Gayaneh* (with 'Sabre Dance') and *Spartacus,* piano and violin concertos.

khaki (Hindi, = dust coloured), term first applied to uniform worn by British army in Indian Mutiny (1857). Similar uniform came into general use during the Boer War.

Khama, Sir Seretse (1921-), Botswana politician. Returned from exile to Bechuanaland (1956) after renouncing claims to tribal chieftaincy. Became (1965) premier of Bechuanaland and president (1966) of new Botswana republic.

Kharkov, city of USSR, railway centre of E Ukrainian SSR. Pop. 1,330,000. Machinery mfg., engineering. Cap. of Ukraine 1920-34.

Khartoum (*El Khartûm*), cap. of Sudan, at confluence of Blue Nile and White Nile. Pop. 648,000. Admin., commercial centre, railway jct., cotton trade, univ. (1951). Founded (1822) by Mohammed Ali. Destroyed after siege (1885) by Mahdists, in which Gordon was killed; recovered (1898) by Kitchener. Khartoum North lies opposite Khartoum, across Blue Nile. River port, dockyards; cotton trade. Conurbation also incl. OMDUR-MAN; combined pop. 648,000.

Khiva, town of USSR, Uzbek SSR; in oasis region of R. Amu Darya. Pop. 22,000. Carpet, textile mfg.

Khmer Republic, alternative name for CAMBODIA; name changed to Kampuchea (1976).

Khomeini, known as Ayatollah Khomeini (1901-), Iranian religious leader. Deposed Shah and set up Islamic republic (1979).

Khrushchev, Nikita Sergeyevich (1894-1971), Soviet political leader. Emerged as dominant figure in Soviet leadership following Stalin's death (1953); became first secretary of Communist Party (1953). Consolidated power by becoming premier (1958). Denounced Stalin and his repressive internal policies (1956); adopted policy of peaceful co-existence with West. Withdrew missiles from Cuba after confrontation with US (1962). Policies embittered China. Deposed 1964.

Khufu or **Cheops** (*fl* c 2900 BC), Egyptian pharaoh, founder of 4th dynasty. Famous for building of Great Pyramid at Giza.

Khyber, mountain pass, between Afghanistan and NW Pakistan, linking Peshawar and Kabul. Hist. route for invading armies and trade, c 45 km (28 mi) long; now carries a railway and road.

Kiangsi, prov. of SE China. Area c 171,000 sq km (66,000 sq mi); pop. (est.) 22,000,000; cap. Nanchang. Mountainous, drained by many rivers incl. navigable Kan flowing NE to L. Poyang. Major rice producer; silk cultivation.

Kiangsu, prov. of E China, on

Yellow Sea. Area c 106,000 sq km (41,000 sq mi); pop. (est.) 47,000,000; cap. Nanking. Rich agric. region consisting mainly of alluvial plain of R. Yangtze. Silk mfg., cotton. Densely populated, with many large cities, incl. Shanghai.

kibbutz, see COLLECTIVE FARMING.

Kicking Horse Pass, in Rocky Mts., Canada; on British Columbia-Alberta border. Height 1627 m (5339 ft).

Kidd, William (c 1645-1701), British pirate, known as Captain Kidd. Commissioned by governor of New York (1695) to protect English ships from pirates, he turned to piracy himself. Arrested (1699), he claimed his actions had official support. Tried and convicted (1701), hanged.

Kidderminster, mun. bor. of Hereford and Worcester, WC England, on R. Stour. Pop. 47,000. Carpet mfg., begun 18th cent. by Flemish immigrants.

kidnapping, illegal seizure and detention or removal of person by force or fraud, often for ransom. In US, public reaction over Lindbergh case led to federal, state reform of law.

kidneys, in vertebrates, pair of excretory organs; in humans, located near vertebral column in small of the back. Separate waste products, *eg* urea, toxins, from the blood and excrete them as urine through the bladder. Also regulate acidity of body fluids and secrete a hormone.

Kiel, city of NE West Germany, at E end of Kiel Canal, cap. of Schleswig-Holstein. Pop. 269,000. Shipbuilding, engineering, fishing; univ.

KIEL CANAL

(1665). Hanseatic League member from 1284, major German naval base 1871-1945.

Kiel Canal, Schleswig-Holstein, N West Germany. Waterway 98 km (61 mi) long, from North Sea to Baltic Sea. Built 1887-95 as Kaiser Wilhelm Canal.

Kielce (Russ. *Keltsy*), city of EC Poland, cap. of Kielce prov. Pop 129,000. Railway jct.; food processing; marble quarries nearby. Founded 1173; under Russian rule 1815-1919.

Kierkegaard, Sören Aabye (1813-55), Danish philosopher. Attacked organized religion, believing that man must work out own relationship with God. Influenced 20th cent. existentialists. Works incl. *Either/Or* (1843), *Stages on Life's Way* (1845).

Kiesinger, Kurt Georg (1904-), West German statesman. Chancellor (1966-9) at head of coalition of Christian Democrat and Social Democrat parties. Defeated in 1969 by Brandt's Social Democrats.

Kiev, city of USSR, cap. of Ukrainian SSR; on Dnepr. Pop. 1,764,000. Indust. and cultural centre. Cap. of powerful medieval Kievan state (*fl* 10th-13th cent.); early centre of Greek Church in Russia. Under Russian control in 17th cent. Hist. buildings incl. 11th cent. cathedral of St Sophia, monastery of St Michael. City devastated in WWII.

Kigali, cap. of Rwanda. Pop. 60,000. Admin. centre; trade in cattle, hides, coffee.

Kigoma-Ujiji, town of W Tanzania, on L. Tanganyika. Pop. 33,000.. Terminus of railway to Dar-es-Salaam; trade with Burundi, Zaïre. Former slave and ivory centre. Stanley met Livingstone at Ujiji (1871).

Kikuyu, African people, belonging to BANTU group. Largest Kenyan tribal group. Led by Jomo KENYATTA, fought British in Mau Mau uprising. Mainly agric. economy.

Kildare, county of Leinster prov., EC Irish Republic. Area 1694 sq km (654 sq mi); pop. 72,000; co. town Naas. Mainly agric., incl. Bog of Allen, Curragh (racecourse, horsetraining). Main rivers Liffey, Barrow. Kildare, market town, pop. 3000. Cathedral, abbey ruins.

Kilimanjaro, mountain of NE Tanzania, highest in Africa. Permanently snow-capped extinct volcano, rises to 2 peaks (Mt. Kibo 5892 m/19,340 ft, Mt. Mawenzi 5270 m/17,300 ft). First climbed 1889 by Hans Meyer.

Kilindini, see MOMBASA, Kenya.

Kilkenny, county of Leinster prov., SE Irish Republic. Area 2062 sq km (796 sq mi); pop. 62,000. Hilly; main rivers Nore, Barrow. Coalmining; black marble quarrying; agric. Co. town Kilkenny, on R. Nore. Pop. 10,000. Ancient cap. of Ossory. Castle (12th cent.), abbeys (13th cent.), Protestant, RC cathedrals.

Killarney, town of Co. Kerry, SW Irish republic. Pop. 7000. Lakes of Killarney nearby; tourist centre.

killdeer, *Charadrius vociferus*, North American bird of plover family, with penetrating cry.

killer whale or **grampus**, *Orcinus orca*, largest of dolphin group, reaching length of 9.1 m/30 ft. Voracious predator on seals, porpoises; birds; will attack other whales. Worldwide distribution.

Killiecrankie, Pass of, in Tayside region, C Scotland. Scene of battle (1689) in which William III's forces were defeated by Claverhouse (who was killed).

Kilmarnock, town of Strathclyde region, W Scotland. Pop. 49,000. Coalmining area; engineering, carpets, distilling. Burns Memorial museum.

Kilvert, [Robert] Francis (1840-79), English clergyman, diarist. Known for *Diary 1870-9* (1938), giving picture of life in rural parishes.

Kimberley, city of NE Cape Prov., South Africa. Pop. 104,000. Major diamond-mining and cutting centre, metal working; railway jct. Founded 1870; besieged 1899-1900 by Boers.

Kincardineshire or **The Mearns,** former county of E Scotland, now in Grampian region. Hilly in W (sheep); fertile along coast and Howe of the Mearns (cereals, root crops). Fishing; whisky distilling. Co. town was Stonehaven.

kindergarten (Ger., = garden of children), a school or class for children before official school age (usually 3-5), using informal games, exercises, crafts to prepare them for later school. Theory and 1st kindergarten formed by FROEBEL.

kinetic art, term referring to sculptured works which involve moving parts, shifting light, *etc.* Examples incl. mobiles of Calder and complex machines of Jean Tinguely.

kinetic theory of gases, explanation of behaviour of gases, which assumes that gas molecules are elastic spheres in continuous motion; their kinetic energy depends on the gas temperature. Impact of molecules on walls of containing vessel accounts for gas pressure. Theory explains all experimental gas laws (Boyle's law, Charles' law, *etc.*).

King, Billie Jean, née Moffitt (1943-), American tennis player. Wimbledon champion 5 times between 1966 and 1973, US champion 4 times, she is known for her efforts to obtain equal prize money for women.

King, Martin Luther (1929-68), American clergyman, civil rights leader. Founded Southern Christian Leadership Council after leading successful boycott of segregated buses in Montgomery (1955-6). Chief advocate of non-violent action against segregation of blacks. Awarded Nobel Peace Prize (1964). Assassinated in Memphis.

King, William Lyon Mackenzie (1874-1950), Canadian statesman, Liberal PM (1921-6, 1926-30, 1935-48). Helped draw up Statute of Westminster (1931) which recognized complete autonomy of Commonwealth dominions.

kingbird, New World bird of Tyrannidae (tyrant flycatcher) family. Species incl. black and white Eastern kingbird, *Tyrannus tyrannus,* of US.

King Charles spaniel, see SPANIEL.

king cobra, see COBRA.

kingfisher, any of Alcedinidae family of fish-eating birds with long sharp bill, short tail. European kingfisher, *Alcedo atthis,* has iridescent blue-green plumage.

Kings, book of OT, called 1st and 2nd Kings in Authorized Version. Relates history of Hebrews from death of David until fall of Judah. Incl. reign of Solomon, division of kingdom into Israel and Judah, and lives of prophets, Elijah and Elisha.

King's [or Queen's] Bench, in UK, one of three divisions of High Court of Justice. Formerly, supreme court of common law.

King's Counsel, *see* BARRISTER.

Kingsley, Charles (1819-75), English clergyman, author. Known for historical romances *Westward Ho!* (1855), *Hereward the Wake* (1866), moral fantasy *The Water Babies* (1863). Christian socialist, involved in controversy with J.H. NEWMAN.

King's Lynn or Lynn Regis, mun. bor. of Norfolk, E England, on R. Great Ouse. Pop. 30,000. Market town, food processing. Medieval port; church (12th cent.); Greyfriars Tower (13th cent.).

king snake, non-poisonous constrictor snake of North America. Species incl. Eastern king snake, *Lampropeltis getulus,* which eats rodents.

Kingston, port of SE Ontario, Canada; at NE end of L. Ontario. Pop. 62,000. Locomotives mfg., textiles. Founded as Fort Frontenac (1673); destroyed 1758, resettled 1782; cap. of United Canada (1841-4). Has Queen's Univ. (1841) and Royal Military Coll.

Kingston, cap. of Jamaica, on the Caribbean. Pop. 112,000. Port with deep harbour. Hq. of coffee trade; tobacco produce, exports; textile, brewing, food processing industs. Founded 1692; became official cap. (1872).

Kingston-upon-Hull, *see* HULL, England.

Kingston-upon-Thames, royal bor. of SW Greater London, England, on R. Thames. Pop. 140,000. Created 1965 from Surrey residential bors. Saxon kings crowned here.

Kingstown, cap. of ST VINCENT.

Kinross-shire, former county of E Scotland, now in Tayside region. Important agric. area. Co. town was Kinross, on Loch Leven. Pop. 3000. Textile mills.

Kinsey, Alfred C. (1894-1956), American zoologist. Famous for questionnaire-based report *Sexual Behaviour in the Human Male/ Female* (1948-53) showing permissiveness was more widespread than previously thought.

Kinshasa, cap. of Zaïre, on R. Congo. Pop. 1,624,000. Admin., commercial centre, univ. (1954). River port, railway to Matadi, airport. Founded (1881) by Stanley as Léopoldville; cap. of Belgian Congo from 1929; renamed 1966.

Kintyre, penin. of Strathclyde region, W Scotland. Extends 68 km (40 mi) SSW from Tarbert. Hilly; main town is Campbeltown.

Kioga or Kyoga, Lake, lake of SC Uganda, on Victoria Nile. Area c 2600 sq km (1000 sq mi). Shallow, swampy; allows water transport in cotton-growing area.

Kipling, [Joseph] Rudyard (1865-1936), English author, b. India. Works incl. novels, eg *The Light that Failed* (1891), *Kim* (1901), poetry, eg 'Mandalay', 'Gunga Din', 'If', in *Barrack Room Ballads* (1892), popular children's books, eg *The Jungle Book* (1894), *Puck of Pook's Hill* (1906). Reflected British imperialism in India. Nobel Prize for Literature (1907).

Kirchner, Ernst Ludwig (1880-1938), German artist. An originator of the Brücke group, he was influenced by Oceanic and primitive art; painted in an expressionist style employing bright colour and simplified form. Also made many powerful woodcuts.

Kirghiz Soviet Socialist Republic, constituent republic of SC USSR. Area c 199,000 sq km (76,500 sq mi); pop. 2,933,000; cap. Frunze. Mountainous, with Tien Shan range along Chinese border. Stock raising, esp. sheep; cotton, wheat grown in valleys. Annexed to Russia by 1876.

Kiribati, see GILBERT AND ELLICE ISLANDS.

Kirin, prov. of NE China. Area c 186,500 sq km (72,000 sq mi); pop. (est.) 17,000,000; cap. Changchun. On fertile Manchurian plain; soya beans, grain grown. Major source of timber, coal, iron, etc. Cities incl. Kirin, pop. 1,200,000.

Kirk, Norman Eric (1923-74), New Zealand politician. PM at head of Labour govt. (1972-4).

Kirkcaldy, town of Fife region, E Scotland, on Firth of Forth. Pop. 50,000. Port; linoleum, textiles mfg.; engineering.

Kirkcudbrightshire, former county of SW Scotland, now in Dumfries and Galloway region. Uplands in N, W; slopes S to Solway Firth. Cattle, sheep rearing; tourism. Co. town was Kirkcudbright, former royal burgh. Pop. 3000. Market town.

Kirkintilloch, town of Strathclyde region, C Scotland. Pop.25,000. Iron founding, engineering.

Kirkwall, town of Orkney, N Scotland, on Mainland isl. Pop. 5000. Fishing port, exports agric. produce;

whisky distilling. Has St Magnus' cathedral (1137).

Kirov, Sergei Mironovich (1888-1934), Soviet political leader. Close aide of Stalin and member of Politburo from 1930, his assassination was excuse for massive Communist Party purges and trials during 1930s.

Kiruna, town of N Sweden. Pop. 23,000. Mining centre of high-grade iron ore, transported by rail to Luleå (Sweden), Narvik (Norway).

Kisangani, city of NC Zaïre, on R. Congo. Pop. 261,000. River port, trade in cotton, rice; univ. (1963). Founded (1883) as Stanleyville, renamed 1966. Rebel govt. estab. here briefly during civil war (1960-4).

Kishinev (Romanian *Chişinău*), city of USSR, cap. of Moldavian SSR. Pop. 400,000. Centre of rich agric. region; food processing. Scene of pogrom (1903). Part of Romania (1918-40).

Kissinger, Henry Alfred (1923-), American govt. official, b. Germany. Secretary of state (1973-7), he negotiated withdrawal ·of American troops from Vietnam, end of Arab-Israeli war (1973) and Israeli withdrawals from Arab territ. captured in 1967. Awarded Nobel Peace Prize (1973).

Kitakyushu, indust. city of Japan, N Kyushu isl. Pop. 1,042,000. Produces iron and steel, textiles, machinery, chemicals. Formed (1963) from 5 towns (Kokura, Wakamatsu, Yawata, Moji and Tobata).

Kitasato, Shibasaburo (1852-1931), Japanese bacteriologist. Authority on infectious diseases, discovered plague bacillus (1894).

Also isolated bacilli of tetanus and developed antitoxin for diphtheria.

Kitchener, Horatio Herbert Kitchener, 1st Earl (1850-1916), British field marshal, statesman, b. Ireland. After reconquering Sudan, became its governor-general (1898). As commander-in-chief (1900-2), introduced successful tactics against Boers, negotiated peace. Secretary of state for war (1914-16), supervised expansion of British army. Drowned en route to Russia.

Kitchener, town of S Ontario, Canada; on Grand R. Pop. 112,000. Tanning, meat packing; mfg. industs. Settled by Germans c 1824 (then named Berlin); renamed 1916.

kite, bird of hawk family, with long pointed wings and forked tail. Feeds on carrion and small animals. Species incl. European red kite, *Milvus milvus*.

kithara or **cithara,** lyre-like musical instrument of the ancient Greeks, with 5 to 7 strings stretched between a crossbar at the top and a sound box at the bottom. Played by plucking.

kittiwake, *Rissa tridactyla,* gull of Arctic and N Atlantic. Inhabits open sea, breeding on cliff faces.

Kitwe, city of NC Zambia. Pop. 290,000. Indust. and commercial centre in copperbelt mining region. Founded 1936.

Kivu, region of E Zaïre, main town Bukavu. Coffee, cotton, rice growing; gold, tin mining. Incl. Albert (or Virunga) National Park, Ruwenzori Mts.; rain forest (W). Scene of heavy fighting in civil war (1960-4).

kiwi, nocturnal insectivorous New Zealand bird, genus *Apteryx*, with small functionless wings, hair-like feathers, and long curved bill.

Kizil Kum, *see* KYZYL KUM.

Klagenfurt, town of S Austria, at E end of Wörthersee, cap. of Carinthia prov. Pop. 74,000. Winter sports centre in mountain lakeland. Produces textiles and leather goods.

Klee, Paul (1879-1940), Swiss painter. Began as a graphic artist; later associated with Blaue Reiter group. Works, characterized by love of fantasy and calligraphic line, incl. *Twittering Machine* (1922). Taught at Bauhaus for many years.

Kleist, [Bernt] Heinrich [Wilhelm] von (1777-1811), German author. Known for plays, eg comedy *The Broken Jug* (1803), tragedy *Prinz Friedrich von Homburg* (1821), novella *Michael Kohlhaas* (1808).

Klemperer, Otto (1885-1973), German conductor. Left Nazi Germany and settled in US in 1933, when he became conductor of Los Angeles Symphony Orchestra. Toured Europe, America extensively; best known for interpretations of Beethoven.

Kleve (Eng. *Cleves*), town of NW West Germany. Pop. 23,000. Food processing, footwear mfg. Castle (11th cent.) associated with *Lohengrin* legend. Birthplace of Anne of Cleves.

Klimt, Gustav (1862-1918), Austrian painter. Leading exponent of art nouveau in Vienna and co-founder of Vienna Secession group, he is known for his richly ornamented decorative work, incl. female portraits and murals.

klipspringer, *Oreotragus oreotragus,* small African antelope of mountainous regions of E and S Africa.

Klondike, see DAWSON, Canada.

knapweed, any of genus *Centaurea* of perennial plants of composite family, esp. *C. nigra*, with purple flowers resembling those of thistle.

knee, joint formed between lower end of femur and upper end of tibia, protected by kneecap or patella. Powerful ligaments and muscles maintain stability.

Kneller, Sir Godfrey, orig. Gottfried Kniller (*c* 1646-1723), English painter, b. Germany. Court painter from time of Charles II to George I. Employed large studio to produce numerous fashionable portraits; best-known work is series of portraits of 42 members of Kit Cat Club.

knighthood, form of feudal tenure involving both a property qualification and code of conduct termed CHIVALRY. Reached zenith at time of Crusades (12th-13th cents.). Feudal landholders who held land directly of the crown were required to provide given number of knights for service in field (in England, normally 40 days per year). Military or religious orders of knighthood, independent of feudal obligations, also existed, eg Knights Templars, Knights Hospitallers.

Knights Hospitallers, members of religious military order founded in Jerusalem during 1st Crusade to protect pilgrims. Driven from Holy Land (1291), they estab. themselves in Rhodes (1310), which they held against Turks until 1522. Moved to Malta (1530) where they continued their wars against Turks. Expelled from Malta (1798) by Napoleon.

Knights Templars, members of military order founded *c* 1118 to protect pilgrims to Holy Land. Driven from Jerusalem (1187), they estab. their hq. in Acre, which they held until 1291. Resentment over their powerful banking role in Europe led to their persecution and dissolution (1314).

knitting, method of making fabric by looping yarn with special needles. Developed in 15th cent.; a knitting machine was invented in 1589 to produce hosiery.

knocking, in internal combustion engine, noise caused by explosion before sparking of over-compressed mixture of air and petrol vapour.

Knossos or **Cnossus,** ancient city of N Crete, Greece, near Iráklion. Centre of MINOAN CIVILIZATION. In Greek legend, home of King Minos and site of labyrinth.

Know-Nothing movement, in American history, popular name for American party (*fl* 1850s) which sought exclusion of RCs and foreigners from public office. Influence declined after split over slavery question (*c* 1855). So called because members professed ignorance of party's activities and membership.

Knox, John (1505 or 1515-72), Scottish religious leader. Converted to Protestantism under influence of GEORGE WISHART. Exiled in Geneva (1544) where he conferred with Calvin. Invited to lead Reformation in Scotland (1559), succeeded in estab. Presbyterianism after abdication of Mary Queen of Scots. Proposed organization of CHURCH OF SCOTLAND in *The First Book of Discipline* (1560).

Knox, Fort, see LOUISVILLE.

Knoxville, port of E Tennessee, US; on Tennessee R. Pop. 175,000. In coal, iron, zinc mining region; livestock, tobacco market. Marble quarrying nearby. State cap. (1796-1812, 1817-19). Hq. of Tennessee Valley Authority.

Knut, see CANUTE.

koala, *Phascolarctos cinereus,* arboreal bear-like Australian marsupial with large ears, grey fur. Tailless, c 60 cm/2 ft long; diet of eucalyptus leaves. Protected since 1936, following intensive hunting.

Kobe, seaport of Japan, on Osaka Bay, SW Honshu isl. Pop. 1,289,000. Produces iron and steel, textiles, ships, chemicals. Expanded rapidly after 1868, absorbing old port of Hyogo.

København, *see* COPENHAGEN, Denmark.

Koblenz or **Coblenz,** city of W West Germany, at confluence of Rhine and Moselle. Pop. 120,000. Centre of wine trade; furniture, piano mfg. Roman Confluentes, founded c 10 BC. Held by archbishops of Trier 1018-1794; cap. of Rhine prov. 1824-1945.

Koch, Robert (1843-1910), German bacteriologist. Developed methods of identifying, classifying and growing bacteria which estab. modern science of bacteriology. Discovered (1876) anthrax bacillus and studied its life cycle. Discovered (1882) tubercule bacillus causing tuberculosis, for which work he received Nobel Prize for Physiology and Medicine (1905).

Kodály, Zoltán (1882-1967), Hungarian composer. With Bartók, collected Hungarian folk tunes. Works, national in idiom, incl. *Háry*

János, Psalmus Hungaricus, Dances of Galanta.

Kodiak Island, off S Alaska, US; in Shelikof Str. Area 13,890 sq km (5363 sq mi). Hilly and forested, indented coastline. Salmon fishing, canning.

Kodok, town of SC Sudan, on White Nile. Formerly called Fashoda, scene of 'Fashoda incident' (1898) when French occupation caused diplomatic crisis between UK and France.

Koestler, Arthur (1905-), British writer, b. Hungary. Works, incl. essays, *eg Spanish Testament* (1937), novels, *eg Darkness at Noon* (1940), studies in history of ideas, *eg The Sleepwalkers* (1959), reflect scientific background, disillusionment with Communism.

kohlrabi, *Brassica oleracea caulorapa,* plant of cabbage family. Grown for edible, bulbous portion of stem.

Koko Nor *(Tsinghai),* salt lake of Tsinghai prov., WC China. Area c 4210 sq km (1625 sq mi). In Tibetan highlands at alt. of 3205 m (10,515 ft); brackish, of little economic use.

Kokoschka, Oskar (1886-), Austrian painter, dramatist. Early work incl. violent expressionist landscapes and portraits expressing psychological tension. Has travelled extensively, painting colourful views of towns, which attempt to capture the spirit of the place.

Kokura, see KITAKYUSHU.

kola, see COLA.

Kola Peninsula, region of USSR, N European RSFSR, between Barents and White seas. Tundra in N, forested in SW. Rich mineral resources. Chief town Murmansk.

Kolar Gold Fields, city of Karnataka state, S India. Pop. 168,000. Chief Indian goldmining centre.

Kollwitz, Käthe (1867-1945), German graphic artist. Work depicted harshness and suffering of proletarian life; specialized in woodcuts and lithographs. Mother and child theme was favourite subject.

Köln, see COLOGNE, West Germany.

Kolwezi, town of S Zaïre in Katanga prov. Pop. 48,000. Commercial and transport centre for copper, cobalt mining region. Site of massacre of Europeans and Africans by Katangese rebels; led to French, Belgian armed intervention (1978).

Kolyma, river of USSR, NE Siberian RSFSR. Rises in Kolyma Range; flows N c 2550 km (1600 mi) to East Siberian Sea. Passes through important goldfields.

Komodo dragon, Varanus komodoensis, world's largest lizard, reaching lengths of 3.7 m/12 ft. Discovered (1912) on Indonesian island of Komodo.

Konakry, see CONAKRY, Guinea.

Königsberg, see KALININGRAD.

Kon-tiki, legendary sun king supposed to have migrated from Peru to the Pacific Isls. See HEYERDAHL.

Konya (anc. Iconium), city of SC Turkey, in rich agric. region. Pop. 228,000. Textile, carpet mfg. Cap. of sultanate of Iconium or Rum under Seljuk Turks in 11th cent. Religious centre of Whirling Dervishes from 13th cent.; has tomb of their founder Celaleddin Rumi.

kookaburra, Dacelo gigas, large Australian kingfisher, with loud laughing cry. Also called laughing jackass.

Kooning, Willem de (1904-),

American artist, b. Netherlands. Major abstract expressionist in 1940s, he is known for his figurative series of 'women', begun in early 1950s. Later reverted to more abstract style.

Koran (Arab., quran,=recitation), sacred book of Islam. Written in classical Arabic, regarded as word of God revealed to MOHAMMED by angel Gabriel. Derived to some extent from Jewish scripture. The canonical version was estab. c 652.

Korda, Sir Alexander (1893-1956), British film producer and director, b. Hungary. Made great contribution to British film indust. Films incl. The Private Life of Henry VIII (1932), Things to Come (1935).

Korea (Choson), historical country of E Asia, divided (1948) into North and South Korea. Mountainous penin., forested in N (gold, iron deposits), agric. in S (rice, barley) with tungsten, coal resources. Language: Korean. Religion: Confucianism. Kingdom 1392-1910 until Japanese annexation. Liberation after WWII led to Russian (N), US (S) occupation and Korean War (1950-3). **North Korea** (People's Republic of Korea) estab. under Communist govt. Area c 120,500 sq km (47,000 sq mi); pop. 16,246,000; cap. Pyongyang. **South Korea** (Republic of Korea) dependent on US aid after invasion by North Korea (1950). Area c 98,500 sq km (38,000 sq mi); pop. 35,860,000; cap. Seoul.

Korean, language of Korea and part of Japan. Appears to be unrelated to any other language, although syntax similar to Japanese. Literature dates from 7th cent. AD.

Korean War, conflict fought (1950-

3) between Communist and non-Communist forces in Korea. Invasion of South Korea by North Korean troops (later backed by Chinese) led UN to authorize support for South Korea by international military force under UN command. Ceasefire negotiations (begun 1951) led to 1953 agreement ending war.

Kórinthos, see CORINTH.

Kos, see Cos, Greece.

Kosciusko, Tadeusz (1746–1817), Polish national hero. Led nationalist revolutionaries against Russian invasion (1794), was captured but freed (1796) to live in exile.

Kosciusko, Mount, highest peak of Australia, in Snowy Mts., S New South Wales. Reaches 2229 m/ 7316 ft. Surrounded by Kosciusko State Park; tourism, winter sports.

kosher (Heb., = fit for use), term for food complying with Jewish dietary laws. Meat must be that of animals which chew cud and have cloven hooves; must be slaughtered by specially trained Jew and cleansed of all traces of blood, and must not be cooked or eaten with milk products. Strict observation of these laws distinguishes ∴ a Jew as orthodox.

Košice, city of E Czechoslovakia. Pop. 146,000. Indust. centre, esp. machinery, textiles, food processing. Gothic cathedral (14th cent.). Part of Hungary until 1920.

Kossuth, Louis (1802–94), Hungarian revolutionary hero. Instrumental in precipitating Hungarian nationalist uprising against Austria (1848). President of short-lived republic (1849); fled to Turkey after

Russia came to Austria's aid. Lived in exile in England and Italy.

Kosygin, Aleksei Nikolayevich (1904–), Soviet politician. Succeeded (1964) Khrushchev as premier and chairman of council of ministers, sharing power with Leonid Brezhnev, secretary of Communist Party.

Kotabaru, see DJAJAPURA.

Koussevitzky, Serge (1874–1951), Russian conductor. Settled in US and conducted Boston Symphony Orchestra (1924–49). Conducted 1st performances of many important works by Stravinsky, Ravel, Bartók and Prokofiev. The Koussevitzky Music Foundation, founded 1943, has encouraged many composers.

Kowloon, seaport and penin. of Hong Kong. Pop. (city) 2,195,000. Adjoins Kwangtung prov., S China. Main indust. area of Hong Kong; linked by rail to Kwangchow.

Kozhikode, seaport of Kerala state, SW India, on Malabar Coast. Pop. 334,000. Exports coconut goods. Formerly called Calicut, once renowned for calico. Site of many European trading posts 16th-18th cent.; ceded to British 1792.

Kra, Isthmus of, narrowest part of Malay penin., in S Thailand.

Krakatoa, small Indonesian isl., between Java and Sumatra. Violent volcanic eruption in 1883 caused much destruction; thousands killed by resulting tidal waves.

Kraków (Eng. Cracow), city of S Poland, on R. Vistula, cap. of Kraków prov. Pop. 590,000. Iron, steel industs.; trades in timber, agric. produce; educational and cultural centre, univ. (1364). Founded 8th cent., cap. of Poland 1305-1609.

Under Austrian rule 1795-1919, except 1815-46 (independent republic). Cathedral (14th cent.) contains royal tombs.

Krasnodar, city of USSR, S European RSFSR; on R. Kuban. Pop. 491,000. Food processing, oil refining, steel and machinery mfg. Founded in 1794 as Cossack fort; called Ekaterinodar until 1920.

Krasnoyarsk, city of USSR, indust. centre of C Siberian RSFSR. Pop. 688,000. Railway engineering, textiles; centre of goldmining region; major h.e.p. plant on R. Yenisei.

Krebs, Sir Hans Adolf (1900-), British biochemist, b. Germany. Described Krebs or citric acid cycle, series of biochemical reactions governing the oxidation of foodstuffs and release of energy. Shared Nobel Prize for Physiology and Medicine (1953).

Krefeld or **Crefeld,** city of W West Germany, on R. Rhine. Pop. 223,000. Textile centre, formerly linen (estab. by Huguenots), now silk and rayon. Also produces steel.

Kreisky, Bruno (1911-), Austrian political leader, chancellor (1970-). Helped negotiate treaty (1955) achieving Austrian independence and neutrality. Formed (1970) 1st single party govt. in Austria since WWII after socialist electoral victory.

Kreisler, Fritz (1875-1962), Austrian violinist. Famous for his brilliant playing. Created cadenza now usually played in Beethoven's violin concerto; also wrote pastiche pieces. Settled in US during WWII.

kremlin, fortified citadel in several Russian towns. Best known is that in Moscow, much of it dating from 15th cent. Contains palaces, cathedrals, bell towers. Now centre of Soviet govt.

Kreutzer, Rodolphe (1766-1831), French violinist, composer. Works incl. 19 violin concertos, over 40 operas and violin studies still in use. Beethoven's Kreutzer sonata is dedicated to him.

krill, small shrimp-like crustacean, main food of toothless whales.

Krishna, in Hindu religion, eighth incarnation of VISHNU. As adolescent, represented as erotic, often sporting with milkmaids. As adult, he is hero of epic *Mahabharata*.

Krishnamurti, Jiddu (1895-), Indian religious leader. Toured England and US (1926-7) as protegé of ANNIE BESANT. Repudiated messianic claims made on his behalf, but continued to write and teach. Works incl. *The Songs of Life* (1931). Settled in US (1969).

Krivoi Rog, city of USSR, SC Ukrainian SSR; on R. Ingulets. Pop. 600,000. Iron mining centre; produces iron and steel, chemicals.

Kronstadt, port and naval base of USSR, on Kotlin Isl. in Gulf of Finland, W European RSFSR. Pop. c 50,000. Taken from Sweden (1703) by Peter the Great and later fortified. Served as port for St Petersburg but importance declined after canal built to latter (1875-85).

Kropotkin, Piotr Alekseyevich, Prince (1842-1921), Russian anarchist. Arrested for spreading nihilist propaganda in Russia (1874). Fled Russia (1876); lived in England for 30 years until returning to Russia after 1917 Revolution. In his *Mutual Aid* (1902), he argued that cooperation is essential to human survival.

Kruger, [Stephanus Johannes] Paul (1825-1904), South African statesman. Secured independence of Transvaal (1881) in the Pretoria Agreement with Britain. As president (1883-1900), opposed Rhodes's policies of unifying South Africa under British rule. Tried to maintain Boer supremacy by excluding non-Boers from franchise.

Kruger National Park, large wildlife sanctuary of NE Transvaal, South Africa. Area c 20,720 sq km (8000 sq mi). Founded (1898) as Sabi Game Reserve; renamed 1926. Tourism.

Krupp, Alfred (1812-87), German industrialist. Built up his father's small forge into the famous iron and steel works at Essen where from 1847 he manufactured arms. His son, Friedrich Alfred ('Fritz') Krupp (1854-1902), specialized in armaments but also built warships. His daughter Bertha married Gustav von Bohlen and Halbach (1870-1950), who adopted the name Krupp and manufactured almost the entire output of German armaments in WWI. Krupp works was centre for German rearmament in period after 1933. Gustav's son, Alfred Felix Krupp (1907-), was imprisoned as a war criminal for using slave labour; he subsequently rebuilt the organization into an international concern.

krypton (Kr), inert gaseous element; at. no. 36, at. wt. 83.80. Found in minute traces in atmosphere (c 1 part per million). Used in fluorescent lights. Discovered (1898) in residue of liquid air.

Kuala Lumpur, cap. of Malaysia and Selangor state, West Malaysia.

Pop. 452,000, mainly Chinese. Commercial, transport centre for tin mining and rubber growing area.

Kublai Khan (1216-94), Mongol emperor of China. Grandson of Genghis Khan; succeeded to empire on death of his brother Mangu Khan (1259). Completed Mongol conquest of China with defeat of Sung dynasty (1279). Invasions of Java and Japan were unsuccessful. Visited by Marco Polo.

Kubrick, Stanley (1928-), American film writer, producer-director. Independent maker of popular films, varied in style, subject, eg *Lolita* (1962), *Dr Strangelove* (1964), *2001: A Space Odyssey* (1968), *A Clockwork Orange* (1971).

Kuching, cap. of Sarawak state, East Malaysia. Pop. 63,000. Port on R. Sarawak, exporting sago flour, pepper.

Kuchuk Kainarji, Treaty of, peace treaty between Russia and Turkey (1774). Ceded certain Black Sea ports to Russia, thus facilitating annexation of the Crimea (1783), and gave Russia rights as protector of Christians in Ottoman Empire.

kudu, *Strepsiceros strepsiceros*, large African antelope, with long spiral horns and striped grey coat.

Kuibyshev, city of USSR, E European RSFSR; port on Volga. Pop. 1,094,000. Indust. centre; aircraft, tractor, textile mfg. Founded (1586) as Samara to protect trade on Volga; renamed 1935.

Ku Klux Klan, in US history, 2 distinct secret societies; original Ku Klux Klan founded (1866) to maintain white supremacy in South. Disbandment ordered (1869), but local organizations continued.

Second Ku Klux Klan (founded 1915) added intense hatred of foreigners, anti-Catholicism, anti-Semitism to its white supremacy policy. At its peak in 1920s, influence has declined, even in South.

Kulturkampf, struggle in Germany to restrict power of Catholic church in politics, as represented through Centre party. Govt. under Bismarck passed series of laws from 1872, incl. measures to remove church control of school system and introduction of civil marriage. Ceased when Bismarck, fearing rise of Socialism, rescinded anti-Catholic policies.

Kumasi, city of SW Ghana, cap. of Ashanti region. Pop. 345,000. Commercial centre; market town in cocoa-producing dist., railway to coast; univ. (1961). Former cap. of Ashanti confederation, captured (1896) by British.

kumquat, any of genus *Fortunella* of shrubs native to China and Japan. Bear small citrus fruits with soft pulp and sweet rind, often candied as sweetmeat.

Kun, Béla (1886-c 1937), Hungarian politician. After becoming Bolshevik in Russia, headed short-lived Communist dictatorship in Hungary (1919). Fell from power after defeat by Romanian troops intervening in counter-revolution (1919). Returned to USSR where he is thought to have died in party purges.

kung-fu, Chinese system of self-defence, similar to KARATE, but emphasizing circular rather than linear movements.

Kunlun, mountain range of C Asia between Tien Shan and Himalayas along Tibet border. Length *c* 1600 km (1000 mi). Highest point 7724 m (25,340 ft) at Ulugh Muztagh.

Kunming, cap. of Yunnan prov., S China. Pop. 1,700,000. Commercial, transport centre; coal, steel complex. Ancient walled city. Bronze temple of Ming dynasty nearby. Prosperity dates from building of rail link to Hanoi (1910).

Kuomintang, Chinese nationalist political party, organized (1912) in accordance with principles of SUN YAT-SEN. Strengthened (1922-4) with aid of Communists. Under leadership of CHIANG KAI-SHEK, Kuomintang troops captured Peking (1928) and set up govt. in Nanking. Engaged in civil war with Communists after 1927. Authoritarian rule lasted until Communist victories forced Chiang and Nationalists to set up govt. in Taiwan (1950).

Kura (anc. *Cyrus*), river of SE Europe. Flows E from Turkish Armenia *c* 1450 km (900 mi) through Georgian and Azerbaijan SSR to enter Caspian Sea S of Baku.

Kurdistan, hist. region of SE Turkey, and parts of Iran, Iraq, Syria. Inhabited by pastoral nomads. Revolts in Turkey suppressed (1920s, 1946); Kurdish revolt in Iraq, begun in 1960s, collapsed 1975 following withdrawal of Iranian assistance.

Kuril or **Kurile Islands,** isl. chain of USSR, stretching from Kamchatka penin. to Hokkaido isl. (Japan). Area *c* 15,600 sq km (6000 sq mi). Of volcanic origin, with several active volcanoes; main occupations lumbering, fishing. Japanese possession (1875-1945).

Kurosawa, Akira (1910-), Japanese film director. Known for dramatic treatments of historical, legendary stories, *eg Rashomon* (1950), *The Seven Samurai* (1954), and *Throne of Blood* (1957), a version of *Macbeth*.

Kuro Shiwo or **Japan Current**, warm ocean current of W Pacific. Flows N past E Taiwan and Japan, moderating climate of both.

Kutch, Rann of, salt marsh region of Gujarat state, W India. Area disputed by India and Pakistan; scene of fighting between their forces (1965).

Kutuzov, Mikhail Ilarionovich (1745-1813), Russian army officer. Superseded Barclay de Tolly as commander after the defeat at Smolensk (1812), and devised the tactics which reversed the French advance and turned it into the disastrous retreat from Moscow.

Kuwait, independent sheikdom of SW Asia, at head of Persian Gulf. Area *c* 18,000 sq km (6950 sq mi); pop. 1,031,000. Mainly desert; major oil producer. British protect. (1899-1961). Shares control of Neutral Territory with Saudi Arabia. **Kuwait** or **Al-Kuwait** is cap. and port. Pop. 80,000.

Kuznetsk Basin, see KEMEROVO.

Kwajalein, atoll in Ralik Chain of Marshall Isls., W Pacific Ocean. Incl. many islets. Dist. hq. of US trust territ. of the Pacific Isls.; missile station. Japanese base in WWII, taken by US (1944).

Kwangchow or **Canton**, cap. of Kwangtung prov., S China. Pop. 2,300,000. Major port on R. Chukiang delta. International airport. China's centre for external trade, site of twice-yearly trade fair. Shipyards, textile mfg., steel com-

plex. Centre of Sun Yat-sen's Kuomintang movement (1911).

Kwangju, city of SW South Korea. Pop. 503,000. Agric., commercial centre; rice milling, cotton and silk mfg.

Kwangsi (-Chuang), auton. region of S. China. Area *c* 220,000 sq km (85,000 sq mi); pop. (est.) 24,-000,000; cap. Nanning. Mainly hills with basin of Si Kiang. Major producer of sugar cane, manganese, tin.

Kwangtung, maritime prov. of S China, incl. Hainan isl. Area *c* 231,500 sq km (89,400 sq mi); pop. (est.) 40,000,000; cap. Kwangchow. Coast has enclaves MACAO, HONG KONG. Fishing, agric., major sugar cane producer, oil refining.

Kweichow, prov. of SC China. Area *c* 171,000 sq km (66,000 sq mi); pop. (est.) 17,000,000; cap. Kweiyang. High plateau region. Produce incl. rice, cereals, timber. Minerals incl. mercury, coal.

Kweiyang, cap. of Kweichow prov., SC China. Pop. 1,500,000. Rail, indust. centre. Important coalfields nearby. Textile and fertilizer mfg.

Kyd, Thomas (1558-94), English playwright. Estab. vogue for revenge tragedy with *The Spanish Tragedy*. Also wrote early version of *Hamlet*.

Kyoto, city of Japan, SC Honshu isl. Pop. 1,419,000. Centre of Japanese art, it retains many craft industs. Founded in 8th cent., hist. cap. of Japan 794-1868 (political power resided in Tokyo after 1603). Buddhist centre with many shrines and temples; has old imperial palace. Univ. (1897).

Kyrie eleison (Gk.,=Lord have mercy), in several Christian churches, invocation forming part of the Mass. Only Greek part of RC liturgy; an English version is used in Anglican services.

Kyushu, isl. of SW Japan. Area *c* 35,600 sq km (13,800 sq mi). Mountainous; mild subtropical clim- ate favours agric. Indust. concentrated in N around country's largest coalfield.

Kyzyl Kum or **Kizil Kum,** desert of USSR, in Uzbek SSR and Kazakh SSR, between Amu Darya and Syr Darya. Name means 'red sands'.